THE ENCYCLOPAEDIA OF SPORTS

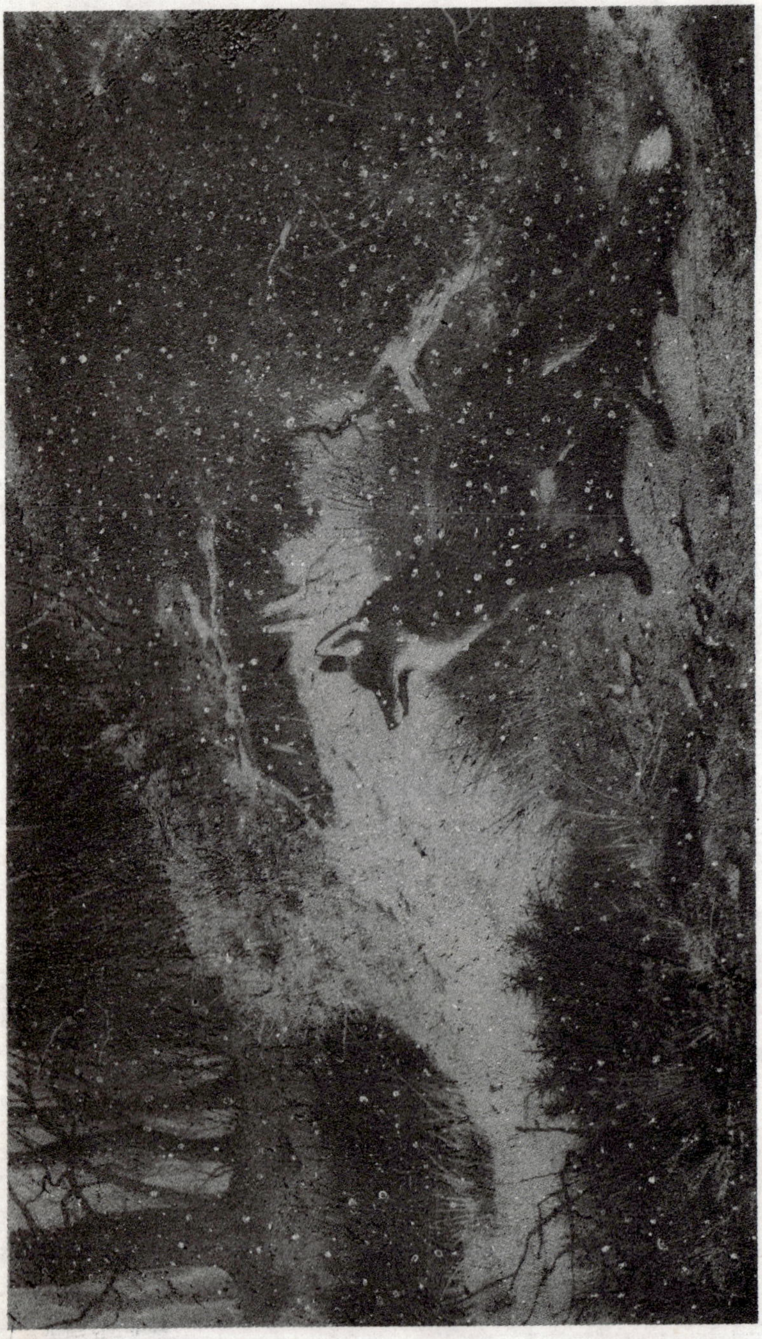

THE

ENCYCLOPAEDIA

OF

SPORTS

(in 4 vols.)

Edited By
HEDLEY PEEK
AND
F.G. AFLALO

Vol I

A-EEL

GYAN

GYAN PUBLISHING HOUSE

NEW DELHI-110 002

THE ENCYCLOPAEDIA OF SPORTS
(Sports, Physical Education)

ISBN: 81-212-0276-0 (Set)
ISBN: 81-212-0277-9 (Vol. 1)

Published in 1997 in India
by Gyan Publishing House
5, Ansari Road
New Delhi-110002

Printed at Goyal Offset Printers, Delhi-110035

PREFACE

LOVERS of Sport cannot complain that in recent years their interests have been neglected by English publishers; but, although books devoted to the consideration of Sport continue to multiply apace, no serious effort has been made to produce a national Encyclopædia of Sport.

Many editions of Blaine's *Encyclopædia of Rural Sports*, which first appeared in 1840, were published down to 1870. Blaine announced that he proposed to describe "the progress of each sport to its present state of perfection," and he acquitted himself creditably. The book was very useful in its day, but its day is past.

Football was so slightly regarded when Blaine's work appeared that he actually makes no mention of a game which is now among the most popular of our recreations. Some sports, Cricket for example, have been completely revolutionised during the last fifty years; and others, Badger-baiting and the like, described by Blaine, have disappeared from the catalogue of national amusements, and are here relegated to the article on Obsolete Sport.

Blaine's predecessor, Strutt, published in 1801 *The Sports and Pastimes of the People of England*, which was frequently reprinted. This valuable and entertaining book, a mine of antiquarian lore, has no pretension to the name of Encyclopædia, though Strutt pursues his investigations even to the chronicling of "the obsolete sports of the young," as deduced from old engravings. Among these obsolete sports one is surprised to find games resembling "Blind Man's Buff" and "Leapfrog"; though, as the latter is apparently being played by monks and nuns, the monks giving the back, Leapfrog in that particular form may fairly be reckoned among obsolete sports.

Strutt, and to a large extent Blaine, worked single-handed; but it is obvious that if an attempt is to be made to cover the whole range of sport, scores of experts must collaborate. The Editor is glad to say that, in answer to his appeal, the leading authorities on every branch of sport have placed their services at his disposal. In not a few cases, indeed, men who have never before published any portion of their complete and carefully acquired knowledge have been prevailed on to break through their habit of silence in favour of this work. Even the less important and unsigned articles have been submitted, to insure all possible accuracy of detail, to the careful revision and scrutiny of experts.

The scope of the present work is very wide, and includes many articles on subjects which, though not in themselves sport, are certainly its corollaries. Such are, for instance, "First Aid," "Taxidermy," and "Veterinary Work."

Of the first-named some knowledge should be in possession of all who take part in sport of any kind; for what sport worthy of the name is free from danger? It is not too much to say that very slight surgical skill on the part of a servant would have prevented a fatal termination to one of the most deplorable of recent accidents on the hill.

Of Taxidermy every big-game hunter, be his object science or sport, should have at least such elementary knowledge as shall insure the preservation of specimen or trophy in presentable condition. And of the perpetual use of Veterinary work there can be no need to remind sportsmen.

Nor has natural history been neglected, though made subservient to sport throughout.

The plan of publication in parts has been adopted in the confident expectation that those who buy the earlier numbers will never rest satisfied without the complete series. The acquisition of a full-blown Encyclopædia is seldom undertaken without the misgiving born of a dread of satiety.

It may at all events be urged that this method of publication has the advantage of affording to well-wishers of Sport an opportunity of giving us the benefit of suggestions in time to correct errors or repair omissions in future numbers. Who can tell that we may not with such assistance expand in due time to the dimensions of the *Dictionary of National Biography!*

In these volumes, without any sacrifice of accuracy or technical detail, a lighter style than is usual in works of this description has been permitted, so as to render the monthly issue to the full as attractive as any of the most popular magazines. It will be allowed that the *menu* thus offered to the public is, at any rate, not lacking in variety.

The glossaries under each subject mu: be claimed as something of a new depa: ture, though, of course, the facilities fc reference must necessarily remain incor plete until the publication of the Inde. with the final number.

There are not nowadays many sport from the enjoyment of which women ar excluded; but some are considered a peculiarly within their province; and fc these, such as Cycling, Lawn-tennis, &c the services of ladies have been secured.

All the Plates, and with few exception the text-cuts, have been specially execute (under the supervision of Mr. Hedley Peek for this work, which, when it reaches com pletion, will be generally recognised as needed and valuable addition to Englis Encyclopædic lore.

It remains to add that the founde and architect of the scheme developed i these volumes is Mr. F. G. Aflalo, wh has devoted himself to his editorial tas with unflagging energy.

SUFFOLK AND BERKSHIRE.

LIST OF PLATES

THE ENCYCLOPÆDIA OF SPORT

AARD-VAARK or **EARTH HOG** (*Orycteropus*)—A South African ant-eater of burrowing and nocturnal habits, of which three species are known. The flesh is said to taste strongly of formic acid, but is nevertheless much appreciated by the natives, who spear or hunt the animal with trained dogs. Strong iron traps are sometimes used.

AGOUTI (*Dasyprocta aguti*)—A small rodent of South America and the West Indies, which has done much damage on the sugar plantations. It is largely eaten by the natives, who beat the undergrowth lining the rivers and shoot from boats as the animals take to the water.

ALBICORE (*Lichia glauca*)—A large ocean-fish allied to the tunny and mackerels, which, from its habit of following for days in the wake of vessels, is much angled for with outrigger bamboo pole and log-line. The latter, reeved through a block, terminates in a fathom of wire rope and a single large hook dressed with two-feet strips of red and white bunting. A small bell is so arranged on a loop-line as to ring when a fish is hooked. This Albicore-fishing is, from the great strain, not successful at any speed over twelve knots.

ALEVIN—The earliest form of salmon-fry as it emerges from the egg with yolk-sac attached.

ALEXANDRA—A large and deadly artificial fly, dressed with silver body and peacock harl, and worked deep like a salmon-fly. It is used in various sizes for salmon, trout, grayling, &c. (No. 1 hook in Yorkshire for grayling), and is found to be especially killing on waters where a silver-bodied fly answers, though the fish soon tire of it.

ALEXANDRA.

It is prohibited on many fly-fishing club waters, as well as in many preserved lochs and chalk streams; but in Scotland and Norway its use, which has been aptly compared to a variation of minnow-fishing, is general.

ALLIGATOR—The name popularly applied to all the species of three genera of Saurians: (1) Alligator, (2) Caiman, (3) Jacare, found only in the New World.

They may always be distinguished from Crocodiles by the presence of a pit in the upper jaw which receives the long teeth of the lower, and by the fact that they have the hind feet webbed to a lesser degree.

Alligator-shooting is treated of under CROCODILE.

AMATEUR—As long as there have been national sports in England there have also been classes of men who have practised them for gain and as a means of livelihood; and these men have been usually termed **professionals**, although in one game, Cricket, the name **player** has always been in vogue. Professional jockeys, professional cricketers, watermen, and runners have been with us always; and in most sports there have been gentlemen of means who have taken part for amusement and not for gain, although they had no objection to ride, play, row or run for money-stakes or bets. This class were long described in contradistinction to the players or "**pros.**" as **gentlemen**, because they consisted entirely of men of gentle birth.

With the rapid popularisation, however, of all sports and games during the last fifty years, and especially in consequence of the introduction of "gate-money" into games, the old vague distinction, drawn between the gentleman who was the patron and the professional who was hired, became obsolete; and the votaries of different sports set to work to divide competitors into two classes, the **professionals** who competed for money, and the **amateurs** (a term borrowed originally from across the Channel) who declined to receive money either by way of remuneration or in the shape of a prize, but who pursued their sport solely for its own sake.

It would be tedious to trace the corruption of so called "amateurism" to its present state. It is here only possible to give a *résumé* of its condition at the present day.

Athletics—Many of the leading amateurs must obviously make a living out of athletic sports, as they travel to distant parts of the country, and win prizes all over the kingdom, and are clearly not possessed of the means to pay for their own amusement.

Cricket — Most amateur cricketers are genuine amateurs, but there are some instances to the contrary of men who, without visible means of spending the entire summer in recreation, must obviously pay their way in life by what they receive under the guise of "expenses."

Cycling—Scores of the leading "amateur" cyclists are directly or indirectly paid by the manufacturers of cycles whose machines they ride, or receive enough for their "expenses" to keep themselves throughout the season.

Football—As soon as there were hundreds of pounds to be made by charging an admission to the ground, the players naturally wanted to share in this. In the *Association* Game, professionalism has been recognised, and there are professional clubs as well as amateur clubs, and competitions in which both play together. It is the custom for amateurs, however, to have their travelling expenses, and often their hotel bills, paid by their own clubs. In the *Rugby Union* Game, the authorities are still making a determined effort to allow no paid footballer to take part with the amateurs; in the provinces, however, scores of amateurs receive, directly or indirectly, remuneration for representing their clubs.

After considerable friction for many years between the Rugby Union authorities and some leading clubs in Yorkshire and Lancashire, there was at length an open rupture in 1895. At that date, a large number of the leading clubs in the two counties seceded from the Rugby Union and formed a Northern Rugby Union. This body comprises at least half, and by no means the least important half, of the clubs in the two great Northern shires. The ostensible reason for the rupture was that the Northern malcontents wished to pay their players for "broken time," that is, some equivalent for the wages they lose by taking part in matches; but most observers are of opinion that the rupture was really due to deeper causes of difference between the North and South.

The players who receive payment for broken time are at present in an anomalous position. They play as amateurs amongst amateur clubs, but are not recognised as amateurs by the Rugby Union, nor as amateur athletes by the Amateur Athletic Association.

Racing (including **Steeplechasing**)—There are many licensed **Gentlemen Riders.** Of these, some spend money on their amusement and are genuine amateurs; others have their expenses paid by the owners whose horses they ride. The latter proceeding is entirely illegitimate, and is usually hidden by some such device as giving the quasi-gentleman the result of an imaginary bet if he wins and of course claiming nothing from him if he loses.

Rowing—In this sport, the amateurs may be described as *genuine* amateurs; they pay for their own amusement. The causes of this are two-fold. Firstly, it is impossible to charge "gate-money" to see races on the rivers. In other sports, the promoters find that it pays them to lure the leading amateurs with bribes, because their appearance increases the "gate." Secondly, rowing at the leading regattas is barred to "mechanics, artisans, or labourers." In real fact, amateur rowing in England is, from the nature of the sport, confined to those who have some means. With athletics, cycling, and football, it is impossible to preserve this distinction. The money for the sport is found by the public, who look on and pay their shillings at the gate. The public wants to see the best men, not merely those who happen to be possessed of private means.

The usual form in which a modern "amateur" receives remuneration for his services is under the heading of "expenses." It is very forcibly contended that few men who play a game are in a position to give up their time and to travel about the country at their own expense; it is only fair, therefore, it is said, that a man who represents his club or county should have his travelling expenses, and even his hotel bills, paid. On the other hand, it is pointed out that if a man is throughout a season boarded and lodged at his club's expense, he is really making a living out of the game he is supposed to be playing for the love of sport; and it is also obvious that if a man is paid his "expenses," or so many pounds for his "expenses," he is well able to save a bit out of what is given to him. The problem is where to draw the line as to payment of expenses.

Another difficulty, which has to be considered, is that things which are no substantial reward to men of one class are so to those of another. If the University oarsmen have their boats and oars paid for by their club, and their hotel bills at Putney defrayed by the same means, it would be hard to say that by so doing they lose their right to be called amateurs; yet if a body of pitmen are boarded and lodged for a month at the seaside at the expense of their football club, the amateur footballer would call them "pros." and would point out that they are getting an excellent gratuitous holiday out of the sport they follow.

It is often asked what is the object of separating the two classes in sports. The answer given is—that to allow paid and trained exponents of a sport to compete against those who are working for their living, and training only in their leisure moments, is to suppress the latter class and to discourage the truest form of sport, that of honest recreation. It is also pointed out that when a sport gets entirely into the hands of people whose only object is to make money out of it, the sport gets full of dishonesty and trickery, and the public at large, instead of taking part in it, do nothing but look on and bet, which is not so good for their bodies or their minds.

A distinguished Irish judge is reported to have been asked by a still more distinguished English statesman what was the solution of the Irish problem, and to have replied, "the Irish problem is just insoluble." It is difficult to give any other answer if one is asked for the correct solution of the *Amateur Question.*

MONTAGUE SHEARMAN.

["An amateur is one who has never competed for a money prize or staked bet, or with or against a professional for any prize, or who has never taught, pursued or assisted in the practice of athletic exercises as a means of obtaining livelihood."—Rule 1, A.A.A.]

AMBULANCE—[*See* FIRST AID].

AMERICA CUP—The America Cup was first offered for racing in 1851 by the Royal Yacht Squadron, under the name of the "Queen's Cup." The course assigned was round the Isle of Wight, and the victory was won by the United States boat *America*, a schooner. In 1857 it was given by the five owners of the w nning boat to the New York Yacht Club, to be held by them against all challengers as an international trophy. In 1870 and 1871 England sent over boats which were defeated. In the first year the *Cambria* came in eighth, amongst twenty-three competitors; in the second the *Livonia* sailed five races against two different boats representing the N.Y.Y.C., and lost four. Canadian boats made unsuccessful attempts to win it in 1876 and in 1881.

Since that date England has made unsuccessful attempts to bring the cup back in 1885, 1886, 1887, 1893, and 1895. [*See also* YACHTING.]

The laws under which the yachts run are subject to constant revision, but two conditions are permanent: the visiting yacht must be built in the country that challenges, and the race must be sailed in the waters of the country holding the cup.

RECORDS OF THE RACE.

	Yacht.	*Rig.*	*Owner.*	*No. of victories.*
1870	MAGIC (winner)	Schooner	Mr. F. Osgood...........	1
	Cambria.................	,,	Mr. J. Ashbury.	
1871	COLUMBIA* (winners)	,,	Mr. F. Osgood...........	2
	SAPPHO* (winners)		Mr. W. P. Douglas......	2
	Livonia	,,	Mr. J. Ashbury	1
1876	MADELINE (winner)...	,,	Mr. J. Dickenson	2
	Countess of Dufferin	,,	Major C. Gifford.	
1881	MISCHIEF (winner) ...	Sloop	Mr. J. R. Bush	2
	Atalanta	,,	Capt. Cuthbert.	
1885	PURITAN (winner) ...	Cutter	Mr. J. W. Forbes	2
	Genesta	,,	Sir Richard Sutton.	
1886	MAYFLOWER (winner)	,,	Gen. C. J. Paine	2
	Galatea	,,	Lieut. Henn.	
1887	VOLUNTEER (winner)	,,	Gen. C. J. Paine	2
	Thistle	,,	Mr. James Bell.	
1893	VIGILANT (winner) ...	Cutter	Messrs. O. C. Iselin and Morgan	3
	Valkyrie II.	,,	Earl of Dunraven.	
1895	DEFENDER (winner)...	,,	Mr. O. C. Iselin	3
	Valkyrie III.	,,	Earl of Dunraven.	

* In this year the N.Y.Y.C. took the right of sending out what representative they chose on each day.

AMMUNITION—This subject may, for convenience sake, be divided into two parts: the first section dealing with the ammunition required for shot guns, whilst the second treats of that used with sporting rifles.

SHOT-GUN AMMUNITION.

Powders—In treating of ammunition, gunpowder naturally occupies the premier position. Black powder for shot guns, if not indeed [illegible]ly obsolete, probably will soon be entirely [illegible]seded by the more modern forms of ex[illegible], except perhaps in very hot climates, and [illegible] therefore no necessity to investigate that [illegible]lar part of the subject. There are many [illegible]d smokeless powders on the market for the sportsman to choose from, and fresh ones are constantly being brought to his notice. The earliest form of smokeless powder was designed to occupy, power for power, the same space in the cartridge-case as did black powder. Powders of this type have done excellent work in their time, but they leave a good deal of solid residue after combustion, which, when shooting against wind, is frequently blown back into the eyes of the shooter. The newer form of concentrated powders are tolerably free from this defect, and most of them really deserve the application smokeless, which is more than can be said of the earlier kinds, and therefore they are gradually winning their way in public favour.

Nitric acid is the active agent in all smokeless powders at present in use. The principal absorbents are wood pulp, cotton wool, and glycerine. These substances, after treatment with the acid and combination with other ingredients, are so manipulated that the combustion is retarded to such extent as to insure that on explosion the pressure set up in the gun shall not exceed three tons per square inch, or about the pressure given by a full charge of black powder, which was taken as the standard of comparison. If it is desired to use smokeless powders in shot guns exceeding 10-bore, one of the primary types of powder first mentioned, which comprise Schultze, E.C., S.S. and Amberite, should be chosen for the reason that sufficient experience has not as yet been obtained to determine satisfactorily as to the action of the concentrated powders in guns of greater calibre.

Smokeless powder may be kept for any length of time without deterioration in a cool dry place, if the temperature is within from 40° to 60° Fahr. In cold weather better results will be obtained if the cartridges are kept in a warm room for a few hours before use, so as to bring their temperature up to about 60°.

Shot—The shot in general use varies in size from about 40 to 1,000 pellets to the ounce, as may be seen by reference to the table annexed:

NEWCASTLE CHILLED SHOT CO.	
Size.	No. of pellets per oz.
Mould Shot.	
S G	8
S S G	11
S S S G	14
Drop Shot.	
A A A	40
A A	48
A	56
B B B B	56
B B B	64
B B	76
B	88
1	104
2	122
3	140
4	172
5	218
6	270
7	340
8	450
9	580
10	850

WALKER'S, PARKER & CO. LONDON.	
Size.	No. of pellets per oz.
Mould Shot.	
L G	5½
M G	8½
S G	11
S S G	15
S S S G	17
Drop Shot.	
A A	40
A	50
B B	58
B	75
1	82
2	112
3	135
4	177
5	218
6	270
7	341
8	600
9	984
10	1726

From the foregoing tables it will be gathered that in some sizes the number of pellets to the ounce varies considerably as between the two makers, and although the anomaly has often been pointed out no revision has as yet been effected.

There are two kinds of shot made; "soft," which is composed of nearly pure lead, and the so-called "chilled," which is in reality an alloy, with lead as the principal ingredient. Chilled shot possesses many advantages over the soft kind, for, as its name implies, the pellets are harder, and for this reason they do not lose to so great an extent their spherical form in the cartridge or bore of the gun, and in consequence of this they keep a more correct line of flight. The pellets are formed by pouring the molten metal through a perforated plate fixed at the top of a high tower. The height of the drop gives time for the naturally-formed globules of metal to harden before falling into a tank of water, which is placed in the base of the tower to receive them. The larger sizes of shot are generally used for wild fowl, against the strong feathers and tough bodies of which they are very effective, often at ranges exceeding one hundred yards. The choice of size of shot is usually regulated by the size of the game and the distance at which it is to be killed. No. 6, of 270 pellets to the ounce, is the size most generally used for ordinary purposes of game shooting in England.

Cartridge Cases—For shot guns these are sometimes made of solid drawn brass; but this more particularly applies to the larger sizes used for wild-fowling purposes. For guns of ordinary size, *i.e.*, 20 to 12-bore inclusive, paper cases are almost universally employed. The principal objection to brass cases is that the sharp edges are liable to cut the fingers of the shooter. Several improvements have been made recently in the paper used in the manufacture of cartridge cases, the most important of these being the "*Pegamoid*" process, which renders the paper waterproof.

Concentrated powders require a special form of cartridge case, having the interior of the base, that is to say the powder chamber, of a conical shape. These bases vary somewhat in form for the several powders, as also do the cap domes, which have one or more flash-holes of various sizes. The fulminate in the percussion cap is somewhat different in composition and in action from that required to ignite the older type of smokeless powder. A question of vital importance bearing on the action and behaviour of present-day explosives is the inequality of power of the percussion caps, many serious accidents having resulted from this cause. In some instances, owing to the small quantity of fulminate in the cap, the shot charge has been moved only a very short distance up the barrel and the next charge fired has burst the gun. An excess of fulminate in the cap gives rise to high gas pressure in the breech, which is likely to injure the weapon, and in any case irregularities of the sort indicated are a barrier to good and regular work.

Wadding—In the shot cartridge the wadding is a very important item, as it must fulfil several requirements. It must act as an effectual gas check, not only at the instant of explosion but also while the charge is passing from the cartridge into the bore of the barrel, thus effectually bridging over that part of the bore of the gun termed the "cone."

From numberless experiments it has been found that in a 12-bore a card wad of medium thickness over the powder, next which is a ⅜ in soft felt with a grey cloth under the shot, gives the best results; the wad over the shot only being sufficiently stout to keep the pellets from shaking loose during transit.

RIFLE AMMUNITION.

Twenty years ago the subject of ammunition for sporting rifles was a very large one. At that period rifles were made by rule of thumb, no two being exactly alike, and as each maker had his own particular charge of powder, shape and weight of bullet, &c., the varieties of ammunition in use were innumerable. In the event of bullet mould being lost or injured only the original maker of the rifle could supply a new one, so that the difficulties under which sportsmen laboured (especially in foreign countries were considerable. This unsatisfactory state of affairs has for several years past ceased to exist and rifles are now made to take ammunition of standard sizes, which can be obtained in all parts of the civilised world.

Powder—The remarks previously made with respect to the use of black powder in shot guns are applicable for the most part to the employment of this form of explosive in rifled arms, though it is still preferred for large bore rifles and modern ball guns of the "Paradox" type. Indeed, owing to the difficulty of obtaining a good smokeless powder abroad, the care with which it must be transported and kept, and the necessity of using a powder easy to load and invariable in its results, many big game shooters still rely on black powder only. But improvements in the manufacture of smokeless rifle powder make it unlikely that this will always be the case.

As stated in the previous section, smokeless powders are of two distinct varieties: first, those that, power for power, bulk the same, or nearly the same, as black powder—for example, S.R. powder, designed originally for rifles of the Martini-Henry class—and, second, those explosives of the concentrated type which occupy a much smaller space in the cartridge case. None of the powders of the former class really deserve the appellation smokeless; and they are all more or less hygroscopic On the other hand the majority of the concentrated powders are absolutely smokeless and impervious to damp, whilst the flame emitted from the muzzle of a rifle on firing a charge of one of these powders is scarcely perceptible. Concentrated powders may be divided into two classes; those that are composed almost entirely of nitro-cellulose or gun-cotton, and those that consist of nitro-cellulose combined with nitro-glycerine. Each of these has its own peculiar advantages and disadvantages which may be briefly summed up as follows:—Those powders containing nitro-glycerine give low and regular gas pressures, and for any given weight of charge the ballistic properties are excellent. The heat of combustion, however, is exceedingly high, and causes severe erosion of the bore, a matter of much importance in the case of a rifle, as the accuracy of shooting rapidly deteriorates in consequence. Powder of the nitro-cellulose class generally give higher and more irregular gas pressures; but the heat of combustion is comparatively low, therefore they do not so quickly destroy the interior of the rifle, and the barrel remains cooler during quick firing. As an example of the last-named class *Rifleite*, and of the former kind *Cordite* may be taken. *Ballistite* holds an intermediate position, as it is principally composed of nitro-cellulose with only a small percentage of nitro-glycerine. Two of the principal advantages accruing from the use of concentrated powders are (1) the great power that can be stored in a small cartridge case, and (2) the considerable reduction in recoil as compared with black powder.

Projectiles—Almost every sportsman holds a different opinion as to the kind of bullet that should be employed on big game. Some hold that a 4-bore elongated bullet weighing 1,880 grs., as propelled by 12 drs. of black powder, is the proper projectile to use. The muzzle velocity of such a bullet is about 1,330 feet per second, and the striking energy at short ranges about 7,000 foot pounds. Others are in favour of a 4-bore spherical bullet weighing 1,250 grs. This projectile when propelled by 12 drs. of black powder would have a muzzle velocity of about 1,460 feet per second, and a striking energy of nearly 6,000 foot pounds. Some sportsmen of experience consider that an 8-bore "Paradox" bullet is powerful enough for anything in the way of dangerous game, for at ordinary sporting range it gives such a smashing blow that the animal is killed or turned over at once; a consideration of much importance when an infuriated animal is charging. The 10-bore brass case "Paradox" is almost as powerful as the foregoing, for as it is practically a 9-bore, the projectile used is only slightly inferior in weight and smashing power, whilst the arm itself is considerably lighter. At the trial of an 8-bore "Paradox" ball and shot gun made by the editor of the *Field* some few years ago, six bullets were placed within a space measuring $1\frac{3}{8}$ in. by $2\frac{3}{16}$ in. the range being fifty yards. The charge used was 10 drs. of Curtis and Harvey's No. 6 grain powder and a hardened cylindro-conoidal bullet of 1,150 grains. The weight of this particular gun was 14 lb., and length of barrel 28 in.

8-Bore Paradox Bullet. (Steel bullet coated with lead.) Cut out of an elephant.

Some sportsmen prefer to have heavy bullets made with a hardened steel point so as to obtain great penetration; others choose a hollow-pointed bullet that will expand on striking, thus expending the whole of its energy in shock. The general consensus of opinion being that an 8-bore, or the No. 10 brass case bullet of the "Paradox" type of weapon is the most satisfactory projectile to use on dangerous game at any range within one hundred yards.

A ·577 bullet weighing 591 grains and propelled by 164 grains of black powder is largely used by those still preferring black powder. It is particularly suited for shooting the largest kinds of African deer, as well as lion, tiger, and giraffe, and even heavier game such as elephant, rhinoceros, buffalo and other Indian and African large game. The muzzle velocity of this bullet is about 1,660 feet per second, and the striking energy about 3,600 foot-pounds. The smaller ·500 bullet weighs 444 grs., and propelled by 138 grs. of powder it has a muzzle velocity of 1,780 feet per second, and a striking energy of 3,134 foot-pounds. A bullet of this kind is suitable for smaller and less dangerous game than that before mentioned. Both the ·577 and the ·500 bullets are occasionally used

·577 CARTRIDGE.

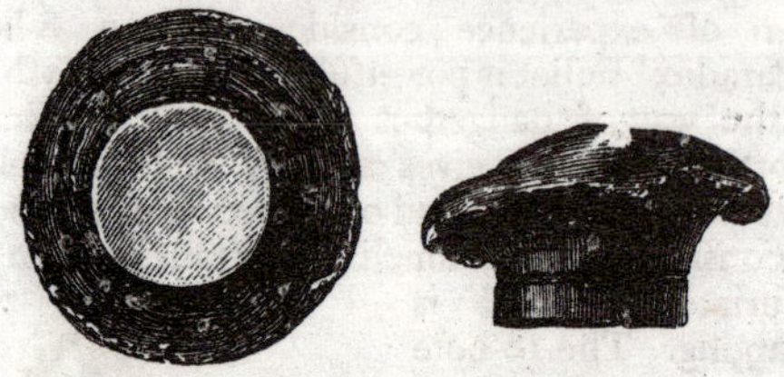

·577 BULLETS. (Cut out of an elephant.)

with a copper envelope, which, by preventing deformation on striking, adds greatly to their penetrative power. A few years ago the ·450 and the ·400 "express" bullets were in great favour, but they are now being superseded by the ·303 Lee-Metford with a nickel envelope, and the ·256 Mannlicher with a steel envelope. These bullets on account of their extreme velocities possess enormous striking energies. For instance, the ·303 with a muzzle velocity of about 2,000 feet per second, has a striking energy of about 1,907 foot-pounds, although the bullet only weighs 215 grs. The ·256 Mannlicher bullet with a muzzle velocity of 2,456 feet per second has a striking energy of 2,070 foot-pounds with a bullet weighing only 155 grains. When these high speed bullets are made to expand on striking, they are very effective against deer and other game not requiring so very weighty a blow to kill them. Undoubtedly

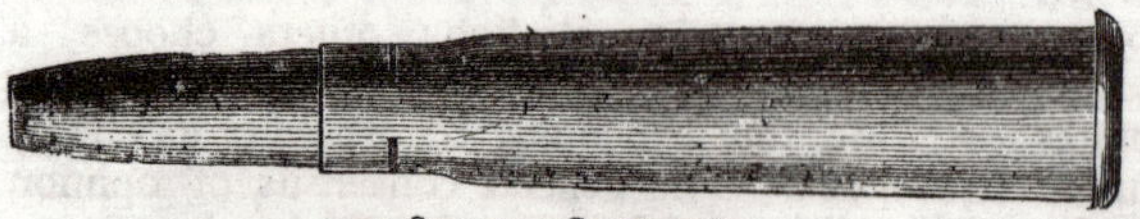

·303 SPORTING CARTRIDGE.

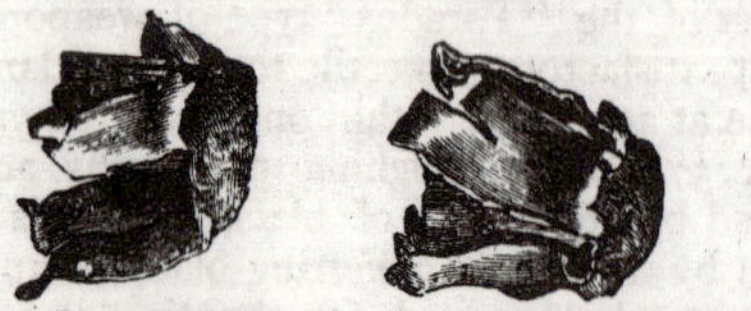

·303 SPORTING BULLET. (Cut out of red deer.)

big game have been killed with projectiles of this class, but apart from the consideration of danger to the sportsman, the chief objection to their employment for the work is the fact that an immense amount of wounding must be done when shooting big game with very small bullets. Notwithstanding the high velocities attained by these small-bore projectiles, their shock-giving properties are not such as to insure the immediate collapse of the larger game, unless hit in heart or brain.

The bullets in general use for rook and rabbit shooting are the ·295, ·250, or the ·220, but most sportsmen are of opinion that the ·250 is the smallest bullet that should be used for rabbits.

The following table gives the weights of these bullets with their powder charges:—

WEIGHT OF BULLET.	CHARGE OF POWDER.
·295, hollow-pointed, 80 grs.	10 grs.
·295, solid, 80 grs.	10 ,,
·250, ,, 56 ,,	7 ,,
·220, ,, short, 30 grs.	3 ,,
·220, ,, long, 30 ,,	4 ,,
·220, ,, extra long, 40 grs.	5 ,,

Cartridge Cases—For rifles, of whatever bore, these should be of brass and solid drawn. For ball and shot guns of the "Paradox" type it is permissible to use paper cases if thought desirable. The selection and mixing of metals for the metallic cases requires the utmost care to insure a high degree of elasticity in the finished cartridge case, so that after it has been expanded by the explosion to fit the chamber of the rifle it will resume its original dimensions, or nearly so. If this important point is not attended to, difficulties will arise with the extraction of the empty cases. When, however, the cases are made of suitable metal they may be resized and reloaded repeatedly without fear of their jamming in the chamber. The cap-dome in the base of the cartridge case is made to suit the nature of the powder to be used. Some have a large or small central flash-hole, whilst others are provided with two or more flash-holes which are placed round the apex of the dome. The percussion caps are also made suitable for the different powders. Some powders, such, for instance, as black, merely require a heating flash; whereas smokeless powders, especially those of the concentrated type, require a special cap composition. The question of percussion caps is at the present time a very vexed one, the igniting agent not having received the attention it deserves in face of repeated issues of new or improved powders.

Wadding—In most cases the wadding made of soft felt and saturated with grease is to be preferred for rifle ammunition, but a grease-proof wad should, in every instance, be interposed between it and the powder. In many kinds of rifle cartridge, the felt wad is dispensed with and a wad formed of a mixture of bees'-wax and tallow, with a thin jute wad to prevent the grease injuring the powder, is used in its place. No wadding whatever is used with the ·303 Lee-Metford and the ·256 Mannlicher, the bullet being made large enough in diameter to act as its own gas check.

H. F. PHILLIPS.

ANGLING—Definition of the Term— Although there may be considerable doubt as to the exact origin of the term, "Angling" may be defined as the art of fishing with rod, line, and hook. Even the derivation of the word is a matter of dispute, but whether it be from the Latin, Greek, or Dutch, we may safely assume that the hook is always indicated as indispensable for the catching of fish. One of the recently published dictionaries describes Angling as "fishing with an angle." About this there is a charming vagueness which leaves abundant room for the exercise of private judgment.

History—In the voluminous and ever-increasing literature of Angling a vast variety of interesting speculation has been compassed as to the history of the art. There are well-known passages in the Old Testament which are quoted as proof that the ancients were accustomed to fish with hook and line, if not with rod; and inscriptions and drawings recovered from unearthed cities leave no doubt that the Greeks, Egyptians, and Romans included Angling amongst their occupations or pastimes. The Egyptians must have brought their practice of the art to considerable perfection, for amongst the wonderful relics excavated from the tombs by Professor Flinders Petrie are well-preserved examples of fish-hooks of admirable shape and make, and in general characteristics not unlike the Limerick pattern beloved by salmon fishers in the present day. Here, again, is suggested food for fancy, and if there is no evidence (as some have alleged there is) that Tubal Cain was the first manufacturer of fish-hooks, and that one of Noah's sons was the first fly-dresser, there is no living person who can authoritatively affirm otherwise. The supporting argument that fish were the only outside animals which survived the flood is, to say the least, ingenious.

The old-world fishing must have been a matter of honest and every-day pot-hunting. It would first become a calling, and then a science. However, early in civilisation Angling was evidently practised as a sport, and there are oft-quoted passages from Oppian that might be, with little alteration, adapted in describing a fight to-day with a big salmon or pike in a British stream.

Older Literature—The character and progress of Angling amongst the ancients are too much matters of conjecture to justify more than a passing allusion; but we are on firm ground in the period which may be said to be represented by the legendary Dame Juliana Barnes, whose treatise was the first published work upon fishing, although it would seem that the earliest known reference to Angling in England is a brief passage in a tract, entitled *Piers Fulham*, supposed to have been written about the year 1420. The *Treatyse of Fysshynge wyth an Angle* goes, however, into particulars, and shows that fishermen of the day were familiar with the use of rod, line, hook, leads, floats, and fishing boats. The Romans undoubtedly knew something about artificial flies, and used them, but it is believed that fly fishing was practised in this country in the fifteenth century, and the aforesaid lady of St. Albans gives a respectable list of the flies to be used in successive fishing months, her season very reasonably beginning with March instead of February, as with us. This list of flies, however, only refers to trout and grayling. In the next century Leonard Mascall published a book on fishing with hook and line, and it contains much practical wisdom about fish culture. The angling pictures were taken from Dame Barnes. Early in the seventeenth century a published angling poem by "J. D." (John Dennys) teemed with sound advice and instruction to anglers. In these old books the development of Angling may be traced, and they indicate that the sport was well established amongst the English people. In the same period Gervase Markham issued his *Art of Angling*, which is to a great extent a rendering into prose of "John Dennys, Esq."

Walton—Walton and his contemporaries may be taken to represent another period, in which the anglers were good all-round sportsmen. More than that, not only Cotton's contribution to the *Compleat Angler*, but Barker's little book which was published before Walton's immortal classic, furnishes internal evidence of proficiency in the dressing of flies and use of the fly rod. Walton probably took not a little of his information from Barker, who appears to have been the first English writer to mention the use of the winch in fishing. The old woodcut illustrations of this period represent the rod without the winch, but some sort of a reel (or as they used to call it, winder) was not unknown to the few. After Walton there is not, for a while, much in literature to indicate in what degree Angling developed; but an active and cultured English Angling School arose soon after the opening of the nineteenth century, and Salter, Davy, Hofland, and others were amongst its head masters. The revolution brought about by steam and cheap literature gave an impetus to our play, no less than to our work, and Angling advanced with leaps and bounds, foremost amongst the leaders of the more modern period being "Ephemera," Francis Francis, Rooper, Pennell, and many others in England; Stoddart and Stewart in Scotland; Newland and Maxwell in Ireland. Anglers are now a great host; their sport has its periodical press; a modern community is not complete without its fishing club, and Westwood and Satchell's *Bibliotheca Piscatoria*, which was published in 1883, catalogues over three thousand works more or less concerning fish and fishing.

Fly Fishing—Although in matters of sport comparisons should never be invidious, by common consent there may be legitimate distinctions. Hence fly fishing is universally regarded as the highest form of angling, and it is a claim which is not advanced without sufficient reason. For example, it appeals most of all to the artistic and imaginative fancy; it demands special knowledge; it requires delicate skill; its exercise is at once costly, and beset with difficulties of an exceptional nature.

On behalf of fly fishing it is further to be said that it is applied to the choicest of our fresh-water fishes, since members of the Salmonidæ, which are, technically speaking, the game fishes of this country, head the catalogue of species which are habitually lured by the artificial fly. These require the purest and best preserved streams for their habitation; sluggish and open waters are not their natural home, though they often do maintain an existence therein. The proper habitat of the game fishes is all that is brightest and best of our rivers and lakes; it is the stream which runs crystal clear and pursues a joyous course that is the ideal home of salmon, trout, and grayling; and not the least of the fascinations which make fly fishing an absorbing pursuit is the association it brings as a matter of course with the most picturesque phases of natural scenery. These are amongst the reasons why fly fishing is always lauded and magnified to an extent not possible with other branches of angling. It is often urged, indeed, with ample justification, that the fly fisher is by his sport brought face to face with sylvan beauties seldom visited by others, and that in his progress in or upon the water, and along its banks, he explores exquisite nooks and corners which even the searching eye of the wandering artist has not the opportunity of discovering.

Salmon—While fly fishing is considered the highest form of the art of angling, it is to be remembered that it is but a section of a general sport, and that it has distinctions within itself offering endless variety of attraction. In glancing at these, the salmon must come first into consideration. With some sportsmen fly fishing means salmon or sea-trout fishing only, just as the word "fish" in Scotland is an exclusive term by which *Salmo salar* alone is honoured. In trout fishing there have of late years grown up definite schools, but the noble sport of salmon fishing does not admit of much divergence from the settled practices of our forefathers; with the exception of developments here and there, not necessarily improvements, in the details of rods, lines, and artificial flies, the general principles of salmon fishing remain what they were fifty or sixty years ago, when there were eminent masters whose wisdom is embalmed in the literature of their day, and whose prowess has never been surpassed.

There are, it is true, other methods than fly fishing for the capture of salmon, and these have in the present day, perhaps, increased rather than diminished. By the fly fisher pure and simple they are viewed with disfavour. But there are excuses to be advanced. It is not always that a salmon will be in the humour to rise to a fly; and there are rivers, of which the Trent, in the Midlands, is the most conspicuous example, where salmon habitually decline to be taken by the artificial fly. They have been tempted with every known composition of fur and feather, yet to no purpose. Even in what are known as the sporting salmon rivers, for which enormous rents are paid, there are pools that are apparently by nature "sulky"; the fish run into them and lie there, and may be caught by spinning baits, prawns, or worms, but as a rule they refuse the fly. Perhaps if salmon fishers would oftener try the experiment of sinking their fly to somewhere near the bottom they might be more successful, but it is not easy to persuade the purist that the wrapping of lead round the body of his Jock Scott or Durham Ranger, or the adoption of any other unusual device for taking the line down to the floor of the pool, consorts with the honourable canons of sport.

The apparatus for salmon fishing and some other methods of angling will be treated of in their alphabetical order as they occur in future numbers; at present we are concerned with the general principles, and the mention of such matters as spinning, prawning, and worming for salmon may be dismissed with the remark that they are not in themselves illegal, that they are operations requiring great skill, and that, under certain conditions, they are legitimate practices if conducted in sportsmanlike manner. The rod is the item of the fly-fisher's equipment of highest importance, and he should aim at selecting one suitable to the size of his hand, the strength of his wrist and the length of his arm, the inches of his stature and his physical strength; he should be equally careful to attach to a reel, in balance with the rod, a line that, being neither too heavy nor too light, will work in harmony with both. These are first principles, and it may be added that the line or collar of gut attached to the winch line should be of a substance in proportion to the rest of the tackle as well as suitable to the kind of fishing to be engaged in; and that the artificial fly should be suited to the character of the water upon which it will be cast. These admonitions are the A B C of the game, but it is necessary to put them in plain words, for one often meets brother sportsmen who have fished long enough to have earned the description of experienced, yet who make their recreation a burden and their sport a failure by non-observance of just such primary considerations.

Choice of Rod—Spite of much written and oral advice, the man himself must be the judge of the rod that will suit him. The discussions which are conducted as to the relative merits of whole cane, split cane, or greenheart rods, should not persuade the purchaser to

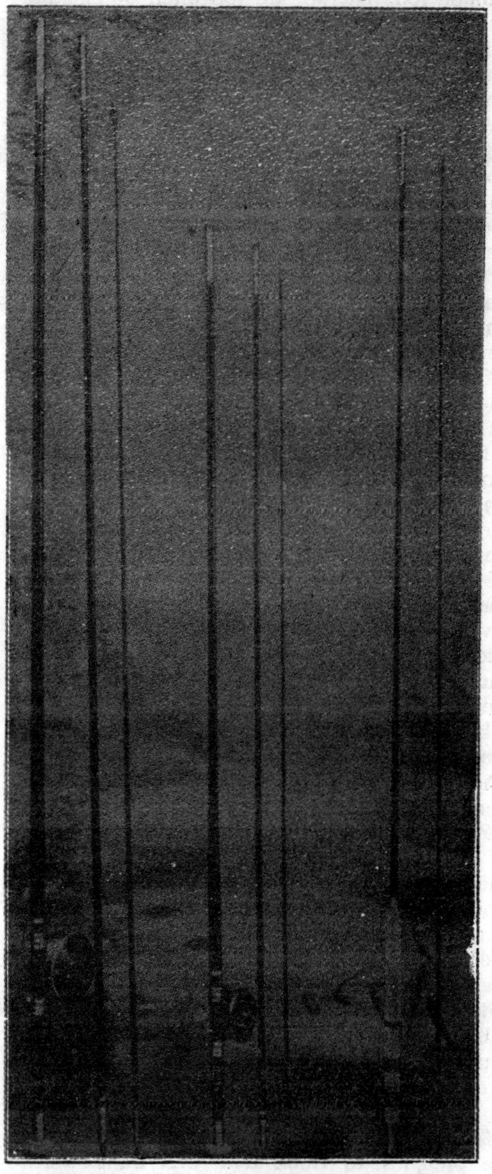

SALMON ROD. 14-FT. TWO-HANDED ROD.* TROUT ROD.

* [The Editors have to thank Mr. C. S. Cummins for assistance in illustrating this article.]

overlook the paramount importance of obtaining the thing that pleases, not his ethical notions, but his hand and arm. In the matter of rods we have learned something from American sportsmen; no longer is it insisted, as a hard and fast law admitting of no amending clause, that the salmon-rod must be eighteen or twenty feet in length. The longer the rod the more power, of course, in the casting of the line, in its recovery from the water, and in the command of a fish when the hook has been driven home. There are, obviously, many advantages which may be claimed for a long salmon rod, but they are too often obtained at the cost of excessive labour. When the angler is either fishing from the bank or wading in the stream, a rod of seventeen feet is, in these progressive days, considered to be adequate for all the purposes of salmon-fishing, and many British sportsmen are adopting the practice of their comrades across the Atlantic, and are content in boat fishing to use a rod of fifteen or sixteen feet; but it is strictly essential that the materials and workmanship should be of super-excellence. A length of line sufficient for all practical purposes can be cast by a rod of this description, and as for the playing of a heavy salmon, if the smaller rod entails upon the captor another ten minutes or quarter of an hour in the struggle, the eager sportsman will not complain of this as a serious hardship. There are well-known salmon rivers where angling is only possible from a boat, and if this is not the most scientific way of catching a salmon with the fly, it is largely practised, with most satisfactory results, and with the knowledge that if the operation of casting becomes in time monotonous, there are compensations in the minimum of tax levied upon physical exertion and mental excitement. The angler, however, whose enthusiasm is most warranted, is he who dons a suit of waders and, with well-spiked brogues, betakes him to the river bed, studying the places where salmon would naturally be found, regulating the length of his cast to suit the situation, and when fortunate, following his fish up or down, fighting him from terra firma. This sort of salmon-fishing offers the chances of many a moving incident on land and water, of perils and obstacles, of the wit of man pitted against the wonderful instinct and pluck of the gamest of fishes; and he is not to be laughed at as rhapsodical who avouches that he would rather hook one salmon in a contest so fought out than half a dozen from the tranquil limitations of a boat. But boat-fishing, like the use of baits other than artificial fly, is at times a necessity.

The British pessimist is occasionally heard to assert in those very desponding moments when he pretends to think that everything worth having is played out in this weary world, that our salmon-fishing, amongst other great institutions, has gone to the dogs; but, as a matter of fact, in our rivers that are properly preserved and managed, this particular sport, taking one season with another, and considering all circumstances, holds its own with that of any other country. For matters of practical comparison, we have to deal with Norway and Canada. In the early years of the century—when Sir Hyde Parker wrote that he sometimes had so much sport with the salmon as to be indifferent whether he fished any more for a week—phenomenal bags were made in Scandinavia, but we seldom hear of anything like such wonders in these days. In the rivers that are least harried by the nets, Norway salmon-fishing is still fine in favourable seasons, but the old flavour is gone. In Canada, also, the results are on the whole enough to satisfy an average appetite for sport; but given a typical river like the Highland Dee, where the riparian owners have wisely taken measures to secure a free ascent of fish from the tidal waters, and taking into account the duration of the season with its spring, summer, and autumn runs of salmon and grilse, there is no better sport in the world, although the size of the fish may leave something to be desired. The legislation for salmon-fishing, which has long ago reached bewildering proportions, has been generally in the interests of the netsmen at the mouth, rather than for the sportsmen in the upper waters. The observer, indeed, who formed an opinion solely from the persistence with which in legislative action the sporting is sacrificed to the commercial interest in the matter of salmon-fishing, would not be much out of order in defending Napoleon's dictum that we are a nation of shopkeepers. The worst drawback to the salmon-fisher in the British Islands is the caprice of the climate, with its alternations or long spells of drought and flood. Over-netting in the tidal waters is also the curse of nearly all the good salmon streams of the United Kingdom, and without early remedy by Act of Parliament even the commercial interests will be ruined by greed. A painfully notorious illustration of a salmon river temporarily ruined for the angler is the Blackwater in Ireland; once the desire of all sportsmen, it is now practically worthless for rod and line. [*See* SALMON-FISHING.]

Sea-Trout—For the main requirements of legal phraseology and official regulations salmon and sea-trout are one; and to the angler the latter is the former in miniature. *Salmo trutta* is angled for in the same way as his bigger relative, but with every item of tackle correspondingly reduced in dimensions. A double-handed rod of fourteen feet, with line, winch, and gut-cast in character, and small flies of bright dressings, present a kind of connecting link between the strong tackle that should be designed to deal with a forty or fifty pound salmon, and the dainty accoutrements of the practitioner who devotes his attentions to the non-migratory Salmonidæ. Sea-trout angling, when the fish are running freely from the sea, and sporting at their best in the streams and pools which they affect as regularly as the seasons revolve, is superlatively delightful; there is no trying labour in handling the rod, and the sea-trout is probably the most sporting of all British fishes in his leaps and bounds, in his undying determination to yield only with his life, and in his bold advances when the right humour is upon him.

Trout—Fly fishing for fresh-water trout (as *Salmo fario* and his kind are termed as a matter of convenience rather than accuracy, since the migratory fish seek the fresh waters, and the non-migratory often drop down to salt) is the pursuit of the many amongst the educated classes; and amongst them there has of late years grown up or developed what is known as the dry-fly school. The word developed is suggested because probably so long as men have fished for trout with the artificial fly, it has been used both wet and dry. In the case of salmon-angling, it is not certain in what light a fish regards the artificial fly. Opinions differ, and doctors disagree upon the question, but the popular idea is that it is taken for some creature pursuing its erratic movement in the water. The acceptance of this theory, however, raises the very vexed question of whether salmon are total abstainers from food in fresh water, and its rejection throws upon us the onus of believing that the mighty boil of the fish is merely playfulness, or an angry attack upon an object which has caught its attention and aroused its irritation. In preparing the fly for, and offering it to, the bonnie brown trout, however, there is substantial foundation to work upon. With many of the movements of the salmon we are unfamiliar; the dark, swirling, heavy, eddying waters of a typical salmon pool forbid observation of its tenants, except when they condescend to break the surface at uncertain intervals. The representative inland trout stream, on the contrary, should be clear and sparkling, flowing over alternating deeps and shallows; and while the life history of *Salmo salar* has yet to be written in its entirety and with certainty, we have little if anything to learn of the common trout from beginning to end. He is under our eye from cradle to grave. Although insect food is not by any means his exclusive, or even principal, diet, it is his choicest dish, and his preference for it is probably only limited by the everlasting question of supply and demand. There are rivers once famous for their good trout-fishing that are losing, or have entirely lost, their reputation. The trout still exist in even larger numbers than in the palmy days of sport, but the insect life has, for reasons which are difficult to define, almost entirely disappeared, and the stream so changed is no more praised as "free rising." With the steady hatch of ephemeridæ a thing of the past, the trout fall into other habits. Though, however, the olive-dun or March brown may float down in single spies instead of battalions, the old instinct remains; the trout will rise to the fly when his keen eye detects the airy form sailing upon the surface overhead. The angler is therefore able to proceed upon tolerably sure knowledge; he knows that his fly must be presented to the fish on the understanding that it is to be in all essentials a colourable imitation of the insects hatched in that particular water, or the land-born flies that are blown to their doom from the sedges and overhanging bushes. In this respect the trout-fisher is a class to himself. There are purists also here; while there are salmon-fishers who never handled a trout-rod, thinking it beneath their standard and notice, so are there fly-fishers for trout who will have nothing to do with what they deem the rougher and coarser wielding of the big salmon rod, with its heavy line and strong cast.

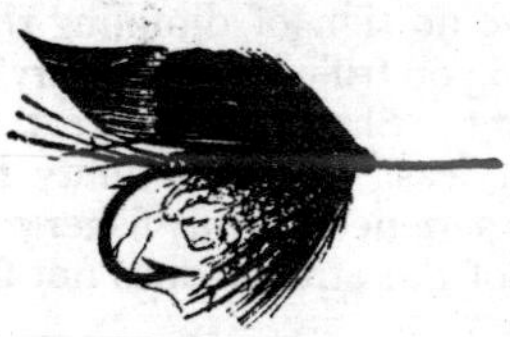

LOCH FLY.

Eyed Hooks—Until comparatively recent times, fly-fishing for trout signified the use of a cast of two or three or more winged or hackled flies, to be cast on speculation and allowed to travel down with the stream, more or less submerged. This is what is now classified as wet-fly fishing. It might be imagined from the prominence given to the contentions and ideas of the new dry-fly school in periodical and permanent angling literature, that all the world is at the present time a dry-fly fisher; yet the dry-fly school, though its members include the most eminent of anglers, is a comparatively limited one in numbers, and its history may be briefly told. A few years ago Mr. H. S. Hall, then, as now, mathematical master at Clifton College, sent a communication to an angling journal advocating the use of artificial flies dressed upon hooks with upturned metal eyes, to which the end of the collar might be knotted, as a preferable plan to the attachment of gut lengths as an essential part of the dressing of the fly. Eyed hooks had undoubtedly been known before in one shape or another, but the universal practice was to tie the fly to a length of gut. The advantages claimed for the eyed hook were: (1) that fewer flies were whipped off in casting; (2) that the liability of the gut attachment at the head of the fly to fray and break was

SALMON FLY.

obviated; (3) that the angler could always make certain that the even continuity of his collar or casting line was not marred by the juncture at the critical portion of a strand of gut out of due proportion; (4) that the fly was always ready for use on gut which could be kept in a proper condition to receive it; (5) that a stock of eyed hook flies sufficient for a day or a week might be kept in a box in a single pocket, and preserved in ease and safety from one year to another without danger of treachery from rotten gut. The communication thus published roused a widespread interest, and kindred ideas that had been previously entertained by a few anglers were gradually made known.

FLOATING FLY.

Dry-Fly School—Out of the discussion arose the doctrine of the education of trout. The chalk streams fishers laid special emphasis upon the virtues of the dry-fly as an antidote to the growing difficulty of angling. They insisted that in rivers where the trout used to rise with regularity and confidence, and where sport might be reckoned upon as a tolerable certainty, the fish had become shy, suspicious, and in point of fact educated. The old-fashioned methods of fishing with a cast of artificial flies for such unnatural trout were deprecated as obsolete, and the superior attractions of a single artificial fly, made very small, dressed with upstanding wings, cast with a scientific calculation of direction and force never dreamt of previously—the *sine qua non* being to deliver the imitation fly in the exact presentment of the natural insect, and in a manner that would ensure its floating upon the stream as if it were the real thing—were urged with eloquent enthusiasm. It was in this way that the dry-fly school began to acquire a name of its own; converts were made, and are still giving in adherence; and one of the results has been the evolution of an entirely different character of artificial fly. The dry-fly school of angling is said to include among its members some dogmatists who will scarcely admit the wet-fly brethren to *brevet* rank, but there is room for all and reason on both sides.

In mountain-born waters, like the trout streams of Scotland, Ireland, and Wales, the fascinating old-fashioned style of fishing with a cast of flies rules as if nothing had happened; the rapid rivers must be fished in that way, and the master fly-fisher for trout is the man who, regulating his methods to the requirements of the day, the water, and their ever varying moods, can adapt himself to circumstances as an adept of all styles.

It is one of the leading instructions of the dry-fly master that the disciple shall remain inactive, possessing his soul in patience, and standing by until the trout are seen to be visibly rising at, and taking, the fly sailing down stream. On Itchen, Test, Kennet, and any other typical chalk stream, the angler may accordingly be observed, for hours together, watching for the rise. The wet-fly fisherman, with his cast of assorted winged, hackled, or spider patterns, like his forefathers, arriving at the waterside, comes into action at once, animated by the hope that the trout, if they give no sign of dimpling ring, are busy below, feeding on trifles borne at varying depths in the current. Should they treat his flies with disdain, at least no opportunity has been wasted. The experienced dry-fly fisherman, where the character of the stream does not forbid, stations himself below the fish, kneeling on the bank to lessen the chances of scaring the shy trout; his aim is to cast his single floating-fly three or four inches above the mentally marked position of a rising fish, and to do this accurately at the first cast. Simple as the operation may appear, it can only be done to perfection by the exercise of long experience and extreme skill. The casting of the line so that the floating-fly shall drop at the precise point aimed at and at once assume the position and appearance of the natural insect, and to do this when and where it will secure the attention of, but without alarming, the alert trout below, is one of the triumphant feats of fly fishing. The

WAITING FOR THE RISE.

whisking of the fly through the air by backward and forward wavings of the rod, and the length of line often necessary for reaching a distant fish, keep the angler in healthy exercise if the rise is protracted. The former tax upon the strength may, however, be lessened, though not quite avoided, by the modern practice of anointing the fly with odourless paraffin, or some other unguent, by a touch of the camel's-hair brush on hackles and wings; a couple of flourishes will then suffice for drying the fly.

The wet-fly fisherman, who cares for none of these things, has the privilege, at any rate, of being constantly on the move, always hopeful that at least one of his flies will find a trout; while in the progress of fishing steadily up or down the stream he is able to change his scene with his chances at every hour. The dry-fly fisherman was a South of England product, and was the effect of which the educated trout of the chalk streams was the cause. In other parts of the three kingdoms, the wet-fly fisherman is the rule, but it is a rule the exceptions to which are becoming more and more numerous. [*See* TROUT and CHAR.]

Artificial flies, either for salmon or the smaller game fish, will be treated of hereafter. [*See* SALMON and SEA-TROUT, FLY DRESSING.]

A general reference to fly fishing does not end with mention of salmon, *salmo trutta*, and fresh-water trout. The grayling must have passing attention. This is a fish which, with many undoubted sporting qualities and one special virtue, is not always popular with trout fishermen. Yet it is one of the freest of surface-feeders, and has all the qualities of a fly-fisher's pet. Having an adipose fin, the grayling is, like the smelt, classed among the *Salmonidæ*, but in bodily appearance there is no other resemblance. It, however, gives the same kind of sport, with, generally speaking, the same methods in fly fishing; and the special virtue hinted at above is that, when trout fishing ceases at the end of September, the grayling is at its prime, and may be fished for throughout the winter. [*See* GRAYLING.]

Besides grayling there are a few of the summer spawners, such as dace, bleak, rudd, roach and chub, which, for want of bettter, are not unworthy the attention of the fly-fisher, the first four with small flies, and the last with large palmers, imitations of moths, bees, and beetles. Only in the hot months, however, is the sport at all worth the trouble of attempting their capture with the tackle intended for higher game. [*See* THAMES FISHING.]

Spinning and Trolling—These may be regarded as synonymous terms since, in the country south of the Trent, the second has fallen into disuse. In Scotland and Ireland, when fishing men talk about trolling, they mean the use of the spinning bait, especially as practised from a boat, and in the majority of instances the reference will be merely to the somewhat mechanical process of trailing from the stern. Trolling, however, is a word once of definite signification to English pike-fishers. It was known two centuries ago—was in use, probably, long before what we understand as spinning was in vogue. One of the quaintest of the older angling books is the venerable Nobbes' *Art of Trolling*. Nobbes was a master of the now discredited method. Its main feature was the dead gorge bait, which is now discountenanced by all respectable angling societies and sportsmanlike persons, except when used as a means of warrantable destruction. As the process, therefore, will not be further described it may here be stated that the bait employed is a dead roach, dace, or gudgeon, through whose body, from mouth to tail, is passed a leaded wire permitting the issue from the caudal fin of a short length of gimp looped at the end for fixture to the reel line. A rank hook, either a double or single, welded into the lead, slightly protrudes from the side of the bait's mouth. The small dead fish thus armed is cast at first close to the bank upon which the angler is standing, allowed to sink head first to the bottom, the angler pulling in short lengths of line in successive coils, working the bait up and down slowly in the water. The silvery fish is thus represented as swimming between and out of weeds, or as darting in spasmodic jerks from the bottom to the top, now sinking and now ascending. It is a deadly method of attracting the marauder lying *perdu* in the subaqueous copses. The pike seizes its prey across the middle of the body, twists it round into its bristling jaws and swallows (or gorges) it head foremost. The art, such as it was, of trolling, afforded wholesome recreation to generations of innocent pike-fishers, who never supposed they were sinning against the light. The secret of it was to ensure the complete gorging of the bait before putting any sort of check upon the line. The pike would sometimes seize the bait with a strong snap, which left the troller in no doubt of the fact, but very frequently the check would be so slight that the unaccustomed hand might suppose the sinking and roving bait was entangled with weed; if he then tightened the line the chances were strong that he would scare his pike. The custom, therefore, was to allow the fish to run unchecked until it stopped of its own accord; this it would presently do in pursuance of its habit of pausing to pouch or gorge. Fishermen used to time this period of expectancy ten minutes by the watch. When the bait was gorged, the gullet of the pike would so tightly encase the bait that the strong, protruding hooks entered its vitals. The victim came in with little fight, and there was no possibility of restoring it to the water after such treatment. Within recent times, as the stock of pike diminished in rivers where they were tolerated for sport, an outcry was raised against the murderous gorge-hook, the principal objection being that under-sized fish were ruthlessly and unnecessarily slaughtered. In many waters the use of the gorge hook, as in the Thames, is therefore prohibited. With this passing description of a method which is now only legitimate in waters where pike are ranked as vermin, and where it is desirable to kill them of all sorts and sizes, we are free to deal with the general subject.

Spinning is the cosmopolitan form of angling. Allowed to rank next to fly fishing as a fine art, it is of wide application, is applied to every description of game fish, is not only popular with the fresh-water angler in Great Britain but with the sea-fisherman who thereby with rod and line obtains spirited sport with such fish as bass, pollack, and mackerel, and is practised by the casual angler in all parts of the globe. Wherever predatory fish are to be found, there the angler may remember the adage in whist, and when in doubt play his trump in the shape of some kind of spinning bait. Mahseer in India, the hucho in Bavaria, the monster trout of the Canadian lakes, the prolific salmon of the Pacific, are alike taken by the spinning rod. The method is capable of varied treatment, and has some of the good points which are enumerated for fly fishing; the spinning man, for example, is not condemned to inactivity in a Windsor chair, or on the camp-stool by the waterside, but like the trout or salmon fisher is in healthy bodily movement during his term of sport. Another recommendation to the hardy sportsman is that spinning for pike affords excellent recreation during the winter months, when all coarse fish are in the height of condition. Even when the grayling rise but seldom to the fly, the pike are in keen humour, in prime colour and form, with appetites often sharpened rather than depressed by the hard frosts and howling north-easters, which put an end to other kinds of sport.

Artificial Baits—The spinning-rod, however, is largely used also for salmon and trout. It is certain that the practice of spinning for salmon has increased during the last quarter of a century; and were all the truth made known, it would be found that many of the bags made upon salmon rivers, and published weekly in the sporting newspapers, are made by the blue phantom, or silver and golden minnow. The principle underlying the art of spinning is to attract the fish by the movement through the water of an object that shall imitate, in shape and action, some form of aquatic life. The artificial baits which have been invented to effect this object are legion. They are of metal, gutta-percha, and of soleskin, in the case of the phantom, which is a collapsible object when out of the water, but a plump imitation of trout, gudgeon, or loach when, set in motion by the spinning-rod, it becomes filled with water. Some of the artificial baits, brightly glittering, or artificially coloured, are armed with fans at the head to ensure the spinning, but these permanent outstanding fixtures are not in unison with the tastes of all anglers; to meet their wishes a very effective pattern of artificial fish is produced, the spin of which is effected by a fixed

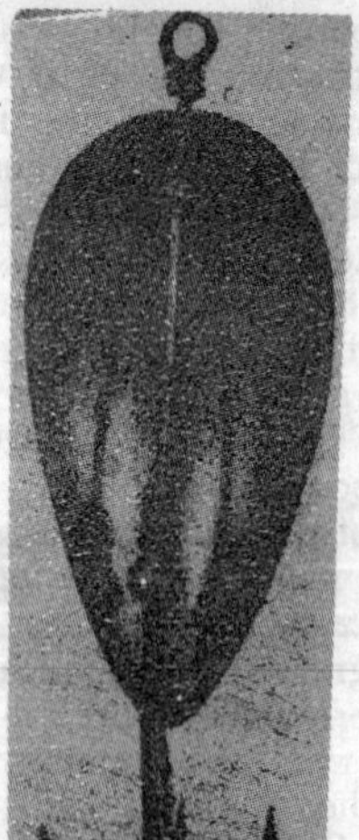

PIKE ROD AND BAR-SPOON.

curvature of the tail. Notwithstanding the host of "notions" which have been placed upon the market as registered or patented inventions, there is probably no better all-round artificial spinning-bait for salmon and pike than the spoon, which spins, as the saying goes, like a flash, is without the complications which often render the ingenious patents useless after a few trials, and which, by the colouring of the inner surface (gold, copper, or even red), presents a brilliantly tempting appearance in the water. In the salmon rivers of Norway, in the estuaries on the Pacific coast, there is no more trusted lure than the spoon. For pike fishing also this rough and ready imitation of a darting fish is most effective, and when the pike run large, a spoon of five inches in length is not a whit oversized. It is maintained that the spoon as a bait for predatory fish was first discovered by accident in the United States, and at the Chicago World's Fair, what was labelled as the first spoon ever used in angling, was exhibited. The rude mother-of-pearl and bone hooks that are used by the South Sea Islanders, and certain devices known to the New Zealand Maories when the white settler first visited them, were the crude originals of the beautifully finished spinning-baits of to-day.

Natural Baits—The small natural fishes upon which the ravenous pike, prowling perch, and dashing trout of our fresh waters largely subsist, are, however, the most reliable baits for general spinning, and for their utilisation there is an ample choice of flights and hooks at the service of the angler. The earlier kinds of spinning flights consisted of two or three sets of strong triangles with perhaps a single hook for insertion in the lip. For salmon or trout such hooks are mounted upon treble or single gut to suit the magnitude of the fish to be caught. The formidable teeth of the pike, and the serrated interior of his gaping mouth, render it necessary, however, to approach him with stronger gear, and the hooks should be fastened to a six-inch length of gimp, or a special adaptation of wire. The two objects which the spinner must primarily keep in view are (1) the employment of swivelled traces and bait fashioned so as to ensure regular spinning, bringing the bait though the water in, as far as possible, a natural course and manner of progression; and (2) regulation of the advancing object at a speed and depth suitable to the habits of the fish and the force, colour, and depth of the water. Spinning, if properly studied, requires intelligent study of the circumstances of the day. In fairly flowing rivers, the current will, in practised hands, like the action of the rod in fly fishing, do much of the work for the angler, while in a lake or dead pool he must rely entirely upon his own dexterity, unless he indulges in the harling or trailing in which the boatmen play a leading part. It must be repeated that the paramount essential is that the bait spins properly. The salmon- or trout-fisher who uses the phantom, spoon, or minnow may reckon upon the encouraging assistance of a lively current, which, in a measure, if he understands how to humour it, will take charge of the bait, and present it in the most perfect manner to the fish over which it travels; when the line is trailed from the stern of a boat a like advantage is ensured by the intelligently-calculated rowing of an experienced boatman. Anglers who have carefully studied the habits of the pike, which is the fish *par excellence* for the spinning-rod, frequently differ in opinion upon one point, viz., is it best that the bait should spin in a straight line, or in a series of jerks and gyrations? In this, as in everything else (notably in wet- and dry-fly fishing), it will be found that the best man in the long run is he who can adapt himself to all conditions. There are times when a pike that will run half-heartedly at the bait which represents a smaller fish moving in a decorously straight track, will rush savagely at the imitation which, by a different fixing of the tackle, is induced to progress in a series of awkward and fantastic evolutions. The theory is that the appearance of a roach swimming at ease was apparently noticed without excitement, while the suggestion that here was a wounded or feeble creature, trying to escape, aroused the sharkish propensities of the wolf of the waters.

The duty devolving upon the angler, any where and at all times, is plain: if one method fails, try another. One of the most important considerations, yet one commonly overlooked in spinning, is the weighting of the bait to correspond with the character of the water fished. The latest tackles devised for spinning with natural baits have been brought to a high state of effectiveness; there are endless contrivances for fastening the hooks to the dead fish, and for concealing the weight necessary for sinking it in its own body. This is without question better than leads, detachable or permanent, affixed a foot or so up the trace; with certain tackles, these are, however, unavoidable, but a double splash is inevitable when the bait is cast forth by the spinning-rod. The bait leaded within itself, on the contrary, may, skilfully treated, be made to fall lightly, with but one disturbance. The detachable lead carries the distinct advantage of enabling the angler to weight his gear to suit the different conditions of water.

Faulty Spinning—Too many spinning men seem to have an idea, if they ever think at all about the matter, that the fish for which they spin are surface or middle-water feeders, and the result is disastrous. Pike lie low, and spring upwards, as their mood finds them. To-day they will not budge for anything but prey that touches their nose; to-morrow they will leap from the deep out of water in pursuit. Mid-water is the happy mean for spinning, but quite close to the bottom is frequently the depth to which the bait should be regulated. There is no more besetting sin in the spinner, above all in the pike-fisher, than to work above the heads of his game. Another mistake frequently made is as to speed. It stands to reason that a fish must be honestly sharp set, and in the true fighting humour, to dart after prey that is scurrying through the water at express speed. The rapid spinner is like the fly fisher who plucks away the fly in over-eager fashion. The accomplished angler always avoids these two dangers, and will never rest until he learns how to weight his bait to a nicety at will, and to accomplish speed upon commonsense principles.

We have mentioned as fish which are systematically caught by spinning, the salmon, trout, pike, perch and sundry sport-yielding sea fish, but at odd times chub, carp, grayling, dace, eels, and barbel are deluded by spinning-hooks fairly taken in their mouths. Barbel are so caught principally in the state of restlessness incidental to recovery from the exhaustion of spawning. At these interesting periods they pack together in the rough water, and it is a daily experience during April and May for Thames trouters, spinning from the weir heads, to have their time and temper wasted by struggles with huge, worthless, out-of-season barbel. The taking of spinning-baits by grayling, and by the minor coarse fish, may be included amongst the things that seldom happen. These remarks upon spinning have of necessity involved frequent mention of salmon, trout, and pike, and it may be added that a so-called spinning-fly has been introduced into salmon fishing; the creation is distinguished by a pair of metal fans at the head of an ordinary salmon-fly, and the trace must be swivelled.

Imitations of small birds cast with spinning or salmon-rod for pike, are often successful in shallow waters, in the late summer months, when the fish are basking among the weeds, but it is only by a stretch of imagination that this method can be described as either fly fishing or spinning. It stands as an independent entry in the methods of pike fishing, and with it may here be mentioned the much practised sport of fishing with live bait upon snap-tackle, by which the fish, struck sharply at the run, is hooked in the mouth, and has therefore the opportunity of return to the water if undersized or out of condition. [*See* PIKE.]

LIVE BAIT TACKLE. ("Jardine Snap.")

Bottom Fishing — In angling, the greatest happiness for the greatest number is yielded by the humbler phase of the sport which has been, not too happily, designated as bottom fishing. The presumption that the plebeian denizens of the lake, river, and pond feed entirely upon the bottom is but partly warranted. As has been intimated on a previous page, some of the so-called "coarse" fish are surface feeders, and the dace is so much so, that it might almost be considered a link between the game fish proper, and those which are specially treated in the Act of Parliament bearing the name of Mr. Mundella, who took charge of the measure in the year when the Fresh-water Fisheries Act became law. The remarkable increase in the number of anglers has chiefly been amongst the wage-earning classes, who fish in the more primitive methods which may be followed at a minimum of expense and expenditure of time. The schoolboy who is born with the instinct of angling first puts his predilections into practice by a simple wand, a length of string, a painted float, a shotted line, and a cheap hook that is nevertheless all-sufficient for impaling the wriggling worm or pellet of paste, and for swishing out behind him the perch and roach which constitute his juvenile triumphs. The unpoisoned rivers in the vicinity of towns are still well stocked with roach and dace, with barbel, chub, bream, and gudgeon; and in the lakes and ponds there are stores of tench and carp, which are also occasionally found in rivers.

The apparatus used in coarse-fishing is cheaper and more simple than that necessary for the more aristocratic branches of the sport, and that is why, since the diffusion of cheap literature and the facilities for travel established by railways, the artisans of Great Britain have in their tens of thousands become patient disciples of Izaak Walton. All anglers are called Waltonians, but it is doubtful whether the old man knew much about fly fishing or spinning. He, however, was an adept in all-round fishing, and his memorable idyll owes its charms to his love for, and knowledge of, angling for coarse fish. The crowds of men and youths who go out of London every Sunday for the Thames or Lea, or from the large provincial towns to the rivers which flow near their homes, may not have read their Izaak Walton, but in the main they follow the directions which he laid down, and which have been adopted from generation to generation with very little alteration. To those who never personally angled for roach in the Thames or Trent, or for bream in the slow-running Midland rivers, the recreation, with its modest appliances, may seem ridiculously simple, yet in its degree there is as much skill required for success with these essentially shy species as with those which have been previously considered.

Rods and Lines—The most general form of bottom-fishing is for roach and dace. These gregarious fish shift their ground in search of food, cruising wide in summer, and retiring to the deeps as the weeds which supply them with food disappear before autumn floods and winter frosts. Their established haunts are the angler's "swims," and by the aid of ground-bait the fish may, when they intermittently rove, be soon attracted back. All fish are easily frightened by disturbance or unaccustomed objects on the bank, but the roach is pre-eminently shy, and to be an adept in catching it demands long experience and infinite patience. There are also schools of bottom-fishermen, and they are in the nature of old foundations. Thames, Trent, and Lea have

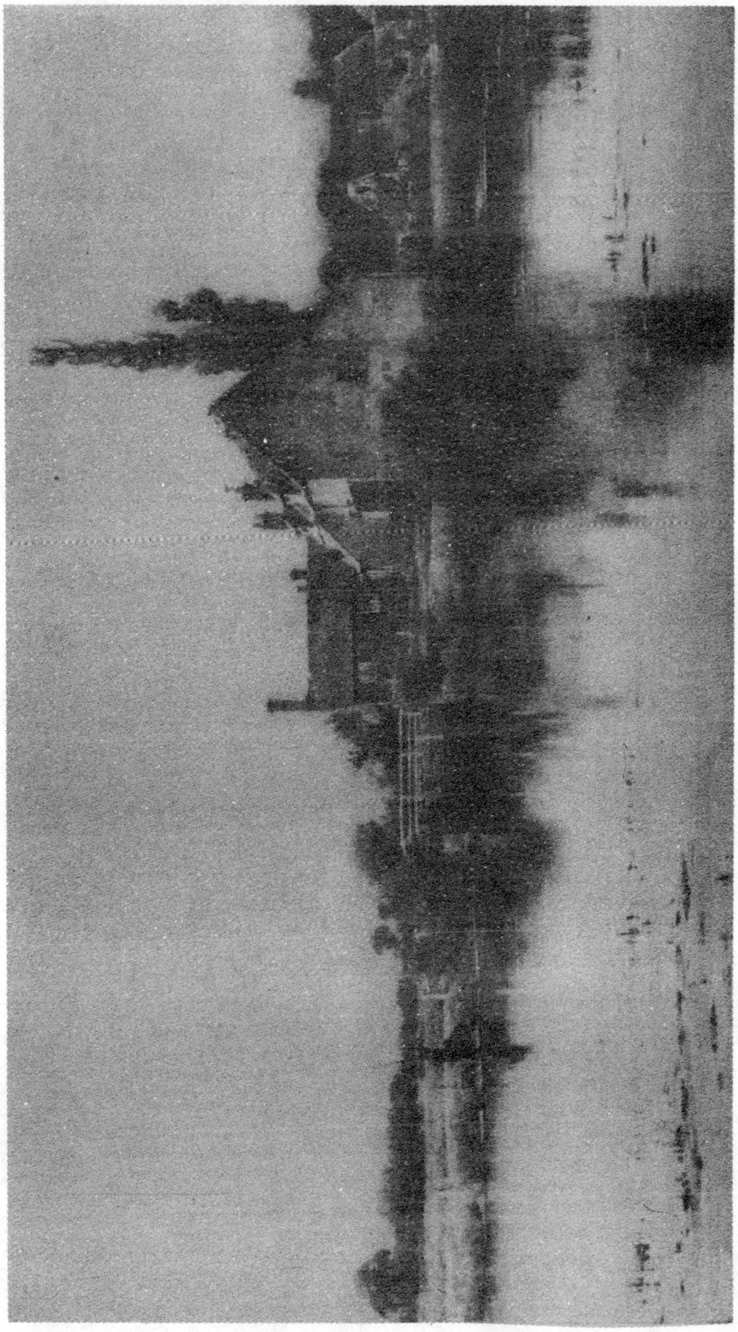

their own curriculum. The bank-fisher's stock begins with a hollow bamboo rod of eighteen or twenty feet in length, without rings or winch fastenings. There being no reel a running line is dispensed with. The line for this rod should be fine, and shorter than the rod, for the fish bites gingerly, and the strike should be instantaneous; this is only possible with a rod that is comparatively stiff, even to the point, and length of line sufficient to permit of angling with the rod held horizontally over the water. Sometimes the roach bites boldly, and the quill float disappearing sharply, a turn of the angler's wrist and a quick uplifting of the point hooks the stricken fish; with such a rod, landing is effected by unshipping the butt and reducing the length.

Until comparatively recent times all the footlines were of horsehair, and many modern roach-fishers use them. To the human eye, horse-hair looks much coarser than the fine drawn gut which has extensively superseded it, but as it keeps free of globules of water, and does not glitter, it is probably least obtrusive to the eye of the fish. Mention has been made of ground-bait, and although it is indispensable, in excess it is destructive of chances. Most professional fishermen indulge profusely in masses of moistened bran, bread, and clay pounded together. The object of ground-bait is to attract and not surfeit, and no more is required in the ordinary forms of bottom-fishing than a few balls so kneaded that the lighter constituents slowly flake off when the bulk has found resting place; small pellets thrown in at intervals are enough to keep the fish, once gathered to the spot, in the swim. Coarse fish, like the bream, may have more liberal treatment, and bushels of grains are often cast forth over night to bring together a herd of fish for the angler at the earliest dawn of day. The favourite ground-bait for barbel, which has habits and haunts of its own, are large dew worms, whole or chopped, and chandlers' greaves.

Float Fishing—The methods of bottom fishing are—float-tackle, legering, and paternostering; and of these, the first affords the popular summer pastime on the river, with legering as the *tour de force* for barbel. The merits of float-fishing are apparent when the weedy bottom of a river is confronted, but when the bed is of gravel, hard sand, or clay, the leger will answer for almost any kind of coarse fish, and it is a method that suits the idle fisherman, who, having cast out his lead, through which the foot line is allowed to pass freely, waits until the "knock knock" at the rod-top signals a fish attempting the bait. In fishing a roach swim, the bait, shotted to trip over the bottom, is always travelling, to be withdrawn for re-travel as it reaches the end of the swim. The float drifts down its allotted course, necessitating no more exertion for the angler than its repeated withdrawal. It is, in summer time, a delightful form of angling, and social in its tendencies, in that ladies indulge in it, though, nowadays, it is growingly the fashion for fair dames and damsels to despise the gudgeon, which beauty draws with a single hair, and to be satisfied with nothing less than trout- or salmon-rod. The different ways in which these plebeians of the coarse-fish streams bite give zest to the sport. The roach nibbles so tenderly that, to an ordinary eye, the float is not disturbed, but the Thames or Lea expert will

PIKE ROD. ROACH POLE. PUNT ROD.

have noticed the faint movement, and, striking at the right time, secured his prize. The dace pulls down the tell-tale with decision; the little gudgeon does the same; the wary carp (when it can be induced to feed at all) is also a bold customer. The perch, beloved of youngsters for his dashing, fearless habits, also leaves no doubt as to his proceedings under water. The tench, one of the least common of the coarse fishes, trifles with the bait before taking it, with leisurely movement. The bream is also a slow biter; and the fish has a habit of playing with the bait for several minutes before the final seizure. The float meanwhile will be bobbing and slanting, and even lying flat on the water, a position caused by the fish rising with the bait in its mouth. Nor is it always safe to strike at this abnormal movement. It is much better to wait a moment or two, when the horizontal position will be gradually changed; the quill will slant off to the perpendicular, and then quickly disappear for final conclusions. The gamest of coarse fishes is the strongly-built barbel. Fishing "fine and far off," is a golden maxim for bottom-fishers, and one of the verities is a thorough acquaintance with the bed of the river. The plummet is the means to this end, and the practised angler would as soon think of going out without this useful article as without his hook.

Nottingham Method—The two high schools of bottom fishers, Thames and Trent, were once sharply defined, but they have learnt to adopt each other's styles. The principle of the Nottingham men was the travelling tackle, or "long corking"; in other words bottom fishing at a long distance from the angler's base. The special tackle for this is a long and supple rod, upright rings, a Nottingham reel without check or complications, the finest undressed silk lines, and quill or cork float. The angler, by this method, keeps absolutely out of sight of the fish. The Nottingham system of casting is flattered by imitations, and has become fashionable in salmon, trout, and pike fishing. It is difficult to master; everything is done from the free running winch, and the difficulty is to so regulate the reel, that there shall be no over-running. The angler in preparing to cast, winds in his baited line until less than a yard length is left hanging from the top ring. He turns partly away from the water to effect the necessary swing over his left shoulder, and the skilful practitioner, bringing his shotted line round with a nicely-adjudged swing, casts an incredible distance. This is one of the approved methods of casting the phantom, or angel minnow for salmon or trout. With the Nottingham style, the coiling of the line on the grass, in the hand, or on the bottom of a boat, as with other methods, is avoided; and the fisherman is able to work without danger or confusion when there are obstacles behind or around him on the margin of the stream.

The Angler's Equipment—To describe in full the paraphernalia which furnish an angler's equipment, would be impossible and profitless. Without any extra encouragement, he is prone to overburden himself with non-essentials. Whatever branch of the sport he favours, he at least cannot do without his rod. There was a time when the ingenious makers of the United States were able, without deadly sin, to boast that we of the old country were centuries behind. Fishing so often as they do from boats in vast waters where there are no obstacles to the play of a fish, they were able to reduce the length of their rods and the corresponding tackle to the smallest proportions. Their special pre-eminence was in split cane rods, generally of six sections of selected cane glued together. We have overtaken them, and have for years produced rods that are not to be surpassed. The split cane rods, spite of their costliness, are highly appreciated, and English patterns are now exported to the Colonies, the Continent and America. Many salmon-fishers nevertheless remain faithful to the stouter, heavier, and cheaper, but not less serviceable, greenheart. It is the same with trout- as with salmon-rods in this respect.

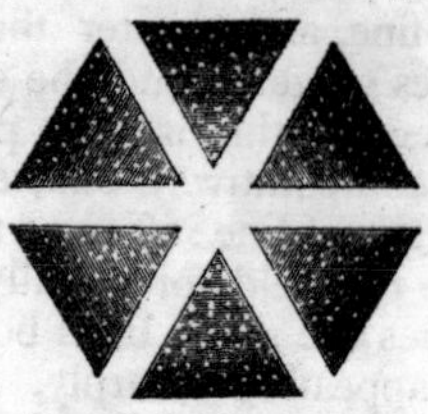

SECTION OF SPLIT CANE.

The selection, as has already been suggested, is a matter to be decided by the angler himself; the neophyte, of course, will take the counsel of a competent adviser; ornamental fittings are no harm if they are no good, and there is no law against buying a rod because it is the latest pattern. But the real desideratum is a weapon that can be handled without discomfort. The middle course lies between the extremes of stiffness and suppleness. With respect to a stiff fly-rod there are almost as many pros as cons. It is true that with a stiff rod the cast may be better delivered, the fly more decisively taken from the water, and a maximum of power obtained in a rough adverse wind, but flies are oftener whipped off, and the physical strength is more severely taxed. The springy rod is not so easily managed, but practice makes perfect; and when the taste has been acquired, as with the devotees of Castle Connell, it lasts for a lifetime. Another consideration in the choice of a fly rod is, ferrule *v.* splice. The advocates of the splice declare that the rod can be put together as quickly as the ferruled, but this is theory and not practical experience with the majority. There is no question that a well-spliced rod offers a harmony of play from butt to point which cannot possibly be obtained with the ferruled; but the balance of argument is on the side of the ferrule, especially in these days when automatic fastenings have been invented, removing the objection often heard to the inconvenience of tying the joints together.

Rod Woods—Although a number of new woods are continually tried for the manufacture of rods, the familiar materials are still the best. Greenheart is the timber most largely imported for rod making. The tree grows in British Guiana, and none but picked selections should be worked up by the rod-makers. Lancewood, with which the top joints were formerly made, being less heavy than greenheart, has gone a little out of fashion, except for the cheaper sort of trout-rod. The hickory used for the common rods turned out by the wholesale firms is the American variety. Ash was once an indispensable butt for all kinds of fishing rods, and when the wood is well seasoned may always be depended upon. Washaba, mahoe, snakewood, and, most recently of all, another West Indian timber, called steelwood, enter into the composition of trout-rods, but do not oust the greenheart. The canes, however, have apparently come to stay, and the whole, or hollow, bamboo or cane, as it is termed in contra-distinction to the solid split cane, is now much used for salmon- and trout-rods. The bamboo rods are very light and remarkably strong, but they are apt to weaken at the ferrule. Canes are mostly shipped from India.

Winches—Next to the rod is the winch; and this mechanism, much more than any other part of the angler's equipment, has monopolised the ingenuity of the patentee. In America, especially, the reel is an affair of complicated and delicate works, very beautiful to look at, delightful to use, so long as its intricate parts act smoothly as per design. But in angling, it is a wise maxim that the simplest is the best, and

NOTTINGHAM: PAST AND PRESENT.

that all inventions should be avoided which increase the risks of disaster when the angler is at the waterside far from means of repairing mechanical break-downs. These exquisite novelties will never lack customers; but most men, having given the patented and registered reels a trial, are content to return to the well-made hard-metal winches, with their serviceable check. The multiplying arrangement of the last generation has been discarded, and the tendency of the moment is towards the winches which are a compromise between the check pure and simple, and the absolutely unchecked Nottingham reel. The salmon-winch, for example, that will be required in a strong water where the fish run large, and where the stoutest of salmon-gut is necessary, will need a strong check action that will tell upon a running salmon without application of the hand to the line. When the streams are shrunken and clear, and the size of the fly has to be reduced to sea-trout size, with a corresponding change from the stoutest to medium gut, the check should be less obdurate. To meet these divers conditions, reels have been furnished with the means of regulating the revolutions of the free runners. The most recent of these is a clever invention whereby the angler, by putting his thumb upon the rim, can reduce the speed of the wheel to almost stoppage point. Reels are made of bronze, brass, gun- and other metals; of wood with light metal protections, and of ebonite. The reel should be, above all things, of the best quality, for it is the gear upon which dependence is direct in critical times. Rod, line, and fish are each and all in danger with an inferior winch.

Lines—In lines, again, the whims and fancies of anglers are encouraged by the makers; the main considerations—after the matter of strength—are the weight of the line as adapted to the rod, and the best of dressings. For casting there was nothing better than the silk and hair formerly used by fly-fishers, but they were liable to hold the wet, to perish prematurely, and to play unpleasant tricks when least expected. Dressed silk lines are in these days thoroughly prepared by scientific methods. It is questionable whether a tapered line is, in the long run, preferable in salmon fishing to one of even substance. A salmon-line should be about 120 yards long, though it is seldom during a lifetime that 100 yards will not suffice. There is an element of excitement, no doubt, in the narrative one occasionally reads of a gallant fish taking 100 yards of line out at a gallop, but, with proper handling of the rod, such an occurrence seldom happens. A cast of 30 yards is a fair distance for the salmon-rod and generally ample for fishing purposes. A trout-line of 50 yards is more than sufficient for the day, as not half the quantity will be in use for ordinary fish. Such lines are now made for dry-fly fishing, tapered at both ends, and heavy in the middle to fit the temper of split cane rods.

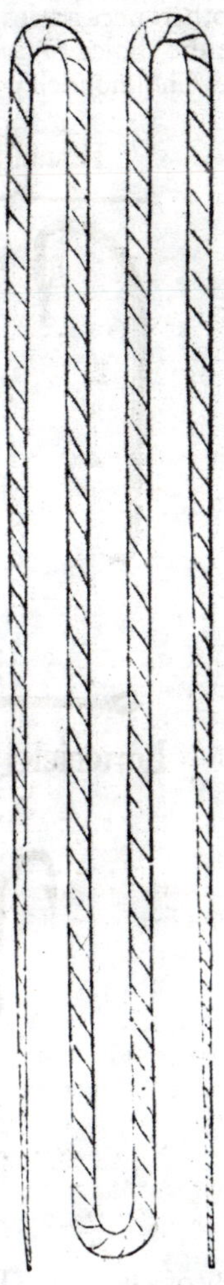

TAPERED LINE.

Hooks—The bulk of the fish hooks used in the world are made in England—Redditch and Kendal being the centres of manufacture. They are exported by millions. The preference of the moment is for the Pennell-Limerick in salmon, and a Pennell-Sneck pattern for the superior class of small trout flies. The sizes vary from the huge salmon-fly affected in the spring, and at other periods for heavy waters and the tiny midge iron, known as 000 or No. 17, according to the custom of the manufacturer. The latter are probably as near an approach to the invisible hook as can be reached with safety; and as they are often required to land trout of two and three pounds, the temper of the steel must be beyond suspicion. Individual fancy, here, as in other necessaries for a fisherman's outfit, will rule the choice of hooks, upon which experts like Mr. Cholmondeley-Pennell have devoted the study of a life-time. Upon the question of hooks, however, anglers are apt to be particularly faddy.

Various—The fly-fisher, besides his rod, line, and winch, his fly-book or his box, requires a net or gaff, a basket or bag, and a set of waders. These are the essentials of his equipment, but the catalogue may be extended *ad lib.* for those who require their spring balance weighing-machine, vaseline, "priest," gag, disgorger, knee-protector, clearing ring, and small bottle of odourless paraffin for the anointment of the cock-winged flies. In case of accidents by the waterside, a little spare silk, scissors, pliers, and wax, are really useful, but the angler's equipment, when overdone, increases his burden without adding to his efficiency. Many anglers are naturally expert in the making and repairing of tackle; others are naturally clumsy with their fingers and never succeed in even the rudimentary mechanical achievements. The incapables, however, need not distress themselves, since everything that is necessary, and with heaps to spare, can be purchased from the tackle makers.

Care of Tackle—There are certain operations, nevertheless, which the angler should try to master; he need not enter into a course of instruction in the mysteries of fly-dressing, but he should be able to whip a hook to a trace, or patch up a broken rod top. And, next to the acquisition of sound simple tackle comes the duty of taking methodical care of it, both when in use and when in inaction. The line should always be taken off the reel to dry at the end of a day's fishing; the ferruled joints should be kept vaselined; and every bit of varnish that is accidentally knocked off should be replaced; flies should be kept in an atmosphere of albo-carbon, or other preventive, to keep out moths; hooks deposited where rust will not corrupt, and gut casts excluded from light and moisture. Precautions like these mean money saved, and efficiency promoted.

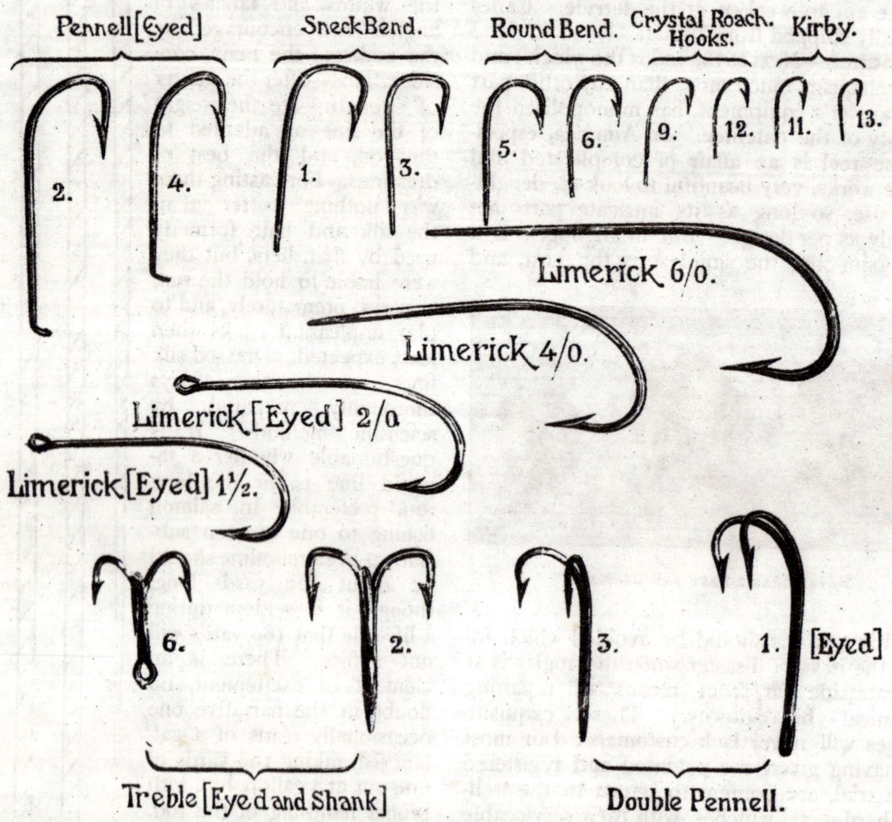

SCALE OF HOOKS.

Seasons and Regulations—By the law of the land, rod-fishing for salmon begins in England and Wales on February 1st and ends on November 2nd; in Scotland, the season is from February 10th to November 1st; in Ireland, the dates vary according to districts, but the close time for netting must never be less than 168 days. The general trout season begins with February and ends with September, but at present in Scotland there is no fence-time for trout. The duration of the close-seasons for salmon is often fixed by the local Boards of Conservators under powers given them by the Salmon Fisheries Act, and the legal limits are only enforced where the rivers are not under local governance. Accordingly, salmon-fishing in Scotland practically extends from January 10th in the north to the end of November in the south, but these are the extreme exceptions affecting a small proportion of the streams. All

MODERN CREEL.

private trout fisheries in England are allowed to fix their own close times, and they vary considerably in different districts. Trout are not in condition before March in any river, and in the choicest streams the opening day is in April or May. The last day of September is the invariable limit of the season. Salmon licences are required in England, Wales and Ireland, but not in Scotland.

By the Act for the Protection of Fresh-water Fish (Mundella's), passed in 1878, a close season is established in public waters from March 15th to June 15th for all kinds of fish other than the migratory species. The middle of June is, however, too early for the coarse fish which spawn in March, April, and May, and the pike and roach have not recovered their condition until July at the earliest. The Lea Conservators, indeed, do not allow angling for pike and perch till August 1st, nor for other coarse fish until the 1st July.

Minimum Sizes—The limits of size for fish caught in angling vary, according to the quality of the streams, and the standard decided upon by societies or individuals. In rivers where the trout rarely run large, the minimum length is often eight or nine inches. The maximum figure is upon the Thames, the trout of which are a special and most gallant variety; and here the limit fixed by bye-law is sixteen inches, representing a trout, in good condition, of about two pounds. A twelve-inch limit for trout and a ten-inch for grayling are generally considered a sportsman-like standard. The average scale of the fishing clubs for other species are—Pike, 18 in.; perch, 8 in.; chub, carp, and bream, 10 in.; rudd and dace, 6 in.; tench, 8 in.; barbel, 13 in.; gudgeon, 4 in.; roach, 7 in.; bleak, 4 in.; pope, 4 in.

Literature—There is no English sport so rich in literature as angling, and it is of al! qualities—theoretical and practical; idyllic and didactic; ranging over the entire watery world, domineering over whale and minnow with equal zest, and abounding with directions, occasionally, perchance, contradictory and impracticable, as to how to capture the fishes of sea and river. The magnitude of the angler's bookshelves has been indicated on a previous page, in the reference to Westwood and Satchell's *Bibliotheca Piscatoria*, a monument of painstaking research, careful compilation, and remarkable accuracy. In the thirteen years which have intervened since its issue by authors since deceased, many practical fishing books have been published, and it only remains in this article to specify the useful works by which the angler, in search of information to assist him in his sport, will be faithfully served. The poetry and lighter literature of angling we may leave for the reader's own discovery. It is not to be supposed that those processes of angling in its various branches, which have been briefly outlined in the foregoing pages, can be wholly learned from books, but the written page is a superstructure upon which experience will rise more rapidly and surely than would otherwise be the case. The following is a recommended selection:—

Fishing for Salmon—"Badminton Library"—*Salmon and Trout* (Longmans); *How to Tie Salmon Flies*, Captain Hale (Sampson Low); *The Salmon Fly*, G. M. Kelson (Wyman and Sons); *Rod and River*, Major Fisher (Bentley); *By Hook and by Crook*, Fraser Sandeman (Sotheran).

Trout and Grayling—*Floating Flies and How to Dress them*; and *Dry Fly Fishing in Theory and Practice*, F. M. Halford (Sampson Low); *Fly Fishing for Salmon, Trout and Grayling*, Dr. Hamilton (Sampson Low); *Fly Rods and Fly Tackle*, H. P. Wells (Sampson Low); *Practical Fly Fishing*, J. Beever (Methuen and Co.); *British Angling Flies*, Theakston, edited by F. M. Walbran (Sampson Low); *North Country Flies*, T. E. Pritt (Sampson Low); *The Fly Fisher's Entomology*, Alf. Ronalds (Longmans); *Favourite Flies* (America), Mary Orvis Marbury (Sampson Low); *The Angler and the Loop Rod*, David Webster (Blackwood).

General Angling—*A Book on Angling*, Francis Francis (Longmans); *The Book of the All-Round Angler*,

John Bickerdyke (Upcott Gill); "Badminton Library"—*Pike and Coarse Fish* (Longmans); *The Practical Fisherman*, J. H. Keene (Upcott Gill); *Angling, and How to Angle*, Burgess, edited by R. B. Marston (F. Warne and Co.); *Fish and Fishing*, J. J. Manley, M.A. (Sampson Low); *The Nottingham Style of Float Fishing and Spinning*, J. W. Martin (Sampson Low).

Monographs—*The Book of the Pike*, C. Pennell (Routledge); *Grayling and How to Catch Them*, F. M. Walbran (Angler Co.); *The Book of the Roach*, Greville Fennell (Sampson Low); *The Book of the Grayling*, T. E. Pritt (Goodall and Suddick); *The Book of the Black Bass*, Dr. Henshall (Clarke, Cincinnatti); *The Ouananiche*, E. T. D. Chambers (Harper Brothers).

Ichthyological—*Making a Fishery*, F. M. Halford (Horace Cox); *The Angler Naturalist*, C. Pennell (Routledge); *Salmon Problems*, Willis Bund (Sampson Low); *Habits of the Salmon*, Major Traherne (Chapman and Hall); *Domesticated Trout*, Livingston Stone (Osgood, Boston, U.S.); *The Angler's Paradise*, J. J. Armistead (Angler Co.); *The Practical Management of Fisheries*, Francis Francis (Horace Cox); *British and Irish Salmonidæ*, Dr. Day (Horace Cox); *Freshwater Fishes of Europe*, H. G. Seeley (Cassell); *British Freshwater Fishes*, Houghton (Dean); *British Sporting Fishes*, J. Watson (Chapman and Hall); *British Fishes*, Dr. Day (Horace Cox).

Fishing Haunts—*The Angler's Diary* (Horace Cox); *The Sportsman's Guide to Scotland* (Watson Lyall); *How and Where to Fish in Ireland*, Hi Regan (Sampson Low); *The Rod in India*, Thomas (Calcutta); *Norfolk Broads and Rivers*, G. C. Davies (Blackwood); *Travel and Trout in the Antipodes*, W. Senior (Chatto and Windus); *Near and Far*, W. Senior (Sampson Low); *Angling Travels in Norway*, Fraser Sandeman (Chapman and Hall).

Legal—*Oke's Fishery Laws*, and *the Freshwater Fishery Acts of 1878 and 1884*, J. W. Willis Bund (Butterworths); *A Treatise on the Law of Scotland relating to Rights of Fishing*, C. Stewart, second edition, edited by J. C. Shairp (Clark, Edinburgh); *Digest of the Irish Fisheries Acts*, Sir Thomas Brady (Eyre and Spottiswoode).

WILLIAM SENIOR.

COARSE FISH—So far as the so-called "coarse fish" are concerned, the art of angling has perhaps reached its highest level among those who frequent the lovely reaches of the Thames. Much persecution has rendered the fish of our premier river shy to a degree, and Thames anglers, being put on their mettle, now practise almost every known method of fishing with rod and line, and display an amount of skill which is not excelled on any river in the kingdom. To be a thorough Thames angler is to be one who can catch fish in almost any part of the world, though certain foreigners, such as the mahseer and tarpon, of course require different tackle from that used in English streams.

Any one who can successfully play a large Thames trout on quite fine tackle in a seething weirpool, will have no difficulty whatever in capturing salmon on the stouter gut which is commonly used for the king of British fishes; and even the art of dry-fly fishing may be acquired by practising on the dace which, in, alas! far fewer numbers than formerly, frequent the shallows of the lower portion of the river. The peculiar method of fishing followed by the anglers of the Trent—viz., of sending float-tackle a considerable distance down stream by running a fine silk line off the reel, is much practised on the Thames, and, as we have already said, there are no methods of fishing of any account which are unknown to the more successful among Thames fishermen.

Trout and **Pike** fishing will be found dealt with under separate headings, so we may well begin here with a description of Barbel fishing. Without having the dash and vigour of a trout, the **Barbel** (*Barbus vulgaris*) ranks among the strongest of fresh-water fish. Being caught commonly in places where the stream runs strongly, and, unless the water be thick, requiring fairly fine tackle in his capture, he gives more sport than perhaps any other fish in the Thames, the trout excepted. He spawns in the spring, and for a while afterwards, develops a most remarkable appetite, often taking the spinning bait

BARBEL.

of the trout fisher in the weirpools. However, by the time the angling season opens, which is about June 16th, he begins to feed on worms and other baits. Greaves, called "scratchings" on the Trent, gentles, and cheese, will all account for a barbel occasionally, and these fish are very fond of the caddis at the commencement of the season. They sometimes take a lampern in the autumn. But of all baits the worm stands first, and, perhaps, greaves come second.

When the water is very low and clear and the fish seem almost unapproachable, clever anglers occasionally make moderate captures of barbel by using a fine line and a small hook baited with gentles. They place a lump of stiff ground-bait immediately above the hook; the few gentles on the hook then look as if they formed a portion of the neighbouring mass. This method cannot of course be used in the ordinary heavy barbel swims, but is more suitable to weir-pools when the water is almost or quite shut off. **Clay-ball** fishing, as it is called, is very similar to this method, but can be practised in stronger streams. Clay into which gentles, greaves, or worms are worked is placed around a tiny cross piece of stick which is tied into the line just above the bait, or the stick is placed a foot or more above the bait and the gut below the stick is wound round and round the clay ball and squeezed into it. This arrangement if carefully made can be cast out like a leger.

The barbel is a remarkably uncertain feeder; and to Izaak Walton's dictum that one can fish neither too early nor too late for him, there is nothing to be added. He is essentially a summer-feeding fish, and on the Thames the angler is most likely to meet with success after a fall of rain, particularly if the river is somewhat coloured. One of the most phenomenal takes of late years was made when there had been a long drought; the river had run low, and quantities of barbel had retired into a certain deep hole. Then came a freshet, the hole was fished, the fish fed eagerly and large numbers were taken.

Considerable care should be observed in choosing a barbel-rod. With coarse tackle, the rod may be fairly stiff, but the water presses heavily on a stout line and, the barbel being shy and fairly well educated, as fine a line as possible should be preferred. A fine line and a stiff rod spell catastrophe; for the weaker the tackle, the more occasion there is for suppleness in the rod. The favourite line on the Thames is smooth and softly dressed, of eight plait silk; and a leger is the most common form of tackle at the end of it. The Thames **leger** consists simply of about a yard of gut with a hook at the end; above it comes a foot of fine gimp on which is slung a bullet with a single shot so fixed on each end of the gimp as to prevent the bullet working on to the gut. Beyond the gimp may be still more gut, but this is not absolutely necessary. This tackle is cast out either off a Nottingham reel or in the Thames fashion in which the line is pulled off the reel and coiled on the floor of the punt before the cast is made. After the leger is cast out the angler awaits a couple of knocks or a steady pull and then strikes when, if the fish is large, he will encounter a determined resistance which is increased by the force of the water.

In most Thames barbel-swims, float-tackle is of little use, but in quieter waters, such as one finds in the Trent, and indeed in certain parts of the former river, heavy float tackle can be used with Nottingham tackle. Of this Nottingham fishing there are practically two kinds. The more common method consists in allowing a float to work down stream and draw line off the reel. Sometimes the float is cast out and held back. In this last-mentioned method, called "tight-corking," the shot has to be heavy enough to keep the bait on the bottom and the float must be at a greater distance from the bait than the water is deep. Practically, the tackle amounts to a leger with a float, shot taking the place of the bullet. It is a particularly deadly method of catching large roach and other fish when a river is in slight flood and the fish are feeding on the bottom. For "long-corking," except where many shot are required, the favourite float is a quill from the wing of some large bird. For "tight corking," cork floats are more often used.

Much success with the barbel is not to be obtained without a considerable expenditure of trouble and perhaps money in **ground-baiting** Several thousands of lobworms are usually placed in barbel-swims, either fixed in clay balls or thrown in loosely, or allowed to crawl into a sod of turf which is dropped into the river. Another plan is to place the worms with a stone or two in a paper bag, and sink the latter. The method to be adopted depends largely on the nature of the swim, local knowledge, and so forth.

SLIDER FLOAT.

The object of baiting is, perhaps, not so much to collect the fish as to get them accustomed to feed on a certain kind of food and to view it without suspicion. Their suspicions being lulled, they take the worm on the angler's hook for a time, but as soon as a few fish have been pricked and lost, or the swim becomes disturbed by other reasons, the effects of the ground-bait appear to wear off. Greaves and cheese should be used very sparingly as ground-bait, as they appear to sicken the fish, and lob-worms should be thrown in whole, otherwise the small fry will get them. It is judicious in an ordinary swim to throw in about 500 worms one morning, 300 twenty-four hours later, and fish it on the morning of the following day. While fishing, worms or pieces of worms should be thrown in from time to time, and the choicest and the best scoured should be selected for the hook. In large pools where barbel are plentiful, many more worms may be thrown in with advantage.

The **Roach** (*Leuciscus rutilus*) is of all fish the one which yields sport to the largest number of English anglers, and is beloved of the clubmen of both London and the Midlands. A bright, handsome fish, playing for a short time strongly if caught on fine tackle, it is shy to a degree in much-frequented waters. In winter, if properly cooked, it is by no means despicable as food.

In the commencement of the season, roach are found in the swiftest streams of a river where they probably go to become re-invigorated after the efforts of spawning. As summer advances,

..hey get into slightly deeper water, and wherever there is a nice, gravelly and sandy bottom, and weeds, reeds or rushes, they may be looked for. In winter, their swims depend largely on the state of the water and the temperature. If it is very cold, they seek the deepest waters, while if it is warm, they work out into streams of moderate depth. Thick water invariably sends them into shallow swims, which is a point to be remembered, while, when the river runs very clear and the frost is severe, they may be looked for in the deepest holes. Under ordinary "summer" conditions the best fish will be found in running water. All fish, it should be noted, rather favour eddies during a flood, for there food is swept and shelter is obtained from the strength of the current.

The baits for roach are simply unlimited in number and variety. There is hardly any kind of paste which they will not take, and they feed eagerly on wasp-grubs, gentles, the larvæ of all kinds of flies, and water insects, and are often caught on the silk weed. To grain, if stewed until it is tender, they are very partial in certain rivers,

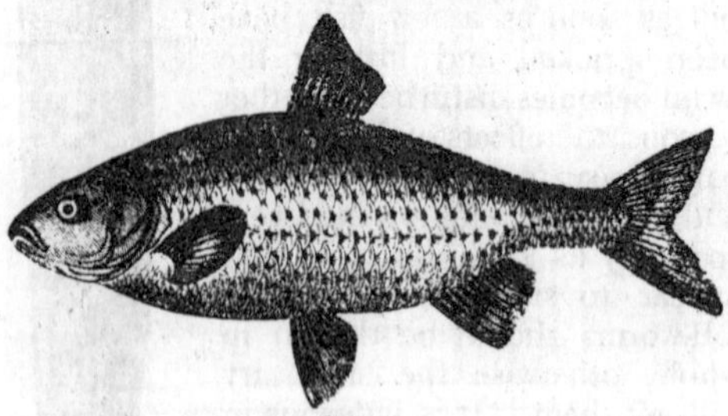

ROACH.

and even in those waters where it is not regarded as a suitable bait the fish can be induced to feed on it by baiting up swims some days in advance.

The most common method of fishing for roach is with float-tackle, and this may be either used with a tight line, that is to say, the line being made fast to the end of a long rod, or with running tackle. Where rivers are shallow and it is desirable to be at some distance from the fish, there the Nottingham method of casting out a float and allowing it to travel with the stream is certainly the best, but in deeper waters where the fish cannot, it may be presumed, see the angler, there the tight line, or Lea method, accounts for the most considerable baskets of fish. Where roach are shy and much fished for, the angler cannot strike too quickly on perceiving a bite. It is obvious that with a tight line and the point of the rod held only a foot or two above the float, the strike can be made quicker than where the float has travelled ten or fifteen yards down stream; not only in the latter case has the elasticity of the line to be overcome, but there is a loss of time between the actual strike and its effect on the fish, during which the bait may be, and often is ejected.

On the Thames, the bank-angler commonly uses a long bamboo roach-pole and tight line; but large numbers of roach are caught from punts moored across the stream by means of poles called ripecks, the angler lowering the line over the side of the punt, letting the float travel three or four yards, then drawing it in and taking a fresh swim. While this is going on, the attendant will from time to time deposit balls of ground-bait over the side, which keeps the fish together and induces them to feed, *if* not given with a too lavish hand.

Roach-fishing is so largely practised, that many refinements of tackle are affected by the professors of the art, one of the most important of which is, in our opinion, the staining of the gut and the colouring of the hook shank. In winter the best colour for gut is brown, in summer, green to match the weeds, while the hook-shank should be coloured according to the bait; that is, if gentles are used, white or a very pale yellow; if wheat, wheat-colour; if worms, a brownish-red, and so on. These colours are easily made by mixing a little French polish with the dry colour obtained of the oil-and-colourman. The mixture will dry very quickly.

It is not every tackle-maker who sells roach-hooks mounted on sufficiently fine gut, for the houses which supply trout- and salmon-fishermen almost ignore this branch of their trade. To obtain the best roach tackle, it may therefore be necessary to go to the houses which are patronised by the London bank-anglers. As to the best shape of hook for roach, there is a diversity of opinion, many anglers preferring the "crystal" bend, while others declare there is nothing so good as the round bend. Silkworm gut is now drawn much finer than horsehair, but not a few anglers still swear by hair on account of its durability, absence of glitter, and for other reasons. A length of drawn gut will fray in the course of a day and, it is believed, is then more visible to the fish than the coarser horsehair, which may perhaps be taken by the fish for a piece of brown weed or some similar natural object.

Baits—To revert to the subject of **baits**—paste, gentles, and creed or stewed wheat, certainly take the highest rank, and it is a singular fact that in many rivers only small roach appear to prefer gentles while the larger fish are caught on wheat or paste. In the early part of the season, a red worm is sometimes found a good bait, and in certain waters, among which the Thames is not one, is regarded all through the year as even better than gentles or paste. In winter, the lobworm is one of the best baits that can be used, provided the water is slightly coloured.

In roach-fishing, ground-bait is all important, and it should be in nature somewhat similar to the hook-bait. One of the best and most commonly used consists of the waste crusts from the bread pan scalded until they are quite soft, the water squeezed out of them, and kneaded into a stiff consistency with the addition of fine bran. To this may be added a little boiled rice, creed wheat, or other food which the roach favour. The amount to be put in depends on the extent of the river and the quantities of fish which are believed to be about. It is obvious that if there is only a shoal of fifty roach it is useless to throw in enough for two thousand. The fifty fish get gorged and refuse to be caught. One of the secrets of success in roach fishing is to put in a little ground-bait frequently and so induce the fish to keep looking about for food. To throw in a quantity of ground-bait at once simply gives them a big feast, after which they retire contentedly to some shady corner out of the way of hooks, floats, and anglers.

A great many roach are caught on the leger, such as described under the head of Barbel fishing, but it need hardly be said that for this fish the gut should be much lighter than that used for fighting the heavier tenants of the weirpool.

In some rivers, roach come on to the shallows during the summer and will take an artificial fly, particularly if the hook is tipped with a gentle. The fly should be allowed to sink and then be drawn slowly through the water, and the angler should not strike until he sees the line tighten, as the roach does not rise like a trout, but swims for some distance after the fly before sucking it in.

The **Rudd** (*Leuciscus erythrophthalmus*) closely resembles the roach in appearance, but it is rather deeper in the belly, has a tail more forked, and its red parts are more brightly coloured. A simple method of distinguishing the two fish is to examine the upper lip. This in the roach will be found capable of a slight elongation and can be pulled down, a convenience which evidently enables the fish to pick up food off the bottom. With the rudd, on the other hand, the upper lip is of a hard, bony, immovable nature.

Rudd are not now, so far as we know, found in the Thames, but are exceedingly plentiful in the waters of Norfolk, Suffolk, and Cambridgeshire, and in many ponds. They will take all the usual roach baits, but are particular favourites with the angler by reason of their readiness to seize (rather than to rise at) an artificial fly. Slapton Lea in Devonshire is a noted water for fly fishing for rudd. In hot weather shoals of these fish love to swim over muddy shallows, the bottom of which is paved with weedy verdure. Approach them cautiously and cast a fly in their midst, and the whole shoal will swim towards it, the largest after following it for a yard or two sucking it solemnly into its mouth. In some cases, skilful fly-fishers will, by exercising great care in their method of approaching and playing the fish they hook, kill half the shoal or more before the fish take alarm. Float-tackle, used when the fish are near the surface, should be cast a long distance, the angler keeping as low as possible.

The **Dace** (*Leuciscus vulgaris*), a bright silvery fish, slimmer in shape than, and lacking the red fins of, the roach. It is caught by much the same methods as its more corpulent cousin, but in addition rises like any trout to a fly in shallow waters, and the young would-be trout-fisher cannot do better than try his hand on these pretty fish. Almost any small fly will tempt them, and if they will not rise to the black gnat or other dark fly a bright Soldier Palmer, or white-winged Coachman should be tried. In some rivers, they commonly disdain a wet fly and are as a rule only to be caught with a carefully dried dun or other floating fly.

Some of the best dace fishing near London is to be obtained in the tidal waters of the

DACE.

Thames, where these fish abound. There, they are usually caught from punts, and it has become a common practice of late years to stir up the bottom behind the punt with a gudgeon rake. This proceeding disturbs various water-insects and slightly colours the water, and the fish, heading up stream towards the source of the discolouration, come upon the angler's tackle and are caught. Very large dace are often taken by the barbel-fisher, and are in fact regarded by him as a great nuisance. When it is found that there are continual bites which are being missed, and that the lobworm is being bruised about the head, the presence of dace may be at once suspected, and the way to clear the swim of a few is to bait with the head of the lobworm alone. Though dace are mainly a fish of the shallows, the larger members of the family are frequently caught in deep waters where their presence would not be suspected.

The **Chub** (*Leuciscus cephalus*) is another fly-taking fish, and though almost worthless as food and treated to words of opprobrium in many a trout stream, is beloved of Thames and other anglers for the fine sport he affords. Like many other fishes, he seeks the shallows at the commencement of the season after spawning, but soon retires to holes beneath overhanging willow trees, where any one peering cautiously over the bows of the boat or punt on some bright sunny day may see a shoal swimming in and out the maze of roots which project into the water. There they lie the summer through, feeding on beetles and caterpillars and other insects which fall into the water from the overhanging branches. In much-navigated rivers, the fly cannot be used with great success except in early morning, because as soon as the first launch or boat has passed, the fish which are

CHUB.

basking near the surface sink to a depth at which they disregard artificial flies. Still, there are many retired shallows and places in which chub may be found until the end of August, and there the fly-fisher still has his opportunity.

In fly-fishing from a boat, success depends as much upon the boatman as on the fly-fisher, the slightest roll of the craft or splash of the oars scaring the fish. The chub indeed is above all famous for his extreme distrust of man. If unaware of the angler's presence, he will take a bait presented to him on tackle of astonishing coarseness, but if he once obtains an inkling that his dread enemy is in the vicinity, no bait, however tasty, presented on the finest of tackle will tempt him. This, of course, as a general rule.

In addition to the flies, which should be large and dressed rather full and heavily hackled, small frogs, lobworms, a bunch of gentles, a piece of beef fat, crayfish-tails, and the large black slugs which come out at night after a showery day, are all placed before this fish by means of a fly-rod.

In deep holes, many a good chub is caught by means of leger-tackle, the bait being greaves or cheese, but perhaps the most general and successful method of angling for these fish is with Nottingham tackle. A large quill float, fairly heavily shotted, is sent by the side of the bank down stream right among a shoal of chub which, owing to the distance between them and the angler, are without suspicion. One of the most favoured summer baits is cheese-paste, while in the winter there is nothing to equal a piece of marrow or pith, previously scalded, from the spine of a bullock. The brains, which have also been scalded, are thrown in as ground-bait. The best line for this particular method of fishing is made of pure undressed silk, either twisted or plaited. The rod should be rather long and powerful to hold the fish from out those roots towards which he is certain to swim when hooked, and the whole proceeding must be conducted with the greatest care and caution. Not many chub are often caught from one spot, and the angler who tries place after place will catch many more than he who sits quietly waiting for the fish to come on the feed.

The **Bream** (*Abramis brama*) is a flat-sided, deep-bellied, hog-backed fish, which abounds in many Midland and East Anglian waters, and is also found in the Thames. Generally speaking, it is a night-feeder, and enormous numbers are caught between the hours of two or three, and five o'clock in the morning during the months of July and August. In the Thames, a few are caught in barbel swims, and these appear to feed during the day. They are taken with the leger, but in the slow-flowing rivers of the Fen country the favourite tackle consists of a rod somewhat akin to a hop-pole, a piece of twine, a float such as a Thames angler would use for jack, and what is commonly known as a "penny hook." The penny hook is tied immediately to the twine, and above the knot is a strip of lead, probably cut off the nearest gutter. With this very primitive tackle as many fish seem to be caught as with the finer gear used by the Thames anglers. But it is to be remembered that the rivers of the Midlands are more highly coloured than the Thames and Lea, and, as we have said, the fishing is carried out in the early morning when the light is not very good, circumstances under which fine tackle is not particularly called for. The float, too, is so arranged that at least a foot of the line lies on the bottom, and thus is but little observed. Even the worm may be more or less covered with mud, and has to

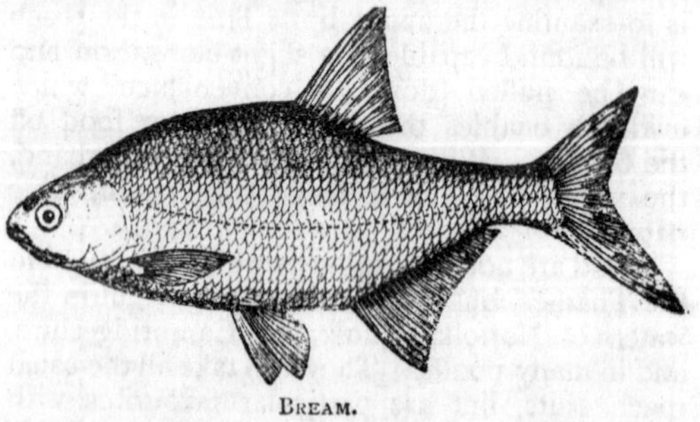

BREAM.

be routed up by the snouts of the fish. As a rule, bream-swims are heavily ground-baited, a favourite bait for this purpose being brewers' grains. The hook bait is usually a worm, but the fish will also take gentles, paste, and creed wheat.

So little do bream feed in the daytime on Midland rivers, that in some of them an angler might fish day by day for a year without discovering that there was a bream in the river. The bream to which we are alluding are the large, bronzy fellows which grow to a considerable weight; but in the Norfolk broads and other waters there is a smaller fish of the same family called the **Bream-flat** (*Abramis blicca*), which is caught in immense numbers and rarely attains a considerable weight. We have taken these fish on paternoster, leger, and other tackle, and when well on the feed there appears to be no limit to the numbers which may be lifted into the boat.

The essentials of bream fishing, in short, are to fish at an exceedingly early hour in the morning, in fact before daybreak, to moor the punt in a bream-hole, to allow a portion of the line to lie on the bottom, to ground-bait sufficiently some twenty hours previously, and also during the fishing. Of course, the angler should be careful not to disturb the swim. That rule applies to fishing of all kinds.

The **Perch** (*Perca fluviatilis*), which may be instantly recognised by his striped sides, hog-back, and prickly dorsal fin, is one of the most sport-yielding, and at the same time best table,

PERCH.

fish found in fresh water. When large, he is by no means easily caught, but in the days of infancy he bites boldly and foolishly, particularly in ponds. Like the roach and some other coarse fish, he is found in the streams in spring and summer, retiring to deeper water in winter, the best time to make a large bag being when the river has been in flood and the water has sunk and cleared a little, and the fish have not yet left the large eddies in which they congregated to avoid the force of the current. If, added to these conditions, there are a few frosty nights to whet their appetites, the captures made are likely to be phenomenal.

In summer time, perch are scattered about the river, and the angler who understands how to use the paternoster will take one here and another there from among holes in the weeds, by the side of the camp sheathing, and near any old wreckage or timber work.

For large perch, there is no better bait than a live gudgeon, but minnows are more commonly used, perhaps because they are more easily obtained. On lakes and ponds, the red worm is very deadly; and in rivers, when the water is much coloured, there is no bait better than the worm. During a summer flood, if a shallow and not too swift swim is baited up with lobworms, good sport may be expected, and the tail of a lobworm is great medicine whenever the water is at all thick. When many anglers consider the Thames quite unfishable, owing to the thick water, there are a few who swim the tail of a lobworm round small eddies close to the bank, taking out a perch here and a perch there, and occasionally chub and roach. In lakes, perch sometimes take flies, such as a large red Palmer, and they will dash at small bright spinning baits at any time and in any water.

The **paternoster**, a piece of tackle rarely used for any other freshwater fish except perch, is to be made in the following manner: Take a three-yard length of fine gut and make two loops in it about eighteen inches apart, the lower one being only three inches above the end of the collar. To this lower end attach a pear-shaped lead of about half an ounce or less, the other end being fastened to the running line. Fasten to the large loops in the upright portion of the gut two No. 7 hooks, the gut of which should be shortened to about five inches. The paternoster is then ready and a very much better one than can be purchased in the shops. In rivers, this tackle is baited with minnows or gudgeons (these necessitate larger hooks) and shot rather than lowered into places where perch are expected. The rod should be held exceedingly steady, and immediately the little tap-tap at the point is felt, which denotes a perch, the point should be lowered for a second or two, then, if it be evident that the fish is feeding, there should be a gentle strike. For a perch of half a pound or upwards it is best to use a landing-net, as these fish have large and delicate mouths from which the hook often comes away in their struggles.

In ponds and lakes, the same tackle may be used, substituting worms for minnows, though minnows are preferable if they can be obtained. Where worms are the bait, it is as well to have a good supply and to throw in a few occasionally to keep the perch round about and on the feed. Almost the same float-tackle can be used for perch as for roach, except that it may be a trifle coarser, and the hook a little larger; but as regards the hook, this should always suit the bait in the matter of size.

If there is some place where perch are known to be and the fish are exceedingly shy and difficult to catch, it is a good plan to use the finest possible float-tackle, and to wait patiently till a perch takes it; and, as we have said, if worms are the bait, a few should be thrown in from time to time. We have known perch caught on leger-tackle in rivers when they could be taken by no other means, the bait being a gudgeon. The reason probably is that the gut of the leger lies on the ground and is not seen by the fish, whereas with float tackle or a paternoster, a very visible line comes from the surface of the water to the bottom immediately over their heads.

Tench (*Tinca vulgaris*) may be easily known by their greenish-bronze colour, small bright red eyes, and minute scales covered with a thick,

TENCH.

tenacious mucus. When of small size in ponds, they are easily caught with paste or worms, but when large, whether in rivers or ponds, they are, as a rule, shy to a degree, but bite well enough when the water is thick. In rivers they should be fished for carefully close to the edge of, but not on, a bank of mud from out of which grow water-lilies and other weeds, and if there is an old root or two about so much the better. They may be caught either on float- or leger-tackle or by the method termed "tight-corking," already described. They feed best in spring and early summer, but are sometimes taken in winter if the weather is mild and the water coloured. One secret of success is to use a small hook, thoroughly well covered with the bait, and give the fish plenty of time. Congealed blood is used as a bait with much success in some canals and other waters. With it, the strike should come sooner than with worms. Those who would catch large tench should be on the water soon after daybreak.

The **Carp** (*Cyprinus carpio*) is perhaps the shyest fish that swims. It is usually angled for during the summer, one of the best baits being a parboiled potato placed on a small triangle by means of a baiting needle. Paste sweetened with honey, worms of various kinds, boiled wheat, green peas, wasp-grubs, cheese, &c., are also used with varying success

Carp are mostly caught in the very early morning or late evening. Ground-bait is essential, and it should resemble the hook bait but be coarser in character. In suitable places the leger answers well, as it is less visible to the fish than other tackle. But those anglers who can cast out a float a considerable distance use that form of tackle with much success in lakes. In enclosed waters, it is a good plan to bait up several spots and, after catching a fish from one, to go to another, so as to give the first swim a rest.

There are few baits which the **Eel** (*Anguilla vulgaris*) will not take, and few waters in which this valuable food fish is not found. The leger and ordinary float-tackle baited with worms are both much used. There is also a method called bobbing, or clod-fishing, which consists of stringing a number of big worms from end to end on a piece of worsted, looping them up into a lump resembling a small mop-head, and lowering them to the bottom by means of a cord and a short stout stick or bamboo. The eel's teeth catch in the worsted and the fish can be lifted up and dropped into a pail in the punt. Bobbing is much practised at the mouths of streams during a rise and discolouration of water.

On hot summer days when eels are lying in holes in banks, sniggling is practised. The sniggler takes a long needle, whips on a piece of fine line to the centre of it and inserts the needle in a worm, just bringing out the point which is stuck into the end of a stick. The needle encased in the worm is then placed in front of the eel's nose, and if it is taken and swallowed the sniggler puts on a gentle but continuous pressure until the eel's strength gives way and he is drawn out with the needle athwart his throat.

Eels are also caught in baskets which should be baited with live gudgeon. The best baskets are made of withies. We cannot recommend those constructed of wire. Thousands of eels are taken in fixed traps or weirs, and in eel-nets placed across the rivers of Norfolk and Suffolk. Spearing eels is very good fun. Sometimes the method is practised indiscriminately over mudbanks, or if the water is clear, the mud

CARP.

is prodded only where blow-holes are seen. In spring-time, the spear is used in the feathery green weeds, beloved of pike, which are seen in masses on the bottom of rivers.

The **Gudgeon** (*Gobio fluviatilis*) is a small, round-bodied, brown-backed fish, which abounds in many rivers and, as a general rule, is very easily caught. Like the barbel, which it somewhat resembles in shape, it is a summer-feeding fish, and is caught close to the bottom. Gudgeon fishing is largely carried on by Thames anglers and is highly favoured by the fair sex, provided some one of sterner mould is at hand to adjust the worm on the hook and remove the resulting fish.

For this branch of angling, fine roach tackle

is most suitable, but the hook should be very small and baited with a fragment of red worm or brandling. At the slightest depression of the float the angler should strike. Ground-bait is rarely used for gudgeon, the better plan being to disturb the bottom from time to time with a a heavy long-handled rake made for the purpose. It is important to plumb the depth and adjust the float with great accuracy. The bait should float down stream as near the bottom as possible without touching it. On the Thames, bags of twenty dozen or more of these fish are sometimes made by two rods in a day. As regards choosing a swim, the fish love a shallow over which the river flows gently, on the edge of a deep hole. As the summer wanes, they gradually get into deeper water. The bottom should be sandy gravel, *i.e.*, not too hard. As a table fish, gudgeon are most excellent, and they make first-rate baits for perch, pike, trout, and salmon.

There only now remain the small fry which are principally used for bait. **Bleak** (*Alburnus lucidus*), however, rise eagerly to a fly, and are

GUDGEON.

caught without difficulty by means of a single gentle, caddis, or piece of paste. They afford grand sport to the young angler during the summer, and, particularly if toughened in spirits of wine, or other preservative, are first-rate spinning baits if mounted on the Chapman spinner or one of its varieties.

The **Minnow** (*Leuciscus phoxinus*), a useful bait, is found in most brooks and rivers, and is best taken by means of a square or round net with fine meshes which is lowered to the bottom. As soon as the minnows swim over, it is rapidly lifted.

The **Stone Loach** (*Nemacheilus barbatula*), Colloch, or Colley bait of Ireland, is also a valuable bait, particularly for salmon and trout, and is usually caught by turning over the stone under which it lies. A tap with a hammer on the stone will sometimes stun it.

The **Ruffe** (*Acerina vulgaris*) or Pope is a kind of miniature perch. It is shaped like the perch, but has the colour of a gudgeon. It exudes a nasty slime, and has some poisonous spikes on the corner of its gill covers. It has a vexatious habit of swallowing the bait and hook.

The **Miller's Thumb** (*Cottus gobio*) is a quaint monstrosity, nearly all head. It is found under stones in the shallows of small brooks.

Of the **Stickleback** (*Gasterosteus spinulosus*), of which there are several varieties, little need be said. From the naturalist's point of view it is highly interesting as to its breeding habits, and urchins may be seen catching them any day by means of a red worm tied to the end of a piece of cotton. The greedy stickleback half swallows the worm and is lifted out before it has time to leave go.

The **Lamprey, Burbolt** or **Eel-Pout** the **Azurine**, the **Vendace**, the **Powan**, the **Gwyniad**, and the **Graining** are other rare fish, of a kind which do not as a rule afford sport to the angler.

(The **Flounder**, which is found indifferently in fresh and salt water, is dealt with under the head of **Sea-Fishing**.)

JOHN BICKERDYKE.

GLOSSARY.

Caddis—The larva of certain aquatic insects which reside in a self-constructed case or shell. A deadly bait for roach and some other fish.

Cast of Flies—The name given to the length of gut with the flies attached.

Coarse Fish—The term applied to all fresh-water fish with the exception of the *Salmonidæ*, the latter being termed *Game Fish*. If the distinction has reference to the mode of capture it is unsatisfactory, as the chub and dace at least give much sport with the fly.

Collar—The knotted length of gut to which are attached the flies. (Called also *Cast.*)

Flights—Combinations of hooks on gimp or gut. *See* PIKE, TROUT, &c.

Floats—Contrivances of cork, celluloid, horn, or quill, designed to keep the bait clear of the bottom, as well as to indicate to the angler when to strike. The sliding-float allows the free passage of the line through its rings until stopped by the lead or a rubber-band. The ordinary float lies flat on the water when there is insufficient weight below to keep it erect, but self-cocking floats are weighted with lead at the lower end.

Fly-Fishers' Club—A high-class social club for fly-fishers, founded in 1884 and having its headquarters at 8, Arundel Street. Hon. Sec., D. Wilson.

Gaff (otherwise **Cleek**, or **Gogger**)—A barbless steel hook, affixed to an ash handle and used in landing large fish. When not in use, the point is generally protected with a brass screw cap. Most modern patterns are collapsible.

Game Fish—*See* **Coarse Fish.**

Gimp—A line composed of a silk cord lapped with fine copper or other wire, and much used in the manufacture of traces and mounted hooks for pike-fishing.

Gorge-fishing—Virtually trolling with a dead bait on a double hook. [*See* PIKE.] It is illegal on the Thames.

Gut—A semi-transparent substance, manufactured from the silkworm. The insect is plunged in boiling vinegar, and its entrails drawn out. It is used either plain or stained in various tints to suit certain waters; and is usually sold in hanks of a hundred lengths (called in Ireland "hairs"), or made up in casts. *Drawn* gut, used in clear-water roach fishing, is drawn through steel plates. *Marrana* is a fine salmon-gut. The bulk of the supply is derived from Spain.

Hooks—Made in a large variety of patterns or, as they are called "bends," the chief being Limerick, Kirby, Round, Sneck, and Sproat. The two principal centres of the manufacture are Redditch and Kendal; and the makers in numbering their hooks work upon systems diametrically opposed, the Redditch scale being from 17 or 18, the smallest, up to 10/0, the largest; whereas, the

Kendal scale runs *vice versâ*, from 0/0 up to 20. For ome fishing, notably live-baiting, two or even three ooks are lashed at the shank, and are known as *doubles* nd *trebles*. *Eyed hooks* are those in which the shank nds in a loop, the latter being straight, upturned, or ownturned.

Landing-net—A net on telescopic or other handle, used for the same purpose as the gaff, but in landing smaller fish. On salmon rivers where the gaff is prohibited, the fish are secured by landing-nets of the largest and strongest pattern.

Leger-Tackle—A tackle that takes its name from the lead, which is either coffin-shaped or a bullet: in either case pierced so that the line passes freely in the direction of the hook, its movement back towards the angler being checked finally by a split shot, which is too large to pass through the lead. Two derivations, each having reference to the fact that the whole weight of the lead rests on the ground, have been suggested, the one from the French *leger*, the other from the German *liegen* (to lie).

Priest—An implement used to give the fish its quietus.

MAHSEER.

Rank Hook—A hook of which the barb projects unusually.

Snap Tackle—A treble or double hook pike-tackle, in using which the angler strikes as soon as the bait is seized. [*See* PIKE.]

Swim—The term used for the length of water to which the angler's operations are for the time being confined, and over which, in bottom-fishing, his float is allowed to travel at each cast.

Trace—A length of gimp or other material to which are attached the lead and spring bait.

AMERICAN ANGLING—[*See* **Black Bass, Ouananiche, Tarpon, &c.**]

INDIAN ANGLING — **Mahseer** — The Mahseer (*Barbus tor*) the largest of the Carp family (*Cyprinidæ*), commonly running to fifty pounds in weight, and attaining as much as one hundred and fifty pounds, has its habitat only in large, rocky, mountain rivers. In such rivers, it is distributed throughout the continent of India, extending into Afghanistan, Chitral, Burmah, and China, and seemingly Japan also. It is the most sporting fish in the East, the violence of its first rush on feeling the restraint of the hook being phenomenal, and constituting a special difficulty in its capture. It does not take the bait, as a salmon or trout ordinarily does, leisurely rising and leisurely returning to its place, but with a sudden blow which takes the angler by surprise, and which will even jerk the salmon-rod out of his hands, if he is unprepared. And this blow is instantly followed by a violent rush to which the run of a salmon can bear no comparison. The rapidity of this rush is accounted for by measurements of the tail and fins as compared with the rest of the body of the fish, which show that the superficial areas of the propelling and directing powers amount together to as much as the superficial area of the whole of the rest of the Mahseer's body. The sudden jerk and violent rush make it necessary to fish for it with a thoroughly *pliable* salmon-rod, that will yield to the first rush more rapidly than it is possible for the angler's hand to do, to yield indeed before the effect of the blow has even reached the angler's hand, and so to allow the line to run out, but for which the strongest tackle that can be well used with a rod must be broken. The tackle too must be good and strong, and the running line, the same as for salmon, should be one hundred and fifty yards long. Other rushes also the Mahseer will make before he yields, but none such as his first for suddenness and rapidity.

Another peculiarity of the Mahseer is that, differing herein from most predatory fish, it has no teeth at all in its soft, leathery mouth. In lieu thereof, it is furnished with great muscular power of jaw, by means of which it can exercise such a violent power of compression, that its prey is stunned and squeezed lifeless at the moment of capture. This is noticeable in a fishing spoon, the size and thickness of an ordinary dessert spoon, being crumpled up by it like a piece of paper. The spoons used must therefore be stout and strong, and the hooks of specially stout wire, not to resist tension, but to stand this violent power of compression. To produce the results it does, the Mahseer must also have a property very unusual in a fish, but with which we are familiar in the pad of the Tiger, of rigidifying the soft parts of the mouth at the moment of delivering its blow.

The smaller Mahseer can be taken with an artificial fly, the size of a salmon-fly, in the smaller tributaries, and in the shallows; but the best lure for the larger Mahseer is undoubtedly a small fish, or its imitation a spoon; and spoons are more used than any other bait, and of sizes varying from three-quarters of an inch to three inches in length, the general preference being for spoons one and three-quarters to two inches long. The three-inch spoon is used only in deep waters, for the rocky pools in which Mahseer delight are often twenty feet deep, and there the larger spoon shows best. The spoons must be mounted with treble hooks made of the specially strong wire above mentioned.

When the water is flood-coloured, Mahseer may be taken legering with a live bait at the bottom. In places where frogs abound, they are also taken with that lure, and if the place has been freely ground-baited, they may also be taken with parched grain bored to receive the hook. But this last style of fishing is only practised in special localities.

When rivers are coloured and chilled with melted snow-water, the Mahseer will take no bait. The best season in the South and on the West Coast is August, September, and October, when the rivers have cleared from the floods; while in Northern India it is, with exceptions, March and October.

In flood time, Mahseer migrate long distances up stream, ascending thousands of feet for the purpose of spawning at altitudes at which the water, though deep enough to hold the parent fish in flood time, will, by the time the spawn is hatched, have so dwindled that only tiny fry can stay in it, and the tiny fry will thus be safe from their larger predatory parents, which have meanwhile dropped down stream to their former habitats in the deeper rocky pools.

Rohu—The Rohu, Rahu, Rohi, or Rohita, as it is variously called in various localities, is the *Labeo rohita* of science, and may be taken as a typical specimen of the genus *Labeo*, of which genus there are twenty-five species. Of these, eight run large, attaining respectively to one and a half feet, two feet, three feet, and nearly five feet in length. The Rohu is distributed all over Northern India, attains three feet in length, is well known for its high edible qualities, and the excellent sport it shows, and it has been caught on the rod up to fifty-four pounds. As fry, it enters reservoirs through the river channels by which they are fed. The manner of its capture bears some similitude to roach-fishing, but the Rohu is as far above the roach in the nicety of skill required for its capture, in the play it shows when hooked, and in its flavour on the table, as it is in size. After ground-baiting for three days, it is fished for with a lump of paste bait from the size of the thumb-nail to the size of the end joint of the thumb, on a No. 1 Limerick hook, resting on the ground, the depth having been taken, and the float adjusted and re-adjusted with such careful accuracy, that the float neither lies down upon the water nor stands straight up, but is tilted so as to ride at an angle of about forty-five degrees with the surface of the water. The float, a special one, much more sensitive than anything used in roach-fishing, known in India as the Detective, is made of six inches of the stem of a peacock's tail feather, selecting the part that is one eighth of an inch thick, with a loop attached at the thin end only, half an inch at the top end is painted vermilion with oil colour, half an inch left white, and then again red and white alternately till there are three half-inch bands of red and two of white, the rest being left white. The rod too is a special one, much stronger than a roach rod, but as light and rigid, made of what is called in the tackle trade "whole cane," though it is not cane, which is a ground-creeper, but bamboo, which is a grass. The bamboo is a special one known as the Ringol, or solid bamboo, and is ten feet long. If longer, the float would be too far off for the bites to be visible. The float is straight under the rod-top. The line is of single stout gut at the end, and no shot are put upon it, only a little soft lead wire is wound round the head of the hook, so that it will rest on the bottom, and be concealed by the bait. The running line has to be fine so that it shall not weight the very sensitive float. In the rains the Rohu bite so freely that any ordinary roach-float would suffice, and the stroke should be made as for roach. But when the periodical rains have passed, or where the Rohu have been much fished, they bite so subtly, that the bite of a ten- or twenty-pound fish would not be perceptible on an ordinary roach-float. With the Detective float the first sign of a bite is given by the float leaving the angle at which it rode, and standing upright, thus attracting close attention to the fine bite that is to follow. Then the float begins to move up and down, but so slowly and so slightly that the eye could not follow the movement but for the aid of the alternate bands of red and white. This may go on for minutes that seem hours, the float going gradually and very slowly deeper and deeper till it nearly goes under, but it is of no use to strike till there comes a *rapid* succession of small bobs, sometimes no more than a vibration or quiver, but *rapid*. Then is the critical second, and the stroke must be delivered instantaneously, or it will be too late, and the same fish will thus steal the bait ten or twenty times, unless the angler is quick at the critical second. If he is, his reward is a fish that may be only two pounds, or may be twenty or thirty or more, and will make a good fight before it can be landed with so light a rod and tackle. The stolen bait serves to keep the fish round the angler, and when once the fish are collected the bites frequently follow each other in quick succession. But it nevertheless requires great quickness of eye and hand to make a good bag. One rod has been known to kill two hundred pounds weight in a day, from twenty-seven pounds and twenty-three pounds each downwards, the smallest being two pounds.

Kalbans—Kălbāns, the usual abbreviation of the more correct vernacular Kālăbāns, is *Labeo calbasu*, the scientific name having been incorrectly adopted from the vernacular. It is a thick, deep fish running to three feet in length, and certainly over twenty pounds in weight, found in the still waters of rivers throughout India; like the Rohu, getting as fry into reservoirs by the channels by which they are fed, flourishing there, and there fished for just like the Rohu. It adds to the sport that the bite of one is so like the bite of the other, that conjecture is busy as to which fish may be biting.

Mirgha—The Mirgha (*Cirrhina mrigala*) inhabits the same waters as the Kalbans, grows to the same size, and is fished for in precisely the same way, but is a more active fish in play.

White Carp—The White Carp (*Cirrhina cirrhosa*) grows to half the size of the Mirgha, but is otherwise similar, in locality, method of fishing, and activity.

Catla—The Catla (*Catla buchanani,*) a thick fish that attains six feet in length, has been caught with a rod up to one hundred pounds in weight, in the same localities, at the same time, employing the same baits and tackle, as for Rohu. It is much esteemed as food.

Carnatic Carp—The Carnatic Carp (*Barbus carnaticus*), though sometimes found in the runs, generally affects the stiller parts of the same rivers as support the Mahseer, though it also strays further into the plains away from the foot of the mountains, not being so dependent on rock for its food supplies. It attains twenty-five pounds, but is more ordinarily taken from two to seven or eight pounds. Swimming in shoals like dace, and rising to a fly in the same manner as they do, it affords excellent sport to the angler fishing with a fourteen feet double-handed trout-rod, casting three flies, the sizes of a medium and a small salmon-fly, and of a large loch-trout fly, on a collar of single salmon-gut. They are chiefly found in the deep eddies under the shade of the forest trees, whose leaves and flowers they largely feed upon. The larger take a small trout spoon readily. Space will not allow of the mention of several sorts of similar fish of which this one may be taken as a fair type in size, habitat, and manner of capture.

Chital—The Chital or Seetul (*Notopterus chitala*), which favours the larger rivers of Northern India, Burmah, and Siam, attains four feet in length. Silver sided, very flat and deep, it feeds on the bottom, but swims horizontally, and is a very game fish to the angler, leaping four feet into the air again and again on being hooked, and otherwise showing great activity. It has a very small head and mouth, the bait therefore must be small, and there is none better than its natural food the small mullet (*Mugil cascasia*), three and a half inches long, mounted on small trebles, and spun very slowly close to the bottom, where it may be allowed to rest from time to time. The bite of this large fish, which runs to eighty pounds, and is very commonly taken at twelve or sixteen pounds, is a very small nibble, which it needs a light hand to feel, and which must be answered immediately. It has a smaller congener in Southern India, *Notopterus kapirat*, which does not run over two pounds, and may be taken in the same way, or with prawn or worm.

Freshwater Sharks—Indian rivers supply many of these Siluroids, of which it will suffice to mention *Bagarius yarrellii*, *Silundia gangetica*, *Wallago attu*, which have no English synonyms, except that of Freshwater Sharks, and each of which attains six feet in length, and two other *Macrones* which run to much the same size. They feed mostly at the bottom, using their feelers as much as their eyes, and should be fished for with a live bait of about half a pound on a line weighted to the bottom, the hooks being such as would be used in England for Pike, mounted on stout gimp or wire, as these fish have very formidable teeth, and a grip so strong that it is very difficult to loosen when once they have closed on an object. For landing them, a gaff-hook is necessary. Though they offer strong resistance, taking out line with no denial, they display no great activity, and therein sink, as a game fish, to the low level of the Pike, though as regards size and teeth, they compare with him much as a tiger might with a cat. Space will not allow of the mention of the numerous species of lesser Siluroids with which the waters of the East abound.

Baril—There are several species of *Barilius*, running about the size of a hungry beck-trout, which are keen takers of a small trout-fly, as many as seven dozen having been taken in a forenoon, but one of the genus Baril (*Barilius bola*) is said to attain five pounds in weight, but ordinarily runs to one and a half pounds, and swimming in shoals, as many as three have, on occasion, been taken at one cast on a collar of three flies the size of a loch-trout fly. Though not of the *Salmonidæ* they bear such a strong resemblance to a Trout, that they are commonly called the Indian Trout, and are held

in very high esteem by the angler as a sporting fish.

Chilwa—The Chilwa (*Aspidoparia morar*), misnamed by science *Chela*, may be called the Indian Bleak. So small a fish (six inches) would not be mentioned, but for its extraordinary numbers and the rapidity with which it may be taken with a small fly, which make it very popular with some; forty, fifty, and even sixty having been taken in an hour by one rod with two flies up.

Bà-min and Begtie—These are sea fish entering estuaries, to be taken similarly, spinning as for Salmon, but with hooks mounted on gimp or wire.

The Bàmin (*Polynemus tetradactylus*) attains six feet in length, and commonly runs from ten to twenty pounds, and is celebrated for the amount of tackle it breaks, on account of its extraordinary activity and strength. The Begtie (*Lates calcarifer*) runs over thirty pounds, and is much esteemed for food. It is known to Europeans as the Cock-up.

Megalops—*Megalops cyprinoides* is estuarial, but accommodates itself to fresh water in ponds, runs to a cubit in length, and may be taken with a white loch-fly or a trout-spoon. It is active.

Marral—The Marral (*Ophiocephalus marulius*) attains four feet; four other species of the same genus attain three feet. They are found in the still pools in rivers, and in ponds, are similar to the Pike in their habits, but are best taken at the surface with a live frog.

Hilsa—The Hilsa (*Clupea ilisha*) is far famed for its specially excellent flavour, and is said to take a white fly. But to treat of these, and Mangoe fish, and Mullets numerous, and Eels of sorts, and Gudgeon attaining a cubit in length and three pounds in weight, space will not allow.

H. S. THOMAS.

ANTELOPES (Characters and Distribution of)—The term "Antelope" is so familiar to all, that it may be a matter of surprise to many to learn it is one totally incapable of definition. Nevertheless, this affords no reason for the rejection of the name, which, in its widest sense, is the most convenient collective title for a large and important group of Hollow-horned Ruminants coming under the designation neither of Oxen, Sheep, nor Goats. By zoologists, the Hollow-horned Ruminants, or *Bovidæ*, are divided into a number of sectional groups, or sub-families, one of which includes the Oxen, and a second the Sheep and Goats, while the others contain among them the various Antelopes and certain forms serving to connect the latter with the Goats. It is thus evident that the term "Antelope" has not the same zoological significance as Oxen, but comprises a number of more or less distinct groups ranking in the same grade as the latter. Some of the groups of Antelopes are, indeed, closely related to the Oxen—with which they are connected by means of the Anoa of Celebes—while others exhibit an equally intimate relationship with the Goats and Sheep.

In its widest acceptation, the term Antelope may, as already said, be taken to include all the members of the *Bovidæ* which are neither Oxen, Sheep, nor Goats. There is, however, an intermediate group connecting the more typical Antelopes with the Goats, and hence termed the Goat-like Antelopes. These are all mountain-dwelling forms, and include the Gorals (*Cemas*) and Serows (*Nemorhædus*) of Eastern Asia, the Himalayan Takin (*Budorcas*), the so-called Rocky Mountain Goat (*Haploceros*) of North America, and the European Chamois (*Rupicapra*);—the latter being the most Antelope-like of all. Eliminating these transitional forms—which constitute a sub-family (*Rupicaprinæ*) by themselves, ranking with the Oxen (*Bovinæ*) and Sheep and Goats (*Caprinæ*)—it is somewhat less difficult to give an approximate definition of Antelopes in a popular sense. True Antelopes, then, are Hollow-horned Ruminants, generally of more or less light and elegant build, and carrying the head raised considerably above the line of the back. Their horns—which may be present either in one or both sexes—differ greatly in relative size, but are quite different from those of either the Oxen or Sheep. As a rule they are more or less cylindrical, while they are frequently somewhat lyre-shaped, and are often ringed for a longer or shorter distance above the base. In most cases their direction is more or less upright; and in certain instances they are spirally twisted. A very general, although by no means universal, feature of Antelopes, is the presence of a gland beneath the eye; such glands being wanting in the Oxen and Goats, although present in most of the Sheep. More important is the circumstance that the bony cores supporting the horns of the Antelopes are nearly always solid throughout, whereas those of the other three groups are extensively hollowed internally. An important distinction between the Oxen (*Bovinæ*) on the one hand and the Sheep and Goats (*Caprinæ*) on the other is to be found in the structure of the upper molar teeth; those of the former being nearly square in section, whereas those of the latter are oblong. Among the Antelopes, both these types are to be met with, the Gemsbok and Sable Antelope group having Ox-like molars, whereas those of the Gazelles, Hartebeests, and Gnus are of the Goat-like form. Moreover, certain Antelopes, such as Eland and Koodoo, have a third type of molar structure; the crowns of these teeth being short—instead of tall—and thus resembling those of some of the Deer. These differences alone are sufficient to show that Antelopes in no sense form a single zoological group, but that they comprise a number of distinct groups which for many purposes it is convenient to brigade together under a common designation. Consequently it will be manifest that no further attempt at a definition of the assemblage can be made.

Exclusive of the Goat-like group, these animals may be divided into the following seven sections, or sub-families, viz:—(1) *Bubalinæ*, Hartebeests and Gnus; (2) *Cephalophinæ*, Duikers and Four-horned Antelope; (3) *Neotraginæ*, Dik-diks, Steinboks, Grysbok, &c.; (4) *Cervicaprinæ*, Rhebok, Waterbuck, Rietbok, &c.; (5) *Antilopinæ*, Pallas, Saiga, Chiru, Gazelles, &c.; (6) *Hippotraginæ*, Sable Antelope Oryx, Addax, and their allies; (7) *Tragelaphinæ*, Nilgai, Harnessed Antelopes, Koodoo, and Eland

The whole of the numerous Antelopes comprised in these seven groups are exclusively confined to the Old World, while the great majority are restricted to Africa south of the northern tropic, or at least to Africa with Syria and Arabia. The first section, for instance, has no representatives beyond the countries named, and it is indeed only one species of Hartebeest that is even found beyond Africa, the Gnus being restricted to those portions of that continent lying south of the northern tropic. In the second section, the Four-horned Antelope is Indian, whereas all the numerous species of Duikers (*Cephalophus*) are restricted to Africa south of the Sahara. The members of the third section—all of which are small-sized creatures—are absolutely confined to the area last named; and none of the fourth section (*Cervicaprinæ*) extend their range beyond the same limits. Skipping section (5), it will be found that most of the members of the *Hippotraginæ* inhabit Ethiopian Africa (as that part of the continent lying to the south of the northern tropic is called), although the Addax is found in Northern Africa and Arabia, and the Beatrix Antelope (*Oryx beatrix*) inhabits the latter country, and is said, indeed, to range as far as Bushire. Both the groups enjoying this wider range are desert-haunting forms. In the sixth section, the Nilgai (*Boselaphus*) alone is Indian, all the other forms being Ethiopian. Reverting to the fifth section, or *Antilopinæ*, we find this the most widely spread of all; most of its representatives being inhabitants of more or less desert districts. Indeed, the only exclusively Ethiopian genus in this group is the one containing the Pallas (*Æpyceros*). Of the others, the one species of *Saiga* is confined to the steppes of Central Asia, the Chiru, which alone represents *Pantholops*, inhabits the highlands of Tibet, while the Blackbuck, forming the sole member of the now restricted genus *Antilope*, has its home on the plains of India. Of the Gazelles, the typical genus *Gazella* has the widest distribution of all the Antelopes, ranging from South Africa (where it is represented by the Springbok) through the eastern and northern districts of the same continent, to Syria, Arabia, Asia Minor, Persia, Baluchistan, northern India, Afghanistan, and Mongolia. Probably this wide distribution is to be accounted for by the desert-frequenting habits of most Gazelles, which has enabled them to traverse districts impassable to the majority of their kindred. The more aberrant Gazelles, such as the Gerenuk (*Lithocranius*), Clarke's Antelope (*Ammodorcas*), and the smaller Beira (*Dorcatragus*), are, however, exclusively confined to Eastern Ethiopia.

It will thus be apparent that by far the great majority of Antelopes are Ethiopian (including in this designation part of Arabia), and indeed, with the exception of the Gazelles the only true Antelopes found elsewhere than Africa, Syria. and Arabia, are the Indian Four-horned Antelope, Blackbuck, and Nilgai, the Tartarian Saiga, and the Thibetan Chiru. Most noteworthy is the circumstance that no true Antelopes are to be found in the countries lying to the eastward of the Bay of Bengal; although Goat-like Antelopes of the genera *Cemas* and *Nemorhædus* range into Burma, China, Japan, &c.

Ethiopian Africa thus being pre-eminently the headquarters of the true Antelopes, it is curious to find that at no very distant epoch of the earth's history many extinct species closely allied to modern African types inhabited India, Persia, Greece, and Hungary. Hence it is evident that there has been a great southern migration of the Antelopes; while it is probable that the entrance of the group into Africa is a comparatively recent event. Possibly the original northern forms may have been suited only to a comparatively dry climate, which would account for their never having been able to effect an entrance into the Malayan countries; but it is extremely difficult to discover any adequate reason for the extinction in India of nearly all its original inhabitants belonging to this group.

Be this as it may, it is evident that when the original migrants from the north (which were probably comparatively few in species) succeeded in establishing themselves in Ethiopian Africa, they found a country so eminently suited to their requirements, that they increased, alike in number and in the development of generic and specific types, in a manner unparalleled in any other part of the world. Although it is quite probable that Antelopes were originally inhabitants of open and comparatively dry districts, their Ethiopian descendants have developed the capacity of adapting themselves to stations of every kind. Whereas the Gemsbok and other members of the genus *Oryx*, together with the Gazelles, and many of the Hartebeests, are still inhabitants of open and more or less desert districts, the Waterbuck, Lechive, and other species of *Cobus*, as well as the Sitatunga and others of the Harnessed Antelopes (*Tragelaphus*), delight to dwell among the reeds fringing the banks of rivers and swamps, or even to stand neck-deep in the water of lakes. Some members of the latter group inhabit the steaming tropical forests of the Congo valley, and in Senegambia it seems not improbable that the Derbian Eland is a forest animal. Not only are the plains tenanted by their special denizens, but the mountains have been invaded by forms like the Klipspringer and Rhebok, which rival, or excel, the Chamois in their jumping powers. Structural peculiarities have accompanied their adaptations, the Klipspringer having its hoofs short and rounded like those of a Goat, whereas those of the Sitatunga are enormously elongated. As regards food, too, Antelopes seem capable of great adaptations; since whereas most kinds live on grass, a Steinbok inhabiting two small islands near Zanzibar lives entirely on leaves and twigs.

At the present day, Africa is undoubtedly the paradise of Antelopes, but it is very doubtful if this would ever have been the case had Deer succeeded in penetrating south of the Sahara. Why Antelopes reached Ethiopia, while Deer were kept out, we shall probably never know.

R. LYDEKKER.

ANTELOPE SHOOTING. **Europe and Asia**—Antelope shooting in various forms is to be obtained in many parts of the world, but it may be said with truth that the natural home of this family lies in Africa, and especially in **South Africa.** Here, magnificent sport is still to be had with antelopes ranging in size from the Eland, whose stature exceeds that of a stall ox, down to the tiny Blue Buck, which is scarcely larger than a good hare. In Europe, the chase of the Chamois, which is stalked or driven among the difficult mountains of the Alps, is well known. In the Caucasus and Mongolia, the wary **Djerân** (*Gazella gutturosa*) is occasionally stalked, but more often coursed with greyhounds upon the great steppes. The curious **Saiga** (*Saiga tartarica*), with its hideous swollen-looking nose, is a denizen of South Russia and the Central Asian steppes; it is nowhere abundant and has seldom fallen to the rifles of English sportsmen. The **Thibetan antelope** (*Pantholops hodgsoni*) is another rare species, hitherto seldom obtained by Europeans, found among hills and valleys beyond the northern frontiers of India and in Turkestan. It carries handsome horns, strongly annulated the best measurement hitherto obtained is 27⅞ inches. In India itself, the well known **Blackbuck** (*Antilope cervicapra*), whose characteristic horns are perhaps more familiar than those of any of the smaller antelopes in European collections, is to be found, often in large numbers, in suitable localities from the north to the south of the country, on wide, open plains or in grassy places near the banks of rivers. Among English sportsmen it is almost invariably pursued by stalking, and affords excellent sport. The natives hunt it occasionally with the Cheetah, and at other times stalk it by aid of trained bullocks or with a bullock cart. The average weight of a Blackbuck is about 85 lbs.; the longest horn measurement hitherto recorded 28¼ inches—straight measurement. The **Nilgai** (*Boselaphus tragocamelus*), which is now usually included among the tragelaphine groups of antelopes, is a large and somewhat odd-looking beast, found in level country varied by bush and light jungle, in many parts of India. As beasts of chase Nilgai are not looked upon with much favour; they can be pretty easily shot, and natives in many localities have a strong prejudice against their being destroyed.

A good blue-bull, as the male of the Nilgai is called, stands from 4 feet 4 inches to 4 feet 6 inches at the shoulder. The horns are short

BLACKBUCK.
Ht. at shoulder, 32 in. Av. horn meas. 22 in. Max. horn meas. 40½ in.

and ox-like, and the best recorded measurement is 9¼ inches. The **Four-horned** Antelope, or **Charsingha** (*Tetraceros quadricornis*), is found sparingly in many parts of India in bush, jungle, and grassy covert. It is a small antelope, and lies very close in covert, and is more often than not snapped with the shot gun, as are the smaller bush-loving antelopes of Africa.

The **Indian Gazelle,** commonly known as the **Ravine deer** (*Gazella bennetti*), is found in ravines and among rocky hills and scrub in many parts of India, Beluchistan and Southern Persia. It carries nice horns measuring from 10 to 14 inches in length and, although sly and wary, can be stalked successfully by the careful gunner. Camels and shooting-horses are occasionally employed to aid the sportsman in his operations with this antelope. [*See* CHICKARA.] The **Thibetan Ravine deer** (*Gazella picticaudata*), found in Mongolia and Western Thibet, is an animal strongly resembling the last-named species, and of much the same habits.

Among Indian antelopes, one can scarcely pass over the mountain-loving **Goral**, or Himalayan Chamois (*Nemorhœdus goral*), and the

RAVINE DEER.
Ht. at shoulder, 26 in. Av. horn meas. 9 in. Max. horn meas. 14½ in.

Himalayan **Serow** (*Nemorhœdus bubalinus*), goat-like antelopes, which afford excellent mountain stalking. Closely allied to the last-named is the Serow of Sumatra (*N. sumatrensis*), found, as its name implies, among the hills of Sumatra, as well as on the mainland.

Gazelle Stalking—The true desert-loving gazelles, which include many species, enjoy a wide range from Persia and Central Asia to Arabia and North Africa. Chief among these may be named the Dorcas, Atlas, Arabian, Persian, Isabella, and Sœmmering's gazelles; *Gazella dama*, *G. rubifrons*, and the Addra gazelle. The Somali lowland gazelle (*G. spekei*) is remarkable for a curious bulging skin formation upon the nose, which easily distinguishes it. The Somali Plateau gazelle bears a strong resemblance to the last-named, but lacks the nasal peculiarity. Grant's gazelle, carrying very beautiful horns extending to 30 inches in length; Clarke's gazelle, remarkable for its long, slender, giraffe-like neck; and Thomson's and Waller's gazelles are all very handsome forms discovered in East and North-East Africa within recent years. All these gazelles are only to be stalked and secured at somewhat long ranges by accurate rifle-shooting. Some of them, in countries where they have been much shot at, are almost unapproachable. Occasionally patches of bush or isolated thorn trees may be made use of in approaching these wary plain-dwellers, but it must be admitted that, as a rule, stalking gazelles upon open flats, under a burning sun, is extremely trying work for the sportsman. By the aid of natives, it is sometimes possible to conduct driving operations, and to push the game within shot of the gunner lying concealed; and occasionally the old South African Bushman plan is resorted to, and, arrayed as an ostrich, the European sportsman is enabled to get right among troops of gazelle and other game and shoot what he requires. This last is an exceedingly deadly method, but the gunner has first to obtain a complete skin, head, and neck of an ostrich, and great care has to be exercised in approaching in a natural and ostrich-like manner and in taking advantage of the wind, which, if blowing from the direction of the stalker, would at once betray him. For gazelle shooting a ·450 or ·303 rifle is the best weapon that can be employed, and as few shots are obtained at less than 200 yards, it is a matter of vital importance that the sighting be adjusted with extreme care and accuracy.

South African Shooting—In South Africa, where during immemorial ages vast numbers of antelopes of many and remarkable species must have wandered and fed in undisturbed possession, much of the game has, as in other parts of the world, been shot off. Yet much still remains. South of the Zambesi, some thirty species of antelope are still to be found; many of them near the southern littoral, others in far, remote places where they are difficult of access. The **Eland**, the largest antelope in the world [*see* ELAND], is now somewhat scarce in South Africa. The **Sable** and **Roan** antelopes (*Hippotragus niger* and *H. equinus*), two of the most magnificent forms in the African Continent, are to be met with in North Matabeleland, Mashonaland, and thence to the East Coast, sparingly in Khama's country, and thence northward beyond the Zambesi. One of the great advantages of hunting in South Africa—although it is, too, answerable for much of the rapid disappearance of the fauna—is the fact that horses can be always, or nearly always, employed (except towards the East Coast, where the Tse-Tse fly abounds), in pursuing the larger antelopes and heavy game. A ·450 or ·500 rifle, or the old sporting Martini-Henry—still one of the most useful of all weapons—is usually employed in shooting the larger South African antelopes. Of late the ·303 has been used, and although differences of opinion have arisen as to its merits, Mr. F. C. Selous and other well-known hunters speak of its results in terms of satisfaction. The sable and roan antelopes are usually found in semi-bushy country, or among the lower slopes of hills and kopjes. Sables run in troops of from a dozen to fifty; Roan antelopes in small bands of from six to fourteen. Both of these great antelopes are possessed of considerable speed and staying power, although they can occasionally be run down on horseback. The magnificent horns of the Sable antelope, scimitar-shaped and strongly annulated, form one of the greatest prizes of the hunter in South Africa. The Roan antelope has horns of a somewhat similar character, but shorter and thicker in growth. It ought to be remembered in approaching wounded individuals of these antelopes, that both are extremely savage, and, unless completely disabled, will charge desperately. Many a good dog has been killed by the deadly sweep of a Sable or Roan antelope's horns. A good Sable antelope bull will stand 4 ft. 6 in. at the withers and carry horns measuring 45 in. over the curve. A Roan antelope averages two or three inches more in height, but bears horns which lack the magnificent sweep of the Sable's and seldom exceed 32 inches over the curve.

It should be borne in mind in shooting antelopes, and especially the larger African

SABLE ANTELOPE.
Ht. at shoulder, 54 in. Av. horn meas. (male), 40 in. Max. horn meas. 46 in.

antelopes, that they are possessed of immense vitality, and will often run clean away from the hunter after having received wounds that to the casual observer would inevitably signify immediate collapse. Even with a bullet through the heart or lungs, an antelope will succeed sometimes in making good its escape. The writer has spoored for miles a blue wildebeest bull, which had been shot clean through the lung with a Martini-Henry bullet, and then had to abandon the pursuit to a Bushman tracker. As few Europeans, unless they have spent many years in the pursuit of great game, are equal to the science of spooring, it is necessary to have at hand a native or two, preferably Bushmen if they can be obtained, who will find and track game and will take up the spoor of animals when wounded. Many a good head of game has been lost for want of a native spoorer.

The **Koodoo**, one of the biggest and noblest of the African Antelopes, is noticed elsewhere [*see* KOODOO], as are the **Gemsbuck** [*see* ORYX] and the black and blue **Wildebeest** [*see* GNU]. The **Hartebeest** is one of the most characteristic of the Ethiopian group of Antelopes, and is represented in South Africa by the Cape hartebeest (*Bubalis caama*) and Lichtenstein's hartebeest (*B. lichtensteini*). In East and North-East Africa are to be found Jackson's hartebeest (*B. jacksoni*), the Tora hartebeest (*B. tora*), Swayne's hartebeest (*B. swaynei*), Cooke's hartebeest (*B. cookei*), and the Senegal and Koba hartebeests (*B. senegalensis* and *B. koba*), which two last are found indifferently in East and West Africa. Besides these forms we have the West African hartebeest (*B. major*) which is only met with in West Africa. All these hartebeests have a strong family resemblance, although there are slight differences in colour, habits, and the shape of the horns. They are all characterised by speed, staying powers, and vitality, so that even when severely wounded they will not unfrequently make good their escape. It is useless attempting to run down a hartebeest, or its near cousin the Tsesseby, in tail-on-end chase. Such an attempt is sufficient to break the heart of the stoutest horse, and, indeed, the writer has seen a good African shooting pony which succumbed from nothing but the effects of a desperate gallop after hartebeest. The Cape hartebeest—often called by the Boers the Rooi (or red) hartebeest—stands about 4 feet at the withers, and has, like most of its kin, very drooping quarters. Its colour is of a reddish-brown, darker upon the back, shoulders, and fore legs. The face is black and extremely long, giving the animal a quaint, old-fashioned expression, while the rugged horns are perched upon an extremely high frontal bone. It is still common in Bechuanaland, the Kalahari, Great Namaqualand, and about the Botletli River, in Ngamiland. It runs in good sized troops, varying from twelve or fifteen to fifty and occasionally even more. It is found indifferently in open, park-like forest country, or upon grassy plains.

These animals, although shy and suspicious, are yet occasionally very stupid. They have a habit of wheeling round and halting in the middle of a run and the mounted hunter can thus often dismount and obtain a fair shot. They are obstinate, too, in sticking to a particular line of flight, and the writer has more than once cut a troop in half in this way and secured an easy shot. They can be turned from their course, as can other South African antelopes, by firing a bullet or two over their heads so as to strike the ground in front of them; and if the leader of the troop can be wounded and turned out, the rest will often become bewildered and afford easy shooting. If it were not for these weak points, the hartebeest would be one of the most difficult of all animals to bring to bag. As it is, it is by no means one of the easiest. Lichtenstein's hartebeest is found in Mashonaland, Gazaland, Portuguese South-East Africa, and thence northward into East Africa. Its habits are very similar to those of *Bubalis caama.*

The **Tsesseby** (*Bubalis lunatus*) is a handsome antelope, averaging in height close on four feet, nearly related to the hartebeest and greatly resembling that antelope in appearance and colouring. The horns, which are crescent shaped, differ, however, a good deal from those of the Cape hartebeest. At the present day the Tsesseby is most plentiful in Mashonaland, Nganiland, and in South-East Africa between the Pungwe and Jambesi rivers. It is the swiftest and most enduring of all antelopes, which is saying a good deal; yet, thanks to the characteristics which have been pointed out in the case of its near congener the hartebeest, it is often brought to bag. **Hunters' Antelope** (*Bubalis hunteri*) is a species lately discovered in East Africa, also related to the hartebeest. The horns are, however, much more prolonged and extend in length to 26¼ inches. Up to the present this antelope has been chiefly found on the Tana River in East Africa.

An extremely interesting group of animals to the sportsman are the water-loving antelopes, which include the **Lechwe** (*Cobus leché*), the **Pookoo** (*C. vardoni*), the **Sitatunga**, or Speke's antelope (*Tragelaphus spekei*), the **Inyala** (*T. angasi*), the **Reedbuck** (*Cervicapra arundineum*), **Penrice's Waterbuck** (*Cobus*

WATERBUCK.
Ht. at shoulder, 48 in. Av. horn meas. 20 in. Max. horn meas. 33½ in.

penricei), and the **True Waterbuck** (*C. ellipsiprymnus*), all of which are found in South or South Central Africa. The **Sing-Sing** (*C. defassus*) is an East African form of the large waterbuck, while the White-eared Waterbuck (*C. leucotis*) and another form *Cobus kob* are smaller antelopes found in Central and East

PALLAH.
Ht. at shoulder, 36 in. Av. horn meas. 20 in. Max. horn meas. 27½ in.

Africa. Of these animals, the True Waterbuck, the Lechwe, the Reedbuck, and the Sing-sing are best known to hunters. The Pookoo is scarce and restricted as to habitat, while the Sitatunga, although flourishing in large numbers in the swamps and reedbeds of the river systems of the interior, is extremely difficult of approach and seldom falls to the rifle. In South Africa, the Waterbuck, the Lechwe, and the Reedbuck all afford excellent rifle-shooting on the river systems beyond the Vaal. Penrice's Waterbuck, a new species, has only lately been discovered by Mr. G. Penrice in the country behind Benguella, Portuguese West Africa. It is a handsome antelope, differing only slightly from the Sing-Sing and the South African Waterbuck. The Inyala, a form between the Bushbuck and the Koodoo, frequents the rivers and swamps of South-East Africa, and is extremely local. It may still be found in the neighbourhood of Delagoa Bay, and is well worthy of the hunter's labours.

The **Pallah**, or **Impala** (*Æpyceros melampus*), is an extremely elegant antelope, bearing peculiarly characteristic horns, which differ from most other species; and it is to be met with in considerable troops from the Limpopo River northwards into East Africa, in bushy and forest country, upon the borders of such of the river systems as are not surrounded by swamps.

Where it has not been much disturbed, the beautiful Pallah roams in large numbers, as many as eighty or a hundred in a troop. Thanks to the nature of its habitat, where covert is abundant, it is not a difficult antelope to shoot. In height the Pallah stands slightly under three feet, while representative horns range from twenty to twenty-seven inches over the curve.

Three small antelopes which give very excellent mountain shooting in South Africa are the **Klipspringer** (*Oreotragus saltator*), the **Vaal**, or **Grey, Rhebok** (*Pelea capreola*), and the **Red Rhebok** (*Cervicapra lalandi*). These antelopes frequent many of the mountain ranges of South Africa, and afford admirable shooting with the rifle. The **Klipspringer** is found as far north as Abyssinia. It is a very charming and astonishingly active little mountaineer, and well deserves its title, "Chamois of Africa."

The well-known **Springbuck** (*Gazella euchore*) is happily still abundant in many parts of South Africa, from the Karroos of Cape Colony to Ngamiland, and even Benguella on the West Coast. This fleet, active, and characteristic antelope affords some of the best stalking in South Africa. It can be driven by approaching in line *downwind*, when it invariably takes up-wind and can be cut off by gunners mounted or in carts; or it can be quietly approached by slowly walking a horse until within four hundred yards and then dismounting and sidling in for a shot. Very accurate shooting is, however, required for the springbuck, which is seldom bagged nowadays at less than three hundred yards range. The **Blesbok** and **Bontebok** (*Damalis albifrons* and *D. pygargus*) are two very handsome and remarkable antelopes, which formerly thronged the plains of South Africa, but are now only to be found preserved on a few farms. As game animals they may be considered, unfortunately, almost extinct.

The **Bushbucks** (*Tragelaphus*), **Steinbuck** (*Nanotragus campestris*), **Oribi** (*N. scoparia*), **Grysbuck** (*N. melanotis*), **Duiker** (*Cephalophus grimmi*), **Natal Redbuck** (*C. natalensis*), and **Bluebuck** (*C. monticola*) are small antelopes, which in many parts of Africa are to be obtained, principally amid bush and thickets, or, in the case of the Steinbuck and Oribi, on grassy plains. As a rule, most of these antelopes fall to the shot gun. They are often bagged when the gunner is in pursuit of feathered game. In the thick bush fringing the littoral of Cape Colony, big drives are organised, in which large numbers of bushbuck and bluebuck are secured. The **Harnessed Bushbuck** (*Tragelaphus scriptus*), a very beautiful form of bushbuck, is found upon the banks of the river systems of South-Central, East, and West Africa, from the Limpopo northwards, and is a prize that any sportsman may well be proud of.

North America—Turning to North America we find but two antelopes to make note of. Of these, the well-known **Pronghorn** (*Antilocapra americana*) has become so scarce as to be now hardly accessible as a beast of chase; while the singular **Rocky Mountain Goat** (*Haplocerus montanus*), an excellent quarry for those fond of the most arduous and difficult mountain shooting, may be classed among the goats almost as much as among the antelopes. Perhaps the best ground at the present day for Rocky Mountain goat is among the snow- and ice-covered ranges of Alaska.

ROCKY MOUNTAIN GOAT.
Ht. at shoulder, 35½ in. Av. horn meas. (male) 8 in. Max. horn meas. 11½ in.

H. A. BRYDEN.

ANTELOPE COURSING—The common Indian Antelope (*Antilope cervicapra*) is so fleet of foot, that it is ordinarily held to be useless to slip greyhounds after it. Even two greyhounds held in leash, the second to take up the running when the first was distressed, have been known to be successively exhausted by one antelope with apparent ease, aided though they were by two riders similarly riding alternately. On soft ground, however, after rain, the pointed hoofs of the antelope sink so that a single greyhound will pull down the fleetest of them. Aware of this, the antelope, if surprised among cultivation, where the fields are divided by ridges, will keep to the hard dry ridges, however rectangular, never cutting a corner across the plough, though the hound be within a stride, and therein showing its wisdom, makes good its escape. But even on hard ground, a fawn well selected from the herd by a practised eye as young enough may be run down if well ridden to. When the herd see the hounds closing up to a fawn, they circle round and cut in between the fawn and the hounds, and dally with them to lead them off. Then the riders must be close up, so as to be able to call off the hounds and lay them on to the fawn again. The herd will repeat the manœuvre again and again. A fawn so young that it had milk in its stomach took a field of well-mounted men with five deerhounds ten miles at such speed that all the hounds were exhausted, and all the horses but two, which only continued the chase by being ridden and saved alternately.

ANTELOPE SNARING—In India antelope snaring is practised in the rutting season after the following method. A tame buck antelope, his horns dressed with nooses, is led in sight of the herd. His instinct prompts him to join the does, a move resented by the black buck of the herd. A fierce combat ensues, in the course of which the horns may become so entangled, that both eventually fall exhausted and in such plight are easily secured.

ARCHERY—The practice of Archery can be traced back to very ancient times, though authorities differ as to when the use of the bow first became common in England. The many statutes for the encouragement and directing of the practice of Archery, the provisions made by them that practically every one should be skilled in the use of the bow, are sufficient evidence of the value which our ancestors placed upon it before "villanous saltpetre" ousted it from the proud position of our national weapon. After fire-arms had taken the place of the bow in war, the practice of archery appears in a great measure to have died out, though it still existed in the north of England, and up to about 1760 in the Finsbury fields.

The revival of Archery as a pastime can be traced to 1780, when Mr. Waring, the Secretary or Manager of the Museum belonging to Sir Ashton Lever at Leicester House, took it up. Finding that it improved his health, he persuaded Sir Ashton Lever to try it. He did so, and, fascinated by it, with the assistance of his friends founded in 1781 the Royal Toxophilite Society which, from that time to the present day, has maintained its position at the head of the sport. Patronised and practised by the Prince of Wales and other Royal Dukes, archery at once sprang into popularity, and numerous Societies were founded, which flourished till the stern reality of war gave people little time to practise the peaceable sport of the bow. On the conclusion of peace, it was again warmly taken up, old Societies were revived, new ones were started all over the country, and in 1844 the first Grand National Archery Meeting took place at York. At the present time, there are numerous Societies all over England, and the five public meetings held annually show the popularity of the sport.

Of the pleasures of archery and the facilities which it affords to both ladies and gentlemen for physical and graceful exercise there can be no doubt, and its fascination is well known to all who shoot. Unfortunately it has the drawback of being difficult, and without regular practice and a knowledge of how to do it, it is not easy to excel, this however in the eyes of its votaries being one of its principal charms.

The object of this article is to give instruction which will assist beginners to commence shooting in the correct way, a great obstacle to success being the assumption of wrong methods at first, faults being thus established which it is difficult afterwards to eradicate. Many books of instructions on the subject have been written, commencing with Ascham's *Toxophilus* in 1545, down to the present day, good, bad and indifferent. It is therefore impossible to write a new essay on archery without repeating much of what has been already said by the writers who come under the first category, notably Messrs. Roberts,[1] Ford,[2] Butt,[3] and the latest exponent of the art, the Rev. Eyre Hussey.[4]

The logical course seems to be first to describe the implements of the craft, and then endeavour to teach their use.

Bows are called "Self" if made of one piece of wood, and "Backed" if made of two or more strips of wood glued together. Self bows are generally made of yew or lance, though the term as applied to those made of the former wood is misleading, as they are almost invariably spliced at the handle. Self-yew is the dearest bow made, self-lance the cheapest. Backed bows are made of various combinations, yew-backed yew, as implied by the name, having both back and belly made of yew, being the best. In all other descriptions the back is made of hickory; yew, fustic, washaba, or lance supplying the belly. In three-piece bows the back is generally hickory, the centre fustic, and the inside of the belly yew.

There is no question that the best bow is either a self-yew, or a yew-backed yew, there being little to choose between them; but both are expensive, require careful handling, and are easily damaged. Beginners are therefore advised to commence with a self-lance, taking to a three-piece yew, fustic, and hickory as their shooting advances, and a self or yew-backed yew, when their skill and knowledge warrant it. A self-lance does not last long, as it soon loses its "cast" or power, but the three-piece will last a long time. The more expensive bows are certainly the most pleasant to shoot with, but it must not be thought that good scores cannot be made with the cheaper backed ones, provided they are made the right shape; indeed many good shots use nothing else.

The shape of all bows should be much the same, namely, it should be quite straight, or slightly follow the string (Fig. 1). If the bow is at all reflexed, as it is called when the back bends forward, it is apt to jar on being loosed, the only exception being when a self-yew is

[1] *The English Bowman.*
[2] *Archery, its Theory and Practice.*
[3] Butt's *Ford.*
[4] *Archery* (The Badminton Library).

made this shape in consequence of the natural growth of the wood.

The length of a lady's bow should be from 5 ft. 5 in. to 5 ft. 7 in., and of a man's from 5 ft. 11 in. to 6 ft. 1 in., the longer bow being the best. If longer arrows than the respective standard lengths of 25 and 28 inches are to be used, the bow should be longer, or the increased strain may break it. The weight marked on a bow is the number of pounds it will take to pull it—25 inches if a lady's, or 28 inches if a man's.

In choosing a bow care should be taken that the grain is close, even, straight, smooth, and free from knots or pins, especially on the centre of the belly, as the rounded part is called, and towards each end. This is particularly necessary with yew, as pins in this wood are liable to develop into "crysals,"—minute cracks at first scarcely visible, but gradually increasing in size, are termed, which eventually cause the bow to break. The grain on the flatter side of the bow or back should be smooth and even from end to end, and in a self-yew the line between the white and darker parts of the wood should be well defined and even.

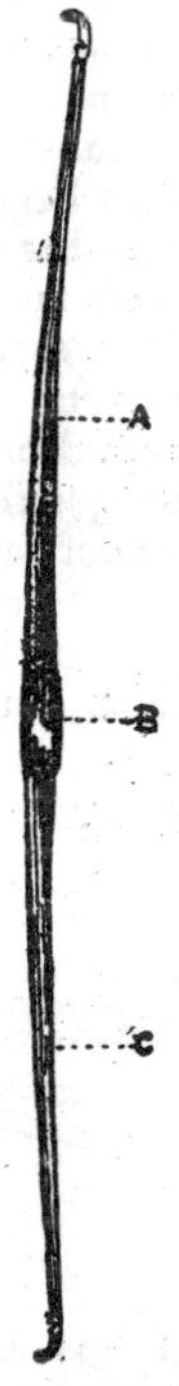

FIG. 1.—THE BOW.
A, Upper limb.
B, Handle.
C, Lower limb.

The weight of the bow to be selected is an important point; it is a common thing to find archers "overbowed"—*i.e.* having a stronger bow than they can manage. The weight of bow that can be pulled is one thing, that which can be properly loosed is quite a different matter. It is a mistake to suppose that the stronger the bow the lower will be the trajectory; unless the bow is thoroughly under control, the reverse will be the case. Ladies are advised to begin with a bow of 24 or 25 lbs. and men with 46 lbs. The longest distance now shot is 100 yards; a properly loosed bow of 48 lbs. will carry it well, and it is far better to be "under" than "over" bowed.

The weight being decided on, the back of the bow should be held upwards to see that it is straight, and that the two limbs are in the same plane. It should now be strung and the bend when drawn up carefully examined to see that the bow is rigid for about 20 inches in the centre, thence bending equally to each end (Fig. 2). It should then be held string uppermost, one end resting on the ground, when the string should appear to divide the bow into two equal parts.

Arrows are made of deal, the best being "footed" with hard wood at the point or pile end, and these alone are to be recommended; for though good shooting can be done with a cheap bow, cheap arrows are in the long run the dearest, besides being unsatisfactory. Arrows are made of four different shapes: the "straight," which should be the same size from end to end, but slightly reduced at the feathers; the "barrelled," which are largest in the centre, tapering both ways; the "bob-tailed," which are gradually reduced from the pile to the feathers, and the "chested," which is largest at about one third of its length from the feather end, tapering thence towards both ends. This last arrow is only used for flight shooting, and it is the others which bespeak our attention. The straight arrow is the steadiest and stiffest, but it is not quite so fast as the barrelled, for which reason several good shots prefer the latter. The bob-tail is a weak, bad shape; it is not sufficiently strong to stand the blow it receives when leaving the bow, and consequently it "flirts" or flies off to the left. The straight arrow is the one recommended, but care must be taken that it really is straight, as many so-called straight arrows are bob-tailed.

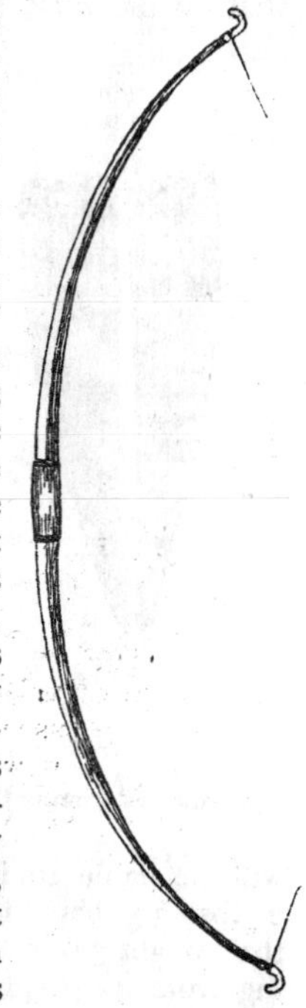

FIG. 2.—A GOOD SHAPE WHEN STRUNG.

The **feathers** are made of two patterns, the straight (Fig. 3) and the parabolic (Fig. 4). They should not be too large, and should be placed as far back as possible, the former shape being perhaps the better. The wing of the peacock supplies the stiffest and most durable feather, turkey's coming next, the "grey goose wing," that poets write about, having lost its charm to the fletcher.

The flight of an arrow, supposing it to be properly shot, is affected by its weight and balance. The weight, which is marked at the nock end of the arrow, represents its equivalent in new silver; thus an arrow marked 3.3. weighs 3s. 3d., 4.6. 4s. 6d., and so on. The balancing point is that part of the arrow on which it will balance on the finger. It will generally be found that all the arrows in a dozen are not precisely alike in these particulars, a variation of 1d. or 2d. in weight not being unfrequent. The arrows should therefore be sorted into sets as nearly as possible alike in weight and balance, to be used at the same time. No doubt the difference in flight caused by the weight and balance not being exactly the same is not very great, but there is no reason for "giving away" anything.

The weight of the arrow should be adapted to that of the bow, as if the arrow is too light it

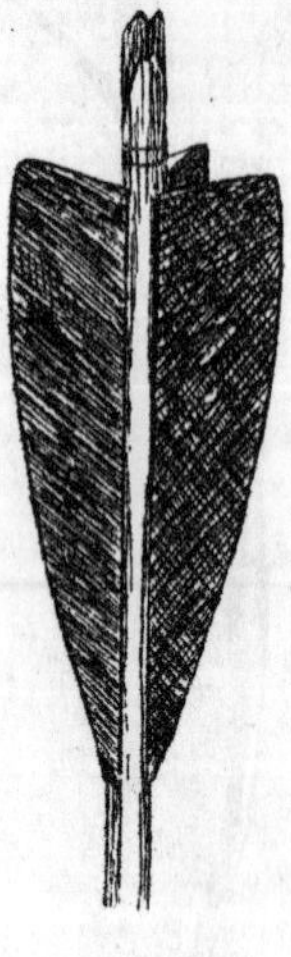

FIG. 3.
STRAIGHT FEATHERS.

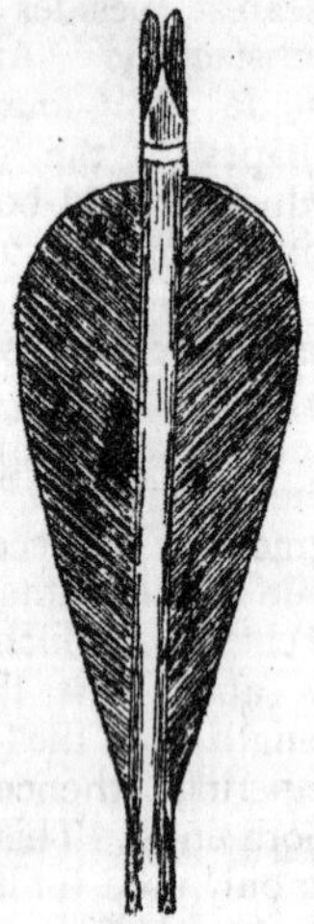

FIG. 4.
PARABOLIC FEATHERS.

will be liable to flirt. For ladies' bows up to 27 lbs. 3.3 should be heavy enough, beyond that weight 3.6 is advisable. For a bow weighing from 45 to 48 lbs. the arrow should not be lighter than 4.6, 4.9 being suitable for heavier bows. Arrows longer or shorter than the regular length should be heavier or lighter accordingly.

In order to ascertain if an arrow is straight, put the nails of the thumb and second finger of the left hand together, place the footing of the arrow upon them, and holding the nock of the arrow with the thumb and finger of the right-hand twist the arrow so as to make it revolve. If it does so smoothly it is straight, if it is crooked it will jump.

Tips, as the leather protection for the fingers of the right hand are called, are made of two

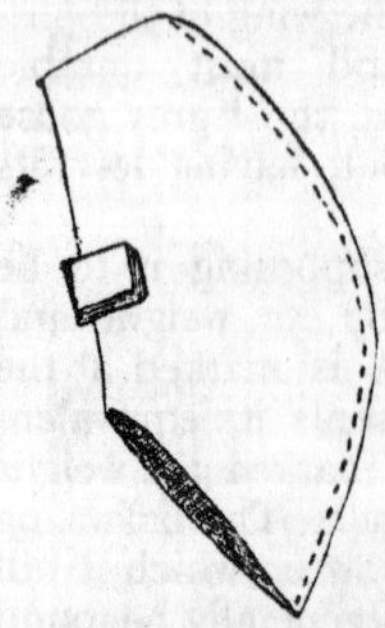

FIG. 5.—KNUCKLE TIP.

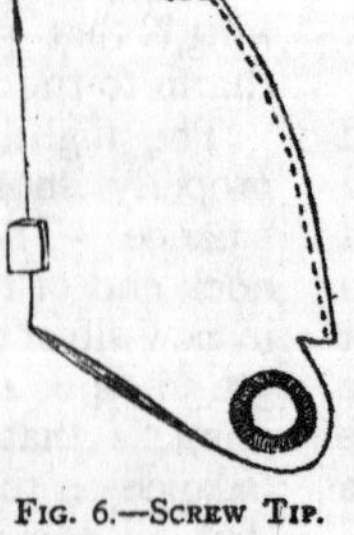

FIG. 6.—SCREW TIP.

patterns, the knuckle (Fig. 5) and the screw (Fig. 6). There is not much to choose between them but great care must be taken that they fit accurately, the top of each finger just showing through the top of the tip. The leather of each tip should be of the same substance and not too thick. It will be found a good plan in order to keep the tips supple, to rub vaseline into them, and before putting them on, the fingers should be moistened and rubbed on glue.

There are many other devices for protecting the fingers and obtaining a good loose; sewing

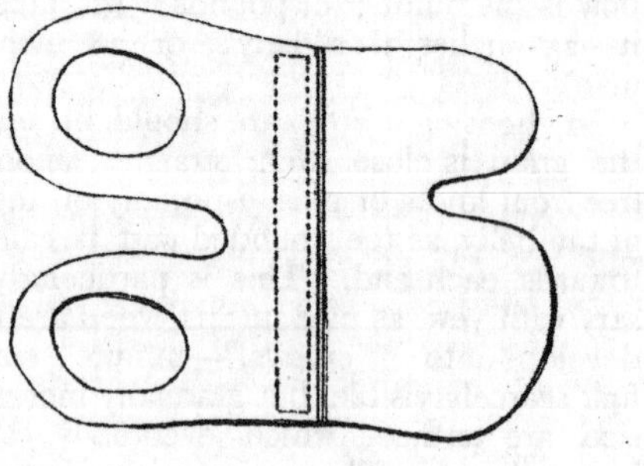

FIG. 7.—TAB.

pieces of leather on the fingers of an ordinary glove is a favourite device among ladies, and is not a bad one, provided the leather is not soft or spongy. The tab (Fig. 7) has many advocates, but it is not easy to use, and the beginner had best be satisfied with tips, or leather sewn on a glove. The tips which are sold fastened together to strap round the wrist are to be avoided, as they never fit all three fingers.

The **bracer** or arm guard is strapped on the left arm to protect it, should the string strike it when the arrow is loosed. It is made of various patterns, the best being that in which the straps and bracer are cut out of one piece of horse butt, and graduated, which is called after its

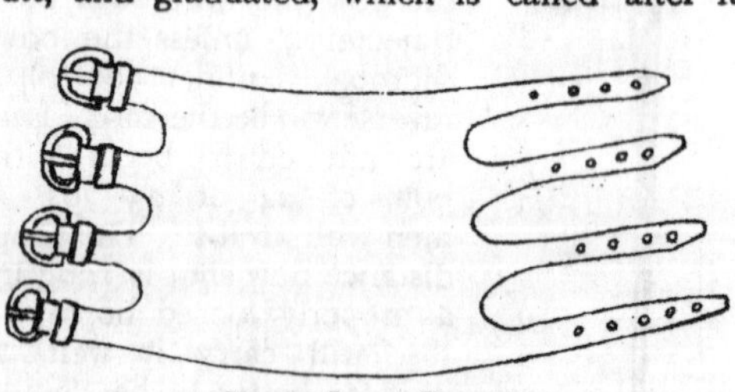

FIG. 8.—LEWIN BRACER.

inventor the "Lewin" (Fig. 8). A less expensive shape, also made entirely in one piece, but of ordinary leather, will also be found satisfactory, but it does not fit so close to the arm.

The belt with quiver attached is necessary for ladies, but men generally now discard it, placing the arrows in a pocket of the shooting-coat. A tassel to wipe the arrows and a scoring-book complete the archer's personal equipment. The **targets** now used are four feet in diameter and made of straw, having a canvas face on which five concentric rings are painted—the centre gold, then red, blue, black, and white. The value of each ring is respectively 9, 7, 5, 3, and 1, and the arrow counts as if it were in the ring of the highest value which it touches. It is usual to have two targets pitched opposite each other at from two to five yards more than the distance to be shot, the centre of the target being four feet from the ground. Each archer stands at the proper distance in front of the target and shoots three arrows, which are called an end. After all have shot, another end is shot from the opposite target, and so on till the appointed number of arrows has been shot. The scoring-book is therefore divided into six spaces, the first four for the ends and the two last for the total hits and score in the dozen. Supposing the first three arrows to have resulted in a blue, the next in a gold and red, the third in a black and white, and the last to have been missed, the dozen would be marked thus—

5 - -, 97 -, 31 -, - - - 5 -25.

A few words are necessary before trying to instruct the beginner how to use his or her newly-acquired weapons. Archery in many respects resembles rifle-shooting, and, as in the latter, position and aiming-drill are highly useful, but of themselves will not make every one a first-class shot, so in Archery, assistance can be given by useful hints, but practice alone will enable an archer to become a good shot.

First of all, it cannot be too strongly impressed on the mind of every beginner that deliberation and strict attention to every detail are absolutely necessary, and that undue haste is to be avoided. It is far better practice to shoot a few arrows carefully and well than a York Round against time. Losing one's temper, or giving up "because I can't shoot," is fatal. Few sports afford so many opportunities for losing one's temper as Archery, and none exacts a greater penalty for its loss.

In Archery, **position** is everything, and though everybody does not shoot in *precisely* the same attitude, still the difference among good shots will be slight. Some archers succeed in making, for a time, good scores in indifferent fashion, but sooner or later they come to dire grief. Many names could be given of promising beginners, who, having made good scores by bad methods, scorned advice, and after a year or two were reduced by their tricks to hopeless mediocrity or worse.

Before attempting to shoot, the bracer should be carefully put on the left arm, the sleeve being drawn back so as to leave it on the inside smooth and free from wrinkles. The next thing is to "string" or "bend" the bow. Grasp the bow at the handle with the right hand, the back, or flat part, being towards the body, and place the bottom horn against the hollow of the right foot. Place the ball of the thumb of the left hand about five inches from the top of the bow, the fingers resting against the eye of the string. Draw the right hand towards the body, at the same time pressing down the left hand, and place the eye of the string in the nock of the upper horn with the fingers (Figs. 9 and 10). The method of unstringing is the same, except that the eye of the string is lifted out of the nock.

Now see that the string is straight by looking at the bow, string upwards, and also observe if the string at the handle is the proper distance from the bow ($5\frac{1}{2}$ inches for a lady's and 6 for a man's). Next, see that the nocking-point is marked exactly opposite the top of the

Fig. 9.—Stringing.

handle, so that the arrow, when "nocked" on the string and resting on the forefinger of the left hand, which should be even with the top of the handle, is at right angles to the string. This is important, as, should the nocking point be too high or too low, the arrow will not fly properly.

Supposing a pair of targets to have been duly pitched opposite each other sixty-five yards apart, the archer should place himself on the mark five yards in front of one of them. He should stand sideways, the feet about eight inches apart, so that a line drawn through both heels should pass to the centre of each target. The body should be perfectly upright, the head erect, but turned to the left, the eyes fixed on the gold of the opposite target.

The handle of the bow should now be grasped, the upper part of the hand even with the top of

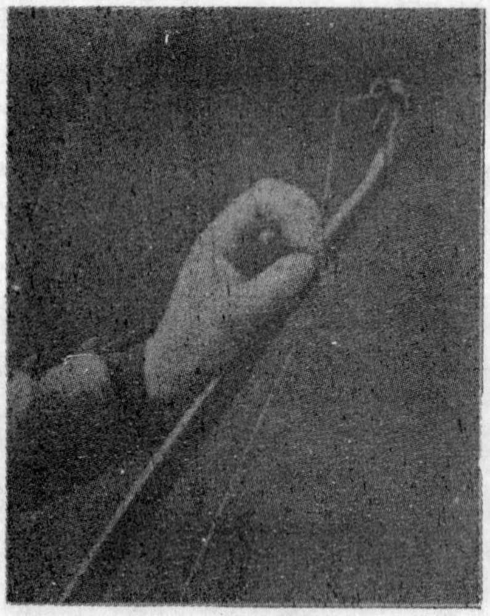

FIG. 10.—POSITION OF THE HAND IN STRINGING.

the handle, the back of the bow parallel with the knuckles of the finger and thumb. Fig. 11 shows both sides of the hand. A line passing through the centre of the bow will, if the grasp be correct, fall just inside the knuckle of the thumb. The wrist must be quite straight; if it is bent back, the string will strike the bracer; if forward, power is lost. Now raise the left hand

FIG. 11.—THE GRASP.

to the full extent of the arm, and, looking over the knuckle, see if the centre of the bow is on the gold. If it comes on it at once, the position will be correct; if it does not do so, raise the toes, turning on the heels slightly to the right or left till it does. If the hand cannot be brought on the required spot without doing so, the right foot may be drawn back slightly. The position of the feet is all important, as it governs that of the shoulders, which should be at right angles to the target or point of aim. Should it be necessary, in consequence of wind, to aim to the right or left of the target, the feet should be moved accordingly; on no account should the required position be obtained by turning the body on the hips.

Having got the correct position, take an arrow with the right hand and place it on the knuckle of the left, placing the nock on the nocking-point, the cock feather (that which is at right angles to the nock) being farthest from the bow, and press the string home. Place the first finger on the string above the arrow, the second

FIG. 12.—BEFORE THE DRAW.

and third below it, holding the arrow without pressing it on the string. Hold the bow as nearly upright as possible, the left arm close to the side, the forearm bent level from the waist and pointing towards the target, and bring the right hand across the body as far as possible (Fig. 12).

Gradually extend the left arm, tightening the grasp on the handle, till the hand is on the point of aim, at the same time bringing the right hand just under the chin, the thumb touching it, the right elbow being slightly raised (Figs. 13, 14, and 15). It will be seen from Fig. 13 that the right elbow should not be raised above the line of the arm, till the arrow has been drawn about three-quarters of its length.

During this motion, the body must be kept

upright, resting firmly on the feet, the weight thrown slightly on the heels. The head must be erect, the face being turned towards the

FIG. 13.—DRAWING.

target. Both wrists should be quite straight, and not turned in or out. This movement should be repeated several times before trying

FIG. 14.—DRAWING.

to loose an arrow, indeed it can be practised with advantage at home before a looking-glass, but it must never be attempted without an arrow in the bow, as the bow might be over-drawn, and broken.

Aim and **loose** now claim our attention. The point of aim will of course vary according to distance, and it is also affected by the strength of the bow, the wind, and above all the loose. This is, however, merely a question of raising or lowering the left hand, as the right should always be in the same place, and practice alone will enable the archer to find the right spot. The bow being drawn as explained above, and still taking the gold as the point of aim, as soon as you are in position, see that the point of the arrow is pointing direct to the gold over the left hand.

Now comes the critical part of the shoot, the loose or release of the arrow from the bow, and truly a good loose is as valuable as it is difficult

FIG 15.—THE BOW DRAWN UP.

to attain. The best loose is obtained by drawing the right fore-arm slightly back, at the same time making a slight outward turn of the right wrist, the thumb remaining against the chin, the fingers remaining closed after the release, as they were before it (Fig. 16). Of course the whole operation takes far less time to perform than to describe, as the arrow should not be held longer than is absolutely necessary to get the aim, nor should it be loosed till the aim has been obtained. Care must be taken that neither the right hand nor elbow is allowed to drop, and that the former does not leave the chin. The left hand should also be kept up till the arrow has hit the target or the ground, as the archer will thus be enabled to ascertain if it has shifted during or after shooting.

The importance of always drawing to the

same spot cannot be too strongly insisted on, and this cannot be accomplished unless some part of the face is touched, the chin for choice. The right hand should never be brought behind the eyes, but should always be in front of them, or a correct aim cannot be obtained. The distance between the right hand and the eye acts as a back-sight does in a rifle, the point of the arrow corresponding to the fore-sight. For this reason, it is necessary that the head should be erect, and that the hand should be brought to

FIG. 16.—AFTER THE LOOSE.

the chin, *not the head brought down to meet the hand*, as if this is done the arrow must fly low to the left. It is also necessary that the right hand should not leave the face at the moment of loosing, as should it do so, the left hand will be pulled out of place. How important it is that the left hand should be kept steady will at once be understood, as should it be moved up or dropped the arrow will of course go high or low, and any lateral motion would equally prevent its going straight.

A common fault is to allow the right hand to move forward when the arrow is drawn up and while the aim is being taken. This is called "creeping," and must be guarded against, as it gives a forward loose which takes all the vitality out of the arrow's flight. Dropping the bow-hand and allowing the body to turn on the hips at the moment the arrow is loosed are also faults which must be avoided.

Attention must be paid to the string, and should any symptom of weakness be observed, a new one should at once be fitted, as the fracture of the string will often cause that of the bow; indeed, a careful archer should always have a spare string ready whipped. To put on a string, place the eye over the upper end of the bow, seeing that it is free from kinks, and push it down about six inches. To make the timber hitch with which it is fastened at the bottom take a turn of the end round the string, and twist it three times round the loop (Fig. 17). The string requires (in order to assist the loose and to protect it should it strike the bracer, which it should never do) to be served or whipped with carpet thread for about two inches above the nocking point and five inches below it. To put this lapping on, string the bow, find the nocking point as before explained, and mark the string two inches above it. Wax the string well for seven inches below the mark, and place the bow, string upwards, on the knees. Lay half an inch of the thread along the string, and wrap the thread tightly round the end and string, till the waxed part is nearly lapped. Now take five or six turns of the thread round the string, in the reverse way, and bring the end of the thread to the lapped part, holding it with the thumb. Lap the reversed turns over the end of the thread and string till they are all undone, and then pull the end through, holding the lapping down with the finger and thumb to prevent its rising (Fig. 18). A nocking-point of silk half an inch long put on in the same way, makes the string ready for use. The nocking-point should fit sufficiently tight to bear the weight of the arrow.

FIG. 17.—THE LOOP.

All Archery materials require careful looking after. The receptacle in which they are kept is termed an Ascham, and it should be so arranged that the bows do not rest on the ground, and that the arrows stand upright on their points, each arrow passing through two corresponding holes cut in two boards about fifteen inches apart. It is needless to say it should not be in a damp place, nor should it be close to the kitchen fire, an equal temperature being required. Should a favourite bow show symptoms of being "crysalled," it is as well to have it looked to at once, as a new belly can generally be put in. The strength of bows can be increased by shortening them, but this is not recommended unless the bow was originally extra long; to weaken bows is a simple matter for the bowyer.

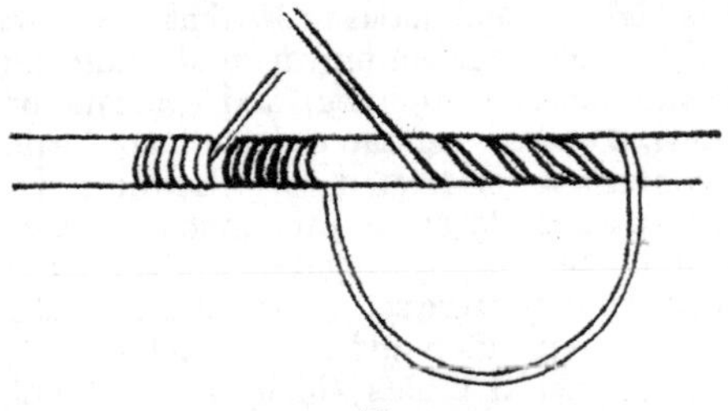

FIG. 18.—WHIPPING.

For going to meetings a bow box, or waterproof canvas bag termed "a pole," should be procured, while the arrows can be conveniently carried in what is called the "Wiltshire" box, which has a compartment for tips, &c., and is made by Messrs. Aldred. Should the bows or arrows get wet they should be carefully dried, the string beeswaxed, and the feathers of the arrows shaken before a fire.

Roving, or shooting at unknown distances is no longer practised, all shooting now taking place at known distances. The York Round, consisting of six dozen arrows at 100 yards, four dozen at 80, and two dozen at 60, is generally shot by men; the National Round of four dozen at 60 and two dozen at 50 being the recognised one for ladies. Longer distances, or "clout shooting," are only patronised by the Woodmen of Arden and Royal Company of Archers at Edinburgh.

Shooting at a Popinjay, or painted wooden bird, was formerly a popular form of Archery. In England it is extinct, but it survived at Kilwinning in Scotland till 1870, where it was called the "Papingo." The papingo was placed on the top of the Abbey tower, and shot at from below, whoever brought it down receiving a "benn" or muffler. This style of shooting is almost the only form of archery still practised in France and Belgium, though the method of shooting is somewhat different to that of the Kilwinning Papingo. In France, outside certain towns, notably Calais and Boulogne, long poles may be seen with wires projecting at right angles, and graduated from the top. On the top of the pole and on the wires, when a meeting takes place, are placed imitation birds decked with ribbons, to each of which a specific value is attached, the highest being that of the top bird. Competitors stand sufficiently close to the pole to be able to rake the wires and top bird, using strong bows, and arrows having a broad flat horn head, receiving the equivalent value of any bird they may bring down. In Belgium somewhat similar competitions take place, a sort of penthouse round the pole regulating the distance the competitors stand from it.

It may be thought that the use of the bow in field sports is a thing of the past. Such, however, is not the case. Of its practical use in the chase and the delights which attend camping out with the bow for one's sole weapon, Maurice Thompson has much to say. The experiences of himself, his brother and others in Florida, Georgia, Illinois, Indiana, &c., while sporting with the bow, are the subject of many pleasant pages in *Scribner's*, *Harper's*, the *Badminton*, and other magazines, and tell us of turkeys, herons, wood-ducks, thunder-pumpers, and other strange birds and beasts slain with the bow; bass or trout of four pounds weight also falling victims to it. The camp life seems to have closely approached the conditions existing before the introduction of firearms.

A member of the Royal Toxophilite Society, Mr. J. Straker, an enthusiastic archer, has for some years, taken bows and arrows as part of his sporting-kit to India, and has met with some success in using them against birds. Of the advantage the bow has over the gun in not disturbing a tract of ground he speaks highly, but he has not, like Mr. Thompson, trusted wholly to the bow.

Mr. H. Peard, M.B., has told us in the *Field* on sundry occasions of his sport in Argentina with a bow and arrows. Small partridges, tinamou ducks, spur-winged plover, nutrias, biscacho, and foxes, "horresco referens," are mentioned by him as falling victims to the "winged shaft."

Even in England, rabbits are shot with the bow, so it will be seen that its practical use is not yet extinct. One thing stands prominently forward, that all who write on this particular branch of Archery vie with each other in its praise.

H. WALROND.

ARMADILLO (*Dasypus pelosus*), a South American burrowing ant-eater, protected by an armour of bony plates. It is much hunted for food, the usual course being to smoke it out of the burrow and then put trained dogs on to it. When attacked, it curls up like a hedgehog.

ATHLETICS, OR ATHLETIC SPORTS

—The wide term Athletics bears at the present day in the sportsman's vocabulary the special or restricted meaning of competition at running, jumping, and putting, or hurling, of weights, as practised on specially prepared tracks or grass fields in the open air. After being practised without much system for many hundreds of years in England for amusement, and for something like a century by paid or professional exponents, athletic sports have gradually, during the last thirty years, been developed upon systematic lines into an organised form of sport for amateurs [*see* AMATEUR]. Every public school and most of the private schools of any size have an annual athletic meeting: each college at the universities has its meeting; there is at each university a meeting open to the whole university; and these are followed by the annual contest between Oxford and Cambridge in London, usually on the day preceding the Boat Race; the hospitals and military colleges follow the example of the universities; and hundreds of clubs throughout the kingdom hold meetings with competitions for their members and with "open" races—that is, open to every approved amateur. In each summer there is an Open Championship meeting held in rotation in London, the Midlands, and the North, under the management of the Amateur Athletic Association, which is the recognised governing body of athletic sports; and this never fails to attract entries from every part of the United Kingdom and occasionally from the United States and the Colonies. A similar system of athletic sports has taken firm root in the United States, where the sports are termed Games; and the system is already spreading in France and to some small extent in Germany. In 1895, there were a number of athletic events included in the so-called revival of the Olympic Games at Athens, several Americans, Englishmen, and Frenchmen being amongst the competitors.

The wide-spread popularity of athletics in this country fairly entitles them to be ranked among the national sports of the country. The fine runner or jumper ranks in popular esteem with the fine cricketer, footballer, or oarsman. At the universities those who compete as "first strings"—*i.e.*, "first choices"—in each event at the Inter-University meeting are entitled, like the members of the Eight, the Cricket Eleven, or the Football teams, to wear the blue coat and cap which are reserved for those who represent one university against the other, and are known as "blues"; and in schools, colleges and clubs, the best athletes are similarly held in high honour.

At the universities, the two winter terms are those devoted to athletics, the summer term being mainly devoted to cricket and boating; and the University athletic season concludes before Easter with the University and Inter-University sports. Most of the public schools follow the example of the universities in bringing off their athletic meeting before Easter. Throughout the rest of the country, however, the athletic season begins in May, and continues throughout the warm weather until the end of September, when the athletes betake themselves to paperchasing, football, or other winter sports. The Amateur Championship meeting is now always held on the first Saturday in July. As the Scottish and Irish Championships usually precede the English Championship meeting by a week or two, the athletes of the three kingdoms are best brought together at this date; but the fact of the meeting being held in the summer operates to the prejudice of the university athletes, as they find it difficult to get into condition at this time of year.

It is perhaps superfluous to say that excellence in athletics demands not only natural ability, but long and arduous training and preparation. Training, so far as diet and conditions of health are concerned, is treated of elsewhere [*see* TRAINING], and does not vary much in essentials from the training required for rowing or other hard bodily exercise. It is with the peculiar features of preparation and the requisites of success in the special events which are commonly included in the programme of an athletic meeting that the following articles will mainly deal. The programme selected for the earlier meetings of the two universities has done much to determine the line on which athletic competitions have developed. At the Inter-University meeting there are nine events—viz., 100 Yards, Quarter Mile, Mile, Three Miles, (all flat races): 120 Yards Hurdle Race over ten flights of hurdles, each 3 feet 6 inches high, High Jump, Long Jump, Weight Putting (16 lbs.), Hammer Throwing (16 lbs.). The Amateur Championship meeting has the same nine events with the exception that the Three Miles is replaced by a Four Miles, and has in addition a Half Mile Race, a Pole Jump, a Two Miles Steeplechase, and a Four Miles Walking Race. In addition there is a Ten Miles Championship Race, which is held in the spring at the conclusion of the paperchasing season.

It is usual at an ordinary club meeting to make most of the races handicaps. By this means, large entries are secured, as the number of superlative athletes is small compared with the hundreds, or one may fairly say thousands, who, though of mediocre ability, are able to win prizes with a moderate handicap.

At the universities and at most of the big towns, athletic sports are held upon a regular running-ground which has a cinder track of a quarter or a third of a mile in circumference, with grass in the centre of the track, and specially prepared places for the Jumps, Weight Competitions, and Hurdle Races, the ground also including seating and standing room for spectators and proper dressing accommodation for the competitors. In most country districts, the venue of the meeting is the local cricket ground.

Of late years, the popularity of athletic sports with spectators has rather tended to discourage the cultivation of Jumping and the Weight Competitions, and to increase the number of flat races. Jumping and Weight Competitions with many competitors take a great deal of time and cannot so easily be witnessed and followed with interest as races round a track. At the present time Jumping and Weight Competitions are not practised in England nearly so much as in Ireland or Scotland.

The governing body of athletic sports is the Amateur Athletic Association, the practical work being done by three committees in the North, South, and Midlands respectively. To this body some 200 athletic clubs are affiliated, and about as many more, without being affiliated, hold meetings under "permits" from the governing body and under their rules and jurisdiction. To give some idea, by rough computation there

A COUNTRY MEETING.

are probably about 1,000 athletic meetings, great or small, held in the United Kingdom, and the number of persons competing throughout the country is certainly not less than twenty-five thousand.

MONTAGUE SHEARMAN.

CROSS-COUNTRY RUNNING—Every year sees an increase in the numbers participating in so-called cross-country running, and clubs spring into existence in bewildering succession, some to flourish with the growth of years, but many either to become absorbed in larger organisations, or else to die a natural death. In spite of this it is doubtful whether more than a small percentage of this number have any conception of the delights of real cross-country running, and it cannot be denied that the pastime has declined in popularity, and has lost caste amongst the educated classes. The reason, so far as London is concerned, is not difficult to understand. The rapid growth of the suburbs necessitates a longer train journey to reach the open country than formerly. Too many clubs are, through the exigencies of circumstances, compelled to have their head-quarters in thickly populated districts; and the appearance of clusters of runners, generally of very poor class and all too airily clad, splashing through muddy thoroughfares, is not an inspiring spectacle, and undoubtedly tends to prejudice the minds of those who have had no opportunity of becoming acquainted with the sport at its best.

Infinitely the most enjoyable and invigorating branch of cross-country running is the old-fashioned paper chase, introduced about the year 1867. It is with sorrow that we have to record the fact that every year the paper chase finds a smaller place in the fixture-card of leading clubs, and that it is being displaced by the ever-increasing number of races with their attendant prizes, which involve traversing two or three set courses so often as to become quite monotonous.

If a paper chase is to be successful, the details cannot be too carefully arranged. Two hares are chosen, preferably of equal calibre, possessing a knowledge of the surrounding country. They should, before starting, have a general idea of the course they mean to steer. Each hare carries a long sausage-shaped bag supported from his shoulders, packed tight with printers' waste strips, which are recommended strongly in preference to squares of paper. It is essential to the success of the chase that a continuous trail shall be lightly laid; and the practice in vogue at our Universities of laying the scent in patches some distance apart is to be condemned. If these ordinary bags are tightly packed, the paper, with judicious laying, will easily last ten miles. A clever pair of hares will lay several false scents to check the too rapid progress of the hounds, and by taking advantage of cover and varying the nature of the country as much as possible the run is made more interesting. The grace allowed the hares is usually ten minutes, but it should not exceed fifteen minutes, and the hounds can be despatched in fast and slow packs if found desirable; to maintain interest the hounds should always have a fair chance of catching the hares. Upon the hounds receiving a check, say in the middle of a field, the pack should at once spread out in fan shape, and on the scent being regained the fact should be notified by bugle or call. The distance traversed will, of course, vary considerably, but it should not exceed ten miles, for there are few runners who can last a longer distance without undue exhaustion. Some runners maintain their stride throughout, and we have even known instances of men who have kept on their toes throughout a long journey, but the majority of runners are not strangers to a temporary feeling of fatigue during some part of the journey—it may be over plough or going up hill—but they are recommended to make the effort to maintain a jog trot rather than indulge in the luxury of a walk, because it is found that alternately walking and running materially increases the fatigue in the long run.

The dress suitable for cross-country running is a pair of twill knickerbockers cut fairly short, so as not to interfere with the action of the knee, a thin merino vest, and sweater if the weather be bad, and indiarubber or spiked shoes, the latter being preferable as giving a better grip on the ground.

Training for the cross-country championships has now been reduced to a science; and the gentleman amateur, though he may be a first-class cross-country performer, is no longer able to hold the position of a few years ago, unless he is prepared to devote the whole of his leisure time to training. The championships are now usually run round race-courses or enclosed spaces, instead of over genuine cross-country, and the question of gate plays an all-important part; this system is followed by betting with its attendant evils. If a competitor is training for

CROSS-COUNTRY CHAMPIONSHIP.

a cross-country championship, say, ten miles, he is advised to take long road walks at a brisk pace, varied by occasional spins of two to four miles on the track or road, with a weekly run across country. Many runners fall into the fatal error of thinking the best form of training is to confine their work to cross-country, and to run from five to ten miles at repeated intervals. There could be no greater mistake, because they will quickly tend to become hopelessly slow, and moreover are likely to overstrain themselves and be quite unable to make the extra effort that is often called for at the crisis of the race.

The question of pace plays an important part in a cross-country race, and our experience is that scratch and back-mark men will find it advantageous to make the pace hot from the start, as, if fit, they are likely to maintain it fairly evenly throughout, whereas it is often difficult to increase the pace after a slow start, and as an illustration of this we may instance a cross-country championship, where it is generally recognised that the leading twenty at two miles will furnish the first fifteen at the finish.

No material alteration in the ordinary diet is recommended, the important point to bear in mind being that the training should be of such a character that the competitor turns up on the day of the race not only fit but anxious for his work.

We have dealt with the practical, rather than the historical, side of the question; firstly, because a record of performances is apt to become somewhat invidious, and, secondly, because there are not, and cannot be, any reliable cross-country records, owing to the marked differences in the nature of courses, and in their ever varying condition.

Over-anxious parents often place a veto upon cross-country running, but experience has amply proved that, given a sound constitution, the fear of over-strain is very little, and certainly no healthier or more invigorating recreation can be found.

HAROLD WADE, L.A.C.

HIGH JUMPING—One of the prettiest of our athletic pastimes has of late years been much neglected by sports-promoters. Popular opinion has always held the view that the high jumper is a freak of nature possessed of wonderful "spring," the seat of which is usually supposed to be in the instep and toes. No view could be more erroneous. High jumping may be, in special cases, a gift, but is almost invariably the result of long and constant practice; nor is the jump accomplished by a spring from the toes. It is in reality done from the knees, off the flat of the foot and, in many cases, the heel. This latter is easily verified by examining the "take-off" on a soft day, when the heel-mark is always very prominent. The methods of jumping are various, but two main types predominate—viz., the straight jump, and the side-way or scissors jump. The pure straight jump—*i.e.*, lifting the knees directly up to the chin and so crossing the bar—is rare, and is more usually combined with the "shoot," or twist. The principle in all methods is the same. The first effort of the would-be aspirant to fame is to get his feet over the bar, and with this end in view, always to practise at a higher bar than he thinks he can clear.

Never allow him to raise the lath himself, as by so doing he is aware of the height he is essaying, and knows exactly when he has reached his usual limit. By employing an assistant to raise the lath, he is unaware as to the exact height and often clears more than he expects. Having learnt to raise his feet, he must now endeavour to raise his body in the air by a muscular contraction and also by using the limb, or limbs, which are over the bar as a lever: at the same time by means of a twist or

HIGH JUMP.

shoot, and a sudden lifting of the arms over the head, he must so alter his position in the air that his feet, which have previously been as high as, and in many cases higher than, his head, now point directly downwards, and by this means he will lift his body and buttocks clear of the bar. It will thus be seen that, instead of a single spring, several separate actions constitute the true jump. In fact, his endeavour should be to climb over the cross-bar in sections, first the feet, then buttocks, and lastly the upper part of the body.

The Take-off—It is essential to find a level spot from which to take off at a given distance from the bar. Practice alone will determine the correct spot for each individual performer. This spot should be fixed, and always adhered to. A simple method in practice is to stick a hair-pin through a piece of paper, which thus catches the eye.

The Run-down—The length of the run varies with each individual, but should be short for the low jumps, and gradually lengthened for greater heights, and should be as long as it can be made without tiring the muscles, as the momentum hereby gained allows more time for executing alterations in position while in the air. The last three steps should be somewhat longer than the others, and of the nature of slight jumps and should, like the take-off, be fixed.

Training—As to training for jumping, all the muscles of the body must be in good condition. Sprinting is excellent: gymnasium work is also good. All toe-exercises are useful, especially skipping; in short, all exercises tending to strengthen the muscles round the knee-joint. One should never jump more than three days a week, and never within four days of a competition, as the muscles are apt to lose elasticity. Stiffness must be vigorously guarded against. High kicking is very useful during the off-season.

One's shoes should be light, strong, and tight-fitting, and should in addition to the ordinary toe-spikes, contain three heel-spikes arranged in triangular form, with the apex of the triangle posteriorly. If possible, a pit should always be used to jump into, as by this means the jar which always follows on landing is greatly diminished.

But infinitely more important than all of these are the qualities of self-confidence and pluck, without which no one need hope to become a successful exponent of jumping.

REGINALD WILLIAMS.

HURDLE RACING has been in vogue since the early days of amateur athletics, and perhaps in no branch of athletic sports is proficiency more difficult to attain.

Hurdle races at various distances, such as 300 yards and 440 yards, are at times included in the competitions at athletic meetings; but from the first, the favourite distance has been 120 yards, with ten flights of hurdles, 3ft. 6in. high, placed ten yards apart, thus leaving fifteen yards from the starting-line to the first hurdle, and the same distance between the tenth and the winning-post. Sprint hurdle races must always be run on a straight course. In this country they are invariably run on grass, which must be perfectly level; but in America it is customary to use the cinder track, which is undoubtedly faster. Hence the American records are slightly better than our own.

The Hurdle—The modern hurdle consists of an obstacle specially made with perfectly level top bars; the result is that flights of uniform regulation height are secured, and no competitor is benefited or impeded by any irregularities in the top bar, as was so often the case in the old style of hurdle. They are fixed on short pedestals of about a foot in length, and are much superior to the old hurdles in that they can be easily moved and the necessity of driving into the ground is obviated.

It was early discovered that in the race of 120 yards with ten flights, each 10 yards apart, three was the requisite number of strides on the flat between the hurdles; and no one can hope to attain even mediocrity as a hurdle racer unless he can accomplish what is generally known as the "three stride" method. This consists in taking three complete strides on the flat, the fourth stride carrying the runner over the hurdle.

To accomplish this the runner must be careful to approach the first hurdle at the highest speed attainable, and in rising from the left foot (jumpers usually preferring to spring from the left) the right knee is raised upward and forward above the hurdle, and the leg (from knee to foot), brought inwards across the line of the body with the foot on as nearly as possible the same level as the knee, traverses the bar in an almost horizontal position, and is then brought to the ground as rapidly as possible. In the meanwhile, the left leg, with the knee pointing outward, is brought up rapidly as the body passes over the bar and is carried forward to the ground, thus constituting the first of the three strides.

The practised hurdler manages to gather up his legs in clearing the hurdle in such a way that

HURDLE RACE.

only an inch or two intervenes between his body and the top bar.

Hints to Beginners—A beginner must remember that the hurdle must be cleared in a stride (*i.e.*, he must rise from one foot and alight on the other), and that he must in no case jump it; he will soon discover that jumping the hurdle will necessitate his taking five strides instead of three. Godfrey Shaw, of the London Athletic Club, probably the finest hurdler this country has produced, clears as much as fifteen feet in his stride over the hurdle, thus leaving the same distance to be accounted for in the three strides before rising at the next, and goes over the ten hurdles without so much as touching one. It will be seen, therefore, that the three strides, which appear almost insuperable to the novice, average only five feet each, or much less than he would be taking if running 100 yards on the flat.

Should the beginner find (as he no doubt will) that the regulation hurdles are too high, he should commence by practising over three or four obstacles of about 2ft. 6in. in height, but always ten yards apart.

When he can accomplish the three strides over these, he should gradually increase the height and number of the obstacles.

There are several qualities necessary for the making of a crack hurdler. He must have speed and jumping power (hence it is that good hurdlers are frequently good long jumpers); he must have, too, dash and determination, and not be afraid of falling or barking his shins. That there are comparatively few hurdlers may be attributed to various causes. Among other reasons this branch of sport is not supported or encouraged by athletic clubs as it should be, by facilities being given for proper practice, or by including hurdle competitions in their programmes. Again, few good sprinters will take to hurdling, as there is little doubt that the mechanical and artificial action necessary in hurdling interferes with speed on the flat.

With regard to training for hurdle races, constant practice is the thing most needed; rigid dieting is comparatively unimportant.

In hurdle handicaps, where men have been known to give as much start as twenty-five yards, the runner most heavily weighted starts so many yards behind the scratch, and is usually described as "owing so much." Thus the limit, or longest start competitor, is usually placed on the scratch; though it sometimes happens that, on account of the length of the course being limited, the longest start man is placed as much as five yards in front of scratch, and has then only ten yards to run before reaching the first hurdle.

Finally, the beginner must remember that in hurdle racing constant practice will probably effect greater improvement than in any other branch of athletic sports. Frequently men who as novices are very slow, and who have the greatest difficulty in mastering the three strides, develop eventually into first-rate hurdle racers.

C. L. LOCKTON.

LONG JUMP—Long jumping ability is made up of two elements, **pace** and **spring**. Pace in the run-up supplies the impetus; spring enables the jumper to lift himself into the air so that this impetus has time to act before the law of gravitation takes effect, and also adds a certain amount of forward motion itself. A man who can jump well but is a slow runner can achieve a certain degree of success in the long jump by virtue of his spring alone; similarly a fast runner without much jumping power can cover a certain distance if he learns to rise a little at the end of his run. The best kind of long jumper is the man who is both a fast runner and a capable high jumper.

Thus it is clear that in training for the long jump, besides practising the long jump itself, a man must cultivate his sprinting and high jumping powers to their highest pitch. Practice at the long jump will enable him to combine the two skilfully.

Before beginning such definite training, it is necessary first to get into general condition by playing cricket, football, or any other game that gives good exercise; or to go through a course of grinding walks. Then should follow a week or fortnight of easy exercise on the cinder-track, consisting chiefly of sprinting and a little high jumping. This preliminary training will have got the muscles used in the long jump into working order, and actual practice may then begin. An experienced performer will not require more than a month's further practice to produce his best effort, though some men prefer to take much longer. Both in preliminary and in actual training for this event, it is absolutely essential not to do too much work a day. Two or three days a week may be given to serious long jumping, prefaced by about three high jumps and two or three short sprints. The other days should be devoted to serious high jumping and determined sprinting. A novice who has to learn the way to long jump must give himself six or eight weeks in order to obtain sufficient practice without overworking himself. Hurdling is an excellent subsidiary exercise for a long jumper, and it is a good thing to run over the entire length of flights or to take three or four flights four or five times. Hurdling and long jumping ability often go together, but if a man wishes to train simultaneously for both events he must give himself long enough to practise both adequately without having to do too much work a day.

The long jumper's sprinting practice should be very much the same as that of a pure sprinter. He should confine himself chiefly to short bursts of forty yards, with an occasional run through the hundred yards, varied by a stride over three hundred or a lap well on his toes.

In his high jumping practice he may follow the methods of the professed high jumper, supplemented with occasional "high-long" jumps—*i.e.* over a lath fixed at from four feet six inches to five feet and taken at the end of a fast run of about twenty yards.

With regard to actual practice at the long jump, he must aim at three things—to learn to take-off with the ball of his foot on the taking-off board; to do that when going at full speed; and to jump as high as possible into the air.

There are two reasons for taking-off on the board: first, that if the jumper takes-off behind it he is not credited with the full distance he has covered, all jumps being measured from the edge of the board nearest the pit to the hindmost heel-mark; secondly, because the board is firmer and more springy than the cinder-track. When a jumper takes-off six inches behind the mark, he loses a foot, if not more. This accuracy in taking-off is partly mechanical and a matter of practice, partly a matter of eye. When a man is fit and in good jumping fettle, his eye, brain and foot work so well together that he takes-off exactly where he intends. At the same time, it is fatal to look at the taking-off mark while running-up. His eyes ought to be fixed eagerly on a spot where he hopes to land —*i.e.* somewhat *beyond* his usual jumping distance. It is most helpful to have a piece of paper put in the centre of the pit about a foot further than he has ever jumped. It not only takes his eyes off the board, but draws him out. In order to gain mechanical accuracy, a mark should be made on the cinder-track. Behind this the jumper should start and, after a few yards run, plant his toe on it, continue at full speed up to the board, and then jump determinedly. In nine cases out of ten he will have taken-off behind the board, as can be seen by examining the track. Before starting for the next jump, the mark should be moved forward as many inches or feet as he took-off behind the board.

It is a great mistake to shorten or lengthen the stride in running up. It not only makes it impossible to acquire and practise mechanical accuracy in taking-off, but lessens considerably the impetus which is the *raison d'être* of the run-up. The length of the run-up should be between forty-five and fifty-five yards. Practice will soon discover the suitable length. A man's run-up to a long jump should be the facsimile of the first part of a hundred yards as run by him. The whole run should be a winding-up for the jump.

The reason for jumping high has been mentioned. The difference between a first-class and a moderate performer in this respect is most marked. It is possible to jump too high, just as a cricket ball may be thrown too high for length; but at the end of a run-up at full speed it is practically impossible. As a working rule, it is safe to advise a long jumper to jump as high as he can—*i.e.* much higher than he feels inclined.

The best kind of shoes for long jumping are ordinary hurdling shoes with one or two spikes in the heel. It is useful to have a pair for practising with thickened heels, as the heel is planted with great violence on the ground in taking-off. *Bruised-heel* is a common complaint with long jumpers. Care should be taken that the pit is well dug up and softened before jumping, and that no rake, spade, or other edged tool is left near the pit, in case of a sprawl or fall out of the pit after landing. It is a good thing, especially in cold weather, to rub the legs and back well before starting work. A gentle sprint and two or three small high jumps as preliminaries should always be taken in order to get the muscles into working order and prevent them being strained or torn by the sudden concentrated effort implied in a long jump.

C. B. FRY.

POLE JUMPING—Owing to a few unfortunate accidents, usually resulting from lack of care in the selection of a suitable pole, this, one of the oldest of our English sports, has practically dropped out of the list of events of most sports-holding clubs. This is deeply to be regretted, as in addition to being a most popular item with spectators, it is in itself a splendid exercise demanding much all-round ability.

Broad Jumping with a pole was for many years a necessity, and subsequently a sport, in the Fen districts of Lincolnshire and Cambridgeshire, and from this doubtless the pole-jumping of the present day had its origin. It seems strange that broad jumping with a pole should never have found its way into our athletic programmes; but as sports-promoters are ever on the look-out for attractive novelties, it is possible that it may yet be seen. Though originating in the Fens, pole-jumping is now almost entirely confined to the Furness district of Lancashire, and is especially associated with the town of Ulverston, from the immediate neighbourhood of which most of our recent champions have sprung. Here it still retains its hold on the people, and may it long do so! He who would attain excellence in this branch of sport must be at once a jumper and a gymnast, and must have no lack of pluck, for strains and bruises are of common occurrence.

There are two distinct types of pole-jumping, the old and by far the more graceful type, and

POLE JUMP.

the new, or what may be called the *gymnastic*, type. The **old type** of jumper, now rapidly becoming extinct, grasped the pole firmly in the lower hand slightly below or on a level with the jump he was about to attempt, took a longish run, and having planted the pole firmly in the ground about one foot in advance of a horizontal line drawn between the bases of the two uprights, sprang into the air, throwing his feet as high as possible and then with a twist raised his body clear of the lath, being careful at the same time to loosen his grip and throw back the pole before the lath became displaced.

In contradistinction to this, the **new type** of jumper, running slowly to the take-off, springs into the air, and the moment his pole assumes the perpendicular, climbs rapidly hand over hand up it, and with a quick lift raises his legs and body clear of the bar. This method, though demanding great ability, is, we think, more in the nature of a gymnastic display and should, we venture to suggest, be confined to such competitions. Though recognised as legitimate pole-jumping by the English Amateur Athletic Association, it has never been recognised or allowed by the A.A.A. of America.

To turn now to practical details. The first thing to do is to procure a good, strong, flexible pole as light as is consistent with safety, not less than eleven feet in height, made of ash or hickory. It should be thickest at the base, which should be shod with three steel spikes arranged in the form of a tripod, and these should be firmly secured by a metal ring. This gives a firmer grip than one spike. The pole should gradually taper from below upwards. The uprights should be square.

Take-off—The take-off should be selected with great care, and a pit of large dimensions provided on the landing side, which should be filled in with sawdust and earth. By these means many a jar and accident will be avoided. High jumping must be assiduously practised and also gymnastic exercises of all kinds, rope- and pole-climbing being essential.

REGINALD WILLIAMS.

RUNNING—Before the days of organised athletics, runners were heard of who had the reputation of being able to beat their opponents at any distance. In the present days of highly specialised effort, a runner who essays all distances is likely to prove the master of none. One never hears to-day of a sprinter who can perform well at long distances, or of a long-distance runner who is anywhere near the front rank of sprinters; and the few all-round athletes who appeared in the early days of the athletic movement would, if they had been competing to-day, have been compelled to devote themselves to one particular class of distance if they desired to acquire championship honours. Nowadays, a runner is either a sprinter—that is, accustomed to run from 100 yards up to 300 yards at full speed—in which case the limit of his special abilities will probably be a quarter of a mile at the outside—or he may run the middle distances—that is, from a quarter to a half mile; or he may be a long-distance runner, with distances from a mile upwards. Men cannot, of course, be measured by exact standards, and he who can run a mile well and he who can run a quarter may often meet together on even terms at a half; but for purposes of rough classification, to divide runners into the three classes of sprinters, middle-distance men, and long-distance men, is to draw the dividing lines as closely as nature will allow them to be drawn.

Sprinting is the name given to the running of short distances at "full burst." Sprinting is perhaps more popular, both with spectators and athletes, than any other class of race, and a sprint handicap at 120 or 150 yards is likely to produce the largest entry of all at a sports meeting. But although the number of mediocre sprinters is large, the number of really fine sprinters is very small, and it is seldom that a man reaches his best form until after two or three seasons of steady practice.

Success in sprinting comes more from the rapid repetition of the stride by bringing up the legs quickly than from artificial attempt to lengthen the stride. The more the runner practises "bursts" of speed the more he will find that his stride is naturally lengthening by his striding from the hips and not from the knees. The natural sprinter is nearly always a man of big thighs and strong back, and the capacity for attaining to really first-class form consists in being able to "put one's back into it," and to keep up a prolonged and vehement burst at high pressure throughout the whole distance one has to go. A great practical exponent of sprinting once expressed an opinion that to win a sprint one should "run like a madman." There is some truth in this: the sprinter has to learn to keep up an abnormal burst of speed or he will be left behind.

To come to practical directions, the sprinter must continually practise short bursts of speed; he must stride well from the hips so as to lose not an inch of his stride; should run as straight as an arrow goes from the bow; and should be careful not to throw his shoulders too far back, as this tends to shorten the stride: the rest must be left to natural capacity and to assiduous practice.

It is of immense importance to a sprinter to start quickly. Until about seven years ago the received method of starting was for the runner to stand on his toes with the right foot seven or eight inches behind the left foot so that it could be brought up quickly for the first stride, the body being kept square to the starting-line. Of late years most sprinters have taken to starting with both hands resting lightly on the starting-line. When the pistol is fired, the runner gathers himself up and darts forward, at the same time rising to the perpendicular. There can be no doubt that the new style is efficacious, as it is now almost universally adopted. It has undoubtedly rendered the starting of sprint races much easier and fairer, for while the runner has his hands on the ground he cannot "break away," from the mark, and if a runner "breaks away," he is, under the A.A.A. rules, put back a yard.

Frequent practising at starts and bursts and an occasional run over the full distance he is

FINISH OF A SPRINT.

training for, should be the regular work of the sprinter; above all, he should never run alone, but have some one to sprint with him. When a man sprints alone, he often gets slow and sluggish without noticing it.

A sprinter must do his best, by one form of exercise or another, to get hard and muscular without getting stiff; for stiffness is fatal to speed. It is undoubtedly a good thing to be well rubbed over the back and legs after each day's practice.

On the day of his race, the sprinter should always take a short "burst" on his way down to the starting post to warm the muscles.

Sprinting requires at least as many weeks' practice as any other form of running; a month, at shortest, is necessary to acquire one's best form.

Middle Distances—*The Quarter Mile*—A great many sprinters, after a little experience and with careful training, develop into fine quarter-milers. In fact, when a man is running four hundred and forty yards in less than 50 seconds, as many amateur runners have done and can do, he must obviously go at full speed nearly every yard of the distance. But there are many runners who are but indifferent sprinters and yet can do marvellous performances at a Quarter. The two best quarter-milers of the present day, E. C. Bredin, of the London Athletic Club, and W. Fitzherbert, of the Cambridge U.A.C., are each of them good enough on their day to beat 49 seconds for a Quarter Mile, and yet as sprinters they are barely in the second rank. The same remark applied to L. E. Myers, the American, and H. C. L. Tindall, of Cambridge, the two best amateur quarter-milers of their day. From this it appears that it is fairer to describe a Quarter Mile as one of the middle distances, for all the men I have mentioned could run equally well at Six Hundred Yards and at Half a Mile. Still, the fact remains that in the Quarter Mile races two runners of an entirely different class often meet; the sprinter, who is strong enough to struggle home over a Quarter, and the middle-distance man, who is running his own distance.

The training for the distance should be entirely different for the two classes of men. The sprinter must be careful not to overdo himself and thus get jaded and slow, but he should frequently run spurts of three hundred yards, or thereabouts, to get used to prolonged effort, and must be very careful in his diet so as to preserve every ounce of his staying power. The regular middle-distance man must train differently: he is usually a lighter man than the sprinter, and he can stand more hard work, but when once he has got moderately fit, what he requires most is speed, and he must assiduously practice sprinting and starting to improve his speed.

Again, when it comes to running the race, the sprinter must use different tactics to the middle-distance runner. He must use his pace when he has got it, that is at the beginning of the race, for after he has covered the third of the distance he will find that his power of "making a burst" is all but gone; the middle-distance man, who can rely on being able to finish out and to keep his stride to the end, wants a pace-maker, some one who will pull him out in the early stages of the race. Let us illustrate these abstract principles by an example. Some of the great struggles of late years at a Quarter Mile have been those between Jordan, of Oxford, and Fitzherbert, of Cambridge: their races are and ever will be memorable historic contests. The Oxonian is a fine natural sprinter; the Cambridge man has only learnt to run short distances fast by assiduous practice: he is not a natural sprinter. The tactics for Jordan are to try and get away from his opponent early in the race; if he does not, his slower opponent can outstride him and cut him down at the finish, as he did in 1895 and 1896. In 1894 Fitzherbert let Jordan get well away from him, and was never able to get up to his shoulder. Many are the races, too, which Bredin has thrown away or jeopardised by starting like a snail, although he can finish like a lion.

The sprinter, then, who wishes to include the Quarter Mile in his repertory must recollect that, although he has to get hard and strong, it is upon his speed that he must rely; and at all hazards he must retain his dash. He can lay the foundation of his staying powers by walking, which hardens the legs and back, or even by rowing, or by lawn-tennis or any hard exercise; but when he begins to train for his races, he must be careful not to get slow and stiff by pounding round the path at longer distances. The middle-distance man can train for his Quarter as he trains for the Six Hundred Yards or the Half Mile, of which we shall now proceed to speak.

Six Hundred Yards—This is a very popular distance which is often run. The pure sprinter cannot last the distance, and the middle-distance men have it to themselves, but it is an interesting race, because a Half Mile race attracts many who are really long-distance runners with staying power and no speed except that which comes from a long natural stride; but a Six Hundred Yards race is necessarily confined to middle-distance men alone. To run fast at Six Hundred Yards, the half-miler has to be careful to push himself along either by a pace-maker or by learning by means of a watch-holder how fast he is going the first half of his distance.

The *Half Mile Race* produces perhaps the most interesting of all athletic contests. It lasts but two minutes, or thereabouts, and therefore cannot grow tedious, and it presents scope for staying power, judgment and spurting. While many long-distance runners can do fine performances at half a mile, they are bound to be outpaced by the really fine middle-distance runner. There are plenty of instances of men who, though good at a Quarter, have not sufficient speed to hold the sprinters, and good at a Mile, yet are unable to keep amongst the first flight of milers, and yet at Half a Mile are magnificent runners. It is unfortunate, therefore, that a Half Mile does not figure in the Oxford and Cambridge programme, as the middle-distance runner has little scope for his abilities at the Universities. There is of course a natural reluctance to interfere with the programme and with the chance it gives to strength, as distinct from speed, in the Weight-Putting, and Hammer-Throwing events, and it is also undoubtedly necessary to have an uneven number of events; but there are many who would not be sorry to see the number of events increased from nine to eleven by the addition of two races at 220 Yards and Half a Mile.

However, to return to the half-milers. The middle-distance men are bound to have a good deal of staying power, and should not be afraid to take a good deal of work. In practising, they must learn to run to a watch, that is, to keep going all through the race by learning to run the first quarter fast. If a man wants to run Half a Mile under two minutes, he should do his first quarter in 58 seconds, and nothing can teach him to know that he is keeping up his pace better than the "running to a watch" held by his trainer. He should frequently run Quarter Miles and Six Hundred Yards in practice, and occasionally the full distance, starting to do his distances slowly when he begins his training, and gradually quickening up as he is approaching fitness and his best form. Nor must he forget to practise bursts of speed, as every runner is the better by improving his pace and by learning to make a sprint, but the main thing a half-miler has to achieve is to go strong and brisk in the early stages of the race. Many half-milers are inclined to be sluggish in the first stage, and for such the best tactics in a race are to start a runner who will "make the

HALF-MILE CHAMPIONSHIP.

pace" for them. The pace-maker can run his first quarter in fixed time, and he will thereby draw out the half-miler, who will hang not far behind him, until he takes up the running after the half distance. The American, Kilpatrick, who holds the amateur "world's record" for Half a Mile, is rarely known to do a fast time without a pace-maker to draw him out.

The pace-maker in such contests should have orders to run the first quarter in about a second faster than the "crack" requires to do the same distance, and this is pretty sure to produce the desired effect.

One Thousand Yards and *Three Quarters of a Mile* are distances occasionally run. Experience has shown that the former is particularly a middle-distance event. Most half-milers can cover the additional 120 yards if called upon. A race at Three Quarters is usually chosen because it makes rather an open thing when a good miler and a good half-miler are matched at a distance which is half way between the two. At this distance the chances are all in favour of the miler, for three quarters of a mile is a distance generally beyond the powers of the middle-distance runner.

Long Distances—All distances from a Mile up to Four Miles are common at meetings at the present day, nor is a Five Miles Race by any means a rarity, and since paperchasing became popular, a Ten Miles Flat Race has formed part of the championship programme. It is hardly possible to separate long-distance runners into classes, and the only general remark that can be made as to the classification of long-distance men is that the lighter their weight the more likely are they to be able to spin over the long distance. The rules for getting fit for long distances are fairly simple; the runner must get down his weight, and do a lot of work. We do not of course mean to say that cases of men overworking themselves and getting stale are not common enough, but the long-distance runners succeed by their endurance and staying power, and are able to stand a lot of work, and every pound of superfluous flesh will tell in a long race.

It is by no means uncommon for a runner to hold the championship at One, Four, and Ten Miles in the same year, which should prove the point we contend for, that all long-distance men belong to one class. To win the championships at One and Four Miles in the same year the runner has to do both races in the same afternoon. The Ten Miles championship is run in the spring at the conclusion of the paperchasing season, at which time all the long-distance men are likely to be as fit and hard as only paperchasing can make them.

For a man to work up to his best form in long-distance races he must "run to a watch" in the way we have mentioned before. His trainer (or he himself after a season or two, for every man should soon learn to gauge his own strength and health) can judge on each particular day whether he should do a little more or a little less work, for this depends on the state of a man's health. It is a fatal mistake to attempt to get fit by doing too much work in a limited number of days. A slow and steady increase of work, which means doing the distance selected at a gradually increased pace, is the safest plan for success.

The runner who confines himself to the Mile race only must possess some considerable speed. The first quarter in a Mile championship is often covered in a minute or thereabouts. In 1885, when the amateur record was made by F. E. Bacon, the first quarter was covered in 58 seconds, and the first half mile in 2 minutes 5 seconds. As the distances get longer, scope is given to the man whose capacity consists almost entirely in being able to keep pegging away. But for all long-distance running the road to success consists in steady training, a quantity of work and a rigid dietary.

Boys' Races—A word should be added as to running races for boys. It should be almost superfluous to say that growing lads should not be put to so severe training as men. The best foundation for training with boys is to let them have plenty of games such as Cricket or Football. By these they harden the muscles and improve the wind. We are no believers in open races for boys. Every boy should be encouraged to run in his own school sports in classes with boys of his own age, but in these school sports there should not be many races of a long distance, and no long races at all for young boys who so often have more energy and spirit than strength. Boys also should be encouraged at schools more than they are at present to practise the High and Long Jump and Pole Jump. They afford plenty of amusement and healthy rivalry and can do nothing but good, and it is as natural for a boy to leap as for a kitten to play. When jumping is taught in English schools, we shall see more and better jumping than is common in England at present.

MONTAGUE SHEARMAN.

STEEPLECHASING—For many years past no athletic sports programme has been considered quite complete without a steeplechase, and at country meetings especially this event provides more interest and amusement than any other. One would naturally have assumed that such encouragement would attract a larger number of cross-country runners to this undoubtedly good sport; yet not only have steeplechases of recent years at athletic meetings produced as a rule thin fields, but the class of competitor, with a few exceptions, has been distinctly poor. The explanation may lie in the fact that steeplechasers have enough discomforts to put up with in any case, and are not prepared to make themselves ridiculous for the amusement of the crowd by being asked to take almost impossible jumps. To a considerable extent sports-managers have only themselves to blame for driving distance runners on to the flat.

A good steeplechaser must combine speed, endurance, and jumping ability, a combination which many of our cross-country runners possess to a marked degree, and which would bring them the highest steeplechasing honours if they turned their attention to the sport. The steeplechase course is generally laid out on a grass enclosure, and comprises a number of artificial obstacles placed at intervals of about eighty yards, generally in the form of hurdles, which should not be too difficult, say three feet in height and tipped with furze. The *pièce de résistance*, however, is the water jump, a ditch about six feet wide by two and a half feet deep, the approach to which is guarded by a solid structure such as a fence, more thickly studded with furze than the other hurdles, and which must be *cleared* and not rushed.

The favourite steeplechasing distances are from three-quarters of a mile to two miles, the amateur championship being at the latter distance.

STEEPLECHASING.

It is surprising to note how few competitors take the obstacles scientifically, that is fly and not jump them. The obstacles should be taken in the stride as in the hurdle-race, so that the runner alights on one foot and at once resumes his stride. The generality of steeplechasers jump the hurdles, often clearing them by several inches, thereby uselessly exhausting energy; but the real fatality of this method lies in the fact that the runner alights on both feet, coming practically to a dead stop and entirely getting out of his stride. It is evident that a recurrence of this at intervals of every eighty to one hundred yards is not only exhausting, but loses an immense amount of time, probably several seconds in a mile. There is no necessity to clear the ordinary hurdle, as, if the timber is topped, the furze will yield to the impact of the body. The chief attraction so far as the spectators are concerned, centres in the water jump, and it is here that the experienced steeplechaser is seen to greatest advantage. Unless he is a jumper of exceptional ability he never attempts to clear the ditch, but jumps into the middle of the water with arms and body slightly bent forward so that he may grasp the edge of the ditch with his hands, and spring out with a minimum loss of time.

There is usually not wanting the competitor who seeks to arouse the enthusiasm of the spectators by clearing the water jump, but the effort is very exhausting, and the exhibition steeplechaser is not to be taken seriously, as he seldom finishes in the first three. The usual rule of athletics as to passing applies to steeplechasing, but special care is needed in approaching the water jump, particularly if the men happen to be in a cluster. It is an unwritten law that the man just behind has the courtesy, to use a mild term, to swerve in his jump either to the right or left, otherwise a serious spiking accident is likely to occur. So many qualities combine to produce a good steeplechaser, that it is to be regretted that more good men do not apply themselves to cultivate the art.

A steeplechase across country differs in many respects from that described above, but primarily in the fact that it is held over country supposed to be open, and the obstacles encountered are natural and not artificial. The courses naturally vary in accordance with the country traversed, but care should be taken to make them as varied as possible; and to apply the term "cross-country" to some courses, mainly consisting of road, is a misnomer. In the cross-country steeplechase of the present day it is seldom that hedges or gates are cleared, though vaulting is an extremely useful accomplishment, and should be more cultivated than at present. Most runners get through a gap in a hedge, or take a ditch very gingerly, whereas with a little more pluck and determination the obstacle could be negotiated much more quickly, and with less personal injury. Racing for a gap is quite legitimate, provided the holder does not wilfully hang back with the object of impeding those behind. Further hints on cross-country running have been already given in an article under that heading.

HAROLD WADE.

THROWING THE DISC has had a precarious existence in Greece since classical times, but cannot be said to have been conformed to rule and formally introduced to the athletic world until the Olympic Games of 1896. Its obvious elegance deserved a better fate.

The disc is circular, having a diameter of 22 centimetres (about 8½ inches), and is composed of wood surrounded by a rim of iron. A nucleus of lead is let into the centre, bringing up the total weight to 2 kilogrammes (about 4½ lbs.).

The performer stands in a square of two metres and holds the disc in both hands above his left shoulder. The fingers of the right hand grip it tightly by the upper edge; those of the left merely support it. The left leg is advanced. Then the body is swung half round to the right, so that the face is turned towards the disc, the latter having been brought round by the right hand to a position above and behind the performer's head. At the same time, the right leg is put forward. It is this attitude which is depicted in the celebrated statue of the "*Discobolos*." The left leg is then brought swiftly to the front again, and the disc is hurled with all the swing of the body. The hand must at the moment of ejection be horizontal, so that the missile may traverse the air horizontally. The distance thrown at the Olympic Games was rather over 95 feet.

THROWING THE HAMMER has always suffered from diversity of rules. We need only concern ourselves with the A. A. A. and American codes, which compel the performer to throw from circles of nine and seven feet diameter respectively. The American circle has a raised rim to keep the thrower safely in. Under both sets of rules the hammer must weigh 16 lbs., must have a total length of not more than four feet, a handle of metal or wood, and a head of any metal. The Inter-University circle of thirty feet will, it is to be hoped, soon vanish, and may therefore be dismissed, as may also the Scotch or stationary method, which is of very limited application. The performer stands generally with his back to the direction in which he wishes to throw, with the head of the hammer resting on the ground outside the ring beside him. He obtains the impetus required by whirling the hammer round above his head as many times as he deems necessary, keeping his feet quite stationary. When he has obtained sufficient

THROWING THE HAMMER.

swing, he brings his whole body round with a jump (some performers contrive to gyrate twice or even thrice within the circle, but this practice is not recommended), keeping his arms and the hammer as far outstretched as possible, and having thus arrived at the front edge of the ring, he discharges the missile. The cardinal points to be observed are (1) keeping absolutely stationary while getting the swing on the hammer, (2) rapidity in jumping round (most important of all), and (3) continuous command over the weapon, so that it may be thrown with the whole force of the body, and not merely with the arms.

G. S. ROBERTSON.

TUG OF WAR—[*See* MILITARY SPORTS].

WALKING, LONG-DISTANCE—Of recent years walking has fallen into desuetude, and nowadays it is rare indeed to hear of feats of endurance approaching those of Captain Barclay or Mr. Ross. This is the age of cycling, nor can it be denied that cycling is a most fascinating and rapid means of getting about. In these days of hurry, the fact of a man's being able to compass on the wheel fifteen miles an hour without any distress to himself, constitutes an incontrovertible argument in favour of the bicycle. At the same time, from the point of view of physical condition, there can be no comparison between the cyclist and the pedestrian, who, in six hours, while the former is travelling his seventy or eighty miles, is content to cover his twenty-five miles on foot.

WALKING RACE.

The late Sir John Astley, one of the keenest of sportsmen, brought long-distance walking into great prominence a few years ago, when some wonderful performances were accomplished. Since his death, however, walking has relapsed into its former oblivion. Still, it is sure sooner or later to revive. Of track-walking the writer does not propose to treat. It is entirely then for the benefit of amateurs who may feel inclined to attempt a long-distance walk that the following hints, the result of some experience, are intended.

Patient and systematic training is the chief consideration: to get condition and keep it. It is of the first importance that the feet should be good. Good feet are indispensable, and without them long-distance walking must never be attempted. Assuming, then, that the intending walker has naturally good feet, they must in addition be well cared for. It is the greatest mistake to suppose that a horny foot is durable in proportion. The skin should be supple and pliant. After the bath the feet must be thoroughly dried, well hand-rubbed, then soaped all over. Some advocate soft soap, but good brown soap is preferable. The socks, too—*lambswool* is the best material—should be well soaped. Strong *shooting boots* or *shoes* are to be recommended, having a long, low heel, with plenty of nails (but large nails are a mistake) at the toes and sides. It is also well to bear in mind the maxim "The heavier the man, the stronger the boot." Flannel underclothing is indispensable.

Training—The preparation should be gradual. The man who attempts only fifteen miles on the first day will at the end of a week cover thirty with infinitely greater ease. The feet must, on returning home, be the first care. Excessive tubbing is not recommended; it is far better to rub them well first with a damp towel and then with a dry one, followed by more hand-rubbing. Regular hand-rubbing also for the legs, back, and loins is the great secret of keeping in condition.

Diet—A man in really hard work can eat

anything. The less he drinks, no matter what the liquor, the better; and the sounder his condition, the less thirsty he will feel. During the early days of training, a man naturally perspires a great deal, becoming, in consequence, very thirsty, a craving that should, however, be fought down. It is an excellent plan to rinse the mouth with water. Sluicing the arms up to the elbows in water will also be found to relieve the thirst to an almost incredible degree; and water which is not fit to drink may still be utilised by standing in it above the ankles for a few minutes. The feet will soon dry, and if the pedestrian keep going, he will suffer no ill effect.

As a practical instance of a long-distance walk, the writer undertook on one occasion to walk from Derbyshire to the north of Perthshire, a distance of 347 miles, in a week. He had trained, it is true, to a certain extent, though not by any means as carefully as he would now, were he fit to undertake what he then accomplished. At the end of the first day, after he had covered fifty-eight miles, his feet went completely to pieces, which may be partly attributed to the fact that for the last seventeen miles the road was paved with great cobblestones. The second day, on which he started in acute pain, put another forty-six miles to his credit; on the third his feet gradually improved, and he ultimately arrived at his destination with three and a half hours to spare. It is significant, as bearing upon the principle of abstinence advocated above, that the writer's bill for wine and spirits during that week did not amount to half a sovereign, and this included a plentiful dose of neat brandy, when on the second day he fainted three times.

FRED COTTON.

WEIGHT PUTTING—The weight should weigh 16 lbs., and in England must be of iron. It is put by A. A. A. rules out of a seven-foot square, in America from a seven-foot circle with a raised rim. Oxford and Cambridge use a ten-foot square. The put is measured in England along a perpendicular, from the pitch of the shot on the side, or side produced, of the square; consequently crooked putting is as disadvantageous in England as it is advantageous in America.

Excellence in shot-putting, as in hammer-throwing, depends entirely on the capacity to bring the weight and strength of the body to bear upon the missile. To acquire this, the elbow of the arm which supports the shot, should be kept directly below the hand, and the hand close to the shoulder, which it should not leave till the very instant of discharge. Further, the performer should stand sideways in respect of the front side of the square, keeping the right shoulder and the shot well back, and being careful to rest the whole weight of shot and body on the right leg. The left leg is raised and held in front to balance the body. A hop forward is taken in this position, the right shoulder being kept as far back as ever; then by a rapid twist of the whole body, the right side and leg are brought to the front, and the shot is propelled. This twist corresponds to the circular jump in hammer-

PUTTING THE WEIGHT.

throwing; and in both cases, rapidity and the continuous application of all available strength and weight to the missile are of the highest importance.

G. S. ROBERTSON.

GLOSSARY.

Amateur Athletic Association—The A.A.A. was founded at Oxford on April 24th, 1880, when the representatives of the chief clubs met and formed a federation. It is the governing body in all athletic matters, and every athletic meeting must be held under its rules. It has taken the place which the Amateur Athletic Club, founded in 1866, tried, but failed, to fill. All the championship contests are now held under its supervision. [*See* Rules *infra.*]

Cinder-track—A running or cycling path made as follows: The surface is dug out to the depth of 12 or 18 inches, according to the soil. Some 6 to 8 inches are then filled with brick rubbish or large gravel. Above this are placed 3 or 4 inches of rough cinders or clinkers, and finally 3 inches of fine cinders. Amongst famous running tracks are, in London, Stamford Bridge, Lillie Bridge, Catford Bridge, and Queen's Club; Aston Manor at Birmingham; Iffley Road at Oxford, and Fenner's at Cambridge.

Consolation Race—A race at the close of an athletic meeting, for which all may enter without extra fee who have competed in previous events but have failed to win a prize. The character of the race varies, but it is usually a sprint of 220 yards.

Corks—Small cylinders, usually, but not always, made of cork, held in the hand to enable the fist to be clenched without straining fingers or palms.

Dead-heat—The result of a race in which two or more competitors reach the finish exactly together.

Event—A completed race, including preliminary *Heats* (*q.v.*), which are not in themselves "events."

Final—[*See* HEAT].

Flights—Each leap that has to be taken over a hurdle, and therefore, by extension, each hurdle, is sometimes called a flight. In the ordinary hurdle race there are ten flights.

Fly—To take the hurdles in the stride without pausing, in contradistinction from jumping them.

Foul—A wilful jostling, crossing, or obstructing of one competitor by another. Also used as a verb. [*See* Law 18.]

Hand-spring Start—A method of starting only employed in the shorter races. The competitor stands, or rather crouches, with his fingers, or corks, upon the line and his feet and body behind it. The first in England to succeed with it was T. L. Nicholas, of Monmouth, the champion quarter miler of 1890.

Handicap—(1) The start which a man gives to another or receives from him. (2) A race in which men receive or give starts. Contrasted with *Scratch Race* (*q.v.*). (3) As verb, to assign starts to competitors in proportion to their capacity.

Heat—A division of a race in which the competitors are too numerous to run all at once. The race is decided eventually by the winners (or winners and seconds) running together in a Final Race or Heat.

Heel and Toe—A description of fair walking, in which the heel of the walker comes to the ground before the toe. It is also sometimes used in a sense equivalent to that of the old "*Toe and Heel*," which meant that "as the foot of the back leg left the ground and before the toes had been lifted, the heel of the foremost foot should be on the ground."

Lap—One complete circuit of the track.

Lifting—Unfair walking, the toe of the back foot coming up before the front heel is down.

Limit Man—The competitor with the longest start in a handicap race.

London Athletic Club—The L.A.C. was founded under another title in 1863, but in 1866 took its present name. Its headquarters are at Stamford Bridge.

Marksman—The official who is responsible for placing competitors upon the proper "mark," which shows their start and the point from which they race.

Mixing—A deliberate attempt to put in a few running strides when in a walking race. To be distinguished from "Lifting," which may be accidental.

Novice—A competitor is a novice if he has never won a prize in the *class* of event for which he is competing, *e.g.*, a quarter-mile champion might be a novice at a walking race, but not in a mile race, even though he had never before run the distance.

Pacing—Going in front so as to quicken the speed at which the race is being run, or at which some particular competitor is running.

Penalise—Strictly speaking, a penalty is a minus handicap, *i.e.*, the man who is giving the other competitors starts, is placed behind the line from which the distance to be run is reckoned. This method of handicapping is usually employed towards previous winners, and is most common in hurdle races.

Pit—The space hollowed out beyond the board which limits the *Take-off* (*q.v.*) in the Long Jump. The result is that if the competitor over-run the line, he cannot get a jump at all.

Run-in—The distance from the last hurdle to the finish of the race.

Scratch Line—The mark from which the length of any race is measured.

Scratch Man—The competitor who gives starts, but receives none from any. Often called simply "Scratch."

Scratch Race—A race in which no competitor gives or receives a start.

Shot—Another name for the Weight.

Shot—A man is said to be "shot on the post" when a competitor just dashes by him as he eases for the finish, or fails from exhaustion.

Side Stride—The common method of taking the High Jump, which consists of running from the side and getting one leg over before the other.

Spin—A practice run.

Sprint—(1) A race whose whole distance can be run at full speed, including the 100 and 220 yards, and, in some opinions, the quarter mile. (2) As verb, to run for a little way at top speed, not only in a short race, but even in a long one, in order to pass or dishearten an opponent.

Standard—The time or distance assigned to each event at a championship meeting, by beating which a competitor becomes entitled to a medal.

Straight—The section of the track between the last bend and the winning post.

Strings—(1) In a hundred yards' race the competitors run side by side between strings fastened to stakes along the course. The width between the strings must not be less than 4 feet, and the stakes not less than 30 feet apart. [*See* Law 33.] (2) "First," "second," and "third" strings are the first, second, and third men chosen to represent a club in any event.

Take-off—The spot from which a competitor rises for the high, or long, jump. The term is also used sometimes for the style of rising from the spot.

Tape—The line held across the track at the winning post, which competitors must touch. It is now general to fasten a thread from side to side, which is broken by the leader. Frequently called the "Worsted."

Waiting—Running behind another man, allowing him to make the pace, and reserving the energies for the finish.

LAWS AND RECOMMENDATIONS OF THE A. A. A.

(1) Laws

FOR ATHLETIC MEETINGS AND COMPETITIONS.

(Rule XXIV. of the Constitution of the A.A.A. enacts, "That if any Club advertise their Sports 'under A.A.A. Laws' and then violate the said Laws, such Club shall be dealt with as the General Committee of the A.A.A. shall think fit.)

1. All competitions must be limited to Amateurs. This Law does not interfere with the right of any Club to refuse an entry to its own Sports.

As to the Qualification of Competitors.

"An Amateur is one who has never competed for a money prize or staked bet, or with or against a professional for any prize, or who has never taught, pursued, or assisted in the practice of Athletic exercises as a means of obtaining a livelihood."

The following exceptions shall be made to this Law, viz:—

(*a*) Amateur athletes shall not lose their amateur status by competing with or against professional football players in ordinary Club matches for which no prizes are given, or in Cup Competitions permitted by the National Football Associations or Rugby Unions of England, Ireland, Scotland or Wales, providing that such competitions or matches form no part of, nor have connection with, any Athletic Meeting.

(*b*) "Competitions at arms between Volunteers and Regulars shall not be considered as coming within the scope of the A.A.A. Laws."

(*c*) "Competitors in Officers' Races at Naval and Military Athletic Meetings (such races being for officers only, and for which money prizes are not given) shall be exempt from any of the laws of the A.A.A. disqualifying runners for competing at mixed meetings."

(*d*) The "Championship of the Army" Race at the Aldershot Sports shall be exempted from the effect of this Law.

(*e*) No person must be allowed to compete while under a sentence of suspension passed by the A.A.A., National Cyclists' Union, Amateur Swimming Association, Amateur Gymnastic Association, Scottish A.A.A. or Irish A.A.A.

(*f*) No one shall be allowed to compete at any meeting held under the Laws of the A.A.A. as "unattached" for more than one season.

(*g*) A paid handicapper is not a professional.

(*h*) A competitor who asks for $\frac{\text{and}}{\text{or}}$ receives expenses ceases to be an amateur.

As to Prizes.

2. No "value" prize (*i.e.* a cheque on a tradesman) must be offered.

3. No prize must be offered in a Handicap of greater value than £10 10*s*.

4. Every prize of the value of £5 or upwards must be engraved (when practicable) with the name and date of the Meeting.

5. All prizes shall be of the full advertised value, that is, without discount, and must be publicly presented on the grounds on the day of the Sports.

6. In no case must a prize and money be offered as alternatives.

Betting.

7. All open betting must be suppressed.

Advertisements.

8. All Clubs must hold their Sports "under the Laws of the Amateur Athletic Association," and so advertise them on all Prospectuses, Entry Forms, Programmes, &c.; and *must* have printed on their Entry Forms "the definition of an Amateur." (*See Law* 1.)

9. That all affiliated clubs shall place on the advertisements, programmes, prospectuses, &c., of their meetings a statement that the club is so affiliated; and that all unaffiliated clubs or managing bodies to which a permit has been granted, shall also so state that the permit has been granted.

Entries.

10. Sports Committees may reserve to themselves the right to refuse any entry, without being bound to assign a reason; or to disqualify a competitor at any time if his conversation or conduct is unbecoming, or if it is shown that his entry was made under false pretences.

11. Entries shall not be tendered or accepted without the stipulated fees. Any competitor winning a first prize in an open handicap shall be penalised for all handicaps in which he may compete during the four days following such wins, Sunday not included. (The scale of penalties may be obtained from this Association.) The penalties not to apply to the scratch mark. No person, other than the handicapper, shall be permitted to alter the starts or to accept additional entries after the starts have been published. Competitors must notify to the Judges before the race is run that they have incurred a penalty, otherwise they will be disqualified and render themselves liable to suspension. Handicappers to state on their Handicaps up to what date they are made, which must be published on the programme. No one shall be permitted to start for a scratch race unless his name is printed on the programme, nor for a handicap event unless his name and handicap allowance are so recorded.

12. Competitors in Handicap Competitions shall be required to send with their entries full and definite particulars as to their last three performances (if any). No club shall be affiliated to the Association or registered as "approved" unless it agrees to adopt the A.A.A. Entry Form.

13. All entries shall be made in the real name of the competitor, and this name shall appear on the programme.

Youths and Novices.

14. Competitors in Youths' races must state their age and previous performances, and, if required, must furnish certificates of birth. Races for Youths, other than club races, shall be confined to boys under 15, resident for three months prior to the sports within a radius of three miles from the ground of the promoting club, and entries from boys under this age shall not be accepted for open events. This rule not to apply to boys attending schools and competing within 20 miles of Charing Cross, London. The age of boys (months and years) must appear on the programme of the day. For Novices' races, a novice is held to be one who, at the time of competing, has never won a prize in a similar class of competition—*i.e.* winning a prize for walking would not disqualify for running, or *vice versa;* but winning a prize for running any distance would disqualify for running. (N.B.—The clause as to Novices does not apply to School and Boys' races.)

Protests.

15. All Protests against a competitor or against a competitor's qualification to compete, shall be made to the Secretary of the Club, in writing, before the prizes are distributed; and if the protest shall not be made good within one calendar month the prizes shall be awarded. Every protest must be accompanied with a deposit of five shillings, which shall be forfeited in case the same shall appear upon investigation to have been made upon no reasonable ground.

Stations.

16. In Handicaps, stations shall be awarded according to the number on the programme.

Attendants.

17. No attendant shall accompany any competitor on the scratch (except in cycle races) nor in the race; nor shall a competitor be allowed, without the permission of the Judges, to receive assistance or refreshment from any one during the progress of a race. In cycle races attendants will be allowed for the sole purpose of lending assistance in starting. Any attendant who steps or follows the machine over the mark of the competitor whom he is assisting to start will cause such competitor to be disqualified.

Fouling.

18. Wilfully jostling or running across or obstructing another, so as to impede his progress, shall disqualify the offender.

Starting.

19. All questions as to starts shall be in the absolute discretion of the starter. All races (except time handicaps) shall be started by the report of a pistol. A start shall only be made to the actual report of the pistol. The starter shall place the competitors on their allotted marks, and shall, if necessary, have the assistance of marksmen for this duty. No competitor shall touch the ground in front of his mark with any part of his body. If any one competitor overstep his mark before the pistol has been fired the starter shall put him back one yard for distances up to and including 220 yards, two yards up to and including 440 yards, three yards up to and including 880 yards, and five yards up to one mile or more. These penalties to be doubled for a second offence, and disqualification to follow a repetition of the same offence. (Committees of Sports are specially desired to print this rule *in extenso* on their Sports' Programme.)

Walking Races.

20. In walking races, cautions and disqualifications shall be left to the decision of the judges of walking,

who may appoint assistants if necessary. A disqualified competitor shall at once leave the track.

The High Jump and Pole Jump.

21. Each competitor shall be allowed three jumps at each height. Crossing the scratch without displacing the bar shall not count as one jump. All measurements shall be made from the ground to the centre of the bar. In the High Jump neither diving nor somersaulting shall be permitted. In the pole jump three attempts, even if the cross-bar be not displaced, shall count as one jump.

The Broad Jump.

Each competitor shall be allowed three jumps, and the best three competitors of the first trial shall be allowed three more tries each for the final. The farthest jump of the six attempts shall win. If any competitor fall back or step back, after jumping, or crosses the taking-off line with either foot, or so swerves aside that he pass beyond the taking-off line, such jump shall not be measured, but it shall be counted against the competitor as one jump. All jumps shall be measured to the taking-off line from the edge of the heel-mark nearest that line, along a line perpendicular to that line.

Steeplechasing.

22. For steeplechases the hurdles shall not be higher than 3 ft. Every competitor must go over or through the water; and any one who jumps to one side or the other of the water jump shall be disqualified.

Throwing the Cricket Ball.

23. In throwing the cricket ball, the distance thrown shall be calculated from the centre of a scratch line; and the thrower, in delivering the ball, shall not cross such scratch line. Three tries only shall be allowed, and crossing the scratch shall count as one try.

Winners of Trial Heats.

24. The winners of trial heats must compete in the finals, unless the consent of the Judges to their abstention has been obtained, or become liable to suspension.

Bye-laws and Regulations.

25. That the N.C.A.A.A. and M.C.A.A.A. and the Southern Committee have power to make and enforce bye-laws and regulations in their respective districts, subject to the veto of the General Committee of the A.A.A.

26. That the Secretary of every race meeting shall send a marked copy of the programme of the meeting to the Secretary of the A.A.A. division within which the meeting is held; and in the event of a mixed meeting, also to the Secretary of the local centre of the N.C.U. These programmes are to be filed and to be open for inspection by all athletes at reasonable hours

27. That all club handicaps shall be made from the actual scratch man in the race.

(2) Recommendations.

In addition to the foregoing, the following Rules for Competitions and the Management of Athletic Sports, adopted by the Amateur Athletic Association, are recommended to clubs holding sports under the Laws of the A.A.A.:—

Officials.

28. The officials of a meeting shall consist of: A committee, in whose hands shall be placed all matters which do not relate to the actual conduct of the meeting itself, and who shall have a final decision in all cases not provided for in the rules of the meeting.

Two or more judges, whose joint decision shall be final in every competition, and with whom shall rest the power to disqualify any competitor.

A referee, who shall decide in the event of a difference of opinion between the judges. The decision of the referee shall be final in all cases.

Two or more stewards, or clerks of the course, whose business shall be to call out the competitors for each event, and to assign to each his distinctive badge.

One or more special judges of walking, a timekeeper, a starter, and one or more marksmen.

Stations.

29. Competitors in level races shall draw lots for their respective places on the post before leaving the dressing room. Each competitor shall be supplied with and wear during each contest a distinctive number corresponding to his number in the programme.

30. Only the winners of the trial heats (first round) in sprint handicaps run over a stringed track shall be eligible for further competition. In cases where the track is not stringed and in distance races the first and second, or first, second, and third, may compete in second round or final heats, at the option of the judges.

Track Measurements.

31. All tracks shall be measured 12 inches from the inner side of the path.

Clothing.

32. Every competitor must wear complete clothing from the shoulders to the knees (*e.g.*, sleeved jersey and loose drawers).

Any competitor may be excluded from aking part in the sports unless properly attired.

Straight Sprint Races.

33. Straight sprint races shall be run on a part of the cinder path or grass so staked and stringed that each competitor may have a separate course. The width between the strings shall not be less than 4 ft., and the stakes shall not be less than 30 ft. apart.

Hurdle Races.

34. The hurdle race shall be over 10 flights of hurdles on a level grass course of 120 yards straight. The hurdles shall stand 3 ft. 6 in. from the ground, and shall have level toprails, and shall be placed 10 yards apart. The first flight of hurdles shall be 15 yards from scratch. Each competitor shall have his own line of hurdles, and shall keep to that line throughout the race.

Throwing the Hammer and Putting the Weight.

35. The hammer shall be thrown from within a circle of 9 ft. in diameter. The head of the hammer shall be of iron and spherical, and the handle shall be of wood. The head and handle shall weigh together 16 lbs. The total length of the hammer shall not be more than 4 ft. Each competitor shall be allowed three throws, and the best three competitors of the first trial shall be allowed three more throws each. The farthest throw of the six shall win. All distances shall be measured from the circumference of the circle to the first pitch of the hammer along a line drawn from that pitch to the centre of the circle.

36. The weight shall be put from the shoulder with one hand only, and without follow from a 7 ft. square. The weight shall be of iron and spherical, and shall weigh 16 lbs. All puts shall be measured perpendicularly from the first pitch of the weight to the front line of the square, or to that line produced. Each competitor shall be allowed three puts, and the best three competitors of the first trial shall be allowed three more puts each. The farthest put of the six shall win.

37. In throwing the hammer and putting the weight, crossing the scratch shall count as a try.

Tug-of-War.

38. The teams shall consist of equal numbers of competitors. The rope shall be of sufficient length to allow for a "pull" of 12 ft., and for 12 ft. slack at each end, together with 4 ft. for each competitor; it shall not be less than 4 in. in circumference, and shall be without knots or other holdings for the hands. A centre tape shall be affixed to the centre of the rope, and 6 ft. on each side of the centre tape two side tapes shall be affixed to the rope. A centre line shall be marked on the ground, and 6 ft. on either side of the centre line two side lines parallel thereto. At the start the rope shall be taut, and the centre tape shall be over the centre line, and the competitors shall be outside the side lines.

The start shall be by word of mouth. During no part of the pull shall the foot of any competitor go beyond the centre line. The pull shall be won when one team shall have pulled the side tape of the opposing side over their own side line. No competitor shall wear boots or shoes with any projecting nails, springs, or points of any kind. No competitor shall make any hole in the ground with his feet, or in any other way before the start. No competitor shall wilfully touch the ground with any part of his person but his feet. If the competition is for teams limited in weight, each competitor shall be weighed before the start. The final heat shall be won by two pulls out of three.

Programmes, &c.

39. The A.A.A. recommend that a programme of any proposed meeting (showing the entrants for, and the starts allotted in each event) shall be forwarded by post to each entrant, to the address given in his entry form, and shall be posted not later than the day before the day appointed for the meeting, or that such a programme as aforesaid shall be advertised the day next before the day appointed for the meeting in one of the public papers circulating in the district of the proposed meeting.

40. It is recommended that all athletic clubs and sports' committees have the following notice conspicuously printed on their entry forms and programmes.

> "The prizes offered at this meeting will be awarded subject to the statements of previous performances given on the entry forms being strictly accurate."

The following Rules must be observed at all Athletic Meetings where Cycling Events are included in the Programme.

All Sports and Festivals throughout England and Wales advertised and carried out as Athletic Sports shall, as regards the general conduct of such Athletic Meetings, be under the Laws and control of the A.A.A., but all Cycle Races competed for at such meetings shall be run under the rules and regulations of the N.C.U., and any competitor in such races shall as regards his entry, and whilst actually competing in any such Cycle Race, be amenable to the N.C.U., as regards all future suspension or disqualification.

On the other hand, all Sports and Festivals advertised and held as Cycle Meetings shall as regards their general conduct, be under the control of the N.C.U., but all Foot Races, or other description of Athletic Sports as at present understood, shall be held under the Laws and Regulations of the A.A.A., and any person offending as to entry or conduct whilst actually competing shall, as regards all future punishment, be dealt with by the A.A.A.

The decision of the Judges or Referee at Athletic Sports or joint meetings to be final, and without appeal to either Association.

The N.C.U. also undertakes not to sanction any professional Cycle Races at any meetings where Foot Races or other Athletic Sports form part of the programme.

In cases where Cycle Races shall be held under N.C.U. Rules at meetings held under the management of clubs affiliated to the A.A.A., the N.C.U. will not (except at the invitation of the A.A.A. club) make any order upon the Committee of the A.A.A. club to alter their decision upon any matter in which the Committee of that club have already adjudicated.

All joint Race Meetings shall be advertised to be, and shall be held under the rules of both Associations.

All suspensions by either body to be binding on the other body.

If a permit be refused by either body to any privately-promoted or speculative meeting, or one that is considered objectionable, it shall be against the laws of both bodies for that meeting to be subsequently, directly or indirectly, carried out under the management of an affiliated club of either the A.A.A. or N.C.U.

Any club refused affiliation by the A.A.A. or N.C.U. shall be ineligible for affiliation to either body without the consent of the other.

That any club after having been members of either body, shall not be elected to the other body, nor granted permits for sports, until communication be made as to the cause of such club's retirement.

N.B.—Clubs affiliated to the A.A.A. and N.C.U. are not required to obtain permits from either body to hold Athletic or Cycling events, but non-affiliated clubs or meetings registered under Rule XVIII. of the A.A.A. code must obtain a similar registration certificate from the N.C.U., for which application should be made to the Hon. Sec. N.C.U., 57 Basinghall-street, London, E.C.

Infringement of A.A.A. Laws.

Any infringement of A.A.A. Laws, or any other malpractice connected with Athletics, should immediately be notified to the Secretary or the representative of the proper Local Association, or to the Honorary Secretrry of the A.A.A. The Amateur Athletic Association undertakes to bear the expense of all necessary prosecutions in the case of charges preferred by an Affiliated Club.

Extracts from the A.A.A. Rules, of Importance to Athletes.

Rule XIII.—The Association strongly deprecates the selling of prizes, and the Committee is instructed to take such action as they may think necessary when such sales are brought under their notice.

Rule XIX.—Any person wilfully competing against one who is under sentence of suspension shall be himself suspended until the expiration of such sentence or for such longer period as the Committee may think fit.

Rule XXII.—Any one taking part in a competition to the winner of which a prize and money are offered as alternatives shall be suspended for such time as the Committee may think fit.

Rule XXIX.—No one shall be allowed to compete at any meeting held under the Laws of the A.A.A. as "unattached" for more than one season.

Rule XXIII.—That the General Committee, the Southern Committee, and the Committee of the N.C.A.A.A. and M.C.A.A.A. shall have power to reinstate any Amateur who shall have competed for money or against a Professional in ignorance of the Laws of the A.A.A.; or shall have otherwise offended against or broken the said Laws.

That no application for requalification to compete under A.A.A. Laws shall be considered unless accompanied by a deposit of 5*s*., such deposit to be only returnable to the applicant at the discretion of the Committee.

Rule XXVII.—(*a*) All clubs affiliated to the A.A.A. shall have the following rule incorporated into their rules, viz.: "That the Committee shall have the power to expel any member whose subscription is twelve months in arrear, provided a notice in writing shall have been sent to such member by a registered letter, addressed to his last known address, informing him of the proposed action of the Committee."

(*b*) The name and address of any person so expelled from a club in the Southern district shall be sent to the Hon. Secretary of the A.A.A.; and of any person so expelled from a Club in the Northern or Midland districts, to the Secretaries of the N.C.A.A.A. and M.C.A.A.A. respectively, and shall be entered by each of such officers in a book (to be called the "Black Book") kept for that purpose. Every person whose name has been so entered in a Black Book shall be suspended from competing at a meeting held under A.A.A. Laws until the liability causing his said expulsion shall have been discharged.

N.B.—Club Secretaries sending up a name for entry in a Black Book must send with each name the Post Office Receipt for the registered letter sent to such person, or the name will not be inserted.

New Record Rules.

1. A Record can only be made in a *bonâ fide* competition (either level or handicap) which has been duly fixed and advertised before the day, and is included in the printed programme, together with the names of the entrants for the event.

2. No one, whether entered or not, may join in the competition after it has been started.

3. In foot races the time must be taken by one or more competent timekeepers, the watch and watches must be proved to be accurate, and the course measured (12 inches from the inner edge of the track) by a surveyor or qualified member of the Association.

4. In competitions other than foot races, the distance must be measured at the time and certified by a surveyor or qualified member of the Association.

Records

Passed by the General Committee to end of 1895.

Running.

Distance.	Name. Record made by	Time. H.	M.	S.	Date.	Club of which a Member.
Yards.						
100	A. Wharton				3 July, 1886	Darlington College.
	C. A. Bradley			10	1 July, 1893	Huddersfield.
	A. R. Downer				4 May, 1895	London A. C.
120	W. P. Phillips				25 Mar., 1882	,,
	C. A. Bradley			11⅘	28 April, 1894	Huddersfield.
	A. R. Downer				11 May, 1895	London A. C.
120 Hur.	Godfrey Shaw			15⅘	6 July, 1895	,,
150	C. G. Wood			14⅘	21 July, 1887	Blackheath H.
	C. J. Monypenny				27 Feb., 1892	Cambridge U. A. C.
200	E. H. Pelling			19⅘	28 Sept., 1889	Ranelagh H.
	A. R. Downer				11 May, 1895	London A. C.
220	C. G. Wood			21⅘	25 June, 1887	Blackheath H.
300	C. G. Wood			31⅖	21 July, 1887	,,
440	H. C. L. Tindall			48½	20 June, 1889	Cambridge U. A. C.
	E. C. Bredin				22 June, 1895	London A. C.
*440 Hur.	T. M. Donovan.........			58⅘	7 Aug., 1894	Queen's College, Cork.
600	E. C. Bredin		1	11⅖	10 June, 1893	London A. C.
880	F. J. K. Cross		1	54⅗	9 Mar., 1888	Oxford U. A. C.
1000	W. Pollock Hill		2	15⅘	8 May, 1889	,,
1320	No reliable record.					
Miles.						
1	F. E. Bacon		4	17	6 July, 1895	Ashton & Reading A.C.
1½	S. Thomas		6	53⅗	13 May, 1893	Ranelagh H.
2	W. G. George		9	17⅖	26 April, 1884	Moseley H.
3	S. Thomas		14	24	3 June, 1894	Ranelagh H. & L.A.C.
4	E. C. Willers............		19	33⅘	10 June, 1894	Essex Beagles.
5	S. Thomas		24	53⅗	24 Sept., 1893	Ranelagh H. & L.A.C.
6	,, ...		30	17⅘	22 Oct., 1892	,,
7	,, ...		35	36⅘	,, ,,	,,
8	W. G. George		40	57⅖	28 July, 1884	Moseley H.
9	,, ...		46	12	7 April, 1884	,,
10	,, ...		51	20	,, ,,	,,
12	S. Thomas	1	2	43	22 Oct., 1892	Ranelagh H. & L.A.C.
15	,, ...	1	22	15⅖	,, ,,	,,
20	G. Crossland	1	51	54	22 Sept., 1894	Salford H.
25	G. A. Dunning	2	33	44	26 Dec., 1881	Clapton Beagles.
30	J. A. Squires	3	17	36½	2 May, 1885	London A. C.
40	G. A. Dunning	4	50	12	26 Dec., 1879	Clapton Beagles.
50	J. E. Dixon	6	18	26⅕	11 April, 1885	L. A. C. and Spartans.
100	No records..............					

* Hurdle Race on Grass, over ten 3 ft. hurdles not less than thirty yards apart.

WALKING.

Distance.	Name. Record made by	Time.			Date.	Club of which a Member.
Miles.		H.	M.	S.		
1	W. J. Sturgess		6	39⅕	24 Aug., 1895	Polytechnic H.
†2	,, ...		13	44	25 Sep., 1895	,,
3	,, ...		21	16⅘	28 Sep., 1895	,,
4	,, ...		29	1⅗	19 Oct., 1895	,,
5	,, ...		36	27	,,	,,
6	,, ...		43	58⅗	,,	,,
7	,, ...		51	27	,,	,,
8	,, ...		58	56	,,	,,
9	H. Curtis	1	11	14⅖	27 Dec., 1890	Highgate H.
10	,, ...	1	19	27⅗	,,	,,
15	*Tom Griffith	2	0	27	3 Dec., 1870	South Essex A. C.
	C. W. V. Clarke ...	2	10	13	26 Dec., 1885	Southampton A. C.
20	*Tom Griffith	2	47	52	3 Dec., 1870	South Essex A. C.
	W. E. N. Coston ...	3	0	9	27 Dec., 1880	Southampton A. C.
25	,, ...	3	53	35	,,	,,
30	,, ...	4	46	52	,,	,,
40	*A. W. Sinclair	6	38	3	14 Nov., 1879	North London A. C.
	J. A. McIntosh	7	1	44	2 Oct., 1886	Ealing H.
50	*A. W. Sinclair	8	25	25½	14 Nov., 1879	North London A. C.
	J. A. McIntosh	8	52	25	2 Oct., 1886	Ealing H.
75	*A. W. Sinclair	14	10	0	27 Aug., 1881	North London A. C.
100	* ,, ...	19	41	50	,,	,,

* In matches against time.

† On June 20 Sturgess walked the distance in 13 min. 33 sec., at Wembley Park, but it has not yet been considered by the Committee.

TIME RECORDS—WALKING.

Event.	Name. Record made by	Distance.			Date.	Club of which a Member.
		M.	yds.	ft.		
2 hours' Run.........	G. Crossland	20½			22 Sep., 1894	Salford H.
1 hour's Walk	W. J. Sturgess......	8	270		19 Oct., 1895	Polytechnic H.
3 hours' Walk.......	Tom Griffith.........	21			3 Dec., 1870	South Essex A. C.
12 ,, ...	A. W. Sinclair......	64	180		27 Aug., 1881	North London A. C.
		H.	M.	S.		
London to Brighton (52¼ miles)	J. A. McIntosh......	9	25	8	10 April, 1886	Ealing H.

ODD EVENTS.

Event.	Name. Record made by	Distance.		Date.	Club of which a Member.
		ft.	in.		
*High Jump	J. M. Ryan	6	4½	15 Aug., 1895	Irish A. A. A.
Pole Jump	R. D. Dickenson...	11	9	1891	Windermere.
Long Jump	C. B. Fry............	23	6½	4 Mar., 1893	Oxford U. A. C.
Putting the Shot (16lb.)	D. Horgan	46	5½	15 Aug., 1894	Banteer.
†Throwing the Hammer (16lb.)	W. J. M. Barry ...	134	7	23 July, 1892	Southport A. C.

* G. W. Rowdon's 6 ft. 5⅝ in., Aug. 6, 1890, at Hayter Camp, is not authentic.

† J. Flanagan, of Kilmallock, threw 147 feet at Stamford Bridge Grounds, London, May 25th, 1896, but it has not passed the General Committee as yet.

Best Amateur Records in America.

EVENT.	RECORD.	HOLDER.	CLUB.	GAMES.	DATE.
100 Yards...........	$9\frac{4}{5}$ sec.	J. Owen, Junr. ...	Detroit	Championships	Oct. 11, 1890
100 Yards...........	$9\frac{4}{5}$ sec.	B. J. Wefers	N. Y. A. C.	N. Y. A. C. v. L. A. C.	Sept. 21, 1895
220 Yards...........	$21\frac{1}{5}$ sec.	B. J. Wefers	Georgetown, U.	Inter-Collegiate	May 30, 1896
300 Yards...........	$31\frac{1}{5}$ sec.	B. J. Wefers	N. Y. A. C.....	Travers Island........	Sept. 28, 1895
440 Yards...........	‖$47\frac{3}{5}$ sec.	W. Baker	Boston A. C. ...	Boston	July 1, 1886
Half-Mile...........	1 min. $53\frac{2}{5}$ sec.	C. J. Kilpatrick ..	N. Y. A. C. ...	N. Y. A. C. v. L. A. C.	Sept. 21, 1895
One Mile	4 min. $15\frac{3}{5}$ sec.	T. P. Conneff	N. Y. A. C. ...	Travers Island	Aug. 30, 1895
Four Miles	20 min. $15\frac{4}{5}$ sec.	W. D. Day.........	S. I. A. C.......	Bergen Point, N. J....	Nov. 16, 1889
Five Miles	25 min. $23\frac{3}{5}$ sec.	E. C. Carter	N. Y. A. C. ...	New York	Sept. 17, 1887
Ten Miles...........	52 min. $38\frac{2}{5}$ sec.	W. D. Day.........	S. I. A. C.......	West New Brighton..	Oct. 26, 1889
120 Yards Hurdles.	*$15\frac{2}{5}$ sec.	Stephen Chase ...	Travers Island..	New York	Sept. 28, 1895
One Mile Walk ...	6 min. $29\frac{3}{5}$ sec.	F. P. Murray	W. A. C.	New York A. C.	Oct. 27, 1883
Two Miles Walk...	13 min. $48\frac{3}{5}$ sec.	F. P. Murray	W. A. C.	Manhattan A. C.	May 30, 1884
Three Miles Walk.	21 min. $9\frac{1}{5}$ sec.	F. P. Murray	W. A. C.	New York	Nov. 6, 1883
Four Miles Walk..	29 min. $40\frac{4}{5}$ sec.	T. H. Armstrong..	N. Y. A. C.	....	Nov. 6, 1877
Seven Miles Walk.	54 min. 7 sec.	E. E. Merrill	Univ. A. C.....	Boston A. C...........	Oct. 5, 1880
High Jump	6 ft. $5\frac{5}{8}$ in.	M. F. Sweeney ...	N. Y. A. C. ...	Manhattan Field	Sept. 21, 1895
Broad Jump.........	23 ft. $6\frac{1}{2}$ in.	C. S. Reber	Detroit	Detroit, Mich..........	July 4, 1891
Pole Jump..........	11 ft. $5\frac{3}{8}$ in.	W. S. Rodenbaugh.	....	Philadelphia, Pa.......	Sept. 17, 1892
Throwing Hammer 16-lbs. (7ft. circle).	145 ft. $0\frac{3}{4}$ in.	J. S. Mitchell......	N. Y. A. C. ...	Travers Island, N.Y.	Oct. 8, 1892
Putting the Weight 16-lbs. (7ft. circle).	47 ft.	G. R. Gray.........	N. Y. A. C. ...	Chicago.................	Sept. 16, 1893
Throwing 56-lbs. (7ft. circle)	35 ft. $10\frac{1}{2}$ in.	J. S. Mitchell......	N. Y. A. C. ...	Travers Island, N.Y.	Sept. 2, 1894

* On cinders; same runner 16 sec., on grass, Sept. 22, 1894. ‖ On a straight course.

AUROCHS—The true Aurochs (*Bos taurus*, var. *primigenus*) is not now found in a wild state. That which sportsmen call the "Aurochs," is really the European bison (*Bos bonasus*). [*See* BISON AND BUFFALO.]

BABIRUSA (*Sus babirusa*)—A wild hog found in Celebes and some neighbouring islands, and distinguished by the extraordinary size and curvature of the tusks in the lower jaw of the male. It is much hunted by the natives, who drive it into a netted enclosure and afterwards secure it alive or spear it.

BADGER (*Meles taxus*)—An unfamiliar, though by no means rare, British quadruped, of burrowing and nocturnal habits. As **Badger-Baiting** [*see* OBSOLETE SPORTS] has long since been forbidden by statute, the "brock," as it is widely known in the north country, affords now-a-days but little legitimate sport. In some districts, however, mainly owing to its falsely alleged taste for game (its real diet consisting mainly of roots, wild fruits, and insects), it is shot by keepers, and also persecuted in various ways. The favourite methods of capturing it at the present day consist either in digging it out; or, on a moonlight night, when the animal is away from home, blocking every entrance to the burrow but one, and, having placed a sack in the free entrance, driving the badger back to this extemporised trap with dogs.

In South Germany, where the hunting of the badger is much more in vogue, the small breed known as Dachshund (*Dachs* = badger) is employed, and two of these animals will keep their tough assailant at bay until their master is able to seize it by the tail and transfer it to a sack.

BADMINTON—The game of **Badminton** is played in a Court forty-four feet long by twenty wide. The **net**, which ought to be as light as possible, and made with a small mesh, should be stretched for twenty feet across the centre of the court, and should not be less than eighteen inches deep. Its lower edge should be five feet from the ground, and as taut as possible.

The Badminton **bat** should not be more than five ounces in weight. The **shuttlecock** should weigh about a quarter of an ounce. The small shuttlecock used by many clubs weighs considerably less than a quarter of an ounce. This small shuttlecock is slower in flight, and the rallies are consequently longer and the game generally easier.

Badminton is best played in a well-lighted room or hall, where the wind cannot affect the flight of the shuttlecock. It can be played very well with the larger shuttlecock in the open air on a calm day. The game is often played with three or four players on a side. This is not, however, the scientific game; for with more than two on a side the players in front cannot help getting in the way of their partners behind.

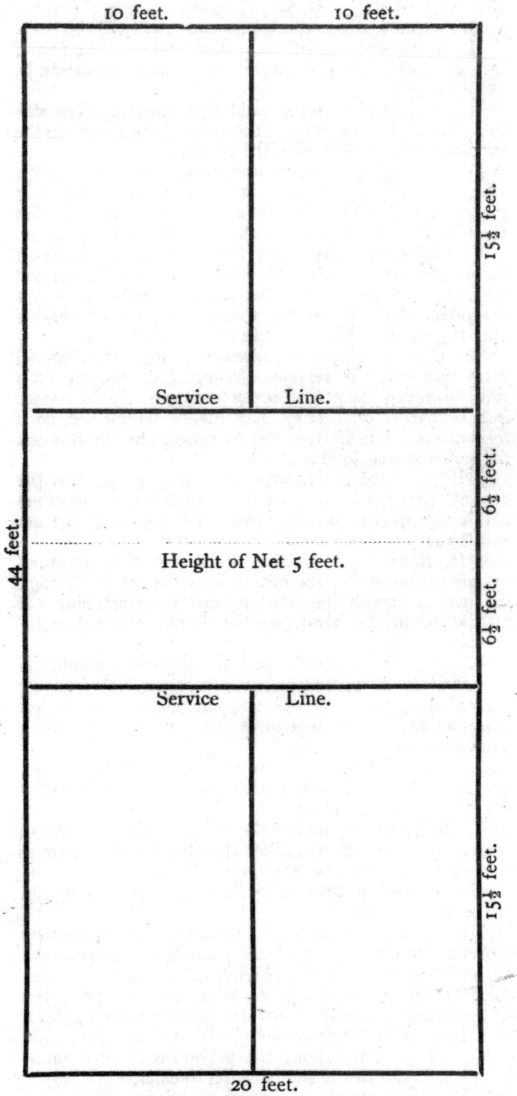

Scale ⅛ inch to a foot.

The **Service lines** are drawn across the court parallel with the net, and six and a half feet on each side of it. A line down the centre, joining the service lines and baselines, forms the four courts.

The **game** is fifteen for one or two players on a side, twenty-one for three players, and twenty-eight for four players on a side.

In beginning a game with two players on each side, the side that goes in first is only allowed one hand in, but after the first round the partners go in one after the other.

In **Serving,** the striker must stand behind the service line, and hit the shuttlecock so as to give it an upward trajectory, and send it over the opposite service line into the opposite diagonal court. There are no faults allowed in serving as in lawn-tennis. Only the player in the diagonal court can take the serve. After the serve, the players can go as near the net as they like, and send the shuttlecock anywhere within the courts, provided it goes over the net and between the poles. If the shuttlecock touches the net in going over, it does not invalidate the stroke, but the striker must not touch the net with his bat.

If the striker send the shuttlecock into or under the net, or outside the courts, it scores against him. If his side be in, the hand goes out; if the other side be in, it scores an ace. If the shuttlecock touch the ground within the opposite courts, or touch the dress or person of a player, the striker scores an ace if his side be in; if the other side be in, their hand goes out.

Whenever an ace is scored, the server changes courts. When the score stands thirteen all, they set five; when fourteen all, they set three. They begin counting again, and the side which first scores five or three wins. The sides cross over when the score has reached eight.

Badminton is a quicker game than lawn-tennis. The courts being smaller, there is not so much running about, but there is more hard hitting, and the exercise to the arm is greater.

It is a great advantage to put the server out at the first stroke, to prevent his side scoring. The policy of the server is to send the shuttlecock high, so that it may drop as perpendicularly as possible into the farthest corner of the diagonal court, and thus make it difficult for the adversary to cut it down and kill it. It is generally good play to keep sending the shuttlecock high at the back of the adversary's court until an opportunity comes to cut it down and kill it. In cutting down the striker should try not to send it within reach of the adversary. When the shuttlecock is being driven hard backward and forward, an ace is often secured by suddenly altering the pace and dropping the shuttlecock just over the net.

In playing **singles,** the player who gets command of the shuttlecock, and is thus able to send it at each stroke far from the adversary, has a great advantage. In such a case, unless the last ace in the game is in question, it is *better deliberately to lose the ace* than to continue playing at such a disadvantage. As an illustration, the writer saw a very good lady-player lose an important match in this way to a skilful adversary. It was towards the close of a severe contest that the lady was forced by her antagonist to run across the courts at every stroke. She ran so well that she must have covered nearly fifty yards before she failed at last to return the shuttlecock. The effort was so great, that she was quite exhausted, and the lady opposed to her made the two or three aces necessary to win the match with the greatest ease.

Badminton is a game of science and strength. The quickest and most active player is almost sure to win, but he must also possess that instinct which enables him in the heat of a rally to decide in a moment where to place the shuttlecock so as to be in the most difficult position for the adversary to reach it.

Badminton, at first played only at Bath, Cheltenham, and other places where retired Indians congregate, is now widely known. Clubs are formed all over the country. The game has stood the test of time, is more popular than ever, and will doubtless continue to flourish.

ARTHUR SOUTHEY.

BADMINTON IN INDIA is ordinarily played in a ground the size of a double lawn-tennis court (78 × 36 ft.), with five players a-side. Instead of the usual shuttlecock, most players prefer a ball of Berlin wool wound on a double disc of cardboard 2¼ inches in diameter, with a central hole of 1 in. The ball flies more quickly than the shuttlecock. When missed by one player, it is not considered dead until it has touched the net or ground, or been taken in hand, but may be returned by any other player, or players, on the same side.

GLOSSARY.

Ace—The unit of scoring.

Base-lines—The lines parallel with the net, which limit the ground at the extremity of the courts.

Court—The ground, a rectangle measuring 44 ft. × 20 ft., is marked out into five divisions. The service-lines are parallel to, and on either side of the net. The spaces between the service-lines and base-lines are subdivided into right and left courts [*v.* diagram].

Fault—An attempted service or return, which either fails to clear the net, or pitches outside the proper court.

Game—This consists of 15 points for 2 players a-side, 21 for 3 a-side, or more.

Hand-in—The player who serves.

Hand-out—The server or striker is out when the shuttlecock does not clear the net, or when it does not reach the proper court or drops beyond the boundary-lines.

Net—This is slung across the shorter transverse of the courts, midway between the base-lines. It should be between 5 ft. and 5 ft. 1 in. in height. It is a light, small-meshed net.

Points—The units of scoring. A point is scored when the opponents fail to return the shuttlecock, or when they send it out of the courts.

Racquet—Must not exceed 5 oz., and is strung with cat-gut.

Service—The opening stroke of a round, the server standing in one court between the service- and base-lines and driving the shuttlecock in a rising trajectory, so that it would pitch, if allowed, in the court *diagonally* opposite him.

Service-lines—Lines drawn across the ground parallel with the net and 6½ ft. on either side of it.

Shuttlecock—The missile employed, which consists of a cork crowned with feathers, from 3 to 5 inches in length. In weight, about ¼ oz.

RULES.

I. Badminton can be played by any number of players, up to four on a side.

II. A full-sized court is 44 feet by 20. The top of the net should be 5 feet from the ground and should be quite straight.

III. Choice of courts is decided by tossing. The side that loses the toss taking the serve; the player in the right hand court beginning the service.

IV. In beginning the game, when there are 2 on a side, only one hand goes in, when 3 are on a side only 2 go in, and when 4 are on a side only 3 go in. After the first service the partners all go in one after the other.

V. The server may serve from any part of his court behind the service line. He must serve over the net and over the service line on the opposite side, into the diagonal court. In serving, the wrist must not be higher than the elbow. No faults are allowed in serving.

VI. Only the player or players standing in the diagonal court can take the service. Where 3 are playing on a side, however, the player at the back can take the service from either court. They may take a wrong service if they choose, but if they fail to return the shuttlecock the server scores an ace.

VII. After the serve both sides may go as near the net as they like, and send the shuttlecock anywhere within the opposite courts, provided it goes over the net and between the poles.

VIII. Should the shuttlecock be served or returned by any player, under the net, or into the net, or through the net, or outside the court it scores against him. If his side is in, the hand goes out, if the other side is in, it scores an ace.

IX. If the shuttlecock touches the ground within the opposite courts, or touches any part of the dress or person of a player in the opposite courts, the striker scores an ace if his side is in, if the other side is in their hand goes out.

X. If a player touches the shuttlecock with his bat, but fails to return it, it scores against him, whether or not it falls outside his courts.

XI. If the striker touches the net with his bat it scores against him, and if he strikes the shuttlecock before it has crossed the net it scores against him.

XII. If the shuttlecock touches the line it is within the courts.

XIII. Whenever an ace is scored the server changes courts; when 2 on a side are playing he changes with his partner; when 3 are playing the player at the back comes to the front to serve; when 4 are playing the server changes courts, with the partner standing level with him in the back or front as the case may be. No change of position among the players is allowed unless an ace is scored by the side wishing to change.

XIV. If the shuttlecock touches the net or the poles in going over the net, it does not invalidate the stroke.

XV. The game is 15 for singles or 2 on a side, for more than 2 on a side the game is 21.

XVI. When the game is called 13 all they set 5, when 14 all they set 3. In each case they begin counting again and the side which makes 5 or 3 first wins. In games of 21 they set 5 at 19 all, and 3 at 20 all.

XVII. In games of 15 points the sides cross over when the score has reached 8, and in games of 21 they cross over when the score has reached 11.

XVIII. The decision of the umpire is final, whether it is right or whether it is wrong.

BANDY—Bandy, or Hockey on the Ice, is a similar game to hockey on the land. It is played by skaters upon broad sheets of ice between goals, with curved sticks called "bandies," and a ball or "cat."

Teams—The players are divided into two parties or teams, and the object of each set of players is to drive the ball through the goal of their opponents.

Ground—A large piece of ice is needed for playing the game satisfactorily. The smallest ground allowed by the rules is 100 yards × 50 yards, and that only when a larger cannot be obtained. The ground should be *quite free from snow*, as even a thin layer spoils the game, and the snow should be swept off at once before it has time to harden.

Goals—The goals consist of two upright posts, 12 feet apart.

Number of Players—The players are eleven a side, but if the field is smaller than 100 yards × 50 yards it is better to reduce their number; thus, six a side make a good game on a field of 75 yards × 35 yards.

The Bandy—The bandy used is a curved ash stick of about 1½ inches diameter and 3½ feet long. It is very similar to the stick used in hockey on land, except that the blade is not so curved, and is not, as in that game, rounded on one side, but has both sides flat.

The Cat—The "cat" used is an india-rubber ball, about the size of a lawn-tennis ball. With such tools on a surface like ice tremendous hits might be given. To discourage this, and also to prevent accidents, the bandy in hitting *may not be raised above the shoulder.*

The Game—The rules of the game are in general the same as those of hockey on land, the rules of offside being the same as in Association football, with the exception that a player cannot be offside in his own half of the ground. There is, however, no rule that all hits must be made on one side of the bandy, or from the right hand; and, in fact, in dribbling the player keeps the ball well in front of him, pushing it forward, now with one side of the bandy now with the other, and often changing hands when dodging an opponent. The teams are ranged in the field much the same as in hockey and football, there being a goalkeeper, backs, half-backs, and forwards; and a combined game of passing across the ground is found effective, especially upon smaller grounds. On larger grounds the dribbling is a special feature of the game, and is far more brilliant and effective than in the games above mentioned. The skilful player can run with the ball in front of him at very nearly his full speed, perhaps at the rate of from twelve to fourteen miles an hour, or even more, and can, almost without slackening his pace, dodge and elude a single player coming forward to "tackle" him; while it is almost impossible for the player when passed to turn round and catch him up again. The way in which a fast and skilful player will sometimes thread his course with the ball through his opponents is astonishing. These facts, and the rapidity with which the ball travels when hit, make the game exceedingly rapid and exciting, and of keenest interest to players and onlookers; and it would doubtless become very popular but for the very limited number of days in the year upon which it can be played, the difficulty of finding a suitable ground, and the necessary uncertainty which attends every fixture, even when made only two or three days ahead, from the changes in the weather.

The game has been described as played in accordance with the rules of the *National Bandy Association* which are given below. But where the field of ice is very small a plain cork bung, covered with leather or bound with string, may be used with advantage; and in some places the thin hockey-stick with bent end of about six inches, formerly used by the Virginia Water and other clubs, is still preferred. On the artificial ice at the Ice Palace (Regent Street), where the space is of course extremely limited, a fairly good game is obtained by using a flat india-rubber disc (3 inches diam. × 1 inch thick) as the cat, and by prohibiting the bandy when used in hitting from being raised from the ice.

The kinds of skates used in the game are various. The members of the *Bury Fen Club* use ordinary "fen runners" (wooden with flat blades), and by preference the "Standard" skates (marked "S. B." with crossed bandies), but the Virginia Water players, and many others outside the fens, use one or other of the varieties of figure-skates with curved blades.

The game, played with the restrictions imposed by the rules against high hitting, tripping, charging, &c., is both safe and delightful; and the writer, after considerable experience, hardly remembers a serious accident occurring. But if played in rude and unrestricted fashion, and in an ill-natured spirit, it becomes dangerous. A great advantage is that it is played with enjoyment and success by men of middle age, and also by ladies, among themselves. The game has for some years been played by ladies on private pieces of water, and by, among others, the Princess of Wales and her daughters. Ladies should, however, use thinner bandies and a lighter ball than those above mentioned. A lawn-tennis or a string ball is suitable.

Among the principal bandy clubs are the *Bury Fen* B.C. who play on Bury Fen, at Earith (Hunts.); the *Virginia Water* B.C. who play on Englemere, near Ascot; the *Winchester* B.C., on Winnall meadows near that city; the *Camberley* club, on the "Staff" lake, and the *Northampton* B.C. Mr. Bryant's lake at Stoke Pogis, and the Duke of Marlborough's lake at Blenheim are also fine bandy grounds. The game was introduced in 1890–91 into Holland, and there are clubs at Haarlem, Amsterdam, and other places. In 1894 Mr. C. G. Tebbutt introduced it into Norway. It is also regularly played in the season at Davos Platz, and at St. Moritz in Switzerland by the English visitors. Further information may be obtained from Mr. H. Blackett, Sunninghall, Ascot, hon. sec. of the Bandy Association. ARNOLD TEBBUTT.

GLOSSARY.

Ball—Of solid indiarubber, diameter between 2¼ and 2¾ in. Usually red.

Bandy—The club from which the game is named. Shaped like a hockey-stick, only with the blade flat on both sides. Length along the outer curve, not more than 4 ft. Width, not exceeding 2 in. at any point.

Corner-hit—A free-hit, given to one side from the corner next their opponents' goal.

Dribbling—Pushing the ball along with the flat of the bandy, as opposed to hitting.

Goal—(1) Two posts 12 ft. apart, connected by a tape or lath 7 ft. above the surface of the ice. (2) The scoring unit, obtained by driving the ball through the posts.

Ground—A rectangular sheet of ice, measuring not more than 200 yds. × 100 yds. and not less than 100 × 50.

Offside—Same as in Association Football (*q.v.*); only a player cannot be offside in his own half of the ground.

Team—Eleven players on each side.

Time—Usually one hour and a half for each match.

RULES OF PLAY.

1. A bandy team shall consist of eleven players.

2 The ground shall be a right-angled parallelogram, 200 yards long by 100 wide; but when it is not possible to provide so large a ground it may be reduced, and also the number of players, by mutual agreement, provided that the ground be not less than 100 yards by 50 yards. The longer sides to be called *side lines* and the shorter lines *goal lines*. A line, or mark, parallel to, and equidistant from, the goal lines shall be called the *centre line*. (The usual and best size for play is 150 yards by 100 yards.)

3. The bandy shall be of wood, not exceeding two inches in width in any part, or four feet in length as measured along the handle and round the curve; and shall have no metal fittings or sharp edges.

4. Players must wear the colours of their side on the playing arm or bandy.

5. The ball shall be of solid indiarubber, not less than 2¼ inches, nor more than 2¾ inches in diameter. It is desirable to have it coloured red. The present regulation lacrosse ball is much used.

6. The goals shall be in the centre of the goal lines, and consist of two uprights or goal posts twelve feet apart, connected by a horizontal tape or lath seven feet from the ice.

7. The choice of goals shall be tossed for at the beginning of the game; and at half-time, and then only, the teams shall change ends. The time during which a match is to last shall be agreed upon beforehand by the captains, the recognised time for play being one and a half hours.

8. To start the game, and after each goal is made, each team being on its own side of the centre line, play shall be commenced by the referee or one of the umpires throwing up the ball perpendicularly in the air from the centre of the ground, and when the ball has reached the ice it shall be in play.

9. A goal is scored when the ball has passed between the goal-posts and under the tape or lath.

10. When a player touches the ball, any player of the same side who at that moment is nearer his opponents' goal-line is offside, and may not touch the ball himself, nor in any way whatever prevent any other player from doing so, until it has been touched by another player; unless there are at least three of his opponents nearer their own goal-line. No player can be offside when within his own half of the ground.

11. Whilst the ball is in play, and when a player strikes at the ball, his bandy may not during any part of the stroke rise above his shoulder.

12. The ball may be stopped with any part of the body or bandy, but not with the hand on the ice, except in the case of the goal-keeper; nor must it be picked up, carried, kicked, thrown or knocked on, except with the bandy. No charging, kicking, collaring, shinning, tripping, throwing the bandy, or rough play shall be allowed. Fencing or hooking bandies shall not be allowed.

13. On the occasion of a free hit, no member of the offending team shall be within five yards of the spot where such hit is made, but he shall not be compelled to go behind his own goal-line. A goal cannot be scored from a free hit, unless the ball just touches another player.

14. On the occasion of a free hit, a corner hit, or when the ball is hit off from a goal-line, or from a side-line, the striker or thrower shall not touch the ball again until it has been touched by another player.

15. When the ball has passed the side-line, it shall be immediately struck or hit in from where it crossed the line, in any direction, except forward, by one of the opposite team to that of the player who last touched it. No other player shall be within five yards of the side-line.

16. If the ball is passed beyond the defenders' goal-line, but not through the goal by the attacking team, it shall be hit out into play by one of the defenders, from any point on the goal-line within ten yards of the nearest goal-post, and on that side crossed by the ball, the attacking side being at least twenty-five yards from the said goal-line. But if the ball has been last touched by one of the defending team before crossing the goal-line, a player of the attacking team shall have a free hit from any point on the side-line within a yard of the nearest corner; and at the moment of such hit, all the defenders must be behind their own goal-line.

17. The penalty for any breach of these rules shall be a free hit by one of the opposite team, from the spot where the rule is broken.

18. Two umpires and a referee should be appointed, each captain appointing one umpire, and the umpires so appointed choosing the referee. When there are only two umpires and no referee, each umpire shall act in one half of the ground as divided by the centre-line, and give decisions only in that half. The two umpires shall not cross over at half-time. In case of umpires disputing, the decision of the referee shall be final. In case there is only one umpire, his decision shall be final. Should there be no umpire, or umpires, the captains shall be arbitrators in all disputes.

19. A match is won by the team which scores the greater number of goals.

20. In the event of an appeal for any supposed infringement of the rules, the ball shall be in play until a decision has been given.

21. The referee shall have power to stop the game for such time as he may think fit, whenever he may deem it necessary to do so; and he shall deduct any time which he considers has been wasted, owing either to an accident or other cause.

22. In the event of any temporary suspension of the play from any cause, the ball not having gone beyond the side-line, or behind the goal-line, the game shall be restarted by the referee throwing up the ball at the spot where the play was suspended; and when the ball has reached the ice, it shall be in play.

[NOTE.—"Touching" in these rules means touching the person or bandy.]

BARBEL (*Barbus vulgaris*)—[*See* ANGLING, (COARSE FISH)].

MEASUREMENTS, ETC.—Length of head 4 to 4⅔, of caudal fin 4⅔, height of body 5 to 6 times in the total length. *Eyes*—rather high up, situated in the middle of the length of the head, 8 to 10 diameters in the length of the head, 3½ to 4½ diameters from the end of the snout, and 3 to 4 apart. Dorsal profile more convex than that of the abdomen, which is almost horizontal. Snout produced and somewhat overhanging the jaws, the maxilla much longer than the mandible. Lips thick. *Barbels*—two thick pairs, the maxillary ones extending to beneath the middle of the eye, while the rostral pair are somewhat shorter. *Teeth—pharyngeal*; curved, hooked at their extremity and pointed, 4, 3, 2/2, 3, 4. *Fins*—dorsal commences about midway between the angle of the mouth and the base of the caudal fin, the extent of its base ¼ shorter than the third undivided dorsal ray, which is the longest, osseous, strong, and serrated along its posterior margin: last ray of the fin half the height of the longest anteriorly. Pectoral inserted low down, broad, and about four-fifths as long as the head, but not reaching the ventrals, which latter do not extend to the anal. Anal narrow, the length of its base being only two-fifths of its height. Caudal deeply forked. *Scales*—about thirty-five rows anterior to the base of the dorsal fin, and seven between the lateral-line and the base of the ventral. *Lateral-line*—complete, continued to the base of the caudal fin. *Gill-rakers*—short. *Colours*—olivaceous, shot with gold, lightest along the sides and lower surface. Dorsal fin with a narrow, dark outer edge. The other fins of a reddish colour.

Day, *Fishes of Great Britain and Ireland* (Horace Cox), vol. ii. 169.

BARRACOUTA (*Thyrsites*)—A name locally applied to more than one family of sea-fish. The finest species, both for sport and food, is found in the waters round Tasmania, where it is caught from a boat up to a weight of 10 lbs. with what is called the "Maori-jig," a simple tackle consisting only of a piece of red wood pierced by a tent nail. The boat is kept in motion and the fish, which seize the bait greedily, are jerked on board by means of a short, stout rod and line.

BASEBALL—Many writers, when chronicling the merits of their own particular sport, seem to consider they cannot do it justice unless they prove by arguments, more or less convincing, that it dates from almost prehistoric times. Baseball, I may say at once, does not belong to Ancient History. What matters it whether the game originated in the days of Alfred the Great or simply dates its birth somewhere in the last half century? If the skill and science of the pastime appeal to the athlete, what does it matter for its antiquity? I may frankly admit then that Baseball, as Baseball, is not yet half a century old.

Similarity to Rounders—An Englishman, witnessing the game for the first time will immediately exclaim, "Why, this is nothing but Rounders!" To a great extent the Englishman is right. Baseball is Rounders made scientific. Using Rounders for their groundwork, our brothers on the other side of the Atlantic started to build the edifice of America's national game. Rules and regulations were made to govern the game. Each year saw something added, something amended. The rough edges were hewn off, the rough surface in time was polished. Useless rules were abolished and useful ones evolved. The result has been that Baseball can now take its stand amidst the finest forms of athletics and its followers can boast of as much skill and science in their pursuit of the game as do the devotees of Football or Cricket in the better known winter and summer sports at home.

The Theory of the Game—Eighteen players are required for a Baseball match, nine on each side. The aim of each team is the same as in Cricket—viz., to make as many runs as possible. To score a run a player must make a complete circuit of the bases, but not necessarily on one hit. For instance, with his own hit he may only get as far as first base. He may get to second base whilst the pitcher (the equivalent of the bowler in Cricket) is delivering a ball to the succeeding batsman. Third base may be reached on the hit of the batsman; and he may reach home plate on a hit by batsman number three. So he would score a run. There are other methods, of course, of getting from base to base, but the above will suffice for an example.

The captain of the home team has choice of innings. To the cricketer such a proceeding would seem to give the visiting team the worst of the bargain. Did the game take as long to decide as Cricket, the argument might hold good: but, as a baseball match as a rule does not last more than two hours and a half at the most, it would be hard to say that either side is unduly favoured. One team takes the field, and the members of the other take their turn at the bat in regular order. When three men are put out the innings is finished, and the other team then takes its turn with the bat. The game consists of nine innings for each side, and the team having the greatest number of runs at the finish wins.

To Lay out the Baseball Field—The simplest method of marking out a Baseball field is as follows:—Procure a heavy cord one hundred and eighty feet in length. In it tie three knots, one at sixty feet five inches, another at ninety feet, and a third at one hundred and twenty-seven feet four inches. When you have found the most suitable position for the home-base, more commonly called the home-plate, drive a peg in the ground and attach the line to it. Carry the line straight out in the direction in which you intend to bat, and knot number three will give you the position of second base. Great care must be taken that the cord be quite taut and absolutely straight from the peg at the home-plate to the centre of the second base. Whilst the cord is so held, the knot at sixty feet five inches will mark the centre of the pitcher's plate. Let one end of the cord be held at the home-plate, the other at second base, and let some one holding the knot at ninety feet, which of course is the exact centre of the cord, walk out with it to the corner of the diamond where first base is to be situated, and when the line cannot be carried further without bringing it away from the home-plate or second base, there fix your first base. Repeat this in the opposite direction and mark third base, and there you have your diamond complete. Herewith is appended a diagram of a Baseball field showing the positions of the fielders, the foul lines, bases, &c.

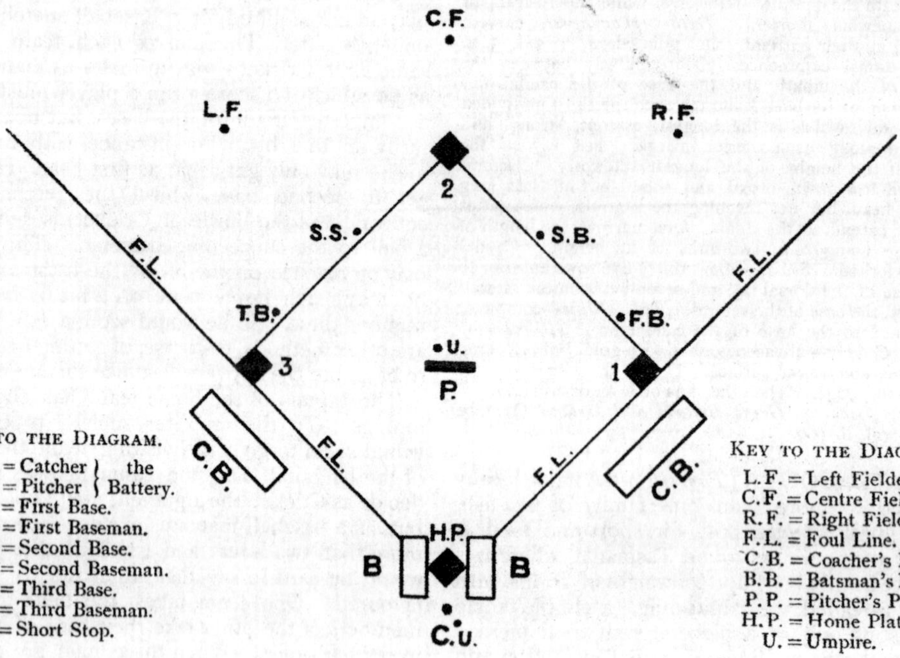

KEY TO THE DIAGRAM.

C. = Catcher } the
P. = Pitcher } Battery.
1. = First Base.
F.B. = First Baseman.
2. = Second Base.
S.B. = Second Baseman.
3. = Third Base.
T.B. = Third Baseman.
S.S. = Short Stop.

KEY TO THE DIAGRAM

L.F. = Left Fielder.
C.F. = Centre Fielder.
R.F. = Right Fielder.
F.L. = Foul Line.
C.B. = Coacher's Box.
B.B. = Batsman's Box.
P.P. = Pitcher's Plate.
H.P. = Home Plate.
U. = Umpire.

PLAN OF GROUND.

Duties and Qualifications of Players —The Pitcher—The pitcher is in Baseball what the bowler is in Cricket, and consequently his first qualification must be a thorough command of the ball. It is true that speed counts for a good deal in both games, but speed is practically useless if eight out of ten balls are sent to the batsmen in such a fashion that they can never be effective. The pitcher is not allowed a run, as is the bowler, preparatory to delivering the ball; but apart from that, his deliveries are practically untrammelled. He may pitch, throw, jerk or hurl the ball provided he does it in such a way that the ball pass over the home-plate not higher than the batsman's shoulder nor lower than his knee. His aim is to deliver three balls answering the above description in such a way that the batsman cannot hit them, and provided he succeeds before he sends up four balls that are not of this nature, he retires the batsman. Should the batsman, however, strike at a ball not coming over the plate and miss it, the pitcher has attained his end just the same. A thorough command of the ball, then, is necessary. When he has got this, he must bear in mind the important fact that the true art of pitching is to deceive the eye of the batsman. That is to say he must send the ball towards the bat in such a way as to lead the striker to believe that it is coming high when it is really coming low, that it is travelling direct for his chest when it is really going feet away from his body, that it is a fast delivery when in reality it is slow, and so on. Like the bowler in Cricket, if he wants to excel in the game he must use his intellect. Brute strength and fast pitching are all very well in their way, but unless allied to sound judgment, to all intents and purposes they are of very little avail. To keep his judgment, he must keep his temper. He must not, simply because his best deliveries are treated with contempt, lose control of himself. When he loses control of himself, he loses control of the ball; and when that happens, he had better vacate his position, or else he will soon lose his side the match.

The pitcher must, above all things, have a code of signals with his catcher. A movement of the hand, an elevation of the head by the latter, lets the pitcher know that this ball is to be an in-shoot, the other an out-curve. A movement of the head may mean that the pitcher is to throw to second base; a nod may mean that the ball is to be hurled to first base, and so on. They must agree upon their signals, and the services that the catcher will render the pitcher, who cannot watch the field as does the man behind the bat, will be invaluable.

It was doubted for some time in England that the Baseball pitcher could curve or twist a ball in the air. That the average pitcher does so there cannot be a doubt. It seems

THE PITCHER.

wonderful that any one can do so without assistance from the ground, but a lesson or two from a good pitcher will give a likely man the knowledge of how it is done, and then constant, steady practice will do the rest. The beginner must be content with ordinary straight balls at first. The science of pitching will be picked up in time. One thing I would impress upon the pitcher, and it is this, study the batsman. If you find that he is timorous of the deliveries that come near his body, you must attack his weak point. If you discover that he cannot hit a low ball, do not be anxious to treat him to high ones. Study the weak points of your adversary. Find where his defence is weakest, and, when you have found the weak spot, turn your attention to scoring off it.

The pitcher, too, must be a man of pluck. In his position the ball will be batted very often to him at lightning speed. He must not be afraid to face it. If he is nervous and timorous he is scarcely likely to pitch with judgment, for he will be so impressed with the idea of avoiding being hit that he will think of little else.

The Catcher—The catcher's position, to my mind, is the most difficult and most dangerous in the game. When there are not any men on bases the position is an easy one, but when "two strikes" or "three balls" are called, then the troubles commence. He must come right up behind the bat and face the fastest deliveries without flinching. It is a position demanding courage. In addition to courage the catcher must have splendid judgment and a sure eye. His duties are akin to those of the wicket-keeper in Cricket, but considerably more varied. He must be able to hold every third strike missed by a batsman, or, if he drop the ball, he must be alert enough to pick it up in time to hurl it to first base so that it will arrive in the baseman's hands before the runner can get to the base. He is bound to keep a most watchful eye on the base runners so as to cut them off when they endeavour to steal a base. To do this he must be a good fast thrower. and must throw with the greatest judgment, for a ball sent flying wildly over the baseman's head might be the cause of a run or two runs being credited to the opposing side.

The catcher must have a ready eye for the weak points of a batsman. He is in a better position to detect them than even the pitcher, and when he has discovered them he must bring the code of signals, of which I wrote above, into play to let the pitcher know exactly what kind of a ball to send in.

Some catchers make the mistake of throwing to a base whenever the base-runner makes a feint at stealing a base. Here the catcher's judgment must again be brought into play. He must know by intuition when the base-runner is feigning, or "bluffing" as they say in America, and when he is seriously intending to steal a base. He must, before he throws, first be sure of his baseman; secondly, be sure of his aim; and, thirdly, be sure that he times his throw well.

First Baseman—The position of first baseman is the one for the tall man, for he has to stop all kinds of throws, straight or wild. All basemen should be able to catch well, but the occupant of first base should especially excel in

THE CATCHER.

this line. More men are disposed of at first base than at any other position on the field. The ball is returned there from every part of the diamond, as the fielders all endeavour to cut off the base-runner at first base. As a result, balls are hurled in every conceivable way at the poor baseman. They come in every possible direction, and he is expected to stop them all. He is expected to catch the high, the low, the wide, and, if it is absolutely impossible for him to catch them, his fellow players consider that he is bound, at any rate, to stop them. No matter how fast a ball is thrown at him he must get in front of it, for if it passes him there is no telling the harm it may do the side.

Not only must he catch well, but he must be an expert thrower. He must throw straight and with speed. He must, too, have quick judgment to know in an instant when his own base is safe and where the ball is to be sent to do the greatest damage to the opposing side.

Second Baseman—The second baseman, being the centre man in the field, is called upon to do his work quickly and reliably. He must be a most active fielder, for being in a direct line with the batsman he receives some of his hottest drives, and must stop them unfailingly. Moreover, he is a target for the catcher, who throws more often to second base to cut off a runner than to any other position in the field. He must be at his base to accept the hottest throws, and prompt to touch at once the base-runner with the ball before that worthy can attain his haven of rest. Catching the ball and stopping it do not cover the duties of second baseman. He must be able to take in the situation at a glance, and be able to throw surely and effectively the very moment the ball is in his hands. A cool head is needed for the position, with judgment and readiness enough to render him equal to any and every emergency.

Short Stop—Short stop is a very difficult position. As regards fielding, I consider it the most important of any of the positions in the in-field. It is one which calls for a very active player to discharge its duties thoroughly. A very great number of batted balls come to this position, and more often than not they travel at a speed that would disconcert a player who was in any way faint-hearted. He must be a sure fielder and an unerring thrower, for very, very often in the game devolves upon him the duty of securing the treacherous grounder and sending it over to first base in time to cut off the swiftest runner. He is also called upon to back up all the positions of the in-field. He must be behind second baseman when the catcher throws to cut off a runner; the same applies to him with regard to third baseman. He must be on the alert to pick up any ball that glances, when hard hit, off the pitcher's person or clothing. No player consequently is fitted for the position who is not quick and lively in his movements. Great judgment, too, is required in fulfilling the duties of the position. Above all things, he must not be liable to lose his head. He can do more harm by a wild throw to first base than any other fielder, for the simple reason that if he sends the ball out of the reach of first baseman he is sending it right away out of the field of play.

Third Baseman—The position of third baseman involves duties quite as onerous as those of first and second baseman or short stop. In nearly every respect he resembles them. In catching, throwing, fielding, and in the exercise of good judgment he must excel. He must be more on the alert, if anything, than the other in-fielders, for the catcher and pitcher cannot give him warning of their intention to throw to him to catch a base-runner who has ventured too far from his base. Consequently he must be always on the *qui vive*. His fielding must be particularly good, as on it will frequently depend the increasing of the enemy's score. The third baseman with short stop and first and second basemen constitute what is known as the in-field. They must all be in complete accord, and each must know the peculiarities of the others' play. They must work in harmony, and with true dependence on one another. By means of this thorough concord and knowledge of each other's ways many brilliant plays may be brought off. In playing third base the aspirant to Baseball honours must be careful in his throwing. Let him before throwing collect his wits, and when he does throw, let the ball travel low rather than high, for a low ball can be stopped if not caught, whereas a ball overhead is calculated to give the opposing team a base or two. Let the third baseman be energetic and active. Indifferent players seldom trouble themselves to field a ball that does not actually come within their province, but a good player does not wait to consider whether the ball is in his district or not. He goes after it and, if it is fielded by another in-fielder, he has the satisfaction of knowing that he is on the spot to rectify any error his brother player may make.

The Out-fielders—Left, right and centre field constitute the out-field, and the occupants of these positions should be equal in their qualifications. Each should be able to throw well. A good long throw is anywhere in the neighbourhood of eighty-five or ninety yards. The out-fielders should not occupy one position all the time. They must use their discretion and judgment. It would be silly to be as far out for the poor hitter as for the heavy slogger. They must study, too, the peculiarities of the batsman. One may have a habit of hitting always in the direction of left field. Another may have a penchant for driving the ball to the other side of the field. A third may have a knack of batting the ball close to the foul lines. A fourth may bat the pitcher's deliveries just over second baseman's head. All these details must be attended to. The out-fielders, too, must be good judges of fly-balls. The ground balls are generally attended to by the in-fielders. In judging fly-balls it is always safer to get well out for a long hit, as it is easier to run in to catch the ball than to run out with it and stand a great chance of missing it. When the out-fielders get a ball, they should not hold it an instant. Throw it at once into the in-field, for a man can never be put out whilst the ball is sojourning in the out-field. Let the novice remember this. No doubt he will feel perplexed at times as to where he should throw. Don't wait. Throw it somewhere into the in-field.

Left Fielder—The player occupying this position will find that the majority of the out-field hits are made to his part. Consequently he must not be lazy. Because he has not had a ball for some time he must not on that account go to sleep. A very great number of batsmen are dismissed by being caught by the left fielder. He must then be a good catcher, and he should also be a good runner. Speed is a great help in left field, for the simple reason that often he has to travel from right out in the distance, to take a catch batted well over third baseman's head. He must be ready, too, to back up third baseman and short stop, for if the ball passes them, he must be behind them to avert serious consequences. Good judgment is necessary to calculate, immediately the ball leaves the bat, where it is likely to travel, and at what speed it is going. If his judgment tells him that the ball will not reach him on the fly, he must not wait for it to roll to him. No, he must run to meet it; and this remark applies to the other out-fielders.

Centre Fielder—This player should act in support of the second baseman. If he gives him good backing up there is no saying what an amount of good he can do for his side. He gives the catcher confidence to throw to cut off a runner, since he knows that even if the ball elude second baseman the centre fielder will be behind him to save serious results. If he plays his position well, he deters the base-runner from trying to steal from first to second base. Good eye and quick judgment are as necessary for him as for left fielder, and like all men in responsible positions—and every position in Baseball is responsible—he must reason for himself. In conjunction with second baseman, if he but use his intellect, he can bring off some very tricky plays.

Right Fielder—The hints given to left and centre fielders apply equally to this position. Sure eye and sure hands for catches, an intellect quick to discern the best possible thing to be done in all circumstances, and a wakefulness to his responsibility of securing the balls that manage to get by the first baseman into the out-field are requisite. So I finish with the fielders. Let us now briefly give a little consideration to the batsman.

The Batsman—To become a good batsman, it is in Baseball as in Cricket. The player must have confidence, nerve, and decision. Of course a good eye is a *sine quâ non*. The batsman, to be a batsman, must keep in constant practice. When at the bat he must study points. He is not the good batsman who, putting every bit of brute strength into his hits, plays purely for applause from the spectators. Such a batsman is no use to his side. Every time he drives the ball away out into the distance, he is giving away a chance for his side, for there are fielders waiting to catch the ball as it descends. The batsman who is of use to his side is the one who strives to place the ball. If he sees an opening between first and second base, he will endeavour to hit the ball in that direction. Or he will strive to drop one just over second baseman's head. At times he will sacrifice his own chance so that some one else on the side may obtain a run or even advance a base. Batting in Baseball is different from batting in Cricket. To begin with, in England's national

THE BATSMAN.

game a bat is used; in America's national pastime a club, by no means so broad as the cricket bat, is brought into requisition. In Cricket the ball is bowled and usually touches the ground before reaching the batsman. In Baseball the ball is pitched like a full toss. However, cricketers as a rule will find that they will soon pick up the knack of using the club to advantage.

Immediately the batsman hits a fair ball, he endeavours to get to first base. If he gets there without being caught, or before the ball can be sent to first baseman in time to retire him, he at once begins scheming how he is to reach second base in safety. He may get there on a safe hit made by the succeeding batsman or he may steal second; that is, that either when the pitcher is off his guard or when he is actually delivering the ball, he makes a dash for second base and arrives there before he can be put out. When he succeeds in making the tour of the bases the run is scored.

If you consult the diagram you will find I have treated of all the figures except the F. L. (Foul Line) and C. B. (Coacher's Box). I shall now proceed to describe them.

The Foul Line—Cricketers who have never seen the game played wonder how so few runs are scored when we have but nine fielders. The reason is very simple. The beautiful cuts through the slips and hits to leg are absolutely useless in Baseball. Every ball, to be of any use, must be hit inside the foul line. When it is hit outside the line it counts for nothing, unless one of the opposing team catch it, and then the batsman is out, provided the man who catches it is not within ten feet of the home-plate. Should however the opposing catcher catch the ball within ten feet of the home-plate a strike is recorded against the batsman.

The Coacher—In the diagram C. B. means the Coacher's Box. A coacher in Baseball is a member of the side at the bat, and it is his object to assist and direct the base-runner. When the runner has not to be worrying himself as to where the ball has travelled to, he can concentrate all his thoughts on whatever his coach bids him do. The base-runner must put implicit trust in him. He has not to think for himself. He has not to decide when to steal a base, and when to slide. His mentor's word is law. Immediately the coacher says, "Go!" the runner must not for the fraction of a second stop to consider. His business is to obey. He will be the more ready to do this if he recollects that it is highly improbable that the coacher, being one of his own side, would counsel any act which would be detrimental to their common interest. Implicit trust must be placed in the coacher.

It must not be imagined, however, that anybody can coach. Such is far from the case. The coacher, like the poet, is born, not made. One might think that the players of most experience would be the best advisers of the base-runner. That is a fallacy. It is the man of quick wit and judgment, the one who evinces a thorough grasp of the points of play, the one who is gifted with the faculty of quick yet sound reasoning that is best adapted for the post. He must, moreover, be gifted with a ready wit, for by a humorous remark or a quaint saying he will often distract the attention of the fielder, and that is precisely what he wants, as he can score off the enemy's unpreparedness.

In coaching, rude and offensive language must be strictly tabooed, and all remarks must be addressed to the base-runner. While doing this, the coacher is often able, if he have tact, to address other people through the man whom he counsels. A humorous coacher, whilst his humour serves its purpose in increasing the chances of his side, is highly diverting to the spectators, and adds life and zest to the game. Abuse of the privilege would soon render the coacher's office a nuisance, but the proper use of it adds a feature to the game, which is entertaining to all, and of the utmost service to a team.

I must not forget to mention the necessity of the base-runner and coachers thoroughly understanding how to receive a command and how to interpret it. There must be a code of voice inflections on the part of the coacher, letting the runner know when he is to obey and when he is to pay no attention to what is merely "bluff." The coacher may shout "Go!" over and over again, but the runner will pay no attention to the injunction, for he knows it is only used to fool the fielders, since the proper intonation or inflection of the voice was not used. When, however, "Go!" is shouted in the stipulated tone, he must not hesitate the fraction of a second in obeying the word of command.

The Umpire—As in Cricket, so in Baseball, the position of umpire is most responsible, and at the same time somewhat thankless. The umpire is the man who must be obeyed. His every word is law, and no player may question his decision. True, the captain of a team, and the captain only, may suggest that he has erred in the interpretation of a rule, but he must do so in a thoroughly respectful fashion. The umpire, to fill the position with honour, must be experienced in the rules of the game, quick to read character, that he may know the man who is "bluffing," and the one who appeals for a decision on honest conviction. He must, moreover, be quick in his decisions and prepared to stand by them when once made. The duties of the umpire are very clearly laid down in the rules, and so I shall not enlarge upon them. This I will say,—when an umpire is to be chosen, let him be such a one as possesses the confidence of the players, and is possessed of an equable temper and disposition. In fact the qualifications that go to constitute a good umpire in Cricket or Football, are requisite for the one who would excel in the same line in Baseball.

Concluding Remarks—It can scarcely be said that in the present article I have given a thorough exposition of Baseball. This short treatise must serve but as a foundation upon which the reader, by help of the rules, by witnessing Baseball games, and by questioning the players on the points of which he is doubtful, may build the edifice of his own Baseball reputation.

There are many inducements to lead the average Englishman to embrace the American sport. The game is admirably adapted to the requirements of the average professional man or artisan, as it does not call for a great sacrifice of time, inasmuch as the game does not last longer than two hours and a half. But what an amount of exercise is crowded into that short space of time! Every one is busy. Every one is on the move. There is no room for the lazy man. Everybody is given a chance to excel both at the bat and in the field. In Cricket, should you get out first ball, your chance is gone, in all probability, of distinguishing yourself at the bat for that day. It is not so in Baseball. As nine innings are played you have five or six chances more of retrieving your honour. From the sportsman's point of view, Baseball should stand ahead of most manly games. It is open to everybody to learn it and become speedily efficient. Application and diligence are the only requirements. With them the average athlete will, after a game or two, learn every detail; and when he has taken to Baseball I can safely say that he will not be in a hurry to desert it. R. G. KNOWLES.

GLOSSARY.

Assist—Any fielder co-operating with another or others in retiring a base-runner is credited with an assist.

Balk—When a pitcher, with a view to deceiving the batsman, makes a motion as if to pitch the ball to him, and fails to do so, the umpire must declare a balk.

Ball—A pitched ball, not passing over the home-plate at an altitude not higher than the batman's shoulder nor lower than his knee, must be declared a ball, provided the batsman does not strike at it.

Base Hit—Any ball so hit that, provided an error has not been made, it cannot be fielded in time to prevent the batsman from reaching his base.

Base on Balls—Is a base accorded the batsman when the pitcher has delivered four balls.

Batsman's Box—The space on either side of the home-plate in which the batsman must stand.

Battery—The pitcher and catcher.

Block Ball—A ball in play touched by a spectator or by one of the batting side when not actively engaged in the game.

Bunt Hit—A ball deliberately batted so slowly to the in-field that it cannot be fielded in time to put out the base-runner.

Coacher's Box—The space in foul territory near first and third base devoted to the coacher.

Dead Ball—A ball delivered by the pitcher which, when it has not been struck at, touches any part of the batsman's person or clothing, or any part of the umpire's person or clothing, while on foul ground, without first passing the catcher.

Diamond—The ground is so called on account of its shape.

Double Play—A play in which the ball is handled quickly enough to retire two men.

Earned Run—When the round of the bases is made without the help of a fielder's error, before the side can be retired, the run is "earned."

Error—Is the mistake of a fielder which helps the opposing side.

Fair Ball—A ball passing over the home-plate not higher than the batsman's shoulder, nor lower than his knee.

Fair Hit—A ball batted within the foul lines and remaining in that territory till it has passed first and third bases, or a ball batted outside the foul lines which rolls inside before passing first or third base.

Fly Ball—A ball batted into the air.

Forced Out—When a base-runner is compelled to make room for his successor and is touched by the ball held by a fielder or cannot reach the next base as soon as the fielder holding the ball.

Foul Ball—A ball batted into foul ground, except in the case of a foul tip.

Foul Lines—The lines running from the home-plate through first and third bases to the extremity of the field.

Foul Strike—A ball batted by the batsman out of position or a ball bunted which rolls into foul ground.

Foul Tip—A foul hit not rising above the batsman's head and caught by the catcher within ten feet of the plate.

Home Run—A complete circuit of the bases made on a hit without the help of a fielder's error.

In-field—First, second and third basemen and short stop.

Out-field—Right, centre, and left fielders.

Passed Ball—A pitched ball which passes the catcher and allows the base-runner to advance a base.

Plate—The home base.

Pitcher's Box—The plate on which the pitcher must have one foot when delivering a ball to the batsman.

Sacrifice Hit—When the batsman purposely hits a ball in such a way that he is put out, with the view of advancing a base-runner.

Shut Out—An innings in which a side does not score a run.

Slide—When the base-runner to avoid being put out slides feet or head first to a base.

Stolen Base—A base obtained by a runner without help from a hit by a batsman.

Strike—When the batsman tries and fails to hit a ball delivered by a pitcher or does not strike at a fair ball.

Strike Out—A batsman strikes out when three strikes have been called upon him.

Triple Play—A play in which the ball is handled quickly enough to retire three men.

Wild Pitch—A ball pitched out of the reach of the catcher, which allows a base-runner to advance a base or bases.

Wild Throw—A ball thrown out of reach of the fielder to whom it was directed.

SIMPLIFIED RULES.

1. Each side consists of nine players.

2. An innings is complete when three men on the batting side are out. Three men being out constitutes an innings.

3. A game consists of nine innings played by each side.

4. The players go to the bat in regular order: the first man on the list of his side being the first man to bat in the first innings. Afterwards the first batsman in an innings is the one next on the list to the third batsman out in the previous innings. But, if a base-runner is the third man retired, and this occurs while a man is at bat, such batsman shall bat first in the succeeding innings.

5. The batsman must not step out of his position, known as the batsman's box, and must strike at every ball delivered by the pitcher that crosses the plate between the knee and the shoulder.

6. If the batsman fails to strike at a good ball so delivered, the umpire must call "One strike."

7. If the batsman strikes at any ball, whether it be a good or bad one, and fails to hit it, the umpire must call "One strike."

8. When the umpire has called "Three strikes," the batsman is out, providing the ball constituting the third strike be caught by the catcher before it touches the ground. If the catcher fails to hold the ball, the batsman has an opportunity of reaching first base, but the catcher may recover the ball and intercept the base-runner by throwing it to first base. If the ball reaches the base before the runner, he is out.

9. If the pitcher delivers a ball which does not pass across the plate between the batsman's knee and shoulder, the umpire must call "One ball."

10. If the umpire calls four balls, the batsman is entitled to his first base.

11. If the batsman hits the ball so that it falls outside

the foul lines, it is a foul hit, and does not count, provided that if a fielder catches it before it touches the ground, the batsman is out.

12. If the batsman hits the ball so that it falls inside the foul lines, it is a fair hit. Any ball hit to ground inside the foul lines is a fair hit, unless it should roll outside the foul lines before reaching first or third base, as the case may be. Any ball hit to ground outside the foul lines which rolls inside the foul lines before reaching first or third base, as the case may be, is a fair hit.

13. The batsman becomes a base-runner immediately he has made a fair hit; immediately after four balls have been called by the umpire; immediately after three strikes have been called by the umpire, provided that the catcher has not held the ball at third strike, as provided in Rule 8; if any part of his person be hit by a ball delivered by the pitcher, unless the hit be upon the forearm; and immediately after the pitcher has illegally delivered a ball.

The batsman is out:—

14. If he fails to take his position at the bat in his order of batting.

15. If he fails to take such position within one minute after the umpire has called for the batsman.

16. If he makes a foul strike. To make a foul strike is to hit the ball when not standing in the batsman's box, as provided in Rule 5.

17. If he attempts to hinder the catcher from fielding or throwing the ball.

18. If, while the first base be occupied by a base-runner, three strikes be called on him by the umpire, except when two men are already out.

19. If, while attempting a third strike, the ball touches any part of his person.

20. If, after two strikes have been called, the batsman obviously attempts to make a foul strike.

21. If the ball struck by him, whether in a fair or foul hit, be caught before touching the ground.

22. If the catcher catches the ball at third strike before it touches the ground.

23. If, after he has made a fair hit, or after the third strike (provided in the latter case that the catcher has not caught the ball before it touches the ground) he is touched by the ball in the hands of a fielder before he has reached the first base.

24. If, after he has made a fair hit, or after the third strike, as mentioned in the preceding rule, the ball is securely held by a fielder who is touching the first base with any part of his person.

25. If, in running the last half of the distance from home-plate to first base, he runs outside the three-foot line, unless to avoid a fielder attempting to field the ball.

The batsman is entitled, without being put out, to a base:—

26. When the umpire has called four balls.

27. If the umpire has awarded a base to a succeeding batsman, and the base-runner is thereby forced to vacate the base held by him.

28. If the umpire calls a balk.

29. If the ball, delivered by the pitcher, passes the catcher and touches the umpire or any fence or building within ninety feet of the home plate.

30. If, upon a fair hit, the ball strikes the person of the umpire standing upon fair ground.

31. If the fielder stops or catches a batted ball with his hat or any part of his dress.

The base-runner must return to his base, and is entitled to do so without being put out:—

32. If the umpire declares a foul hit.

33. If the umpire declares a foul strike.

34. If the umpire declares a dead ball.

The base-runner is out:—

35. If, in running from first to second base, from second to third base, or from third base to home plate, he runs more than three feet from a direct line between such bases, to avoid being touched by the ball in the hands of a fielder.

36. If he in any way obstructs a fielder attempting to field the ball, or intentionally interferes with a thrown ball.

37. If, while the ball is in play, he is touched with the ball in the hands of a fielder, unless some part of his person is touching a base he is entitled to occupy. The ball must be held by the fielder while touching him. In running to first base, he may overrun the base, and will be allowed to return to it without being put out for being off his base. Provided he must return at once and retouch the base, and afterwards he may be put out as at any other base. And if, after overrunning first base, he should attempt to run to second base or should turn to the left as though about to do so, he may be put out To return to and retouch an overrun base, the runner must turn to the right.

38. If he should start to run on a fly ball and he is touched with the ball after it is caught before he has returned to his base. The base-runner must not run on a fly ball until it has been momentarily held by a fielder. A fly ball is a ball caught either in fair or foul territory before it touches the ground.

39. If he is put out when forced to vacate his base under the following circumstances: when the batsman becomes a base-runner, the players occupying the bases in advance of him must vacate those bases in favour of the batsman or succeeding base-runner, and cannot return to such bases unless the batsman is put out at first base. Then they have the privilege of returning to their bases.

40. If he is hit by a batted ball before it touches a fielder.

41. If, when running bases or returning to a base, he fails to touch each intervening base.

42. If, when the umpire calls "play" after any suspension of a game, he fails to return to and retouch the base he occupied when "time" was called.

43. A run is scored by a base-runner running one hundred and twenty yards and touching first base, second base, third base and home plate in succession.

Bibliography—*The Art of Pitching and Fielding; The Art of Batting and Base Running*, H. Chadwick (New York, 1886); *Baseball Guide for* 1876, R. M. De Witt; *Baseball* (Oval Series, 1896), R. G. Knowles and R. Morton; *Baseball*, J. M. Ward (Philadelphia, 1888).

BASKET-BALL—[*See* UNIVERSITY CONTESTS.]

BASS, BLACK—There are two species of Black Bass, the small-mouthed Bass (*Micropterus dolomieu*, Lacépède) and the large-mouthed Bass (*Micropterus salmoides*, Lacépède). The methods of angling for them are the same. Their appearance and habits are similar, though the small-mouthed Bass prefers swift and rocky streams, while the large-mouth is more at home in lacustrine waters and sluggish streams. When inhabiting the same waters their game qualities are equal, though the small-mouth in swift streams is more active than the large-mouth in still waters.

In England—Several years ago, the small-mouthed Bass was placed in several small lakes in England, but the experiment was a failure, as it is not suited to such waters. Had the large-mouthed been substituted, the broads and lakes of England might now be teeming with one of the gamest fish.

There exists an unwarranted prejudice against the Black Bass among British anglers which originated (as my friend Mr. R. B. Marston informed me) through the over-zealous assertions of the late George Sheppard Page and Professor

G. Brown Goode at a meeting of British anglers during the Fisheries Exhibition in 1883. In their efforts to convince their auditors of the grand game qualities of the Black Bass, they unwittingly conveyed the impression that it was a very predatory and voracious fish, as bad as the Pike, if not worse. This idea, of course, is entirely erroneous. The Black Bass is not at all a piscivorous fish in the true meaning of the term. The character of a fish's teeth indicates its food. The Pike, having sharp, conical teeth, is pre-eminently piscivorous, as such teeth imply. So, in a measure, is the Brown Trout, which has sharp, conical teeth, though not so numerous or strong as those of the Pike.

Food.—On the other hand, the Black Bass has villiform or brush-like teeth, much like the surface of a tooth-brush, which are incapable of wounding or cutting: such teeth indicate a diet of crustaceans and insects. As a matter of fact, seventy-five per-cent. of the natural food of the Black Bass consists of crayfish, but like all carnivorous fishes, the Bass occasionally swallows small fish, frogs, &c., especially if they are found in a disabled condition; and this explains why a minnow proves a good bait, and is eagerly taken by a Black Bass when he may ignore a school of lively minnows swimming near him. Those of the school are hard to catch, while the one on the hook is easily captured.

There are countless small lakes in America where the Black Bass, Trout, and many other species of fishes have co-existed from time immemorial, showing conclusively that the Black Bass is not the enemy of other fishes, and does not militate against their increase in the same waters, even when of an isolated character. On the contrary, the Black Bass, under such circumstances, does not multiply so rapidly as the other species, notwithstanding that it guards its eggs and young. The unfortunate introduction of the German Carp in American waters has been very disastrous to the Black Bass, owing to the spawn-eating proclivities of the intruder. It astonishes the American angler to learn that the English are so prejudiced against the Black Bass, although tolerating such a marauding fish as the Pike, to say nothing of spawn-eaters like the Carp, Tench, Dace, Perch, &c.

Game Qualities—The Black Bass is a percoid fish and much higher in the scheme of evolution than the Salmon or Trout, and in game qualities is their peer—"Inch for inch, and pound for pound he is the gamest fish that swims." "He has the arrowy rush and vigour of the Trout, the untiring strength and bold leap of the Salmon, while he has a system of fighting tactics peculiarly his own." These words seem to me, after twenty-five years' experience, as true as ever.

Distribution—The Black Bass is capable of a much wider geographical distribution than most other game fish. In America, its range extends through twenty-five degrees of latitude and thirty degrees of longitude, which shows that it can withstand very great variations of temperature and vicissitudes of aquatic life.

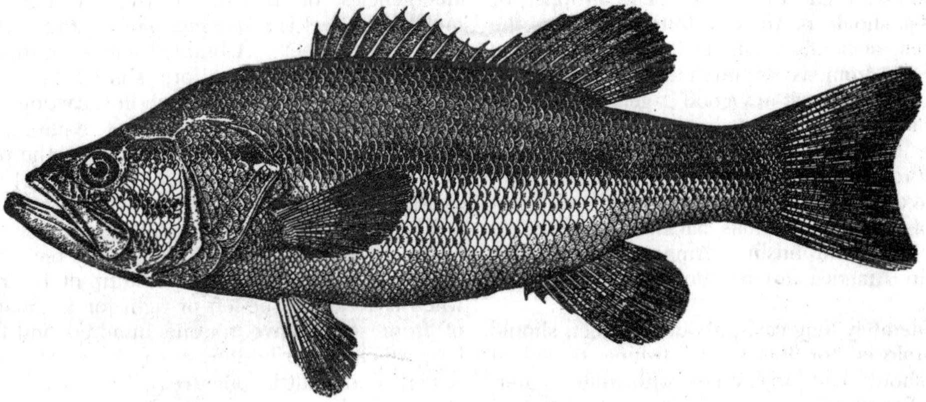

BLACK BASS.
(By kind permission of the Editor of *Forest and Stream*).

In Germany its introduction has been very successful, especially that of the large-mouthed Bass. It has also been transplanted to France, the Netherlands, and other countries.

Fly-Fishing—The methods of angling for Black Bass are fly-fishing, minnow-casting, still-fishing, and trolling. Fly-fishing, of course, comes first in importance. The Black Bass rises to the artificial fly as eagerly as the Salmon or Trout, and perhaps under more varying conditions. While it has the boldness of either, it is more wary and intelligent, and must be fished for with corresponding caution, for inasmuch as it is only in comparatively shallow water that any fish rises to the fly, it follows that all due caution must be exercised to keep out of its sight.

If fishing from a boat, the angler should keep in deep water and cast toward the shallows or shore. If fishing from the bank, he should stand well back from the shore and make long casts, or be screened from observation by trees, bushes, &c. If wading, which is the preferable plan, he may fish either up or down stream, but fishing down stream is preferred in America, particularly in swift streams, as the line is thereby always straight and taut, and a more natural appearance is given to the fly.

The best time for fly-fishing for Black Bass is late in the afternoon, toward sunset, and during twilight. The early morning hours are also favourable; but, except on very dark, cloudy days, the angler will catch nothing for his pains during the hours of mid-day. The reason for this is that all fishes feed mostly at night, and in shallow water; consequently, they are found in such situations at the times mentioned, approaching or departing from their feeding grounds.

The method of casting is about the same in vogue for wet-fly fishing for Trout. One or two flies may be used in the cast. The dropper, or hand-fly, should be three or four feet above the stretcher, or tail-fly. The leader, or casting line, should be from six to nine feet of good, round, single gut. Almost any good "general" Trout fly of large size, tied on hooks No. 4 to 7, will answer for Black Bass. The Coachman, Red Ibis, Professor, Grizzly King, Alexandra, Montreal, &c., and small Silver Doctor are all good flies, as also the various hackles (Palmers), if made large and bushy. Among the best flies used in America are my Polka, Henshall, and Oriole.

Moderately long casts, about fifty feet, should be employed for Black Bass fishing, though if there should be a brisk breeze with ruffled water, somewhat shorter casts will answer. The line should be always straight and taut. After the cast is made the flies should be gently roved or drawn from side to side with jerky or tremulous motions, to simulate the movements of a natural fly. They should be permitted to sink frequently for several inches, or a foot, in likely-looking places, especially in lake or pond fishing.

The angler should strike upon sight or touch; that is, he should instantly strike upon feeling the slightest touch of the fish, or upon seeing its swirl. Striking is merely a turn of the wrist with a taut line, which is sufficient to set the hook. After the fish is hooked, he should be kept on a bent rod and taut line, never under any circumstances having slack line. When the Bass leaps from the water, which he may do half a dozen times before he is in the landing-net, the straightening of the bent rod is sufficient to keep the line taut while he is in the air, but he should be followed into the water by slightly lowering the tip, if necessary, to prevent the hook from tearing out with the weight, and the instant he reaches the water he should again feel the spring of the rod. He should be reeled into close quarters as soon as possible, and kept near the surface of the water. The spring of the rod will eventually cause him to turn on his side, when he should be taken into the landing-net.

The most suitable rod is ten feet three inches long, and weighs not more than eight ounces. Any good Trout fly-rod of about this description will answer. The line and click-reel ordinarily used for Trout fishing do very well for Black Bass fishing.

Minnow-Fishing—Casting the minnow for Black Bass is a very artistic mode of fishing. It requires special tools and tackle. In America the short, single-handed rod known as the "Henshall" rod is universally employed. It is eight feet three inches long, and weighs eight ounces for an ash and lancewood, or greenheart rod, or seven and a half ounces for a split bamboo. It is somewhat stiffer than a Trout fly-rod, but pliable enough for all the emergencies of playing a fish. A first-class multiplying reel is a *sine quâ non*, as the bait is cast from the reel. A braided line of undressed silk of the smallest calibre should be used. Twisted lines kink too much for casting. A leader, or casting-line of gut, is not required, the swelled hook being attached directly to the reel-line by a small brass swivel. A sinker of the smallest size may also be affixed, if necessary.

The minnow, from two to four inches in length, is hooked through the lips, and reeled up to within a foot or two of the tip of the rod, when it is cast to the left or right for a distance of from seventy-five to one hundred and fifty feet, which is easily done with the tackle mentioned, and a little practice. The cast is not made over-hand or over-head as in fly-fishing, but under-handed—that is, from below upward —the tip of the rod being a foot or two from the ground or water at the beginning of the cast. The running of the reel must be controlled by the thumb, which should maintain a gentle, but uniform, pressure upon the spool to prevent over-running or backlashing, and when the bait reaches the desired spot the thumb stops the reel by a stronger pressure. The bait is allowed to swim about, if lively, and the line slowly reeled in, giving a natural, swimming motion to the minnow; a new cast is then made in another direction. The playing and landing of the Bass is the same as in fly-fishing.

Still-Fishing—Still-fishing is about the same as Perch fishing in England, and the best Perch tools and tackle may be employed, when of sufficient strength. A float may be used, though it is generally dispensed with in America, except where the bottom is grassy or mossy. Usually still fishing is practised from an anchored boat. Any time of day will answer for still-fishing or minnow-casting, though the Bass will be found in deeper water during the middle of the day.

Trolling—Trolling is practised with a stiffer rod than that for minnow-casting or still-fishing, and a somewhat larger line—one of flax will answer—about the size used for large Perch. The bait may be a large minnow, hooked through the lips, or a trolling spoon or spinner of small size. One hook is all-sufficient. A minnow, hooked through the lips with a single hook, presents a more natural appearance and is far more effective than the most approved spinning-tackle, with its forbidding array of flying hooks.

Trolling is practised from a boat, which is propelled over the feeding-grounds at a speed varying according to local conditions.

From fifty to one hundred and fifty feet of line are let out from the reel. The Bass hooks itself when it strikes.

JAMES A. HENSHALL.

BASS, SEA (*Labrax lupus*). [*See* SEA-FISHING.]

MEASUREMENTS, ETC.—Length of head $3\frac{3}{4}$ to 4, of caudal fin $5\frac{3}{4}$, height of body $4\frac{1}{4}$ to $4\frac{2}{3}$, in the total length. *Eye*—diameter $4\frac{1}{2}$ to 5 (or even proportionately larger in very small examples) in the length of the head, $1\frac{1}{4}$ to $1\frac{1}{2}$ diameters from the end of the snout, and $1\frac{1}{4}$ apart. Posterior edge of the preopercle strongly serrated, the largest tooth being at its rounded angle, and three more forwardly directed along its lower limb. Two opercular spines, the rest of the bones of the head unarmed. Jaws of about the same length anteriorly; the maxilla reaches to beneath the first, third, or middle of the orbit. Nostrils patent. *Teeth*—villiform in the jaws, the outer row in the upper somewhat larger than the rest: in an almost crescentic spot on the vomer, in a band on the palatines, and also at the base of the tongue. *Fins*—occasionally the first spine in the anterior dorsal fin is absent, the first two are short, the third two-thirds the length of the fourth, which is equal to the two succeeding which are the highest and slightly exceed the length of the rays of the second dorsal. Third anal spine slightly longer than the second. Caudal forked. *Scales*—ctenoid. *Lateral-line*—nearly straight, passing from the upper edge of the opercle to the centre of the base of the caudal fin. *Intestines*—five short cœcal appendages. *Colours*—gray on the back, becoming silvery on the sides and beneath. A dark spot at the upper half or two-thirds of the opercle, darkest posteriorly. Dorsal, anal, and caudal fins stained with gray externally; pectorals and ventrals yellowish-white. The young have usually some fine dark spots scattered over the body.

Day, *Fishes of Great Britain and Ireland*, vol. i. p. 9.

BEAGLES. [*See* DOGS.]

BEAGLING. [*See* HUNTING.]

BEAR-SHOOTING

AMERICA, NORTH—Bears are the most widely distributed of all North American big game, and may be encountered at any moment almost anywhere in the Rockies.

There are three species of Bear in North America, the Grizzly (*Ursus horribilis*), to which the following notes chiefly apply, the Black Bear (*U. americanus*), a much smaller and less formidable beast, and the Polar (*U. maritimus*) [*See* BEAR, POLAR]. The so-called Brown Bear of North America is a variety only, though many sportsmen insist on regarding it as a distinct species.

Grizzly Bears are not nowadays to be found east of the Rockies, and even in that range there is sometimes considerable difficulty in procuring a trophy.

They constantly change their quarters according to where the best food supply is to be found. In the early spring, when the skunk cabbage shoots forth its handsome yellow flower, Bears are high up the mountain sides digging at the roots. Later on, when putrid salmon strew the river banks, they will be found revelling in a nauseous meal. Where salmon do not exist, they will pick up a living on beetles and other insects until the berries ripen in the fall, when they claw down the luscious fruit and lay on their supply of fat preparatory to hibernating.

Baiting—Of the various modes of hunting Bears, by far the most successful and pleasant is baiting for them. This can, however, only be accomplished in a country plentiful in deer; which should be killed and left in suitable places, care being taken to select spots which the sportsman can easily approach unperceived.

Bears make little use of their eyes, but are keen-scented, quick of hearing, and surprisingly active.

The bait must be inspected within two or three days, and should it be found partially eaten or buried, the hunter should lie in wait at dawn or nightfall for the Bear, taking care to approach up-wind and noiselessly. In places where Bears have been much hunted, they become nocturnal in their habits, but otherwise they frequently wander abroad during the daytime.

A wounded or seemingly dead Bear should be approached with caution; for even when shot through the heart, it can still prove dangerous at close quarters.

Vulnerable Points—Through the neck, if it be sufficiently exposed, is the best shot: otherwise spine, shoulder, or head is good enough.

If, as sometimes happens, the hunter comes upon a grizzly with cubs, let him pay due attention to the old Bear before meddling with the cubs.

Hunting with Dogs—Another mode of hunting Bears is with well-trained dogs, which quickly "tree" the black Bear, while a grizzly, being unable to climb, will be held at bay until the sportsman comes up.

In Canoes—On certain rivers whose banks are composed of mud flats, or fringed with berry-bearing bushes, Bears are hunted in canoes which are paddled noiselessly in and out of every irregularity of the bank, until either a Bear is seen grubbing in the mud or eating ad salmon, or can be heard dragging down rries. If a clear view of him cannot be obtained, there is nothing for it but to wait patiently until he appears, for the underwood in districts usually haunted by Bears is so dense that to approach unheard would be impossible.

Choice of Ground, &c.—The best furred Bears come from the north coast of British Columbia and up the Skeena river, where they are mostly killed in May just after leaving the *cache*, when the fur is at its prime.

Bears are in the finest condition from September to May, according to climate; after the end of May the wool falls out, the long hairs slip, and the pelt becomes valueless until the end of September.

The mode of hunting is most arduous and uncomfortable. While the snow is still deep in the timber, but rapidly melting on the mountain side, a likely valley must be sought, the sides of which rise almost perpendicular in this country.

Here, on swampy ground surrounded by patches of snow, the tent must be pitched and no fire lighted. Morning and evening the hunter scans the steep rocky sides of the valley or cañon until high up he spies a bear. Carefully locating it, he starts on a perilous climb of an hour's duration, and is usually unable to see the Bear at the end of it.

Sometimes from a spot below he may see as many as seven Bears, but on getting close to them, all are hidden by great boulders of rock.

If the sun shines, it becomes too dangerous for climbing; warning avalanches come crashing down, and if one does not fall on a man, his weight is sufficient to start another. This class of hunting is suitable only for Indians.

Bears' *caches*, as they call the holes wherein they spend the winter in a more or less torpid condition from about December to April or May, are often discovered during the summer, and if the exact spot can be found when deeply covered with snow it is almost certain to contain a Bear; here, too, the she-bear gives birth to her young.

The largest Bear in the world, excepting the Polar Bear, inhabits Alaska, and does not appear to have received due attention from any naturalist. It differs somewhat from the grizzly in uniformity of colour and in the shape of its claws, and is said to be plentiful in the dense country around Mount Elias.

A ·500 Express is, taken all round, the finest weapon for the work.

No one who can handle a rifle should requre to give his Bear more than one bullet. The grizzly being an animal of uncertain temper, it is well to reserve the second barrel, in case of accidents.

J. TURNER TURNER.

INDIA.—The Sloth Bear (*Melursus labiatus*) is the only species found throughout India to the south of the Himalayas. It is common in the hill ranges and jungles, more especially where the ground is rocky. Its habits are nocturnal; during the day it lies up in thick jungle or in caves and recesses among the rocks. It may occasionally be met with by sportsmen out stalking early in the morning or late in the afternoon; but as a rule, except when driven out in the course of a beat, it will not be observed during the day. Its food consists of the jungle fruits, ants, beetles, and other insects, and it is also fond of honey, and climbs the forest trees to procure the honeycombs which hang from the boughs. Instances have been known of its eating flesh, but they are rare. Like all wild animals it avoids man, but may attack when suddenly come upon; and many natives are mauled by bears that they have disturbed. In a beat, bears coming out of holes in the rocks at the last moment, when the beat is close to them, often charge the beaters. On the whole, however, this bear is by no means a dangerous animal before it has been fired at and wounded, but when wounded and followed up, it will often charge. The writer discredits the popular idea that the bear rises on its hind legs and hugs its adversary. He has never seen a charging bear rise on its hind legs. Bears can stand erect, and do so to look about them in long grass or jungle that they cannot see over on all-fours. The soles of their feet leave a print not unlike that of a child's foot. Their cylindrical bones resemble the same bones in a human skeleton more closely than those of most other animals; and this formation enables them to assume the erect position. Their claws are long, and with them they dig up the ground for roots, ants, and termites, and turn over stones to get the beetles and insects that lodge there. The female has generally two cubs, sometimes three, which remain with her till nearly full-grown. When young, she carries them on her back. In a beat, a she-bear will often be seen galloping along with her cubs hanging on to her. The cub clings to the long hair on her shoulders with his fore-legs, the hind-legs hanging down her side well clear of the ground. The "Indian Black Bear," as it is also called, has long and shaggy hair, especially on the top of the shoulders; and on the breast is a large yellowish crescent-shaped mark. The muzzle is of a dirty white. As the hair is very coarse, an Indian bear's skin is not of much value as a trophy.

Bears in India are not usually made a special object of sport. They are generally shot when men are out tiger-shooting—on days when no tigers are abroad. A chance beat on suitable ground often produces a bear or two. Bears are turned out in the course of a beat for tiger, but on such occasions they are not fired at. They are driven in the same way as all large

game has to be driven in India. A crowd of beaters are collected from the nearest villages, a few of whom have tom-toms and other native musical instruments, useful not only in waking up the animals and keeping them moving, but also in keeping the beaters in line. A large number of stops have to be placed in trees on either side of the intended drive to prevent the animal breaking out at the side. The sportsman is placed in a tree or on a rock in front, and if the drive has been properly planned and carried out (the chief, if not the only, secret of success in this kind of shooting), the animal passes within a few yards, and, whether walking or galloping, affords a very easy shot.

Another way of shooting bears is to visit before daylight the rocks, in which they are known to lie up, and to intercept them as they return from their nocturnal rambles. They are also shot by sportsmen when stalking bison or deer. The sportsman, walking through the jungle, sees them by chance and stalks them; but it is no good going out with the special object of stalking bears, as they are not numerous enough to make it worth while, so far, at least, as the Indian Black Bear is concerned, though it is different with the Himalavan Black Bear and the Brown Bear.

Weapon, &c.—Every sportsman has his own fancy as to the best rifle for the work. The writer prefers a good double-barrelled ·500 Express to any other rifle for all kinds of soft-skinned big game. It is comparatively light, can be quickly manipulated for a running or snap shot, and better shooting, especially with running shots, is made with it than with a heavy rifle. The shot, if at all properly placed, will certainly kill the animal in a few seconds. The only objection to it is that, in the case of a charge, an Express bullet

SLOTH BEAR.

Average height at shoulder, 2 ft. 6 in. Average length from head to root of tail, 5 ft.

does not give the knockdown blow of a heavier solid bullet, and is therefore less likely to stop the charging animal. On the other hand, the proportion of charges to animals fired at is extremely small, and the weapon that will bring most game down is the preferable one. At any rate, a ·500 Express is quite big enough for a bear. In firing at a bear it is necessary to remember that the animal is not so large as it looks, and that a good deal of the apparent size is due to its long hair. All shots should be aimed so as to enter the cavity of the chest. Behind the shoulder, through the point of the shoulder, and in the centre of the yellowish mark on the chest, according to the position of the animal, are the usual shots. Through the back of the skull or neck is also fatal, but the body shot is recommended, the mark being greater.

J. D. INVERARITY.

[The other Indian Bears are the Black (*U. torquatus*) and the Snow, or Isabelline (*U. isabellinus*), both of the Himalayas. The former is chiefly to be found in the forests at the base of the range, where it lives on fruits, acorns, the crops of the villagers, and occasional carrion. It feeds at night and is usually shot as it comes to or leaves its feeding-ground.

The Isabelline Bear, on the other hand, is chiefly encountered along the snow-line. Like the foregoing species, it hibernates; and its food also differs little, except in a preference for roots.]

POLAR (*Ursus maritimus*).

Habitat—It ranges over the whole of the discovered tracts of the North Polar regions, but to a greater extent in the southern part of the Arctic zone than further North. In the expedition of Sir George Nares in 1875-6, no bears were seen north of lat. 79°, although travelling parties reached the latitude of 83° 20. Previous to this, however, bears had been seen, and killed, though not in great quantities, by the United States exploring expedition under Captain Hall as far north as 81° in the locality visited by Nares. They are found in great numbers in Franz Josef land, in Novaya-Zemlya, in Spitzbergen, along the east coast of Greenland, in Davis Straits and Baffin's Bay, and in the numerous channels and inlets leading thence, and they are encountered as far south as Hudson's Strait and Bay, and along the Coast of Labrador. They might, with a fair show of reason, be regarded as aquatic rather than terrestrial animals; for not only have they been found on icefloes and icebergs hundreds of miles from any land, but I have come across them swimming unconcernedly in the water with no ice in sight and more than eighty miles from land!

Colour, Size, Habits, &c.—Their colour is sometimes of a very pure white, the tip of the fur in places being tinged slightly with a yellowish hue. Their feet are large, flat and muscular, being armed with formidable claws, and they have very strong and powerful teeth. They do not hug, as is alleged of their congeners the brown bears, but bite and use their claws freely. It is averred that they never eat their victims until life is extinct, but will play with them as a cat with a mouse.

The Polar bear attains a great size. I have myself killed them over 10½ feet in length, and weighing something like half a ton, and they have been known to exceed even 13 feet in length; but this is, I believe, quite an abnormal size, the average being about 7 or 8 feet from the tip of the nose to the end of the tail. They possess enormous strength. On one occasion we disturbed a bear in the enjoyment of his feast on the ice, which proved to be the entire body of a white whale, fifteen feet in length and weighing about 3 or 4 tons. This whale was presumably found by the bear floating dead in the water, and must have been dragged by the bear on to the ice where we found it. It is difficult to conceive how this could have been accomplished, for it would have taken at least half-a-dozen strong men with ropes and other appliances to have hauled it up on to the ice-floe.

The flesh of the bear is eatable when nothing better can be obtained, but it is coarse and rank and terribly tough; the liver, however, is to be avoided as an article of human food, for it has the reputation of producing severe bowel complaints.

Their rate of progression over soft snow is wonderful, and when once alarmed, unless stopped by a bullet, they speedily place a safe distance between themselves and their pursuers. Their powers of locomotion in the water are also marvellous, and it is by no means an uncommon incident to see them plunge after a seal, and pursue it in its own element, but whether with a successful result I have never yet been able satisfactorily to determine. They will watch a seal for hours together on an icefloe, and if unable to approach it without being observed, have been known to slip quietly into the water, and swim towards it *under the ice*, and then emerge suddenly alongside of their prey, so that if it takes to the water it falls into the clutches of the bear, and if it remains on the ice it soon falls a victim to its powerful adversary.

Unless rendered fierce by pain or hunger, they will very rarely attack man. On one occasion only can I call to mind their assuming the offensive, not being themselves attacked or wounded. In that instance, it was a female accompanied by her cub. We first sighted them on a piece of ice, and immediately pulled lustily towards them in our boat. Without, however, waiting for us to come to close quarters the bear, followed by her little one, plunged into the water, swam vigorously towards us, and would certainly have succeeded in getting into the boat had not a bullet from my rifle terminated her existence. The cub we captured alive and took aboard the ship. It was a most ferocious little beast, and was just as wild and untameable after it had been on board three months, as on the day of its capture. It sounds somewhat unnatural, but the only food

which wounded him badly and caused ! slink away behind some hummocks. R up somewhat imprudently in my haste to his skin, I suddenly came across the which at once rushed at me open-mouthe fortunately for myself, I succeeded at ab yards in planting a bullet in his head

POLAR BEAR.
Average height at shoulder, 4 ft. 3 in. *Average length from head to root of tail, 8 ft.*

it had for the first few days after it came on board was the flesh of its own mother, which it devoured greedily and with apparent enjoyment.

On another occasion we had observed a bear reposing apparently asleep on the ice. I proceeded to stalk it, but the noise made by my breaking through a piece of rotten ice disturbed the animal in his slumbers and caused him to get up. Thinking he was contemplating a retreat, I took a hasty and long shot,

effectually put a stop to any ments.

These are the only instance under my personal observatio Polar bear has assumed a disp the offensive. On all other occ been exceedingly timorous danger.

The majority of bears that a vessels engaged in sealing

in the water, for on the approach of a boat, unless they happen to be on an extensive field of ice, they invariably endeavour to effect their escape by swimming. As a boat can be propelled at double the speed at which a bear can swim, the poor beast is very soon overhauled, when a bullet through its brain kills it.

This, however, is the poorest of sport; in fact, it is no sport at all, for the element of danger, which makes the pursuit of savage animals so attractive, is altogether wanting.

Pursuing a bear on a large icefloe, or pack, is, however, altogether different. Prudence has then to be exercised in approaching the quarry; care has to be taken to avoid stepping on treacherous pieces of young ice; and when after, perchance, much trouble and exertion, the hunter succeeds in approaching within the desired range, more skill, care and dexterity are required in handling the rifle in order to ensure killing, than would be the case if the beast were swimming in the water, where it would be comparatively harmless.

Vulnerable spot—My experience has taught me that the only vulnerable part of a Polar bear is the forehead. I have known several instances of bears being hit in other parts of the body, and they have either succeeded in making good their escape, or required another bullet to finish them. The head is, of course, a small mark, but a shot in it is instantaneously effective.

Rifle, &c.—I have always used a small Martini-Henry rifle with a ·45 solid bullet; but I am inclined to think that a good magazine rifle carrying a ·4 expanding bullet would be the best and safest for Polar bear shooting.

Range—Unless a bear is actually making off at speed over the ice, I should deprecate firing at a greater distance than 15 or 20 yards; the nearer you are to the animal, the greater the chance of hitting it in a vital spot. They are wonderfully tenacious of life, and unless hit in the head will scamper away over the ice and through soft snow with perhaps two or three bullets in them, leaving behind a bright crimson trail on the otherwise spotless snow with which the ice is covered.

To sum up, the Polar bear is by no means a formidable beast to contend with, if the hunter is armed with a good magazine rifle, is a fairly reliable shot, and is prepared to undertake a trip to the "regions of thick-ribbed ice" in quest of his prey.

A. H. MARKHAM.

RUSSIA (Bear=*Russ. Mědvyed*)—Though the number of bears killed within reasonable distance of St. Petersburg has of late years steadily diminished, these animals still abound in outlying Governments, such as Olonetz, where any sportsman able to spare a month or more, and to afford the expenditure of a considerable sum of money, may still be certain of a bearskin or two.

Bear shooting is a winter sport, for without snow to track them in, these shy rovers are not easily found; luckily for the sportsman, however, the Bear is a hibernating animal, and the first fall of snow not only drives him hurriedly to seek his winter-quarters, but also enables his enemies to track him to his chosen retreat.

Finding the Bear—The usual method is for the local sportsman to sally forth about the first fall of snow, in November, either alone or with his dog; that is, if he has one endowed with the gift of silence. He knows from experience how to mark down each animal to the sanctuary in which it had hoped to sleep through the winter; and having made careful note of the whereabouts of a number of occupied *berlogi*, as these hibernating dens are called in those parts, he hastens with his secrets to St. Petersburg, where, as the bears are not likely to emerge when once they have settled down for the season, he is able to dispose of each *berloga* for a sum of from 40 to 70 roubles (£4 to £7), according to the estimated size of its occupant. It is not improbable that he will thus sell his whole batch of bears, from one to a dozen, to a single amateur, who will then, as soon as convenient, set out from town well equipped with heavy rifle and small arms, or, if he be of an enterprising disposition, with no more than a bear-spear, though the practice of engaging the beast so lightly armed is well-nigh obsolete.

He must drive to his destination, the vehicle being in all probability the *Kibitka*, a tented sleigh drawn by a pair of horses, the latter being changed *en route* at the post-stations. At the end of his journey, a matter of a week or considerably more, according to the distance traversed and the state of the roads, he will lodge at his guide's house; and, unless he is prepared to live on black rye-bread and *vodka*, with now and again a dried herring and a cup of weak tea, he should take with him a store of provisions.

Snowshoes will be found necessary, but they may generally be had of his host, and those of Olonetz, shaped like Norwegian *ski* (long and narrow, and not after the Canadian model), are perhaps the very best obtainable.

Then comes the march for the nearest *berloga*, a function in which a trained dog is of use in supplementing his master's memory; and at last the supreme moment arrives when the sportsman stands, rifle in hand, at the den mouth, having secured good foothold for his snowshoes, in order that they may not slide at an awkward moment.

Meanwhile the guide, aided by his dog, if he has one, begins the work of driving the bear from its retreat, a feat accomplished by either sending in the dog to bark at and worry it, or stirring up the sleeper with a pole pushed through the frozen snow and piled brushwood that form the outer wall of its den.

Sooner or later, a question of seconds or minutes according to the disposition of the tenant, the walls of the sanctuary will part suddenly and, with a roar of rage or a howl of terror, the bear will, in nine cases out of ten, bolt for the nearest cover. In the tenth case he will charge. Either way, this is the moment to fire, and, if possible, kill at a shot, otherwise an accident, or at best a long snow-chase, ending possibly in disappointment, will follow.

Spearing—When bear-spears were in vogue, the sportsman would stand at the mouth of the *berloga*, receiving the brute's rush upon the steel-tipped point, and wrestle with the impaled monster until it succumbed. Sometimes the bear would succeed in hurling its assailant to the earth and tear savagely at his flesh before expiring.

Occasionally a bear is seen and shot in the vicinity of St. Petersburg, or a solitary marauder may at still rarer intervals fall to the axe of some peasant infuriated by the spoliation of his oat-patch or rye-field.

This being the first of the articles dealing with various forms of sport in Russia, it may be convenient to offer a few hints as to the several ways of reaching that country, and how to proceed when arrived there. Firstly, then, let the intending traveller provide himself with a passport, and let him have this properly *visé* by the Russian Consul, in Great Winchester Street, E.C. Armed with this necessary document, he may set out with an easy mind. St. Petersburg may be reached by sea or overland, as preferred. If the sea-route be chosen, there are frequent sailings from Hull during open navigation time, that is, roughly, between April 30 and October 30. It is advisable to obtain permission before attempting to pass firearms into Russia.

Without friends in Russia, or introductions to sportsmen, it is difficult to obtain sport near St. Petersburg; intending shooters are therefore warned to make full inquiries beforehand, through friends in the country, to prevent disappointment.

FRED WHISHAW.

BEARS, SCANDINAVIAN—The **Brown Bear** (*Ursus arctos*) of Northern Europe is distributed, though in gradually diminishing numbers, over the greater part of Norway and Sweden. It is, however, rarely, if ever, now met with south of latitude 59°.

Many hunters consider that there are two distinct kinds of Scandinavian Bear, whereas most naturalists are now agreed there is but one, though two skins are seldom found exactly alike. Some are black-brown, dark-brown, light-brown, yellow-brown, some grayish-brown with silver-tipped hairs, and others of a light yellow.

The Northern Bear retires into winter quarters about the middle or end of October according to the season, and at this period he falls into a lethargic state and ceases taking food. He comes out again about the middle of April, but this depends greatly on the season and locality.

On first coming out, he is lean and scraggy, and has only ant grubs to depend upon for food, which cause his flesh to smell strongly of formic acid. At this time he greedily devours any putrid carcass which happens to be in the neighbourhood. Later in the spring and summer the alpine sow-thistle (called *Tort* by the peasants), angelica and cow-parsnip afford him a good meal. Berries of every description from juniper to mountain ash, cloudberries (*Molte bær*), wild raspberries, whortleberries, cranberries, crowberries, &c., wasp and wild-bee grubs and combs, beetles, slugs, frogs, shell-fish near the fiords, barley, oats, and rye in the peasants' clearings in the forests, to say nothing of cattle, sheep and goats, all find a place in his bill of fare.

In Norway, Bears are more or less numerous in North and South Throndjem, Nordland, Hedemarken, Nedenæs, Bratsberg and Romsdal, Amts, also in Sætersdal, Thelemarken and Finmarken. In Sweden, in the forests of Jemtland, Dalecarlia and Vermeland, and in Swedish Lapmarken generally.

Of the various modes of hunting and killing the Bear, the most sporting way is with a good bear-hound in leash, in summer and autumn, accompanied by one follower only. In winter time several dogs may be used to range the woods and find the "*Hie*" (winter lair), the hunters traversing the snow on "*Ski*."

Dogs are absolutely necessary for the first-named mode of hunting, and prices ranging from five pounds to twenty-five are often given for a first-rate animal; an indifferent hound is worse than none at all. They may be bought in Jemtland and Ljusnadal in Sweden, and at various places in Norway.

The dogs should be fitted with a light leather harness round the chest and shoulders, to which a leading strap three yards long should be attached. They are most intelligent animals, with remarkably good scenting powers, and will lead the hunter straight up to his game. They should never be beaten.

Bears have a very keen scent, but neither their sense of sight nor hearing is so well developed. Should a Bear once realise that he is being hunted, he will travel down wind in the most provoking manner all day, keeping a few hundred paces to leeward of you, and unless you can reverse the situation, it is almost hopeless to follow him.

Being a wonderful stayer and first-rate climber (though rarely climbing trees), he can beat any dogs at clambering up or down rocky hill-sides.

Haunts of the Bear—During hot weather

he lies up for many days at a time, picking out a cool, swampy dell in the recesses of the forest, where he makes several large holes in which he wallows like a hog. He also retires to the high ground, above the timber-line, and digs out a bed in a secluded snow-patch, where he will remain for days, safe from flies and mosquitoes.

On cool days, with a northerly wind and drizzle, during August and September, he is usually out feeding, and the hill-sides where berries grow in profusion should be carefully scanned early and late.

When the first snow falls in mid October, the hunter has a good chance of tracking him and ringing him in his "*Hie.*" When this is found, it should be approached with caution and invariably upwind.

Stalking, &c.—Get as close as possible to a feeding Bear, keeping above him all you can. If his broadside be toward you, aim just behind his right or left shoulder as the case may be. If he be running from you, shoot anywhere, at his rump or tail; load quickly, and fire into his chest as he turns round to charge. If below you, aim between his shoulders or loins, or at the centre of back. Should you suddenly come on a she-Bear with cubs kill the old one first; if the cubs escape, fix up the mother's carcass and wait near, you will then probably bag them also. In the event of shooting a cub at some distance from the mother, load immediately, and hide near the body, for she will certainly turn up sooner or later. Should she rush in on you, making a loud angry "huff, huff," keep your nerve and shoot straight. Never approach a dying or apparently dead Bear with unloaded rifle, but go up cautiously with both barrels at full cock. Do not smash the skull with your finishing shot, as one in the neck or behind the head is equally effective.

BROWN OR SCANDINAVIAN BEAR.
Average height at shoulder, 3 ft. Average length from head to root of tail, 6 ft. 6 in.

Measurements—Scandinavian Bears will run up to nearly 900 lbs. in weight, and a skin has been measured 9 ft. 3 in. long and 6 ft. wide. The largest shot by the writer weighed about 800 lbs., having a skin 7 ft. 11 in., from nose to tail, by 4 ft. 8 in. in width. Thirty-five years is about the limit of age.

Guns and Ammunition—A ·500 or ·450 express, by a good maker, firing a conical expanding bullet with a thick solid base and small, shallow hole at apex is a very useful weapon, being accurate at long ranges and effective at close quarters.

GERARD FERRAND.

BEAVER—[*See* TRAPPING.]

BIG GAME—

AFRICA—Although shooting in Africa has vastly changed since Captain Cornwallis Harris (the forerunner of the great hunters) first entered the present Transvaal country in 1836, and discovered a wilderness teeming with game, where the sound of the rifle had never yet been heard, there is still, if the sportsman will travel far enough, plenty of sport to be got among the great fauna. But the wonderful plenty of what may be called the great game-slaying epoch—1836 to 1890—is not nowadays to be found except in a few remote and difficult places. The sportsman, then, must be prepared to work much harder, and to travel very far before he can find and bag big game. He will discover, as a general rule, that heavy game in Africa is much wilder and more suspicious than of old, and that its pursuit involves much more difficult hunting. Many species of game that forty or fifty years ago grazed quietly in vast legions upon the open plains, and merely stared at the wagons as they plodded slowly across the Veldt, now drink by stealth during the night, feed across the flats at very early morning, and then betake themselves to the bush, where they find sanctuary during the hot hours. The mere pursuit of many of these animals frequently involves long and weary days in the saddle, starting from the wagons before sunrise, and often not coming up with the game until after several hours of steady spooring, which is undertaken by a native hunter or bushman. Perhaps another two hours are occupied in the actual chase, and the operations of skinning and cutting up, after which ensues a long ride of possibly another five or six hours back to the wagons. Not infrequently, after leaving camp at dawn, the hunter does not reach it again until dusk or even darkness has set in. To hunt successfully in South Africa nowadays, therefore, the sportsman should possess patience, endurance, an even temper, and a hardy frame. The actual shooting of the game, in itself not always an easy operation, is by no means the most difficult part of the business of modern South African hunting. The mere fatigue of riding under a burning sun for from eight to ten hours, or even more, day after day, over a rough, and often parched and waterless country, is no light matter. And even with good and willing native servants (not always to be counted upon), the labours of the day are by no means ended when the camp fire is reached. The skinning of specimen heads, and perhaps rare birds, which should never be entrusted to raw natives, cleaning guns, changing camera plates, writing up the diary, seeing that horses and dogs are fed, and many other necessary matters, have to be attended to before the wanderer can settle himself down by the fire, and enjoy in quiet his pipe and cup of coffee.

If, however, the sportsman is possessed of patience and a determination to succeed, he will find at the end of a week's hunting that his labours are becoming somewhat lightened. Every succeeding day hardens him and puts him in condition. The irksome detail of carrying a heavy rifle in the right hand during a long day while riding, which at first seemed so wearying, becomes a mere trifle as the muscles of the arm grow hardened to the task; and so with the rest of the labour. In some parts of Africa, where Tse-Tse fly abounds, and horses cannot be used, the fatigue of hunting on foot, no light operation in Africa, has to be faced. In these districts, however, bush and covert are more abundant, the game has been less disturbed, and shots are more easily obtained.

Hunting Grounds and Game—Thanks to the advance of railway communication in South Africa, the traveller can get within hail of his hunting ground, at the present day, with far more ease and at considerably less expenditure of time and money than was the case a few years back. It is not worth while lingering in Cape Colony, unless it be intended to shoot the smaller antelopes, such as springbok, klipspringer, steinbok, duiker, rhebok, bushbuck and bluebuck, or in the Orange Free State and Transvaal until close on the Limpopo River. If the sportsman is minded to shoot in Khama's Country, Eastern Matabeleland, the North Kalahari, and towards Lake Ngami and the Zambesi, his best plan will be to proceed by rail direct from Cape Town to Mafeking, and fit out there. In another year he will be able to rail direct to Palachwe (Khama's Town), or even to Buluwayo. If he mean to hunt in Mashonaland he will do best to rail to Johannesburg, and there procure his waggon, stores, and equipments; while for hunting the country between Beira and the Zambesi—on the whole the richest hunting ground now left to South Africa—he should proceed to Beira by sea from Cape Town or Natal. In this latter country buffalo are extraordinarily plentiful, and roan and sable antelope, eland, blue wildebeest, Lichtenstein's hartebeest, waterbuck, reedbuck, spotted bushbuck, inyala, koodoo, eland, pallah, tsesseby, Burchell's zebra, warthog, bushpig, lion, leopard, and hippos are abundant; while elephant, black rhinoceros, and giraffe may be occasionally encountered. Hunting, however, must be performed on foot. Some useful information as to outfit and cost of hunting in this country is to be found in the article on **Buffalo**.

In Mashonaland and parts of Matabeleland—especially towards the Zambesi in the latter country—the big game to be found is almost identical with that just above mentioned. I may, however, except the inyala, which is only found in the bush country fringing the littoral between the Zambesi mouth and Amatongaland. In Khama's Country, Ngamiland, and the districts towards the Zambesi, giraffe, lion, leopard, cheetah, hippo, ostrich, Burchell's zebra, eland, gemsbok, koodoo, roan and sable antelope, waterbuck, lechwe, sitatunga, pookoo, pallah, hartebeest, blue wildebeest, tsesseby, and spotted bushbuck, klipspringer, steinbuck, duiker, and warthog are all to be found. Elephants and rhinoceros are, however, now nearly shot out, plentiful as they were in all these regions not very long since. In the Barotse Country, Upper Zambesi, and the neighbouring regions, buffalo will be found almost as abundantly as in any part of Africa. Many of the water-loving antelopes, such as lechwe and sitatunga, are also extremely plentiful in this region. Beyond the Zambesi, towards Central Africa, elephants will be again encountered. In the North Transvaal, in the bush country near the Limpopo, koodoo, pallah, and reedbuck are still to be found. In South-West Africa some good hunting grounds are still to be met with in the Kaoko Veldt (Damaraland), and in the Ovampo, Okavango River, and Cunene River Countries. Here game of much the same description as in Khama's Country and Ngamiland is to be encountered. Behind Benguella and Mossamedes, in Portuguese South-West Africa, elephant, plenty of buffalo, lion, leopard, zebra, eland, roan and sable antelope, koodoo, and other large antelopes, are to be found. Here, however, bush is prevalent; the country is most difficult to work in; native servants are bad and hard to get hold of; and neither horses nor wagons can be reckoned upon.

THE HIGH VELDT OF THE PAST.

Outfit, Expenses, &c.—For hunting in all Africa south of the Zambesi, except in the Beira country and a few districts close to the river itself, wagons, oxen and horses can be employed. If the sportsman fit out at Mafeking or Palachwe for Khama's country, the Zambesi, Matabeleland, and Ngamiland, or at Johannesburg for Mashonaland, he may reckon upon buying a good second-hand wagon outright for from £80 to £100. Oxen in average times cost from £6 to £7 10s. per head; but since the plague of rinderpest has fallen upon South Africa, the price of oxen has risen greatly, and may continue high for the next two or three years. The latest reports of rinderpest seem to point to more serious consequences. It should be remembered, too, that rinderpest has played sad havoc with game in all parts of Eastern and South Central Africa. A wagon and oxen can be hired in normal times for from £15 to £20 per month; a full span of oxen for a Cape hunting wagon is eighteen. Good, useful, South African horses, suitable for hunting purposes, can be bought at Kimberley (a capital market), Vryburg, Mafeking, or Johannesburg for from £15 to £25 each. A *salted* horse will cost the purchaser from £60 to £100. If the hunting trip take place in winter—the best season—from May to October, a *salted* horse is not necessary. The wear and tear of horseflesh is very considerable, and each sportsman should take with him not less than three reliable hunting-ponies. Mealies (Indian corn) should be carried on the wagon for feeding the stud, and nosebags save waste and are always useful. When travelling among native tribes, mealies and Kaffir corn can usually be purchased. These vary from 10s. a bag (205 lbs.), in an average season, to 35s. and occasionally more in time of drought and scarcity.

With each wagon are required a driver, whose wages should not exceed £2 10s. per month, and leader, from 10s. to £1 per month. Horse boys get from 10s. to £1. A native cook should be got for from £2 to £2 10s. per month. A small waterproof, oblong, canvas tent is a useful thing if the trip is to be a prolonged one. This can be lashed on to the buck-rail of the wagon. Every necessary article required for a hunting expedition (tea, coffee, sugar, tinned milk, tinned fruits and meat, mealie meal, Boer meal, pots, pans, &c.) can, nowadays, be procured at the stores at Mafeking, Johannesburg, and even Palachwe. Messrs. Whiteley, Walker & Co. of Mafeking, Palachwe, and Buluwayo, may be cited as among the most reasonable and reliable store-keepers in South Africa. Stores, horses, oxen, and waggons, if the expedition is made from South-West Africa, can be procured from Messrs. Mertens & Sichel, and other traders, of Walfisch Bay. It is a mistake to use heavy saddles; light English saddles, furnished with plenty of "dees," and bridles, should be taken out from England. Half a common cotton Kaffir blanket, folded small and placed under the saddle, saves horses many a sore back. Breeches, or knickerbocker breeches, of velvet cord, mole-skin, or strong khaki, are best for the veldt. Strong brown boots and pigskin gaiters, or field boots, are best for foot and leg gear. A broad-brimmed felt hat, plenty of flannel shirts, and a strong cord coat for hunting in thorn and bush country, when following giraffe, complete the outfit. The coat can be strapped on the saddle bow; and a compass, a box of matches, and a full water-bottle should never be omitted when leaving the wagon in search of game. A small case of medicines, preferably in tabloids (Burroughs and Wellcome's tabloids can be strongly recommended) in case of fever or dysentery should be remembered. Warburg's Fever Tincture is excellent for both these complaints and should be included. When hunting in the waterless deserts of the Kalahari and Western South-Central Africa, where the loss of one's horse may mean disaster, it is a wise plan to fasten one's mount to the hunting belt by means of a cord or thin hide *riem*, the other end of which is made fast to the cheek-ring of the bridle. With a little practice, a South-African horse will almost always stand quietly for the shot. A few mongrel dogs are useful for baying lion, leopard, or other dangerous game, and guarding the wagons. A pointer should certainly be taken for finding feathered game. It may be noted that, at the end of a hunting trip, the whole outfit, including spare guns, horses and stores, can usually be sold, for about the prices paid for them, on the hunter's return to a frontier town and semi-civilization. With average luck and judgment, therefore, a South-African hunting expedition need entail nothing like the extravagant expenditure hinted at by luxurious travellers.

In East and Central Africa, where neither horses nor ox-wagons are used, the cost of hunting is a good deal increased by the number of native carriers required to convey stores, ammunition, guns and camp equipment. The actual cost—for food and wages alone—of a caravan of between fifty and sixty carriers will amount to from £65 to £75 per month. The sportsman will have further to bear the charge of native hunters, body servants and interpreters, as well as of arms and ammunition for the whole expedition, and other incidental expenses. It may be stated as a fact that a much longer purse is, nowadays, needed to hunt in East, Central, and North-East Africa—mainly owing to the cost of native transport—than in South Africa. In Somaliland, camels are now used for crossing the waterless desert which separates the coast line from the hunting country.

In addition to a large number of antelopes, such as koodoo, lesser koodoo, various hartebeests, blue wildebeest, pallah, eland, roan and sable antelope, Hunter's antelope, waterbuck, sitatunga, bushbuck, reedbuck, oryx, beisa, Clarke's, Waller's, and Thomson's gazelles, klipspringer, duiker, steinbuck, oribi, &c., lion, leopard, buffalo, giraffe, Burchell's and Grévy's zebra, and ostrich are to be found in these regions. Elephant and black rhinoceros, as well as hippopotami, are in some parts numerous. But it is to be remembered that hunting has to be conducted on foot;

and, as a general rule, it may be stated that the climate, especially near the equator, is much more exhausting than in South Africa.

Battery.—I come now to that most important subject, the choice of guns. For South Africa, at the present time, a useful battery would be the following:—

(1) A ·450 double Express rifle by a good maker, accurately sighted for shooting on the plains; this is a most useful weapon for all ordinary shooting; (2) a single ·303 Lee-Metford sporting rifle; (3) a single sporting Martini-Henry. This is one of the most useful rifles for all kinds of game in South Africa or elsewhere. Government ammunition can be procured at every up-country store, in itself a fact well worth remembering; (4) a double ·577 Express; (5) a 12-bore shot gun for bird shooting.

Such a battery is sufficient for all needs of the present day in South Africa. If, however, the gunner mean to hunt buffalo, and possibly elephant, or a stray rhinoceros, he may prefer a weapon of larger calibre. In such a case, a double 8-bore, carrying spherical bullets, may be recommended. For the ·450 and ·577 rifles solid, but not hardened, bullets, as well as hollow bullets should be taken. Many gunners have, like the late Sir Samuel Baker, much greater faith in the solid than the Express bullet. A very useful weapon for giraffe hunting is the Afrikander double rifle, carrying the ordinary Martini-Henry ammunition. Giraffe are usually shot from behind, at pretty close quarters, by the mounted hunter, and for this form of sport the Afrikander is an excellent weapon. In East, Central, and North-East Africa, where elephant, rhinoceros, and buffalo are almost certain to be met with, the double 8-bore should most certainly form part of the equipment. Some sportsmen even recommend the single 4-bore, a most formidable weapon, which may be almost absolutely relied upon to stop the charge of the heaviest and most dangerous game. As the weight of the 4-bore is very great—about 21 lbs. —and its recoil, backed by the huge spherical bullet and 12 drams of powder, proportionately heavy, only a man of the strongest physique and nerves is likely to employ so tremendous a fire-arm. For the rest, the battery recommended for South Africa will be found sufficient for other parts of the continent.

Hints on Shooting.—As regards the actual shooting of game, it may be said that only experience in the field can teach a man the knowledge of which he stands in need. Spoorers and native hunters may be relied upon to take the gunner up to the game he seeks: the rest of the business lies entirely with himself. In shooting lions, leopards, and other thin-skinned game at close quarters, the Express is a very deadly weapon. A broadside shot through the heart or lungs, or a chest shot, if the beast is facing the gunner, is pretty certain to kill or turn dangerous carnivora. The head shot for elephant, often resorted to in India, is seldom relied upon against the African elephant, and the point aimed at is the heart, or lungs. Rhinoceros are, as a rule, not difficult beasts to kill, and are often surprised and shot at close quarters; a shot from a 4-bore, 8-bore, or a ·577 solid bullet, through the lungs may be confidently relied upon to bring this gigantic beast to bag. In shooting heavy game, most beginners usually make the mistake of firing too high for the vital parts. The aim should be, if possible, directed just behind the point of the shoulder, a trifle below the middle of the body. It should always be remembered that for thick-skinned game, such as elephant, rhinoceros, buffalo, and giraffe, only *solid* bullets should be used.

It ought to be remembered that game laws now obtain in most parts of South Africa. In Cape Colony neither buffalo nor elephant, which are still found near the coast, can be shot without a permit from the governor. Zebra, koodoo, hartebeest, gemsbuck, bontebok, reedbuck, blesbuck, wildebeest and hippopotamus are similarly protected. Enactments for the preservation of the smaller antelopes vary in different districts and for different periods. These can be ascertained at the offices of the Agent-General for Cape Colony, Victoria Street, Westminster, or on landing at the Cape. In Natal the larger game is specially protected, as in Cape Colony. The close time for smaller antelopes extends from 30th June to 31st December. In the Orange Free State all game is protected from 1st September to 20th January. In the Transvaal the close season extends from 15th September to 1st February. Elephant and hippopotamus are absolutely protected. A licence to shoot giraffe, buffalo, rhinoceros, or ostrich costs £10; for zebra and large antelopes, £3; and for small antelopes, £1 10*s*. In the Bechuanaland Protectorate, including Khama's Country, and Ngamiland, there is a close season from 1st September to the end of February; in the Tati district from 1st October to 1st April. Special permission to shoot elephant, giraffe, or eland must be obtained from the British Resident for the Bechuanaland Protectorate. Hunting parties of five or under are required to pay a license of £75 to shoot large game; and £25 to all chiefs whose permission is required. Game may, however, be shot for food by travellers within a mile of the road. In the territory of the British South Africa Company there is a close season from 1st October to 1st March. But farmers may shoot game on cultivated land, and prospectors and travellers may shoot game actually required for food, if distant more than ten miles from a township. In Portuguese South-East Africa, strangers entering the country to hunt require a license which costs £50. Residents pay about £6 for a license to shoot big game. In Zululand, whites are not allowed to shoot game without a special permit. In Nyassaland a permit to shoot heavy game costs £25, but it has now been decided to protect all game in the well known Elephant Marshes and for some time to come no shooting will be permitted in that area. Elephants are now protected in German East Africa. In Somaliland a reserve for elephants has been formed by the British authorities.

H. A. BRYDEN.

AMERICA, NORTH—With the exception of British Columbia, the North American continent is, in spite of a few remaining districts where good sport may still be had, practically played out from the sportsman's point of view.

In British Columbia the sportsman must be prepared for downright hard work in a dense, rugged country. Here we shall find in far greater quantity than elsewhere every description of game common to the States, save the **Prong Buck**, to compensate for which we meet the true **Black Tail** deer, unknown in any part of America except along the Pacific coast.

Wherever we strike into the mountains, game of some description is nearly certain to be found. But the country is frequently so densely timbered, that little can be seen. Of well-known districts not yet exhausted, East Kootenay is the best and very easy of access. Here can be obtained in a three months' trip Caribou, White Tail, and Mule Deer; the Rocky Mountain Sheep; the Black and the Grizzly Bear; also the wretched Rocky Mountain Goat, which never can realise its danger. Here, too, lives one of the very few professional hunters of British Columbia. Every one must first gain his experience under a good hunter; and then, if he feel equal to it, let him start out northwards on his own account.

The **Woodland Caribou** (*Rangifer tarandus*), the female of which carries antlers, is distributed throughout British Columbia as far north as the head-waters of the Fraser River, where it gives place to the **Moose.** Further north, and inland, we come to the **Barren Ground Caribou** (*Rangifer grœnlandicus*).

Continuing still further north, we fall in with **Bison**; and finally meet the **Musk Ox**, which is only to be secured by some more than usually tough and enterprising sportsman. Those who hunt the **Woodland Caribou** should do so in the northern districts in September and November, for they shed their antlers remarkably early. They are very keen of scent and hearing, though, if the hunter succeeds in getting into a band of them, they appear to lose their heads and can be shot down right and left. They are also very locally distributed. [*See* CARIBOU.]

The mountains of the western side of the Kootenay Valley hold only Caribou and Mule Deer, while those on the east contain no Caribou at all, but plenty of Sheep, Goats, and Deer.

The **Wapiti** (*Cervus canadensis*), commonly known as **Elk** in America, is a magnificent deer formerly abundant in the States, but fast becoming scarce. At the present time, a specimen head is as likely to be procured in Wyoming as anywhere. The Wapiti is easily stalked and easily killed. It carries its antlers throughout the winter. There are a few examples in Kootenay and plenty on Vancouver's Island, but insular heads run small. [*See* WAPITI.]

The **Mule Deer** (*Cariacus macrotis*), known in America as **Black Tail** deer, is, after the Caribou, the most widely distributed and plentiful deer of British Columbia and the States. Its habitat in British Columbia extends on and off from the extreme south to Stuart's Lake in the north. Its antlers vary in formation and beauty considerably, and the hunter may always hope to kill yet a finer head than the last. Around Quesnell, on the Fraser, is a favourite locality. It is easily hunted and very plentiful in East Kootenay.

The **White-Tailed Deer** (*Cariacus virginianus*). These lovely little deer have, perhaps, the widest range of any deer in the world. They penetrate from the Atlantic to the Pacific, but do not extend far north in British Columbia. They are very abundant in East Kootenay, and are well worthy of all the hunter's skill, which in fair stalking will be taxed to the utmost.

The **Black-Tailed Deer** (*Cariacus columbianus*) are unknown save along the Pacific coast. They never wander far inland. From Vancouver into Alaska, many islands and the whole coast abound with them. They are easily approached.

The **Moose** (*Alces machlis*), known in Europe as the Elk, is the largest and most ungainly deer in the world, and one hideous head should suffice to satisfy most hunters. They are not difficult to obtain either in Canada or a district north-west of Winnipeg, but a whole season given up to their pursuit would be wasted, so far as the prospect of obtaining other game is concerned.

The **Bighorn**, or **Rocky Mountain Sheep**—[*See* BIGHORN].

The **Prong Buck** (*Antilocapra americana*) is exclusively confined to the southern prairies, and even there its numbers are rapidly decreasing. It is hunted with dogs, but affords good stalking and requires straight shooting. It has the peculiarity of shedding its horns about October.

The **Rocky Mountain Goat** (*Haploceros montanus*)—Throughout British Columbia comparatively few mountains are without these tame, foolish creatures which afford no sport save the risk of a broken neck. The hunter has only to discover one to secure it, and by the time he has butchered the first, he will probably consider a second not worth climbing after.

Hints on the Trip—Unless the sportsman is content to risk entire failure, or only possible success in some unknown district, he should, before leaving home, obtain information as to the latest discovery of a good locality for sport, and then secure a reliable hunter. All else is plain sailing.

The best route to British Columbia is *via* New York, and on to Montreal and westward by the Canadian Pacific Railway.

Little game exists east of the Rocky Mountains. If a good hunter be secured, the sportsman need not trouble himself about anything save rifles and clothing. All can be obtained with the hunter's assistance at the last town or Hudson's Bay port, where the hunter should be in waiting.

Expenses, &c.—The cost of a three-months' trip would be, for a hunter £2 per day, to include horses and outfit, and cook £10 per month; in addition to these a suitable supply of cheap provisions, such as flour, rice, canned milk, coffee, sugar, salt, &c., must be taken.

Season—The sportsman should leave England about the 15th of August and must, if hunting in British Columbia, first procure a £10 license.

Shooting Memoranda—When stalking any animal on a mountain side, the hunter should circle round to leeward and get above it, especially when after Bighorn.

By taking up a position between the setting sun and an animal, it can be easily approached unseen. On coming suddenly upon game, should it not be too much scared, it is best to remain perfectly motionless, until it commences to feed, or looks away. The most timid deer will often pass within ten yards of a stationary person without suspicion. A wounded animal should not be followed immediately, but rather be given time to lie down and stiffen. It is advisable to hunt only early and late, resting, as do the animals, in the middle of the day. When upon the hunting-ground, shots should never be fired at winged game, or anything save good heads. The sportsman should learn to skin before going on a hunt, and do all such work himself if the trophies are to look their best. Skins should *not* be dried in the sun or before a fire; and plenty of neck skin must be left on the masks of deer. A good deerhound will find much game and seldom lose that which is even slightly wounded, but he must always be fastened to the belt. Careful bearings should be taken on leaving camp, and if the hunter be lost, there is no need for alarm; it is only the camp that is lost, for a man with a rifle should always be able to exist until he either find his camp or be found. Two shots fired rapidly are usually considered signals of distress. More than one hundred rifle cartridges are unnecessary, and they should never be lost sight of or given over to any official on the way out. It requires an especially strong box to resist the rough handling of porters; and great care should therefore be taken in packing rifles.

Requirements—A **Winchester** is the rifle of the country; it is good and cheap, and cartridges can always be obtained; but the most perfect and satisfactory weapon is a double ·500 hammerless ejecting Express.

If geese and ducks are likely to be met with *en route* to the hunting-ground, a **Paradox** is advisable; its possession likewise renders any mishap to the rifle of little consequence.

A revolver is useless.

The best way to carry a rifle is in a sling over the back.

As for the remaining requisites, ordinary winter clothing will be wanted; as well as about five pairs of common sand-shoes with thin rubber soles, which are the most comfortable and noiseless for climbing and stalking.

A strong leather belt with two knives, whetstone, and compass, as well as a good pair of field-glasses, are necessary. An excellent skinning and hunting-knife is made, the handle of which closes on the blade; the latter fits neatly into a sheath. A second knife should be carried, commonly known as a shoemaker's knife, the blade of which has an upward turn; it takes a rough edge, and is excellent and quick for skinning. A roll valise is very handy for sleeping upon and carrying blankets, &c. The sportsman should be careful not to burthen himself with more than he absolutely requires, and that is very little. [*See also* CAMPING OUT.] A fishing-rod and large trout flies will often come in handy.

J. TURNER TURNER.

INDIAN—India affords as large a variety of animals for the rifle as any country in the world. Some of them are not met with elsewhere. Tiger, Panther or Leopard, Bear, the Gaur (always called in India Bison), Buffalo, Samber, Swamp Deer, Cheetul, Hog Deer, Barking Deer, Nilgai, Black Buck, Gazelle, Four-horned Antelope, Neilgherry Wild Goat (called in India Neilgherry Ibex), Rhinoceros, and Elephant, are the principal animals in India. In the Himalayan ranges, there are the Markhor, Ibex, Serow, Tahr, Gooral, Shapoo or Oorial, Burrel, Snow Leopard, Musk Deer, Brown and Himalayan Black Bear, and Cashmere Stag. In the hills to the west of Sinde, are a wild goat (*Capra ægagrus*), the same animal that is found in Crete and the Caucasus (it is known to Indian sportsmen as the Sinde Ibex), and a variety of the Markhor with a straight horn having a spiral twist. The Striped Hyæna, Wolf, Indian Wild Dog, Cheetah or Hunting Leopard, the Lion, Lynx, Wild Ass, and Wild Boar complete the list of what are usually styled the "big game" of India, though, to the old shikari, the smaller deer and antelopes are not reckoned as such.

The Indian **Lion** is now represented only by a few animals in Kathywar. They are very properly preserved and not shot, except occasionally by some one specially privileged to do so. The writer sees no difference between the Indian and the African Lion and believes them to be identical. **Tigers, Panthers,** and **Bears** are found throughout India, generally speaking, though there are many thousands of square miles without any, and a stranger to the country, unless he has information as to the exact localities and the assistance of some experienced friend, could easily spend months without seeing a single example. All the large mountain ranges of the Indian Peninsula hold the Indian **Bison**: the Satpoora and Vindhyan ranges, the Mysore and Travancore Hills are the best. The **Buffalo** is found only in Assam, parts of Bengal and certain limited portions of the Raepore, Sambalpore, and Chanda districts of the Central Provinces. **Samber, Cheetul, Swamp Deer,** and **Hog Deer** are jungle deer, the two former being found in suitable localities throughout India. The range of the **Swamp Deer** is more limited, its principal habitat being in the heavy grass and forest land in Assam and the foot of the Himalayas. It occurs also in the Mundla, Raepore, and Sambalpore districts of the Central Provinces. The **Hog Deer** is found in Sinde, Assam, and Northern India; but does *not* extend, as stated by Jerdon, into Central India. The **Barking Deer** is also a jungle deer, and is found throughout India. Of the Antelopes, the **Black Buck** lives in the plains; the **Nilgai** in the jungles and also in the open country; the **Four-horned** Antelope in the jungles; the **Gazelle** in the jungles and in open ground. The Neilgherry **Ibex** only occurs in the Madras Presidency, in the Neilgherry and Annamallay Hills, and in Travancore. The only other member of the same genus (*Hemitragus*) is the **Tahr** or Himalayan Wild Goat. The **Elephant** is still numerous in Travancore and Mysore, and in the large forests at the foot of the Himalayas. It is not now found in Central India. Shooting Elephants is prohibited in British territory. In the native states of Travancore and Mysore, also, they cannot be shot without permission from the State. There are two kinds of **Rhinoceros**, the larger and lesser. The former occurs in the Terai and Assam, and the latter in the Bengal Sunderbunds. The **Wild Ass** is only found on the Rann of Cutch, and is not shot. The **Hyæna** is also not an object of sport, and is common. The **Wolf** and **Wild Dog** are not uncommon, and are found throughout the country; the former generally in the open country; the latter do not leave the jungles. The **Hunting-Leopard** is not often met with when out shooting. Some of the native Rajahs keep them for coursing Black Buck. [*See* CHEETAH.] The **Lynx** is also seldom seen. Jerdon states that it is unknown in the Himalayas and in Bengal. That it occurs in Sinde is certain, as one was pulled down there by a couple of greyhounds belonging to a friend of the writer. The **Wild Boar** is found throughout India. In all suitable localities it is killed with the spear only.

The best season for Tiger, Panther, and Bear-shooting in Western and Central India is March, April, and May; after the monsoon breaks, usually the second week in June, nothing can be done. The jungles are then very feverish till about the end of November. In December, January, and February, which are the best months in the writer's opinion for stalking Deer, the jungle is too thick and the water too plentiful for much to be done with the *felidæ*, though some can, no doubt, be procured at that season. Bison and Buffalo-stalking on foot, which is the only sportsmanlike way of attacking these animals, is best followed in April and May, and for three weeks, or a month, after the rains commence. In Northern India, where the long grass necessitates the use of elephants, the shooting is generally done in the hot weather, March to June. In Southern India, on the other hand, the feverish time in the hills is the hot weather, and October and November are safe, although much discomfort is experienced from the rain. In the hot weather the stags have mostly shed their horns, and about Christmas is the time to stalk them. In the Central Provinces, rules have been framed which establish a close-time for Deer, and this includes the hot weather. A copy of such rules should be obtained from the Secretary to the Chief Commissioner Central Provinces by all who wish to shoot in the Central Provinces. Large tracts of country, forest reserves, are also closed to the sportsmen in the Central Provinces; and in other parts also it is necessary to obtain permission from the forest officer in charge to enter the jungles for shooting.

For big game shooting it is necessary to have one horse at least, and it is better to have two for each gun. As in the hot weather it is much cooler in the open air than in a tent, an 80 lb. Cabul tent for each sportsman is sufficient; this will keep things dry in case of the rain and heavy thunderstorms that sometimes occur at this season. A double-barrelled ·500 Express rifle is all that is necessary, but for a battery, the writer recommends two ·500 Express rifles, an 8-bore gun built for ball (not a rifle: a gun is as good and not so heavy) and a 12-bore gun. Bullock-carts can be hired by the month at about 12 annas a day. Beaters' pay varies in different places, from 2 to 4 annas a day. It is usual to give *double* pay if a tiger is killed. The shikaris' pay is from 4 to 8 annas a day. The rewards given by Government for tigers, &c., killed, should be distributed among the shikaris and men. (The Indian rupee equals 16 annas, and at the present rate of exchange is equal to about 14 pence.)

J. D. INVERARITY.

MEASUREMENTS—Probably no subject has given rise to more controversy than the measurements of animals which, in hunters' parlance, are classed as "Big Game," and of trophies of the chase. The reason for this is not far to seek; for the question is dominated by that exceedingly elastic quantity, the "personal equation." Sportsmen, generally, are not too exact in their methods of calculating size or weight, and this inexactitude may arise, not so much from pardonable anxiety to secure a trophy whose weight, length, or girth will rival or exceed that of any other particular trophy, as from the difficulties which attend the exact mensuration of animals killed in situations such as confront the adventurous hunter all the world over. Nevertheless, the means to greater exactitude in measurement are simple in the extreme, and may be summed up by saying that with a five-foot rule, a two-foot rule—some part of it divided into millimetres—a tape-measure of any length over ten feet, a large pair of calipers, and a notebook and pencil, one ought to be able to achieve absolute accuracy.

At present, few of the tables of measurements found in books of sport detail the methods adopted. Some sportsmen measure along all the curves of a carcase (even pressing the tape into inequalities), whilst others measure in a straight line. Obviously, the difference between the two

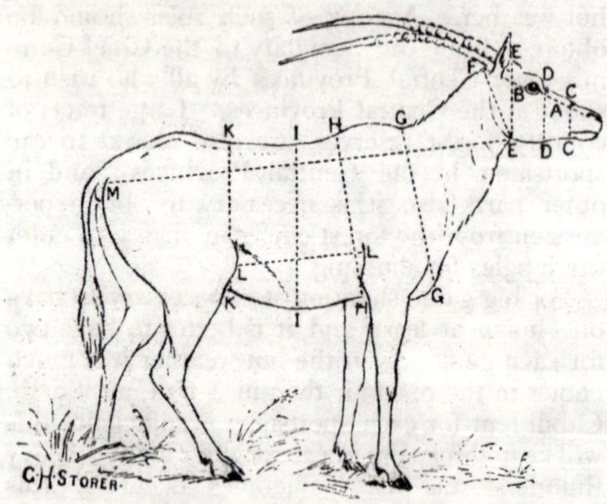

Fig. 1.

methods sometimes amounts to feet—a serious matter when the measurements of two animals, each taken by a different method, are compared, and therefore the method adopted should in all cases be stated: otherwise, confusion worse confounded arises when it is sought to institute comparisons.

Perhaps an indication of what the present writer considers a proper method of measurement may be acceptable to sportsmen generally. For ordinary mammals the method should be to measure, as shown in the diagram, Fig. 1, which is that of the Sabre-horned Antelope (*Oryx leucoryx*).

In a direct line along back from tip of nose to end of tail.

The same along under surface from end of lower jaw to end of tail.

Length of tail, measured underneath from anus to tip, the deduction of which gives the length of body above and below.

Length along top of head, following all curves from nose to just behind and between ears.

Length from proximal angle of nostril to distal angle of eyelid on dotted line A.

Length between distal and proximal angles of eyelids.

Length from proximal angle of eyelid to insertion of ear on dotted line B.

Breadth of head between eyes.

Breadth between ears.

Length and breadth of ears.

Girth around muzzle at proximal angle of jaws (C, C).

Girth around muzzle in front of eyes (D, D).

Girth around head, under throat, in front of ears (E, E).

Girth of neck behind ears (E, F).

Girth of neck in front of shoulders (G, G).

Length of neck, on upper surface, from back of ears to distal edge of shoulder (F, G). Also, on under surface, from throat (E) to point G.

Girth of body just behind fore limbs (H. H).

Girth at greatest depth of abdomen (I, I).

Girth just in front of hind limbs (K, K).

Length of body between posterior edge of fore, and anterior edge of hind limbs.

Extreme length along *side* from throat (E) to below spring of tail (M).

Extreme height from ground to shoulder or withers.

Extreme height from ground to above hip.

Length of limbs as separate items where practicable.

Girth of limbs in three places: at foot, "knee," and junction with body.

Note colours of muzzle, eyes, and all soft parts, and also any peculiarities.

The weight, if possible, to be recorded, and in many cases this may be calculated by the method detailed in certain works for ascertaining the weight of cattle.

Place and date in all cases to be given.

If a horned head, the position of horns in relation to the muzzle, eyes, and ears should be noted, and the width on top of head between their insertions.

The antlers of such an animal as a stag should be measured as shown in the diagram, Fig. 2, drawn from the horns of a Wapiti (often misnamed "Elk").

Length of beam of each antler, following all curves along back of beam to tip of highest posterior tine (see dotted line A).

Length in a straight line from burr to tip of same tine (see dotted line B).

Length along centre of beam to crown.

Distance from burr to spring of first or "brow-" tine.

Length of brow-tine along under surface.

Distance between brow-tine and next or "bez-" tine.

Length of bez-tine.

Distance between bez- and "tres-" tines.

Length of tres-tine; and so on, measuring length of each successive tine, and distance from

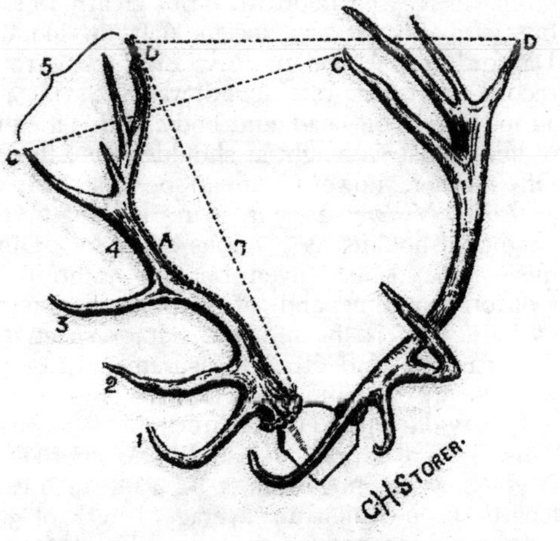

FIG. 2.—ANTLERS OF AN ELAPHINE DEER.

1. Brow-tine. 2. Bez-tine. 3. Tres-tine. 4. Royal-tine. 5. Sur-royals.

this to next. Also note if any anterior sur-royal makes, with the beam, a greater length than that along the dotted line A.

Span between burrs.

Span between tips of brow-tines.

Span between tips of bez-tines.

Span between tips of tres-tines.

Span between tips of anterior sur-royals on dotted line C, C.

Span between tips of posterior sur-royals on dotted line D, D.

Greatest span at crown.

Girth of beam at burr.

Girth between brow- and bez-tines.

Girth between bez- and tres-tines.

Girth between other tines.

The length and girth of any other noticeable tines should also be taken.

It should be noted that the apparent beam above the tres is the "royal tine," and that all points springing therefrom are called sur-royals, anterior and posterior, and often form a cup—the "throstle's nest" of the Scot. Six points on each antler constitute a "royal head." In horns of other than Elaphine deer there is no bez-tine, and the next anterior one above the brow-tine is, therefore, the tres—(sometimes, although erroneously, called the "royal").

The diagram, Fig. 3, shows the different types of antlers, for all of which, except the last, the foregoing method of measurement must be modified.

Twisted horns such as those of the Antelopes and of various sheep should be measured along their front, back and side curves in the manner described by Sir Victor Brooke and other authors, together with girths and distances between the various points.

The length, width and girth of the skull at various points is desirable.

The following tables of Big Game measurements have been compiled from various works, but, as will be observed, in scarcely any case is the exact method indicated, and therefore those measurements for which the writer is not responsible must be taken on their merits. Probably no *skin*-measurements are of the slightest avail, skins being stretched out of all proportion in the process of pegging-out and drying.

In an article like the present, which is necessarily limited, it will be readily understood that not a tithe of the measurements to be found in books of sport, travel or reference can be given, nor, indeed, can all the animals known as beasts of chase be even mentioned, this omission being particularly noticeable in the great order of the *Ungulata*, or hoofed animals. The reader is referred, therefore, to the various works by Anderson, Baillie-Grohman, Baker, Blanford, Sir Victor Brooke, Buxton, Caton, Chapman, Gordon-Cumming, Danford and Alston, Dodge, Jules Gerard, Harris, Jerdon, Littledale, Lord, Lydekker, Lord Mayo, Peek, Percy, Clive

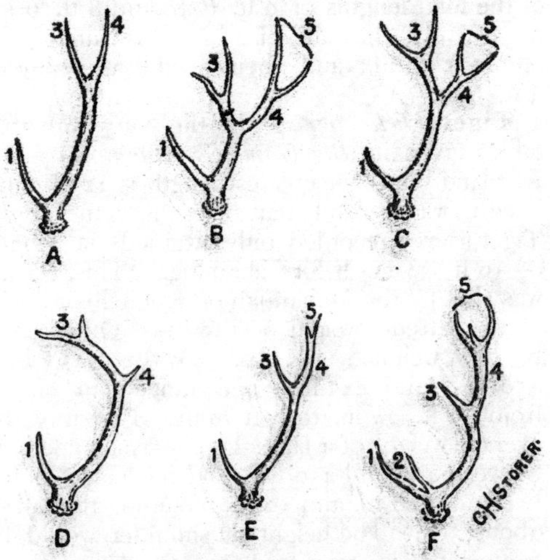

FIG. 3.—TYPES OF ANTLERS (modified from P.Z.S.).

A. Rusine type.
B. Normal Rucervine type.
C. Intermediate Rucervine type.
D. Extreme Rucervine type.
E. Sub-Elaphine type.
F. Elaphine type.

Phillipps-Wolley, Pike, Roosevelt, Sanderson, Sclater, Selous, Sterndale, Ward, Williamson, and a host of others, pre-eminent amongst which, for wealth of measurements, stands out

Rowland Ward's *Horn Measurements and Weights of the Great Game of the World*, which contains nearly all records prior to 1892.

CARNIVORA.

Taking the mammals from highest to lowest form, the Lion heads the list, and although sportsmen imagine specific differences to exist between the African and Asiatic Lion, and between those of various parts of Africa, nevertheless, maned or unmaned, small or large, ruddy or pale, these are but slight or local variations, and there is really only one species.

Lion (*Felis leo*)—Sir Samuel Baker appeared to consider that Lions of 500 to 600 lbs. were by no means uncommon, but the heaviest as yet recorded is one, mentioned by Mr. Lydekker in the recently published *Royal Natural History* as having been shot in the Orange Free State in 1865, which is stated to have weighed 583 lbs. The next in weight is one recorded in *The Field* of July 13, 1890, weighing 563 lbs. A fine, black-maned menagerie Lion, of abnormal size, is stated to have weighed 434 lbs., its length from nose to root of tail being 6 ft. 10 in., tail 3 ft. 2 in., girth behind shoulder 4 ft. 9 in., girth of upper arm 1 ft. 10 in., and height at shoulder 3 ft. 6 in. Selous mentions three, of the respective weights of 410 lbs., 385 lbs., and 376 lbs.; the extreme length of the largest was 9 ft. 11 in., and standing height to top of shoulder-blade 3 ft. 8 in. Indian Lions are generally the smaller, but Sterndale gives two of the total lengths of 9 ft. 6 in. and 8 ft. 6 in. respectively, the tails of which measured 3 ft. and 2 ft. 6 in., and their height at shoulder 3 ft. 6 in.

Tiger (*Felis tigris*)—In the very valuable tables given in *Big Game Shooting* and by Mr. Rowland Ward, the greatest length is 12 ft. 2 in., but this was probably that of a skin, as the largest Tiger as yet recorded only attained the length of 10 ft. 2½ in. before skinning. This, which was shot by the Maharajah of Kuch Behar, was of the extreme weight of 540 lbs. Others shot by him weighed 493 lbs., 467 lbs., 455 lbs., 450 lbs., and 445 lbs., and ranged in length from 10 ft. 2½ in. to 9 ft. 6 in. Probably the average weight of a large Tiger may be taken as between 400 and 450 lbs., and its length as between 9 ft. 6 in. and 10 ft., including the tail of about 3 ft. The height at shoulder would be from 3 ft. 6 in. to 3 ft. 8 in. Sanderson, however, in his *Among the Wild Beasts of India*, mentions that a very bulky, old, well-fed, powerful Tiger was but 9 ft. in length, and weighed only 349½ lbs. The Tigress, as the Lioness, is of less length and of considerably less weight. Tiger cubs of one year old are from 4 ft. 6 in. to 5 ft. 6 in. in length, but at the age of three years attain a length of from 7 ft. to 8 ft. 6 in.

Leopard (or **Panther**) (*Felis pardus*)—Sportsmen, as with the Lion, attempt to differentiate between the Leopard and the Panther, and, indeed, contend for specific differences. The Leopard or Panther of Africa and India are, however, not specifically distinct, although they vary greatly both in size and colour, even to melanism, and, more rarely, albinism. Sanderson, who regards them as varieties, but yet gives each a specific name, says: "The Panther varies in size from 6 ft. to 8 ft. from nose to tip of tail," whilst "the Leopard varies greatly in size, but probably never exceeds 6 ft. in length." Danford and Alston in *Proc. Zool. Soc.*, 1880, record one whose total length was 8 ft., viz., 4 ft. 11 in. length of head and body, and 3 ft. 1 in. of tail, whilst its height at shoulder was 2 ft. 2 in. Of another, however, mentioned in *Cassell's Natural History* as 7 ft. 6 in. in length, the height at shoulder is given as 2 ft. 7 in. Other measurements are given on the authority of Gordon-Cumming and of Captain Fergusson, as being 7 ft. 10 in. and 7 ft. 8 in. respectively. Unfortunately, no other measurements nor any weights are to hand.

Snow-Leopard (or **Ounce**) (*Felis uncia*)—This, the great prize of the Indian sportsman, is given as ranging from 7 ft. 4 in. to 6 ft. in length, from which an average length of 3 ft. must be deducted for the tail. The height at shoulder is given by Sterndale as 2 ft.

Jaguar (*Felis onca*)—This South American cat, locally known as the "Tiger," is stated by Mr. Lydekker (*op. cit.*) to have attained a length of 5 ft. from tip of nose to root of tail; and another, measured by Azara, attained a length of 6 ft. 9 in., from which 2 ft. 2 in., for length of tail, must be deducted; the average, however, may be taken as 6 ft. 2 in., including the tail of 2 ft. 1 in.

Puma (or **Cougar**) (*Felis concolor*)—Another South American cat—locally called the "Lion"—is stated in *Big Game Shooting*, vol. i., to have attained a length of 8 ft. 2 in. including the tail, of about 3 ft. Weight about 150 lbs. A large male, killed in Arizona, says Mr. Lydekker, measured 7 ft., including tail 3 ft.

Clouded Leopard (or **Clouded Tiger**) (*Felis nebulosa*)—This Asiatic cat is stated by Jerdon to grow to a large size, and Mr. Lydekker records one of 6 ft. 6 in. Sterndale gives another whose length was 6 ft. 4 in., including the tail of 3 ft. Mr. Lydekker gives another—a male—which measured 5 ft. 7½ in., including the tail of 2 ft. 6 in.

There are many smaller cats known to science which cannot be included here.

Lynx (*Felis lynx*)—Apparently the European and Asiatic Lynx, although so variable in size and coloration, are to be considered as of one species only. Blanford gives the body length as 2 ft. 9 in., and tail 7¾ in.; probably, however, larger specimens than this are found. *Cassell's Natural History* mentions their length as from 3 ft. 4 in. to 4 ft. 2 in., exclusive of tail 6 in. to 9 in., but these may be skin-measurements.

Canada Lynx (*Felis canadensis*)—Mivart gives this as not exceeding 2 ft. 6 in. in length from snout to root of tail, which is 5 in., but in the *Museum of Natural History* one is recorded as 3 ft., with 4½ in.

Hunting Leopard (or **Cheetah**) (*Cynœlurus jubatus*)—Jerdon states that an adult attains a length of 7 ft., of which the tail comprises 2 ft. 6 in. The height at shoulder is given as from 2 ft. 6 in. to 2 ft. 9 in.

Striped Hyæna (*Hyæna striata*)—Sterndale gives the measurements of one as—Length of head and body 3 ft. 6 in., tail about 1 ft. 6 in.

Brown Hyæna (*Hyæna brunnea*)—*Cassell's Natural History* mentions a specimen as having a length of 4 ft. 10 in., including tail of about 1 ft., and a height at shoulder of 1 ft. 4 in.

Spotted Hyæna (*Hyæna crocuta*)—In the same work, measurements of one are given as—extreme length 5 ft. 10 in.; height at shoulder 2 ft. 8 in.

Wolf (*Canis lupus*)—Whether the Indian Wolf (*Canis pallipes*) is to be considered as specifically distinct from *C. lupus*, it is certain that both the European and American Wolf are to be regarded as one species, and this in spite of the extreme variability of their coloration. Sterndale gives the length as 5 ft. 2 in. to 5 ft. 8 in., including the tail of 1 ft. 8 in. Cassell gives height at shoulder as 2 ft. 8 in.

There are several of the smaller Cynoidea which need not be included here.

Polar Bear (*Ursus maritimus*)—The weight has been variously estimated as from 600 to 700 lbs. (see *Royal Natural History*, vol. ii.), and as 1,500 lbs. (see *Big Game Shooting*, vol. i.), and its length, from snout to tail, as from 8 ft. to 9 ft. 6in.

Brown Bear (*Ursus arctos*)—No exact measurements appear to have been recorded of large European specimens, but it is believed that they sometimes attain a length of fully 8 ft. from nose to root of tail. In the Himalayas, the average length is 5 ft. or 5 ft. 6 in., although examples of 7 ft. are met with, and the length of one has been recorded as 7 ft. 6 in. whose height was 3 ft. 5 in. The tail does not exceed 2 in. or 3 in.

Isabelline Bear (*Ursus isabellinus*)—Major Fitz Herbert appears to have met with a male specimen measuring 5 ft. 5 in. from nose to tail; height at shoulder, 3 ft.; girth, 4 ft.; forearm, 1 ft. 5 in.; and a female whose extreme length was 4 ft. 9 in. According to Major Ward, the length of another specimen was 6 ft. 10 in.

Grizzly Bear (*Ursus horribilis*)—Messrs. Lewis and Clark measured a specimen which had attained a length of 9 ft. J. C. Tolman gives the dead weight of one as 1,656 lbs., and measurements of fresh skin as follows:—Length from nose to anus, 13 ft. 6 in.; from ear to ear,

SNOW LEOPARD.
Average height at shoulder, 2 ft. Average length from head to root of tail, 3 ft. 8 in.

1 ft. 1 in.; poll to nose, 1 ft. 8 in.; length of hind foot, 1 ft. 6 in.; breadth of forefoot, 1 ft. The weight of a female is given as 900 lbs.

American Black Bear (*Ursus americanus*)—Adult male specimens frequently weigh from 600 to 700 lbs., whilst their length rarely exceeds 5 ft., and their average height is 3 ft.

Himalayan Black Bear (*Ursus torquatus*)—The average length from nose to root of tail is given as 4 ft. 9 in. to 5 ft. 6 in., although one is recorded, on the authority of Major Ward, as measuring 6 ft. 6 in.

Malayan Bear (*Ursus malayanus*)—Average length of head and body, 4 ft.; never exceeds 4 ft. 6 in. Length of adult female recorded as 3 ft. 6 in.; weight, 60 lbs.

Sloth Bear (*Melursus labiatus*)—Length of head and body varies from 4 ft. 6 in. to 5 ft. 8in.; tail, exclusive of hair, 4 in. to 5 in.; height at shoulder, 2 ft. 2 in. to 2 ft. 9 in. Average weight of large males probably 280 lbs., although the weight of one has been recorded as 320 lbs.

Southern Sea-Lion (*Otaria jubata*)—Sometimes called Captain Cook's Sea-Lion, and

WALRUS.

Average length from snout to root of tail, 10 ft. Average length of tusks (male), 1 ft. 9 in.

stated by him to have attained, in his day, a length of 12 ft. or 14 ft., and a girth of from 8 ft. to 10 ft., but males are now said to attain a length of only 7 ft. from tip of muzzle to root of tail.

Northern Sea-Lion (*Otaria stellari*)—Adult males vary in length from 11 ft. to 13 ft., including the tail of 3 in. to 4 in., girth from 8 ft. to 10 ft.; estimated weight, 1,000 to 1,300 lbs.

Northern Sea-Bear (or Fur-Seal) (*Otaria ursina*)—The extreme length of adult males is given as 7 ft. to 8 ft.; girth, 6 ft. to 7 ft.; estimated weight, 700 to 800 lbs. Females: Length, 4 ft.; girth, 2 ft. 6 in.; weight, 80 to 100 lbs.

South American Fur-Seal (*Otaria australis*)—The average length of male specimens is said to be 6 ft. to 7 ft., that of females 5 ft.

Walrus (*Trichechus rosmarus*)—Adult males appear to range in length from 9 ft. 6 in. to upwards of 12 ft. from snout to root of tail, but Elliot mentions one from the Behring Sea whose length was 13 ft. and girth 14 ft., whilst their weight is variously estimated at from 2,250 to 3,000 lbs. and even more. Tusks have been recorded of a total length of 2 ft. 7 in. and a weight exceeding 8 lbs. each; such examples are, however, exceptional, tusks of 4 lbs. weight and 2 ft. in extreme length being considered very fine. Tusks of females rarely exceed 1 ft. 8in.

There are many others of this group—the Carnivora pinnipedia—of which mention is here unnecessary.

UNGULATA.

Aurochs (*Bos taurus*)—No small confusion appears to exist in the nomenclature of European wild oxen. The Aurochs, which, in a sub-fossil condition, is known to palæontology as *Bos taurus* var. *primigenus*, is now only represented by the half-wild Chillingham and other park cattle, and by our domestic breeds descended therefrom. That which sportsmen term the "Aurochs" is really the European Bison (*Bos bonasus*).

The horn measurements of a Chillingham Bull are stated to be—Length 1 ft. 6½ in.; girth 10⅜ in.; span at tips 1 ft. 8 in.; width inside 1 ft. 9⅛ in.

Indian Humped Cattle (*Bos indicus*)—Semi-wild in some parts of India, and the Galla Ox of Africa may not be specifically distinct.

Gaur (*Bos gaurus*)—Known to Indian sportsmen by the incorrect designation of "Bison," this is stated to attain a height of 6 ft. 0 in. (18 hands) at the shoulders, and one is recorded by Sir Walter Elliot as measuring 6 ft. 1½ in. at shoulder, 5 ft. 3 in. at rump, 9 ft. 6½ in. in length from nose to root of tail, tail 2 ft. 10½ in., length of dorsal ridge 3 ft. 4 in., height of dorsal ridge 4½ in., muzzle to frontal ridge 2 ft. 1¾ in., breadth of forehead 1 ft. 3½ in., ear 10½ in., spread at tip of horns 2 ft. 1 in., girth of horns 1 ft. 7½ in. The longest horns recorded were 3 ft. 3 in., with a circumference of 1 ft. 7 in. The greatest circumference is 1 ft. 10 in. with a length of 2 ft. 8 in. The greatest spread at tips recorded is 3 ft. 1¾ in., with a length of 2 ft. 4⅜ in., circumference 1 ft. 3¾ in., and widest spread, inside, 3 ft. 4½ in.—which is also the maximum record.

Gayal (*Bos frontalis*)—Found genuinely wild in some parts of India, and smaller than its ally, the Gaur. Ward mentions two pairs of horns measuring respectively 1 ft. 3 in. and 1 ft. 0⅝ in. in length, 11½ in. and 1 ft. 1¼ in. in circumference, and 2 ft. 2⅜ in. and 2 ft. 3¾ in.

from tip to tip, but Blanford records that the horns of an old wild bull measured 1 ft. 2 in. both in girth and length.

Banting, or **Javan Ox** (*Bos sondaicus*)—Sometimes known as the Burmese Wild Ox. The maximum height recorded of an adult bull is 5 ft. 9½ in., at withers, whilst the longest pair of horns measured 2 ft. 0¾ in., with a girth of 1 ft. 0¼ in., spread at tips 1 ft. 3¾ in., and widest span, inside, 2 ft. 0¼ in. The greatest spread at tips, however, and the maximum span, are given as 1 ft. 6⅛ in. and 1 ft. 10⅛ respectively, combined with a length of 1 ft. 8⅝ in. and a girth of 1 ft. 0¼ in.

Yak (*Bos grunniens*)—The adult bull is said to weigh about 1,200 lbs., and to average 5 ft. 6 in. in height, but one is stated to be in the Leeds Museum measuring 6 ft. 0 in. in height at shoulder; 10 ft. 10½ in. in length of head and body; tail 3 ft. 1 in.; girth at shoulder 10 ft. 1 in.; girth at belly 9 ft. 4 in; at thinnest part of neck 4 ft. 2 in.; length of horns 3 ft. 0 in.; basal girth 1 ft. 6 in. This length of horns appears, however, to have been exceeded, one pair being said to measure 3 ft. 2¼ in., with a girth of 1 ft. 5 in., spread at tips 1 ft. 7 in., and widest inside span 2 ft. 7½ in., whilst these were exceeded in spread at tips by a pair of 2 ft. 10 in. horns which attained a spread of 1 ft. 8½ in.

European Bison (*Bos bonasus*)—Although truly wild in the Caucasus, and known as the Caucasian Bison, and semi-domesticated in Lithuania and known as the Lithuanian Bison, there is really no specific distinction.

Of a Caucasian bull the following measurements are given:—From nose to root of tail, 10 ft. 1 in.; top of hoof to top of withers, 5 ft. 11 in.; circumference of leg below knee, 10 in.; knee, 1 ft. 4 in.; below hock, 10½ in.; round hock, 1 ft. 7 in.; girth of body, about 8 ft. 4 in. The horns of a Lithuanian bull and cow are said to have measured respectively, from tip to tip, 1 ft. 6½ in. and 6 in.; base to tip around curve outside, 1 ft. 5½ in. and 1 ft. 3¼ in.; around curve inside, 1 ft. 1½ in. and 10 in.; circumference at base, 10 in. and 8 in.; across forehead, 1 ft. 1 in. and 10 in.

American Bison (*Bos americanus*)—Called "Buffalo" by one of those errors which seem to dog the footsteps of sportsmen in dealing with wild oxen, this is stated to have attained, in the bull, a length of 8 ft. 6 in. from tip of muzzle to root of tail and a height of 5 ft. 8 in. at withers. The weight of an adult bull has been recorded as 1,727 lbs., which is probably not exceptional, as another is said to have reached 2,000 lbs. Good-sized horns measure 1 ft. 4 in. to 1 ft. 6 in. in length, but one pair measured nearly 1 ft. 9 in., with girth 1 ft. 3 in.

Cape Buffalo (*Bos caffer*)—The following weights and measurements of different animals have been given by various authorities:—Length of body 9 ft. 0 in., tail 3 ft. 0 in. Height at shoulder 4 ft. 7 in. to 4 ft. 8 in. Weight 45 stone and upwards. Horns:—Extreme span at greatest width 3 ft. 8 in., depth on forehead 1 ft. 3 in., total length of each horn along curve 3 ft. 0 in. Besides these, the maximum measurements recorded, of various examples, are:—Width, inside, 3 ft. 6 in. Width, outside, 3 ft 11 in. Tip to tip, 3 ft. 1⅛ in. Width of palm, 1 ft. 5 in.

Indian Buffalo (*Bos bubalus*)—The bull of this species, known as the "Arna," is said to have attained, in one instance, a length of 10 ft. 6 in. from nose to root of tail. In height it is supposed never to exceed 5 ft. 4 in. (16 hands) at withers, and actual measurements of one specimen are given thus:—Length, from nose to root of tail 9 ft. 7 in., tail 3 ft. 11 in., height 5 ft. 0 in., girth 8 ft. 3 in.; horns from tip to tip along greater curve, 8 ft. 3 in. The longest horn recorded—one in the British Museum—is accredited by one authority with a "length of 6 ft. 6½ in., which indicates a span of about 14 ft. from tip to tip in the pair," whilst another gives its length outside curve as 6 ft. 5⅝ in., and basal girth 1 ft. 5⅞ in.

Of other measurements of various horns, the maximum records are:—Girth 1 ft. 9 in. Spread at tips 4 ft. 7½ in., with greatest width, inside, 4 ft. 10 in.

Musk Ox (*Ovibos moschatus*)—The horns are said to average about 2 ft. or 2 ft. 1 in. in length, but examples have been recorded ranging up to 2 ft. 3¼ in., one pair of this length having breadth of palm 1 ft. 0½ in. and spread at tips 2 ft. 3 in. Maximum breadth of palm 1 ft. 1⅛ in. with a length of 2 ft. 2¼ in. Maximum spread at tips 2 ft. 6 in., with length 2 ft.

American Wild Sheep (*Ovis canadensis*)—Known as the "Bighorn." Average weight of rams, 350 lbs. or less; of ewes, about 233 lbs. Of an adult ram these dimensions have been recorded:—From base of neck to root of tail, 3 ft. 6 in.; girth under forelegs, 3 ft. 9 in.; height at shoulder, 3 ft. 2 in. Approximate height of ewes, 3 ft. Horns range in length from 2 ft. 8 in. to 3 ft. 5 in.—the maximum record, accompanying the maximum girth of 1 ft. 5¼ in. and spread at tips of 2 ft. 4 in.

Kamschatkan Wild Sheep (*Ovis nivicola*)—Closely allied to, and possibly not specifically distinct from the preceding, this sheep is said to attain an average height of about 3 ft. 4 in. at shoulder, the maximum height recorded being 3 ft. 5 in., combined with a length, from nose to tip of tail, of 5 ft. 5 in. The maximum length is 5 ft. 7 in., and the only record to hand of girth of chest is 4 ft. 6 in., with height 3 ft. 4 in. and length 5 ft. 6 in. Of another specimen, standing only 3 ft. 1 in. at shoulder, these additional measurements were made—Skull, from between horns to end of præmaxillæ, 10 in.; greatest width across orbits, 6¾ in. Horns, length round curve, 2 ft. 9 in; circumference, 1 ft. 0¾ in. Maximum length of horns recorded, 3 ft. 2 in., with basal girth 1 ft. 1½ in., and spread at tips 2 ft. 2 in. Maximum girth 1 ft. 2½ in. Maximum spread at tips 2 ft. 2½ in. Horns of adult female, 9 in. in length.

Mongolian and Tibetan Argalis (*Ovis ammon* and *O. hodgsoni*)—These animals, whose differences may be rather of variety than of species, are said to be comparable in size with a large donkey, but no actual weights or dimensions appear to have been recorded except the height of two specimens of *O. ammon*, which were respectively 3 ft. 10 in. and 3 ft. 7 in. at shoulder, and the length of skull of the latter—1 ft. The approximate height of the Tibetan ram is given as from 3 ft. 6 in. to 4 ft. at shoulder. Horns range in length from 1 ft. 8¼ to 4 ft. 1 in., in girth from 7⅜ in. to 1 ft. 8 in., and in spread at tips from 1 ft. 2 in. to 2 ft. 8 in., but one pair has been accredited with a length of 4 ft. 5 in., and a girth of 2 ft. or 2 ft. 1 in.! Of ewes' horns, the maximum record is a length of 1 ft. 6 in., girth 7 in., spread 1 ft. 7¾ in., although they are supposed occasionally to attain a length of 2 ft. 0 in.

Pamir Wild Sheep (*Ovis poli*)—Known also as Marco Polo's Wild Sheep. The weight of an adult ram has been estimated at about 500 lbs. The height of one has been given as 3 ft. 10 in., and Mr. Blanford measured another whose length, from horns to root of tail, is given as 4 ft. 8½ in., tail 5½ in., height at withers 3 ft. 8 in., horns 4 ft. Of horns, the maximum length recorded is 6 ft. 3 in., with girth 1 ft. 4 in., and spread at tips 4 ft. 6½ in.; and the greatest girth is 1 ft. 5⅜ in., with length 4 ft. 11½ in., and spread 3 ft. 9⅝ in.; horns, however, with a length of 4 ft. 5 in. to 5 ft. are considered good specimens. Horns of ewes are small and upright.

Oorial, or Sha (*Ovis vignei*)—The typical form, found in the Punjab and known as the Oorial, has an average height of about 2 ft. 8 in. at shoulder, whilst a variety, found in Ladak and called the Sha, attains a height of 3 ft. or upwards. Maximum length of horns 3 ft. 2⅝ in., combined with maximum girth of 1 ft. 0¼ in., and spread at tips 11¼ in. The greatest spread—1 ft. 11½ in.—accompanied a length of 2 ft. 2½ in. and girth of 9½ in. Horns of ewes are short and nearly straight.

Armenian Sheep (*Ovis gmelini*)—Height at withers, usually about 2 ft. 9 in. The British Museum possesses an extremely large head, with horns said to measure 3 ft. 6¼ in. along curve of fronto-nuchal edge; 10½ in. in basal circumference; and 5½ in.—the smallest record—in spread at tips. Other horns have been recorded as measuring 3 ft. 0¼ in., 2 ft. 6½ in., and 2 ft. 5⅝ in. in length; 2 ft. 2 in. is, however, a very good length. Maximum circumference given, 10⅝ in Maximum spread, 1 ft. 9 in.

Cyprian Sheep (*Ovis ophion*)—Of this form, which may be but a variety of the preceding and not a distinct species, the ram barely exceeds 2 ft. 2 in. in height at withers, whilst, of the few horns noted, the maximum length is 2 ft., with a girth of 8 in. and a spread of 4½ in. or less. Other lengths range down to 1 ft. 10¼ in. Greatest spread, 1 ft. 0¾ in.

Mouflon (*Ovis musimon*)—The dimensions of a living male, formerly in the Zoological Gardens of London, were recorded as 3 ft. 3 in. from nose to tail; tail 5 in.; from nose to base of horn 7 in.; ears 4 in.; neck, from posterior base of horn to abrupt angle of insertion, 8 in.; thence to base of tail 1 ft. 9 in.; height at shoulder 2 ft. 3 in. Horns range in length from 1 ft. 8 in. to 2 ft. 4 in. or 2 ft. 5 in., with a girth of 7 in. to 9 in., and a spread at tips of 5⅛ in. to 1 ft.

Bharal (*Ovis nahura*)—Approximate height of ram, 3 ft. at withers; ewe, altogether smaller. Horns measuring 2 ft. along curve, and about 11 in. in girth are considered good, but examples have been recorded ranging in length to 2 ft. 8 in.; in girth to 1 ft. 0⅝ in., and in spead at tips to 2 ft. 2⅛.

Barbary Sheep (*Ovis tragelaphus*)—Height 3 ft. or rather more. Horns—of both males and females,—which, although finely wrinkled in the young animal are almost smooth in the adult, range in length from 1 ft. 4 in. to 2 ft. 2⅜ in.; in basal girth from 7½ in. to 10¾ in., and in spread at tips from 5 in. to 1 ft. 6½ in.

Pallas's Tur (*Capra cylindricornis*)—This wild Goat of the Eastern Caucasus, known also as the Caucasian "Burhel," is said to stand about 3 ft. in height at shoulder. Horns measuring 2 ft. 7 in. along curve are considered good, although specimens have been recorded ranging in length up to 3 ft. 2¼ in. with girth 1 ft. 0½ in. The greatest girth, 1 ft. 3 in., accompanied a length of 3 ft. Greatest span at tips 1 ft. 7¾ in., with length 2 ft. 9⅝ in., and girth 1 ft.

Caucasian Tur (*Capra caucasica*)—Inhabiting the Central Caucasus, and known locally as the Ibex," yet doubtfully of a distinct species from the preceding. Horns have been recorded ranging in length from 9 in. to 3 ft. 4⅛ in., the latter being combined with the maximum girth—1 ft. 0⅝ in.—and a spread at tips of 1 ft. 3¼ in. The greatest spread—2 ft. 3⅝ in.—was found in a pair of horns 3 ft. 0⅞ in. in length.

Spanish Wild Goat (*Capra pyrenaica*)—Erroneously called an "Ibex," being more nearly related to the Turs. Said to stand about 2 ft. 2 in. in height at shoulder. Good-sized horns measure about 2 ft. in length, but specimens have been recorded ranging up to 2 ft.

7 in., this length being combined with the maximum spread of 2 ft. $2\frac{1}{2}$ in., and a girth of only $8\frac{3}{4}$ in. Maximum girth recorded $10\frac{3}{8}$ in., with length 2 ft. $3\frac{1}{2}$ in. and spread 1 ft. $7\frac{1}{2}$ in.

Persian Wild Goat (*Capra ægagrus*)—This species, termed the Pasang (*i.e.* rock-footed) by the Persians, is said to be the chief ancestor of the different breeds of domestic goats. The height of an adult male is given as 3 ft. 1 in. at shoulder. Of horns, a length of 3 ft. 4 in. along curve is considered good, although one pair of 4 ft. 5 in. has been recorded. The maximum girth—$9\frac{3}{4}$ in.—accompanied a length of 2 ft. $9\frac{5}{8}$ in., and a span of 1 ft. $2\frac{1}{2}$ in.. this span being exceeded by a pair measuring 3 ft. $3\frac{7}{8}$ in. in length, $7\frac{7}{8}$ in. in girth, and 2 ft. 3 in. from tip to tip. The *smallest* span at tips is $1\frac{1}{4}$ in., in horns of the same length as the last.

Alpine Ibex (*Capra ibex*)—The Ibex, Steinbok, or Bouquetin has now disappeared as a truly wild animal, it is therefore a matter for concern that no weights nor body-measurements appear to have been ascertained. and but four horn-measurements are to hand. One pair in the British Museum are said to measure 3 ft. $7\frac{3}{4}$ in. in length, and Mr. Rowland Ward records three as measuring respectively 2 ft. $7\frac{3}{4}$ in., 2 ft. $2\frac{3}{4}$, and 1 ft. $9\frac{1}{2}$ in. in length; $9\frac{1}{8}$ in., $8\frac{3}{8}$ in., and $8\frac{5}{8}$ in. in girth; and 1 ft. $6\frac{3}{8}$ in., 1 ft. $10\frac{1}{8}$ in., and 1 ft. $2\frac{7}{8}$ in. from tip to tip.

Himalayan Ibex (*Capra sibirica*)—The respective weights of a male and female are given as 188 lbs. and 104 lbs. The height of one male specimen was stated to be 3 ft. 4 in. at shoulder; that of a female 6 in. less. Another male was 3 ft. 2 in. in height; 4 ft. 6 in. in length of head and body; tail 8 in. Horns vary in length from 4 ft. $3\frac{1}{2}$ in. (Lydekker records a pair of upwards of 4 ft. 6 in.) to below 3 ft., the girth being from 1 ft. $0\frac{1}{2}$ in. downwards. Greatest spread, 3 ft.

Arabian Ibex (*Capra sinaitica*)—No weights nor body-measurements given, but horns range in length from 4 ft. $3\frac{1}{4}$ in. down to 3 ft. $2\frac{7}{8}$ in.; in girth from $9\frac{1}{4}$ in. to $7\frac{1}{4}$ in.; span 1 ft. $0\frac{1}{4}$ in.

Abyssinian Ibex (*Capra walie*)—No weights nor body-measurements given, but a pair of horns are said to have had a length of 2 ft. with girth $9\frac{3}{4}$ in.

Markhor (*Capra falconeri*)—Several varieties are known, but there appears to be only one species. Heights are given of 3 ft. 8 in. and 3 ft. $2\frac{1}{2}$ in. at shoulder, and lengths of horns around curve are recorded as 5 ft. 3 in., 5 ft. 1 in., 4 ft. 11 in., 4 ft., and under. Measured in a straight line, the greatest length appears to be 3 ft. $6\frac{1}{2}$ in. Greatest circumference 1 ft. $0\frac{3}{8}$ in. Span at tips from about 4 ft. 4 in. downwards.

Tahr (*Hemitragus jemlaicus*)—Males are given as weighing 200 lbs., and as standing from 3 ft. to 3 ft. 4 in. at shoulder, with a total length of 4 ft. 6 in. Greatest length of horns 1 ft $2\frac{1}{8}$ in. Greatest circumference 9 in.; span $11\frac{1}{4}$ in.

Nilgiri Goat (*Hemitragus hylocrius*)—Called "Ibex" by Indian sportsmen. Has a height of from 3 ft. 3 in. to 3 ft. 6 in. at shoulder. Greatest length of horns recorded, 1 ft. 7 in. with a girth of $9\frac{5}{8}$ in. Greatest span $7\frac{3}{8}$ in.

Goral (*Nemorhædus goral*)—Sometimes called Himalayan Chamois. Height at shoulder 2 ft. 4 in. to 3 ft.; total length 4 ft. Weight from 45 to 63 lbs. Greatest length of horns given, $11\frac{1}{4}$ in., with a perpendicular measurement of $7\frac{3}{4}$ in., a girth of $3\frac{1}{2}$ in., and a spread at tips of $6\frac{1}{2}$ in. Lengths of others are given as $8\frac{1}{2}$ in. to $7\frac{5}{8}$ in., with a much less girth and spread.

Himalayan Serow (*Nemorhœdus bubalinus*)—Called also Forest Goat. Height of one recorded as 3 ft. 2 in. at shoulder; weight as 190 lbs. Greatest length of horns recorded, 1 ft. $1\frac{1}{2}$ in. A specimen, $10\frac{1}{2}$ in. in length, had a girth of $5\frac{3}{8}$ in. and spread of $3\frac{1}{2}$ in.; $5\frac{5}{8}$ in. girth, and $5\frac{1}{4}$ in. spread are, however, recorded.

Takin (*Budorcas taxicolor*)—Height, 3 ft. 6 in. at shoulder. Of horns, the greatest length recorded is 2 ft., and a pair 1 ft. $10\frac{3}{8}$ in. had a girth of $10\frac{5}{8}$ in. and a spread at tips of 1 ft. $2\frac{3}{4}$ in.

Rocky Mountain Goat (*Haploceros montanus*)—Girth around chest after skinning, 4 ft. 8 in. Weight is given as averaging 100 lbs. Greatest length of horns given, $11\frac{1}{2}$ in.; girth $6\frac{1}{2}$ in.; spread at tips, $6\frac{1}{2}$ in.

Chamois (*Rupicapra tragus*)—Weight from 50 to 70 lbs. Greatest length of horns given, $10\frac{1}{4}$ in.; girth, $4\frac{1}{8}$ in.; spread at tips, $5\frac{1}{4}$ in

Eland (*Orias canna*)—One of the few species of Antelopes in which the horns of the cows exceed in length, though not in thickness, those of the bulls. Selous shot one 5 ft. 9 in. in height at withers. Weight 800 to 1,100 lbs.; old bulls sometimes attaining to 1,500 lbs. Maximum length of horns, according to F. Coburn, 2 ft. 10 in., combined with the maximum girth of 1 ft. $1\frac{1}{2}$ in. Greatest spread at tips recorded, 2 ft. $1\frac{1}{2}$ in.

Derbian Eland (*Orias derbianus*)—The horns of the male in this species are larger than in the preceding, but those of the cow are smaller. Sir Edmund Loder possesses a pair 2 ft. $10\frac{1}{2}$ in. in length; 1 ft. $\frac{5}{8}$ in. in girth; and 1 ft. $10\frac{3}{4}$ in. in spread at tips, but this spread has been exceeded by a pair measuring 2 ft. $5\frac{7}{8}$ in. between tips.

Kudu or **Koodoo** (*Strepsiceros kudu*)—Males may stand about 4 ft. 4 in., and even 5 ft., at shoulder. The length of body is stated to be 9 ft. Selous shot one whose horns measured, in a straight line from base to tip, 3 ft. $9\frac{3}{8}$ in.; around curve, 5 ft. $0\frac{5}{8}$ in.; basal girth, $11\frac{1}{2}$ in.; spread between tips, 2 ft. 9 in. Another pair taken by him had a length, from base to tip, of 3 ft. 5 in., with the maximum measurement around spiral turn of 5 ft. 3 in.

Lesser Kudu or **Koodoo** (*Strepsiceros*

imberbis)—Maximum measurements of different horns are: Length in straight line, 2 ft. 1½ in.; length around curve, 2 ft. 7½ in.; circumference, 6⅞ in.; spread at tips, 1 ft. 3¼ in.

Harnessed Antelope (*Tragelaphus scriptus*)—Under this designation are to be found four varieties formerly considered as species—the present, the typical variety of West, Central, and South-Central Africa; the second from Abyssinia; the third from East Africa; and the fourth, the "Bushbuck" of the Cape. Stated to stand 2 ft. 8 in. at shoulder, and to measure about 5 ft. in length. The maximum measurements recorded of different horns are: Length, 1 ft. 5⅞ in.; girth, 6⅝ in.; spread at tips, 9¼ in.

West African Harnessed Antelope (*Tragelaphus gratus*)—Height at shoulder, 3 ft. 6 in.; length from chest to rump, 3 ft. 6 in.; tail, 11½ in.; ears, 5½ in. Maximum length of horns, from a specimen in the British Museum, 1 ft. 7 in. A pair in the late Sir Victor Brooke's collection measured 1 ft. 6 in. in a straight line; 1 ft. 11½ in. around curve; 7⅞ in. in circumference, and 11¾ in. in spread at tips.

Central African Harnessed Antelope, Situtunga, or **"Nakong"** (*Tragelaphus spekei*)—Height of male at shoulder, 3 ft. 7 in. Maximum measurements of different horns are: Length around curve, 2 ft. 8⅝ in.; in straight line, 2 ft. 3 in.; girth, 8⅛ in.; spread at tips, 1 ft. 7⅜ in.

Nilgai (*Boselaphus tragocamelus*)—Height of males, 4 ft. 4 in. to 4 ft. 8 in., or even 4 ft. 10 in., at shoulder; length, 6 ft. 6 in. to 7 ft.; tail, 1 ft. 6 in. to 1 ft. 9 in. Maximum measurements of different horns are: Length, 11¾ in.; circumference, 9½ in.; spread at tips, 7¾ in.

Addax (*Addax nasomaculatus*)—Height, 3 ft. Maximum measurements of different horns: Length along curve, 2 ft. 11¾ in; length in straight line, 2 ft. 4⅜ in.; circumference, 6⅜ in.; spread at tips, 1 ft. 5⅝ in.

Gemsbok (*Oryx gazella*)—Height, 4 ft. Horns of the female usually longer than those of the male. Maximum records of different horns: Length, 3 ft. 11½ in.; circumference, 8⅜ in.; spread at tips, 1 ft. 1⅞ in.

Beisa (*Oryx beisa*)—No body-measurements nor weights appear to have been ascertained. Horns of the female, as in the preceding, longer than those of the male. Maximum measurements of different horns are: Length (female), 3 ft. 3 in.; circumference, 8⅞ in.; spread at tips, 10½ in.

Fringe-eared Oryx (*Oryx callotis*)—No body-measurements nor weights appear to have been recorded. Maximum measurements of different horns are: Length, 2 ft. 6½ in.; girth, 7⅛ in.; spread at tips, 1 ft. 1 in.

Sabre-horned Antelope (*Oryx leucoryx*)—No body-measurements nor weights are to hand. The longest horns recorded are a pair in the British Museum with a length of 3 ft. 3⅝ in.; girth, 4⅞ in.; spread at tips, 1 ft. 2⅛ in. Shorter horns, however, have measured 5½ in. in girth, with a less spread.

Roan Antelope (*Hippotragus equinus*)—Height at shoulder, 4 ft. 6 in. Maximum measurements of different horns: Length, 3 ft. 6 in.; girth, 10½ in.; spread at tips, 1 ft. 2 in.

Sable Antelope (*Hippotragus niger*)—Height at shoulder, 4 ft. 6 in.; extreme length nearly 9 ft.; tail, 2 ft. 1 in.; ears, 10 in. Maximum measurements of different horns: Length, 3 ft. 10 in.; girth, 10½ in.; spread at tips, 1 ft. 7½ in.

Springbuck (*Gazella euchore*)—Height, 2 ft. 6 in. Maximum measurements of different horns: Length on curve, 1 ft. 3¼ in.; girth, 7 in.; spread at tips, 5⅞ in.; widest span inside, 8½ in.

Dorcas Gazelle (*Gazella dorcas*)—Height at shoulder, about 2 ft. Of different horns, the maximum measurements recorded are: Length, 1 ft. 1¼ in.; girth, 4¼ in.; spread at tips, 4¾ in.

Indian Gazelle or **Ravine Deer** (*Gazella bennetti*)—Height at shoulder, 2 ft. 2 in. Of different horns, the maximum measurements are: Length, 1 ft. 2¼ in.; girth, 4⅝ in.; spread at tips, 7⅞ in.

Swift Gazelle (*Gazella mohr*)—Height at shoulder, 2 ft. 6 in.; at croup, 2 ft. 8 in.; length, from nose to root of tail, 4 ft. 2 in.; head, from nose to root of horn, 7 in.; tail, without terminal tuft, 7 in. The longest horns—those of a female—are 1 ft. in length, 3¼ in. in girth, and 5⅛ in. from tip to tip.

Clarke's Antelope (*Ammodorcas clarkei*)—Several specimens of this new (1891) Antelope have been procured, but it is much to be regretted that no sportsman appears to have taken the trouble to ascertain the body-measurements or weights. Maximum measurements of different horns: Length, 11¾ in.; girth, 5 in.; spread at tips, 5⅛ in.

Waller's Antelope or **Gerenuk** (*Lithocranius walleri*)—No body-measurements nor weights to hand. Of different horns, the maximum measurements are: Length, 1 ft. 3⅜ in.; girth, 5⅞ in.; spread at tips, 6 in.

Thibetan Antelope or **Chiru** (*Pantholops hodgsoni*)—Height at shoulder, 2 ft. 11 in. Of different horns, the maximum measurements are: Length, 2 ft. 4½ in.; girth, 5⅞ in.; spread at tips, 1 ft. 4½ in.

Saiga Antelope (*Saiga tartarica*)—No body-measurements nor weights are given except of a skeleton, which is said to stand 2 ft. 7¾ in. at shoulder, and to measure 3 ft. 2 in. along "spinal cord." Maximum measurements of different horns: Length, 1 ft. 2⅜ in.; girth, 5⅜ in.; spread at tips, 5⅝ in.

Impala Antelope (*Æpyceros melampus*)—Height about 3 ft. Maximum measurements of different horns: Length, 1 ft. 9½ in.; around bend, 2 ft. 3½ in.; circumference, 6 in.; spread at tips, 1 ft. 5⅝ in.; widest outside, 1 ft. 8 in.

Black-buck or **Indian Antelope** (*Antilope cervicapra*)—The height at shoulder is given as 2 ft. 8 in., and the average weight as 85 lbs.; the size, however, varies considerably in different localities, the smallest variety being found in Mysore, where, according to Sanderson, horns average 1 ft. 2 in. in length and rarely exceed 1 ft. 6 in., although, in other parts of India, the average length is 2 ft. 2 in. or 2 ft. 3 in. Maximum measurements of different horns: Length in straight line, 2 ft. 4¼ in.; around curve, 3 ft. 4½ in.; circumference, 5⅞ in.; spread at tips, 1 ft. 9¾ in.

Reedbuck (*Cervicapra arundineum*)—Height about 2 ft. Maximum measurements of different horns: Length, 1 ft. 3⅞ in.; girth, 7⅜ in.; spread at tips, 1 ft. 2⅜ in.

Water-Buck (*Cobus ellipsiprymnus*)—Height, 4 ft. Maximum measurements of different horns: Length, 2 ft. 9½ in.; girth, 9⅝ in.; spread at tips, 2 ft. 1½ in.

Sing-sing Antelope (*Cobus defassus*)—Height at shoulder is given as 3 ft. 9¾ in.; length, rump to front of shoulder, 4 ft. 4 in.; head, from between horns to tip of muzzle, 1 ft. 1½ in.; tail, 1 ft. 4 in.; ears, from 1 ft. 8 in. to 2 ft. Maximum measurements of different horns: Length, 2 ft. 3⅜ in.; girth, 8⅝ in.; spread at tips, 1 ft. 9⅜ in.

Rhebok (*Pelea capreola*)—Height about 2 ft. 6 in. Maximum measurements of different horns: Length, 8⅝ in.; girth, 2½ in.; spread at tips, 3½ in.

Klipspringer (*Oreotagus saltator*)—Height, 1 ft. 10 in. Maximum measurements of different horns: Length, 4⅜ in.; girth, 2½ in.; spread at tips, 3¼ in.

Steinbuck (*Nanotragus campestris*)—Height, 1 ft. 11 in. The largest horns are recorded as 5⅜ in. in length and 2 in. in girth, with 1¾ in. spread at tips, this spread being often exceeded, however, by smaller horns, the maximum being 2⅝ in.

Kirk's Antelope (*Neotragus kirki*)—Measurements of the female only are to hand, which are: Length of head, 4½ in.; of ear, 2¼ in.; of body and neck, 1 ft. 1 in.; of fore-leg from elbow-joint, 7⅓ in.; hind-leg from knee, 10 in.; hind-foot from heel, 6¼ in. Weight only a few pounds. The short horns are only 2 in. to 3 in. in length, about 1½ in. in girth, and 1½ in. to nearly 2 in. in spread at tips.

Duikerbok (*Cephalolophus grimmi*)—Although it is supposed that only the males are horned, yet Mr. Selous has met with three examples of horned females. Height about 2 ft. 2 in. Maximum measurements of different horns: Length, 5⅜ in.; girth, 2½ in.; spread at tips, 3 in.

Four-Horned Antelope or **Chousingha (Charsingha)** (*Tetraceros quadricornis*)—Height of male, about 2 ft. 2 in. at shoulder, and slightly higher at croup. The remarkable horns, which are only found in the male, have greater length in the posterior than in the anterior pairs. Maximum measurements of different horns are: Of the posterior pair, length, 4¾ in.; girth, 3 in.; spread at tips, 3 in. Of the anterior pair, 2½ in., 2⅜ in. and 2⅞ in. respectively.

White-Tailed Wildebeest or **Gnu** (*Connochœtes gnu*)—Height, 4 ft. 6 in. at shoulder. Maximum measurements of different horns: Length, 1 ft. 10⅜ in.; breadth of palm, 10⅝ in.; spread at tips, 1 ft. 6⅝ in.; width inside, 1 ft. 11⅛ in.

Blue or **Brindled Wildebeest** or **Gnu** (*Connochœtes taurina*)—Maximum measurements of different horns: Length, 2 ft. 2⅛ in.; breadth of palm, 9⅞ in.; girth, 1 ft. 2½ in.; spread at tips, 1 ft. 7½ in.; width inside, 2 ft. 4½ in.

Hartebeest (*Bubalis caama*)—Height, 4 ft. Maximum measurements of different horns: Length, 2 ft. 0¾ in.; girth, 11½ in.; spread at tips, 10⅜ in.

Hunter's Hartebeest (*Bubalis hunteri*)—Height, 4 ft.; length of body, 4 ft.; of tail, 1 ft. 3 in.; of ears, 6 in. Maximum measurements of different horns: Length, around curve, 2 ft. 2¼ in.; in straight line, 1 ft. 10 in.; girth, 8⅜ in.; spread at tips, 1 ft. 4 in.

Tsessebe, Sassabi or **Bastard Hartebeest** (*Bubalis lunatus*)—Height, 3 ft. 10 in. to 4 ft. Maximum measurements of different horns: Length, 1 ft. 3⅝ in.; girth, 8⅛ in.; spread at tips, 1 ft. 1⅝ in.

Blesbok (*Bubalis albifrons*)—Height about 3 ft. 2 in. Maximum measurements of different horns: Length, 1 ft. 6¼ in.; girth, 6½ in.; spread at tips, 1 ft. 0¼ in.

Bontebok (*Bubalis pygargus*)—Height, 3 ft. to 4 ft. Maximum horn measurements, which are those of one pair in the British Museum, are: Length, 1 ft. 4⅜ in.; girth, 6¾ in.; spread at tips, 9⅛ in.

Prong-horned Antelope (*Antilocapra americana*)—Height about 2 ft. 10 in. at shoulder, and 3 ft. or rather more at croup. Length of tail, 3 in. Weight, about 80 lbs. clean. Maximum measurements of different horns: Length, 1 ft. 5 in.; with spread, 1 ft. 8 in.: girth, 6½ in.

Giraffe (*Giraffa camelopardalis*)—Height of males, 18 ft. to 19 ft. to crown of head; females about 2 ft. less. Horns, a few inches in length.

Red Deer (*Cervus elaphus*)—Height of a good stag, 4 ft. at shoulder. Weights of Scotch specimens range from 280 to 420 lbs., but one killed at Woburn sixty years ago weighed 476 lbs. = 34 stone. Greater weights are, however, attained by stags of Eastern and Northern Asia. Maximum measurements of different antlers: Greatest length around outside, 5 ft. 8 in., with a spread inside of 5 ft. 5 in.; this pair had forty-four points, and their weight was 74 lbs.; they were from Central Europe, probably Austria. The greatest spread, however—6 ft. 3$\frac{6}{10}$ in.—has been attained by a pair now in the King of Saxony's collection at Moritzburg, whose history dates back to 1586. Some of the prehistoric stags had antlers which carried astounding numbers of points, ranging from that given above to sixty-six. Between 1611 and 1656, the Elector of Saxony killed 24,563 stags, ranging from one of thirty points to 1,192 of fourteen, of which the heaviest stag weighed 61 st. 11 lbs.; 59 exceeded 56 stone; 651 exceeded 48 stone; 2,679 exceeded 40 stone; and 4,139 exceeded 32 stone. Since that time, the deterioration of the German stags has been as marked as that of the British. In Northern Hungary, and in the Carpathian Alps, stags are still sometimes met with of the clean weight of from 35 to 40 stone.

Of British stags, two only are recorded which carried twenty points; one (11 + 9) which was alive in Ireland, and the property of the late Sir Victor Brooke, and the other (10 + 10) shot by Lord Burton, in 1893, in the forest of Glen Quoich, Scotland.

Kashmir Stag or **Hangul** (*Cervus cashmirianus*)—Height, 4 ft. 4 in. The weight of one is given as 400 lbs. as shot. Maximum measurements of different antlers: Length, 4 ft. 7 in.; girth, 8 in.; spread, from tip to tip, 2 ft. 11 in.; width inside, 4 ft. 1 in. A pair recorded by the late Sir Victor Brooke had sixteen points.

Sikkim Stag or **Shou** (*Cervus affinis*)—Height up to 5 ft. Maximum measurements of different antlers: Length, 4 ft. 7$\frac{3}{4}$ in.; girth, 9$\frac{1}{8}$ in; spread between tips, 3 ft. 3$\frac{1}{4}$ in.; width inside, 3 ft. 9$\frac{3}{4}$ in. Greatest number of points, thirteen.

Wapiti (*Cervus canadensis*)—This, which is called in America, of course erroneously, the "Elk," attains large proportions, and is probably not specifically distinct from the Asiatic Thian Shan Stag and its varieties. Height of stags from 5 ft. 4 in. to 5 ft. 8 in. Length, from tip of nose to tail, 9 ft.; girth of body over heart, 6 ft. 8 in.; weight, from 700 to 1,000 lbs. Williamson, however, records the abnormal weight of 1,200 lbs. Maximum measurements of different antlers: Length along beam, 5 ft. 5 in. (right), 5 ft. 4 in. (left); girth, 1 ft. 4$\frac{1}{2}$ in. (but ?, 12 in. being an abnormal girth measurement between bez and trez); spread between tips, 4 ft. 1$\frac{7}{8}$ in.; width inside, 5 ft. 1 in. Greatest number of points, twenty-five.

Japanese Deer (*Cervus sika*)—No body-measurements nor weights are to hand. Maximum measurements, which are those of one pair of horns: Length, 2 ft. 7$\frac{1}{4}$ in.; girth, 5$\frac{1}{4}$ in.; spread between tips, 2 ft. 3$\frac{1}{8}$ in.; width inside, 2 ft. 3$\frac{3}{8}$ in. Greatest number of points recorded, sixteen.

Axis, Indian Spotted Deer, or **Chital** (*Cervus axis*)—Height very variable, that of a buck in Northern or Central India being from 3 ft. to 3 ft. 2 in., whilst in Southern India the height attained is from 2 ft. 6 in. to 2 ft. 8 in.; weight, about 145 lbs. Maximum measurements of different antlers: Length, 3 ft. 2$\frac{3}{4}$ in.; girth, 6$\frac{1}{2}$ in; spread between tips, 2 ft. 6$\frac{1}{2}$ in. Greatest number of points, twelve.

Sambar (*Cervus unicolor*)—Height, 4 ft. 6 in.; weight of large specimens, 600 to 700 lbs. Maximum measurements of different antlers: Length around outside, 3 ft. 10$\frac{1}{2}$ in.; girth above brow-tine, 7$\frac{7}{8}$ in.; spread between tips, 3 ft. 8$\frac{7}{8}$ in.; width inside, 3 ft. 9$\frac{7}{8}$ in. Greatest number of points, thirteen, but, in nine-tenths of the specimens recorded, the number is 3 + 3.

Hog Deer (*Cervus porcinus*)—Height, from 2 ft. to 2 ft. 3 in; total length, 4 ft.; weight as shot, 96 lbs. Maximum measurements of different antlers: Length, 1 ft. 9 in.; girth above brow-tine, 3$\frac{1}{2}$ in.; spread between tips, 1 ft. 6$\frac{3}{4}$ in.

Swamp Deer (*Cervus duvauceli*)—Height of bucks, 3 ft. 8 in. to 3 ft. 10 in; weight of large specimens, up to 570 lbs., *i.e.* 40 st. 10 lbs. Maximum measurements of different antlers: Length around outside, 3 ft. 5 in.: girth, 5$\frac{3}{4}$ in.; spread between tips, 3 ft. 2$\frac{3}{8}$ in; width inside, 3 ft. 1$\frac{1}{2}$ in. Greatest number of points, fourteen.

Fallow Deer (*Cervus dama*)—Height, about 3 ft. Length: head and body, 4 ft.; tail, including hair, 1 ft. 2 in.; caudal vertebræ, 9 in.; head, 1 ft. 0$\frac{1}{2}$ in.; ear, 6$\frac{1}{2}$ in. Maximum measurements of different antlers: Length, 2 ft. 4$\frac{5}{8}$ in.; girth, 4$\frac{3}{8}$ in.; width of palm, 6 in.; spread between tips, 2 ft. 2 in.; width inside, 2 ft. 2 in. Greatest number of points, twenty-two.

Indian Muntjac, Barking Deer, or **Kakar** (*Cervulus muntjac*) — Height, from 1 ft. 8 in. to 1 ft. 10 in. Average length of antlers, 3 in. or 4 in. on pedicels of 4 in. or 5 in.; but a maximum length of 11 in. is said to have been attained.

Reindeer or **Caribou** (*Rangifer tarandus*)—Notwithstanding the constantly reiterated opinions of sportsmen as to the specific distinctions between the Old World Reindeer and the New World Reindeer or Caribou, whether Woodland or Barren-ground, it will be better to consider that there is but one species, variable in size and coloration according to geographical distribution. Curiously, no body-measurements nor weights of the Old World form appear to have been recorded, but those of a "Woodland Caribou" bull are: Length from nose to root of tail, 6 ft. 7 in; height at shoulder, 4 ft. 5 in.; height behind saddle on rump, 4 ft. 7 in.; girth behind forelegs, 5ft. 1 in.; length of neck (along top), 1 ft. 5 in.; weight (estimated), 400 lbs. Of the horns—which, unlike those of other deer, are borne by the female as well as by the male—the maximum length is given as 5 ft. Maximum girth, 7$\frac{1}{4}$ in.; spread between tips, 3 ft. 4 in.; widest inside, 4 ft. 0$\frac{5}{8}$ in. Greatest number of points, 20 + 27 = 47; this in a New World specimen in the British Museum. Norwegian antlers, which appear to be smaller, have attained 32 points, and their measurements, in the order given above, are 3 ft. 2⅜ in.; 5⅜ in.; 1 ft. 9¾ in.; and 2 ft. 6⅛ in.

Elk or **Moose** (*Alces machlis*)—This, the greatest of all living deer, known in the Old World as the Elk, and in the New World as Moose, sometimes attains a height of 18 hands or more. Average body-measurements of Scandinavian specimens over seven years old are—Height at withers, 5 ft. 8 in. to 9 in.; at quarters, 5 ft. 5 in. to 6 in.; from ground to belly, 3 ft. 4 in. Length, from crest to tail, 9 ft. 5 in.; crest to nose, 2 ft. 5 in. Greatest girth, 6 ft. 11 in. to 7 ft.; around thigh, 3 ft; around forearm, 1 ft. 11 in. Weight (uncleaned), estimated as occasionally exceeding 1,400 lbs. The horn-measurements of one Scandinavian example are: Height of horns from tip of central brow point to tip of highest back point, 3 ft. 1 in.; height of palmation, exclusive of said points, 2 ft. 6¼ in.; 2 ft. 5 in.; curve of inner edge of horns, from coronet to tip of inside back points, 2 ft. 0½ in.; between tips of inner back points, 1 ft. 11¾ in.; between inner brow points, 11½ in.; between tips of fifth points on either side, following curve and across brow, 4 ft. 5⅞ in.; the same measurement, taut, 3 ft. 5¾ in.; across skull at brow, 7½ in.; fifth point (right), 6¼ in.; fifth point (left), 7¾ in.; around coronet, 10¼ in.; around base of horn, 6$\frac{7}{10}$ in. Maximum measurements of various other European antlers are:—Length of longest tine, 2 ft. 8 in.; girth above burr, 7½ in.; spread between tips, 3 ft. 4 in; greatest width, 4 ft. 1⅞ in.; breadth of palm, 1 ft. 0½ in. Number of points, twenty-four. A pair of antlers, which appear to have no parallel, are of the American variety, and are stated to have attained a spread, from tip to tip, of 5 ft. 6 in.; and another abnormal pair, which were but an inch less in spread, measured 3 ft. 5 in. along palmation, with a corresponding width of 2 ft. The next greatest measurements of different antlers (American) are: Length, to longest tine, 3 ft. 3½ in., with girth above burr, 8½ in. Spread between tips, 3ft. 6in. Greatest width, 4 ft. 11¼ in. Breadth of palm, 1 ft. 8 in. Maximum number of points, twenty-seven.

Roe Deer (*Capreolus caprea*)—Height, 2 ft. 2 in. Weight of buck, about 60 lbs. Maximum length of horns, 1 ft. 3 in. (Austria); anything over 9 in. is, however, exceptional, and the next largest pair recorded—from Dorsetshire—have a length of 9⅞ in., a girth of 5 in., and a spread of 5 in. between tips, the last measurement being exceeded by 1 in. in another pair, also from Dorsetshire.

Pampas Deer (*Cariacus campestris*)—Height, about 2 ft. 6 in. Maximum measurements of different horns: length, 1 ft. 2⅝ in. Girth, 3⅞ in. Spread between tips, 1 ft. 2¼ in. Points, normally six.

Virginian or **White-Tailed Deer** (*Cariacus virginianus*)—Very variable in size. Weight, 180 lbs. to 200 lbs. Maximum measurements of different antlers: Length of one antler in British Museum, 2 ft. 3⅝ in., with girth, 5⅜ in., exceeded in last measurement by a pair, 5⅝ in. Greatest spread between tips, 1 ft. 2½ in. Widest inside, 1 ft. 7⅞ in. Points, fifty-two.

Mule-Deer (*Cariacus macrotis*)—Often called, in Colorado, the "Black-tail," which can only be properly applied to the next species. No actual body-measurements nor weights are given. Maximum measurements of different antlers: Length, 2 ft. 8 in. Girth, 6¾ in. Spread between tips, 2 ft. 3⅜ in. Width inside, 3 ft. 5 in. Points, thirty-three.

Black-Tailed Deer (*Cariacus columbianus*)—Weight, about 200 lbs. Maximum measurements of different antlers: Length, 2 ft. 4⅝ in. Girth, 5½ in. Spread between tips, 1 ft. 9⅜ in. Width inside, 2 ft. 2 in. Points, twenty.

There are many small deer, such as the Musk and the Chevrotains, characterised by the replacement of horns by tusks, which may be passed over here, as, indeed, may be the camels, which are only found in a semi-wild state, or escaped from an ancient captivity.

Guanaco (*Lama guanacus*)—Height of full-grown male, about 4ft. Length, from 7 ft. to 8 ft.

Wild Pig or **Wild Boar** (*Sus scrofa*)—Whether the European Wild Boar is specifically distinct from the Indian is rather a vexed question, but Mr. Lydekker, who is an accomplished biologist, and in the best position for judging, inclines to that belief; it is, therefore, to the former that the following measurements belong:—Height, about 3 ft. 5 in. Extreme weight, 600 lbs. Maximum length of tusk round outside edge, 11½ in.

Indian Wild Pig or **Boar** (*Sus cristatus*)—Height, from 2 ft. 6 in. to 3 ft. 4 in. (one of 3 ft. 7½ in) at shoulder. Weight, from 200 lbs. to 300 lbs., or over. Maximum lengths of tusks of lower jaw, 10 in. and 1 ft.; girth, about 2½ in.

There are certain other pigs, such as the Red Bush Pig, the Babirusa, &c., the length of whose tusks sometimes exceeds 1 ft. 2 in., and the Wart-Hogs and Peccaries, which lead to the—

Hippopotamus (*Hippopotamus amphibius*)—Height at shoulder, about 3 ft. 8 in. An old male, measured by Sir Samuel Baker, was 14 ft. 3 in. from snout to end of tail, this being about 9 in. Weight of fresh hide, about 5 cwt. One of a length of 12 ft., kept in confinement, weighed about 4 tons. Maximum tusk-measurements: Length around outside curve, 2 ft. 7⅝ in. Girth, 9½ in. Weight of a large pair, 15 lbs.

Malayan Tapir (*Tapirus indicus*)—Height at shoulder, 3 ft. to 3 ft. 6 in.; at croup, about

4 in. more. Length from snout to root of tail, along curves, about 8 ft.

South American Tapir (*Tapirus americanus*)—No measurements nor weights to hand.

Indian Rhinoceros (*Rhinoceros unicornis*)—Height at shoulder, 5 ft. 9 in. Length, head and body, 10 ft. 6 in.; tail, 2 ft. 5 in. Girth at chest, 9 ft. 8 in., of forearm, 3 ft. 2 in. Horn-measurements: Jerdon mentions one 2 ft. in length, and there is one in the British Museum 1 ft. 7⅛ in. in length, and 1 ft. 10⅜ in. in girth.

Javan or **Lesser One-horned Rhinoceros** (*Rhinoceros sondaicus*)—Sterndale gives the height at shoulder as 5 ft. 6 in.; length, head and body, 12 ft. 3 in., including tail of 2 ft. 4½ in. Horn of one in British Museum measures: Length, 10⅝ in.; girth, 1 ft. 7⅝ in.

Sumatran Rhinoceros (*Rhinoceros sumatrensis*)—Height at shoulder, 4 ft. to 4 ft. 6 in.; length, tip of snout to root of tail, 8 ft.; weight, about 2,000 lbs. Maximum length of anterior horn, 2 ft. 8⅛ in., with girth, 1 ft. 5⅝ in. The posterior horn is often very small, not more than 2 in. or 3 in.

African Rhinoceros (*Rhinoceros bicornis*)—Sir Samuel Baker and Selous state that the males may attain a height of from 5 ft. 6 in. to 5 ft. 8 in. at shoulder. An adult female stood 4 ft. 8½ in.; length, tip of snout to root of tail, 4 ft. 11½ in.; tail, 1 ft. 9½ in. Maximum measurements of anterior horn: Length, 3 ft. 7 in. and 3 ft. 8 in.; girth, 2 ft. 2¼ in. Posterior horn: Length, 1 ft. 7½ in.; girth, 1 ft. 8½ in.

White or **Burchell's Rhinoceros** (*Rhinoceros simus*)—Height at shoulder, maximum 6 ft. 6 in. One, a male, mentioned at p. 329, P.Z.S. 1894, measured 6 ft. 1½ in. at the withers; length between uprights, 12 ft. 1 in.; from lip along base of horns up between ears and following curves of back to root of tail, 13 ft.; to tip of tail, 15 ft. 8½ in.; girth behind shoulders, 10 ft. 3½ in.; round fore-arm, 3 ft. 4½ in.; the width of the lip between the greatest depth of the nostrils is just under 12 in.; anterior horn measures 2 ft. 3 in. Maximum length of anterior horn, now in British Museum, 4 ft. 8½ in., with girth, 1 ft. 11½ in. Others measure 3 ft. 8 in., with girth, 1 ft. 8 in.; 3 ft. 6¾ in., with girth, 2 ft. 1⅜ in. Posterior horns are noted of 1 ft. 5⅞ in. length.; maximum girth, 1 ft. 7¼ in.

Passing over the **Tarpan** or **Wild Horse** of Central Asia we come to—

Zebra (*Equus zebra*)—Height at withers, 4 ft. to 4 ft 2 in.

Burchell's Zebra (*Equus burchelli*)—Height, 4 ft. 4 in. to 4 ft. 6 in.

The **Quagga** and the **Wild Asses** may be passed over. There remain the two largest of beasts.

Indian Elephant (*Elephas indicus*)—Average height of adult male, about 9 ft.; of adult female, 8 ft. A first-class "Koomeriah" or thorough-bred, which was probably sixty years of age, is stated by Sanderson to have measured 9 ft. 2 in. at shoulder. Sterndale gives 10 ft. 7½ in. as the maximum authentic record, but a specimen killed by the late Sir Victor Brooke is said to have stood 11 ft.; and for another, whose skeleton now stands 11 ft. 3 in. in the Museum at Calcutta, an original height of 12 ft. is claimed, the same height being also attributed to a Ceylon example. An elephant's height is normally double the girth of its forefoot. The length of an animal, which stood 9 ft. 7 in. at shoulder, is given by Sanderson as 26 ft. 2½ in. from tip of trunk to tip of tail. The weight of an adult specimen does not appear to have been recorded, but a young male at the Zoological Gardens in 1881, whose height was 8 ft., weighed 2 tons, 17 cwt., 1 qr., 23 lbs.; and another, 7 ft. 6 in. in height, weighed 2 tons, 11 cwt., 0 qr., 23 lbs. The maximum tusk-measurements pertain to the only perfect tusk of the fine animal killed by Sir V. Brooke: Total length, outside curve, 8 ft., *i.e.* outside socket, 5 ft. 9 in., inside socket, 2 ft. 3 in.; greatest girth, 1 ft. 4$\frac{9}{10}$ in.; weight, 90 lbs.

Greater weights have, however, been attained; a tusk of 6 ft. in length is stated to have weighed 100 lbs., and others, from the Garo Hills, are said to have reached 155 lbs. and 157 lbs. respectively.

African Elephant (*Elephas africanus*)—The dimensions and weight of a male specimen, killed by H.R.H. the Duke of Coburg, are given as: Height at withers, 10 ft.; length, from tip of trunk to tip of tail, 23 ft. 5 in.; from crown of head to tip of trunk, 11 ft. 3 in.; girth, 16 ft. 6 in.; girth of head, 10 ft.; from ear to ear, 9 ft.; length of ear, 4 ft. 6 in; entire weight, 4 tons, 8 cwt., 4 lbs. Of another male, killed by Sir John Kirk, the dimensions were: Height, 10 ft. 3 in.; total length, 25 ft. 2 in.; crown of head to tip of trunk, 9 ft.; tail, 4 ft. 2 in.; maximum girth, 18 ft.; girth of fore-foot, 5 ft. 1 in.; width of ear, 3 ft.; length, 5 ft. 9 in. The respective dimensions of two elephants, shot by Selous and Jameson are given as: Height at shoulder, 10 ft. and 10 ft. 4 in.; length of ear, 5 ft. 5 in. and 5 ft. 6½ in.; breadth, 3 ft. 3 in. and 3 ft. 4 in.; girth of fore-foot, 4 ft. 4½ in. and 4 ft. 7½ in. The renowned "Jumbo" stood 11 ft. at withers, and weighed 6 tons, 10 cwt.; and even this height is exceeded by one recorded in the *Museum of Natural History*, whose height is given as 12 ft.

The dimensions and weight of a baby elephant, aged one hour, are stated to have been: Height at shoulder, 2 ft. 10½ in.; length of trunk, 1 ft.; tail, 1 ft. 8 in.; girth at thorax, 3 ft. 9 in.; at abdomen, 4 ft. 1 in.; at base of trunk, 9 in.; of fore-foot, 1 ft 5 in.; weight, 213 lbs.

Maximum tusks recorded: Length of one, 9 ft. 5 in.; and 1 ft. 10½ in. in girth, which weighed 184 lbs.; weight, 173 lbs.; but this weight is said to have been exceeded by a tusk weighing 188 lbs The next weights are 172; 160; 110; and 103 lbs., of the three last of which the respective lengths and girths are 9 ft. 4 in. and 1 ft. 8½ in.; 9 ft. 4 in. and 1 ft. 6 in.; 7 ft. 9 in. and 1 ft. 7 in. The length of 20 ft. 9 in. given for a tusk by Gordon Cumming must be a mistake, inasmuch as its weight was but 173 lbs., and this is shown to be exceeded by other tusks, not half its length. Weight of cows' tusks, 12 to 14 lbs.

MONTAGU BROWNE.

Bibliography—AFRICA—*Wild Beasts and their Ways*, Sir S. Baker (Macmillan). **North**: *Short Stalks*, E. N. Buxton (Stanford); *Western Barbary*, J. H. Drummond Hay (Murray). Soudan: *Life with the Hamran Arabs*, A. B. R. Myers (Smith, Elder). **West**: *Travel and Adventure in the Congo Free State*. "Bula n'Zan" (H. Bailey) (Chapman & Hall). **East**: *East Africa and its Big Game*, Capt. Sir J. C. Willoughby (Longmans); *Through Masai Land*, Jas. Thomson; *Seventeen Trips through Somaliland*, Capt. H. G. C. Swayne (Rowland Ward); *Lion Hunting in Somaliland*, Capt. C. J. Melliss (Chapman & Hall); *The Nile Tributaries of Abyssinia*, Sir S. Baker (Macmillan). **South**: *African Hunting and Adventure from Natal to the Zambesi*, W. C. Baldwin (Bentley); *Gun and Camera in Southern Africa*, H. A. Bryden (Stanford); *Kloof and Karroo, Sport, Legend, and Natural History in Cape Colony*, H. A. Bryden (Longmans); *Five Years' Hunting Adventures in South Africa*, R. Gordon Cumming (Simpkin, Marshall); *Travels into the Interior of Africa* (1796), John Barrow; *Lake Ngami*, C. J. Anderson (Hurst & Blackett); *A Breath from the Veldt*, J. G. Millais (Sotheran); *In Haunts of Wild Game*, F. V. Kirby (Blackwood); *The Sportsman in South Africa*, J. A. Nicolls and W. Eglington (Simpkin, Marshall); *A Hunter's Wanderings in Africa*, F. C. Selous (Bentley). *Travel and Adventures in South-East Africa*, F. C. Selous (Rowland Ward); *Portraits of the Game and Wild Animals of Southern Africa*, W. Cornwallis Harris; *Wild Sports of Southern Africa*, W. Cornwallis Harris; *Men, Mines, and Animals in South Africa*, Lord Randolph Churchill (Sampson Low); *The Okavango River*, C. J. Anderson (Hurst & Blackett); *The Hunter's Arcadia*, Parker Gillmore (Chapman).

AMERICA—**North British**: *On Snow Shoes to the Barren Grounds*, C. Whitney (Osgood McIlvaine); *Sport, Travel, and Adventure in Newfoundland and the West Indies*, Capt. W. R. Kennedy (Blackwood); *The Barren Ground of Northern Canada*, Warburton Pike (Macmillan); *Ten Years' Wild Sports in Foreign Lands*, H. W. Seton-Karr (Chapman & Hall); *A Sportsman's Eden*, C. Phillipps-Wolley (Bentley); *Saskatchewan, and the Rocky Mountains*, Earl of Southesk (Edinburgh: Edmondston); *Caribou Shooting in Newfoundland*, S. T. Davis (Lancaster, Pennsyl.). **United States**: *Sport and Photography in the Rocky Mountains*, A. Williamson (Edinburgh: Douglas); *Camps in the Rockies*, W. A. Baillie-Grohman (Sampson Low); *The Antelope and Deer of America*, J. D. Caton (New York: Hurd); *On the Frontier*, J. S. Campion (Chapman & Hall); *Three Years' Hunting and Trapping*, J. Turner-Turner (Maclure & Co.); *Life in the Backwoods*, J. Turner-Turner (London: Stereoscopic Co.); *The Hunting Grounds of the Great West*, R. T. Dodge (Chatto); *The Big Game of North America*, various authors, edited by G. O. Shields (Chicago: Rand, McNally); *Cruisings in the Cascades*, G. O. Shields (Chicago: Rand, McNally); *Hunting in the Great West*, ed. G. O. Shields, (Chicago: Rand, McNally); *The Camp-Fires of the Everglades*, C. E. Whitehead (Edinburgh: Douglas); *American Big Game Hunting*, various authors, edited by T. Roosevelt and G. B. Grinnell (Edinburgh: Douglas); *The Wilderness Hunter*, T. Roosevelt (Putnam); *Hunting Trips of a Ranchman*, T. Roosevelt (Putnam). **South**: *Sporting Sketches in South America*, Admiral Kennedy (Porter); *The Naturalist in La Plata*, W. H. Hudson (Chapman & Hall); *Wanderings in South America*, C. Waterton (Nelson). Nicaragua: *A Ride across a Continent*, F. Boyle (Bentley).

ARCTIC REGIONS—*Yachting in the Arctic Seas*, J. Lamont (Chatto); *Seasons with the Sea-horses*, J. Lamont (Hurst and Blackett); *Fridtiof Nansen* (1861–1893), W. C. Brögger and W. Rolfsen (Longmans); *The Big Game of North America*, ed. G. O. Shields (Chicago; Rand, McNally); *Farthest North*, F. Nansen (Constable).

ASIA—**Asia Minor**: *Short Stalks*, E. N. Buxton (Stanford). **Northern**: *The Cruise of the Marchesa to Kamschatka*, F. H. H. Guillemard (Murray); **Southern**: *The Large and Small Game of Bengal and the Northern Provinces of India*, Capt. J. H. Baldwin (King); *Thirty Years of Shikar*, Sir E. Braddon (Blackwood); *Sporting Days in Southern India*, Lieut.-Col. A. Pollok (Horace Cox); *Fifty Years' Reminiscences of India*, Lieut.-Col. A. Pollok (Edward Arnold); *Sport in Burmah*, Lieut.-Col. Pollok (Chapman & Hall); *The Rifle and the Hound in Ceylon*, Sir S. W. Baker (Longmans); *The Highlands of Central India*, Capt. J. Forsyth (Chapman & Hall); *Indian Game from Quail to Tiger*, W. Rice (Allen); *Sport and Work on the Nepaul Frontier*, J. Inglis (Macmillan); *Sport on the Pamirs and Turkistan Steppes*, Major C. S. Cumberland (Blackwood); *Hindu-Koh, Wanderings and Wild Sport on and beyond the Himalayas*, Major-Gen. D. Macintyre, V.C. (Blackwood); *Large Game Shooting in Thibet, the Himalaya and Northern India*, Col. Kinloch (Thacker); *In and Beyond the Himalaya*, S. J. Stone (Edward Arnold); *The Sportsman's Manual*, Lieut.-Col. R. H. Tyacke (Calcutta: Thacker); *Thirteen Years among the Wild Beasts of India*, G. P. Sanderson (Allen); *My Indian Journal*, Col. W. Campbell (Edinburgh: Douglas); *Tiger Shooting in India*, W. Rice (Smith, Elder); *Shikar Sketches*, J. Moray Brown (Hurst & Blackett).

AUSTRALIA—*Wild Life and Adventure in the Australian Bush*, A. Nicols (Bentley); *Bush Wanderings of a Naturalist*, H. W. Wheelwright (Routledge).

EUROPE—*Field Sports of the North of Europe*, L. Lloyd (Colburn); *Scandinavian Adventures*, L. Lloyd (Bentley); *Ten Years in Sweden*, H. W. Wheelwright (Groombridge); *A Spring and Summer in Lapland* (H. W. Wheelwright (Groombridge); *Sport in the Crimea and Caucasus*, C. Phillipps-Wolley (Bentley); *Wild Spain*, A. Chapman and W. J. Buck (Gurney & Jackson); *Short Stalks*, E. N. Buxton (Stanford); *Ten Years' Wild Sports in Foreign Lands*, H. W. Seton-Karr (Chapman & Hall); *Yachting in the Arctic Seas*, J. Lamont (Chatto).

GENERAL—*Big Game Shooting* ("Badminton"), ed. C. Phillipps-Wolley (Longmans); *Short Stalks*, E. N. Buxton (Stanford); *Ten Years' Wild Sports in Foreign Lands*, H. W. Seton-Karr (Chapman); *Wild Beasts and their Ways*, Sir S. W. Baker (Macmillan)

BIG HORN (*Ovis canadensis*)—This magnificent animal ranks high from a sportsman's point of view among the Big Game of North America. Although becoming scarce elsewhere, it is still very plentiful in British Columbia, especially in the district of Sheep Creek, East Kootenay, where it is preserved by a close time and a limit on the quantity to be killed.

Probably no animal is keener of scent, sight, and hearing; often, high up the mountain side, it will spend hours upon a solitary rock gazing into the depths below where no movement escapes its notice. Most necessary is it therefore to circle widely round one which may have been sighted, and approach it only from above, and that with the greatest caution, lest a dislodged pebble should give the alarm. At certain seasons large bands of rams herd together high up the mountains; at other times most mixed bands contain at least one old ram, and occasionally two or three old rams appear to wander about by themselves.

Shooting—There are three modes of hunting these sheep. The most legitimate of these is by fair stalking, when the man who scores a fine head will have many reasons to remember the exciting climb it entailed. In some districts

BIG HORN.
Height at shoulder 3 ft. 2 in.; av. horn meas. 35 in.; max. horn meas. 45 in.

trained dogs are used, and when a ram is sighted these are laid on, quickly bringing the animal to bay on some projecting rock, where, if the dogs know their work, they will detain him until the hunter arrives within range. A ram is easily approached under these conditions, for it seems to see nothing but the dogs.

The third method entails constantly watching "Licks," whither sheep make periodical excursions, singly and in bands, from the mountain tops to gorge themselves with clay. They may remain from an hour to two days, and when killed their stomachs will be found full of nothing but the clay formed from denuded limestone, which they lick and gnaw until sometimes deep tunnels are formed in the steep cliffs large enough completely to hide six or seven sheep. The hunter standing over one of these warrens may bolt them like rabbits within two yards of him. Although many big rams may be killed at licks, it scarcely repays the time wasted in fruitless visits. In the dead of winter sheep often come into the valleys and feed off fallen fir trees. At such times they may be seen mixed with white and black tailed deer, low down on a river's bank, and I have known them approach within forty yards of an inhabited log hut.

No North American animal affords better sport, none carries a handsomer head; but it is rare to secure a fine one with perfect tips to the horns, about three inches being nearly always worn off from constant contact with rocks. It is scarcely necessary, however, to mention that the old idea of sheep leaping down precipices and alighting on their horns is one of the many fallacies long exploded.

J. TURNER-TURNER.

BIRD'S NESTING—This favourite hobby of boys, and to a lesser extent of their elders, has, on account of much real, and some imaginary, cruelty, been condemned on all sides. While considering it desirable to give some few hints on the subject of successful collecting, it is not proposed to go into the details of individual nests. The scientific interest in the pattern of eggs lies in their "protective" colouring; and at a very early stage of his rambles the collector will not fail to observe this, more especially in connection with those laid on the ground. Nor will it escape his notice that all eggs laid within hollow trees, and similar situations in which protective colouring would be of no use, are pure white, or at most faintly marked with pale red.

Apparatus—This may be of the simplest, comprising a small tin box of cotton wool (a nest of three boxes is economy of space and is recommended for whole-day excursions), a forked stick, an egg-drill which can be purchased at natural-history stores for threepence, and a blower, easily made over a gas-jet from a penny piece of fine glass-tubing. With this unpretentious equipment, added to twelve feet of knotted rope and a small bottle of clean water, the writer collected over three hundred British eggs, most within five miles of his door.

Not but that the paraphernalia can be multiplied so as to suit the longest pocket and most extravagant tastes; and there are writers on the subject who freely advocate the use of expensive climbing-spurs, field-glasses with which to survey distant nests, and mirrors to reveal the contents of nests hidden in hollow trunks. That these are adjuncts to comfort few will deny; but it is at any rate doubtful whether this elaborately equipped collector derives half the pleasure experienced from a more rough and ready mode of procedure.

Binoculars indeed may be discarded, for they merely encourage laziness; while as climbing-spurs often bring disaster to the climber and ruin to the tree, they may also be rejected in favour of a stout rope.

Method of Collecting—A keen eye and soft tread, unflagging patience and a steady hand are the qualifications of a successful collector. Given these, the rest is a matter of practice. Some slight knowledge of sites affected by the various bird-families, a sense of discrimination between the denizens of tree, hedge and ground, with some idea of the different breeding-seasons—these are the groundwork of the practical experience gained later.

A regular system should be followed at the outset. The best method is to map out a fixed area for each day's operations, and thoroughly search it each morning or evening.

To take an example: at Bexley, where the writer obtained the bulk of his collection, each day in the week was devoted to a particular ground, the chief being the north and south portions of Dartford Heath, Baldwin's Park, the dense shrubberies bordering the Cray Valley, some wild ground near Sidcup, and a thick wood, now fenced in, on Cold Blow. The intervening fields were much built over by larks and pipits.

Blowing—Each egg should be blown when taken, the only exception being an occasional "hard-set" specimen of sufficient value to take home and empty at leisure with forceps and fine crochet-hooks.

For the soft eggs, one hole only is necessary, and it should be drilled in the middle of the egg, not at either end. The shell is first carefully pierced with a clean needle, then the arrow-head of the drill is inserted and a rotary motion imparted so as to make the hole perfectly circular and clear its edge of the inner membrane. Next, stir up the yolk and white with the needle, being careful not to enlarge the hole further.

The pointed end of the blowpipe is then rested lightly in the aperture, and, on blowing gently, the mixed contents soon escape. When the shell is nearly empty, a little clean water is injected with the aid of the blowpipe and the egg is turned in every direction in such a manner that the water reaches every point in its interior.

Poisoning—The egg is then relegated to the wool-lined box; and immediately on reaching home, the collector should inject a few drops of solution of corrosive sublimate. A separate blowpipe should be used for this, and a very convenient form will be found in the pen-fillers (fitting in a glass bottle) supplied with stylographic pens. *Sucking* a short tube, the other end of which lies in corrosive sublimate, is not recommended. The final stage is the drying of the egg, hole downwards, on a clean sheet of white blotting-paper.

Varnishing and Waxing—Two further processes are advocated by many writers ere the egg finally rests in the cabinet. These are varnishing and waxing.

The first-named, imparting as it does a polish that is not, save in certain eggs, found in nature, is not desirable. One might as well decorate the white eggs with fancy patterns!

Waxing is more legitimate, since it counteracts to some extent the rapid fading of the exquisite transparent tints. It is not by any means a complicated process, consisting in the introduction of a *little* suitably tinted melting wax, the egg being revolved so that it shall dry in a coating of uniform thickness over the interior.

Stocking—When not being inspected, all eggs should be kept from the light which soon attacks their delicate colouring. The most pleasing way of stocking them is a matter of individual taste. Some prefer spending considerable sums in elaborate cabinets of many drawers with glass lids, simply resting the eggs on cotton-wool. Others paste them, hole downwards, on cardboard. In any case certain particulars should be recorded on a label corresponding with each egg (*not* gummed on the egg itself), such as species, date and locality of collection, position of nest, &c.

Should a complete *clutch* of eggs be deemed necessary, it is best, with the birds at all events (the starlings, hawks, crows, &c.) that mate for life, to remove one egg at a time and allow the hen to lay twice the usual number. In national collections, where things are done on a large scale, the whole nest is taken and preserved along with the full complement. For scientific purposes this wholesale robbery of our woodlands may be perfectly legitimate; for private collectors, however, having no other purpose to serve than to acquire a representative collection, with the accompaniment of much pleasant outdoor rambling, it should be tabooed.

It is this very tampering with the nest that has cost the birds so much time and labour and skill that has brought bird's nesting into such disrepute.

F. G. Aflalo.

Bibliography—F. A. Capen, *Oology of New England*; O. Davie, *Nest and Eggs of North American Birds*; C. Dixon, *Nests and Eggs of British Birds* (Chapman & Hall, 1894); R. Kearton, *Birds' Nests, Eggs, and Egg Collecting* (Cassell, 1890), and *British Birds' Nests* (Cassell, 1895); Rev. F. O. Morris, *Nests and Eggs of British Birds* (Bell); R. Bowdler Sharpe, *British Birds and Birds' Eggs* (Sonnenschein).

BISON AND BUFFALO—Bison and Buffalo form two very distinct groups of the great Ox tribe, so different from the more typical oxen, that by many writers they are severally assigned to two separate genera—**Bison** and **Bubalus**. All the members of the group are, however, so intimately connected that it seems preferable to include them in the typical genus **Bos**. Both the English names have, unfortunately, been applied to animals to which they do not belong, the American Bison in its native country being almost invariably termed the Buffalo, whereas by Anglo-Indian sportsmen the Indian Gaur is as generally spoken of as the Bison. Properly speaking, Bison include only the **European** and **American Bison**, whereas under the title of Buffalo are comprised the **Indian Buffalo**, the **Cape Buffalo**, and the Short-horned **West African Buffalo**, together with a small form from the Philippines, which is not improbably nothing more than a hybrid between the Indian species and a small buffalo-like animal inhabiting the island of Celebes, known as the **Tamarao**.

The two species of Bison have their nearest relative in the Tibetan **Yak** (*Bos grunniens,*), which serves in some respects to connect them with the more typical oxen. An essential feature by which the Bison are allied to the Yak and the typical oxen is the possession of fourteen or fifteen pairs of ribs. Their horns, too—although smaller—have the cylindrical form of those of the Yak; but in the setting-on of these appendages Bison differ markedly from the latter. Not to enter into details on this point, it will suffice to state that Bison have their horns set lower down on the skull; while the skull itself—in addition to certain other features—is characterised by the marked convexity of the forehead and the tubular form of the sockets for the eyes. The external form of the Bison is too familiar to need much mention. The characteristic elevation of the withers—and the consequent lowness and apparent weakness of the hind-quarters—is the result of the great height of the spines projecting from the upper surface of the vertebræ of the fore part of the trunk. This elevation of the withers is enhanced by the mass of long hair clothing the fore-quarters, which also extends on to the neck, head, and fore-limbs. Elsewhere the hair—in the winter coat—is comparatively short and curly; and since in spring this coat is shed in large irregular patches Bison at this season present a peculiarly ragged and unprepossessing appearance.

The European, or True Bison (*Bos bonasus*)—frequently miscalled the **Aurochs**—appears to have been on the wane ever since the glacial period, soon after which it disappeared from the British Islands. As a wild animal, its range has been gradually contracting on the Continent, and now, apparently, it remains only in certain parts of the Caucasus—where it appears to be rare—and in a protected condition in the forest of Bielowitza, in the Government of Grono—the ancient Lithuania. There are, indeed, reports of its survival in parts of Wallachia and Moldavia, but these it is difficult to verify. A small herd is, it is true, kept by the Prince of Pless in Silesia, but this appears to be composed

YAK.
Height at shoulder 5 ft. 6 in.; av. horn meas. 31 in.; max. horn meas. 38¼ in.

of introduced animals, and has been replenished from Russia. In Bielowitza and the adjacent forest of Swisslotsch, the Bison have been steadily on the wane since the year 1857, when they numbered 1898 head, although the rate of decrease has been by no means regular, and has at some periods been accelerated by popular disturbances, disease, and other adventitious causes. Of late years the decrease in numbers has been very marked, the herd (inclusive of a small number confined in the Zoological Gardens at Bielowitza) having declined from 600 in 1882 to 380 in January, 1889, although by 1892 (since which date the numbers do not appear to have been published) it had again risen to 491. In-and-in breeding seems to be producing the usual results—namely, infertility on the part of the cows and the birth of an unusually large percentage of bulls; and it is only too probable that the term of existence of the Bison in Lithuania will be very limited. Information is lacking as to the prospects of the survival of the Bison in the Caucasus.

In place of being a forest-dwelling species, the nearly allied **American Bison** (*Bos americanus*) is—or rather was—a dweller on the open prairies, although a variety known locally as the "Wood-Buffalo" has accustomed itself to a different mode of life. The American species is so closely allied to the European that it is a somewhat difficult matter to define the points of distinction; although when the two animals are seen side by side, their points of difference are manifest enough. Although, on the whole, a more heavily built animal, the American Bison is less tall than the European species, with weaker hind-quarters; but the deficiency in height is largely veiled by the much more abundant hair on the head, neck, and fore-quarters.

The story of the practical extermination of the American Bison is told elsewhere, so that very few words must suffice on this occasion. The marvel is that an animal which existed in such countless thousands, and enjoyed such a vast geographical range—a range far greater than that of any other of the *Bovidæ*—should have been wiped out in such a short space of time. In 1869, when the Union-Pacific Railway was completed, the Bison still flourished almost in its original numbers. After the division of the animals into two great herds by the railway, the great period of the slaughter of the southern herd occurred between 1872 and 1874, and in the following year the herd, as such, had practically ceased to exist. Not but what numerous smaller herds remained for several years, although by 1880 Bison-shooting came to an end, for the very good reason that there were no animals to shoot. By the same date the northern herd had been decimated, and in the winter of 1882–83 it was reduced to a few straggling parties, all of which were soon after killed off, save for a small band which reached the Yellowstone Park, where they and their descendants have since received Government protection. These, and a certain number of the southern herd which fled to the wilder parts of Texas, were all that remained of the millions that formerly populated the prairies of the North-West.

Whereas Bison, as we have seen, have high withers, shaggy fore-quarters and heads, and cylindrical horns, the animals to which the name **Buffalo** should properly be restricted are characterised by the nearly uniform height of the back, the comparatively sparse coating of hair over the entire skin, and the more or less markedly triangular horns. So thin, indeed, is the hair in aged individuals, that in many instances the skin of the greater part of the body is almost completely bare. As further "points" of Buffalo, may be noticed the broad muzzle, the large, flapping ears—often heavily fringed with long bristly hair—the deep and short neck, and the moderately long and tufted tail. More important than all these features, is, however, the reduction in the number of pairs of ribs to thirteen. All the Buffaloes are old-world forms,—as, indeed, are all the oxen, save the American Bison.

Although Buffalo form a well defined group of the genus *Bos*, the differences existing between the various species are very much more accentuated than is the case with the Bison; the African species forming one section of the group, and the Oriental another. Of the former, the largest and best known is the **Cape Buffalo** (*Bos caffer*), whose typical range extends from the Cape to about the equator. Among the especial distinctive features of the typical form is the enormous development of the bases of the much-curved horns, which in old bulls form a huge mass covering the whole of the upper part of the forehead, and separated only by a narrow groove at their junction. Furnished with enormous, flapping ears, thickly fringed at their margins with hair, the head is remarkably short, with its profile deeply concave in the region of the eyes, and having a distinct hollow near the inner angle of each of the latter. Whereas in cows and young bulls the black skin is fairly well clothed with short dark brown hair, in old bulls it becomes almost completely naked. On the ears and tail-tip the hair, however, always persists. [*See* BUFFALO, CAPE.]

Such is the typical southern form of the Cape Buffalo. When, however, we cross the equator and proceed towards Abyssinia, an animal of a somewhat different type is met with. This is the *Bos centralis*, or *Bos æquinoctialis* of the older writers. In this form the whole build is much lighter and the size smaller, while the hair is lighter coloured and the horns have their bases much less thickened, and separated from each other by a median line of hair. Although some of these Abyssinian Buffaloes differ very markedly from the typical Cape form, yet in the intermediate regions the two seem to intergrade so completely that it appears impossible to regard them in the light of anything more than varieties of a single very variable species.

Passing into Western Africa, we meet another somewhat small and lightly-built Buffalo, which, although showing considerable resemblances to some examples of the *Bos æquinoctialis*, is generally admitted to the rank of a distinct species, under the name of the **Red** or **Short-horned Buffalo** (*Bos pumilus*). The colour of the hair is generally some shade of reddish or yellowish, although occasionally showing a brownish tinge, and the horns, which are relatively small, are completely separated from one another in the middle line. Two races of this species have been described—the one from the Congo district, and the other from Sierra Leone and its neighbourhood. In the Congo race the upwardly-curved horns are very distinctly flattened at their base; and it is this race which approximates so closely to the so-called *Bos æquinoctialis* of Equatoria, and thus gives rise to the suspicion that the Short-horned Buffalo is, after all, nothing more than a highly aberrant modification of the Cape species. On the other hand, in the Sierra Leone, or north-western type, the horns show extremely little trace of basal flattening, and are very widely separated from one another on the forehead, while the direction of their curvature is different.

With the Oriental Buffaloes we come to a very distinct type, which probably includes only one true species. This is the **Indian Buffalo** (*Bos bubalus*), whose proper habitat is formed by the lofty grass jungles of certain parts of India and Ceylon. It is true that reputed wild Buffalo are found in Burma and the Malayan peninsula and islands, although it is probable that these are really descendants from animals originally introduced by man. Many of these feral races—as they are scientifically called—have become very much dwarfed in size, this being especially the case with those inhabiting Java.

The distinctive features most easily recognised in the Indian Buffalo—the *Arna* of the natives—are the length and comparative slenderness of the head, and the enormous dimensions attained by the widely-spreading horns, which are always separated from one another by an interval of great extent and show no trace of a basal expansion. They are, too, much more distinctly triangular throughout their length than are those of the African species, from which they also differ in their direction. There is a marked sexual difference in the direction taken by the horns, those of the females extending almost directly outwards from the head for a long distance, whereas those of the males curve upwards in a bold sweep immediately after rising from the forehead. Apparently, however, in the Assam race the horns of the bulls are directed much more outwardly than is elsewhere the case. Equally distinctive of the species are the smaller and more compact ears, of which the margins are devoid of a distinct fringe of hair. Although the usual colour of the sparse hair and skin is blackish-grey, a dun-coloured variety is found in parts of Assam.

In addition to being domesticated throughout the Oriental countries, the tame Indian Buffalo has been introduced into Asia Minor, Italy, and Egypt, where it appears to flourish as well as in its native home.—[*See* BUFFALO, INDIAN.]

A small sturdily-built Buffalo from Mindao in the Philippines, locally known as the **Tamarao**, has been described as a distinct species, under the name of *Bos mindorensis*. In colour it resembles the Indian species, with which it likewise agrees in its markedly triangular horns. Instead, however, of curving outwards and upwards, the horns are directed upwards, with a marked divergence, but with little or no curvature. The whole appearance of this diminutive animal—which is only about 3½ feet in height—is strongly suggestive of its being a cross between the small Malayan race of the Indian Buffalo and the little **Anoa** of Celebes. That it breeds true at the present day, and thus forms a well-marked race, may be freely admitted; but its claims to rank as a valid species are doubtful in the extreme.

Although the **Anoa** (*Bos depressicornis*) of Celebes can scarcely be regarded as a true Buffalo, yet its affinities are clearly with that group. The upright direction of its horns, and other features, indicate, however, a decided approximation to the Antelopes. To a young Buffalo the Anoa presents a more decided resemblance than to the adult. The small size of this species (3 feet 3 inches at the withers) is in harmony with the small area of its habitat.

R. LYDEKKER.

BISON (*Bos americanus*)—The American Bison, like its European congener, is on the verge of extinction, and as a beast of the chase it has already practically vanished, though a dwindling remnant of the northern form may still occasionally yield a trophy to the sportsman hardy enough to brave the wintry desolation of Athabaska. A very few head are left in the Yellowstone National Park, but are being killed out by poachers. There are several small tame herds here and there; and there are one or two spots in the Rocky Mountains, and possibly one on the Mexican border, where two or three individuals still linger in a wild state. These are all.

Yet, fifteen years ago this was the characteristic animal of the plains, and still swarmed in the Upper Missouri Basin. It was hunted in two ways: by running it down on horseback, in which form of chase the heavy revolver was the weapon usually preferred, and by still-hunting, or stalking, on foot. The last was the method by which the great slaughter of the herds was accomplished. The hunters used long-range rifles, Sharps being probably the favourite weapon. These rifles were usually of ·40 or ·45 calibre, with a long heavy bullet, backed by about 100 grains of powder; they were very accurate long-range weapons, and as the buffalo (as the bison were always miscalled) were slow and stupid animals, a good marksman and skilful hunter could often slaughter twenty or thirty at a "stand," as it was termed.

I never came in contact with buffalo myself until at the very end of its existence as a species, and shot only two; one an unusually large solitary bull on the Little Missouri in 1883, and the other a very fine herd bull in South-western Montana in 1889. The first I stumbled across, and slew out of hand, with one of the ordinary buffalo rifles. The second was procured only after very careful tracking through a mountain forest and was killed with a single bullet from my Winchester.

My brother was in at the death of the southern buffalo herds early in 1877 in North-western Texas. He had full experience of both kinds of chase. Running buffalo on horseback was by far the most exciting method of killing them. The secret of success consisted in racing at full speed from the very outset, since the buffalo, though not very fleet, possessed marvellous endurance; and in riding up almost within arm's length of the brute before firing. It is a very difficult thing to shoot with any accuracy from a horse running at full speed, and especially at another object going at a somewhat different rate of speed. If the shots are fired from any distance, they are apt to miss or only wound. The true method was to push right alongside and fire with the muzzle of the weapon but a couple of feet from the animal's back. It was important that the horse should be trained to sheer off as soon as the shot was fired, as the buffalo sometimes turned and charged with great fury. On a well-trained hunting pony there was little danger, for the buffalo had neither the pace nor agility of the horse. An untrained horse, however, was generally afraid to come to close quarters, and moreover turned clumsily. I know of one instance where riding a large untrained Eastern horse caused a hunter to lose his life, the buffalo making good his charge and inflicting fatal

BISON.
Height at shoulder 5 ft. 6 in.; av. horn meas. 16½ in.; max. horn meas. 20¾ in.

injuries on both horse and rider. Even in this branch of the sport, however, accidents to life and limb from the quarry were not common, though there was no little risk from the falls naturally incident to riding at full speed over rough and broken country. It was a splendid sport, full of excitement, and it is melancholy to think that it is gone for ever.

Still-hunting the buffalo did not differ materially from still-hunting any other kind of game, except that it was rather easier when once the haunts of the bison were reached. Most game animals are adepts at concealing themselves, but the buffalo never sought concealment, and its huge black body could be seen against the yellow prairie as far as the eye could reach; its sense of smell was very acute, but its eyesight was poor, and so stalking was easy. Occasionally the beast charged, but against heavy rifles in skilful hands his prowess availed nothing, and the danger was so inconsiderable, that with anything like proper caution it could be disregarded.

Pursuit by sportsmen had practically nothing to do with the extermination of the bison. It was killed by the hide hunters, red, white, and half-breed. The railways, as they were built, hastened its destruction, for they gave means for transporting the heavy robes to market; but it would have been killed out anyhow, even were there no railroads in existence, and, once the demand for the robe became known to the Indians, they were certain to exterminate it in time, even had the white hunter refrained. Not even in South Africa has there been an instance where so many large game beasts of one species have been slain within so short a time. Originally the bison ranged between the Rocky Mountains and the Alleghanies and from Mexico to the Peace River; but its centre of abundance was the vast stretch of grass land reaching from the Saskatchewan to the Rio Grande. All the earlier explorers who crossed these great plains, from Lewis and Clark and Pike onward, dwelt upon the astounding multitudes of the bison, who furnished the entire means of subsistence for the tribes of Horse Indians. The herds were pressed steadily back, but the period of greatest slaughter did not begin until after the Civil War; then the commercial value of the robes became fully recognised, and the Trans-Continental Railways rendered the hunting-grounds more accessible. The slaughter was almost incredible, for the buffalo were slain literally by millions every year. They were exterminated first from Canada and from the Southern plains; it was not until 1883 that the last herd was killed from the Great North-western plains; and when the fierce greed of the skin hunter and skin buyer had exterminated the last of these great herds, there passed away what was perhaps the most imposing feature of American wilderness life.

THEODORE ROOSEVELT.

BITTERN (*Botaurus minor*), though only shot in this country by collectors, is in some favour with gunners in the neighbourhood of North American swamps, where it is found to lie well to dogs. [*See* WILD BIRDS' PROTECTION.]

BLACK GAME (*Tetrao tetrix*)—British sportsmen are generally alive to counteract, if possible, any danger which may threaten the extinction of a creature of the chase in which they take special interest. This, we are happy to think, has been the case with the black grouse, for there is not the slightest doubt that, on the whole, there has been a marked increase in their numbers since the agitation occurred in their favour a few years ago. Nowadays the gray hens are seldom shot, save by accident; and though the birds have vanished from many of their old haunts, there are now in Scotland, their chief home, an equal number of fresh districts in which they have become more or less plentiful. Close observation tells us that the gray hen breeds for two or three seasons only, after which she becomes barren and useless; and the introduction of square mouthed drains on moor edges accounts for the destruction of a large percentage of young birds.

Distribution—The best districts in Scotland for black game are Dumfriesshire, Roxburgh, parts of Perthshire, Invernesshire, Ayrshire, Aberdeenshire, and Argyllshire. In England they are numerous in the counties of Westmoreland, Cumberland, and Northumberland, whilst good bags are occasionally still obtained in Somersetshire; and until very recently the birds have been killed in every county from Cornwall to Caithness. In Wolmer, the New Forest, and Staffordshire, black game were formerly plentiful, but are now practically extinct. Re-introduction is, in their case, a failure; for the repeated efforts to re-establish the species in Norfolk, the New Forest, Wolmer Forest, and Ireland have met with no success.

Habits—Black game love the rough and broken country bordering cultivated and arable land. Though wandering in early autumn far out into the open moors, the first breath of winter sends them to their true home amongst the deep heather and rough grass lying beneath the birch and fir woods. From this cover they emerge in early morning and in the evening in search of their food supply, which, to such omnivorous feeders, practically comprises everything in the shape of grain, seeds, fruit and insect life that the various seasons afford. As the winter comes on, and the birch buds, a favourite food of theirs, give out, they will sometimes take to the Scotch firs and devour the youngest shoots, but will not do so unless driven to it by stress of weather. A lack of food supply frequently causes vast migrations of these birds in Norway, Sweden, and Russia; but in our islands, a movement on their part

is uncommon except for short distances, and then only confined to individuals and small parties.

The first signs of spring awake the martial instincts of the black cock. By nature, he is a warrior, and those who have watched him in his spring battles cannot fail to have the greatest affection for him, for he is such a veritable *preux chevalier* and settles his little differences so like a gentleman. By the end of March, the black cocks come regularly adorned to their playing-ground, generally an open space of short green grass on the fringe of the moor. The noise made by the birds, each of which selects a station some fifteen or twenty paces from his neighbour, can be heard on a still frosty morning at a distance of nearly two miles; it is a gentle purring sound not unlike the word "whirroo." At intervals too, the black cocks, particularly if a gray hen has been observed near the battle-ground, set up a loud screeching noise not unlike cats fighting at night. In April, when the gray hens begin to come regularly to the lists, there to be fought for and appropriated, the black cock who first observes a possible spouse approaching, throws himself up in the air and flutters up perpendicularly like a lark to a height of twenty or thirty feet. His example is immediately followed by all the other black cocks who, each and all, endeavour to screech the loudest to attract her attention. Black cocks fight long and savagely, often till one or other of the combatants is disabled, though, as with our species, there is a good deal of talk before they begin. No immature cock is allowed to enter the ring. On fine days, in late autumn, black cocks frequently go through their spring pantomime, exhibiting many of their previous antics and calls, but this exhibition is but a subdued version.

By the middle of May, the gray hen has formed a nest of loose dry grass, and in it she deposits her eight or ten eggs, the first brood being seen generally about the beginning of June. Though the gray hen is an excellent mother, the young are extremely delicate and more than half, as a rule, fall victims to various causes. When the chicks are no larger than thrushes, they can fly well, and, if flushed, will readily alight in the trees, where, by the way, the mother generally takes them to roost for safety's sake.

With the moulting of his glorious plumage, the black cock's fiery nature vanishes; he becomes shy, and spends much of his time, with a few companions, hiding in the thick bracken; and as the autumn advances, the regular winter parties are formed. The breeding hens and young of both sexes go together in small or large numbers, whilst the old black cocks form a separate pack or party, sometimes numbering as many as three hundred, as the writer has seen at Doune, in Perthshire. The barren hen, like the emancipated woman, goes on her own, though it does not, of the least necessity, follow that the single hens which are so noticeable in covert shooting are unfertile.

Shooting—The flight of black game is very rapid when they are once under way, about the same as that of grouse, but performed with greater ease and less scurry, and capable of being extended to a much greater distance. The law permits shooters to butcher black game as early as August 20th, but no one who is anything of a shot or has any appreciation for the beauties of nature should ever kill his birds before the middle of September, unless they are actually wanted for the pot. Till this time, when walked up, they are neither an attractive nor difficult mark, whereas, if driven later on, they fulfil every necessary qualification of a high class bird of the chase.

Driving—When driving, it is well to remember that black game are not too easy to kill; their pace is slightly deceptive, and it is best therefore to take both one's shots in front if possible: the gunner too must be well on the alert to observe their approach, as they are so silent when coming forward, and he must be ready to shoot very smartly in case they resort to the dodging header, a ruse they often attempt if frequently driven.

Black game are as obstinate as government mules when they do not wish to go. With a few trained beaters, a good keeper who knows their lines of flight and passes will put them to the guns better than an army of irregulars. Lying in the stooks in an October evening is capital sport, and a few old black cocks shot as they come in to feed afford almost as much fun as duck, shot during flighting. Dull misty weather is the best for black game shooting, as the birds go straight ahead, and do not get into large packs coming on all at once.

There is very little poaching of these birds in Scotland beyond snaring on the stooks, but in England silk net is used to some extent in the border counties. Their strength, speed, and fine sight, too, gives them a fair immunity from the attacks of vermin, the Peregrine alone stooping and killing one occasionally; and then but for sport, for their flesh is not esteemed by the raptorials. A black cock makes a charming pet and becomes very tame, and his attitudes in the spring are interesting and amusing to watch.

Black game have been known to interbreed with Capercailzies, Pheasants, Grouse, Willow-grouse, Bantam, and common Fowl, the hybrids usually being very dark and taking after the black cock, whose progeny they generally are. As with most hybrids, the young are generally males, the most frequent cross being that with the Capercailzie, which may be said to be almost common. Gray hens too, not infrequently, partially assume the plumage of the male. Whole or partial albinos are extremely rare. [*See also* GROUSE.]

J. G. MILLAIS.

BLACKCOCK TOURNAMENTS—A custom prevails in Russia of shooting the male birds of the black-game family during the mating season, a practice excused by northern sportsmen on the ground that the males of this species greatly exceed in numbers the female birds, and that, in their rivalry for the latter's favours, the cocks destroy numerous sittings of eggs by fighting over the very nest. Those who know the blackcock only in the broad light of day may be surprised to learn that in the early hours of a spring morning—from about 2.30 a.m. until sunrise—these birds hold what is to all intents and purposes a tournament in some selected clearing between the forests, or in convenient belts of open woodland. Hither flock the gray hens from their nests, each one watching from bush or tree on the borders of the lists, and flying off anon with her victorious knight.

In the lists, however, the blackcock rarely comes to blows, though serious fights are said to take place afterwards over the nests of the fair.

In order to discover the chosen tourney-ground of the sable warriors, it is essential to pass a night or two in the forest, a function generally performed by the keeper, who may hear from a mile away the hectoring and crooning of the combatants, and will then creep to the edge of their battlefield in order that he may select the exact site for his pine-bough shelter (*Russicè*, *Shalashka*) in which the sportsman is destined afterwards to crouch. The pine branches are placed end-up in a circle, their tops converging to a point, the base enclosing a space about five or six feet in diameter.

Within this space, shortly after midnight, the sportsman takes up his position and waits until, with the earliest indications of coming dawn, the black-plumed champions arrive one by one with a rush and a whirr through the darkness, and alight unseen with a thud close to his ambush, the site of which the keeper has chosen with care. Presently a great crooning arises from many throats, growing in volume until the sound becomes absolutely oppressive. Suddenly, a champion issues his challenge: *chu-wish! chu-wish!* and in an instant the defiance is taken up from every side. The knights close in to the fray, and the bloodless tournament commences, each pair fighting, or pretending to fight, like any two pugnacious barndoor cocks in a farmyard.

It is then that the sportsman may, when the light becomes strong enough, shoot many times without clearing the field, the spectacle of slaughtered companions neither alarming nor even, to all appearance, surprising the survivors.

No sooner, however, does the blazing forehead of the rising sun appear, than all hasten from the lists, and the sportsman should remain concealed until the very last bird has disappeared, otherwise his ambush will not avail him a second night.

FRED WHISHAW.

BLACK FISH—(1) An American sea-fish, also known as Tautog, caught in the autumn months near sunken wreckage. (2) An Australian fish occurring in both river and sea, and caught with rod and line, the only bait being a weed that grows on the local wharves. It is of no use as food.

BLUE FISH (*Pomatomus*)—A game sea-fish of the Eastern seaboard of the United States, caught in large numbers by railing under canvas with any bright spinning tackle.

[BLUES, *see* UNIVERSITY CONTESTS].

BOAR, WILD—Luckily for hunters as a class, the range of the wild boar (*Sus scrofa*) is almost world-wide. On the American Continent, indeed, he has no place, although in Old Mexico, and it is said as far north as Arizona, he is represented by a small variety of his race known as the *Peccary* (*q.v.*), which though neither as large nor as well armed as the true wild boar, has some of the attributes of that grand beast and (making due allowance for western exaggeration) must be endowed with very considerable pluck and pugnacity. Another distant cousin of the true wild swine has his haunt in South Africa, where he is known as the *Wart Hog* (*q.v.*), a beast furnished by nature with tusks alongside of which the record tusks of Indian or Caucasian boars would look utterly insignificant; but occurring as he does in a country where there is such a prodigality of the more important great game, little is known of him as a sporting beast, and none but casual notice of him occurs in most of the African works on sport. From these, however, he appears to possess some of the pace and his share of the pluck and fighting qualities of his race. W. C. Baldwin, for instance, in his *African Hunting*, mentions, in passing, that his big staghound "Hopeful" was carried bodily away on the points of a wounded wild boar's tusks for full fourteen yards.

But the true Wild Boar is *Sus scrofa*, and though he is found in Northern Africa, in the Hawaiian and most of the South Sea Islands, and in other somewhat unexpected places, his true home is in India and Europe.

In very early days wild swine were plentiful in England, and Mr. J. E. Harting, in his *Extinct British Animals*, writes that "to judge of the remains of the animal which have been found in various parts of the British Islands, Wild Boars at one time must have completely overrun the country. In Ireland they were even more plentiful than in England, though small and misshapen, and in Scotland also they were abundant.

They grew to such a size that we have a record of one pair of tusks taken about 1124 which measured 12 inches in length and three in their greatest width. But the wild boar, like a good many better things in England, has had to make room for civilisation, and though his admirers have made several efforts to re-establish him in his old haunts, their efforts have been in vain." Public opinion, which will hardly tolerate the existence of a rabbit, rises in indignation against the wild boar, whose ideas or farming are certainly peculiar. It is of course impossible to fix the exact date at which any given animal became extinct in England, but from documents quoted by Mr. Harting it may fairly be assumed that there were wild boar in abundance in the forests round London in 1174: that the King and Prince of Wales hunted them near Windsor in September, 1617: that in that year boar were still to be found in Lancashire, and that almost at the end of the century (1683) wild swine still existed in England.

In France they exist still, and in Germany, Austria, Russia, and Spain they are plentiful, and still form a prominent feature in the great game drives of those countries.

From Europe eastward, the tracks of the wild swine are by every sluggish stream, his lair in every reed-bed, and his routings the ruin of every peasant's crops. From the Black Sea to the Bay of Bengal there is a ringing of bells by night, a blowing of horns and sounding of clappers, together with an irregular musketry fire all through the ripening time of the grain, and all this in honour of the great wild boar, who as soon as the dusk comes, steals out from the wooded foot-hills or the stony gorges, and trots down to the cultivated grounds to dine.

And the boar deserves all honour. He was England's noblest beast of chase in England's manliest days; and in England's great schooling-ground for soldiers to-day, what beast is his equal? Let some of the men who know him speak. In the *Wild Sports of India*, Major Shakespear says, "I consider that hog-hunting is the very first sport in the world." Col. Heber Percy in the Badminton volumes calls the boar "the pluckiest of all beasts," while Col. Kinloch, in his *Large Game Shooting in Thibet*, endorses both these opinions.

Undoubtedly, if the boar has his due, he must take high rank amongst the beasts of the chase. It is even doubtful if he be not entitled to take the first place. For courage, he has no superior: it is much to say that he has any equal. I have myself seen a comparatively small boar fight his way through a pack of hounds; I have seen a broken-backed sow worry a dog nearly as large as herself; I have known a mortally wounded boar to lie in ambush for his enemy and kill him just before the dawn came and his own life was spent, while Major Shakespear (in the *Wild Sports of India*) writes of the boar's "utter recklessness of life" and of the "fierceness that will make him run up the hunter's spear, which has passed through his vitals, until he buries his tusk in the body of the horse," &c. And again, the native Shikarees affirm "that the wild boar (of India) will quench his thirst at the river between two tigers." This is even more strongly put by Col. Heber Percy, who writes in the Badminton volumes on Big Game that several cases are on record in which an old boar has beaten off a tiger, and some in which the latter has been killed by a boar. As a matter of fact the old wild boar knows no fear, and whenever he does condescend to trot away from an intruding sportsman, he goes somewhat leisurely, under protest, and with an exceedingly savage gleam in his eye, plainly hinting that he would rather stop and fight, than get up and run. And in this estimate of the boar's courage both ancient and modern authorities are agreed, from Holinshed, who speaks of boar-hunting as "a verie dangerous exercise," to Col. Kinloch (*Large Game Shooting in Thibet*) who proved that it was so by "about fifty wounds from one boar" in a single round. Nor is the boar's courage his only claim to high rank amongst beasts of the chase. He has not only courage but pace, and in India offers to the sportsman that perfection of sport known as pig-sticking, in which riding, racing, hunting, and fighting are so happily blended, that even an Irishman would be content with its glorious opportunities for fun and sudden death.

Naturally, with all these good qualities, English sportsmen delight in killing him, and have surrounded his obsequies with many rules and much ceremony. In India it is a maxim that the only sportsmanlike way of killing him is with a spear: it is a law that no boars shall be shot within forty miles of rideable ground. And to the average Englishman these laws and customs will at once appear to be founded on right reason. There is probably more danger in pig-sticking than in any other form of sport. The ground over which the riding has to be done is as little adapted to riding as it well could be; nothing annoys an old boar more than to be hustled at top pace before he has had time to digest his food; a spear is infinitely more difficult to kill with than a rifle; and if the hunter is in real luck, an angry boar may give him fifty wounds in five minutes that take nearly forty minutes to sew up and dress; a sow may run up his spear and fasten on his horse's chest, or at any rate his horse will be so knocked about by the rocks amongst which he has ridden, that he won't be able to go out of the stable again for a fortnight. Hence it comes that hog-hunting is the most popular sport in India, and for those anxious to study it in all its details, numerous volumes have been written.

Here it must suffice to say that the boars are either intercepted in the early morning on their way from their feeding-grounds to their lairs in the foot-hills, or are driven from their lairs by beaters. Along the edges of the covert, horsemen armed with spears are stationed in dumb expectancy until the boar breaks. Then the signal to ride is given, and such as are within reasonable distance of the quarry, lay into their boar, press him as hard as their horses can before he has time to get his wind or gain covert, and despatch him, if they are lucky enough to get within range of him, by spear thrusts, delivered from the saddle, the honours used both on foot and on horseback; and in Hawaii, where they claim an indigenous pig and good rideable country, it is used to-day. In Britain it would seem from certain paintings and written records which have been preserved to us that the boar was not ridden down in the open as in India, but was first driven to bay by hounds and then killed with a heavy jobbing spear, a sufficiently dangerous pastime even so, as is in some sort proved by the records of lands granted to certain gentlemen and corporations by the King for the destruction of notable boars

BOAR.
Ht. at shoulder, 35 *in.* *Av. length of tusk*, 8 *in.* *Max. length*, 12 *in.*

of the run going to the man who draws first blood, or, as they say, takes the first spear, although it is by no means probable that the first spear will finish the business. On the contrary a good boar is likely to give employment to most of those engaged before he dies. The spear used in this sport varies in the different districts from six and a half to seven feet long in Bengal, to eight or nine feet in the Bombay Presidency. [*See* PIG-STICKING.]

There would seem at all times and in all countries to have been a remarkable consensus of opinion as to the propriety of killing wild swine with a spear. Formerly in Britain it was which had committed great depredations, and by a curious clause, quoted by Mr. Harting from the *Book of the Rights and Privileges of the Kings of Erin*, which restrains one of the kings of Ulster from going into the wild boar's hunt or "being seen to attack it alone." One cannot help wondering whether, being Irish, that good king did not avail himself of the companionship of courtiers who were discreetly blind upon occasion. In Spain, in the old days (according to Mr. Abel Chapman), the "javato" was hunted on horseback with spear, pike, and lance, and even now in Estremadura is hunted with horse and hound "during the stillness of a moonlight night when the acorns are falling from the oaks in the magnificent Estremenian woods."

But there are many places where the boar cannot be ridden down even by Englishmen, places where no horse could gallop, and in these the boar gives very fair sport with the rifle, either to the stalker or the leather-lunged sportsman who with a small pack of hounds (three or four) drives him to bay in such mountain fastnesses as may be found on the shores of the Black Sea, or through such forest tangles as abound on the Caspian. In Russia, as I believe in Austria and Germany, the wild swine are shot in the great forest drives, but though they form a fine picture crashing through the frosted undergrowth, it is a poor way of killing them. The Caucasian peasants' methods are better. Like most other forest beasts, the boar is more or less nocturnal in his habits; and it is in the stillness of the night that those who watch learn most about him. When the moon is up and the pears are down, in August, the natives sally out with their old muzzle-loaders and catch the boar feeding under the pear trees, or with a white string knotted round their gun's muzzle for a sight, lie in wait by his path through the reeds to the water. Many of the guns used are poor things, the bullets and charges both light, the shooting inaccurate, and the light bad, and as in addition to this the boar's hide is at certain seasons almost impenetrable in places, this hunting is dangerous work. Not a few of the old Cossacks who indulge in it are badly scarred, and as for their hounds, unless they develop a phenomenal degree of caution and activity early in life, their careers are short.

Appearance and Habits.—Throughout his wide range, the wild boar varies little in habits, size, or appearance. As a youngster, he is of a reddish-brown striped with darker colour; as he grows older, he loses the stripes; and as an old warrantable boar, he becomes a grizzled grey with an undercoat of black. As far as my own knowledge of him goes in the Caucasus and Russia, he is at all times a clean feeder, living upon roots, chestnuts, acorns, and the different fruits and crops, but some authorities maintain that he will devour a carcass if he comes across it. Night is his feeding time. In the day-time, he lies up in thick scrub, generally near some soft ground in which he can wallow, and not necessarily near his feeding ground, for he is a great traveller.

Measurements and Weight—In weight and size he varies perhaps more than in any other particular, and from such data as I have been able to obtain I should imagine that the Caucasian boar, amply fed upon the fallen chestnuts and maize-fields by the Black Sea, is perhaps the largest of his race. Professor Radde, of the Tiflis Museum, once wrote to me as follows: "The largest solitary boars, measured at the shoulder, and measured straight, stand about 105 centimetres, and their total weight, not dressed, rarely exceeds 15 puds (*i.e.*, 600 lbs.)." In India, on the authority of Captain Baldwin, Major Shakespear, and others, we have it that a boar which stands 40 inches high at the shoulder has attained to the maximum size of his race. In Hawaii, I have a record of a boar killed and weighed by my friend Mr. Purvis, which *dressed* 325 lbs., and judging (at hazard) from the records of certain tusks taken, the old English wild boar was not far behind the Caucasian beast.

Captain Baldwin, a very careful writer, gives the measurement of a boar killed by him in the Himalayas as five feet ten inches in length and over three feet at the shoulder, but adds that boar in the Himalayas frequently exceed this.

Tusks—As to the size of tusks, the principal trophies of the boar, Baldwin writes that "the tusks of a very fine Indian boar sometimes reach eight and a half and nine inches in length, but anything above this is exceptional;" whilst in Mr. Rowland Ward's book on Horn Measurements a pair of 10 inch tusks, secured by Sir Samuel Baker in India, are the largest recorded.

I have reason to believe that larger tusks than these have been taken in Hawaii, and I have myself measured a pair in the possession of a Caucasian Governor (Col. Verubof of Naltchik) which went 11½ inches round the outside curve. Certainly 9 inch tusks, and even 10, are not uncommon there; and I have myself secured a pair not unduly curved, well over 9½ inches. When the upper tusk has been lost by accident, it not unfrequently happens that an abnormal growth takes place, the lower, or fighting, tusk growing round and so attaining greater length, whilst it becomes useless as a weapon.

But perhaps there is no tusk on record at present to surpass those recorded by Boethius as taken from a boar killed in Scotland 1124 (or thereabouts), twelve inches long and three in their greatest width.

CLIVE PHILLIPPS-WOLLEY.

BOAR SHOOTING—In considering the pursuit of the boar with the rifle on foot instead of with horse and spear, according to the orthodox fashion, it must be borne in mind that there are large tracts of forest in India swarming with pig that are absolutely unrideable from a pig-sticking point of view. These are so remote from ground on which that grand sport may be obtained that it cannot even be contended that they act as nurseries to maintain the supply of pig for the rideable districts. In these forests, Indian though they be, wild boar are perfectly fair game for the rifle.

In all forest-stalking it is hopeless to hunt in the middle of the day; the animals are then lying down, and if stumbled upon by accident, a rush through the scrub and a confused vision of vanishing sterns offer the sole chance of a shot. Early in the morning it is very different. The hunter, moving slowly and noiselessly in his india-rubber or felt-soled boots, either catches sight of a sounder feeding on some grassy glade, or hears them rooting among the bamboos at the bottom of a ravine; sometimes he will intercept an old gray hog returning from his night's foray among the crops in the jungle clearings, or catch the sharp clashing sound of a heavy boar whetting his tusks, and be able to creep up within easy range for a shot.

BOAR SHOOTING.

Weapon, &c.—It may here be observed that a ball gun of the Paradox type is about the best weapon to use. Express bullets are too apt to glance from twigs to be absolutely reliable in forest shooting, and the writer has lost several beasts from this cause. Small-bore bullets also often leave no blood trail, and wounded animals are frequently lost through this defect in forest shooting.

The chief element of risk in boar shooting is having to follow up a wounded beast in thick covert. The main rules to be remembered in such an event are—to avoid approaching any dangerous animal up hill, and not to be in a hurry, but to give time for the wound to tell on the animal's strength.

The unparalleled courage and ferocity of wild boar are referred to in the foregoing article. Still, it is only fair to admit that a boar will rarely attack unless something has occurred to ruffle its proverbially short temper. The writer, riding on one occasion unarmed over some open downs in Central India, espied a goodly boar making his way home after its night's ramble, and he trotted up to within about forty yards of it. The boar stood still and chucked up its chin defiantly. There was nothing more to be done; it was folly to risk a charge with only a switch to protect the horse; so each party drew off.

Another time, when after other game with a brother officer and two hunters, the sound of a boar whetting its tusks was heard; and on the party advancing in the direction of the noise, a sounder of pig was disturbed. The old sow and her family made off at once through the grass, but the boar came trotting back as if to cover their retreat. As it was essential for sport not to disturb the ground by unnecessary firing, no notice was taken of him, and he presently followed the others. The party had not, however, proceeded another twenty yards when the veteran came back again and barred the way with such evident malevolence that the sportsmen had to cock their rifles and place the natives behind them in case of attack.

It was rather a curious sight; on one side of a grassy glade stood four men, two of them armed with rifles, and on the other stood the huge old boar, almost white from age, shaking his head and daring them to come on.

The utter unreasonableness of the whole affair was too ludicrous. The men had not the smallest intention of hurting him, except in self-defence; and if he declared war and charged across that open glade up to the muzzles of two rifles, the only possible result would have been his death.

At last the old fellow seemed to make up his mind either that he had asserted his own authority, or that the enemy were too strong for him, and trotted off again; but on the party resuming their advance he at once turned and faced them a third time, but only for a few seconds, when, considering he had wasted enough time over them, he trotted off and rejoined his family.

Another rather absurd adventure befell the writer once when, intent on procuring pork for the larder, he had carefully selected a promising squeaker out of a sounder that were feeding among some bamboos at the bottom of a steep ravine. After shooting his selection through the head, so as not to spoil the meat, he clambered down to inspect his prize. He had barely time to examine it when there was a crash among the bamboos, and the long lean head of an evil-looking pig appeared, facing him, some ten yards off. There was no time to deliberate. The bottom of the ravine, where the writer was standing, was barely two feet wide: the sides were steep, and it was certainly no place to stand a charge, while avoiding one seemed out of the question. So a quick shot, which placed the bullet between those fierce little eyes, had to settle the matter. It was the old sow, unfortunately; but the place was too tight for careful discrimination.

R. HEBER PERCY.

BOWLS—If this ancient and historic game did not originate in England, it must have been introduced not long after the Norman conquest. Strutt, after all his researches, could only say that it was probably an invention of the middle ages, confessing his inability to ascertain the time of its introduction, but he traced it back to the thirteenth century, and in his *Sports and Pastimes* gives a copy of the earliest pictorial representation he had found. The original may now be seen in the British Museum in a MS. (20 D. IV. p. 187) in the Royal Library. It is a well-preserved coloured drawing and shows two players and two bowls and two small cones, one of the latter being placed at either side of the playing ground and evidently serving as alternate marks to bowl at. By the fourteenth century the cones had been superseded by a single small bowl, now and for ages past called "jack," as the object played at, for in a spirited drawing of that period, also copied by Strutt, we find three players with three bowls and a jack. Nowadays each player uses two or more bowls, and, allowing for changes in costume and more numerous players, the game seems to have been played in much the same way then as now.

Abundant records of the intervening centuries show the position held by the game in public estimation. During the sixteenth and seventeenth centuries and the early part of the eighteenth, it was in great favour with royalty, the nobility, clergy and the well-to-do, but after Queen Anne's time a reaction set in, which continued down to our own day. Of recent years, however, the game has experienced a great revival, and now bids fair to attain and hold the high position it deserves as a gentle and healthful recreation.

The game was established in England long before its introduction into Scotland, where the practice of it has been modified and differs in many important respects, though the main principles and objects of play remain the same. [*See* BOWLS, SCOTTISH.] It is played upon what are called "bowling greens," grass plots of varying extent usually taking the form of a square or oblong with a width or length of from 40 to 60 yards. Such a space affords ample scope for play, a stretch of 35 or 40 yards from "trig" to "jack" being quite enough to play over, if nicety of play is to be regarded and fatigue avoided. The trig (or "footer") is an essential implement in the game, and the starting point of all play. It is usually a piece of leather or matting about 18 in. square, upon which the leading or first player places one foot when throwing off jack, which he must do to a distance of 20 yards at least, but not nearer than a yard to the edge of the green. If the first throw fails he is allowed a second, but failing again, his opponent is entitled to one throw, and if he also fail, the throw reverts back to the first player, but the order of play is not interfered with by such failures.

The jack is sometimes made of ivory, but commonly of wood or earthenware, and is from 2½ in. to 4 in. in diameter. On some greens biassed jacks are still used, but earthenware straight-running ones are superseding them. The bowls (of which each player uses two in ordinary English play) are of globular form and much larger and heavier than the jack. They are made of *lignum vitæ* or other hard and heavy wood, and vary in size and weight; the largest seldom exceeds in circumference the Scotch limit of 16½ in. and the average weight is about 3 lbs., but there is no *minimum* limit of size. The most peculiar and interesting feature in bowl-playing is that the bowls are purposely made with a "bias," i.e., a tendency to diverge from the straight line when set running. Every bowl is practically round in the largest circumference or running part, but is shaved down very carefully and evenly on one side by the turning lathe, the effect being to cause the bowl when slackening speed to incline and turn (or draw) towards the reduced side, the divergence corresponding in intensity to the amount shaved off. Formerly the bias was brought about by inserting lead on one side of the bowl, but not so now. Perfectly straight-running bowls are not allowed, so that the player has, in sending a bowl on its journey, to allow for this created bias, the distance to jack, and the amount of force necessary to accomplish the object of his play. Inequalities in the surface of the green must also be taken into account, otherwise elevations, depressions, or slopes will inevitably tell tale by impeding the bowl or carrying it out of the contemplated course.

The usual complement of players in the English game is six, who divide into two sides of three either by choice or by drawing lots. Each side agrees upon one of their number to lead or play first, and we may call him No. 1; he is supposed to be the weakest player and is followed by the medium player as No. 2, the rear being brought up by the most experienced and skilful player, No. 3. Nos. 1 on each side toss to see which shall lead, and the game commences by the winner throwing jack within the prescribed limits, and when it has come to rest and is in all respects a valid mark he proceeds to play one of his bowls and is followed by No. 1 of the opposing side with one of his; they play their second balls in the same order and Nos. 2 and 3 on either side alternately so continue the play until all the twelve bowls are played, when an "end" is said to be finished, and the side owning the bowl lying nearest jack are said to have the "cast," which reckons one point in the score and they are allowed another point for every additional bowl of theirs which lies nearer jack than any bowl of their opponents.

The number of available players of course varies. Two may play, opposing each other in what is called "single-handed" play, or four can play, two on each side, after the same manner that six do, but the play single-handed or two of a side being more continuous and involving frequent crossing of the green is apt to become fatiguing, especially in warm weather. If more than six play in a set, the ground in the neighbourhood of jack becomes so encumbered with bowls that the hindmost players have few openings left for their skill, and their enjoyment is correspondingly lessened.

The game does not consist merely in playing the bowls so as to rest as near jack as possible in unobstructed ground, for second or third player often finds his course obstructed by the bowls already played and that his own can only approach by passing, sliding from, or removing one or more of them, whilst third player has additional responsibility, the final result of the "end" depending on his play. He is generally equal to the occasion and by a well-played bowl insinuates his own or a partner's into a winning position or "saves something." His only resource often is "firing" (playing with much force) at jack or bowls or both, either to send jack off the green and so "void" the end altogether, or to scatter the bowls to drive away his opponents or let in one of his partners. Leading players should never be "short," i.e., by playing their bowls so as to stop short of jack; to go beyond it is better, as the jack can be driven to them if desired; the second players should play "well up" unless it is advisable to "block" the ground against the opponents in order to maintain a favourable position.

It is most important that the beginner should adopt a good position and attitude for delivering his bowls. If a right-handed player, he should place his right foot firmly on trig, then advance the left about a yard, and, bending the left leg and stooping, bring his body down nearly parallel with the green, leaving just sufficient space to swing his right arm with the bowl in hand clear of the grass, so that the bowl may glide from the hand and strike the turf at the slightest possible angle, the nearer trig the better. In this position the player has complete command of the bowl, and his eye can detect any unevenness in the ground requiring allowances. A left-handed player places left foot on trig, and advances the right in the same manner. A right-handed player naturally plays on the right-hand ground, that is, to the right of an imaginary line drawn from trig to jack, and ought to play both bowls on that ground unless blocked by other bowls, when he should "change his ground" by playing to the left of the line. It becomes necessary to change the ground in many cases. For instance your opponents may have a "short" bowl lying a little to the right of jack, and, should your bowl touch it, it may be driven nearer to jack; in such a case you play on the left-hand ground. This changing the ground is necessitated by a variety of circumstances too numerous to specify. In play the bowl should be firmly grasped in the hand, in right-handed play the little finger resting near the biassed side and the thumb on the other side, which is called "playing finger." If the player decides to change his ground he turns the bowl in his hand and plays with the thumb on the biassed side, and this is called "playing thumb." Beginners often feel a difficulty in playing on both sides, but should never give way to the natural inclination to play only on one side; there never was a good player who did. Occasionally the green is so encumbered with bowls on both sides of the imaginary line that to succeed it is necessary to reduce the natural curve caused by the bias, and this may be done either by playing with extra force, or by "setting up" the bowl so that its circumference inclines a bit to one side or the other, a manœuvre in which some players excel.

On the completion of each "end" the players cross over and a fresh one is entered upon by the winning leader throwing jack again from trig, which is placed within one yard of the spot from which jack was taken up in the completed end; the bowls are played as before and ends succeed each other until one or other side scores seven or any agreed number of points for game.

England has not yet a national or central association of bowling clubs, and consequently there is no uniform standard of playing rules applicable to the whole kingdom, though there are local associations of clubs in Lancashire, Yorkshire, Durham, Norfolk, Suffolk and elsewhere which have framed sets of rules for their respective districts. In these and other parts many clubs exist and flourish independently under their own sets of rules, but scarcely any two of them are alike in all respects. In Scotland, however, the Scottish Bowling Association has provided a set of rules which are generally acted on throughout the country. Scotland has about 35,000 players and 400 greens, with district associations for Edinburgh, Leith, Glasgow, Midlothian, &c. The number of English clubs is unknown, but there are several hundreds of them. They are very numerous in Newcastle, Manchester, Lancashire, Yorkshire and Norfolk, and the colleges at Oxford and Cambridge have several.

The English greens are not usually so level as the Scottish, and several sets may cross each other's lines of play, so that great variety may always be had owing to the constant shifting of the play and the inequalities of the green. English players use only two bowls apiece except in the more northern districts, where three or even four are sometimes allowed. In their club matches a team of twelve players is selected and divided into four sides of three each, and in matches independent of the associations the contest is usually in two parts, the first taking place on the green of the challenged club, the second on that of the challengers. The visitors, of course, have to find out as best they can the peculiarities of each green and must be skilful to win both out and home. If each club gets a win a deciding match is played on a neutral green. In Lancashire, however, there are never more than two of a side, and their matches are usually played single-handed, the points gained by each player being added to those gained by the other players of his party, and the club making in all the highest total of points wins. Every club has its own prize meetings and the associations promote contests between clubs and single-handed tournaments for individual merit open to all members. The players are generally attended by lads, who pick and clean the bowls for them, receiving 1d. each evening from every player; in this way the players are saved much time and trouble and their attention is not distracted from the game by doing the work themselves. Some clubs, however, dispense entirely with these "helps."

The game is not much played in Ireland, but we hear of it as practised in some form or other in most European countries, and in the United States, Canada, South Africa, Calcutta, Kurrachee, Japan, Australia and New Zealand (where there is a Bowling Association) it is rapidly advancing.

E. T. AYERS.

BOWLS, SCOTTISH.—Bowl-playing is one of the oldest games now practised, and statistics could very easily be produced to prove that year by year it is still growing in popularity. In the fifteenth century it was unquestionably very popular, and in the next century an Act (33 Henry 8, c. 9) was passed, whereby it was declared to be an illegal pursuit, and it was further enacted that no person "by himself, factor, deputy, servant or other, shall for his or their gain, lucre, or living, keep, have, hold, occupy, exercise or maintain any common house, alley, or place of Bowling." It was alleged that it interfered with the practice of Archery, and it was only allowed to exist in the land as a luxury and for the rich. Thus, by the same Act of Parliament, artificers, servants, &c., might play at Christmas time, and a licence might be granted to those worth over one hundred pounds per annum to keep a bowling-green for private play only. Curiously enough, this Act remained unrepealed until 1845, when by 8 and 9 Vict. cap. 109, sec. 1, "any game of mere skill, such as Bowling . . ." was declared to be quite lawful.

Long before the embargo of Henry VIII.'s parliament was removed, the game was widely popular. In the north its progress was more extended and rapid than elsewhere, and in Lancashire, Yorkshire, and Scotland it speedily obtained a hold upon the affections of the people which it keeps to this day. According to Mitchell, the first bowling-green in Scotland of which we have any account is that of Glasgow. So popular has the game now become that some corporations, notably that of Edinburgh and Newcastle-on-Tyne, have provided public bowling-greens. On these greens it is usual to make a charge of one penny an hour, and it is only necessary to mention that during the summer of 1895, no less than 57,646 pennies were collected by the Edinburgh Corporation. Queen's Park, Glasgow, is the home of Bowling in the north, and is the chosen venue for the final stages of the annual championships in connection with the Scottish Bowling Association.

The game of Bowls varies in point of detail in different parts of the country, and even its title is not always the same. According to Mitchell and all the older authorities, the correct name of the game is *Bowl-playing*, although Mitchell uses the terms Bowl-playing, Bowling, and Bowls indifferently.

The game as played in Scotland differs widely from that played in Lancashire and Yorkshire. (Southern English Bowls has been explained in the foregoing article). The chief differences between the two games are these :—

In Scotland the greens are absolutely level, or as nearly level as skilled experts can make them ; spherical earthenware jacks are used to play to ; the play must be confined to the rink that is, a space usually about seven yards wide, extending the full length of the green ; the players in single and double-handed matches invariably use four bowls ; and club matches are invariably played with four men a side, as in curling, each player using two bowls.

In Lancashire each green has a "crown" varying in rise and slope, so that it is almost impossible to find any two greens alike ; the jacks are of wood with bias, much the same as the bowls ; the first player can throw the jack to whatever part of the green he likes, the different lines of play thus frequently crossing each other ; players only use two bowls ; and matches are decided by a series of single-handed games, the rink form of contest being practically unknown.

The Scottish game is gradually extending its sphere beyond Scotland, and in London, Northumberland, Cumberland, Durham, Westmoreland, Ireland, Australia, and New Zealand, greens have been made and the game played as in Scotland.

Greens vary considerably in size, from thirty-five to fifty yards square being the usual extremes. Where grounds can be obtained at all, they should never be less than forty yards square, and five yards more each way is a very great advantage. That area permits of plenty of variety in the matter of length, and prevents the ends from becoming worn out, as they inevitably do when the green is so short that the mat has almost invariably to be on the same spot. In laying a green, particular care must be taken so as to ensure efficient drainage, and the turf used must be fine and wiry in substance, and such as to stand plenty of wear. Experience has taught that the turf found growing on the sand by the seashore is incomparably better than any other for a bowling-green, and so great is the demand for it, that a price quite equal to the value of the freehold of the land has to be paid before a sod can be turned. For many years the Ayrshire coast was the chief source of supply, but of late that has become exhausted, and nowadays we frequently hear of turf being brought from such distant isles as Colonsay and Islay. Of course all bowling-greens must be kept closely cut and rolled ; and to obtain the best results it is necessary to mow it a few times each season with a specially set scythe. An expert mower with a proper scythe will cut barrowfuls of grass after the closest-set machine can get no more ; and the advantage to be obtained, both in the way of keener play and a healthier green, can only be appreciated by those who know from experience.

The aim of every player is to get his bowls—"woods," they are sometimes called—nearer to the jack than his opponent, and immense variety is afforded by "drawing," "guarding" a shot or a road, "trailing" a jack to alter the position of an end, "striking" to remove an opponent or clear the way, and so on.

Up to a few years ago there was no recognised central authority on the Scotch game, but in 1891 one of the best bowlers in the north, Mr. James Brown, acting upon a suggestion dropped by the present writer, founded the Scottish Bowling Association. Already it has organised a couple of championships each season, one for single-handed play and the other for rinks, and the prizes offered are looked upon as the highest honours in the Bowling world. In Scotland all inter-association, inter-county, and inter-club matches are played in rinks, but at tournaments the play is almost invariably single-handed, although there are occasionally some for "pairs," and there is also the Association rink contest. Never a season passes but several tournaments take place, and at some of the larger meetings it is not uncommon to find more than five hundred entries, and the play extending over the best part of a month. It remains to add that the present practice of giving money-prizes is being opposed by an ever-increasing host of bowlers, who warmly approve of the strictly amateur position taken up by the Association.

J. B. Little.

BOWLING—"Booling with bouls," as it is pronounced by Northumbrians, is played on a course whose length varies from 1,150 yards to one mile. The object is to cover the course in the fewest possible throws. For each throw a short run may be taken up to the "trig," which is a line fixed by the referees at right angles to the course, at the point where the ball last fell. The length of the trig is about two yards. The arm may be swung completely round before the bowl leaves the hand in the final lurch. The weight of the balls, which are mostly of stone, sometimes of concrete, varies from 3 oz. to 50 oz. Weights are, of course, specified before a match. Where the players are to be handicapped, the heavier balls are given to the better players.

In Newcastle the game is played largely by pitmen on the Town Moor, which consists of 927 acres of undulating grass land. Saturday afternoon is, naturally, a favourite time. Another Northumbrian course is at Newbiggin. The knots of pitmen who play it are extraordinarily keen and excited over it, and it is well not to balk them by ill-timed crossing of the course.

GLOSSARY.

Alley—Properly a covered green, but sometimes used for any ground on which the game is played.

Auld-bowl—The bowl lying nearest the jack. Sometimes called Cast-bowl.

Baby—[*See* JACK.]

Back-hand or Cross-hand—The left-hand side of a right-hand player and *vice versa*. Used also in description of a throw when the hand is across the body at the moment of delivery and the bias on the right side of the bowl.

Bares—The old name for *Greens*.

Blocking—(Also **Guarding** and **Obstructing**.) Playing a bowl so that it shall come to rest between the next player and the jack, or any bowl at which he may wish to aim.

Burned—The jack, or bowl, is said to be "burned" when touched, accidentally or deliberately, by any player, or spectator after coming to rest. If by the former, the opposing side choose whether they will begin the "End" (*q.v.*) again or not, but if by the latter, it *must* be recommenced.

Cast—The unit of scoring; a ball lying within six feet of the jack and nearer to it than any opponent.

Charging—[*See* FIRING.]

Cot—[*See* JACK.]

Cote—A sliding touch upon another bowl. [*See* KISS.]

Cross-hand—[*See* BACK-HAND.]

Dead length—A bowl stopping exactly on a level with the jack.

Dead bowl—A bowl which is out of the game because:—

(1) It did not travel three yards from the "footer" (*q.v.*);
(2) It travelled off the ground, or
(3) It was moved by its owner or a partner.

Directors—The captains of sides; also called **Drivers** and **Skips**.

Ditchers—Bowls that at the first cast, or in the subsequent play, are driven off the green.

Drawing—Playing slowly up to an unobstructed jack, so as to rest close by it. In Scotland, placing a bowl a little beyond jack in the direction in which it is expected to be driven.

Drivers—The last players of a side, and usually the captains. [*See* DIRECTORS.]

Duggler—A bowl at rest touching the jack.

End—One delivery of all the bowls upon the two sides, after which the jack is again "set." Also called Head.

Firing—Sending the bowl with great force in order to carry away the jack or an opponent's bowl; or to disarrange the mass upon the chance of improvement. In Scotland it is known as **Riding**.

Footer—The square cloth or mat set by the place from which the jack was thrown. Each player must have one foot upon it at the moment of delivery. Also known as **Trig**. [*See* HOB.]

Fore-hand (also **Open-hand**)—The right-hand side of a right-hand player and *vice versa*. Used in description of a shot in such direction, with the bias on the left side of the bowl.

Green—The level grass surface upon which the game is played. It should be not less than forty yards square.

Guarding—[*See* BLOCKING.]

Head—[*See* END.]

Hob—The straight stick formerly used instead of the "footer" (*q.v.*). Each player must have one foot behind it when delivering the bowl.

Jack—The object at which all the bowls are aimed. It is usually turned from light-coloured wood, or from darker wood and painted white. Not infrequently, it is made of white earthenware; the diameter should be within the limits of 3¼ and 3¾ inches. Sometimes called **Cot** or **Baby**.

Kiss—[*See* COTE.]

Land—A local expression for the ground over which the ball is to travel (*e.g.* "Come this land.")

Lead—To throw the jack for a "mark" (*q.v.*).

Leaders—The first players upon a side.

Lurch Game—A game in which one side has scored five before the other has scored one.

Mark—A "mark" is *set*, *thrown*, or *led*, by the winners of an end after the score has been settled. It is obtained by throwing the jack, which should run not less than twenty and not more than forty yards from the footer.

Marred—If a bowl or jack in motion is impeded or has its course altered by any obstacle other than a bowl in play, it is said to be marred. If the jack be marred by a foreign article, or by a partner of the striker, the end is void, but if by an opponent, the striker may take his choice. If a running bowl be marred by the player or his partner, it is dead, and must be taken off the green; if by an opponent after passing the jack, the player may have his throw again, or may put the bowl where it would have gone; if by an opponent before passing the jack, he must have his throw again.

Narrow throw—A throw in which insufficient allowance has been made for bias.

Nutmegs—Very small bowls.

Obstructing—[*See* BLOCKING.]

Odd—Extra bowls played by a member of the side fewer in number to make the total throws equal.

Open-hand—[*See* FORE-HAND.]

Over—A throw which goes past the jack.

Play-finger—To deliver the bowl with the little finger resting on its inner or smaller side.

Play-thumb—To deliver the bowl with the thumb resting on its inner or smaller side.

Points—The unit of scoring. [*See* CAST.] The number required for a game varies according to agreement. Generally the total is from seven to eleven, but in matches sometimes as high as twenty-one.

Raking—Scottish for "Stiff-drawing" (*q.v.*).

Riding—Scottish for "Firing" (*q.v.*).

Rink—(1) A narrow section of a bowling-green, some twenty feet in breadth taken by one party for their game. (2) All the players upon the two sides. (Both terms are more common in Scotland than England).

Rub—Any obstruction to the bowl's course from inequalities of the ground or natural obstacles; also used of a running bowl sidling from another.

Score—[*See* POINTS.]

Short bowl—One that does not reach the jack.

Side—Varies in number. In Scotland usually four, and in East Anglia three. In the north of England single matches are common. There are rarely more than four.

Skip—[*See* DIRECTORS.]

Skittling—"Firing" (*q.v.*) without judgment and without necessity.

Standard—The light reed or cane usually employed to measure the distance between rival bowls and the jack. It is only used up to one yard. The reed is shortened until it will no longer rest upon the first tested bowl and the jack. If it can then be made to rest upon the second and the jack, the latter wins the cast.

Stiff drawing—Playing with such strength as to move the jack a few yards onwards, or to push out another bowl. It shades into "Firing."

Still bowl—A bowl at rest.

Through the house—A delivery that goes through a mass of bowls without touching any.

Trig—[*See* FOOTER.]

Turning the jack—"Means a player doing any palpable act to indicate that he claims the game to be up as the bowls then lie, and his opponent allowing the claim. The only period at which this can be done is when the claimant or his partner has one bowl to deliver after all the bowls of the opposite side have been played."—ROYLE.

Void end—A round which does not count anything to either side owing to some accident, *e.g.* the jack knocked off the green, or interfered with by a spectator.

Welshman—A handicap match. Adopted from Cock-Fighting.

Wide throw—A delivery which allows too much for the bias.

Woods—Another term for the bowls. The jack is said to be "wooded" when surrounded by bowls.

RULES.

The Game of Bowls as played by the Norfolk and Suffolk Bowling Association.

1. No player shall change his bowls after commencing a game, unless with his opponents' consent. The circumference of a bowl not to exceed 16½ inches.

2. On commencing a game, the footer must be placed by the leader before he throws the jack.

3. On changing ends, the leader, before he throws the jack, must place footer within one yard of the spot previously occupied by the jack, and from thence play must be resumed.

4. The footer must not be taken up until the last bowl has been played. If the footer has been taken up, and the last bowl by reason of a rub or set, has to be played again, it must be replaced as nearly as possible in its former position.

5. If the jack is struck off the green, the footer must be placed one yard from the edge opposite to where it had been struck; but if half the bowls have not been played, they must be returned, and play resumed from where the footer lay.

6. If the player who has to throw the jack fails in two trials to throw a mark, one of the opponents must then throw it. The defaulter (not the thrower) must play the first bowl. If the opponent at one trial fails to throw a mark, the defaulter again takes the lead.

7. If the jack in its course be impeded in any way, or stops on the land of any other players, it must be removed or thrown again.

8. If two jacks are thrown near the same place, the one that is last stationary must be pronounced not a mark, and must be removed or thrown again.

9. If a bowl be played before the jack is at rest, it must be taken off the green.

10. If a played bowl has reached its destination before the jack is pronounced not a mark, the end proceeds.

11. The jack must not be thrown so as to stop near the centre of the green and obstruct other players.

12. A jack, if delivered a yard from the boundary of the green, must not be played along the edge of the green, so as to rest at the same distance from the boundary. If the jack is at rest four yards from the edge, in a line with its course, it is a mark. A jack delivered four yards from the edge may rest at a distance of one yard.

13. The player on delivering a bowl must place his right or left toe on the footer, according as he plays with his right or left hand. Any bowl not so played may be stopped and played again. Any bowl not so played a second time, must be taken off the green.

14. A player after delivering a bowl must not follow it up in such a manner as to impede the sight of his opponent; if, after being cautioned, he persist in doing so, the opponents shall have the option of playing out the end, or declaring it void.

15. If a bowl be played out of turn, it may be stopped by an opponent; or, at his request, be played again in its proper turn; if, however, it has reached its destination, it must remain, and the opponent may play two bowls in succession if he has them.

16. If an opponent's bowl be played by mistake, it may be stopped; but if it has reached its destination, it must be replaced by the right bowl if requested.

17. If a bowl be played whilst the preceding one is in motion, it becomes a dead bowl.

18. A player may retain possession of the footer until his bowl has ceased running.

19. Players, when at the end where the jack lies, must not stand within the radius of the bowls as they are played, or directly behind the jack, so as to obstruct the sight of the other players.

20. When an end is finished, neither the jack nor a bowl that scores must be removed (unless with the consent of an opponent) until the casts are all counted and the players satisfied; otherwise the end may be declared void.

21. A person may be chosen to keep the score and declare it at each end; but if no scorer be chosen, the leader, before he throws the jack, must declare the state of the game by pronouncing his own score first, and loud enough to be heard by his opponents.

22. If a running bowl be impeded by an opponent, or any other cause, before it reaches the jack, it must be played again; but if impeded by the player or his partner, it must be taken off the green.

23. If a running bowl be impeded by the player or his partner, after passing the jack, it must be taken off the green; but if impeded by an opponent, or a bowl of the player's, it must remain where it stops.

24. If a still bowl be displaced by an opponent, or any other person, or by a bowl or a jack of any other players, it must be replaced as nearly as possible in its original position.

25. If a player touch or displace a still bowl of his own or his partner, it must be taken off the green.

26. If a player take up or remove one of his own, his partner's or an opponent's bowl, to give himself or partner an advantage in play, he forfeits the game.

27. Before delivering a bowl, a player or his partner, on obtaining permission, may remove a bowl belonging to any other foreign set of players, if it obstructs his play, or they may take it up to prevent a running bowl of their own (but not an opponent) striking it.

28. If the jack is displaced by a bowl or the jack of any other players, or by any exterior cause, or taken up by one of the players whose bowl was nearest to it, before the last bowl is played, the end is void.

29. A player may block an opponent at hand whenever he thinks proper, but he must not play his bowl a less distance than four yards from the footer. The bowl must be played, for, if placed, it becomes a dead bowl.

30. If a player strike the jack with his bowl, and the jack rub or hit his partner, or any other person, or a bowl or the jack of any other players, the end is void; but if it rub or set on a bowl of the player's, it must remain where it stops, and the bowl nearest to it (when the end is finished) scores first cast.

31. Whenever the jack is struck off the green the end is void.

32. If a player touch the jack for the purpose of claiming the game, before the opponents have played their last bowl, or before he has a sufficient number of casts to win, the end is void.

33. The jack must not be turned, but may be touched gently with the finger.

34. If the last player and his partner have a sufficient number of casts laid to win the game, he may decline playing his bowl, or he may request his partner to touch the jack; and if, by then playing, he change the position of the jack or bowls, it does not alter the game.

35. If he play his bowl without the jack being touched, it must not be stopped or the jack touched; and if the position of the jack or bowls is changed, and the casts reduced to less than will make the game, or if he set an opponent's bowl first, it scores, and the game proceeds.

36. If a bowl so played be stopped, or the jack touched by the player or the partner, the end is void.

37. When it is doubtful which bowl is nearest the jack, it must be decided by a standard, if the distance is less than a yard. After the standard is taken by the leader or his partner, the bowl must be removed; then, if the opponents can make it rest on their bowl and the jack, they win the cast.

38. Whenever a bowl rests against another, and the bowl rested against has to be removed to allow the other to be measured from the point nearest the jack, it must be removed by an opponent or a disinterested person, and measured as it settles after such removal.

39. No measuring is to be permitted until the end is finished.

40. A player may instruct his partner, but he must not stand or place any object between him and the jack for the purpose of indicating the land to be taken when he is in the act of playing.

41. Bowls played or struck off the green, or prevented going off by resting against anything at the edge or in the channel, must not be scored.

42. If, during the course of the game, it becomes so dark that the jack cannot be distinctly seen from the footer, any player may have a light exhibited at the jack if he so request.

43. Spectators are not permitted to instruct, or give any intimation whatever to players, and are amenable equally with the players to the rules of the green and the game.

44. No persons, other than players, are allowed on the green, except measurers, at such times as their services are required, and dogs are not to be brought on the green by any person.

45. No bowl to count that is more than six feet from jack.

46. If a bowl be carried by the player four yards from the footer, the bowl to be forfeited.

NOTE.—The rules of the game vary considerably in different parts, but the foregoing may be accepted as typical.

BOXING—This art, of great antiquity and undoubted usefulness, whether looked upon as a most interesting and perfect branch of gymnastics or as a means of defence which supersedes the use of artificial weapons, has always been held in high regard in England; and, notwithstanding the decay of the prize-ring as an institution, probably at no period in the history of the country was the "noble art of self-defence" in greater vogue than it is at the present time.

Boxing, in this country at all events (for in what is called "la boxe française" the use of the foot as a weapon is admitted and encouraged), consists essentially in striking with the closed hand or fist, covered for purposes of practice with the boxing glove of soft leather, stuffed with horse-hair, to act as a necessary buffer between the face and the attacking knuckles.

There has grown up, round what would appear to the uninstructed mind a simple matter, a very complicated and artistic system of attack and defence, subject to such rigid prescriptions, as shall insure immunity from brutality and unfairness.

An extraordinary development of glove-fighting has been seen of late years, and, instead of the old battles with bare knuckles which were so frequent in the early Victorian age, we have seen that a great deal of encouragement, pecuniary and social, has been bestowed upon glove-contests between professional exponents of the art.

Whether this has resulted, as might at first sight have been expected, in an increase of scientific development as distinguished from mere endurance and power of giving as well as receiving punishment, or whether something has not been sacrificed in the way of general efficiency to the desire to terminate a contest abruptly by a "knock out," is a question which requires some consideration.

It is certain that the majority of boxing matches in the present day are so terminated, whereas in the old days of knuckle-fighting, the days of the Fives-court, Nat Langham's, Jem Shaw's, Bill Richardson's, and other well-known resorts of the old fashioned fighting-man and his patrons, this seldom occurred; and the fact may be attributed, we cannot but think, to their "shaping" in the manner we shall endeavour to describe when treating of position, and to the jealous care with which a straight use of the left-hand was taught and practised.

The object now seems to be in too many instances to endeavour by hook hits and round half-arm hitting to "send to sleep" an antagonist as soon as possible, risking in the process the reception of hits which, if made with the bare knuckles, could not but stop the most thorough "glutton" for punishment.

An example of the brilliant and successful use of the straight left against these attempts is to be found in the case of an accomplished coloured boxer, Peter Jackson, whose style shows more of the old form than that of most of his colleagues.

It is a notable fact, upon which we may perhaps be allowed to congratulate ourselves without being charged with too much chauvinism, that England and her colonies, notably Australia, have produced so many able exponents of the art of boxing and that the majority are of Anglo-Saxon or Hibernian blood, whether hailing from this country or the United States; and that several boxers of eminence from the last-named country have to acknowledge the United Kingdom as their native home.

The general enthusiasm for the art of self-defence has spread from the civil population to the military forces, and there is something very remarkable in the rapid strides that have been made of late years in this direction in the army, the navy also, as might be expected when anything combative is toward, being well in evidence.

The Brigade of Guards some four years ago showed the way by engaging efficient instructors, and now, thanks partly to this good example, at such great military centres as Woolwich, Chatham, Aldershot, Portsmouth and the London barracks, regimental and garrison competitions are held each winter, and an annual championship meeting takes place at Aldershot. That this manly and healthy sport possesses the sanction and good-will of the higher authorities is shown by the fact that the present commander-in-chief, Lord Wolseley, stated when presenting the prizes at Chelsea Barracks, that he hoped that boxing would very soon form part of every soldier's education.

We can only wonder that the authorities at Scotland Yard and the chiefs of police throughout the country have not insisted upon instruction in boxing forming a part of every policeman's education. The time is probably not far distant when this will be the case, no doubt to the great advantage of a fine set of men who have very arduous and dangerous duties to perform with an equipment of arms much inferior to that used by any other police force in the world. Even if they use the comparatively inefficient weapon which they carry, the truncheon, except in circumstances of the greatest pressure, they have to run the risk of severe censure.

We have said that the English race, using the term in its widest sense, appears undoubtedly to possess a marked pre-eminence in the theory and practice of the "noble art of self-defence;" but let us caution the aspirant, proud in the confidence of youth and strength and flushed with a sense of racial predisposition, that skill in boxing does not come by the light of nature; and that, if he desire to use his "natural weapons" to the best advantage, he will be well advised in seeking the tuition of some accredited master. It is only by assiduous practice and imitation of well chosen examples that proficiency is to be attained in what is a highly complicated and scientific sport.

None of the arts of defence can be learned from books, though books may be useful as adjuncts to practical demonstration, in fixing principles, maintaining what is of value in tradition, and furnishing useful hints and necessary cautions.

This being premised, we will endeavour to explain as succinctly as possible those different positions, leads-off, counters, guards, stops, and means of avoiding hits by ducking, slipping, and getting away which experience has taught to be most useful.

We shall adopt the following classification:—

Position—Getting About and Breaking Ground—Lead-off at Head with Left Hand—Guard for Lead-off at Head with Left Hand—Guard with Right-hand and Counter with Left-hand—Lead-off and Guard Left-hand Counter—Counter at Body with Left Hand—Counter at Body with Right Hand—Lead-off with Left Hand and Duck—Left-hand Lead at the Body—Guard for Left-hand Lead at the Body—Stop for Left-hand Lead at the Body—The Upper Cut—Double Hit at Body and Head with Left Hand—Guard for above—Right-hand Cross-Counter—Stop for Right-hand Cross-Counter—Feints—Draws—Ducking—Slipping—In-Fighting.

Position—Place the left foot in front, pointing straight towards your opponent, the left

FIG. 1.—POSITION.

knee slightly bent and foot flat on the ground, the right foot about once its own length in rear of the left with the toes slightly turned to the right, but not nearly so much as to form a right angle with the left foot, the ball of the right foot on a line with the heel of the left, the right heel slightly off the ground, the weight being chiefly on the ball of the right foot.

The body is turned three-quarters towards your opponent, the head being slightly inclined to the right and not presented full-face, but in such a manner that you maintain your view of your opponent chiefly with the left eye. This position diminishes greatly the chance of the point of the jaw, the mark for the right hand cross-counter, being reached.

The right hand and fore-arm are to be placed across the lower part of the chest, nearly horizontally, so as to cover that part of the pit of the chest which is known as "the mark." This is a point of major importance, as a severe punch in this part is both painful and disabling, and if unchecked might bring a friendly sparring match to an abrupt end.

The left hand and fore arm are to be held horizontally on a level with the elbow, so that arm and forearm form a right angle, the hand pointed towards the opponent, the elbow kept close to the side.

Let the shoulders be well kept down, the right slightly lower than the left. Stand easily and avoid any fixing or tightening of the muscles; let your whole attitude be free and unconstrained; a great deal depends upon the suddenness of the attack and, if the muscles are rigidly strained, quickness and ease are rendered impossible. This, however, will be better seen when we come to consider the next point.

Getting About and Breaking Ground—The beginner, being placed in proper preliminary position, or "on guard," must now be taught to shift his ground in accordance with the varying needs of the situation. Let it be impressed upon him that the relative position of the feet is to be rigorously maintained, except in the case of some attacks and counters, to be described in due course, after the delivery of which he immediately returns to the original position. This position, which undergoes some slight alteration in accordance with the idiosyncrasies of various teachers, is, in the main, the best as a point of departure for attack or defence, the left hand being ready for immediate use in leading-off or countering, the right hand guaranteeing the most vulnerable portions of the body, ready to guard the head and mark, and held as a crushing reserve to be used when opportunity presents itself.

To Advance, the pupil is taught to step forward about the length of his own foot with the left foot, the distance traversed being naturally regulated by his length of limb, the left heel being distinctly the first portion of the foot to touch the ground, and to follow it up smartly with the right foot.

In Getting Back, the right foot is moved to the rear, about the above named distance, followed by the left foot. In this and the preceding case the distance between the feet and their relative positions are to be carefully maintained.

Boxers are in the habit of circling round each other, or in other words "breaking ground" either to right or left, but the beginner is to be taught that breaking ground to the *right* is safer as by that means he keeps out of danger of his adversary's right hand, and his feet are less likely to be crossed, a thing which might be disastrous to the combatant if attacked when in that position.

To Break Ground to the Right, the boxer steps about twelve inches to the right with the right foot and immediately places the left foot in position in front of it.

To Break Ground to the Left he steps to the left with the left foot, and without loss of time, places his right in position in rear of it, but this mode of procedure, as stated above, is considered fraught with danger and must be used with caution.

Sometimes the boxer may jump back with both feet off the ground at once, taking care to maintain the proper position. This jump may be repeated when hard pressed and when there is sufficient floor room. When out of distance, the left hand may be dropped to ease it, but when within distance it must immediately be brought up to the proper position.

The beginner must be taught to get about easily and lightly, moving his feet smartly and retaining his balance and the proper distance and relative position of the feet. The hands are not to be kept immovably in the attitude described but to move easily backwards and forwards in unison with the movements of the feet.

Lead-off at the Head with the Left Hand—This is the most frequent and the most useful and safe of all attacks, and upon its proper execution, smart and quick, with the weight of the body assisting the force of the

Fig. 2.—Lead-off at Head with the Left and Guard.

blow, must the whole system of sparring be founded. It must be made with quickness and determination, otherwise the task of your adversary in countering is rendered dangerously easy.

Step in, in the manner described for the

advance, striking with the left hand at your adversary's head, letting hand, body, and foot work simultaneously with as much rapidity as you can possibly command. Take care that the left hand and elbow are in proper position—at the beginning of the attack, the left elbow is to be close to the side and the hand is to be shot out smartly with the palm slightly upward, so that the knuckles will be the part to come into contact with the face.

Your left foot should touch the ground at the same time as your hand reaches your opponent's face, and should bear most of the weight, the right foot resting lightly on the ground. Take care that, in stepping in with the left foot, the heel is distinctly the first portion of the foot to touch the ground and that the foot points straight towards your antagonist, as the hand will instinctively follow the direction of the foot. Immediately after the delivery of your attack step smartly back, your left hand in position to meet any emergency. If hard pressed you may spring back, both feet off the ground at once.

It may here be pointed out that the boxer must in all cases hit with that part of the glove which covers the knuckles and not with the point or the inside of the glove; striking with the inside, or "heel of the glove" as it is sometimes called, would entail disqualification in competitions, and hitting or flicking with the point of the glove is an attempt to gain reach at the expense of all efficiency.

Hits are to be directed at the head and face and any part of the body above the belt.

Guard for Left Hand Lead-off at the Head—Raise the right hand in front of the left side of the forehead, half extend the arm, and maintain your view of your opponent over your right fore-arm, keeping the elbow down and the palm of the hand outwards. You will find that in this position you get a pad of muscle before the bones of the fore-arm which will break the force of the blow considerably. Whilst this attack and guard are being practised, as they should be, assiduously, so as to make them a good basis of departure for the other movements, care should be taken that the eyes are kept open (a matter not always so easy as it would seem) and fixed upon the adversary, so that no movement of his may be lost, and that the mouth is kept shut. A blow upon the partially unclosed jaw shakes it terribly and might even dislocate it. The hands must not be kept constantly clenched, which would only fatigue the muscles and cause slowness and stiffness. In getting about or sparring round, in what is known as "out-fighting," the hands are to be kept partly open and are to be firmly closed on the delivery of a blow and, in some instances, on the formation of a guard. The left hand lead-off at the head may be met in other ways to be described in due course—as by the left hand counter at the head, or left hand counter at the body with a duck to the right, or by the right hand counter at the body with a duck to the left, or by that most effective of manœuvres, though difficult of execution, the right hand cross-counter.

Guard and Counter with Left Hand on the Lead-off at the Head with the Left—Form your head-guard as before described with the right hand, and strike out at your adversary's face with your left at the same moment of time. The position of the left hand and arm is precisely the same as in the lead-off but the movement of the feet is different: you will keep the right foot firmly fixed on the ground and step forward with the left about once its own length. You here combine the two movements of guard and return, and must be careful to time them accurately and start at the same time as your opponent.

Lead-off and Guard the Counter—Should you anticipate that your opponent will counter at your head with his left on your lead-off, you will, as you lead off, guard with your right hand.

Counter at Body with Left Hand—Step in with the left foot inside your opponent's,

FIG. 3.—COUNTER AT BODY WITH LEFT HAND.

the ball of your foot coming on a line with that of his, keeping your right foot in place, firmly fixed on the ground, and helping the forward impetus of the body as in a fencing lunge. Incline body and head well to the right so that his hand in the lead-off may pass harmlessly

Fig. 4.—Counter at Body with Right Hand.

over your left shoulder and hit with the left hand at the mark, hand and foot working together. The palm of the hand is to be turned downwards. Here we have an example of that other position of the feet to which we have referred at the beginning of the article, and great care should be taken that the movement is correctly executed, and that the body is brought forward and downward as well as to one side sufficiently to bring the head out of danger without risking the loss of balance.

This movement has a certain kinship with a lunge in fencing but will be seen to differ in material particulars. It constitutes what is termed a "Duck," and we shall have frequent need to refer to it.

Counter at Body with Right Hand—To counter with the right hand at the body, bend the body and incline it and the head to the left, step forward in the same way as before with your left foot, the heel of the right off the ground, bring forward your right shoulder and hit with the right hand slightly below the heart, the palm of the hand turned down, keeping the left hand in position.

There is no possibility of stopping the right hand counter at the body when leading off with the left hand at the head, if the counter is aimed at the spot directed (just below the heart), your right arm, which protects the mark, not reaching sufficiently far to stop this blow, and your left arm being placed by its movement of attack in an impossible position for guarding.

Lead-off at Head with Left Hand and Duck—Lead-off at the head with the left hand, retaining your hold of the ground with your right foot as in the case last described, incline body and head to the right (duck) so as to allow your opponent's fist, should he counter, to pass over your left shoulder. The palm of the hand is to be slightly downward at the time of delivery. The right hand is to be kept in position over the mark.

Lead-off at Body with the Left Hand—This is made in the same manner as the preceding attack, with the right foot fixed. The duck is to the right in this instance. The blow is delivered at the mark. The knuckles are turned up (palm downwards), the elbow slightly inclined outward. After the blow is delivered you are to spring back well out of distance. It will be observed that all these attacks with ducks bring you much nearer to your opponent than the left-hand lead-off at

Fig. 5.—Lead-off at Head with Left Hand and Duck.

the head, and there is increased necessity for smartness in getting away to avoid what is known as an upper cut, to be described presently.

Guard for the Above—This is guarded by the right arm, simply kept in its original position across the body, carefully and efficiently covering the mark.

Stop for Lead-off at Body with the Left—Immediately your opponent commences to move, if you are able to judge his intentions correctly, which practice will enable you to do, counter straight at his head with your left hand. This will effectually check the completion of his attack and form what is very aptly termed a "stop." It is in fact a time hit and if delivered with judgment is an exceedingly effectual and pretty manœuvre.

Should you not have attempted to stop him upon this attack, you can guard it in the ordinary way with your right hand, and before he has time to spring back out of reach, upper cut him with the left hand.

The Upper Cut, as its name implies, is a hit delivered in an upward direction with either hand; with the arm bent and the elbow kept down. As your adversary is brought close to you by his movement of attack, there is neither need nor opportunity for you to advance on him, but the blow can be swung upward with great force, every muscle in the body seeming to aid its impetus, and if the right time is seized, the position of your opponent's head and body will insure his getting its full force.

Fig. 6.—Double Hit at Body and Head with the Left Hand.

This very useful hit may be used as a counter under several circumstances, especially upon your adversary's leading off with the right hand at the body (a practice not to be recommended), or, upon his leading off at the head with either hand, holding his own head down. Form a body guard with the left arm or a head guard with the same, according to the circumstances of the attack; and cut upwards at your opponent's face with the right hand, the arm bent and elbow down. In case of a wild and ill-judged rush on your opponent's part, with head down and arms flapping wildly like the sails of a windmill, the upper cut may advantageously be administered with either hand according to the position of his head, and will probably have a markedly deterring effect.

It may be well here to notice that methods are taught by skilful professors for "drawing" these upper cuts, and for dealing with them when so drawn by various movements of great practical interest.

These would come under the designation of "Feints," of which we shall endeavour to give a summary description in due course, but they are only to be learnt by careful practice in sparring with an able instructor.

Double Hit at Body and Head with the Left Hand—Lead off at the body in the manner just mentioned above and, instead of making the rapid retreat there described, bring forward your right foot to its ordinary distance from the left in the guard position and step in again with the left, striking at the face as in leading off with the left, except that here in both instances the palm of the hand should be turned down. In this case, the assault at the body is what is called a "draw," and acts as a feint by drawing off your opponent's attention from his head, which is your real objective.

Guard for Double Lead-off—Form a body guard with the left arm by placing the forearm across the body in such a manner as to cover the mark, elbow close to the side, and form your head guard with the right hand in the usual manner.

This double guard is exceedingly useful, and one may often use it when hard pressed or puzzled by a sudden and unexpected rush of an antagonist. It is well in this case to combine it with a movement of retreat.

Right Hand Cross-Counter—We have now to deal with a movement which, while it forms a most tremendous weapon in the hand of the boxer who knows how to time and execute it with perfect precision and absolute appropriateness in point of time, will land him in great difficulties if attempted at the wrong moment and without sufficient powers of execution. For this reason it is not to be attempted by the tiro until he has achieved a proper degree of proficiency in the various other attacks, stops and counters. It may be thus described:—Upon your opponent's moving to lead off with his left hand at your head, step in with your left foot inside his, so that the ball of your foot comes into line with that of his, and at the same time duck to your left, so that his hand may pass over your right shoulder, and strike with your right hand, knuckles turned up, at the point of his jaw, bringing your right shoulder well forward, by that means and the forward movement of your body in the duck, throwing the whole of your weight into the blow. The right foot is naturally drawn forward towards the left as this blow is delivered.

The position at the finish, if the movement has been well timed, is that your opponent's blow has passed harmlessly over your right shoulder, whilst your right hand has crossed over his left arm to land upon the point of the jaw. This blow, the force of which is increased by the momentum of the forward movement of both men, very often puts a final stop to an assault by "knocking out" its recipient. Even with muffled hands it comes with tremendous force and should be rather indicated than actually driven home in friendly sparring.

When the learner has sufficiently educated hand, eye, foot and, last but not least, judgment, to be able to bring this counter-hit to a satisfactory conclusion he may flatter himself that he has nearly passed out of his novitiate.

Stop for Right Hand Cross-Counter—If you can catch your adversary on the beginning of his movement, before he has had time to duck, hit straight at his head with your left hand and his movement will be effectually stopped. It is upon slow and tame attempts at leading off that the counters can be safely used and a determined and straight delivery renders them too difficult and dangerous to be properly executed.

Feints—The feint is, as its name implies, a feigned attack or simulacrum of attack made to enable you to judge of the plan of defence likely to be adopted by your adversary. It is also made at a certain point preliminary to the real attack, with a view to induce him to cover that point, and in so doing necessarily to uncover some other part at which the real attack will be delivered.

For instance, you may feint a left hand lead-off at the head by making a quick partial extension of the arm at the same time that you make a short step forward with the left foot. Should your opponent move to a head guard, you can then deliver a left hand body-blow.

Should he cover the head for a moment and immediately return to his ordinary guard you can follow up your feint at the head by a real attack made at the same spot.

Should he show a tendency to counter at the body or cross-counter at the head, you may find an opening for an upper-cut.

If your opponent, priding himself upon the possession of a good right hand, makes repeated attempts to cross-counter, you can make a feint at the head with the left hand to draw his counter, and follow it up with a determined

FIG. 7.—RIGHT HAND CROSS-COUNTER.

lead-off at the head with a duck to the right, which will entirely spoil his game.

Feints are also made with the right hand, but the beginner is warned to be sparing of either feints or lead-offs with this hand. Should it be desired to employ them, feints with the right are made by suddenly drawing back the arm as though preparing to hit, the hand not being "placed" for attack like the left (and this alone would serve to show the danger of leads with this hand). At the same time that you draw the arm back, the left foot is to make a short advance.

Draws—A draw is but a kind of feint, having for its object to draw your adversary's attack with the intention of countering upon his movement. It is not unlike what is sometimes termed a "combined attack" in fencing.

Ducking—This has already been described in various appropriate positions; its essence is to avoid a blow by moving the head to one or other side at the same time that it is carried upon a lower plane than that of the general guard. Examples of it have been given in the description of the right hand cross-counter, the left-hand counter at the head, that at the body, &c. It is an exceedingly useful manœuvre, but it must be used with caution, as if a man can be induced to duck upon a feigned attack, he is very likely to become the recipient of some unwelcome attention in the way of an upper-cut.

Slipping—This affords a way of getting out of an awkward position, such as, for instance, occurs when you have been forced into the corner of a ring, or may be useful in the case of your being subjected to the rush of a man carrying heavier metal than yourself. Upon your opponent's advance, feint a lead-off with your left, duck to the right, and, instead of recovering backwards in the ordinary way, bring up your right foot and make another step forward with the left foot, passing under his left arm. This will bring you on the left side of your opponent instead of his front, and to face him again you must, of course, turn smartly to your left once more.

In-Fighting—We have so far dealt with what is termed 'out-fighting,' and have now to describe what happens when two men come to really close quarters: here we have done with all finessing and manœuvring, and the only thing possible is to try to hit quicker and harder than your opponent and to endeavour to get your hands inside his, as by that means you gain a considerable advantage.

In-fighting is brought about generally by one of the men getting cornered and setting to work to fight his way out like one "rightly struggling to be free," or simply obeying the natural law which dictates combat to every hunted animal whose retreat is cut off, and is often forced by a boxer who finds himself over-matched at out-fighting by an adversary gifted with a better left hand than his own.

When this happens, you will bring your right foot nearly in line (front line) with your left, the ball of the right foot on a level with the heel of the left and with an interval of about 12 inches separating the two; you will keep your head down by well sinking the chin, while you keep your eyes fixed on your opponent's and strike with right and left hands as quickly as may be at the head, not drawing back the arms too far, and throwing the weight of the body into each hit by bringing the shoulder forward as you strike. Both knees are slightly bent. In beginning in-fighting, the left hand should be aimed at the face, the right hand at the point of the jaw. This gives the desired position inside your opponent's arm. Holding your adversary is not allowed in competitions, and it is better, irrespective of this, to have both hands free and busy in hitting. Blows should mostly be aimed at the head, the mark being visited when occasion offers; they are delivered with a bent arm, and constitute what is termed "half-arm-hitting."

After the delivery of four or five effective blows you must get away smartly. Nothing is more distressing to the onlooker than to see two men, exhausted and out of breath, tumbling up against each other and feebly pushing their gloves each into the other's face.

The above description, although it makes no claim to be exhaustive, will give, we hope, to the inquirer a sufficient idea of the various modes of attack and defence which are most sanctioned by experience.

Other methods of attack there are, no doubt, and some of them, such as the lead-off at head or body with the right hand, have been deliberately omitted, as we consider that they lay the boxer dangerously open when opposed to a man with a good left hand; and it is well, in accordance with the ancient precept "never despise your antagonist," always to behave as if you had a good man in front of you.

It used to be the custom in works on boxing to describe various wrestling movements such as the "cross-buttock," "back-heeling," &c., &c., and also what is named, by a kind of inuendo against the legal system of this country, "getting into chancery," from which it was as difficult to extricate a pugilist as a litigant; but since the well-nigh complete extinction of the old system of prize-fighting, these, with all sorts of holding and gripping, have been excluded from the field of legitimate boxing and particularly tabooed by the Amateur Boxing Association.

Training—It may be expected that we should say a few words as to the mode of preparation for boxing, although we cannot lay down a complete system of training for boxing competitions.

The boxer who wishes to maintain himself in good and tolerably hard condition and to develop quickness and activity, is, in the first place, recommended to avoid such exercises as tend to produce a huge and unwieldy development of muscle, which, however imposing in appearance, would only make him ponderous and slow in his movements. The rapid motions of the torpedo-boat are rather to be imitated than the slow, if majestic, progress of a first-class ironclad, and while the weight of the body should be employed in driving home the force of a hit, inert weight is of but little use. Weight-lifting, practice with heavy dumb- or bar-bells, Indian clubs, and slow gymnastic exercises, are therefore to be carefully avoided.

Quick movements with dumb-bells weighing from two to three pounds each, stepping in and striking at a suspended football and getting away smartly from its recoil, or, following the example of many distinguished boxers, skipping with a skipping rope, with plenty of walking exercise and occasional sprinting or running a distance of about sixty yards at top speed, are exercises admirably adapted to develop the breathing power and to induce quickness and alertness on the feet. Fencing and sabre or stick-play might be looked upon as excellent practice for sparring, were it not that they themselves demand so large a share of the attention of their devotees. Lawn-tennis, no doubt, requiring as it does, quick movements and a watchful and attentive eye, is an admirable preparation for boxing. In fact any exercise which tends to increase the respiratory powers and to develop the muscular system by a series of active movements not entailing too great an expenditure of force at a given moment may safely be recommended. [*See* TRAINING.]

Above all, let the learner never throw away any chance that may present itself of engaging in friendly sparring with the best men he can induce to put on the gloves with him; and let him rest assured that he will always find the best performers the best tempered and the most opposed to slogging and roughing.

Let it not be forgotten that it has been claimed for the exercise which we have endeavoured to describe, and, no doubt, rightly claimed, that its influence upon the physique and general health of the body is not more potent than its disciplinary effect upon the "morale" of its exponents: and that it has been supposed to teach endurance, fortitude, courage without swagger, and generous forbearance.

Should it continue to do this in the future as it has in the past, it cannot but be considered a powerful agent in the formation of what is best in the national character.

B. JNO. ANGLE.
G. W. BARROLL.

GLOSSARY.

Break away—To get away from an opponent.

Break ground—To take up a fresh position to the right or left.

Bye—In a competition where the number is uneven, the odd man is said to draw a "bye," and has to box the usual number of rounds with a non-competitor.

Corner—The opposite angles of the ring in which contestants sit during the intervals between the rounds.

Catchweight (To box at)—Boxing without restrictions as to weight.

Counter—A blow given in response to an opponent's lead-off, as nearly as possible simultaneously.

Cross Counter (Right Hand)—A blow at the head delivered with the right hand, across an opponent's left lead at the head.

Draw—A feigned attack, to cause an adversary to expose his tactics.

Duck—Inclining the head to left or right to avoid a blow.

Feint—A show of attack made at one spot, in order to make an adversary guard that, and in the act uncover some other point.

Foul—An act committed contrary to the rules of boxing.

Gloves—Leather gloves padded with horsehair used in boxing.

Guard—Defence with either arm to protect the head or body.

In-Fighting—Fighting at close quarters.

Judges—Two officials placed at opposite sides of the ring. If their opinions agree the winner is declared, but should they disagree, the judgment of the Referee is demanded.

Knock-out—A blow which, in the opinion of the Referee, decides a bout by the temporary disablement of a contestant.

Lead-off (Left hand)—A hit with the left hand (not a counter) at the head or body.

Mark—The pit of the stomach.

Out-Fighting—Leading off from a distance and preventing your adversary from getting to close quarters.

Point—Either side of the chin.

Position—The attitude taken by a boxer when facing his opponent.

Referee—The official whose judgment is appealed to in the event of the judges disagreeing. He is invested with supreme power, and his decision is without appeal. He can disqualify a competitor in the event of a foul, or stop a contest when he decides that sufficient punishment has been administered.

Ring—A roped enclosure, of not less than fourteen feet square in open competitions.

Round—A period of time, usually of three minutes' duration, during which the boxers are continuously engaged. In competitions governed by the rules of the Amateur Boxing Association, three rounds are contested, two of three minutes and one of four, with an interval of one minute between each round.

Seconds—Men, generally professional boxers, appointed to attend on the contestants in the intervals between the rounds. During the progress of the rounds they must be outside the ring.

Side Step—Consists in drawing the left foot slightly behind the right foot, and springing sharply off the ball of the left foot towards the right front.

Slipping—On the adversary leading off, a long step forward, combined with a duck, is taken with the left foot, thereby avoiding the line of attack.

Stop—Frustrating the adversary's intention by a more rapid attack.

Time—The call to commence or conclude boxing.

Timekeeper—The holder of the watch, who times the duration of the rounds and of the intervals between the rounds.

Timing—A blow delivered simultaneously to the opponent's attack.

Upper Cut—This blow is in reality a counter, delivered upwards with either hand, when an opponent leads off or rushes in with his head down.

Weights—Boxers are divided by the Amateur Boxing Association into five classes, according to their weights, as follows:

Bantam Weight,	not exceeding	8 stone	4 lbs.
Feather	,,	9 ,,	
Light	,,	10 ,,	
Middle	,,	11 ,,	4 lbs.
Heavy	,,	...	any weight.

Bibliography—E. Donelly, *Self-Defence* (1879); B. J. Doran, *Science of Self-Defence* (1893, Toronto); John C. Earl, *Handbook of Boxing* (1893); Pierce Egan, *Boxiana* (4 vols. 1818–24); F. W. J. Henning, *Recollections of the Prize Ring* (1889); E. B. Michell, *Boxing* (Badminton Library, 1889, Longmans); H. D. Miles *Pugilistica* (3 vols. 1880–81); "Pendragon" (H. Sampson), *Boxing* (1878); E. E. Price, *The Science of Self-Defence* (1879); J. C. Trotter, *Boxing* (Oval Series, 1896).

BREAM (*Abramis brama*). [*See* ANGLING (COARSE FISH).]

Length of head 5 to 6, of caudal fin $4\frac{1}{3}$ to $4\frac{2}{3}$, height of body 3 to $3\frac{2}{3}$ in the total length. *Eyes*—diameter $4\frac{1}{2}$ to $5\frac{1}{2}$ in the length of the head, $1\frac{1}{2}$ diameters from the end of the snout, and 2 diameters apart. Body oval, elevated and strongly compressed. Head small, snout short and obtuse, mouth protractile and small, upper jaw slightly the longer and reaching posteriorly to below the anterior nostril, lips moderately developed. *Teeth*—pharyngeal; 5/5 compressed and notched at their extremity. *Fins*—the dorsal commences slightly behind the base of the ventral, and about midway between the front edge of the eye and the base of the caudal fin, and just below the end of the highest point of the dorsal profile, while its last ray is on a line with the first of the anal; it is highest anteriorly. Pectoral inserted low down, and as long as the head excluding the snout, it reaches to above the commencement of the ventral, and the latter to the origin of the anal. The anal fin is falciform, and highest anteriorly. Caudal deeply forked. *Scales*—of medium size, higher than wide, $6\frac{1}{2}$ or $7\frac{1}{2}$ between the lateral line and base of ventral fin. On the edge of the abdomen between the ventral and anal fins, the scales do not pass across, forming a sharp keeled edge. *Lateral-line*—curves downwards, passing along the lower third of the body to the base of the caudal fin. *Colours*—back of a dull olive or sea-green, lighter on the sides and beneath, the abdomen being silvery tinged with pink. In old fish the body becomes more of a yellowish colour. Fins brownish, the pectoral rays being often tinged with scarlet, which colour may be seen in the first few rays of all the other fins. Day, *Fishes of Great Britain and Ireland*, vol. ii. p. 193.

BREAM-FLAT OR WHITE BREAM (*Abramis blicca*). [*See* ANGLING (COARSE FISH).]

Length of head $5\frac{1}{3}$ to $5\frac{3}{4}$, of caudal fin 5, height of body $3\frac{1}{4}$ to $3\frac{1}{2}$ in the total length. *Eyes*—diameter $3\frac{1}{4}$ to $4\frac{1}{4}$ in the length of the head, $1\frac{1}{3}$ diameters from the end of the snout, and $2\frac{1}{2}$ diameters apart. Body oblong, elevated and compressed; dorsal profile in an almost regular curve to the commencement of the dorsal fin, from whence to the caudal it is somewhat concave; head rather small; snout short and obtuse; upper jaw slightly the longer, extending backwards almost to beneath the front edge of the orbit; mouth protractile, lips rather thick. *Teeth*—pharyngeal in two rows, 5-4, 2-3/3-2, 4-5. *Fins*—dorsal commences behind the insertion of the ventral and about midway between the front edge of the eye and the base of the caudal fin, and just beyond the termination of the highest point of the dorsal profile, while it extends usually to above the third or fourth anal ray, but occasionally not quite so far. Pectoral inserted low down, and as long as the head from behind the nostrils; it reaches to above the commencement of the ventral, which latter does not extend to so far as the anal. Anal falciform, highest anteriorly. Caudal forked. *Scales*—of medium size, higher than wide, five to six rows between the lateral-line and the base of the ventral fin. On the abdominal edge, between the ventral and anal fins, the scales do not pass across, forming a keel. *Lateral-line*—passes downwards and is continued to the base of the caudal fin. *Colours*—silvery, darkest along the back, sides tinged with rose-red, fins of a bluish colour, the dorsal, anal and caudal, with dark outer margins, the pectorals and ventrals tinged with red. Day, *Fishes of Great Britain and Ireland*, vol. ii. p. 197.

BREAM, SEA (*Pagellus centrodontus*). [*See* SEA FISHING.]

Length of head $3\frac{3}{4}$ to 4, of caudal fin 5 to $5\frac{1}{2}$, height of body $3\frac{1}{4}$ to $3\frac{1}{2}$ in the total length. *Eyes*—$3\frac{1}{3}$ to $3\frac{1}{2}$ diameters in the length of the head, 1 diameter from the end of the snout, and also apart. Interorbital space flattened. Preorbital wider anteriorly than it is posteriorly, its greatest depth being scarcely equal to half its length; it is unnotched over the posterior end of the maxilla. Opercle about twice as high as wide. Jaws of equal length in front; the maxilla reaches to beneath the front edge or even anterior third of the eye. Posterior nostril the largest and obliquely oval. *Teeth*—three or four irregularly placed rows of rounded teeth of different sizes laterally and posteriorly in either jaw, none on vomer, palatine, bones or tongue. *Fins*—dorsal spines rather strong, the fourth and fifth the longest, from whence they decrease in length; rays shorter than the spines, the last two somewhat thickened but not scaled nor adherent together; Donovan observes that in his example there were thirteen spines and eleven soft rays in the dorsal fin, the same number being shown by the artist. Pectoral as long as the head. Ventral not extending so far as the vent. Third anal spine somewhat longer than the second. Caudal deeply forked. *Scales*—finely ctenoid, seven rows between the eye and the angle of the preopercle. *Colours*—orange-scarlet, becoming lighter beneath. A large black spot on the shoulder intersected by the lateral line, but is absent in the young. Couch believed that it does not appear till they are twelve months old. Day *Fishes of Great Britain and Ireland*, vol. I., p. 36.

BROADSWORD—This weapon—designed for both cutting and thrusting, but pre-eminently for the former, as the rapier for the latter—has been the typical arm of the Englishman for four centuries, during which it has varied considerably in form. In its early days it had only a plain cross hilt sometimes accompanied by an outer ring, and a double edged blade; it was then used for attack only, and the defence was made with its faithful companion the hand buckler. Later on, this little shield, being irksome to carry on the person, went out of use, and the sword had to be employed both for offence and protection. The masters of the Elizabethan period had to teach the use of "verie manye weapons" mostly accompanied by an arm of defence carried in the left hand, but among their lessons they all laid considerable stress on the management of the "short syngle sword," which in course of time came of necessity to be provided with a "close" or basket hilt. In the last three centuries we find but very few works on the subject. The men who practised the art professionally were rough fighting fellows, skilful in the use of their weapons, and some of them possessed of the rare faculty of imparting their knowledge to others, but they were mostly unlettered men and unable to record it in book form. What we know of the earlier stages of the art we owe mainly to enthusiastic amateurs.

We must consider first the man who should be regarded as the father of English broadsword play, George Silver, who published in 1599 a little book named *Paradoxes of Defence*, which contains interesting matter but no instructive details. He afterwards wrote—and wrote only, for the works exist but in MS. form—two other books, *Brief Instructions on my Paradoxes of Defence*, and *Rules of Defence to be observed in open Fyght, &c.*, which are full of clear and concise information. In Silver's time the *lunge*, as we understand it, was unknown. Two hostile men "drew on sight," they approached each other by "passes" or steps, each manœuvring to place his enemy in a disadvantageous position when he would make a sudden rush upon him. Silver advises three principal "fyghts"—we call them "guards"—although he had many others: the "*Gardant fyght is to carry your hand and hylt above your hed w^t your poynt downe towards your left knee, w^t your sword blade somewhat neer your bodye, not bearing out your poynt but rather declynynge it a little towards your said knee, y^t your enemye crosse not your poynt and so hurt you."* The second is the "*Bastard gardant fyght, wch is to carry your hand and hylt below your hed brest hye or lower w^t your poynt downwards towards your left foot.*" The third is "*forehand, y^t is w^t poynts high, and hands and hylts lowe*"; in this guard the point was held quite upright. The "wards" or parries the lunge made its appearance, and the rough methods of running about and "charging" became tempered into the more refined school of later times. In the seventeenth century we find very little to help us. There appeared in 1639 a little book *Pallas Armata*, which treats of the sword, but is far less complete than Silver's *Brief Instructions*, and towards the latter end of the century we have the numerous works of Sir W. Hope of Balcomie, another famous amateur, who gives us, unfortunately, but very little of the broadsword. In the

SWORD AND GAUNTLET.

were made from these middle positions by moving the sword to the right or left, and they had no other distinctive names. Silver is the first author of any nationality who distinctly advocates parrying and riposting, to which he devotes an entire chapter "*of div^rs advantages y^t you may take by stryking from your wards at ye sword fyght*"; and he also gives a chapter on "*The manner of certaine gryps and clozes to be used at the syngle short sword fyght.*" These grips were methods of overpowering the enemy by seizing his sword hand when he ran in close enough to make it possible. After Silver's day eighteenth century, however, we get more light in the beautiful album of engravings by Captain James Miller (1737) which relate to the work of the "gladiating" prize-fighters, who fought their battles with weapons sharp enough to cut the calf of a man's leg so badly that "it hung over his heel like a flap." We now find Silver's "gardant fyght" still surviving under the name of the "hanging guard" but with the point much more advanced than formerly. The gladiators held this guard in high contempt, dubbing it the coward's guard, being a good one for a timid man to shelter under, but a bad one for a bold man to attack from. Then we have Silver's "forehand," exactly reproduced under the name of the "medium," with varieties in the form of the inside and outside guards, in which the points were still kept very high though not "bolt upright." Concerning the practices of the gladiators we learn a great deal from another enthusiastic amateur, Captain John Godfrey (1747), a practical man who says, "I have purchased my knowledge in the backsword with many a broken head and bruise in every *garian and Highland Broadsword Exercise*, and Roworth's *Art of Defence on Foot with the Broadsword and Sabre*, neither of which differ materially in their methods from Miller and Lonnergan, and both of which contain the useful *Ten Lessons of Mr. John Taylor*, a sturdy swordsman of the good old school whose name is recorded only in these two books.

In 1804 a new edition of Roworth came out in which the "medium" guard disappeared, and in the "inside" and "outside" guards the point

MEDIUM GUARD. (MILLER.)

part of me"—in his day there were no such luxuries as fencing masks. In 1771 there was published a valuable though unillustrated work by A. Lonnergan, this time a professional, and certainly the most accomplished master of the gladiator period, for whose precepts Miller's beautiful plates still serve as illustrations. He embodies all Miller's ideas in a series of very practical lessons, and he also holds to some of the rough work of Silver's day, notably the blow in the face with the pummel. We now reach the closing years of the eighteenth century, when we have in 1798 the Angelo-Rowlandson *Hun-*

is lowered into the positions of quarte and tierce as now understood.

In 1817 the first edition of Angelo's *Sword Exercise* was issued to the army by "authority," and after this point we notice the decadence of English swordmanship, when the teaching of it was taken out of the hands of the highly-trained fencing master and transferred to those of the mere drill sergeant.

In 1880, however, Professor J. M. Waite, a retired non-commissioned officer of the 2nd Life Guards, who, being of necessity much resident in London, was able to profit by gaining in struction from two famous masters, M. Pierre Prevost and Mr. Platts, produced a highly practical manual *Lessons in Sabre and Single-stick*, &c., in which he dismissed the old hanging guard and retained the inside and outside, but used in preference to all three the "High Seconde" which was at that time the guard most in fashion; it was good to shelter under, but very fatiguing to the arm if maintained for any length of time. It is worthy of note that the fencing sabres used in Waite's day were very heavy, quite equal to the Infantry officer's sword, and his book was written with the view of training the swordsman for war purposes.

In 1889 I myself endeavoured to transmit in my *Cold Steel* the old English play with certain additions from modern Italian masters, especially Parise and Cesarano; but the engaging guard which I find most useful for general purposes is a "medium" I adapted from the "Guardia mista" of Alfieri (1640), in which the upper arm and especially the deltoid muscle is in very reasonable repose, and I added to this a "Resting Medium" with the sword hand lowered a few inches until the pummel rests on the thigh, which thus supports the whole weight of both arm and sword, and the man's physical resources are held in reserve until they are required for action.

Now compare this with the guard ordered at present by the military authorities, in which the arm is raised horizontally to the height of the shoulder, and is held quite straight, a position most fatiguing to any man not endowed by nature with a *deltoid* the size of a shoulder of mutton (p. 144). Which of these two guards, then, is the best for a man of ordinary physique? Then again, compare the *lunge* of the old school, which is that accepted by the French and most of the Italians, with the lunge as enforced in the army by the Adjutant-General at the instance of the professor selected by the War Office. In the former (p. 144), the body is upright and in perfect balance, the position best adapted for facility in recovery; and the increase of reach, gained only by stepping forward with the right foot from the position of guard, is twice the length of the sole of the foot. In the lunge ordered by the Adjutant-General (p. 145), the feet when on guard are in an unnecessarily wide position, so that the increase of reach obtained by the lunge is very slight, and the man is obliged to filch a little more by stooping forward with his body. The official instructions are, "push the body forward to the fullest extent," &c.; thus the trunk is "pushed" into a position actually out of balance, and can only be recovered by excessive muscular exertion.

The good sound English school still exists, and, despite their efforts, I do not think that would-be reformers will succeed in killing it.

ALFRED HUTTON.

GLOSSARY.

Advance—The advance is made when the opponent is beyond the reach of a lunge, and is effected by stepping forward with the right foot about six inches, and then bringing up the left the same distance.

Arrest—The arrest is a direct point delivered during the development of some action of attack.

Attack—The attack (or **appel**) is the preliminary tap of the right foot before attacking. It may be single or double. The latter is a beat with the heel and then the flat of the foot in rapid succession.

Backsword—Old term for Broadsword (*q.v.*).

Beat—A movement which strikes the opponent's blade, in order to force it aside, and thereby to acquire an opening.

Broadsword—A sword which is sharpened upon one edge and blunt upon the other, with the exception of a space extending some eight inches from the point towards the hilt. This is also sharpened, and is termed the **False edge**. Also known as **Sabre**, and formerly as **Backsword**.

Carry Swords—The order to hang the arm at full length, holding the sword upright, so that the edge faces

MEDIUM GUARD. (HUTTON.)

the opponent, and the back rests upon the hollow of the right shoulder.

Centre of percussion—"Is that part of the blade which should strike the object at which the cut is directed. It is situated at about three-quarters of the length of the blade from the hilt. A cut given with any part of the blade above or below this point loses its effect from defective leverage."—(*Fixed Bayonets*, Hutton.)

Commanding is the seizure of an opponent's weapon or person. Now obsolete.

Corps à Corps—The term used to describe the position when the combatants have come so close that they can grapple with each other.

Counter—A hit delivered at the same moment as an opponent's. Similar to a counter in Boxing. Also used as verb.

Counter-time—A blow delivered at an opponent's arm, when he attempts a **time-hit** (*q.v.*).

Cut.—A stroke delivered with the edge of the sword. There are seven primary forms :—

(1) A diagonal downward stroke at the left side of the opponent's head.

(2) A diagonal downward stroke at the right side of his head.

(3) A diagonal upward cut at the inside of his right knee.

(4) A diagonal upward stroke at the outside of his right knee.

(5) A horizontal stroke at his left side.

(6) A horizontal stroke at his right side.

(7) A vertical downward stroke at his left side.

An eighth is sometimes added by Italian swordsmen :—

(8) A vertical upward stroke at the fork.

Cutlass—A short broadsword chiefly used by sailors and marines.

Disengage—To quit that side of the opponent's blade on which one is opposed by his guard, in order to effect an attack where there may be an opportunity.

Distance—[*See* MEASURE].

Draw—A deliberate exposure of some point in order to attract the opponent into delivering a stroke, for whose defence and reply one is fully prepared. Also called **Invite**.

Draw swords—The order to draw the swords from the scabbards and range them perpendicularly with the full stretch of the arm, the edge being to the rear.

Drawing cut—A stroke in which the edge, instead of falling motionless, moves along the surface which it meets, thereby increasing its cutting power.

Engage—To touch the opponent's sword as a preliminary to a contest, in order to ensure the readiness of both.

Engaging guard—[*See* GUARD].

False edge—[*See* BROADSWORD].

Feeble or **Foible**—The half of the blade from the point, which is the weaker.

Fort or **Forte**—The half of the blade from the hilt, which is the stronger.

Gain—A swordsman is said to make a "gain" when after a lunge he recovers his position, not by withdrawing his right leg, but by bringing up his left.

Grip—That part of the sword which the hand grasps.

Guard—The position of body and sword which is safest for defence and most ready for attack. There are four chief guards to one or other of which the swordsman should constantly return after an interchange of blows, and these are known as **Engaging Guards**.

(1) The **Medium Guard**, in which the elbow is about in. from the right hip, the edge inclined downward, and the point towards the opponent's face.

(2) The **Hanging Guard**, where the arm is raised above the head, the edge of the sword upward, and the point directed downward and toward the left. A variety of this is the **Low Hanging Guard**, in which the arm is held lower, but the sword points in a similar direction.

(3) The **Inside Guard** formed by keeping the wrist about the level of the waist, and the point about the level of the eyes, with the edge turned inward.

(4) The **Outside Guard** is similar to the above, except that the edge is turned outward. The special

MILITARY GUARD.

defensive movements against the various cuts are sometimes called "guards," but are more properly Parries (*q.v.*).

Hilt—The part by which the sword is grasped, and which affords protection to the hand.

Invite—[*See* DRAW.]

Loose Play—A contest in which the combatants deliver strokes and effect parries, not in any regular sequence, but as they think each may be most effective.

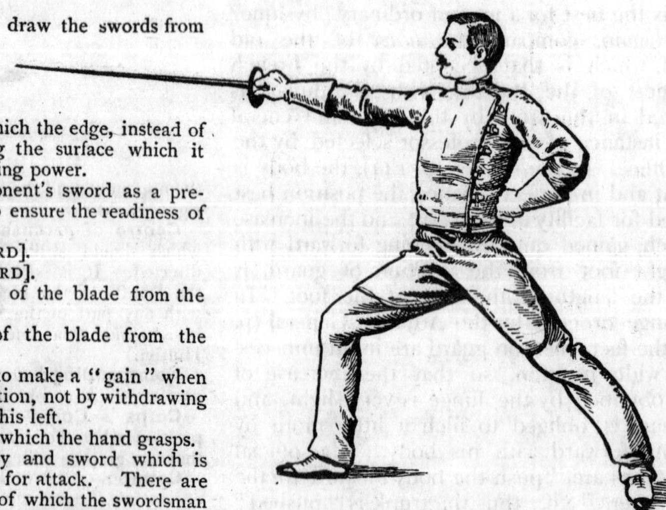

THE LUNGE. ("THE SWORDSMAN," 1891.)

Lunge—The completion of the attack, which is effected by stepping forward with the right foot two soles, length beyond the position of guard.

Mask—A helmet of wire netting protecting the face from injury, but giving full sight of an opponent.

Measure—The exact space in a direct line between the combatants, which must be traversed by a lunge. Hence **Perfect Measure** is when an opponent can be fairly struck without previously moving the left foot. **Out of Measure,** when one must advance at least a step to touch an opponent. **Within Measure,** when one can touch an opponent without lunging. (Also called **Distance.**)

Moulinet—A rehearsal of various cuts in one continuous swing of the sword.

Opposition—The covering one's self with the **Shell** (*q.v.*) of the sword when making an attack, so as to ward off a counter hit from an opponent.

Parade—[*See* PARRY].

Parry—A defensive movement against some particular stroke of an opponent's; sometimes confined to a defence against the point.

set lessons, such as 'les quatre reprises de Jean Louis;' 3rd, in a duel it means a series of attacks, parries and ripostes which occur whether ending in a hit or no."—(*Fixed Bayonets*, Hutton.)

Retire—To give ground intentionally by withdrawing the left foot six inches, and bringing the right a similar distance after it.

Return—A blow delivered immediately after parrying an opponent's blow, also called **Riposte.**

Return swords—The order to replace the swords in their scabbards.

Riposte—[*See* RETURN].

Sabre—[*See* BROADSWORD].

Saint George—The special name attached to the seventh parry (*q.v.*) which guards the head.

Shell—The part of the hilt which protects the hand from injury.

THE LUNGE. ("INFANTRY SWORD EXERCISE.")

The parries in reply to the Cuts (*q.v.*) are

Against Cut 1. Parry quarte.
,, ,, 2. ,, tierce.
,, ,, 3. ,, septime or low prime.
,, ,, 4. ,, seconde.
,, ,, 5. ,, low quarte or prime.
,, ,, 6. ,, low tierce or seconde high.
,, ,, 7. ,, high quartre or high tierce, or the St. George.
,, ,, 8. ,, horizontal quarte.

Pass—The pass is the stepping forward with the rear foot and bringing it one pace in advance of the other. Now obsolete.

Point—A thrust delivered with the point of the blade. There are two chief forms.

(1) Delivered with the hand in supination.

(2) Delivered with the hand in pronation.

Pronation—The position of the hand when the knuckles are uppermost.

Pummel—The lump of steel at the end of the hilt which balances the weight of the sword.

Recover swords—The order to drop the wrist from the "draw swords" position, to the level of the chin, the blade upright, and the edge to the left.

Redouble—To deliver a second blow very quickly after recovery if the opponent does not at once make a Riposte (*q.v.*) after parrying the first. Not to be confused with **Remise** (*q.v.*)

Remise—A second stroke made upon the same lunge as the first, when an opponent does not reply at once after parrying.

Reprise—"This word has three meanings: 1st, in an assault it is a second thrust made on the same lunge, but after having previously found the opponent's blade; 2nd, in a treatise on fencing it is a term applied to a series of

Slip—To withdraw the part of the body at which an opponent aims in order that, finding no resistance, he may overbalance himself, and give an opening for a cut.

Slope swords—The order to carry the weight of the sword upon the right shoulder, the elbow close to the body, and the arm bent straight forward at a right angle.

Spadroon—A light broadsword, now obsolete.

Stop-thrust—A thrust delivered at an opponent at the moment when he advances for the attack.

Supination—The position of the hand when the palm is uppermost, or, if the fist be closed, the nails.

Tang—The narrow piece of soft metal which is attached to the blade of the sword, and fits into the hilt.

Target—A circular or oval piece of wood or linen about 14 inches in diameter, with the cuts and guards marked upon it, before which the learner can rehearse by himself; also that part of the body and limbs on which hits are allowed to count.

Thrust—A stroke delivered with the point and not the edge of the sword.

Time cut, hit, or thrust—The putting in of a cut or thrust at the exact moment when the opponent is shifting his position, especially when he does so in preparation for an attack. To be distinguished from a **Counter,** which is a stroke delivered, not before, but at the moment of, an opponent's attack.

Transport—"The transport is the passing of an opponent's blade from one position to another, describing a conical movement." (F. V. Wright.)

Traverse—The traverse is a shifting of the ground circular-wise to either side, and is effected by moving either foot outward a distance of six inches, and bringing the other opposite to it.

Under Stop-thrust—A thrust delivered to meet an

opponent's advance, the left foot being allowed to glide backward, and the whole weight falling on the right leg.

Volte—Any sudden leap to avoid a stroke. Especially a turning of the whole body upon toe or heel.

A. B.

Bibliography—F. Cesarano, *Trattato teorico-pratico di scherma della sciabola* (Milano, 1874); Captain A. Hutton, *Cold Steel* (W. Clowes and Sons, 1889); Captain A. Hutton, *The Swordsman* (H. Grevel and Co., London, 1891); M. Parise, *Trattato teorico-pratico della scherma di spada e sciabola* (Roma, 1884; 4th ed., 1889); Carl A. Thimm, *A Bibliography of Fencing and Duelling* (John Lane, 1896); J. M. Waite, *Lessons in Sabre, Singlestick, &c.* (Weldon and Co., London, 1880).

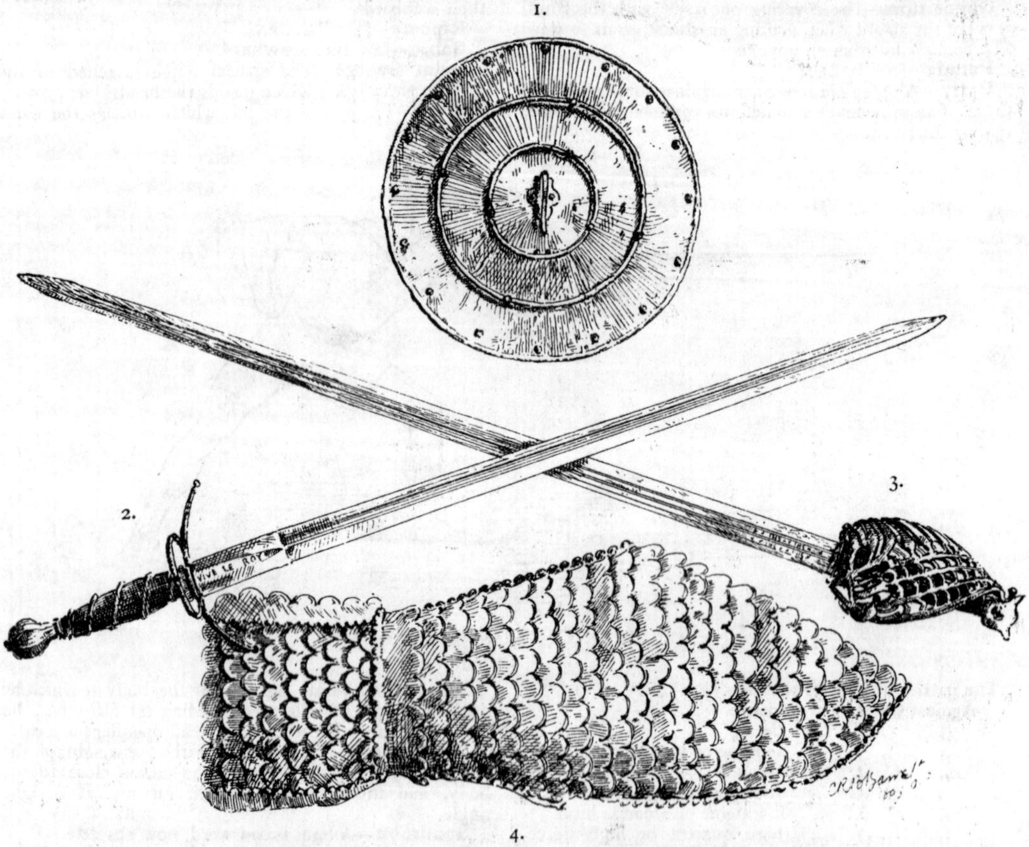

1. Hand Buckler, Time of Henry VIII., with Sword-breaking Rings and Belt-hook.
2. Double-edged Broadsword, Time of Henry VIII.
3. Basket-hilted "Schiavona," 17th Century.
4. Great Parrying Gauntlet of Buff Leather, worn on the Left Arm. (*See* p. 141.)

BUFFALO, CAPE (*Bos caffer*)—Zambesi name, *Nyati* or *Mboga*; Bechuana name, *Nari*. Height, 4 ft. 8 in. to 4 ft. 10 in. Body massive and covered with black hair. Skin of belly and inside of thighs a blackish red, very sparsely covered with hair.

The horns of an average full-grown bull should measure 36 inches in width (outside measurement) across the widest part; 25 inches from tip to tip, and 14 to 15 inches depth of palm at base.

The African Buffalo is generally described as the most savage and vindictive of all ruminants, but it is doubtful whether he fully deserves this character. His aspect is certainly ferocious, but this is caused by the massive weight of his body, the great breadth and thickness of his heavy horns, and especially by the savage expression of his little bloodshot eye. Unless wounded or suddenly disturbed, a Buffalo will seldom charge. As a rule, whether come upon singly or in a herd, they prefer to seek safety in flight; but a cow with a calf will often charge, and keep on charging after the remainder of the herd has fled. Old bulls which have been driven out of the herd and compelled to wander about alone, or in company with two or three other unfortunates, will occasionally charge if suddenly disturbed; and many a hunter has found himself in an unpleasant position on coming suddenly and unexpectedly in front of an old bull standing dozing in high grass. The first impulse of the startled animal is to rush blindly forward, and whatever happens to be in the way has to go, as nothing weaker than a wire rope will stop him. Except from cows when they have calves running by their sides there is no danger in approaching a large herd of Buffaloes in the open; and the bigger the herd the less the likelihood of a charge. In 1894 the writer, accompanied by two native boys, came across a herd of fully 700 Buffaloes feeding on the short grass of the Manamtoi plains near Sarmento. Burchell's Zebra, Blue Wildebeeste, and Lichtenstein Hartebeeste were feeding with the Buffalo, each species keeping pretty well together.

Not being in want of meat, and having already secured several good heads the writer walked out of the high grass which fringed the open plain on which the game was standing, and made straight for the dense mass of animals; without any intention of firing a shot, and merely to see how near they would allow him to approach them in the open. The Zebra and the Wildebeeste were the first to run; the former with many a kick and prance, and the latter frequently halting in their lumbering gallop to wheel round and toss their comical heads; but after both Zebra and Wildebeeste had disappeared into the high grass and palm scrub, the Buffalo remained standing motionless, with noses pushed forward, gazing stolidly at the writer and his two boys as they walked briskly towards the herd. Not until we were within 120 yards of them did they move, and then of a sudden they wheeled round, and the forest of evil looking heads and horns in front of us was transformed into a mass of black sterns and waving tails rapidly retreating amid a cloud of dust. Not one of these evil-looking brutes thought of charging the three attenuated and fever-stricken bipeds who walked up to them in the open.

CAPE BUFFALO.
Ht. at shoulder, 4 ft. 9 in. Av. horn meas. 36 in. Max. horn meas. 49½ in.

But in the case of a *wounded* Buffalo it is a totally different affair. It is then that the almost supernatural cunning and devilish ferocity of the animal shows itself. A beast is hit, perhaps only an inch or two from a vital part (or he *is* hit in a vital part by a bullet from that questionable implement the ·303 rifle), but not dropped, and disappears in the high cover. Beware then how you follow him; for while you and your boys are slowly picking out the blood spoor with eyes fixed on the ground, watching for the red splashes on the grass, the brute will have run back 100 yards or more parallel to his forward tracks, and is lying in wait ready to spring up and charge out on you as you come opposite him, and the odds are that he is upon you before you have time to raise your rifle. The sense of smell possessed by Buffaloes is very acute, and when wounded they will hunt a man through thick cover by this means just as a spaniel will follow the track of a rabbit; but the Buffalo, unwieldy looking though he be, is far quicker than the spaniel, and as long as a trace of scent remains he will follow it, eager to avenge, while his strength remains, the death wound he feels he carries in him.

A Buffalo does not charge blindly with head down, as do the European members of the bovine family. He carries his head at an angle of only a few degrees off the horizontal, and it is only at the moment of striking that the head is lowered and the horns brought into position for a sidelong thrust—consequently a charging Buffalo offers very little chance of being stopped by a bullet, even if there is time to aim; for, though he may be struck on the very small mark offered by the lower part of the forehead where unprotected by the massive horns, the bullet (if of ordinary calibre) is certain to glance off owing to the angle at which the head is carried. The nose is the part to aim at; for even if the brain is not touched by this means, the bullet will penetrate the neck and chest, and so disable the animal as to stop him in his charge. If a wounded Buffalo escapes into thick bush or high grass the wisest plan is to wait an hour before following him. He is certain to lie down before going far, and will become weak and stiff from loss of blood, and therefore less likely to make a sudden charge.

The greatest caution should be exercised when approaching an apparently dead Buffalo. So long as the slightest movement of the sides (caused by respiration) is visible he is capable of staggering to his feet and annihilating his pursuer. The writer once had a narrow escape in this way. Being in want of meat for the camp he went out in the early morning to secure it, and from the top of an anthill sighted five Buffaloes on a small patch of short grass, slowly feeding towards some heavy thorn and palm scrub in which they probably intended to lie up during the heat of the day. It was easy to run through the long grass up to within forty yards of them, and a bullet from the first barrel dropped a cow stone dead, while that from the second barrel appeared to have the same effect upon a scarcely full-grown bull, for both animals rolled over and lay motionless. The cow was inspected first, and proved to be dead, but on getting within twenty yards of the young bull he scrambled to his feet and charged. A hurried shot aimed at the nose hit the base of his left horn and glanced off into the air with a loud hum, doing nothing towards checking him in his charge. The second barrel drove a bullet through his nose, chest, and intestines, smashing the heart, killing him instantly, and causing him to turn a complete somersault. His rump hit the writer a heavy blow on the face and brought him to the ground with a bloody nose and cut lips. The incident probably occupied no more than ten or fifteen seconds; but it seemed longer to the writer; and ever since then he has been very careful, when walking up to an apparently dead buffalo, to do so from *behind* the animal. In this case the first shot of all (which brought it to the ground) was found to have struck forward of the shoulder, grazing the vertebræ of the neck, and causing temporary paralysis, without otherwise injuring the beast.

The rifle used in this instance was a double ·500 bore Express, by Westley-Richards, carrying the long 570 grain soft lead solid bullet and 120 grains black powder. It is the best weapon for general purposes, but hardly heavy enough for the larger descriptions of African game. The rifle most suitable for Buffalo is the ·577 Express, using 6 drams of black powder and a solid 648 grain soft lead bullet. The 10 bore paradox gun (made by Messrs. Holland and Holland) is also an effective weapon in bush country where shots of no greater distance than 70 or 80 yards are likely to be called for. Nothing of less calibre than the ·500 bore should be used on Buffalo; and it is scarcely necessary to remark that the use of hollow bullets is dangerous on these heavy and thick-skinned animals.

When stalking Buffalo, the hunter should always endeavour to reach a position from which he may obtain a fair broadside shot, and then put his bullet *rather low down* immediately behind the shoulder. This is the most effective shot, and indeed the only one almost certain to be fatal, but it frequently happens that natural obstacles, such as tree stems, grass, &c., prevent the hunter from getting a sight of anything but the head and neck. The neck shot may then be attempted, if the animal is standing broadside (or nearly so) to the hunter, but caution must be exercised in approaching it, although it may have dropped instantly to the shot, for a bullet in the neck is seldom fatal unless the vertebræ are broken.

Until recent years Buffaloes were to be met with in vast numbers all over Southern and Eastern Africa, but the advance of civilisation has caused their gradual disappearance from Cape Colony, Natal, and the greater part of the Transvaal; while in South, Central and Eastern Africa they have been greatly reduced in number by the outbreak (in 1890) of an epidemic disease closely resembling anthrax, which rapidly decimated the vast herds which, up to that date, were to be found in those districts. Two years subsequent to the appearance of this disease (viz., 1892), when a railway surveying party were at work in the Kilimanjaro district, no Buffaloes were seen or killed by the hunters attached to the expedition, but the ground was thickly strewn with the skulls of those which had succumbed to the epidemic. It is to be hoped that the disease has not penetrated to the more northerly districts of German East Africa, and that a sufficient number may have been left there to ensure the eventual restocking of the districts which have been ravaged by it; but many years must elapse before the hunter can again encounter vast herds of these noble black cattle similar to those which until 1890 roamed at will through the swamps and high grass of this part of Africa. A few herds are still in existence in the bush country adjoining the sea-coast near Port Elizabeth. These are protected by the Cape Government, permission to kill a limited number being occasionally given, but the bush is so dense and the animals so wary that it is difficult to obtain a shot.

In the Transvaal only a few small herds are to be found along the banks of the Olifants and Limpopo Rivers, and it is probable that they will continue to exist for some years to come, as they keep to the Tse Tse fly district, and are therefore free from molestation by Boer skin-hunters, who never hunt on foot, and are of course unable to take their horses into the fly country.

In North Matabeleland and Barotzeland Buffaloes still exist in considerable numbers, and in fact all along the Chobé and Zambesi Rivers herds numbering up to two hundred are met with; but it is in the low, swampy country adjoining the coast line between the mouths of the Zambesi and the Limpopo that they are still to be found in herds numbering occasionally as many as one thousand animals.

The district around Beira (in Portuguese territory) is without doubt the finest hunting ground in Africa for Buffalo, and indeed for almost every description of African big game.

In the flat swampy lands on each side of the Pungwé, Busi, and Urema Rivers, Buffaloes are to found in great numbers, and sportsmen desirous of experiencing the excitement of Buffalo shooting on foot, and in high grass, cannot do better than proceed to Beira, *via* the Cape, there hire a flat-bottomed decked boat, and proceed up the Pungwé River. Stores can be purchased in Durban; but a Weissman tent should be brought out from England, so that excursions inland of three or four days, or more, can be made from time to time.

The country is, for the most part, covered with dense grass from seven to ten feet high, which makes it almost impossible to see the game until close upon it; but open spaces occur every now and then on which the grass is short and sweet. It is upon these open glades that the game is to be found feeding in the early morning. As soon as the sun is up the Buffaloes and antelopes retire into the shade of the high grass and palm trees, and it is then difficult to see or approach them.

One of the flat-bottomed boats obtainable in Beira makes a fairly comfortable home. The hold is divided into a forward and an after cabin, the former being used by the crew, and the latter by the members of the shooting party. There is room to stow a large number of trophies; and the great expense entailed by the large number of carriers required for a trip by land is saved. Such a boat can be hired in Beira (inclusive of crew's wages) for £35 a month; whereas the wages and food of, say, sixty native carriers required for a purely land trip would amount to £80 a month. The Pungwé River is navigable in a flat-bottomed boat nearly as far as Sarmento, a distance of one hundred miles from Beira; but it is unnecessary to push so far up stream. At 'Mpanda (fifty miles up the stream from Beira) the river divides, the right-hand stream being named the Madinguedingue and the left the Pungwé. These streams again unite about twenty-five miles further north, thus enclosing a large tract of flat swamp land which is full of Buffaloes and other game. The Urema River joins the Madinguedingue ten miles above 'Mpanda, but is too shallow for navigation in a large boat. By means of canoes (which can be hired at 'Mpanda) it is possible to ascend the Urema River, and so reach Barrato's Kraal (distant about forty miles from 'Mpanda), and from there the Lake Sangue district can be hunted. Here Buffaloes (and, in the months of September, October, and November, elephants) are to be found in vast numbers. Barrato is a half-caste Portuguese, and chief of a large native tribe. He is hospitable to Englishmen, and generally willing to give them permission to shoot in what he considers his territory. He has fifty or sixty native hunters armed with good guns engaged in ivory hunting; and when staying at his kraal in 1894 the writer saw about 1,000 lb. of ivory which had been brought in by these men during the previous hunting season.

Buffalo and other game are numerous also along the Busi River, up which a trip could be made by boat from Beira.

The country lying on each side of the Sabi River (which runs into the sea about sixty miles south of Beira) is also good buffalo ground.

The whole of the country above referred to—viz., that lying between the mouths of the Limpopo and the Zambesi Rivers (roughly four hundred miles of coast line)—is within the Tse Tse fly belt; so no domesticated animals can be employed, and all stores and baggage have to be carried by native bearers; while the European sportsman has to walk every inch of the way. It is also the most unhealthy and worst fever country on the East Coast. Sport is therefore attended with more hardships and sickness than in other parts of Africa; and it is to be hoped that by reason of the deadly climate and the difficulties of travelling through such a country, it may long remain, as it is now, the finest Big Game preserve in the world. During the rainy season no European could survive the dangers of the climate, and it is only in the months of August, September, October and November that it is possible to travel through the country. The date of commencement and the duration of the dry season are very uncertain, but the probabilities are that at some period during the four months referred to, the grass will be dry enough to burn; and when this is possible, grand sport may be obtained. Within four or five days, after the heavy grass has been burnt off, the young green blades shoot up, and the game flocks in from all directions to feed upon it. It is then easy of approach under cover of the unburnt grass and scrub.

A. M. NAYLOR.

BUFFALO, INDIAN (*Bos bubalus, vel Bubalus arni*)—The vast tracts of swampy jungle at the foot of the South Eastern Himalayas, the Delta of the Ganges, and the plains of the Central Provinces, drained by the Mahanadi and its tributaries, comprise the districts which the Indian Buffalo frequents.

The wild animal differs but slightly in appearance from his tame congener. He looks plump and well cared for, instead of being lean and scraggy: and his nice brown coat and tidy white stockings, as compared with the patchy tints of so many of the domesticated kind, only mark the difference between the free man and the slave.

The usual habitat of the wild Buffalo being swampy ground covered with tall reeds, they are chiefly hunted on elephants; and the density of the cover may be imagined when (as the writer has sometimes experienced) the sportsman, standing up in his howdah, can see nothing of the elephants on either side of him, though only some fifteen yards away, the top of the reeds being higher than his head.

Buffaloes roused by a line of elephants frequently show fight, a solitary bull, or a cow with a young calf, being especially pugnacious; the bulk of the animal and the short range at which the action is fought (generally fifteen to twenty yards) render effective shooting fairly easy, particularly with staunch elephants; but large bore

INDIAN BUFFALO.
Ht. at shoulder, 5 ft. Av. horn meas. 50 in. Max. horn meas. 77½ in.

rifles, taking heavy charges, should be used for these as for all other thick-skinned game.

An occasional stalk on foot may sometimes be indulged in, where broad sandy river beds divide the masses of heavy cover, as Buffaloes frequently come out on to these to drink and wallow in the clear water. As, however, a wounded beast invariably betakes itself to the thickest cover near, elephants are necessary to follow it up and bring it to bag.

On the plains of the Central Provinces the grass during the hot weather is less dense; and as a great deal of it is regularly set on fire by the villagers every year to produce better grazing, Buffaloes may be regularly hunted on foot without the aid of elephants. Water at that time is scarce, being only found in pools along the river beds, and the game is consequently confined to its vicinity. Good trackers are indispensable for this sport and, given these, the best thing that the sportsman can do is to interfere with them as little as possible; they should be allowed to go ahead and carry on the trail, the sportsman remaining fifty or a hundred yards behind them till the game is sighted, when they should be placed in safety, and the hunter undertake the action.

The chief reason for this mode of procedure is that few Europeans have the keen senses of sight and hearing that jungle-bred natives possess: their movements are also attended with a certain amount of noise, and their presence tends to distract the trackers, who have not the smallest intention of blundering into close quarters with a dangerous animal, and to whom every sign and sound are of the gravest importance.

Naturally the above only refers to tracking an unwounded animal, as, after a beast has been fired at, the trackers must be accompanied by and protected by the sportsman.

Buffaloes thus tracked, and stalked in the early mornings while they are feeding, seldom give much trouble; they are fairly easy to approach. Usually a deliberate shot may be obtained at about fifty yards range, and a heavy bullet, well placed, knocks the fight out of them at once.

A single bull is always easier to tackle on foot than a herd, as the smell of blood from their stricken comrade may, and very likely will, make them charge *en masse* it they happen to detect the firer. Forsyth in his delightful book, *The Highlands of Central India*, gives a vivid account of how he and his gun-carrier had to effect a retreat on account of the threatening demeanour of a herd whose leader he had shot. "A semicircle of pawing hoofs and snorting nostrils, surmounted by forty pairs of monstrous horns," was certainly formidable odds against two men in grass three feet high. When, however, he opened fire again from a more secure position, the buffaloes seem to have made no attempt to attack, but took to flight after a few shots had been fired at them. Williamson, in his *Oriental Field Sports*, written at the commencement of the century, narrates many quaint adventures with Buffalo, which he held in great respect; but it must be remembered that there is a considerable difference in power between the ball guns of those times and the heavy rifles of the present day. He gives a capital account of hunting Buffalo from boats, during the inundations of the Ganges. He describes the hunters as a motley gang of villagers, armed with matchlocks, swords, and spears, mobbing in the water the various animals that had taken refuge on the islands which were gradually being submerged. The Buffaloes, from his account, appear to have been almost harmless, as long as they could be enticed into water deep enough to hinder them from lowering their heads to use their horns.

This sport in a higher form has on several occasions been enjoyed in the Sunderbunds, or Delta of the Ganges, during the rainy season. The sportsmen usually engage a large boat to live in, with small boats attached, in which they are able to follow the smaller watercourses, and so penetrate a considerable distance among the swamps and islands that Buffaloes frequent. The sport is described as magnificent, wounded Buffaloes often charging up to the boats, and requiring heavy metal and straight shooting to stop them.

But the writer has never heard a single instance of one of these parties having escaped malarial fever, and usually the expedition has been forced to return after a brief sojourn in that deadly district, paradise of sport though it be. The absence of wholesome drinking water is the chief cause of jungle fever, and though the Europeans may escape fever by taking extraordinary precautions, their native servants are almost sure to be attacked by it.

R. HEBER PERCY.

BULLS AND BULL-FIGHTING—Although Bull-Fighting is not a sport in which Englishmen commonly engage, it may fairly, as the national pastime of more than one European country, claim a place in an Encyclopædia of Sport.

From the time when the young bull is tended on Andalusian plains to the closing moments of his life in the National *Corrida*, a vocabulary of special words, a separate form of expression illustrates the science of all pertaining to *Tauromachia*. In Spain these terms form part of current expression, as the bull-fight forms part of current existence. This, without penetrating to the inner life of "the fancy" where a language half gipsy, half slang—rich and racy as you please—is the medium of the Matador and his *entourage*. For the hybrid lingo of this set no equivalent could be found, but for some technical terms of the art it is necessary to give a fairly accurate rendering. This, when possible, will be attempted.

The river Guadalquivir after passing Seville forms between its different channels the islands known as Isla Mayor and Isla Menor, and these islands are in their turn subdivided into the far stretching plains of Las Cabezas and Lebrija. It is from the fine herds of fighting cattle specially bred on these plains, that the bull-rings all over Spain are principally supplied. On the adjacent *vegas* of Utrera, are the herds of Muruve and Miura, this last of singular ferocity and sinister reputation. Three times in recent years have *Toros de Miura* overmatched their foes. Thrice has the life-blood Matadors mingled with this *sangre fiera* in open fight. The classic arena of Madrid bore witness to their death-dealing horns, when the Cordoba man José Rodriquez (Pepete) fell, to be followed later by Mariano Canete. The shock which galvanised the public there on the 27th of May, 1894, when poor Espartero died, yet seems to thrill all Spain, for he was a universal favourite. Besides the Seville owners there are breeders in various parts of the country. The bulls are kept separate from the cows in enclosed pastures, each calf (male or female) being given a name at birth and entered in the herd-register. When the calves are a year old, the branding process takes place. This forms almost as important an epoch as the trials for courage which take place later on. It is a rural festival, and a kind of open house is kept at the ranch during the days it lasts. A year passes, or even two, before any further steps are taken with the young stock. In some herds they are tested at two, in others at three years of age. The separation has then to be made between the good and the bad, or in other words, "the cowardly and the courageous"; those which the overseer passes as good, return to their pastures, while those found wanting are condemned to the slaughter-house or the ploughshare. This *tentadero* is again a *fête*, crowds appear, the amateurs are now expected to take an active part, and he who would pose as a sportsman must be more than a fair rider and bestride a speedy nag well broken to the work. With the assistance of a number of trained oxen (each carrying a large bell) the youngsters are herded up on the plain, which extends as far as the eye can reach and offers no impediment to a race between mounted men and themselves. Half the "decoy" cattle are then removed from the mass and rounded up at some few hundred yards' distance. The owner, overseer, and his friends, each wielding a heavy wooden lance, called a *garrocha*, some twelve feet long, with short blunted metal point, similar to that used in the bull ring, rein up their horses for a start, with them being also a professional spearman (*picador*). On a given signal, the herdsmen who are surrounding the beasts to be tried, allow one of the animals to escape, whereupon he or she, for the two sexes are tried indiscriminately, makes headlong for the distant group of tame kine. Immediately two spearmen urge their horses in pursuit, one lying on either side and each riding hard to get in first lance; he on the right endeavours to place his spear, if one may call it such, on the bull's right flank and he on the left *vice versa*. If successful the bull is thrown to the ground; he rises, again to start and once more to be overthrown; then, infuriated, he turns to face his pursuers. These give way to the professional spearman who, with couched lance, awaits the onset. The beast charges repeatedly if he be of the right sort; each time baffled and kept at spear's length, as the metal point fixes in his withers. It is at this critical moment his fate is decided. By the number of times he faces the spear, so is his merit recorded. An inferior or soft animal will refuse, or charge but once, the pluckier ones attacking repeatedly. The whole herd is tried in the same manner. The horsemen, mostly friends of the owner, take their turn in pairs to wield the lance. Bad falls are not infrequent.

The ordeal to which the young bulls are subjected is sometimes even further extended by men on foot giving them *pases*. To "pass" a bull is to induce him to charge by holding open before him some coloured material, which may be a rug, a cape, or something similar. As a matter of fact, the lures used in bull-fighting are made in the shape of a cape, so that when not in use they may be worn by the expert. When the bull lowers his horns in the charge, the texture is cast on one side or the other, the bull follows it and the man is safe. A bull will be brought to the charge several times before he tires of the intangible result. Many breeders condemn this practice, and consider that no bull should be "cheated with the rag" till necessary in the bull-ring. It is easy to understand that he would learn before long to leave the shadow for the substance. Instances of "educated" bulls, which have been extremely dangerous to the matador, are not wanting

The selected bulls pass two years uneventfully until at four or five years of age they are ready for the ring. They are now worth £40, £60, even £70 each, according to the reputation of the herd, though bulls for a *novillada* or second-rate bull-fight cost far less. The breeder's liability does not end until the bulls sold are safe in the ring, or in the railway station booked for a distance. In the enclosures or "surrounds," some of which are many thousand acres in extent, curious scenes are sometimes witnessed. Thus, two bulls fight, and the entire herd ring them round to look on. The loser is pursued by the rest, is badly hustled, sometimes killed. Even if not, the beast will ever after be of evil temper; boycotted by the others, he keeps himself aloof from them. This moroseness is also noticeable in bulls which are sick, lame, or wounded. Another curious fact, in an enclosure containing eighty bulls or more, there is always one master of the rest—one Cæsar. This continues till the herd will stand it no more; then six or seven unite, and together attack the tyrant and kill him. The whole herd then surround the defunct and bellow mournfully, until the stockman removes the body.

The enclosure which contains the cows with the calves is very dangerous ground; should you draw their attention the whole lot will be upon you instantly, and, unless you can put the fence between you and them, you are in a bad way. If caught in the open there is one means of escape, which is to seize a calf, and, keeping it between you and the infuriated cows, to edge back to the railings; as long as you are thus protected you are safe. In entering an enclosure of fighting bulls always keep near the railing or the riverside, even should they be near the former or drinking in the latter—never pass behind them in such a way as to

block their escape. If they should stop and look at you, as they will do after moving a few steps, continue your way and do not stop; barring the sullen, solitary animals mentioned previously, there is no danger of a charge. The better bred they are the quieter they will be in the pastures. When a contractor comes to buy bulls for a *corrida*, or fight, he or his deputy rides through the enclosure with the overseer, and picks out what he wants; these are driven by the stockmen into a separate enclosure by means of the decoy cattle, *cabrestos*, which go with them. They are then driven by easy stages to the town of the fight, following the decoys without a thought of evil, and rest on some pasture in the neighbourhood.

Apart from the bull-fight proper and preceding it by some eight or ten hours there takes place in the same locale a diversion called the *Brandy Bull*. Early in the morning an animal of inferior quality, but possessing most of the attributes of the fighting class, is loosed in the arena. The points of its horns are bound in wooden knobs to prevent loss of life. The public is admitted on payment of a sum equal to about twopence; and any one may jump into the ring and try his hand with a *capa*, that is, draw the attention of the bull to himself. All the rabble of the town is present, and accidents (principally from the throng of people in the ring) are frequent. The bull sometimes gets his horns free, and then many serious wounds are given. After an hour of this baiting, the animal is removed and killed outside. This early excitement puts the people in a suitable frame of mind for the anticipation of the professional contest to take place in the afternoon: as the *corrida* always occurs on holidays, the whole time is absorbed by its ever renewed interest.

With the first morning light the bulls and their "traitorous kin" are roused by shouts of mounted men. Soon the whole herd of bulls and decoys is rattled along the lanes and byways, at a gallop, in the direction of the bull-ring. The horsemen are assisted in this operation, called the *encierro* ("enclosing"), by numerous amateurs. As the ring is approached the road is enclosed by strong post-and-rail fencing. At the end of this open the wide doors of the *toril*, or circular corral surrounded by high solid walls. Through the opening rush the herd, *cabrestos* and *toros* together. The wide door swings to, and all are safe. A passage leads from the corral to the bull-ring, and one by one the animals are admitted to this section. Doors swing conveniently open before each *cabresto*, and he walks quietly to liberty without, free to betray once more. An equally convenient door opens before each bull, but not to liberty. Snorting and panic-stricken, impatient of control, he follows the opening way. Onward through secret panels till he can go no further—a bolt is drawn, a wall falls behind, and he is caught. Between his cell and the arena there is but a board.

The arena, or *redondel*, may be seventy yards across or less. A barrier of wood about six feet high encircles it; then comes a corridor of seven feet, round which the first circle of seats are ranged. These are the places sought by the foremost patrons of the sport. The space between the two circles is called *entre barreras* ("between barriers"), and here in this corridor the bull-fighters not actually engaged in the fray stand at rest; it is here also that the police and the military have their representatives. So, when a bull jumps the barrier, as frequently happens, an amusing *sauve qui peut* occurs. Then the track is closed by throwing a section of the inner barrier to the outer circle, forming a stop. The bull is thus compelled to return to the arena. Some rings are provided with upright screens of wood called *burladeros*, placed at intervals close to and flush with the barrier—a refuge for the experts when hard pressed. From the first row of seats, or *tendidos*, the lines rise in widening circles back to the enclosing walls of the *plaza* or bull-ring. All is open to the sky except on the shady side of the amphitheatre, where a roofing covers the privileged seats at the top, the boxes and presidential balconies; as the spectacle usually takes place in the afternoon no inconvenience in this quarter is caused by the sun's rays. The composure of the *élite* in the boxes, where the bride-like costumes of the ladies give a strange refinement to the scene, indeed the coolness of all in the shady side or *Sombra*, is strongly contrasted by the close packing of the roaring "people" in the *Sol*. On that side the glare and heat are combated by myriads of fans of all colours. These, mixed with bright mantillas and flower-decked heads, make a blaze of tints, the blue sky over all, not easily equalled. The *Sol* has the life and glow of popularity, the *Sombra* the stamp of fashion, both combining the enthusiasm of the Spanish race.

The equipment for an ordinary *corrida* or bull-fight is six bulls. Two *espadas* or *matadors* are engaged to kill alternately, the elder commencing with No. 1. Each "master" has his own band of assistants called a *cuadrilla;* this troupe consists of four men on foot, known as *banderilleros* or *chulos*, and two horsemen called *picadores*. The sacrifice of horses varies; sometimes only ten suffice, at others twenty or more are required. The cost of an average *corrida* would be approximately one thousand pounds. Each matador is responsible for the performance of his party, The senior takes the management of the ring-details. The word of the chief is law to his followers, who usually have great respect and affection for him. In some cases there are three *espadas* engaged; then two bulls fall to the lot of each.

THE OPENING PARADE.

The total number of spectators varies according to the size of the ring, a fair average being 8,000 seats (that of Madrid contains 12,500).

The assemblage is presided over by persons in authority—in provincial capitals by the civil governor, in smaller towns by the *alcalde* or mayor.

The changes in the spectacle are directed from the presidential chair. When nothing goes wrong, the waving of a white handkerchief suffices for the purpose. A red one is the sign of disapproval.

The fight is divided into three stages, first, the *suerte* or hazard play of the *picadores* or horsemen; secondly, that of the *banderilleros* (men on foot), and lastly, the crowning and principal scene, the *suerte* of the swordsman (*matador* or *espada*). The spectacle commences with a procession of the entire "cast," issuing from the gate opposite to the president's balcony. The *matadors* lead the show, walking in line abreast some three yards apart, behind them in Indian file follow the *cuadrillas*. The *picadores* ride in couples behind. The *espada* of highest fame leads the left wing, and the rear is brought up by two teams each of three mules harnessed abreast in gaudy trappings, accompanied by grooms and attendants. The *espadas* wear their gala capes in stately fashion. These garments are soon to be exchanged for less expensive ones for use in the conflict.

Preceding this imposing parade two *aguacils*, or warders, in sixteenth-century costume ride across the ring and go through the form of asking the president for the key of the bulls. This is thrown from above. The retirement of the *aguacil* with the key is the prelude to the fight. The vast arena is now clear save for the *picadores*, who are ranged some twelve yards apart on the left of the door from which the bull will emerge. Their horses are so placed that, if charged by the bull in his first rush, the impetus will be received on the right side. Each man grasps tight his *garrocha* or lance. There is a lull in the roar of thousands. The fatal handkerchief is waved, a herald trumpets the command to unswing the double doors, and the noble beast bounds to his fate. Encompassed on all sides by glaring moving colour, maddened by all he sees and hears, the call on his ferocity is not made in vain, and fain would he wreak his vengeance on all at once. His eye takes in several victims, hardly can he decide which he will first attack. He swerves in his career from one to another, then darts at one and charges home. The efforts of the *picador* with his lance seldom serve for aught at this first charge; the guard is broken through, and horse and man are hurled to the ground. Frequently the *picador* is jammed between the saddle and the barrier. Then the *toreadors* come to the rescue by trailing capes before the bull, and his attention is taken from the fallen man, who may be within a few inches of his horns. The coloured *capa* takes his eye, he turns to catch it on his horns, then sees another horse and man, and on these vents his fury, usually with the same result as before. The object of the *picador* should be to turn the charge of the bull by firmly placing the point of his lance between the shoulder-blades as he wheels his horse to the left in safety.

Whatever may be said in answer to those who claim for the second and third sections greater proficiency and skill, the first part (that of the *picadores*) is but a prostitution of the original finished display of horsemanship. It must be borne in mind that the first *espada*, the *matador*, has completely absorbed the interest of the public. He has become the monopolist of *plaza* favour.[1] As two of rival rank are usually performing at the same fight they are the centre of all eyes, and not infrequently daring competitive efforts are made to draw applause. Thus the *picador* is of secondary interest. The object of the *Suerte de Varas* (lance play) is to tire the bull sufficiently (not too much) to render him a more facile plaything in the use of the *banderilla* and the sword (second and third acts).

As the president (assisted by an expert) gives more or less time to this part of the performance (the *picadores* punishing more severely a strong bull than a weaker one)—wounded horses, terribly wounded horses, are brought up again and again to receive the bull's charge. Only animals unable to bear a man are mercifully brained by the grooms of the ring. After each charge the bull is less inclined to continue the work; then the horses are spurred to where he may be standing and he is urged to charge again by a movement of the bridle or by shaking the lance. This is called *citing* the bull. It is notorious that the *picadores* do not try to save their horses—poor refuse and cast-offs as they are. The men have direct interest in riding a number to death. The public no longer require them to save the horse; rather are they applauded for taking the risk of the falls, and these are considerable. The fame of the breeder is augmented by many slain, while the *espada* scores by achieving the death of a bull which has killed many horses. Should the bull be of soft description and refuse to charge a third time (which seldom happens), the red handkerchief is waved. *Banderillas de Fuego* (darts with fireworks attached) are then implanted in the bull's withers. This is a terrible disgrace to the herd from which he comes. The *picadores* are fined if they place the lance in any but the proper spot or injure the bull in an unorthodox way.

All through the *corrida* the cape or *capôte* is ever cheating the bull—the never-failing lure—flaunted, and trailed, fascinating and fixing his attention. By it the expert stops or directs his charge. Of the two things, the man or the cape, the bull will almost invariably go for the cape. This gives many opportunities for the bull-fighter to show off. In it is involved the first principle of bull-fighting. By the *capôte* or long cape the bull is tired and beguiled during the first two episodes. It is by the small red cloak, or *muleta*, that the *matador*, unaided, encompasses his death in the last act. Not infrequently at the *sortie* of the bull, before he has even charged the first horse, a *matador* will face him in the centre of the ring with extended *capôte*. Between outstretched hands he holds the lure well up; when the bull with furious rush appears almost to have caught him, he swings his arms to one side; with unmoved feet and a sway of the body, the folds of the cape are thrown open on the right, the bull bends his head and follows the trail of colour. He stops his charge and turns to seek the phantom anew. Again the cape is stretched—another rush—again the bull is baulked as the slippery

[1] As their importance has increased, so has their emolument. A hundred years ago each bull was paid for at the rate of about a sovereign—fifty years ago (in the time of the great Cuchares) at £10. To-day Guerrita or Mazzantini will look askance at anything less than £50 to kill a bull.

silk goes slithering across his horns. This *coup* is called *La Veronica*. The movement called *Navarra* is of similar risk.

Another trick called *de Tijerilla* is of still greater danger. In this exhibition the *matador* has the cape crossed over his breast and held beneath the arms. He has to await the charge and yet free himself and divert the bull's attack. The leap of the lance (*Salto de la Garrocha*) is performed by the expert awaiting the bull in mid-ring with one of the lances used by the *picadores*—as the bull lowers his head in the charge he leaps over him. Another risky performance, seldom seen, is to place the foot between the horns and spring over the bull as he charges (*Salto del testus*). In order that the horses may not shrink from the onslaught, their right eyes are invariably blindfolded. When the president considers the bull has been sufficiently "brought down," the bray of the trumpet heralds the next act, the horsemen retire from the ring, and for a few seconds the bull and the slain are in possession. The *banderilleros*, each with a pair of darts, now advance. The *banderilla* consists of a wooden shaft an inch in diameter and $2\frac{1}{4}$ feet (or less) in length, covered with bright paper frilling, having at the end a short sharp iron barb. By waving these at arm's length aloft, the *banderillero* cites the bull to charge. As the bull lowers his head to gore his tormentor, the darts (one from each hand) are deftly implanted between the shoulder-blades, as nearly touching one another as possible, the man reaching over the horns in the act. At the same moment, by a graceful movement of the body he avoids the beast's thrust. This is doing the "turn" well, and indeed a quick and careful calculation of distance is necessary; so much so, that a start with the wrong foot might easily be fatal. The different modes of "putting in the darts" may be divided in two forms. First—awaiting the bull face to face, and second—coming up from behind, when the bull receives them in the act of turning to charge, and before he actually has time to do so. Each form embraces a variety of *coups*, though, it is needless to say, the best is the face to face system. To go into these and other details would require a volume. With the smart of the first pair of *banderillas* the bull roars with fury, and bounds hither and thither, frantically trying to rid himself of the unwonted encumbrances, the shafts of the *banderillas* falling and rattling on his horns to and fro, but firmly attached by the barb, which only pierces skin deep. While in this state he presents a more favourable mark for the second *banderillero*, who fixes with greater ease a second pair; this is called putting in a pair *al relance* (on the rebound). The darts are usually fixed by the *chulos*, but on some occasions the public demand that the *matadors* themselves should do this. By an almost universal custom, the *matadors* affix the darts in the fifth bull. This is always the pick of the six, and hence comes the Spanish proverb "No hay quinto malo," the fifth is ever good. Should only one dart remain sticking, or the pair be badly placed, the public express their disapproval by loud whistling (as in all cases of bungling or cowardice). Four pairs of *banderillas* sometimes decorate a bull before the *séance* changes. Should the beast advance at a trot, he affords no chance, and the *banderillero* must escape to the barrier and wait a better opportunity. Herein lies a fruitful cause of accidents, as he has then no *capôte* for defence, and must trust to speed or his comrades' *capas* to draw off the bull.

REVERTÉ, THE RISING STAR.

A feat introduced by El Gordito, and since emulated by a few others is the "hazard of the chair" (*Suerte de la Silla*). The *banderillero* takes a cane-bottomed chair to the centre of the ring, and, seating himself, awaits the charge. On this taking place he swiftly "plants" the darts and glides to one side, the bull meanwhile tossing the chair on high; this looks very effective. But to resume; the trumpets sound once more for the third and great scene, and an expectant hush falls on the vast gathering as the *matador* steps alone into the arena, and approaching with stately stride beneath the presidential stand, makes an impromptu speech, of which the following may be quoted as an example:—

> Your Grace, to you, this bull I pledge
> To slay, and stake my life,
> Whereof in token, here's my badge
> Ere ent'ring on the strife.

Then, turning sharply on his heel, he casts his *montera* or betasselled cap behind him defiantly, sworn to do or die. Slowly he advances to the bull, grasping in his left hand the *muleta* or small red cloak, a hole in the centre of which admits one end of a short stick for the better extension of the cloth; and in his right the long, rapier-like sword. As he steps out, his wiry and athletic form is well shown up by the bright silken attire of faultless fit, gleaming with gold or silver embroidery and precious stones. At a distance stand his satellites, their *capôtes* ready in case of need. By the *muleta* the bull is induced, with his eye constant to the lure, to charge again and again, the *matador* "passing" him now on one side now on the other, till the panting animal stops in wonder. Raising and depressing the *muleta*, the man observes whether the beast is still obedient to its influence. All this time he has been studying the bull's peculiarities, for on this much of his success depends. When the bull assumes a suitable angle and position the *matador* raises his sword shoulder high, takes a steady aim and makes his running lunge (that is, in the case of the *Volapié*—see later). If successful and rightly placed, the bull falls dead, the sword left in to the hilt. The spot aimed at (just in front of the withers) is only a few inches in size. A small deviation is sufficient for failure, and the bull may require several thrusts; to kill the beast with one counts the highest merit, that is, if properly administered, though thrusts are reckoned good, even if the bull is not killed, provided they are well placed, as the bone often obstructs the sword. The following are the lunges or thrusts of the *matador*:—

UP TO THE HILT—A PERFECT 'SUERTE DE VOLAPIÉ.

GOOD.

Recibiendo or *Aguantando*—Receiving the bull's charge, *matador* motionless, only swaying body to avoid horns.

Á un tiempo—Both bull and *matador* meet midway.

Volapié or *Vuelapies*—The usual method—the bull steady, *matador* kills with running thrust.

INFERIOR.

Á paso de banderillas, Al revuelo de un capôte, Al relance, Á la media vuelta—When the bull is taken in motion on half turn (four variations).

BAD.

Mete y Saca or *Metisaca*—A defective stroke used only with cowardly bulls as a last resource—to kill without regard to rules, care being taken to remove the sword to avoid bad impression.

The *matadors* are recruited from the *banderilleros*, but the *picadors* always remain *picadors*. An interesting ceremony is sometimes to be witnessed in a large ring, when a first-class *matador* elevates a junior colleague to the highest grade. To do this, instead of killing the first bull, his by right of seniority, he formally hands *muleta* and sword to the aspirant, who, having achieved the feat, is ever afterwards of premier rank. This is called "taking the alternative."

The prominent *matadors* of recent years are the following: Bocanegra, El Gordito, Chicorro, Lagartijo, Frascuelo, Angel Pastor, Mazzantini, Espartero, Guerrita, Reverté, Bombita, Lesaca, El Algabeño. Each of these was or is the exponent of a particular school. (In *Wild Spain*, by Abel Chapman and myself, readers will find some account of the Bull Fight as it was in the old days and of the earliest professionals in the art.)

In Portugal a popular spectacle prevails—a so-called Bull Fight, which however partakes more of the nature of a circus entertainment, and is consequently held by Spaniards in very low esteem. In these shows a variety of feats are gone through; the *banderillas* are "put in" as in Spain, but some of the other tricks are of the clown order; one skilful performance deserves praise—a humane adoption of the Spanish *picador's* rôle accomplished by skilful riders mounted on well-trained horses, which indeed is well worth seeing. Finally, when the bull has given sufficient amusement the *cabrestos* are driven in and the beast makes its exit with them. The Portuguese Bull Fight, though presented in a Spanish setting, differs almost entirely in its execution, as the risk to man or beast is small, owing to the round wooden knob which covers the point of either horn.

WALTER J. BUCK.

BULL-FIGHTING WEAPONS.

Sword. Banderillas. Braining dagger. Point of a lance. Wand of a *muleta*.

VOCABULARY OF WORDS REFERRING TO BULL FIGHTING.

Aficionado—An enthusiast, a devotee.
Aguacil—A mounted official, a messenger.
Anillo (or *Redondel*)—The arena.
Arrastre—Dragging by mules the slain animals from the arena.
Banderillero—Expert who places darts or *banderillas* in the bull.
Barrera—Wooden partition encircling arena.
Becerro—A bull calf.
Burladero—Screen for safety or refuge in arena.
Cabrestos (or *Cabestros*)—Tame cattle used in removing bulls.
Capa (or *capôte*)—Cloak, cape, mantle.
Capeador—An expert with the *capa* or cloak.
Castigo—Punishment inflicted by the lance.
Chiquero—Cell or cage for the bulls.
Chulo—An assistant bull fighter.
Cojido—Caught, overcome.
Coleta—Plait of back hair worn by *toreros*.
Cornada—Thrust or wound of a bull's horn.
Corrida—A bull fight.
Cuadrilla—Troupe or following of a *matador*.
Descabello—Act of braining the bull with a sword, sometimes permitted.
Desecho—Inferior, discarded.
Diestro—An expert, a professional.
Divisa—Rosette sometimes placed on the bull.
Embolado—Bulls' horns thus described when points are covered.
Encierro—Enclosing bulls in the ring (*toril*).
Engaño—Lure, deception. Applied to bull fighter's cape.
Entrada—Fee for entering the bull-ring.
Entre-barreras—Between the two barriers round arena.
Ganaderia—A herd, or breed.
Garrocha—Heavy wooden lance with short iron tip.
Gitano—A gipsy.
Humillar—Lowering of the bull's head to toss.
Jurisdicción—When the bull is within striking distance of the expert he is said to be *à jurisdiccibn*.
Lid (*Lidia*, or *brega*)—Action or turmoil of the bull fight.
Matador (*espada*, *toreador*)—The chief bull fighter, he who kills the bull.
Moña—Round padded ball worn at the back of the head by the men during the fight.
Monos sabios—Boys and men employed in the service of the bull fight.
Montera—Cap or headgear worn by all except the horsemen (*picadors*).
Muleta—Small cape without collar used by *matador* on killing the bull.
Novillada—An inferior bull fight, in which the animals are young or defective.
Novillo—A young bull.
Pase—Action of passing the bull from one side to another by using the *muleta*, or small cape.
Paseo—Parade of the bull fighters.
Picador—Horseman armed with lance.
Pinchazo—Half completed sword-thrust.
Pinta—Colour or marking.
Plaza—The bull-ring building.

Puntillero—He who ends the bull (if necessary, after the *matador* has given a mortal wound), by using a braining dagger.
Quiebro—Movement, twist of the body.
Quite—Act of enticing bull from fallen man with cape.
Rejon—A kind of dart or spear.
Res—An animal, applied to a bull.
Sol—Sunny or cheap side of ring.
Sombra—Shady side of ring.
Suerte—Fashion, mode, form, hazard, attack.
Tablas—First wooden barrier round the arena.
Torero—A bull fighter.
Toril—Yard enclosing bulls on their arrival at the ring.
Toro bravo—A fighting bull.
Trastos—*Matador's* tools (sword and small cape).
Vaca—A cow.
Vaquero—A herdsman.
Viaje—A movement or course taken by bull in the ring.

BURREL—The Burrel, Burrell, Burhel Bharal, or Blue wild sheep. *Ovis nayaur*, Hodgson, *Asiatic Rev. XVIII.*, pt. ii., p. 135, (1833); *Ovis nahoor*, Hodgson, *P.Z.S.* 1833; Sclater, *P.Z.S.* 1860; *Ovis nahura*, Blyth, *Cat.*, p. 178; Jordan, *Mam.*, p. 296; *Ovis burhel*, Bluth, *P.Z.S.* 1840, p. 67.

Native Names—*Na, Sua;* Ladak. *Wa, War;* Sutlej valley. *Nirvati;* Nepaul. *Nao, Gnau;* Bhotan.

Measurements—Height of full-grown male 30 to 36 inches, being considerably shorter than Ovis ammon and of a stouter and less graceful build.

Horns, &c.—Average length, 22 to 24 inches; girth at base, 11 inches. Hodgson records a pair of 32 inches: *P.Z.S.* 1840, p. 66. The horns are moderately smooth, with a few wrinkles, and are of a peculiar shape. They are set on the head close together and spring at first outwards in a rounded arch from the head; the points then curl backwards, outwards, and upwards in a manner unlike any other head unless it be that of the Caucasian burrel or the Pyrenean Ibex. The head is somewhat coarse and distinctly sheep-like. No mane or ruff. Ears short. No sub-orbital glands or lachrymal fossæ; but feet pits are present in all four feet.

Colour—Brownish grey in summer: slate-grey in winter. The lower parts, inside of limbs, and buttocks, white. The male has black face and chest; a black stripe down the front of the limbs and along the side of the body. The female is much smaller and insignificant in colour, with rudimentary horns.

Distribution and Habitat—The Burrel from a sporting point of view is an example of the blessings of mediocrity. He has an enormous range. He inhabits practically the whole of the higher portion of the main Himalayan range, from Shigar in Baltistan to Sikkim and Bhatan; together with an indefinite range of country to the North as far as the Yarkund country, the Kuenlan and the Altyn Tagh (Prejwalski). Much of this country is open to the sportsman; the Burrel is not a very difficult animal to find if patience be exercised; nor is he, as a rule, on ground which presents very great difficulties to an experienced stalker. On the other hand his head, though handsome, is not

BURREL.
Ht. at shoulder, 36 in. Av. horn meas. 22 in. Max. horn meas. 32 in.

a very striking trophy, and as he usually dwells within ken of Ovis ammon or Ibex, the average sportsman does not devote the whole of his time and energies to stalking Burrel, but generally hopes to obtain a head or two on his way to or from the home of superior game. At the same time Burrel show very pretty sport. They live upon the highest ground, being seldom found in summer lower than 10,000 feet. Much of the best ground is above 17,000 feet. The pursuit of Burrel therefore requires sound heart and lungs besides mere leg power. At times, owing to the colour of the base rock on which they are lying, and to the indescribable "mirage" of a Ladak summer's day, they are very difficult to spy. Old-time sportsmen have described them as being not easily alarmed. Wilson and Kinloch both relate instances of most confiding behaviour on the part of Burrel in remote districts. Nowadays, it is safe to say that the Burrel, like all wild sheep, has remarkably acute senses of sight and smell and takes the fullest advantage of both, as well as of its powers of speed and endurance, in order to secure its own safety.

Shooting—Like other wild sheep, too, it is very tough to kill and requires to be hit in the right place. A good Balti dog may be a useful addition to the party. Ward in his excellent *Guide to Kashmir and Ladak* mentions a case in which a Balti dog cornered a wounded Burrel under a rock and lay out all night watching it till the sportsman returned with the daylight to put in a finishing shot. This happened in 1881, and a few years later the story was confirmed to the present writer by the owner of the dog.

In some aspects the Burrel is allied to the goats as well as to the sheep. Hodgson at one time classed him as a *Pseudovis*. His horns have a peculiar twist which suggests the goat, and have a strong resemblance to the Caucasian Burrel (*Capra pallasi*), and also to the Pyrenean Ibex.

On the other hand he has no beard and no caprine smell. Indeed, one of the best points about the Burrel is his mutton, which is excellent. Unless it be his congener, the Big-horn of the Rocky Mountains, few animals can supply a better joint than the saddle of a fat Burrel ram, not too young, killed in September or October.

S. H. WHITEHEAD.

BUSH PIG (*Potamochœrus africanus*)—The *Bosch Vark* of the Boers, sometimes called the **Southern River Hog**, is found in various regions of Africa, usually in the neighbourhood

BUSH PIG.
Ht. at shoulder, 28 in. Length, 60 in.

of thick bush and forest. It seldom wanders far from water, and is, therefore, not known in many parts of the dry interior of South Africa. In the bushy parts of the eastern provinces of Cape Colony, and in Natal, Zululand, and the jungly regions of South-eastern Africa, it is not uncommon. It is found sparingly in Matabeleland and Mashonaland. In height, the bush pig stands about 2 feet 4 inches or 5 inches. Its extreme length, from snout to tail-tip, is rather more than 5 feet. The general colour is reddish-brown, mingled with grey. The body carries a great deal of coarse hair, especially upon the back and neck. The ears are long and strongly tufted with bristles. The tail, which is about a foot in length, is also strongly tufted. The tushes resemble those of the wild boar of Europe. The canine teeth are all strong and pronounced. Upon the chaffron is a remarkable bony excrescence. The bush pig is, from its extremely shy habits and the difficult nature of the jungles in which it secludes itself, not often bagged by the white sportsman. It is however, occasionally shot in the periodical drives for small antelope organised in the bush-veldt country of South and South-East Africa. The flesh is fairly good. The **Red River Hog** of West Africa is a near ally, and strongly resembles this wild boar in appearance and habits.

H. A. BRYDEN.

BUSTARD — Thirty species of Bustard, separated into twelve genera or imaginary groups, have been described; we are content to omit these perplexing names and refer them all to the typical genus *Otis*. (The numerals given below after the specific names represent the average length in inches of the males, and serve to show the proportionate size of each species.) In most the males are much larger than the females, but this is reversed in the **Floricans**, the females being the larger. Of the thirty different Bustards, two, the **Great Bustard**, *O. tarda*, 42, and the **Little Bustard**, *O. tetrax*, 17, are resident in Europe, Central Asia, Persia, and North Africa.

Five are Asiatic, and four of these, *O. edwardsi*, 50, the **Bengal Florican**, *O. bengalensis*, 25, the **Lesser Florican**, *O. aurita*, 19, and the **Eastern Ruffed Bustard** or **Houbara**, *O. macqueeni*, 28, are resident in India; the last-named, occasionally wandering to Europe, has been obtained in England. One Bustard, *O. australis*, 48, very similar to the Indian *O. edwardsi*, is peculiar to Australia, and known to Colonials as the **Wild Turkey**.

Twenty-two species are resident in Africa, one of which, the **Western Ruffed Bustard** or **Houbara**, *O. undulata*, 28, occasionally wanders to S. Europe, and is found in the Canary Islands; twelve of the others are S. African, including the largest, the **Gorri-Paaver** of Colonists, *O. kori*, 50, and the **Koorhaan**, *O. afra*, 19.

Bustards are unknown in the American regions. The **Great Bustard** was formerly resident in England, the last of the British race being killed in Norfolk in 1838. Since then occasional visitors appear, generally in winter. Always frequenting open country, this fine bird is found in great numbers on the vast plains of Andalusia, where sometimes flocks of as many as seventy may be seen. The best, but not, perhaps, the most sporting, way of shooting them is by driving, usually in spring. It is difficult in some parts to find any shelter for the guns. Where there are dry watercourses it is, of course, easy work, and in May the wheat is high enough to squat behind, while in some spots it is necessary to make screens of dead thistles and other rubbish. On suitable ground, the gunner can lie flat near the top of the reverse side of any slight hill over which the birds are to be driven. The chief object is to keep perfectly immovable, for no bird has a keener sight than the Great Bustard, and the faintest movement will send it swerving.

It is usual only to shoot the males; the old ones, sometimes weighing up to 36 lb., are called by the Spaniards, "*Barbones*," from the tuft of long bristly white feathers which grow like whiskers on each side of the throat.

These Bustards usually fly very low, within twenty yards of the ground; but, with the wind behind them, much higher. Considering their size they are easily brought down; No. 4 is quite large enough shot to use, but, wonderful to relate, I have seen good shots clean miss them within twenty yards, perhaps because, from their apparently laborious flight, they seem to fly more slowly than is really the case.

When they do not fall to the shot they always, if mortally wounded, void their excrement.

The drivers need not be numerous. The best driver I knew, one "Perico," or Pedro Molina, of Algaba, a village on the Guadalquivir, a few miles above Seville, never used more than two men to assist him as flankers in driving, but his knowledge of the country and consequent judgment of the course the birds would probably take were wonderful. The late Lord Lilford (*Birds of Northamptonshire*, vol. i., pp. 342–4) gives a graphic account of Perico, under whose guidance both himself and the writer shot their first Bustard many years ago. Bustards are also shot in the hot months by the Spaniards at drinking places; but they kill most at night in the way adopted for many small ground-roosting birds, viz., with a lantern and bell. With the Bustards, however, a horse and gun are also used, the gunner walking by the side of his horse, while his confederate rings the bell and shows the light, till it shines on the birds, which are then killed, some times three or four at a shot.

BUSTARD.

Another tedious method, a stratagem practised in almost all countries with Bustards and many other birds, is to approach them with a cart. The most sporting way is stalking them with a rifle, when, if the ground be unfavourable, a shot may occasionally be got by gradually circling round them.

The **Little Bustard**, a straggler to the British Islands in autumn and winter, is also found in Andalusia and Morocco in great numbers, but is a shy and very difficult bird to circumvent. Though usually frequenting more undulating ground than the Great Bustard, I have always found it useless to attempt to drive them, as when flushed they rise at once, sometimes to such a height that unless seen to rise from the ground it would be hard to recognise them. They are also very difficult to detect on the ground, though, when flying, the white of the wings is very conspicuous.

The only season in which they can be easily shot is during the great heat of August, when, at midday, they lie well; but the heat is then too much for ordinary mortals.

Occasionally, without any apparent cause, they will, like Golden Plover, fly past within easy reach, and, keeping very close together, offer a good "browning" shot.

Even when nesting amongst the well-grown corn, they are very wary; and I have found it troublesome to obtain specimens.

When rising from the ground they make a loud rattling noise with their wings, whence the Spanish name of "*Sison*" and the Moorish "*Bou-zerat*," "father of the armourer"; another Moorish name is *Sirt sirt*, from their peculiar call in the breeding season. Their flesh, unlike that of the Great Bustard, is excellent, almost equal to that of the Bengal Florican, and in Spanish hotels figures on the menu as "*faisan*."

The larger Bustards, which frequent open ground, are wary and difficult to approach, needing all sorts of stratagems to obtain a shot; but some of the smaller kinds, like the Bengal Florican, which are found in thick grass, lie close and are easy to shoot.

L. H. Irby.

BUSTARD SHOOTING IN ANDALUSIA —The Great Bustard, banished from Wiltshire Down and Norfolk "Breck," must nowadays be sought in wilder lands beyond the sea, in Danubian province or in the rolling corn lands of Southern Spain.

In Spain the Bustard is not regarded as game, and in autumn and winter is seldom molested. In June, however, a considerable number are shot over pointers in the corn, mostly females and young birds. The peasants also form ambuscades near the wells where the cattle are watered, and whither the Bustard come daily at dawn to drink. Another plan during the great summer heat is to shoot the birds from a bullock-cart, covered with esparto-matting, which is pierced with loopholes. The hunters gradually circle round till within range and fire a volley. These methods all, however, smack of the pot-hunter, and as such do not commend themselves to Englishmen. The real pleasure of Bustard shooting centres in a day's driving in winter. For this, every one must be mounted, as thousands of acres will be traversed during the day; besides, it allows of a far nearer approach to the birds themselves. On spying a flock the object is to "horseshoe" the guns as near as possible to the birds without being seen, advantage being taken of any suitable cover to hide oneself, though the spot is often a bare hill side, with nothing but the slope to conceal one till the birds are within shot. On these occasions it is absolutely necessary to remain quite motionless, as on the smallest movement the keen-sighted birds swerve off. When the guns are placed, three beaters ride round, one to put up the birds, and the other two, by galloping with them, to prevent their breaking out, a frequent occurrence in spite of all precautions.

Should it be necessary to place the guns in full view, the following tactics are useful: the whole party ride round the birds in a wide circle, and as each man in turn reaches his appointed place, he slips off his horse, and, handing the reins to the man in front, flattens instantly on the ground. The man who places the guns should have a thorough knowledge of the lie of the land. In shooting it is necessary to aim much farther ahead than the apparently slow flight seems to warrant, as a Bustard, though falling easily to a single AAA pellet if hit forward, even at long range, will otherwise carry away a lot of shot; indeed, quite as much "allowance" is necessary as at a rocketing pheasant. Clothes harmonising in colour with the surroundings are also indispensable, for so much depends on utilising every possible means of concealment in view of the absence of cover. As specimens, Bustard should be shot in May and June. The females are small, 10 to 12 lbs., and are seldom seen, but the cock birds, "packed" at this season, and with their beautiful neck-ruffs, often weigh 30 lbs. The largest I know was obtained by Mr. Abel Chapman in 1893 and weighed 37 lbs. Three to five guns are the most suitable number, and, with luck, should average a brace each. For a single gun, a brace is a good day's result, though the present writer on one occasion got four brace.

Bertram F. Buck.

BUSTARDS, AFRICAN—Bustards are to be found in many parts of the African continent, but, up to the present, the various species have only been determined with anything like exactness in the countries between the Cape and the Zambesi. Even here, it is probable that one or two new species may yet be established. In South Africa, where at least ten species are at present known, very excellent sport is to be enjoyed with the many bustards to be found almost everywhere throughout the country. The Paauw, or Kori Bustard (*Otis kori*), is the largest bustard in the world, and attains occasionally a weight of 40 lbs. These noble game-birds are usually secured with the rifle. The Stanley Bustard (*O. caffra*), and Ludwig's Bustard (*O. ludwigi*), rank next in size to the Paauw. Following these, come the smaller Bustards, usually known to the colonists as "Koorhaans," many of which are extremely plentiful all over the country especially upon the open plains—and afford capital sport for the shot gun. The Black Koorhaan (*O. afra*), Black and White Koorhaan (*O. afroides*), Vaal (grey) Koorhaan (*O. scolopacea*), the Bush Koorhaan (*O. ruficrista*), the beautiful Blue Koorhaan (*O. cærulescens*), the Senegal Bustard (*O. senegalensis*), Rüppel's Bustard (*O. ruppeli*), and the Black-bellied Koorhaan (*O. melanogaster*), are all handsome and extremely interesting birds known to the South African sportsman. The great Kori Bustard (Paauw) is a magnificent table bird, and most of the others afford excellent eating as well as good sport. The gunner may identify these birds by reference to Layard and Sharpe's *Birds of South Africa*.

H. A. Bryden.

BUTTERFLY AND MOTH COLLECTING—That butterfly and moth hunting is a sport, no one will deny who has ever chased a strong flying fritillary over rough country, or tried to snare over the treacle a restive rarity that refuses to become intoxicated. We therefore give a few practical hints for its successful pursuit.

Capture, Apparatus, &c.—To obtain the perfect insect in its wild state is the finest side of the sport, and the demand is not so much for elaborate apparatus as for activity and energy on the part of the pursuer. For the apparatus, a folding net, of the largest size possible, the ring fitting in a Y socket, is advised, and a broken golf-club makes an admirable stick. For killing purposes one may use a bottle or tin, the latter having the advantage that, if the lid is hinged, one hand can do the work of slipping in the insect. The poison may be *potassium cyanide* contained in a solid basis of plaster of Paris, or chloroform dropped on cotton-wool. Chloroform tends to stiffen the insects, but is quicker in action. The great objection is that one may at any moment find the stock exhausted, and the bottle empty, when far from all chance of obtaining the drug. In any case let the bottle or tin be filled with *very loosely* packed cotton-wool, to prevent insects rubbing on one another. When in pursuit, mark the point of settling, and come up against the sun, so that no shadow may fall and startle the quarry. Almost all butterflies rise *perpendicularly;* therefore get the net well above them.

Localities—For *butterflies*, the best possible place is a rough open common near a wood, and if possible, surrounded by woods. These should be worked thoroughly, as should the ridings of the woods themselves. For those who can spare the time, a week or more in the **New Forest** is bound to yield much sport in all the entomological branches. Clover fields should be watched and the hedges around them carefully beaten, for many moths lie there during the daytime. Disused quarries and railway cuttings are also found attractive.

The *Hawk Moths* are generally bred, but they may be caught with net and light about two hours after dusk, as they come to feed on such flowering shrubs as rhododendron, ivy, &c. A sharp look-out should be kept, during the months in which they come from their pupæ, upon fences, tree-trunks, &c., near their favourite food-plant. In the daytime, once seen, they are secured without difficulty. *Geometers* may be obtained in the daytime by beating hedges and skirts of woods, or by walking over rough ground. It is advisable to try to catch them on the wing as they rise, for, when they get to cover, they are extremely hard to find. They start of their own accord to fly by hedgerows, in gardens, and in the ridings of woods just after sunset, when for an hour and a half the net may be used with success. The usual method for the capture of *Noctuæ* is *Treacling*.

Time—Moths may be captured all through the year, some few appearing only in the winter, but the season for butterflies rarely lasts for longer than from the middle or end of April to the end or middle of September. The best time of day is from about nine till eleven, and from one till three. At midsummer, a hunt before breakfast is sometimes well rewarded by a large capture of some of the rarer flies.

Treacling—It is quite unnecessary to go in for elaborate boilings of treacle, sugar, beer, &c. The simplest recipe is by far the most effective. Take a pound of the best treacle, *not* "foots"; put in a few drops of jargonel, enough to make the scent perceptible at a distance of several yards, a tablespoonful of rum, and mix thoroughly. As dusk falls, put the treacle on rough-barked trees with clear bottoms (so that fallen insects can be seen at once) and always to leeward. The same trees should be used again and again, to prevent the treacle from sinking in too fast. One cannot do better than settle upon a circuit about a mile in length, with some twenty-five selected trees roughly at equal distances. The night must be warm, and, if possible, dark. Two work treacle much better than one, for it is advisable that one should hold the lamp, whilst the other taps the insect into tin or bottle. A *sugaring net*, which can be pressed against the tree and held beneath the treacle, is very useful. It is not often of much use to remain out watching the treacle more than two hours: the attractiveness has usually disappeared after that time.

Breeding provides the finest specimens and gives most scope for experimental work. Larva-cages can be bought, but are easily made, the essential point being to keep them clean. For fairly common larvæ, the escape of some of which is not important, there is nothing better than a grocer's orange box three-quarters filled with mould and carefully planted beforehand with suitable food-stuff. The top may be covered with mill-silk or perforated zinc.

Pupa Digging may be carried on throughout winter and spring, but it is not wise to expect very abundant results. The best spots are around the trunks of big trees which stand at the edges of a wood.

Setting—First, and most important from the start, are **entomological** pins (*No.* 9 is a very handy size for most purposes). A badly-set insect may be relaxed afterwards, but a bad pin remains an eyesore, and its removal is a very delicate operation. It may happen that in the first year of collecting the best variety or the greatest rarity in the collection falls to the net, and is eternally disfigured. The needles used for extending the wings should be fine, but strong, and they will be found very handy if the head be thrust well up into the centre of a stout wooden match.

Of **Setting** there are many methods, the commonest being with strips of thin transparent paper passed over the wings and pinned down beyond them. Another, which can be strongly recommended, is to use only short setting boards, with room for one, or at most two insects. Instead of straps, soft, and fairly fine wool is passed lightly over the wings. One turn should first be taken over the wings close to the body, so as to bring them flat upon the setting boards for the needles to adjust them. Then wind round the board as many turns of the wool as seem necessary to keep the wings absolutely steady. It should be mentioned that this plan is not found to work so well with the micros, for whose setting microscopic slides are sometimes used with success. The chief cause of bad setting is the taking of the insects from the boards before they are *absolutely dry*. Five weeks is by no means too long to leave them. A relaxing-box can easily be made by affixing sheets of cork to the bottom of any air-tight box. If these be damped and the insect pinned to them, it will be ready for re-setting in two days.

For **Identification**, two books that can be strongly recommended are W. S. Coleman's *British Butterflies* and E. Newman's *British Moths*. Other valuable works are mentioned in the Bibliography.

Preservation and Exhibition—Albo-carbon, or its refined form, naphthaline, will preserve insects from mites, and should be kept in every drawer or box in which they are. Light must be jealously excluded.

When a collection is begun a careful note should be made of the species likely to be found, and the available space accurately measured. A "Watkins and Doncaster" label list should be purchased and a proportionate space left with a label for each probable insect in case of capture. It is advisable to leave a considerable interval between each group, in order that an unexpected success may not involve the re-arrangement of the whole.

A good cabinet is almost the only part of his equipment for which the collector is necessarily dependent on others, but it is great unwisdom to attempt the saving of a few shillings in this department. The usual price for the best quality is 15s. each drawer, measuring 16½ by 19½ inches, and they can be obtained from any entomological firm.

Bibliography—C. G. Barrett, *The Lepidoptera of the British Islands*, in monthly parts at 5*s*. each (in progress), (L. Reeve & Co.); W. S. Coleman, *British Butterflies*, 3*s*. 6*d*. (Routledge & Co.); W. Furneaux, *British Butterflies and Moths*, 12*s*. 6*d*. (Longmans & Co.); W. F. Kirby, *Butterflies*, two vols., 6*s*. per vol. (W. H. Allen & Co.); W. F. Kirby, *Moths*, two vols., 6*s*. per vol. (W. H. Allen & Co.); Leech, *British Pyralides*, 16*s*.; W. J. Lucas, *The Book of British Butterflies*, 3*s*. 6*d*. (Upcott Gill); E. Meyrick, *Handbook of British Lepidoptera*, 10*s*. 6*d*. (Macmillan & Co.); F. O. Morris, *History of British Butterflies*, 21*s*. (Longmans & Co.); F. O. Morris, *History of British Moths*, four vols, £6 6*s*. (Longmans & Co.); E. Newman, *British Butterflies*, 7*s*. 6*d*., *Moths*, 19*s*. (W. H. Allen & Co.); H. T. Stainton, *Manual of British Butterflies and Moths*, two vols., 10*s*. (Van Voorst); T. W. Tutt, *The British Noctuæ and their Varieties*, four vols., 7*s*. per vol. (Swan Sonnenschein & Co.); J. O. Westwood, *Butterflies of Great Britain*, 10*s*. 6*d*. (Orr & Co.)

C. S. COLMAN.

CAMPING OUT—AFRICA, SOUTH—

To ensure the success and enjoyability of a sporting trip it is essential that the "creature comforts," as regards both food and lodging, should be carefully attended to; and a few words on the subject may be useful to those who have not had experience of the somewhat difficult task of remembering beforehand and providing every requisite for an expedition into uninhabited country far away from shops or stores.

Wagon Outfit—If it is not proposed to enter the Tse Tse fly country, the best and most comfortable mode of locomotion in South Africa is by Cape wagon. A good full tent wagon costs from £80 to £100, and in this there is ample room for two comfortable *kartel* beds, and the stores, rifles and ammunition requisite for two hunters. Such a wagon requires twelve trek oxen or fourteen donkeys. The writer prefers the latter; donkeys being more tractable and very much hardier than oxen. Trek oxen cost about £9 each; donkeys about £5. A few extra oxen or donkeys should be provided to be used when any of those in the regular teams are sick.

Although the cost of each wagon and team entails a serious outlay (£200 at least), it is cheaper in the end to buy outright than to hire, for if the wagon is a good one and stands the test of, say, six months' work, the price originally paid ought to be obtained for it at the end of the trip.

It is best to regard the price paid for the *teams* as money sunk, for the chances are that, through sickness and accident, very few of the animals will be worth much when the journey is over. The best wagons are those made in Durban and Grahamstown. Second-hand ones are generally obtainable in Mafeking and Johannesburg, the former of which towns is the most convenient starting-point for the Kalahari and Chobè countries; the latter for a point of departure for the bush veldt of the North-east Transvaal. A piece of canvas, ten feet by fifteen feet, will be found most useful to form a shelter from the sun; either thrown over the roofs of two wagons drawn up abreast, and five or six feet apart, or rigged as a lean-to tent against the side of one wagon.

Each wagon requires one driver at about £3 per month, and one "forelouper," or leader, at about £1 per month, in addition to rations. Cape boys and half-breeds make the best drivers.

A boy is required to look after the horses of each member of the party, and to each wagon there should be attached a couple of boys to do odd jobs, such as collecting wood and bringing water to the camp. A cook is, of course, indispensable.

When the game country is reached any quantity of natives can be engaged at 10s. a month and as much meat as they can eat (that is what they really come for), to find and track game.

Each member of the party should be provided with two horses, which can be obtained at from £20 to £25 apiece.

"Salted" horses (*i.e.*, horses which have taken and recovered from horse-sickness) cost from £60 to £100.

A couple of pointers should be taken for partridge and koorhaan shooting, and a pack of mongrels (the more numerous the better) for lions, leopards, &c. These mongrels can be bought at the Johannesburg dog pound at a few shillings each.

Carriers—The following remarks on provisions and camp furniture in the Tse Tse fly country apply equally to the outfit for a wagon expedition.

If the scene of the hunting trip lies within the fly belt, or in British or German East Africa, wagons, oxen, horses and dogs must be dispensed with. The party have to travel on foot, all stores, tents, &c., being carried by native carriers. If a large number of these is required some difficulty and trouble will be experienced in obtaining them.

Zanzibari or Inhambane boys are the best carriers, the latter for choice. It is advisable to write out beforehand and get some one to engage the required number of carriers and ship them to the port from which it is proposed to start.

The recognised weight of a man's load is 60 lbs., but they will carry 70 lbs. or more.

From 20s. to 25s. per month and two pounds of rice per day is the wage of a Coast Kaffir carrier.

Camp Furniture—In any case, whether the start be made from Johannesberg, Mafeking, or Kimberley by wagon, or from Beira, Chindè, Mombasa or Lamoo with native carriers, it is best and cheapest to bring out from England *everything* necessary for the comfort and support of the European members of the expedition. The best tents (these are not required on a wagon trip) are the Weissman tents. One of these, seven feet six inches by six feet, made of stout Willesden canvas with double roof and canvas floor-cloth, costs £9, weighs 100 lbs., and affords comfortable accommodation for two Europeans. Messrs. Edgington provide comfortable camp-bedsteads fitted with hair mattresses and mosquito curtains, which pack into a very small compass in waterproof covers, at a cost of £3 10s.

A strong folding-table should be taken, and, *most important*, each member of the party should have a folding deck-chair with detachable canvas seat.

It is when the long day's march or hunt is over, and the party sit around the camp fire, that the man with the best chair experiences the greatest amount of comfort. For him who has neglected to provide himself with this hunter's luxury, there are only the alternatives of going to bed away from the jovial chat around the fire, or of laying his aching bones upon the ground, with a very good chance of a sting from one of the numerous scorpions who have had notice to quit from the burning logs.

Stores—The writer strongly recommends the Army and Navy Stores as a place where everything may be obtained.

Write out a list of what is required and ask the manager of the Export Department to appoint a clerk to go through it with you. Have the stores packed in half-inch deal boxes with lock, iron hinges, and rope handle at each end, each to weigh 60 to 70 lbs. when filled. Each box should be numbered in large figures, and packed with a small amount of the several articles required for daily use, so as to necessitate the opening of as few boxes as possible each day. A list should be carried showing the contents of each box. By this means any article required can be found immediately.

No vegetables being obtainable in the wilds it is essential to take plenty of desiccated vegetables, dried fruits, figs and raisins. Lard for cooking is most important, the game in some districts being devoid of fat. Danish butter in tins (the smaller the better) keeps well, and is a great luxury. Cheese should be encased in bladders in order to keep well. Bacon should be packed in salt. Tea, coffee, Swiss milk (unsweetened), in tins; jams, golden syrup, soap, spices, salt, candles and lime-juice should be included, and a bag of oatmeal and another of lentil beans will be found useful. Macaroni, arrowroot and essence of beef should be taken as food for fever patients.

Flour should be packed in 14 lb. tins, and care should be taken that the supply of baking powder is ample.

Saccharine should be taken in preference to sugar.

The best and safest mode of carrying whisky or other spirits is in stoneware jars encased in wickerwork, with a metal cover over the bung which locks with a padlock.

In addition to plates, cups, knives, forks, saucepans, &c., a mincing machine should be provided, also a large iron three-legged pot with lid for baking bread.

Messrs. Silver and Co. supply very good folding lanterns with talc sides. Two one-gallon filters, axes, saws, hammers, gimlets, knife-sharpeners and files should be included. A few pounds of six-inch French nails will be found useful for pegging out skins. They do not make such unsightly holes as wooden pegs do.

Skin Preserving—Napthaline tablets prevent the ravages of insects among skins, and for curing the latter nothing is so good as salt and alum mixed in the proportion of two parts of salt to one part of alum. This preparation should be well rubbed on to the raw side of the skin immediately it is stripped from the animal; the skin should then be folded into as small a compass as possible, and left *for not longer than* six hours in that state. When opened out it will be found that the skin is thoroughly cured and ready for pegging. On no account let it be exposed to the sun when pegged out. Arsenical soap and all other taxidermical preparations are costly and dangerous, and not nearly so effective as salt and alum.

The white ash of the camp fire forms an effective substitute for salt and alum when the latter are unobtainable.

Medicine—A medicine chest is, of course, an important part of the outfit. Messrs. Burroughes, Wellcome, and Co. know all about the medicines requisite for Africa, and they supply all drugs in tabloid form. These keep better and are more portable than powders or liquids.

Quinine, calomel and opium are the most important drugs, to which should be added iodoform, carbolic acid, carbolic oil, strong ammonia, sticking plaster, lint and a clinical thermometer.

A. M. NAYLOR.

AMERICA, NORTH—To the ordinary mortal, camping out means roughing it, but to an old campaigner it signifies, if not absolute comfort, something akin to it, and this at no extra cost or additional paraphernalia; in fact comfort is as easily obtained as the reverse, if only you know how to set to work.

The most useful pattern of tent for North America is the A shape, which is obtainable in most American towns and costs but a few dollars. The advantage of this tent is that nothing but the bare canvas need be carried, as the ridge pole and two supports can be cut on every suitable camping ground throughout the Rocky Mountains.

For winter work, the Indian Tepee cannot be improved upon: it is cone-shaped, supported by thirteen poles, and permits of a good fire inside, the smoke escaping through the open top. This tent can only be procured from Indians and would be useless in a district destitute of small trees, unless inhabited by those tribes of Indians who always leave their Tepee poles standing when they move camp.

Another useful form of tent is the Lean-to, very serviceable in the mountains when a man may have to carry his whole outfit on his back; it simply consists of a sheet of canvas 8 ft. by 5 ft., which is fixed to windward in the same fashion as the A tent, and represents when erected half the roof of this tent. It serves well as a shelter from wind, snow, or rain.

Tents should not be taken out to America, but procured on the spot. What should be carried in the way of cooking utensils and luxuries entirely depends upon the mode of conveyance, and that is regulated by the nature of the country. It is sometimes possible to manœuvre a wagon, otherwise the ordinary means is by pack horses, canoes, or pack Indians. In any case, however, some experienced person will be required to superintend the arrangements, and the only serviceable articles which cannot be procured on the spot are a good canteen and air bed. Anything else brought from England will only prove an additional expense and encumbrance.

Camping in the States and Canada is simpler work than in British Columbia, where the further we penetrate north, the greater become the difficulties. There is a marked difference between riding with a pack train of horses along a good trail in the beautifully timbered, park-like mountains of Wyoming, and plodding on foot behind a party of Indians through the almost impassable forests of Northern British Columbia. But the requirements for a good camping ground are the same, and consist of three essentials: namely, water, dry firewood, and sufficient level ground to pitch a tent on. No one who has not tried it could imagine the difficulty of remaining all night in a tent pitched on an incline. Fortunately in America, except upon the Prairies, there is rarely any difficulty about wood and water. The former is an important object and necessitates a good axe-man, who knows how to lay his logs Kentucky fashion in order that the frying-pan bread may be properly baked beneath. Where wood abounds there is no occasion to economise it, and therefore when a dead tree is felled, it is cut into eight-feet lengths which are laid upon two short cross-pieces for dogs. Then, if a birch is handy, some bark is stripped off and placed beneath. This burns furiously, and the whole is soon ablaze and in condition to cook the fresh trout just caught, and the venison which will have been killed *en route*.

Camp life is exactly what you choose to make it, and the fussy man and grumbler are an abomination. It is a curious fact that, charming though it be, camp life brings out all the worst traits in nature, and fortunate is the party which can produce four friends who have camped together for a week without at least a coolness between some of them. "Be certain of your man, or woman, before asking either to camp out," is excellent advice, but very difficult to follow. Persons camp out for one of three reasons—Big-game shooting, fishing, or an idle life of pleasure. In the last case it may be presumed that the camp is supplied with servants and every possible luxury, though what people would find to amuse them after a couple of days of this life it is hard to say.

The fisherman may furnish his camp luxuriously, when once on lake or river bank it becomes a permanency, and can usually be accommodated with anything desirable from no great distance. A very delightful time can be spent thus, and often free from America's greatest curse, the mosquito, which renders an otherwise perfect summer unendurable. By selecting an open spot in a breezy situation on the bank, and guarding it with mosquito-netting, no great discomfort from these pests need ensue.

Camping after Big-game requires the judgment only obtained from experience. The all-important object is reduction in weight, which necessitates baggage being restricted to the absolute minimum. A horse carries on the flat a pack of 300 lbs.; an Indian 100 lbs.; and a squaw twice as much; but for mountain climbing these weights are reduced. Pack-horses must be packed by an experienced hand intimate with the intricacies of the diamond hitch. A hunting outfit will be wanted as follows: Tent, blankets, frying-pan, canteen, three round pots fitting into one another, flour, baking-powder, sugar, bacon, tinned milk, salt, pepper, tea or coffee, and rice; soap, towels, dish-cloths, and also hobbles for the horses. As it is often impossible to camp high up a mountain, lightly equipped expeditions from the main camp must be undertaken. On these excursions, a hunter will carry his own pack of about 50 lbs. weight, consisting of Lean-to, blankets, frying-pan, coffee-pot, round pot, flour, bacon, coffee, sugar, and salt.

Find a snug spot to camp in, and if the weather is fine and the thermometer above zero, the Lean-to can be dispensed with, a large fire supplying sufficient heat. A comfortable bed is made by plucking a quantity of tips from fir branches and laying them carefully one upon the other to a depth of seven inches. This also forms a most satisfactory bed upon snow. If bare ground is slept upon, a spot should be selected with slight hollows to fit the hip and shoulder, for they add greatly to comfort, or such hollows can be scooped out for one's self. Late in the season there will be no water, and snow has to be melted in the round pot. To roast fish and grouse, clean and split them, then fix them on sticks, stuck into the ground close to the fire. They will be found delicious. Bread is baked in the frying-pan.

J. TURNER TURNER.

CAMPING OUT. (NORTH AMERICA.)

INDIA—There is no difficulty in procuring tents in India, as they can be readily purchased or hired. For shooting purposes the less camp equipage that is taken the better. For-a single sportsman a Cabul tent weighing 80 lbs. and a Rowtie for the servants is sufficient. In the hot weather it is cooler to sleep in the open air, and even in the day time it is pleasanter to have one's meals and to sit out under the shade of a tree, so that a tent is not much required for living in. It is, however, convenient for keeping things together and is also useful in case there should be rain: heavy thunderstorms occasionally occur in the hot weather. A Cabul tent has a double roof and keeps rain out well. It is also a good protection from the sun in the heat of the day should the shade of the trees, under which a tent can almost always be pitched, not be sufficient. About half of such a tent is taken up by the bed, which is placed along one side. A piece of netting should be sewn along each wall of the tent so as to form three or four large pockets, which are very convenient for holding clothing, books, and other articles in constant use. Another tent which gives more room and is light, is the Bechoba, a square tent with light bamboo framework and no pole. A small place outside the tent can be screened off for a bath with boughs or mats. In the cold weather, the nights are very chilly and there is heavy dew, and it is necessary then to sleep inside the tent.

A good bed is of great importance when out shooting, as nothing rests one more. Folding up camp beds, as sold in shops, are all uncomfortable. The best plan is to have a strong bedstead made, 7 feet by 4 feet, with cotton webbing, costing about ten rupees. No mattress is required; a *resai*, a kind of quilt stuffed with cotton (cost five rupees), answers that purpose. Such a bedstead is easily carried on a cart if placed on the top of the baggage, and the *resai* is rolled up with the rugs. If a folding bed is required, a good one is made with a stout piece of canvas. Each side is sewn round a bamboo and the ends of the bamboos project and fit into stout wooden legs. Another bamboo at each end of the bed fits into these wooden legs, keeping them apart to the full width necessary to stretch the canvas tight. The two ends of the canvas are furnished with straps and buckles which pass round the end bamboos, and pull it tight in that direction. The objection to this kind of bed is that the canvas gets stretched with the weight upon it and bags down. It is convenient to carry, for the bamboos can be slipped out of the legs when the straps are undone and the legs are rolled up inside the canvas. An ulster should always be taken. In the cold weather, at night, and in the early morning, it is most comfortable in camp. Even in the hot weather, the air is frequently chilly if there is rain. In the cold weather, plenty of warm coverings for the bed are necessary, and in the hot weather a good blanket or rug is often wanted in the early morning before sunrise. Carriage is easily procured; the most usual is the bullock cart. A sufficient number of carts should be hired for the trip at so much a day (about 12 annas = 1*s.* each). It is a little more expensive, but much more comfortable than hiring locally for each move. In some places camels are used for transport, in others everything has to be carried on men's heads. For supplies, fowls and milk can generally be obtained, but it is a good plan to buy two or three dozen live fowls and take them with you. Sheep or goats can also be got, but the sportsman will find that the less he draws on local supplies the more popular he will be. In any case he should make a point of paying in person a full price for everything got from the villagers, as native servants are apt to give less than what is due, if payment is left to them. When moving camp, the Patel or headman of the village should be seen and asked whether every one is satisfied. A small tip to the village officials and to such of the villagers as have attended to the camp requirements, should not be neglected, for then the visit of the Sahib and his retinue will be a subject of congratulation. A butler, cook, and a third servant to make himself generally useful, is sufficient for the ordinary sportsman. A good water-filter is essential. At least three *chaguls* (as the leather water-bags are called) are required for each sportsman to have with him when shooting. Two should be taken out on a day's shooting in hot weather, and one in cold, the remainder being left in camp so as to have a supply of filtered cold water in the evening. Water in leather bags becomes quite cold. In order to sweeten new chaguls and remove all taste of leather, fill them with butter milk, put in a handful of turmeric, and allow them to stand for two days.

When out shooting in camp for more than a week or so, it is advisable to take a Bania or native grain dealer with you, who will carry food for your men and feed them at 2 annas (about 2*d.*) per head per day at your expense. Everything that is required in the way of tinned meats, stores, liquor, cartridges, ammunition, and supplies generally can be bought in any of the Presidency towns as well as in England. If horses are used, a supply of grain, which is a substitute for oats in India, must be taken.

J. D. INVERARITY.

CANOES AND CANOEING—Cruise the world around, and there is not a place or port you can visit without encountering some form or type of canoe. Go back in history beyond the memory or records of man, and you will still find canoes. The early naval engagements, whether by State against State, or by individuals or clans or syndicates against any body or any State they could come across, were fought in canoes, or in craft of canoe type; indeed, we can hasten down to modern, up-to-date war, and find that one of the most destructive craft afloat at the present day is distinctly of canoe form—the torpedo boat.

There are those who will define a canoe as a craft that is propelled by paddles wielded by man or men; but there are many types of canoes, belonging to countries thousands of miles apart, in which the paddle, except for steering, is an unknown implement. In these craft, sail is the furnisher of motive power by agency of the wind, or *vice versa*. Then, for civilised modern times, why not steam or electric propulsion?

If the craft is in type, form, and utility a canoe, and is propelled by a man wielding a paddle, she does not change her nature when the man ceases to paddle and hoists a sail, or when he, by suitable machinery, waggles a differently formed paddle, such as a screw propeller. I think there may legitimately be paddling-canoes, sailing-canoes, and motor-canoes; and, further, that the mode of propulsion should not determine the classification of a craft; but that model and capability to do work commonly assigned to canoes and canoeing is the true guide. No matter where you make your choice of investigation on the millions of miles of sea shore of this world, you will find the "canoe" of that place is formed "sharp at each end"; she is a light draught craft, capable of being navigated in very shoal, and also in very rough water; of as easy propulsion astern as in going ahead; except in a few rare cases she is always transportable by manual power from water to water overland; she is long, narrow, and of light construction.

As to the canoes of savage peoples, any well fitted museum will furnish quite a bewildering assortment of models thereof, if historical research be the aim. We want, however, to get to canoeing as a sport at the present day; and in order somewhat to classify the type of craft which can legitimately claim to be a canoe, we may as well suggest "what is not a canoe."

You may have a canoe, and they exist in many parts of the world, of one hundred feet or more in length; you may have a canoe which carries fifty men; or you may have a canoe which will sail under five hundred square feet of sail, or down to fifty feet on small craft. But each of such craft can be paddled by her crew at or over her sides, by hand-worked paddles, without fixed boat-fulcrum; or she can be sailed under easily removable sails and spars; and she will be able to navigate into waters barely ankle deep, and she will be sharp at each end.

Therefore it is obvious that a small yacht, even though her hull be long and shallow and pointed at each end, if she be of deep fixed draught, with heavy spars and gear not immediately removable, and herself so weighted as to be too heavy for manual transportation, cannot rightly claim to be a canoe.

Coming now to modern times, we may take it as settled that the sport of canoeing, that is, river canoeing under paddle, and travelling abroad chiefly under paddle, but with a small sail for use in fair winds, was brought in and popularised by John MacGregor in his *Rob Roy* cruises and books thereon between 1866 and 1869. And canoe sailing in small canoes was similarly introduced by the writer's voyages in the *Nautilus* in Sweden and the Baltic during 1870 and 1871. Here it may be said that possibly there were other canoes more or less rigged; but with the exception of Mr. Tredwen's *Pearl*, which came into public notice immediately afterwards, there were none in evidence.

Clubs were constituted and held regattas, and the effect of the racing competition, which was extremely keen, soon showed itself in the improvement of model, rig, and fitment, which progressed by leaps and bounds and brought the sailing canoe up to such perfection that, though comparatively a tiny craft, there were several sailing clubs which then barred canoes from competing in their races, because they were too successful.

Canoeing, both paddling, sailing, and cruising, quickly became an acknowledged branch of sport, and it rapidly spread to the Continent and to America; and one soon heard of Englishmen, stationed away in far distant parts of the world, building and using canoes. *Canoe Travelling*, a book published by the writer of this article in 1871, was the first book on canoe design, rigging, and fitting, and it gave drawings thereon; and thereby the sailing canoe of those early days was known as of *Nautilus* type. The *Pearl* above mentioned, which came out shortly afterwards, was of somewhat different lines, or shape, but only so in detail, and of the *Nautilus* and *Pearl* new specimens of improved model and rig were steadily produced year by year, and led the fashion in building. They continued so to do, and to race, up to 1890, and since that year up to this date, 1897, *Nautilus* designs have been from time to time published. Of course there are many men who have produced designs and built canoes which, in their opinion, are of original design; but distinct type they can hardly fairly claim, and it matters not here, nor indeed at all, to seek in them family likeness to *Pearl* or *Nautilus*. I will merely, in regard to the history of the sport, say that when these two sailing canoes were produced there were no existing sailing canoes of any practically valuable nature to copy, and the only book dealing with such craft at that time was *Canoe Travelling*; but since then canoeing, in technical articles and books, has been constantly before the public here and in America. The well-known technical book, *Yacht and Boat Sailing* (Horace Cox), has, in each of its eight editions, contained a complete up-to-date "Canoeing Section," with designs, and drawings, and articles from the pens of "Nautilus," "Pearl," "Cassey," and many other canoe men. (The 6th and 7th editions give the fullest amount of designs and details, the advent of small yachts' designs having rather crowded the canoeing in the eighth edition.)

At all times in the life of the sport of canoeing there has been a marked line between sailing and paddling; there have always been in each of the clubs, both in England and in America and Canada, paddling men who never sailed a canoe, and men who owned canoes built entirely for pleasure paddling, or for racing only. In like manner, there has always been a division of men in each club who never used a paddle in their canoes except when a dead calm overtook them out sailing. But naturally also there have been a few instances of canoeists who have raced successfully both in the sailing classes and in paddling; and on the two £50 challenge cups of the Royal Canoe Club, the sailing and the paddling, may be found three or four double championship holders in the twenty years' existence of the cups.

The racing paddling canoe is very like the hull of the sculling wager-boat, but without the rowing fittings and seat; the racer is built of two streaks only, one on each side, of cedar less than one-eighth of an inch thick. As to size, they of course vary according to the size and weight of the men they are built to carry, but probably an average size would be 20 ft. long by 22 in. wide at top-side. They are decked fore and aft, retaining a bulkheaded "well" or open section of about 4 ft. in length, guarded by a narrow side deck and shallow coaming. In this "well" the man sits on the floor, and has at his back a suitable back-board to press back upon, and an adjustable foot-board or stretcher forward. The paddles used in England are very short, 7 ft. 6 in. to 8 ft. long, with broad spoon blades; the stroke is made close along the side of the canoe, with the body kept sitting erect. In America, the racing paddlers sit on comparatively high seats, some kneel, some even stand up; they use very long paddles and usually have the blades set up at right angles to one another, so that the one passing through the air is doing so edgewise while the other is square in the water. Moreover, the American canoes used in paddling races are much larger, *i.e.* wider and deeper, though shorter than the English "single-streak"; indeed, the single-streak could not be "sat" if a raised seat were used, and it is only by careful practice that one can sit her for effective work—that is, in the extreme models.

The open Canadian model, in which single blades, or half-paddles, are used, is decidedly the favourite river canoe of the present day. Though a considerable number of *Rob Roy* type, or quasi-*Rob Roys*, may be seen on any of our large rivers, they are dropping out. For real travelling, the Canadian type, with its open body, lends itself so easily to ample stowage of camp gear, to quick stowage or discharge, and to easy transportation, that it is only the inexperienced who will, for river or small lake travelling, take the small "decked" canoe of *Rob Roy* type or the later modifications thereof.

Where, however, the tour is to extend to crossing large lakes or to cover some open estuary work, the decked canoe is almost a necessity; but then it is advisable, for such work, to go to the sailing canoe type for safety and comfort. I have had experience on large lakes, in a small decked canoe of semi-*Rob Roy* type, of being wind-bound on an island with food supply growing short and seas running too heavy to allow even a hope of crossing to main land; luckily, the wind gave in before the man had to. A fine summer evening is apt to tempt one to make camp on an island, so as to be free from inquisitive visitors, both of man and of animal nature; but morning may break with a summer gale blowing, and then is the time to appreciate the value of every detail of the complete sailing cruising-canoe. In the first place, her reserve of stores will, or may be, ample, but even if the rough water has to be faced, she will do it, if properly handled, in anything less than a real hurricane.

With regard to travelling in canoes on inland waters, it is well to point out that such work is of two distinct kinds, and that to accomplish each in perfection needs a totally distinct canoe type for each. For the quick-running, shallow, rocky river, with vicious rapids and dangerous falls, with forest portages and the necessity of camping out each night, there can be no question that the open or partly decked Canadian type is the best. The *Rob Roy* type is well enough on easy rivers, canals, ditches, and such like; but in a really bad rapid, and for rough portaging, she is a poor craft. The camp kit, clothes and stores that can be stowed in canoes of the *Rob Roy* type are about fit for a doll, certainly not reasonable for a man, unless an hotel is more or less a certainty every night; even then, in addition to the time wasted in minute packing and unpacking there is the frequent experience of getting all the cargo soaking wet, and stores spoiled after a wet passage through a rapid, or by the leakage common after a few days of bumping on rocky shallows.

In the Canadian type all the perishable stores, clothes, bed-clothes, charts, &c., can be stowed in waterproof "kit-bags," *i.e.* long, cylindrical bags with an internally flounced mouth, which can be fastened so as to be quite watertight. The tent, preferably furled on or around its poles, so as to be ready for immediate setting up, can be stowed lengthwise in an open canoe, whereas it must be disjointed and packed away

in parts in a decked canoe. The kit-bags, cooking gear and other stores stow amidships; and the two men (preferably two) are stationed, one in the bow and the other in the stern quarters of the canoe. In this way, when she grounds on a shallow, the crew jump out and guide her or partly lift her over; or in a few moments the cargo can be lifted right out and landed, and the canoe can be carried over any obstruction. Everything should be lashed in, so that in the event of a capsize nothing is likely to fall out. In this connection, a plan of mine, which will take a lot of beating, is—fit a removable 6 ft. canvas compartment to the middle third of the canoe. It is made thus: One sheet of fine, close-woven duck, either "in the piece" or built in cloths 6 ft. wide, is cut to a length sufficient to lie close across and around the inside and bottom of the canoe, and then across to meet in the centre at the level of the gunwale or top-sides. Two pieces of duck are cut to form bulkheads or ends, of the exact form and size of the transverse section of the canoe; the top of the after one is cut at about 1 ft. above the level of the gunwale height so as to leave this 1 ft. to fold in; the other forward bulkhead is preferably left at its top 6 ft. long, so as to act as flap or cover overalls in wet weather. The edges of the bulkheads, so far as they represent the cross-section of the canoe, are then closely and strongly sewn to the edges of the sheet which forms the bottom and sides and lids, and these edges should be neatly roped and have suitable beckets for lashing down to the bottom and sides of the canoe. When packed with all the bags of stores and gear the two flap edges, having eyelet holes, can be laced or tied together, and the forward bulkhead flap part is then folded aft over all and forms a roof. The whole thing may be waterproofed with linseed oil, or the top flap only; in the former case this "bag-well" will be found very useful as a waterproof ground-sheet for sleeping on. Or, on a pinch, when caught out at night without the proper tent, the canoe can be bedded on shore beneath suitable tree branches, and the bag-well suspended therefrom and spread by a few bent sticks around its real bottom (now its roof). A very fair bed-room is made, and the front flap will just about cover the kit. If the canoe has a fair amount of end decking, say 2 ft. 9 in. or 3 ft. on a 16 ft. canoe, the open body of the canoe will be thus covered in, and be pretty nearly, if not quite, rainproof. Such quarters, of course, are rather cramped for two men, though ample for one; but it is far better to sleep dry in a semi-sitting posture than to have to drag through a wet night with no shelter.

The first point to which an experienced canoe-cruiser looks, after assuring himself of a suitable canoe and an expert companion, is a reliable night camp-kit. There is no such thing as a "standard camp-kit"; what is a perfect kit for one man may be the very reverse for another. One man will fiddle over an intensely wonderful mechanism for cooking—a spirit-stove surrounded by a swarm of little pots and instruments (of about half of which he will lose tally in a two weeks' trip) and take an hour morning and evening in packing and unpacking a sort of Chinese puzzle; while another man does the whole work of cooking over a fire of drift wood with a tin Billy-pot, a fry-pan, a tin mug and a tin dish. As to clothes, the experienced man will have nothing but flannel and wool. The only linen fabric in his outfit will be handkerchiefs and perhaps a white cap cover for hot, sunny days. The bedding may be summed up thus: two thick blankets, one to go folded as a mattress for warm nights, or both to be used on cold wet nights; one inflatable pillow covered with blanket bag (which can be taken off and dried at the camp fire). A suit of pyjamas of thick wool must be taken, and a pair of old fishing wading stockings, cut to knee-boot length, are very useful for early morning wet grass movements, when packing and launching.

Matches should be kept in corked bottles, and tea, tobacco, sugar, salt, and many other stores which are liable to suffer from damp, should be kept in carefully fitted tins stowed in waterproof bags; especially biscuits, which are the most convenient bread stuff that can be carried. As to adjuncts to camping, those essential are an efficient lamp with store of wick and oil, a small axe, and several sailor's sheath-knives. A can of petroleum is not a bad thing in camp for quick fire-getting in wet weather, but it is a fearful nuisance in the canoe unless it is absolutely oil-tight in every way. If a gun is taken, it should be provided with a bag-cover like a sponge bag, absolutely watertight when its neck is tied tightly; and the cartridges can be carried tied in a sponge bag—indeed, sponge bags of mackintosh are extremely useful in many ways in canoeing, where rain and duckings are not unknown.

We will now turn to what is really the leading feature of present day canoeing as a sport—and that is, undoubtedly, canoe sailing. Canoe sailing, with one exception, which we will mention and then leave altogether out of consideration, is now clearly divided into two branches, namely, the sailing canoe and the canoe yawl. There is a further claim upon the title "canoe" which is in no way legitimate. It arises when some small yachts, heavy, bungling, deep-draughted chunbungoes, claim, because they have a sharp ended stern, that they are canoes. If this were admitted, is not a first class battleship, with her sharp ended stern, "a canoe"? Form, as we said in opening this article, must be taken in conjunction with capability of performing the duties common to all canoes, such as navigating shallow waters, and with portability. Here it might be retorted—"You opened by bringing in a torpedo boat as of canoe form." Yes, but bear in mind that small torpedo boats can navigate in shoal water, can be hoisted on board larger ships, and can be portaged from water to water by railway train—whereas a battleship cannot.

Now the class to be wiped out is remarkable in its way—it is the racing machine class. It has grown upon the sport of canoeing as barnacles grow on a ship's bottom; it has grown upon fair canoeing, upon true excellence of model and rig, and upon good seamanship; it has engrafted the athlete and the acrobat upon the sport of canoeing. Neither of them was wanted, and the result has proved very bad for the sport,—to a degree never anticipated when the old stringent rules of classification were relaxed.

While retaining canoe form of great excellence in the body of the canoe, and even in many of her fittings, such as centre plate and rudder

FIG. 1.

and sail area, the relaxation permitted the use of the effect of unlimited beam as a sail carrying power, while the rule at the same time limited the actual beam to a ridiculous minimum. The rule limited the beam of canoes to 30 in. (at the present moment 36 in.), and with the man sitting on his deck and leaning out to windward as the puff struck his craft, sail had to be carefully handled, the rig had to be perfect in all its working parts and more or less get-at-able; therefore there was necessity for a practical "well opening"—indeed, the early sailing racing canoes were as fully fitted and as able cruisers as any could be under the knowledge of the time. The relaxation came in, and though the beam of the canoe remains limited, the acrobat is permitted to use a sliding seat across the deck whereby he slides his whole body, legs and all, right outside to windward and thus obtains such an amount of sail-carrying power that he is more in actual danger of capsizing to windward than in the ordinary way of to leeward; he gains the advantage of nearly 8 ft. of beam without its disadvantage in surface, and yet this is over a limit of 3 ft. of beam, *i.e.* 5 ft. advantage in a size of craft in which an inch tells as much as a foot does in a yacht.

In addition to the acrobatic plan or balance seat allowed by the rules, the racing machine is not required even to have a hole in her deck. Some canoes have been produced in England without any "well," or hatchway even; some here and in America had sails of standing rig, *i.e.* not hoisting or lowering or reefable, but stuck in—as in model yachts. In these craft the sheets are trimmed for the leg of the course, and off she goes at gun-fire; the man is out on his slide, 4 ft. outside his canoe, and he can do nothing but steer and balance till he comes to the turning mark on the course. Here he quickly snatches a fresh trim of sheets for the new leg of the course, and off he goes again. If she gets an extra heavy knockdown puff and capsizes, all the agile acrobat has to do is to jump out on to the centre plate, which is now lying horizontal on the top of the water, and to prise the canoe up, using the slide-seat plank as a lever.

The true canoe, fitted to be useful and comfortable, otherwise than for mere "pot-hunting," has no chance in racing against this machine type of canoe and man. The infinite harm done to sailing and racing by these machines since about 1889 is now beginning to be universally admitted here and in America, but the corrective measures are far too tardily imposed. They are creeping on, however, and it may be quite on the cards that by 1898 racing machines will be impossible in English canoe racing. The racing class is now, by the legislation passed at the autumn meeting of the Royal Canoe Club, held in November, 1896, so well overtopped by the "cruising canoe" class that, "machine racing" being no longer a certain road to winning the chief cups and prizes, intending competitors will have at least the option of building a useful, comfortable craft with a very fair chance of winning prizes by sailing skill and merit, rather than by mere acrobatic skill and luck.

Of the various canoe clubs in England, unfortunately, no two have the same rules in entirety; there is no governing power, no canoe racing association. Of late, however, the senior club, the Royal Canoe Club, has thrown all its races open to members of all other recognised clubs, and to gentlemen amateurs. As such visiting competitors must build under R.C.C. definitions, the production of craft within these rules is steadily insinuating through the outports. The following are the leading definitions of canoes and canoe-yawls, which practically govern the production in 1897.

"The definition of a **canoe yawl** is a

follows. Beam not less than 3 ft. Rating $\left(\frac{\text{length of load water line} \times \text{sail area}}{6000}\right)$ not to exceed 0·5. She shall be sharp at each end, with no transom or flat stern, and no deck seat shall project beyond the perpendicular of the sides. Each canoe yawl shall be fitted with two fixed transverse bulkheads to be approved by the sailing committee such bulkheads shall not be more than 10 ft. nor less than 6 ft. apart and shall have between them a suitable well or hatchway opening. Such bulkheads shall neither of them be placed within 3 ft. of either end of the yawl if she is of or under 18 ft. in length, or not within 4 ft. from the ends in yawls of over 18 ft. length. (*Note*—other bulkheads may be fitted but shall not be placed between the bulkheads above mentioned.)

"A **cruising canoe,** to be classified for racing purposes, shall be sharp at each end; with no transom or flat stern. Any metal keel, centre plate, or ballast shall be detachable from her; and any 'bucket well' fitted within the sleeping compartment shall be detachable. *Maximum dimensions.* Length overall shall not exceed 16 feet. Beam not over 42 inches. Sliding seat, if any, when rigged in to be within the beam of the canoe. Her fixed draught including keel, or drop keel when hauled up, shall not exceed 14 inches. Extreme length of any spar shall not exceed the load water line length or rating length. Rating $\left(\frac{\text{length of load line} \times \text{sail area}}{6000}\right)$ not to exceed 0·3. *Minimum dimensions.* Depth *inside* from deck to skin (to be taken at any distance within 3 ft. of mid overall length and at not less than 10 in. out from the middle line) shall not be less than 12 in. Depth *outside* from top of deck at mid line to underside of keel (taken anywhere up to 1 ft. from either end) shall not be less than 12 in. Sleeping space not less than 5 ft. 6 in. in length, with hatchway thereto of not less than 18 in. in width for a distance or length of 3 ft. (*Note*—Any canoe built prior to and not altered since 1894, as to beam, depth, or well opening dimensions, and not over 42 in. of beam, shall be allowed to sail in races which admit the cruising class, irrespective of depth measurement, but otherwise complying with such qualification.)

"A **sailing canoe, for racing purposes,** shall be sharp at each end, no transom or counter or flat stern shall be allowed, and the rudder shall be hung abaft the stern. Each sailing canoe shall be fitted with two fixed transverse bulkheads, to be approved of by the sailing committee. Such bulkheads shall not be more than 8 ft. or less than 5 ft. 6 in. apart, and shall be placed one forward and the other abaft the 'well.' Neither of such bulkheads shall be placed within 3 ft. of either end of the canoe. (*Note*—Other bulkheads may be fitted but shall not be placed between the bulkheads mentioned in the above rule. Spar doors are allowed in such bulkheads but they must be made watertight to the satisfaction of the sailing committee.)"

Such are the rules which govern the Royal Canoe Club's racing for 1897, and as they can only now be varied or amended by a majority vote of four-fifths at any autumn meeting, it is highly probable that they will stand unaltered until autumn, 1898, when, for following years, the present majority requirement will end if not re-enacted. It is also well to note here that the rules further require the load water length or line to be marked conspicuously at each end thereof in "usual racing trim," with crew on board, and all gear, &c., used in racing. The rules of classification in other canoe clubs in England differ only in a few details, and these only need attention from those who intend racing. I take it that it is only possible to show at present what the canoe has developed to in the present day, leaving variations of detail, whether of construction or of club definitions, to be looked up in the technical books by those interested therein.

All the clubs have the two distinct classes of canoe-yawl and sailing-canoe. The variation of the definitions in different clubs is minute, and probably the sport would all round be better served were the present local peculiarities dropped and one set of rules followed. Taking the canoe-yawl first, the only real distinction between such craft and sailing canoes is her size, but it was found convenient to name the classes differently. The term "yawl" has nothing to do with rig, though it has been for years improperly applied in yachting by some to a class of rig known to sailors as "dandy rig" or "jiggers." The "yawl" proper is, and always has been, a type of hull or model used both for sailing and rowing, in which the rig has nearly always been "main and mizen," with the mizen inboard or forward of the rudder. Therefore she is a "ketch" proper, never a "dandy" or "jigger" as to rig or name. Boat "yawls" on our coasts are always long, shallow draughted, and sharp at each end, rowed or sailed as there is calm or wind, and beachable and portable—indeed, of canoe nature all round; they vary from 40 to about 18 ft. length, and about five beams to length.

A "canoe-yawl" in 1897 is very loosely defined by rule, but in practice she is kept pretty well within canoe nature. In size she is a "half-rater" under the racing rules, which can be set out in "size" to mean just about 16 to 18 ft. water line, 4 ft. 6 in. to 5 ft. beam, 12 in. lowest freeboard, and a depth of immersed body amidships of 9 to 12 in. Below the body may be a few inches of keel for grounding on, but "canoe nature" is at once removed from such craft when they are fitted with fixed deep keels, whether ballasted or not; they then have no rightful claim to the titles "canoe" or "yawl." Of course all canoes obtain their lateral resisting powers from centre plates or drop keels, and the form does not matter so long as they are capable of being hauled up for beaching or shallow navigation. The overall length of canoe-yawls is not fixed by rule, and considerable overhang may be given; the amount depends on the nature of work contemplated. For instance, for river and small lake work very little overhang is needed, and weight is thereby saved and the craft is more easily portable by train or cart; but for open sea, large lakes, and estuary sailing, reasonable overhang is essential. In this connection it is curious to note that all the canoes on the great lakes of Africa have overhang at each end, especially so at the bow; so also, in marked degree, along the N.E. coast of the Pacific, and in all surf boats the world over. The main objection to overhang usually heard in this country is the extra first cost in building, but there always have been men who would "spoil a good ship by the saving of a ha'porth of tar."

The use of the canoe-yawl is that she can (or she is faulty in design if she can't) do all the sea-going work which can be got out of a small yacht, say, up to three or four tons; she can accommodate her one or two "crew" (according to her size). She can be hoisted on a yacht's davits, or on to a railway truck, or be carted for transportation to any part of the country, or on a steamer, or on her own wheel-carriage; she can be housed in a shed or boat-house; she needs no professional crew. Where the yacht cannot go the yawl can go, that is, into harbours which are all but "dry"; she can also go up shallow creeks and rivers. In short, she gives the least expensive and the most extensive form of yachting. So far as open sea is concerned, a well-built and fitted canoe-yawl with a liftable bulbed centre-plate would do all the work that has been done by small boats crossing the Atlantic, and at about one-third the risk that they encounter.

The "cruising canoe" (see the details of dimensions given above) can do very nearly all the work which a "yawl" can do, but of course must be put to it with greater caution. Those who "fears nothing 'cause they knows nothing," as was said of the Brighton trippers when out sailing, have no business to go canoe-sailing; they only bring a bad name on the sport and a silly end to themselves. It does not follow that an expert yachtsman can sail a canoe; quite the reverse is my experience, but an expert canoe-sailor is seldom at fault in yacht-sailing—indeed, many of our best yacht-racing men have graduated in sailing canoes.

As before said, it would be too long a matter to give description and drawings of the numerous types and models of sailing canoes of the present day, or of all their fittings. I therefore confine myself to giving a scale drawing of the latest general purpose type, the "cruising class" canoe. More properly it is the "sailing canoe," in which both cruising and successful racing may be enjoyed. The same model enlarged makes an excellent canoe-yawl, and

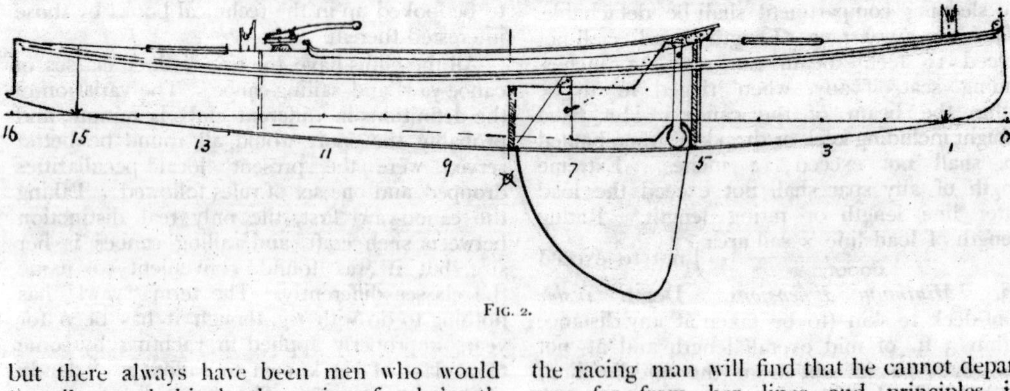

FIG. 2.

the racing man will find that he cannot depart very far from her lines and principles in attempting to produce a racing machine—that is, a successful machine,—so she may be taken as typical of canoe-sailing in general, leaving variations of detail to those who desire special racing or special cruising qualities. In the elements of design which go to make a sailing canoe the leading principle to which the designer has to give way is "compromise." Every item in the above design is fixed to an eighth of an inch by reason of compromise; if one went boldly for one desirable quality, probably half a dozen other useful, if not actually needful, qualities would be sacrificed.

It will be seen, of course, that the body plan from which the building moulds for sections are taken is drawn at double the size of the other plans; this is on account of space in the publication. The sections given are 2 ft. apart, commencing at 1 ft. from the fore side of stern. There are watertight transverse bulkheads at No. 5 and at No. 12 stations. There is just comfortable space to sleep in (that is, for any one accustomed to canoe-camping). The masts step in watertight cases so as not to let rain drain into the stowage spaces, which, it will be seen, are got at through the two hatchways. The centre-plate can be unpinned and then lifted clear out of the canoe; it should be 80 or 100 lbs. in weight, especially in case the owner is not an expert in working the sliding deck-seat. The canoe is preferably built in the manner known as ribband-carvel; that is $\frac{1}{4}$ in. or $\frac{3}{8}$ in. planks are brought edge to edge as in ordinary carvel building, but here ribbands of $\frac{3}{8}$ in. × $1\frac{1}{4}$ in. mahogany are laid fore and aft on the inside and cover the plank joint,

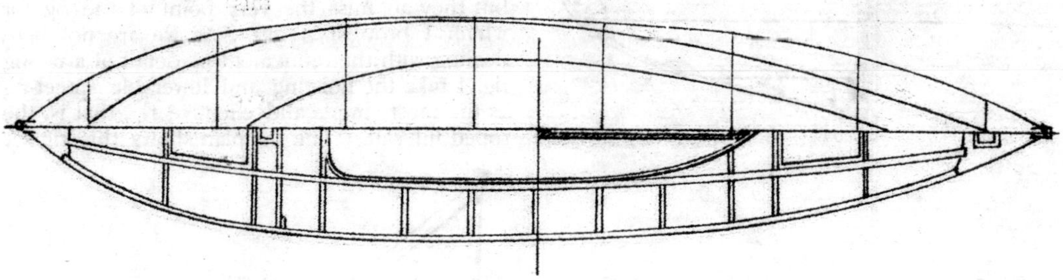

FIG. 3.

the plank edges being riveted or screwed into the ribbands. It forms the strongest light build, and if well done is least liable to leak or crack; the only "timbers" or frames required, are one at each bulkhead and one at ×. Sometimes, as in canoe-yawls, small steamed ribs are let in next the plank to help it stand bumps, but they weaken the ribbands for a certainty.

All such fittings as hatch-covers, drop-plate rudder, deck-steering yokes, tillers, wheels, cleat racks, centre plates, spar doors, indeed a hundred and one important little fittings have from time to time been perfected till their working is now certain, but a description even of the necessary fitments would be far too long for this article.

Possibly the sail plans will give those who are novices to canoe detail the best general idea of the canoe as a whole. As to any particular sail plan, or even type of sail, it is extremely difficult to decide which is better than another—it depends so essentially on the proficiency of the man who is to use it. Simplicity in rigging is often as dangerous as can be the greatest complication of strings and blocks: I have myself worked out six distinct types of sail, and among them I have even now difficulty in picking the one likely to be most suitable all round; but taking that which I have myself found very effective for sailing and handy for cruising, I give a drawing of it here, and remind my readers that the rigs of all kinds are fully represented in all detail in *Canoe Travelling* and in *Yacht and Boat Sailing*.

There is one elementary point in regard to canoe sails which should always be present to the mind of any one about to rig a canoe or desirous of criticising any given canoe rig design: it is that a boat's perfect rig may be a canoe's poison; the crew of the boat or yacht can stand about and move fore and aft in her, but the crew of one man in the canoe must do everything from one position and must handle the boat at the same time that he man-handles the sails. This may be appreciated on looking at the sectional sketch of the canoeist sitting out on his slide deck seat (Fig. 1); he steers with a "flail" handle to his tiller. Assume that an extra heavy streak of wind now lays his canoe flat; he must either "spill" his sail by letting go his peak halliards or he must jump on to the centre-plate to right her. The "sheets" must be kept fast, otherwise the sail goes into the water more and more, and when he rights her by balance, the boom with the sail full of water swaggers out on the opposite side and probably capsizes her again; indeed, it will do so time after time.

There are many who say the sail should be on single halliard so as to come down on one string being let go. I am certain from long experience that, at the "agony angle," it never will come down, and therefore prefer a main, or jaw-halliard, and a peak halliard. The peak halliard on a puffy day can be carried in hand from tack to tack and be worked far more effectively than the sheet, provided the boom is held by its topping lifts. In such weather the mizen of course must be reefed, that is to say except in close racing.

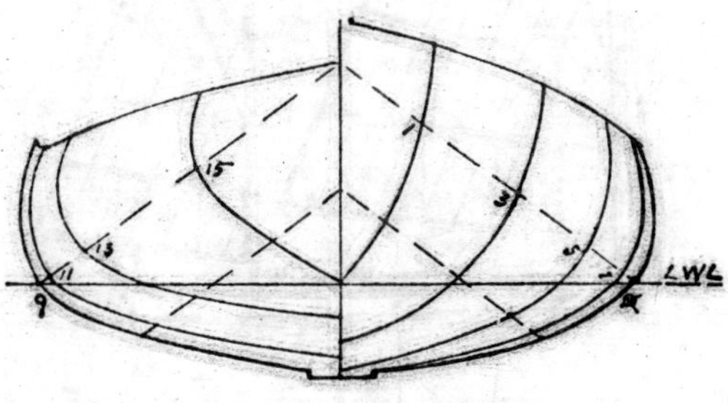

FIG. 4.

Caution is the first quality of a seaman—dash and daring go with caution, but there is no such thing as a foolhardy seaman; a foolhardy man is no seaman. On the mizen no jaw-halliard is necessary, but it may well be fitted, and I prefer to have it; it is only one extra line, and it has many uses. Perhaps, however, this is going too far into refinement of sailing.

Of the many rigs which have been used, the

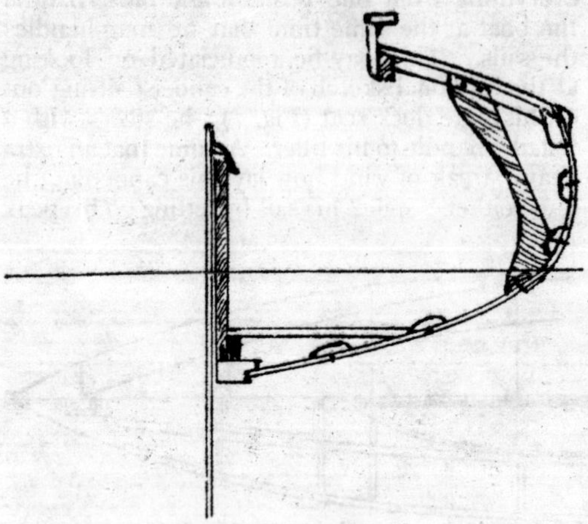

FIG. 5.

balanced battened lug is probably the most popular and possibly the most effective, but it has some decided faults for those who sit high on a deck seat. It is the most dangerous in "jybing"; the boom does not top up, and it either hits the man in swinging across or it goes smash into the water. Hence abaft-the-mast rigs are growing in favour from the handling point of view.

Of all the rigs I have tried and have seen tried, the hoisting-spreet rig is about the best; it gives the shortest spars for area, and if neatly

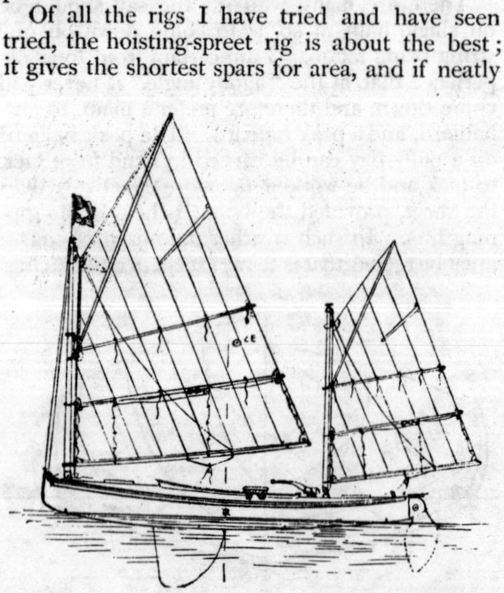

FIG. 6.

rigged is the most capable of many changes and uses. In 1870 I brought out a hoisting-spreet, but it had the fault then of being practically a standing-spreet so far as its spreet was concerned; it was really a sliding-gunter spreet. Since that time, finding it a most effective sail, I modified or improved the idea till I got to what may be called the lowerable-spreet, and in 1885 and 1886 I rigged sails of this nature, only differing in that one was a proper spreet-sail hoisted by the luff-rope and head-rope at the throat angle, (see Fig. 7), and the other had a luff-yard and a spreet so as to use a shorter mainmast. In effect, that rig was a gaff main-sail with a jib-headed top-sail, the yard of which did the duty of a topmast. This sail has since been produced, we will not say copied, on several American canoes, but they all miss the very point of the rig for which I brought it out. As we are not here dealing with the refinement of detail of a racing rig, I take the hoisting and lowerable spreet-rig as the most simple and effective rig, that is, the roped luff-sail. The sail plan shows this rig set

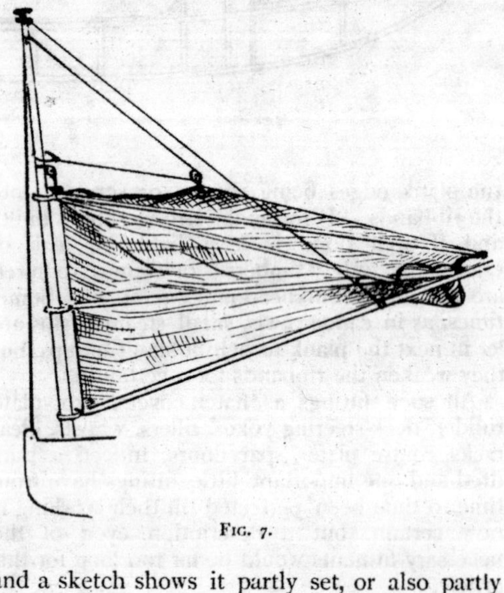

FIG. 7.

and a sketch shows it partly set, or also partly lowered, as it can be for a heavy squall or a bad jybe, or for coming into port among a lot of craft. In this case the main or jaw-halliard is kept fast, and the peak is lowered. The luff-rope on the sail must be strong, and dressed with linseed oil so as not to stretch or be affected by wet or weather.

The sail plan shows a big mizen; this can be shifted into main position and a small mizen can be then set aft, the mainsail and spars meanwhile lashed along on deck; this is specially useful in bad weather or when a night trip has to be made. All the riggings and the semi-automatic reefing gear are fully described in the books I have already mentioned, and they are of the first importance to the successful working of the rig.

The drawings here given of an open canoe, of Canadian type, show a canoe 16 ft. long by 32 in. beam, $7\frac{1}{2}$ in. freeboard, and 4 in. draught of water. She would on that draught displace about 480 lbs., so that, if the canoe comes out, say at 72 lbs., with all her gear, canvas, pack, &c., and the crew at about 308 lbs., she would carry about 100 lbs. of camp and other gear. The midship pack of gear, spoken of above, would fit between the two cross-beams, with 6 in. of it tucked under each. The cross-beams are built into the canoe, but the seat thwarts, shown shaded, are dropped in, dove-tail fashion, so as to be removable; the cross-beams can also be so fitted if it is intended to sleep in the canoe, and to remove them.

Paddles, single blade, are usually 5 ft. 6 in. long; but a much longer one is often useful, and at least a couple of spare paddles should be carried on a cruise. A jointed double blade paddle is often favoured, but is only advisable when a single hand is to work the canoe, and the journey is mostly on quiet flowing rivers or canals. For navigating rapids or lakes with two men in the canoe, far more effective work can be done with "single blades"; these should be of the toughest wood, even at the expense of being a trifle heavy, and they should be protected at the blade end by copper Λ-shaped bands riveted on each side, as shown in the sketch.

For ordinary river work, nothing looks better than varnished cedar or mahogany, built up ribband-carvel fashion, such as may be obtained to perfection at Turk's, at Kingston-on-Thames; they are amply strong enough for all but the roughest camping cruise. These Thames canoes are run very close in build and finish by the canoes of the Stricklands of Lakefield, Ontario (which can be got at Strickland's depot at West Drayton, England). But for rough, knockabout work, probably the Macatawa sheathed canoe, of North American Indian model, would be found the most lasting; and of course for real cruising work, appearance goes for nothing compared to efficiency.

The Macatawa is a wooden-built and planked canoe, sheathed with a tough prepared fabric, cemented over the outside and finished with repeated coats of paint; the life of such a canoe among rocks and snags must be immensely superior to that of the ordinary wooden canoe. G. Harris, of Laleham-on-Thames, imports these canoes.

As to price, a 16 ft. open canoe with three single blades, should not exceed £18. Many of them can be got at "a guinea a foot," and the best of finish, with carpets and cushions, comes to about £20, complete.

The institutions for the promotion of the sport of canoeing, though not very numerous in England, are sound, going concerns with solid capital; they have, or the sport has, suffered much in the last ten years from the rapid growth of small yacht sailing and cycling. The small yachting, in half-raters, was injurious to canoeing; but many men are now finding out to their cost that a half-rater racing machine is not a bed of roses, even for the pleasure of sailing, and is a little heap of expenses out of all proportion to the sport it furnishes, and such men are coming back to canoe sailing and cruising.

The Royal Canoe Club, with His Royal Highness the Prince of Wales as commodore, leads canoeing in England; its headquarters, or club house, is on the Thames at Kingston, and in 1897 a new and permanent club house was erected with all conveniences for housing members and their canoes. The paddling regatta, including some sailing, is held annually on the Thames at Kingston, and the sailing regatta, a week's racing, is, in 1897, again to be held at Burnham-on-Crouch, a salt water, and

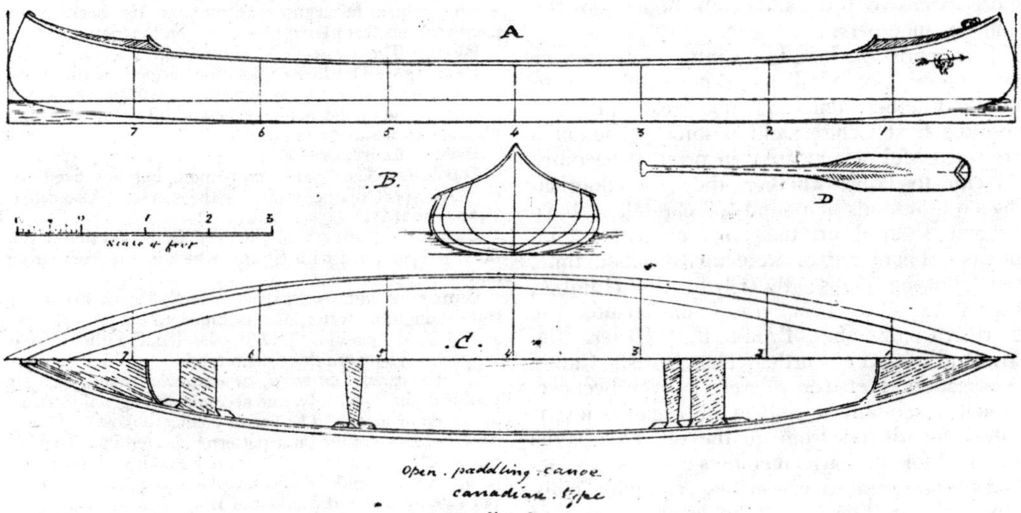

FIG. 8.

fine, open, sailable estuary in Essex. The club has two £50 challenge cups, one for paddling, the other for sailing, and gives a large number of prizes for all classes of canoes.

The Mersey Canoe Club at Liverpool is almost as old as the Royal, and is a very stable and sporting institution. The "Mersey" has not given way to racing quite so extensively as the older club, but none the less it has produced some very excellent canoe sailors, and some canoes and canoe-yawls of considerable merit. Knowing the Mersey well, I have no doubt that were the Mersey Canoe Club now to institute a useful class of sailing canoe, and to give a substantial programme of Saturday racing for the season, the canoe would, on the Mersey, above all places around our coast, show itself in front of small "raters" and open boats in giving sport and pastime for money expended, and the club would have to look for a more extensive boat and club house on the influx of members.

It is impossible here to go into the history or even description of all the canoe clubs, or to decide whether some are not more properly "sailing boat" clubs; and as some of the clubs are so bashful of appearing in print, it becomes difficult to know whether they are flourishing on thousands of pounds of capital, or have become shelved on the glory of past attainments. There are, or were up to a late time, the following clubs: the Clyde, the Humber, the Wear, the Tyne, the Sunderland, the Northern (on the Tyne), the Ulster, the Midland and the Forth. The British Canoe Association is of course well known because, though essentially a club in its organisation, it caters for visitors from all the other clubs as well as for its own members; it is by its constitution only a cruising or camping club. Once a year, however, it holds some races at a regatta during the camp meet; these races are handicapped events and therefore, though furnishing some good sport to those at the meet, they do not in any way represent speed or quality in the canoes or men who compete; indeed, under the circumstances of a cruising meet of men from various clubs owning canoes produced under widely differing classification rules, some ancient, some modern, it is impossible for the B.C.A., without any classification rules of its own, or the adoption of some leading club's rules, to do otherwise than sail handicap races, if races are needed.

The real commanding charm of canoeing over all other aquatic sports is that where there is water there is the canoe's sphere of action. It matters not whether the water be sea or a mere brook, a lake or a fish pond, canoeing can be more or less enjoyed, especially if the right type of canoe for the nature of the water is chosen. The canoe, in one form or other, may be an adjunct to yachting, to fishing and to shooting; she may be useful for travel, for exploration or even for war; but, above all, the sailing canoe on moderately open water is the finest of health-givers, and is so at the least cost. The canoeist can at his own will sail alone or elect to sail in company; not so the yachtsman, who must have a crew, if not guests also. The canoeist can carry his hotel with him; not so the shooting or fishing sportsman, the hunting man, the cyclist or the golfer. All these are dependent on house or hotel when the sport is over, whereas living in a canoe is part of the sport of canoeing.

WARINGTON BADEN-POWELL.

GLOSSARY.

Apron—The macintosh cover put over the canoe "well" opening when the canoeist is seated in the "Well" (*q.v.*), in order to prevent waves from splashing into the body of the canoe. It is not infrequently replaced by a sliding wooden **Hatch.**

Back-board—A board usually hung from the deck coaming, or the bulkhead directly behind the paddler, against which he leans, and presses his back when paddling; his feet giving pressure from the foot-stretcher.

Beam—The greatest width of a boat.

Bearings—The line of flotation formed by the water upon a boat's side and bottom when, with all on board, she has come to the angle of best stability for such displacement, or sail pressure.

Brace [*See* STRETCHER].

Burdens—The boards laid upon, but not fixed to, the lower part of the frame of the canoe. Also called **Floor-boards.**

Camber—The arch of the deck from one side to the other; contrasted with **Sheer,** which is the curve fore and aft.

Canoe—A light boat, sharp modelled at each end, of light draught of water, and destined to be propelled by a paddle or paddles held in the hand without fixed support. There are three main types.

(1) The *open*, *Canadian*, or *undecked* canoe, used for paddling purposes only, and accommodating any number up to ten or more. The native boats are mostly of *birch bark*, but those of the same pattern imported into England are usually of *bass wood*. They are all built with a smooth skin, *i.e.*, the planks do not overlap one another, but are put side by side and caulked or ribboned.

(2) The *Rob Roy*, called after the pseudonym of Mr. John Macgregor, the father of modern canoeing. This is a decked canoe, generally built of oak or cedar, for one or two persons, and able to carry a small sail, but chief reliance is placed upon the paddle. The average length of this type is 14 feet by 26 inches wide. It is always clincher-built.

(3) The Nautilus type and the developments from it. A larger *Rob Roy*, designed by Mr. Baden Powell, with a view to improve the sailing powers and quality of the craft. Like the *Rob Roy* it is generally clincher-built, but the larger sailing canoes are now built with smooth skins, and approach very closely in general character to the ordinary sailing boat.

Paper boats are extensively used in America, but have not been adopted generally in Europe, and canvas canoes are frequently built by amateurs, though seldom seen from boat-yards; the canvas canoe is, with suitable internal structure or frame, about the toughest for real rough work.

Carvel-built—A boat with flush, edge-to-edge planking.

Coaming or **Combing**—A thin plank on its edge fastened around the "well" (*q.v.*), to prevent the water on deck from running below.

Cock-pit—[*See* WELL].

Drip-cups—Leather cups set around the shaft of the paddle to catch the drippings from the blade.

Dug-out—A boat consisting of a log with the interior dug-out or hollowed, the primitive form of the canoe.

Floor-boards—[*See* BURDENS].

Monkeying—Patching up or arranging hastily some fitting for a canoe (American slang).

Nautilus—[*See* CANOE.]

Paddle—A short kind of oar, held in the hand, and not resting in a rowlock, provided with one or two *blades* or *palms*. The usual length is about 8 feet and the width of the blade about 6 inches; they are usually made of pine or spruce, and consist of blade, round or shaft, and ferrule.

Palm—[*See* PADDLE].

Portage—(1) The carrying of a canoe round overland past an impassable bit of river or sea.

(2) The place of such carrying.

Rob-Roy—[*See* CANOE].

Round—The shaft of the paddle.

Stretcher—The board against which the feet are pressed to steady and enforce the stroke.

Well—The opening in a decked canoe to admit the putting in of cargo and to accommodate the crew.

N.B. For other technical terms, which are also used in rowing or sailing, see under those sports.

Bibliography—*Canoe and the Flying Proa*, W. L. Alden (New York, 1878, 2*s.* 6*d.*); *The Cruise of the Canoe Club*, W. L. Alden (Harper, 1883, 5*s.*): *Paddle and Portage, from Moosehead Lake to the Aroostook River, Maine*, T. S. Steele (Estes and Lavirat, Boston, 1882, 7*s.* 6*d.*); *Practical Boat Building and Sailing*, A. Neison, Dixon Kemp, and G. C. Davies (Gill, 1881, 7*s.* 6*d.*); *Canoe and Camp Life in British Guiana*, C. B. Brown (Stanford, 1876, 21*s.*); *Yachts, Boats, and Canoes: their Design and Construction*, C. S. Hicks (Low, 1887, 10*s.* 6*d.*); *Practical Canoeing*, Tiphys (*pseud.*) (Nories and Wilson, 1883, 5*s.*); *An Inland Voyage*, R. L. Stevenson (Kegan Paul, 1878, 7*s.* 6*d.*); *Canoe Travelling*, W. Baden Powell (Smith and Elder, 1871, 6*s.*); *Encyclopædia Britannica*, 9th ed., article "Canoe," J. Macgregor (1876); *Description of the New "Rob Roy" Canoe*, J. MacGregor (Low, 1866, 1*s.*): *The "Rob Roy" on the Jordan, &c.*, J. MacGregor (Murray, 1874, 7*s.* 6*d.*); *The "Rob Roy" in the Baltic*, J. MacGregor (Low, 1879, 2*s.* 6*d.*); *A Thousand Miles in the "Rob Roy" Canoe*, J. MacGregor (Low, 1879, 2*s.* 6*d.*); *A Voyage Alone in the Yawl "Rob Roy" from London to Paris, &c.*, J. Macgregor (Low, 1867, 5*s.*); *Voyage of the Paper Canoe*, J. R. Bishop (David Douglas, Edinburgh, 1878, 10*s.* 6*d.*); *Historic Waterways*, R. G. Thwaites (Maclurg and Co., Chicago, 1888, $1·50); *The Canoe and Boat Builder*, W. P. Stephens (Spon, 9*s.*); *Family Canoe Trips*, F. W. Snedeker (New York, 1892, 2*s.* 6*d.*); *The Canoe and the Saddle*, T. Winthrop (Paterson, 1883, 2*s.* and 1*s.*); *Canoeing in Kanuckia*, C. L. Norton and J. Habberton (Putnams, 1878, 7*s.* 6*d.* and 2*s.*); *Camping out with the British Canoe Association*, J. D. Hayward, *Canoeing with Sail and Paddle*, J. D. Hayward (All England Series, Bell, 1893, 2*s.*); *Canoeing and Camping Out*, J. D. Hayward and A. A. Macdonell (*Bell's Handbooks of Athletic Sports*, Bell, 1893, 3*s.* 6*d.*); *Rowing, Canoeing, &c.*, Captain Crawley (Ward and Lock, 1878, 1*s.*); *The Ethics of Boxing and Manly Sport*, J. B. O'Reilly ("Canoeing Sketches," pp. 243–303) (Trübner, 1888, 7*s.* 6*d.*); *Rowing, Canoeing, Sculling, &c.* (Ward and Lock, 1882, 6*d.*); *Canoe Handling*, C. Vaux (New York, 1888, 5*s.*); *Camping and Cruising in Florida*, J. A. Henshall (Clarke and Co., Cincinnati, 1884, 7*s.* 6*d.*); *Four Months in a Sneak Box*, J. R. Bishop (Davis Douglas, Edinburgh, 1880, 12*s.* 6*d.*); *Canoe "Aurora" Cruise from the Adirondacks to the Gulf*, C. A. Neidé (Forest and Stream, 1885, $1); *Canvas Canoes: How to Build them*, P. B. Field (Forest and Stream, 1887, 50*c.*); *Boat Sailor's Manual*, E. F. Qualtrough (Scribner, 1886, 10*s.* 6*d.*); *Cruises in Small Yachts and Big Canoes*, (Nories and Wilson, 1883, 5*s.*).

CAPERCAILZIE [Cock o' the Woods;

Tetrao urogallus; Coq du bois, Fr.; *Tiur*, Nor.; *Tjäder*, Sw.; *Auerhahn*, Ger.; *Gluhăr*, Russ.]—This magnificent bird, the largest of the grouse-tribe, among English sportsmen termed shortly "the Caillie," is distributed over nearly the whole of Northern Europe wherever large forests of pine or fir exist, and over portions of Central Europe, where the same trees abound at a considerable elevation. Woodlands consisting solely of deciduous trees, however extensive, it never inhabits. But although common in parts of Germany, Austria, Switzerland, and elsewhere, the vast tracts of North-west Russia and the Scandinavian Peninsula may be regarded as its peculiar home.

In Scotland—Said to be indigenous in Scotland, it there became extinct, until early in the present century the then Marquis of Breadalbane re-established the Scandinavian breed in the woods of Taymouth Castle, whence it has spread over various parts of the country similarly suited to its habits.

Favourite Haunts—Its favourite haunts are ranges of pine forest broken by rocky ravines and low cliffs, with open tracks of mossy swamp, coarse herbage, and frugiferous shrubs, whither it can resort for food at early morn and before dusk. It is also partial to wandering on the borders of forest clearings, and makes such habitual use of cattle-paths and other rough woodland tracks as to be easily trapped. Great numbers of frozen Capercailzie are exported during the winter from Russia and Scandinavia. At that season, when the snow lies deep, it feeds on the shoots of the pine until its flesh becomes unpleasantly impregnated with turpentine, but in Northern countries affording abundance of wild forest fruit, bilberries, cow- and bear-berries, cranberries, and the like, the young birds are, in the autumn, delicious eating, and the old ones at least well-flavoured and free from taint. The richly sombre plumage of the cock Capercailzie, its defiant head and eye, strong beak and marked beard, all suggestive of its notorious pugnacity, render it one of the most strikingly handsome and game-like of birds, and its great size and weight make it one of the noblest feathered prizes that the sportsman can secure. It is the stag royal of the winged race.

Driving—In Scotland and most Caillie-producing countries it is often customary to drive the birds over the guns, and the ease with which driven Caillie may be killed is by no means proportionate to their conspicuousness as a mark. To a novice, at least, their flight is most deceptive, inasmuch as they appear, from their bulk, to be moving but slowly, whereas they are, in fact, travelling at a great pace. Many sportsmen, however, will derive greater satisfaction from bagging the giant grouse under conditions less artificial and demanding more individual patience and woodcraft There are, indeed, few wild creatures more wary than a truly patriarchal cock Capercailzie; he can on occasion run like a hare, and even when taking wing within distance, either from the ground or the branch of a tree, has an instinctive knack of interposing obstacles between himself and the gun. His pursuer, whether searching the pine-clad ravine, the depth of the forest, or the borders of the morass, cannot be too cautious or noiseless. Elk-dogs of the smaller breed are in Scandinavia occasionally trained to work up to Capercailzie in a leash, a deadly method of approach.

The Hen [*Röc*, Nor.; *Tjäder-höne*, Sw.]—The hen Caillie, also of noble size, but often wholly out of proportion to her gigantic and polygamous mate, is a careful mother, keeping the young brood together at the commencement of the shooting season, and exhibiting, like the grayhen, much noisy, self-exposing anxiety when danger threatens.

In favourable localities, as when the brood has run down into a willow-swamp to feed, the young cocks will lie well, and may be killed over a steady dog. A hard-hit Caillie will, after a considerable flight, possibly out of sight, almost invariably fling himself under the first, even inconspicuous, bank or ledge on either side of his course, and there die or lie still; he may, therefore, by observation of the flight and the ground, often be gathered without difficulty.

In the spring courting-season the cock Capercailzie's wariness is intermittently dominated by amorous ardour. Posting himself at daybreak on the branch of a selected tree, he thence utters his love-call to the hens, and during each brief repetition thereof becomes absolutely deaf and blind from passion. The watchful gunner has therefore as many correspondingly brief opportunities of approach, but must, when the call ceases, remain instantaneously rigid in his then position, for his intended victim suddenly regains his acute senses, and the slightest sound or motion proves fatal to the stalk. Devotees of this sport describe it as intensely exciting and fascinating, which is naturally a matter of taste. *Tetrao urogalloides* (*Rakkelhane*, Nor.) is the hybrid between the Blackcock and hen Capercailzie.

HENRY POTTINGER.

CAPERCAILZIE, STALKING—This is good sport in countries where the close time for belligerent gamebirds does not include the mating season. The amateur must, to start with, pass the night in the forest; and in Russia, where the sport in question is recognised, he will require the thickest of fur-lined coats and long, wadded boots. Proceeding to the forest in the dusk of an April evening, he must light a good fire and sleep from 9 p.m. until 2 a.m., or converse in hushed tones with the keeper or the village sportsman who is his guide. At the latter hour, or shortly after, he must quit his fireside and move quietly to that portion of the forest which is known as the tourney-ground of the capercailzie warriors. Presently he will hear, if all goes well, a curious and unfamiliar sound, *tok, tokka, tokka*, which will send the keeper's finger in warning to his lips; for during this first challenge he must remain still as death. Soon there falls upon his ear a second sound, a chirping as of some tiny finch, lasting but a few seconds and succeeded by a repetition of the first refrain. It is during the brief spell of chirping, that the sportsman may spring with impunity towards the tree upon the summit of which is seated the love-blinded capercailzie. Should the bird, after issuing the first half of its challenge, stop short without proceeding to the chirping, the stalker must stop short also, no matter how uncomfortable the position in which he may have remained after his last rush.

Thus, by a series of scrambles and wild leaps, he arrives presently within shot, and may, with care, shoot half-a-dozen capercailzies in the same manner, before sunrise puts an end to the sport.

FRED WHISHAW.

CARIBOU—Owing to the inaccessible nature of its haunts, the life history of the Caribou is involved in some obscurity, and it is not quite certain whether there are two species, the Woodland and the Barren Ground, (C. tarandus and C. tarandus arcticus), or whether they are not both merely varieties of the European and Asiatic Reindeer. The forms certainly seem to intergrade, so as to make it difficult to draw any specific line; but the extreme varieties have very different habits.

The **Barren Ground Caribou** wanders far beyond the Arctic Circle, into those desolate regions which it shares with the Musk Ox, and it indulges in very curious and extensive migrations in the spring and fall; these migrations being in some respects different for the two sexes. When migrating, the herds assemble in enormous numbers, as the Bison used of old on the great plains of the West, and the Spring Buck in South Africa. In fact, this is the only American mammal which can still, at certain times and places, be found in the same incredible numbers as of old; for it is protected, as Bison, Elk, Deer, and Antelope are not, by the remoteness and frozen desolation of the wastes where it dwells.

The **Woodland Caribou**, on the other hand, is a beast of the dense Northern forests; in most localities it does not possess any very marked habit of annual migration, though at all times a restless, wandering beast; and it is usually found in small parties, and never in immense herds. The Woodland Caribou is found here and there in the forests of Canada, from the Atlantic to the Pacific, and in two or three places penetrates across the border of the

United States. Like all other large game, it retreats before man, but nevertheless it holds its own against him better than most of its congeners. Caribou are more plentiful in Maine at present than they were thirty years ago. They have one very great advantage in the struggle for life over their giant cousin, the Moose, who so often dwells in the same forest with them. The Moose's long legs and vast power enable him in winter to go through snows where an ordinary deer flounders helplessly; but, when the snows are very deep and a crust forms, he can be run down and killed, with no difficulty beyond the severe toil involved, by any hardy man who is an expert snow-shoer. In many localities, in consequence, the settlers have completely killed out the Moose by this villainous habit of "crusting." The Caribou, however, is not, like the Moose, forced to plunge his legs through the snow to hard ground; he possesses huge splay hoofs and very limber joints, so that he himself has snow-shoes, as it were, and only under very peculiar conditions of crust is it possible for any man to get near him. When plunging at a gallop through the snow, the tracks he makes are not unlike those of a gigantic Rabbit; for the limber hind legs take his weight almost up to the hock. I have seen a Caribou run right away from a party of expert snow-shoers without showing any distress, though in snow where a Moose would have been overtaken in half a mile. This capacity tells immensely in his favour, and more than offsets the fact that under ordinary circumstances he is less wary and more stupid than the Moose.

CARIBOU.

The best time for hunting the Caribou is when there has been a light fall of snow, and he can be tracked while the footfall of the still-hunter is muffled. But in good ground he is not a very difficult beast to kill earlier in the season. He is very fond of lurking about the barrens and cranberry bogs which dot the Northern forests, and, if the hunter can see him here, there is always a good chance to creep up on him. In thick timber, where the trees are close together and there is much brush, with crisp, dry leaves on the ground, it is exceedingly difficult for anyone but an Indian to get up to the Caribou, or indeed any other kind of game. In open forests of large conifers, however, I have found it easy to track and still-hunt Caribou, whether they were feeding or lying down. If one is close on the game, they will often be so panic-struck by the first shot that it is an easy matter to kill several if there is need of the meat. I have had a young bull, whose companion I had just shot, stand looking at me fully half a minute in paralysed terror before it made up its mind to run off unmolested, as I did not want to kill it.

The sight of a Caribou seems scarcely as quick as that of the ordinary Deer, nor are its other senses so sharp, though like all game it has a good nose. It is not so wary as the Moose; but I may remark in passing that my own experience has been that under like conditions the common American or White Tail Deer is the most difficult game on the continent to circumvent; doubtless it is for this reason that it holds its own in the land better than other beasts of the chase.

Caribou are great swimmers, and it is a very common thing to kill them in the water. Of course, however, no man would kill game swimming for sport, although, when exploring and travelling in the wilderness, any man must kill the animals he needs for food, just as he happens to come upon them. It must be remembered that the wilderness hunter, the man who roams through far-off wilds in chase of big game, cannot afford to give law to the beasts of the chase, as can his brother of civilized regions, who does not depend for his dinner, and perhaps for his life, upon the result of a single shot. Where parties of sportsmen merely take a three weeks' trip into the woods for Caribou, they of course kill only the bulls, and these only in legitimate fashion; but a man who travels for three months without seeing a single white face, or who spends his winter alone 500 miles from the nearest human habitation, cannot afford to take chances. If he finds a favourite pass in a lake, across which Caribou swim, he will kill them at this pass; and if, during the time of short rations in midwinter, the conditions of the snow enable him to run up to a herd on snow-shoes, he takes all possible advantage of the opportunity. [*See also* REINDEER.]

THEODORE ROOSEVELT.

CARP (*Cyprinus carpio*)—[*See* ANGLING COARSE FISH.)]

MEASUREMENTS, &c.—Length of head 4 to 4⅝, of caudal fin 5⅝ to 6, height of body 3 to 4½ in the total length. *Eyes*—small, situated a little before the middle of the length of the head, 2½ diameters from the end of the snout, and 3 apart (in an example nearly 17 inches long). Opercle strongly striated. The proportions of the various parts of the fish are exceedingly diverse, dependent upon age, sex, and locality. *Barbels*—of moderate length, those at the maxilla the longest, and almost equalling one diameter of the orbit. Lips thick and leathery. The maxilla reaches to beneath the front edge of the orbit. *Fins*—dorsal commences rather nearer to the snout than to the base of the caudal, its first two or three, or rarely four rays are bony, the last being serrated posteriorly, while the anterior portion of the fin, which is the highest, equals about two-fifths of the height of the body below it. Pectoral situated low down, its length equals about that of the head without the snout, and it does not extend to above the ventral, which latter reaches half-way to the anal. First two or three anal rays osseous, the last being serrated posteriorly. Caudal deeply forked. *Scales*—large, 5½ to 6 rows between the lateral line and the base of the ventral fin. *Colours*—vary, usually brownish or with a bluish tinge along the back, with golden or coppery reflections along the sides. Some have been described of a whitish tint due, perhaps to age, others as having black spots caused, perhaps occasionally, by parasites. Day, *Fishes of Great Britain and Ireland*, vol. ii. p. 158.

CATAPULT SHOOTING—Ever since the Romans used it as their great engine of war, a series of weapons of greater accuracy and greater shock have gradually ousted the Catapult from its first stage of importance, until it has degenerated to the mere plaything of schoolboys.

In the big schools of England, France, Germany, and America, the Catapult is still as popular as it was with our grandfathers. For the most part, a coarse inaccurate weapon, used in hurling small stones, and combining economy and inaccuracy, is in favour.

In a large public school, probably twenty per cent. of the boys have at one time or another used catapults; and though probably only two or three ever really master the science, yet the little weapon is, when properly made and used, and taking into consideration the rough materials of its construction, capable of a wonderful degree of accuracy.

If the history of many of the very best sportsmen and shots could be written, it would be found that the foundations of their skill with gun or rifle were laid in early days by the use of this insignificant weapon. To youths who have not yet attained to the use of large weapons, there is no finer training for judging distances on a small scale than shooting with the "tweeker," the small Catapult to which I shall presently allude. Every shot fired can be seen by the shooter to the top of its parabolic curve, and even when it has begun to drop.

What, it may be asked, has the Catapult got to do with the sportsman who has arrived at years of maturity? And of what practical use is it? None, certainly, to any one who only *begins* to shoot with it in days when the muscles of the arm have become rigid, for there is a certain knack about its use not to be acquired in after years. But to the big-game shooter who may find himself in some out-of-the-way corner of the earth, such as Western America, Newfoundland, Iceland, Spitzbergen, and other places, where the various species of grouse and ptarmigan are plentiful and *tame*, it is of every use. There is not a big-game hunter in search of large animals, who has not, at some time and in such a country, been confronted with the difficulty of supplying his pot with fresh meat without having to bang off his gun or rifle at the risk of disturbing the whole neighbourhood and his particular quarry. A man who knows how to use a Catapult, even though he may not be a first-class shot with it, will find the little weapon of immense help under such circumstances. The various species of grouse, particularly the blue Rocky Mountain grouse (*Dendragapus obscurus*), will, with care, readily allow a man to approach to within eight or ten yards, a distance at which, after a few shots, the catapulter ought easily to be able to strike a blow effectively in either the head or neck. It is not difficult to avoid striking the bird in the body, as the necessary elevation can quickly be obtained against the clear sky. Every shot can be seen, and the shooting is practically noiseless, so that it does not disturb the birds, who only raise their necks and look about, even when a pellet may have touched the feathers in their neck. During a trip to the Rocky Mountains in 1886, I found the blue grouse very plentiful in the Big Horn Mountains, and could generally manage to supply the pot for the day when bigger game was scarce. For this purpose I used elastic about $\frac{1}{8}$ inch in thickness, which is nearly double that of "tweeker" calibre, and gives a greater shock without perhaps the same degree of accuracy.

Materials—Catapults are like rifles in one respect: the thinner the elastic, or the smaller the bore, as one would say, the greater the accuracy. But then, again, range is curtailed by too thin an elastic. Although not giving sufficient shock to kill outright so large a bird as a grouse, the best elastic for all-round use, combining accuracy and shock, is a $\frac{1}{16}$ inch thick, and used in lengths of 9 inches, with a single No. 1 shot, dog-skin pouch, and fork of privet, which should be peeled, dried, and hardened in the smoke of a candle. With such a weapon properly made, it is not difficult for an expert to put ten pellets in a three-inch circle at ten yards. Nearly the whole art of shooting properly with so delicate a weapon is to get the force required. This can only be done by the shooter finding out for himself exactly how to give the pull back of the left hand, holding the shot in the pouch, and letting go as the *right* hand gives the forward jerk to the fork. But no man can be taught to shoot with a Catapult, or any other weapon, by means of a book, though certain hints may be of use, and accuracy is obtained only by constant practice.

The elastic should never be used cold as it is bought. The best plan is to carry it in the breeches pocket two days before using, or steam it for an hour or two in hot water to make it soft and pliable. The writer knows of one boy who was so devoted to his sport, that he always carried a strand or two of the elastic in his mouth, ready for immediate use.

J. G. MILLAIS.

CHAMOIS (*Rupicapra tragus*)—Chamois stalking is with the Austrians what fox-hunting is in England. It is the favourite sport of the Austrian Kaiser, and of all who can indulge in it. But the number who follow the Alpine goat is small compared to the number who follow the stag, partly on account of the expense incurred, and partly on account of the dangerous and fatiguing nature of the work. The first question the huntsman asks the stranger is whether he is *schwindlig* (giddy). If the latter can fearlessly answer in the negative, and proves on his first essay that he is possessed of the necessary nerve in negotiating dangerous places, the *Jäger* is satisfied and—beyond giving a hand in places where only a son of the Alps could manage to progress at all—will confine his attention to the game.

The chamois is hunted by the *Birsch* method, or stalked, both in summer and winter. In the warm weather he keeps to the highest summits of the Alps, but the deep snow brings him down almost to the valleys in search of food, and those who can stand the cold and the fatigue prefer to stalk him in winter. When the snow is very deep, however, stalking is out of the question, and one is reduced to driving.

Habits—He is a very peculiar animal in his movements. The stag will hurry from place to place, only stopping to feed, and thus traverse miles in a day and night; but the chamois will often remain feeding for days together in an area as confined as that of an ordinary dwelling-house. Yet it must not be supposed that he remains quiescent. On the contrary, he is never still for a minute together, but is continually imbued with an unconquerable restlessness that prompts him to take little quick jumps between almost every nibble at the herbage. He is ever on the alert for a foe, and this wariness makes stalking very difficult. His scent is keener than that of the stag, which again enhances the difficulty. In the deepest snow, with a wild wind raging, the chamois will spring unhesitatingly at the face of an apparently perpendicular wall of rock. He makes for the patches of snow visible on the face of the rock, for either instinct or experience has taught him that where there is room for snow to catch he can find footing.

Local Knowledge, &c.—There is no sport that requires such perfect and unerring local knowledge as chamois stalking. In many places during one day a sportsman's life is absolutely in the hands of the *Jäger* who conducts him. The *Jäger* must know every inch of the track, for one false step may mean almost instantaneous death. Consequently, only picked men of undoubted local knowledge are chosen, generally those who have served a long apprenticeship as beaters or drivers. I may here mention, as it is not generally known, that the

CHAMOIS.

Jäger is a servant of the State, for, although paid privately by the gentleman who employs him, he is bound to pass a qualifying examination, and take an oath, before his license is granted him. Moreover, there are regiments recruited from the ranks of these *Jäger*, similar to the *Chasseurs* of France.

Buck and "Geiss"—One of the principal difficulties in chamois shooting is to distinguish between the buck and the *Geiss*, or female. The general contour of their form is alike; they are much the same size, and the horns are very similar in male and female. The only, or at least, the main difference, is that in the buck the horns are wider apart at the tips and thicker at the base than in the female. In the *Jägersprache*, or hunting slang, which is very elaborate in that country, the word *Geiss* has come to be applied only to a female without young, although it really only means "goat."

Clothing—The sportsmen and *Jäger* wear short breeches made of the skin of the chamois, preferable to cloth or leather, for the former gets wet and the latter is generally too stiff to be manageable. The *Jäger's* dress is very quaint, but very practical, which is everything. The breeches, as just mentioned, are of chamois skin, barely reaching to the knee, in order to leave the leg free for climbing, and prettily decorated with designs worked in thread of emerald green. In summer bright green stockings are worn, not quite as high as the knee ; but in winter many pairs of long thick stockings are worn right up to the thigh. The coat is of dark green cloth, with many pockets, and buttons of horn. The more pockets one has when chamois stalking, and the more one manages to get into them, the better one is satisfied. Thick, heavily-shod mountain boots, and a hat decorated with trophies of the chase, generally the feathers of the capercailzie, or a chamois "beard," complete the costume.

This chamois "beard" as it is called, is *the* trophy of the chamois chase. The name is given to the hair which grows along the spine, and which is exceedingly long and handsome. In winter it is a rich dark brown colour, tipped with silver-grey points, but in summer it turns to a greyish tint. The huntsmen pull it out most carefully, and arrange it in the shape of a plume, binding the root ends very firmly together with a green thread. This plume is worn in the hat, generally fixed with a silver brooch stamped with the figure of a chamois. The task of picking, arranging, and binding the hairs, is a slow and tedious one, and makes these trophies very valuable. Between three and four pounds sterling, or their equivalent, are given for a fair trophy of this description, and considerably more if the specimen be a really fine one. In addition to this trophy, the *Jäger* generally extracts the two front teeth, called the *Grandl*, and these are worn in scarf-pins. It is no uncommon sight to see a *Jäger*, or even a peasant landholder, wearing as trophies all that remains of several stags, chamois, and *Auerhahn*, or capercailzie.

On account of the glaciers to be crossed, slippery rocks to be traversed, and similar obstacles, the huntsman must have his feet shod with climbing irons, bound firmly to the foot with stout leathern thongs, and furnished with sharp spikes to grip the ice or rock. He also carries a *Bergstock*, or mountain stick, a long pole with a spike at the end, which is really and truly as necessary in some places as the man's own legs.

Chamois Ground—To show that the chamois requires some room, I may mention that my chamois ground, by no means a very large one, covers an area equal to fifty English square miles. A little lumbering is done on the ground, and some of it is given over to peasant holdings, but the bulk of it is virgin Alp land, roamed over by the chamois, my *Jäger*, and poachers.

Poachers—These are very numerous, and form a powerfully antagonistic element to sport. Poaching as they do from sport and not from want, they are very hard to deal with, and as it is an easy matter for them to find out in what part of the country you will be shooting at a certain time, it is no uncommon thing for them to be enjoying themselves simultaneously at a conveniently remote distance. They do not even stop at human bloodshed when pursuing their illegal sport, but will open fire on the *Jäger* if molested, and many are the reports that come in from the more remote and lawless districts of *Jäger* being tortured or murdered whilst endeavouring to do their duty. On one of the last occasions that I was out stalking, we heard rifle shots not very far from our position, in consequence of which my *Jäger* had to leave me and go and prospect. He was away that day and night, returning next day at noon, but could discover nothing.

Dangers of the Sport—One of the greatest dangers encountered in chamois stalking arises from the frequency and suddenness of the *Lawine*, or whirlwind, accompanied generally by an avalanche of snow, which will come upon the huntsman suddenly and without warning in deep gorges of the Alps, roaring down the mountain side with terrific force, or catching him as he breasts some steep bluff. Such is the force of the wind, accompanied by blinding snow, that the sportsmen are often in danger of being whirled bodily away by the strength of it, and from generations of experience and sad fatalities have learnt to throw themselves face downwards on the ground when it is heard approaching.

A day's sport—To give an idea of what a day's chamois stalking means I will briefly describe a day on one of my last outings.

We rose hours before the dawn on a December morning, with a world of snow around us such as is only seen in Alpine and Northern lands. Breakfast was the first consideration, and full justice we did to the meal. The very prospect of going through a fatiguing day's work in such cold induces one to eat, if only from motives of physical economy. Then, the *Jäger* having bound on our irons, and our *Buckel-sacks* loaded, we put on our strong leathern gauntlets, and, climbing pole in hand, followed our *Jäger* bearing the rifle slung at his back, and carrying a collapsible lantern to light the way till such time as it should brighten. The snow was half-way up our thighs even in the valley (if the gorge round our hut, three or four hours' march from the nearest hamlet, and high up among a chain of Alps, can be called a valley), and we speculated curiously as to what it would be like higher up. Meanwhile, all we had to do was to tread in the *Jäger's* capacious footsteps, and take care not to slip or fall into some unseen cavity. Four hours' stiff climbing, during which our clothes were saturated with perspiration, brought us to a point that we could easily reach in one hour in summer. The lantern had long been extinguished and packed away, and a cold white glare hung over the peaks. We were now half way up one side of a vast gorge, scalloped out of the mountains by centuries of recurring winter snows and spring floods. On a perilous-looking bluff on the opposite slope, just below the line of the eternal snow, is a substantial hut of pine logs, reared by an adventurous Englishman who had come prospecting in the rugged gorges around for precious stones and, what is more, had found them.

The *Jäger* drew his long *Hirschfänger* ("stag-catcher") and proceeded to chop off some pine boughs with it for me to sit on. This knife is very powerful, with a heavy horn handle, and is carried bayonet-wise in a belt around the waist. It is used for despatching the game, gralloching, and pioneering through the undergrowth. He removed my climbing irons, produced from the depths of his haversack my felt overboots, and made my lower man comfortable. My air cushion was inflated, and having donned my thick fur coat, I sat and enjoyed a second breakfast, with the strongest of schnapps, a brand called *Slivovitz*, introduced from Turkey. It is really astonishing how much coarse fat and raw spirits a man can eat when chamois stalking.

Breakfast was nearly over when we sighted a herd of chamois at some considerable distance. I raked them with my glasses, and could make out several fine bucks, jumping every few seconds, as they fed, in their jerky, nervous manner. We packed up and started stalking, but it was no good. We could not get anywhere near them. Later on we sighted a solitary old buck with a fine pair of horns on the wrong side of a rather dangerous glacier. To reach it we must scale flight after flight of *escaliers* built of rough pine logs, and clamped to the face of the rock with iron. It is a beautiful but a terrible pathway. One looks down seemingly miles to the gorge below, and speculates on the results of a false step. In the crevices the Edelweiss blooms gaily, raising its little white star in emulation of the white around. We crossed the glacier, bending nearly double, feeling our way inch by inch, and taking care to get a good grip with our irons before making a single step. The chamois was feeding in a patch of cover near the farther edge. The wind suddenly changed, veering towards him. He became suspicious instantly, although he could see nothing, and came down towards us. While he paused after a run, as is the custom of the animal, I took aim, although he was nearly four hundred paces away, for I knew my only chance had come, as the path he was striking would take him further from me. Simultaneously with the report, and to my intense chagrin and mortification, he went down the slope, skirting the glacier as fast as he could.

We ascended the gorge above the glacier with dampened spirits, when suddenly around a bend came a herd of some fifteen or sixteen, bucking along in a straggling line. I fell upon my knees and waited. Fortunately the wind held good, and they came within range all unsuspecting. I singled out, as I thought, two fine bucks, and fired, succeeding in dropping both. The rest turned, sprang at the rocks and disappeared. On investigation one turned out to be a good buck, the other a very well-developed *Geiss*; but we were not undeceived regarding the latter till we had it in the skinning house. That night, according to hunting custom, the *Jäger* drank and smoked much, telling long yarns of the chase, and ending up with a dance to the strains of a guitar and a mouth-organ, dear to the hearts of all mountain people.

To show what skill a veteran *Jäger* can acquire I may mention that on one occasion his Majesty the Emperor shot twenty-seven chamois in one day, of which *nineteen* were bucks. To anybody who can appreciate the difficulty of distinction this constitutes a record. To the late Count Meran, son of the Archduke John, belonged the honour of having dropped two thousand.

In conclusion I can thoroughly recommend chamois stalking as a sport that brings out all the true qualities of a sportsman, and to any of my readers who may chance to embark on it I wish most heartily *Waidmannsheil!*

SCHLICK.

CHAMPIONSHIPS—This is a word which is frequently used, and also frequently abused, in connection with the various forms of sport which give scope for competition between individuals. We believe the word first came into vogue as a sporting term in the days of the Prize Ring, when a pugilist who had beaten all comers was styled the Champion of England, and held his title until he was beaten in a match arranged to test his claim to the honour, and thereupon the winner took over the title of Champion until he was beaten by a better or younger man. Thus for years there was a legitimate succession of Champions in the Prize Ring, and a record of succession is supposed to be kept by the sporting press up to this very day. A similar system was pursued with regard to professional Sculling, there being a lineal succession of Champion Scullers of England, until Sadler was beaten by Trickett the Australian, since when the struggles go on for what is termed the Sculling Championship of the World.

In modern times, since various forms of Athletic Sport have been organised, it has been customary for the Governing Bodies of each amateur sport to hold an annual meeting, and to award to the winner of each event at that meeting the title of Amateur Champion for that year. A list of the chief amateur bodies who are recognised as being legitimately entitled by common consent to award such a title is given below. It would be impossible to give an exhaustive list, as there is nothing but public opinion to judge of the right of any body to claim to control any sport.

In addition, the title of Championship is used in Cricket, Football, and other games which do not lend themselves to individual competition, but only to competitions between County or Club Teams; and there are scores of competitions in different places, which are said to be for the Championship of the County, or of the District, or even of a particular club. Of the making of so-called champions there is nowadays no end.

Athletics—The Amateur Athletic Association holds an annual Championship meeting in London, the Midlands, and the North in rotation.

Boxing—The Amateur Boxing Association holds a similar meeting every year.

Cricket—The governing body is the M.C.C. The only Championship recognised is the County Championship, which is the prize of the County which is most successful during the year. Amongst cricketers "the Champion" means Dr. W. G. Grace, a title which none can question.

Cycling—Annual Championships at various distances are held by the National Cyclists' Union.

Football—The Football Association holds an annual competition for the Cup, the clubs playing against each other in pairs, in a succession of rounds, until two are left in who compete in the final tie for the Cup. This is practically the Championship for the year, although the term Championship is not used. The Cup is open to both professional and amateur teams. There is also a similar competition for the Amateur Cup, which is confined to amateur players.

The Rugby Union supervises an annual County Championship.

Golf—There is an Amateur Championship, also a Professional Championship and an Open Championship (for both "pros" and amateurs) held at different places under the joint management of several leading clubs.

Lawn Tennis—There is an annual meeting at the grounds of the All England Lawn Tennis Club at Wimbledon, under the management of the Lawn Tennis Association.

Rowing—The Amateur Rowing Association hold no Championship, but the title of amateur Champion of the Thames is recognised as belonging to the winner of the Wingfield Sculls. In other respects the winners of the four great races at Henley (Grand, Stewards, Goblets, and Diamonds) are practically in the same position as amateur Champions at other sports.

Skating—The National Skating Association supervises Skating Championships on the rare occasions when weather permits.

Swimming—The Amateur Swimming Association supervises Championship races held at different places and times during the season.

CHAR (from the Gaelic *ceara*—red or blood-coloured), *Salmo alpinus*, *S. salvelinus*, *S. willughbii*, *S. cambricus*, Welsh *torgoch*. This, the rarest of our non-migratory salmonidæ, has been very much subdivided by naturalists without sufficient cause. The chars which inhabit various waters in England and Wales, Ireland, and Scotland are all of the same species, slightly altered by the different surroundings under which each has lived. Those from Windermere and Coniston (Westmorland and Lancashire) are without doubt the finest in the British Isles, not only in size, but in flavour. When transferred from these larger lakes to smaller sheets of water, such as Hawes Water and Goats Water, the char have changed in outward appearance very much. In these latter places they fail to find the

CHAR.

same food, larvæ, water beetles, &c., upon which they thrive in what may be called the parent waters; they therefore degenerate in size, and rise more or less freely to the fly, both natural and artificial. In such places it is to the char of Windermere just about what the brown and yellow tiny burn trout is to the lusty trout of larger rivers and lakes. Notwithstanding what has been said to the contrary and its nomenclature, "*alpinus*," it is indigenous to this country, and there is no proof of its naturalisation with us. As a sporting fish it does not rank high, rising most freely to the fly in the smaller lakes. In those of Cumberland, Westmorland and Lancashire, where it is found in greatest abundance, it is mostly taken by nets, which are drawn in deep waters on to the shallows. It is also commonly caught by means of "plumb lines," which were invented in order that the artificial baits—spoons or pieces of metal, bright on one side, coloured on the other, cut out in the shape of a fish—used on them, might be spun steadily at varying depths. Two lines are used from each boat, one on each side, and each line has from four to six baits on it. To keep them down, a sinker of about $1\frac{1}{2}$ lb. weight is used, so adjusted that it will not spin round and entangle the line. Each line is fastened to a somewhat stiff rod of about ten or eleven feet long, which is fixed upright in the boat, and to which a bell is attached. When a bait is struck the "tinkle-tinkle" warns the fisherman, who is slowly plying his oars, of the fact. In the English lakes—Windermere, Coniston, Derwentwater, &c.—char are caught in a similar manner, and are seldom nowadays taken with fly or worm. In Llanberis Lake they have occasionally been taken in large quantities with the worm at night. In the Irish lakes, Loughs Conn and Inagh to wit, char are occasionally taken with fly when trout fishing. They used to be so taken on Ulleswater (Westmorland), on Loch Leven, and on Lough Neagh, but from all these places they appear to have disappeared, no doubt exterminated by pike, by destruction during spawning time, and by pollutions. Char vary in weight from six to the pound to a pound and a half each, although fish over 2 lb. have occasionally been caught in this country. An ordinary trout fly, rather bright in colour, will take it best, but the char is an uncertain riser. Some time ago a gentleman was trout fishing in Loch Lubnaig, in Perthshire, and saw a number of fish rising in a curious way close to the bank. He threw over them, and in a short time caught, mostly with a teal and red body, a dozen fish, which he failed to recognise. They were char, and the natives had not known one taken with fly for many years previously. In Lapland and Norway the char grows to a larger size than with us, 2 lb. and 3 lb. fish not being rare, and they take fly freely. It is also more or less plentiful in European rivers and most of the European lakes, especially such as are situate at a high altitude. It is found in America and in Canada.

The char spawns at the same periods as trout, sometimes on the shores of the lakes, sometimes in the adjoining streams. It comes under the same law as trout as to close season. Where a license is required its cost is usually 2*s.* 6*d.*; the charge for a "plumb line" license is 5*s.* The char may not be taken in Windermere and Coniston between October 2nd and March 31st. In Scotland there is no close time. In Ireland it is from November 1st to January 31st. During the season char is considered a great dainty, and "potted char" is one of the luxuries to be obtained at the English Lakes. The char, owing to its delicacy, is not a useful fish for the pisciculturist, and seldom becomes thoroughly acclimatised in waters where it has been artificially introduced.

R. B. LEE.

MEASUREMENTS, ETC.—Length of head $4\frac{3}{4}$ to $5\frac{1}{4}$, of caudal fin 6 to $6\frac{1}{2}$, height of body $4\frac{1}{2}$ to $5\frac{1}{2}$ in total length. *Eyes*—size depends much upon age, sex, and locality from whence procured: usually situated just in front of the middle of the length of the head, from $1\frac{1}{4}$ to 2 diameters from the end of the snout and the same distance apart. In some the comparative height of the body is much greater than in others, and dependent on food, health and the breeding season, the kelts becoming emaciated. The maxilla in some extends to beneath the last third of the orbit, in others to beyond the vertical from its hind margin, while it is likewise slightly more strongly developed in some than in others. The lower jaw in some varieties, as in the torgoch of Wales, may be longer anteriorly than the upper jaw. The opercular pieces are of as diverse shape in the char as the trout, and frequently are dissimilar in the opposite sides of the head. *Teeth*—present in the jaws and in a line across the vomer near its anterior extremity, and opposite the teeth of the palatine arch, none along the body of the vomer. *Fins*—dorsal usually commences about midway between the end of the snout and the base of the caudal fin, in some examples a little nearer the snout. The pectoral and other fins are of varying lengths according to locality, sex, and other varying conditions. *Scales*—small, and a much larger number of rows descending from the back of the lateral-line than there are of pierced rows along its whole extent. *Cæcal appendages*—these vary considerably, in Loch Inch 38 (Thompson): L. Rannoch 28: the Lakes 28 to 44, Dr Günther detected from 36 to 52, and the smallest number in those from Windermere, 36. From the same locality I possess an example with 28. They are as inconsistent as in the trout.

Colours—These again vary, but as a general rule the belly, prior to spawning, becomes of a crimson or claret colour, while there are generally some light-coloured orange or black spots on the body and head. The front edge of the dorsal, ventral and caudal as well as the upper edge of the pectoral are often of a pure white or orange colour. The variation in tints and shades is not so great as in the trout. In some, the ventral, anal, lower portion of the pectoral and hind edge of the caudal partake of the scarlet colour of the abdomen.—Day's *Fishes of Great Britain and Ireland*, vol. ii., p. 114.

CHEETAH (*Cynælurus jubatus*, Hindustani, *Chita*). The Cheetah, or Hunting Leopard, is a member of the great Cat-family (*Felidæ*), allied to the common Leopard, but differing from it in so many essential points that it is now regarded as generically distinct. It stands higher on its legs than an ordinary Leopard, and has relatively a more slender body and a longer tail; ears short and rounded; the face shorter and the crown more elevated than in the Leopard. The upper flesh-tooth is without the cusp on the inner side which is characteristic of the true cats, while the claws are shorter and only partially retractile.

The length of an adult Cheetah is about 7 ft., including the tail, which measures about $2\frac{1}{2}$ ft. The height at the shoulder will vary from 2 ft. 5 in. to 2 ft. 7 in.

The Cheetah occurs throughout Africa and South-Western Asia from Persia to the countries east of the Caspian, but not further east than India, where it is most common in Jeypur and Hyderabad. It has not been met with north of the Ganges nor in Ceylon.

Its usual haunts are the low rocky hills bordering the plains on which are found the Antelopes which form its chief prey; although, like the Caracal or Desert Lynx, it will likewise capture hares and game birds.

The employment of this animal for the chase seems to have been known in the East from a very early period. It is figured on Assyrian bas-reliefs in the act of seizing an Antelope, and is represented also on Egyptian monuments about 1700 B.C. Amongst the animals brought in by way of tribute to the Kings of Thebes by the black tribes of the Upper Nile is a Cheetah led in a slip with a very ornamental collar.

We learn from Baron de Noirmont that both Charles VIII. and Louis XII. of France kept trained animals of this kind, with which they killed hares and roedeer. After a kill, the Cheetah, on being shown a little blood in a tin bowl, would leave its prey and jump on the horse's crupper behind its master. One would imagine that the horse would require as much training as the Cheetah to stand quiet under such very trying circumstances. Francis I., who ascended the throne of France in 1515, also had his Hunting Leopards which, according to Gesner (*Hist. Anim.*), were of two kinds. From his description the smaller kind must have been a Lynx. They must have been very docile, for, he says, the keeper scarcely mounted his horse before the beast jumped up after him, and seated itself on a cushion behind the saddle. Henri II., the successor of Francis I., in 1547 continued this kind of sport, and it appears to have been patronised at the French Court until the days of Henri IV., when the last trained Leopards seen in France were those brought by Marie de Medici from Florence in 1601. After that date, says Baron de Noirmont, they were no longer to be seen either in France or Italy, although in Germany the sport was revived by Leopold I., who died in 1705.

There is no record of the successful use of the Hunting Leopard in England. Even James I., great sportsman as he was, drew the line there. But an experiment was once made in this direction by the Duke of Cumberland, brother of George IV., with one of two Cheetahs belonging to Tippoo Sahib, which were brought to Windsor in 1799. The Duke made a large inclosure in the park with strong netting 15 ft. high, into which he turned a stag from Windsor forest. The Cheetah was then brought in by two Indian attendants and unhooded. The stag showed fight, lowering his horns; and the Cheetah, disliking the look of his opponent, bounded over the nets, and, dashing through the terrified crowd of spectators, pursued and killed a fallow deer at no great distance; and so ended what was probably the first and last attempt at hunting with the Cheetah in this country.

The sport as practised in India at the present day is conducted somewhat as follows:—The Cheetah, hooded like a falcon, and held by a stout collar and cord, is carried to the field on a bullock cart, on which he sits side by side with the native keeper who has charge of him, and who pats and caresses him from time to time. The cart proceeds across country, until deer or antelope are seen. The driver then advances circuitously, gradually narrowing his circle until he gets within one or two hundred yards of the nearest antelope, which, accustomed to see the native carts of the country, does not at first take much notice of that which carries the Cheetah. As soon as he is near enough, the driver stops, and the keeper removes the hood of the Cheetah, which springs lightly from the cart, and commences his stalk, availing himself of every bush and hillock between himself and his prey as he stealthily approaches it. When within forty or fifty yards he jumps up, and in a series of magnificent bounds dashes at the nearest antelope, and generally brings it down,

CHEETAH.
Av. ht. at shoulder, 2 ft. 7 in. Av. length from head to root of tail, 4 ft. 6 in.

fastening at once upon its throat and killing it. It sometimes happens, however, that the intended victim gets too good a start, and the Cheetah, failing to overtake it within a reasonable distance, gives up the chase and returns sulkily to his keeper, who feeds and re-hoods him. In the event of a kill, the keeper runs up with a tin bowl, and, cutting the deer's throat, fills the bowl with the blood, which he allows the Cheetah to lap up, until, watching a favourable opportunity, he slips on the hood, and leads the animal back to the cart. The sportsmen who go out on these occasions are either mounted on horseback, or go in pairs, in bullock carts like that which carries the Cheetah.

J. E. HARTING.

CHEETAH, AFRICAN—The African Cheetah (*Felis jubata*), Leñau of the Bechuanas, Luipaard of the Boers, is a shy, nocturnal beast, which seldom falls to the rifle of the white sportsman. It figures very rarely indeed in the records of English hunters in South Africa. Many Europeans spend years in the country without setting eyes on this animal. Yet, from the Cape Colony northwards, the Cheetah is not an altogether uncommon beast of prey. In Bechuanaland the natives snare annually a considerable number of these animals, and hunt them with dogs. Karosses or rugs made from the handsome skins of the Leñau are well known at the up-country stores, where they are taken in barter. The Cheetah is nothing like so dangerous a beast to tackle as the leopard, and is killed even by the natives with their knobkerries, or club-sticks. The African Cheetah much resembles its Asiatic congener. It stands high upon the leg, and has the dog-like foot and non-retractile claws, which distinguish it at once from the true leopard. Its high skull, somewhat woolly fur, a slight mane, and the differences in marking, which may at once be noted on comparing its skin with that of the leopard, serve further to accentuate the dissimilarity between the two animals.

It feeds on the smaller antelopes, hares, game birds, and occasionally sheep and goats, and is extremely devoted to the springbuck, of which it kills a good many. A peculiar local variety of Cheetah (*Felis lanea*), known to naturalists as the Woolly Cheetah, has been found in the Karroo district of Cape Colony, in the neighbourhood of Beaufort West. In this variety—an example of which was formerly exhibited in the Zoological Gardens—the fur is extremely dense, and the markings are tawny instead of black.

H. A. BRYDEN.

CHEETUL or **CHEETAL** (*Cervus axis*), commonly known as the Spotted Deer of India. It much resembles the Fallow Deer of Europe, except as regards its horns, which are never palmated like those of the Fallow. Its colour, too, a light reddish brown, is darker, and the white spots along its back and sides are more distinctly defined. The stag has three distinct points on each gracefully curved horn, often with one or two short snags just above the brow antler. The ordinary length of horn is about 30 inches, and the circumference of beam about 3½ inches, but the writer has shot a Cheetul with horns over 36 inches, and as they were in velvet and their points quite soft, they would probably have grown an inch or two longer. The span within the bend was 30 inches, but such width is exceptional. In height the Cheetul stands from about 30 to 34 inches, its size varying in different localities.

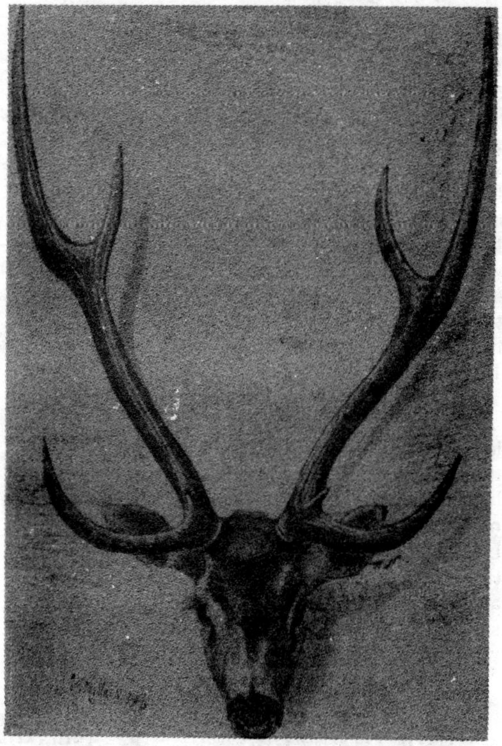

CHEETUL.

Ht. at shoulder, 32 in. Av. horn measurement, 30 in. Max. horn measurement, 38¾ in.

Habitat—It is usually abundant in large tracts of dense forest, interspersed with glades of high grass, where water is fairly plentiful (such as the Terai, for instance), or on the extremities of the forest-clad spurs of the Himalayas, which run down into that tract. It is very common in the Dehra Dún Valley, and on the Sewalik range of low-wooded hills which flank it on the west. In fact it is more or less common in almost all the level or low-hilled jungles it affects, from the foot of the Himalayas to Cape Comorin, and even to Ceylon, but never where deep shade. long grass, and water are absent.

Characteristics—In habits the Cheetul is timid and shy, and it seldom, if ever, attempts to show fight, even if approached when wounded. Yet it may frequently be found quite close to small hamlets where patches of ground in heavy jungles have been cleared for cultivation, especially when the cereals are young and green. Its cry of alarm, a short high-pitched sort of bark, is more often heard at night when the animal is alarmed by some prowling beast of prey. Where its haunts are in more or less level localities it is almost invariably shot from elephant back, but the most sportsmanlike way of hunting it is, where possible, to follow it on foot in broken or low-hilly ground.

Cheetul sometimes congregate in large numbers, but they are mostly found in herds of from five or six to a dozen or more, and usually with a good stag or two in a herd.

A singular characteristic of this deer is the irregularity with which it sheds its horns. The writer has hunted Cheetul at many different times of year and found them with horns in every stage of growth. But the best time for hunting them is from December to March, when the jungles are most free from malaria and the heat is not too oppressive. Moreover, some of their favourite resorts are now strictly closed from April to October by the Government Forest Department.

Armament—A double express rifle of from ·450 to ·500 bore, carrying a projectile of *soft* lead about an inch long, hollowed to not more than half its length, the hollow plugged with a bit of wood, is about the most suitable implement for Cheetul-shooting. The cartridge should be loaded with the strongest charge of powder the rifle can stand. Many a wounded wild animal is lost in dense jungle from want of smashing power and a flat trajectory in the weapon used for shooting at it.

DONALD MACINTYRE.

CHUB (*Leuciscus cephalus*)—[*See* ANGLING (COARSE FISH)].

MEASUREMENTS, &c.—Length of head $4\frac{1}{2}$ to 5, of caudal fin $5\frac{1}{4}$, height of body 4 in the total length. *Eye*—diameter of each $5\frac{1}{2}$ to 6 times in the length of the head, 2 diameters from the end of the snout, and 3 to 4 apart. Snout obtuse. Mouth rather deep, the upper jaw slightly overlapping the lower, and the posterior extremity of the maxilla reaching to beneath the front edge of the eye. The hindermost bone of the suborbital ring the largest. *Teeth*—pharyngeal teeth pointed and hooked at their extremities (in some slightly denticulated), 5, 2-2, 5. *Fins*—the dorsal commences midway between the end of the snout and the base of the caudal fin, its height exceeds by one-third the extent of its base. Pectoral as long as the head excluding the snout. Ventral inserted on a line slightly anterior to the origin of the dorsal fin, its length equalling about half that of the head. *Lateral-line*—slightly concave, three rows between it and the base of the ventral fin. *Colours*—muddy bluish or greenish colour along the upper surface of the head and body, becoming lighter on the sides and beneath. Dorsal and caudal fins dusky or greenish and externally dark: ventrals and anal bluish white tinged with red. Cheeks dashed with red and gold. —Day, *Fishes of Great Britain and Ireland*, vol. ii., p. 179.

CLOSE SEASONS—Angling, *see* FENCE MONTHS. Shooting, *see* GAME LAWS.

COACHING—Coaching may be divided into business and pleasure coaching. Under the former may be ranked those vehicles—they are sometimes large wagonnettes—which run to places of popular resort in connection with the trains, or between places which as yet have no railway connection, or, third, the coaches which are run for the benefit of tourists on a certain round tour, as in the Lake district, from Riggs Hotel and elsewhere. In the old days, all the coaches earned a great deal of money by the carriage of small parcels; but what with trains, sample, parcel, and book posts, few packages now find their way into the coach boot or into the way bill. As compared with those of former times—save when the opposition was so keen that a coach would carry people for nothing or "for any sum the public please," as an old Bristol coach bill put it, rather than they should travel by any rival concern—the present fares of a business coach are low, and consequently the expenses have to be cut down. The result is that the pace is often slow, the horses have to go long stages, and there is none of the spick and span appearance which characterised the coaches of the "thirties." And even the business conveyances are one by one being run off the road as new lines of railway are opened.

Moreover, nearly every business coach or wagonnette runs for the summer season only, while tourists are on the path; and as soon as October sets in, the different proprietors begin to think about taking their coaches off the road. Formerly some of the coachmen who had driven in the olden days took service on some of the out-of-the-way coaches, and if they sorely lamented that the "light of other days" had grown dim, they made the best of the changed surroundings. Those ancient artists, however, have long since gone to rest, and the few who do survive are far too old to think of driving; so a new school has arisen, and, though its exponents are in very many instances safe coachmen enough, they have never been taught by men who were either old coachmen themselves, or who learned under them, so that they have not the style of the true four-in-hand coachman. This subject will, however, be fully treated under the head of DRIVING.

These remarks, it must be distinctly understood, apply solely to those coaches which are entirely unconnected with amateurs and are run to make a profit. In the olden days so many horses were quickly knocked up by fast work that it was sometimes a difficult matter to

make both ends meet, especially if the proprietors had to pay fines for offences against any Act of Parliament—and informers were always on the look out for infringements—and damages for injury to passengers or for collisions. Now it seems quite impossible for any coach, however well it loads, to be turned out in first-rate style out of the passengers' fares, or it may be that where a fair amount of money is earned, the proprietors taking less interest in the appearance of the coaches, horses, and harness, especially as competition has died out, prefer to spend as little as possible on the turn-out, and to put as much money as possible to the profit side of the undertaking. For this view proprietors can scarcely be blamed in these cutting days, when every one desires to be carried cheaply, and to the passenger who has not been bred to coaching, or to the niceties of turning out a four-in-hand, it perhaps matters little if the standard of purely business coaching falls some way short of the ideal.

Taking leave then of purely professional and business coaching, we come to that in which the amateur element largely prevails. This phase of coaching was one entirely unknown in olden days. Amateurs, it is true, used frequently to drive the coaches of a former day when they had their "driving gloves on," which being interpreted meant that they had half a sovereign in their pocket for the coachman who would let them drive a stage. Other amateurs there were who really became professionals. Sir St. Vincent Cotton, Mr. Stephenson, who was educated at Eton and Cambridge, and who eventually drove the London and Brighton Age, and Mr. Charles Brindley, who is better known perhaps under his *nom de plume* of "Harry Hieover," were amongst those who took to horsing and driving stage coaches as a means of livelihood; while Captain Barclay of Ury (the 1000 miles in 1000 hours hero), Mr. Charles Jones, the Hon. E. Jerningham, the Dukes of Beaufort and Somerset, busied themselves about the affairs of the road. Those whilom amateurs who turned professionals made a very good thing of it, their incomes being something like £700 or £800 a year, though that did not last long.

Except in connection with trains, all stage coaching had died long before 1866, in which year the coach between London and Brighton was started by the Duke of Beaufort, Mr. Charles Lawrie, Mr. Angel, and a few others who remembered coaching as it was. Their example was followed by Mr. Charles Hoare, Colonel Stracey Clitherow, Lord Bective, and Colonel Hathorne. These coaches were started for the fun of driving them, but of course it was hoped that they would be so far patronised as to make the passenger fares pay a decent proportion of the outgoings. It may, however, safely be asserted that none of the modern coaches ever came near paying their expenses. In every case there has been a large deficit, which had to be taken out in pleasure. At the end of the season the horses were sold in several instances. In fact, in the majority of cases, the proprietors of a coach did not buy their horses, but contracted with some large dealer or job-master to supply as many horses as might be requisite to work the coach, but in those instances in which the proprietors did buy they sold at the end of the season, and if the horses were well bought, they made some money over the stud. A good many of the horses were hunters, and people, who were in want of a horse to ride with hounds early in the season, knew that in buying a hunter out of a coach they were purchasing a horse in the best possible condition, and fit to go to work at once, and this fact accounts for some of the remunerative prices which were occasionally obtained.

Frequently two or three friends ran a coach together, and shared the driving, and no one else had a chance of "taking hold," unless they were known to the proprietors, and were given a stage or two by them. In the year 1878, however, a new departure was made. Major Dixon and one or two more put on the St. Albans Wonder coach, of which James Selby was one of the professionals. Selby, who had been professional on the Tunbridge Wells coach, by and by started a subscription coach; that is to say, a coach to which several amateurs subscribed a fixed sum, and in return for their money they had the privilege of driving one day a week, or on other days, if they went, provided no other subscriber was present. The passenger fares, of course, went to the proprietor, that is to say to Selby in this case, and so, if there were six subscribers paying £100 each, the proprietor had the nice little sum of £600 to work upon, irrespective of what he might take in passenger fares. This, of course, made all the difference between profit and loss, and since that time subscription coaches have

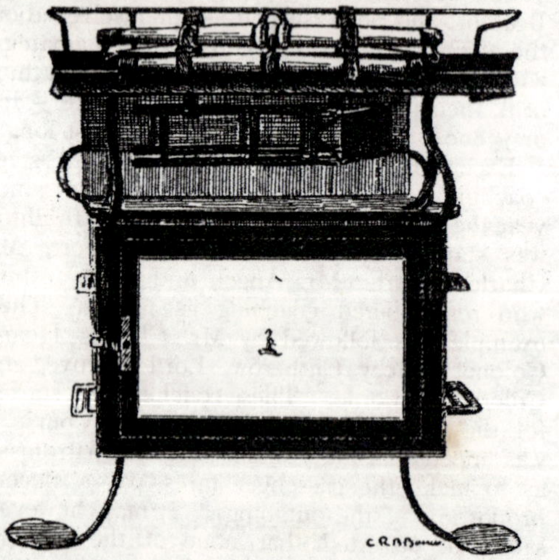

Back Seat of Park Coach or Drag.

increased and multiplied, until at the present day there is but one single coach which dispenses entirely with outside assistance. That coach is the Guildford New Times, run by Mr. Walter Shoolbred, who buys his own horses, pays all expenses, and takes no subscribers, and there is no better equipped coach running out of London, nor has there been its equal for very many years, if at all.

One by one the private proprietors have dropped out, and their places are taken by coaches to which amateurs, ambitious of driving, contribute. During the season of 1895 there were running out of London about a dozen coaches. In point of horsing the modern coaches would compare favourably with any of the older vehicles; in fact, many of the proprietors regard their annual sale at the end of the season as a means of making money. Being for the most part connected with the horse trade, they buy well. In point of number the coaches are rather over horsed, so that the teams have not too much work to do; they are carefully put together, and at the season's end bring, as a rule, prices very much in excess of those which were given for them.

In the old days the usual allowance was one horse per mile, or "one side of the road" as it was termed; that is to say, if the coach were put on from London to Brighton, taking the distance to be fifty-two miles, fifty-two horses would be required; but this allowance is greatly exceeded in modern coaches, since those which run a journey of about thirty miles out and thirty miles home have sometimes forty or fifty horses to work the coach. During recent years the system of contracting for the horses has been adopted by some proprietors, but the sale takes place just the same, he who finds the horses selling in expectation of his own benefit.

That a change has come over modern coaching is indisputable. When the coaching revival first began, the movement was entirely in the hands of amateurs, whereas now the supporters of coaching are not, with few exceptions, of the same social position as those who set coaching on its legs in the "sixties." For some reason or other, coaching does not now occupy the same *status* as it did. The subscribers and their friends form a goodly number of the passengers, but the bulk of the support comes from our American visitors. Many of these on coming to England put up at one or other of the hotels in and about Northumberland-avenue, and it is from there that all the coaches (except the Guildford New Times, which sets out from the Berkeley Hotel, Piccadilly) start. The booking offices are at the Hôtel Métropole and Hotel Victoria, and in fine weather the coaches load very well. No sooner, however, does rain set in, than the patronage visibly drops off, for coaching is now an amusement and nothing more, while in the winter, though three or four coaches are generally kept running, it is no uncommon sight to see coachman, guard, and the subscriber for the day, with the vehicle to themselves.

With the one exception of the Brighton Comet, all the coaches running out of London return on the same day; but the Comet runs from London to Brighton on Tuesday, Thursday, and Saturday, and travels to London on the three intervening days. On Saturdays it is that the coach is most crowded, so any one to whom one day is as another would do well to select Tuesday or Thursday.

At different times in the history of the coaching revival there have been coaches to Portsmouth, Colchester, Eastbourne, and Oxford, and these, like the Brighton Comet, run down on one

BACK SEAT OF ROAD COACH

day and up the next; but in each case the down journey was the more in favour with travellers.

The other coaches, as already mentioned, make the double journey in one day, reaching Northumberland Avenue about six in the evening. The length of the stages varies from about five to ten miles in length, and the changing of the horses makes some pleasant breaks in the journey, for there is always time for a passenger to stretch his legs while the fresh horses are being put to. The above were the arrangements for 1896; but it by no means follows that the summer of 1897 will see the same coaches on the road, or the same routes adhered to. These matters change every year in some detail or another in consequence of some new proprietor coming to the fore, or because some change in the route becomes necessary or is considered expedient.

Now that coaching, being no longer a necessity, is carried on practically for the benefit of those desirous of seeing the country round London, it can at least be said of it that it has made a good many people familiar with districts to which they had previously been strangers. Places within five and twenty miles or so of town are as a rule reached by a very slow train service, and few persons used to book themselves for any but the favourite riverside resorts. It was not until the coaching revival was set on foot in 1866 that Londoners, the majority of them at least, knew what the country between London and Brighton was like, save in so far as they could see it from the railway, while it was not until a few years later that the routes to Dorking, Guildford, West Wickham, High Wycombe, St. Albans, and other places were opened up. In the main the modern coaches have been run upon the lines which governed the older affairs, and perhaps in the earlier years of the revival old fashions were more adhered to than at the present time. The essence of stage coaching is punctuality, and this was fully recognised so long as it was managed in part by those who remembered the road as it used to be. To-day there is, on some routes, too much time spent at the changes—always excepting the New Times and one or two others—with the result that some coaches are late in arriving at their respective destinations.

[*See* DRIVING.] W. C. A. BLEW.

Bibliography—*Autobiography of a Stage-Coachman*, T. Cross (Hurst and Blackett, 1861, 3 vols., 31*s.* 6*d.*); *A New Book of Sports* (Bentley, 1885, 6*s.*); *Brighton and its Coaches*, W. C. A. Blew (Nimmo, 1894, 21*s.*); *Chronicles of the Coach*, J. D. Champlin (Chatto, 1886, 7*s.* 6*d.*); *The Brighton Road*, C. G. Harper (Chatto, 1892, 16*s.*); *The Dover Road*, C. G. Harper (Chapman, 1895, 16*s.*); *The Portsmouth Road*, C. G. Harper (Chapman, 1895, 16*s.*); *Coach Drives from London*, B. Hounsell (*Road* Office, 1892, 1*s.*); *Coach Drives from London*, B. Hounsell (*Sportsman* Office, 1893, 1*s.*); *English Coach Drives*, B. Hounsell (*Sportsman* Office, 1894, 1*s.*); *Autobiography of an Old Passport*, Rev. Alfred C. Smith (Digby and Long, 1893, 21*s.*); *Old Coaching Days*, Stanley Harris (Bentley, 1882, 16*s.*); *The Coaching Age*, Stanley Harris (Bentley, 1885, 18*s.*); *Annals of the Road*, H. E. Malet (Longmans, 1876, 21*s.*); *Old Coaching Days in Yorkshire*, Tom Bradley (Jackson, Leeds, 1889, 4*s.*); *An Old Coachman's Chatter*, Colonel Edward Corbett (Bentley, 1891, 15*s.*); *Tally Ho! Sketches of Hunting, Coaching, &c.*, F. F. Whitehurst (Tinsley, 1878, 9*s.*); *Hark Away! Sketches of Hunting, Coaching, &c.*, F. F. Whitehurst (Tinsley, 1879, 9*s.*); *Road Scrapings*, M. E. Haworth (Tinsley, 1882, 10*s.* 6*d.*); *Coaching: with Anecdotes of the Road*, Lord W. P. Lennox (Hurst and Blackett, 15*s.*); *Down the Road*, C. T. S. Birch Reynardson (Longmans, 1875, 21*s.*); *The Chace, the Turf and the Road*, Nimrod (Murray, 1870, also earlier editions, 5*s.* and 7*s.* 6*d.*); *Highways and Horses*, A. Maudslay (Chapman. 1888, 21*s.*); *History of Coaches*, G. A. Thrupp (Kerby, 1877, 6*s.*); *The World on Wheels*, Stratton (Trübner, 1878, 30*s.*); *Treatise on Coach Building*, J. W. Burgess (Lockwood, 1881, 2*s.* 6*d.*); *Carriages, Roads and Coaches* (Scratch Team of Essays), S. Berdmore (W. H. Allen, 1883, 7*s.* 6*d.*); *Driving* (Badminton Library), Lord St. Maur (Longmans, 1889, 10*s.* 6*d.*); *An American Four-in-Hand in Britain*, A. Carnegie (Low, 1883–84, 10*s.*; new ed. 1*s.*); *Sports and Recreations in Town and Country*, Frederick Gale (Sonnenschein, 1888, 2*s.*); *Where the Rail runs now: a Story of the Coaching Days*, F. F. Moore (M. Ward, 1876, 2*s.* 6*d.*); *Sports and Anecdotes of Bygone Days*, C. T. S. Birch Reynardson (Chapman, 1887, 12*s.*); *Coaching Past and Present*, W. Wilson (J. Garnett, Windermere, 1885, 6*d.*); "*Comet*," *London and Brighton Coach*, H. H. S. Pearse (Plantagenet) (Haddon, 1895, 63*s.*); *Hints on Driving*, C. S. Ward (published by Author, London, 1870); *The English Mail Coach*, T. De Quincey; *Her Majesty's Mails*, W. Lewins (Low, 1865, 6*s.*); *Forty Years at the Post Office*, F. E. Baines (Bentley, 1895, 2 vols., 21*s.*); *On the Track of the Mail Coach*, F. E. Baines (Bentley, 1895, 7*s.* 6*d.*); *A History of the Post Office*, Herbert Joyce (Bentley, 1893, 16*s.*); *The Royal Mail*, J. W. Hyde (Blackwood, 1885, 6*s.*); *Driving for Pleasure*, F. T. Underhill (Heinemann, 1897, 28*s.*).

Note.—For Glossary of Coaching terms, see under DRIVING.

COALFISH, or GREEN COD, or GREEN POLLACK (*Gadus virens*). [*See* SEA-FISHING].

MEASUREMENTS, ETC.—Length of head $4\frac{1}{4}$ to $4\frac{2}{3}$, of caudal fin 6, height of body $4\frac{1}{4}$ to $4\frac{2}{3}$ in the total length. *Eye*—diameters $3\frac{1}{2}$ in the length of the head, 1 diameter from the end of the snout, and $\frac{2}{3}$ to 1 diameter apart. Lower jaw prominent. The maxilla reaches to below the first third of the eye. A rudimentary barbel beneath the chin. *Teeth*—cardiform in the jaws, present on the vomer, absent from the palatines and tongue. *Fins*—the first dorsal triangular, its third ray the longest and equals the extent of its base; a distinct interspace between the first and second dorsal fins, the highest ray of which last equals half the length of its base; an interspace between the second and third dorsal fins, the latter not extending on to the caudal. Anal commences below the last rays of the first dorsal, and terminates below the end of the second dorsal; second anal similar to the second dorsal. Ventral on the throat inserted anterior to the base of the pectoral, which rather exceeds half the length of the head. Caudal slightly forked or truncated. Vent situated on a vertical line beneath the last rays of the first dorsal fin. *Colours*—superiorly gray, becoming silvery on the sides and beneath. Fins gray, the dorsal and caudal dark-edged. Usually a black spot at the axil of the pectoral fins, by which it is mostly concealed. As they get older the dark colour deepens. *Lateral-line*—white, which at once distinguishes it from the haddock, where it is black.—Day's *Fishes of Great Britain and Ireland*, vol. i., p. 294.

COD (*Gadus morhua*). [*See* SEA-FISHING].

MEASUREMENTS, ETC.—Length of head $3\frac{2}{3}$ to $4\frac{1}{2}$, of caudal fin $6\frac{1}{2}$, height of body 4 to 5, or even more in the young, in the total length. *Eyes*—diameter $4\frac{1}{4}$ in the young to 7 in the adult in the length of the head; $1\frac{1}{2}$ diameters in the young to 2 in the adult from the end of the snout, and $1\frac{1}{4}$ in the young to 2 in the adult apart. Body much thickest anteriorly. Nostrils nearer to the eye than to the end of the snout. Snout conical. Mouth wide, with a deep cleft. Upper jaw the longer; the posterior extremity of the maxilla reaches to beneath the first third or middle of the eye. A barbel, generally as long as the eye, but sometimes shorter, is situated below the chin. *Teeth*—cardiform with an outer and much enlarged row in the upper jaw, in a V-shaped patch on the vomer, absent from the palatines and tongue. *Fins*—the first dorsal somewhat triangular; it commences over or slightly posterior to the base of the pectoral, its fourth ray being the longest and about equal to the extent of the base of the fin; from it they diminish in height to the last, which is very short. There exists a very short interspace between the bases of the two first dorsal fins, the fourth ray being somewhat the longest, but not quite equal to half the length of the base of the fin. They decrease in height to the three last, which are short. A very short interspace exists between the second and third dorsal fins, and a longer or shorter interspace occurs between its termination and the base of the outermost caudal rays. The anterior anal fin commences on a vertical line below the fourth or fifth ray of the second dorsal, and a short interspace exists between it and the origin of the second anal, which is similar to the third dorsal. Caudal slightly emarginate, or square, at its extremity. Ventrals small, inserted rather before the base of the pectorals, which are as long as the postorbital portion of the head. Vent situated on a vertical line beneath the first rays of the second dorsal fin. *Scales*—small and cycloid. *Lateral-line*—passes backwards from opposite the upper edge of the orbit, attaining below the centre of the second dorsal fin nearly the middle of the depth of the body, from whence it is continued straight to the centre of the base of the caudal. *Cœcal appendages*—numerous and short. *Colours*—greenish or grayish, or olive, and occasionally covered with yellow or brown spots along the back and upper two-thirds of the body, its lower portion pure white. Lateral-line white, especially in its lower half. Fins gray, darkest towards their outer edges.—Day's *Fishes of Great Britain and Ireland*, vol. i., p. 277.

CONGER (*Conger vulgaris*). [*See* SEA-FISHING].

MEASUREMENTS, ETC.—Length of head 7 to 8, height of body 16 to 20 in the total length. Body anteriorly rounded, becoming compressed in its posterior portion. Head depressed. Mouth wide, the upper jaw very slightly the longer, its cleft extending to below the middle of the orbit. The posterior nostril patent, the anterior tubular. *Teeth*—cardiform in the upper jaw, one regular row of teeth of the same size and placed close together form a cutting edge; a short band on the vomer; cardiform likewise in the lower jaw similar to those in the upper *Fins*—the dorsal commences above the last quarter or end of the pectoral: the anal in the middle of the total length. *Colours*—generally grayish, becoming lighter or even white beneath. A row of white spots marks the openings from the lateral-line The margins of the vertical fins black.—Day's *Fishes of Great Britain and Ireland*, vol. ii., p. 251.

CONSERVANCY OF RIVERS—The United Kingdom is to a large extent mapped out into Fishery Districts, both as regards the sea-coast and inland portions of the country, and Boards or Committees have been formed to administer the law. As regards fresh waters, however, there are not many districts in which it can be said that the Boards have worked much or any improvement, and in not a few cases the majority of seats upon them have been obtained by men who represent the netting or commercial interest, and not only totally neglect the interests of sport, but have laid themselves open to the charge of allowing the netsmen to kill an excessive quantity of fish.

We propose to give a few suggestions as to the best means of increasing the stock of fish in rivers, &c., suggestions which we trust will be taken to heart not only by riparian owners, but also by the members of Fishery Boards. It should be stated at once, however, that as regards sea-fishery districts not a few committees have acted most wisely and beneficially in putting a stop to inshore trawling, a course which will, it is hoped, work great things for the sea fisheries adjoining our coasts. England does not stand alone in this action. The Government of Denmark owns valuable fisheries in territorial waters adjoining the Faröe Islands, which are now frequented by English fishermen who have, thanks mainly to the steam trawler, fished out the formerly prolific banks of the North Sea. In these Faröe fisheries Denmark has strictly prohibited trawling of every kind and description, and has made it an offence to be in possession of a trawl while in those waters. As a matter of fact, Continental and English fishermen have lost nothing by this salutary legislation, for they find themselves able to make immense takes of fish by means of long lines, whereas, had steam trawling been allowed, those fisheries might have been worked out in the course of a few years.

As regards salmon rivers, netting is prohibited by Act of Parliament for a short period once a week, with the object of enabling the fish to ascend to the upper waters. But where rivers are long, and nets are used for a considerable distance above the tideway, the only result of this arrangement is that the fish which are missed during the weekly close time by the fishermen of the estuary get caught on Monday, when the close time ends, by the netsmen higher up. In such rivers it would be most beneficial to make different weekly close times for different portions of the river, for instance, making Saturday and Sunday a close time for the tidal portions, and Monday and Tuesday for a certain number of miles above the tidal portions. Or the weekly close time could be lengthened on all rivers, a proposed change which found favour with a recent Fishery Commission.

In cases where Fishery Boards derive an income from the sale of licenses to netsmen and sportsmen, a large portion of the money so raised should be devoted to the artificial culture of salmon in salmon rivers, trout in trout streams, and coarse fish in other waters. River pollution, which is a standing disgrace to England and Scotland, should be most sternly dealt with, not so much as regards mere household sewage, but as regards the destructive chemical waste products which flow from mills and manufactories of all kinds. Nor must the upper portions of salmon rivers, which are the breeding grounds of the river, be neglected. These require to be made accessible by the removal of obstructions, the shallows in which the eggs are deposited kept clean, and the fish protected from poachers when spawning.

Another point to which too little attention is given is the disturbance of fish by steam traffic in estuaries. It may be that an Act of Parliament would be required to deal with this matter, but it would be highly desirable in the interests of salmon and other fisheries that a limit of speed should be placed on big steamers entering those of our ports into which flow important salmon rivers. As the steam traffic increases in any river estuary, or other inlet of the sea, fish of all kinds, which are very shy creatures, as certainly decrease, and having regard to the importance of the fishing industry and the large rents paid by sportsmen for fishing rights, it only seems reasonable that restrictions of this kind should be placed upon the steamship owners.

With regard to trout streams, given a reasonably suitable extent of water and a not too severe climate, almost anything can be done within fair limits, thanks to fish culture. In some waters the stock is maintained by making a rather high weight or size-limit and returning everything beneath that weight or length, as the case may be, and most certainly the stock of fish can be maintained by this means, provided other conditions are favourable. But one result of this method is that the fish, being caught several times over during their youth, become, when over the size-limit, so exceedingly cautious and difficult to capture that all but very first-class fishermen sometimes despair of making a reasonable basket.

We have more than once suggested that the stock could be equally well maintained by having a much smaller size limit, and making it the rule to turn into the stream one or two yearlings or two-year-olds for every fish taken out. The fish would then rise more freely and better bags could be obtained (for, after all, the object of fishing is to catch fish), and by the continuous introduction of new blood the breed of fish would probably be improved. Yearling trout can be purchased at as low a rate as £10 a thousand, so that the outlay is inconsiderable. A man who gives a £100 or more for his fishing rights should not hesitate to spend an extra £10 in restocking. Given suitable water, there is, as a matter of fact, no reason why he should even buy his fish, for they are very easily bred, as will be gathered from the article on PISCICULTURE (*q.v.*).

Where some suitable pond is available, fishery owners can hardly do better than stock it with yearlings and net it at the end of one or two years for the benefit of the main stream. But it should be a pond which can be run dry, for unless it can be emptied of water a certain number of trout will inevitably be left in, and these, on its being restocked with yearlings, will levy a heavy toll upon the new arrivals. Other details in connection with the preservation of trout are the prevention of pollution; the netting of all coarse fish, particularly pike and chub; the removal of mud if it collects in too large quantities on gravelly shallows, and the judicious cutting of weeds. When streams are very bare of cover they can be greatly improved by placing "hides" for the fish, such as drain-pipes, rocks, and the like. Very shallow streams can easily be deepened by means of dams, or can be widened out here and there into lakes. Ponds, moreover, containing only coarse fish can be emptied, cleared of mud, and stocked with trout. Many reservoirs have been stocked with great success.

As regards coarse fish streams, such as the Thames, the Trent, the Bedfordshire Ouse, the Welland, the rivers of the Norfolk Broads, &c., much can be done to maintain a head of fish and provide a certain quantity for annual destruction by anglers, without going to much expense. In navigable rivers the steam traffic is perhaps the deadliest enemy of the fish, which, in the egg and early stages of fryhood, are destroyed in millions by the wash caused by launches or other steamers. Where it is possible, and the fisheries are valuable, steam traffic should be altogether prohibited, but where that course cannot be followed it should at least be prohibited during the spring months when coarse fish are spawning, or a rule could be made that no steamer should then be allowed to navigate the water at more than a certain number of miles an hour, or, as an alternative, that any one in command of such a vessel driving it at a speed which creates any swell or wash should be guilty of an offence and be liable to a penalty. There is certainly no river in England in which the speed of the steam traffic might not without difficulty be limited during the spawning season.

The next greatest enemies to coarse fish are probably swans and ducks, the latter no less than the former. It is of the greatest importance that these be kept off the water from the first of March to the first of June. The amount of eggs which are picked off the weeds by half a dozen ducks in the course of a day is something astounding. I have seen a small brood of ducks work the side of a river for a mile or more in the course of an afternoon, and, so far as I could see, eat up every grain of the perch spawn which had been deposited there in considerable quantities. If these birds cannot be debarred from swimming in the river during the spawning months, the next best plan is to afford some protection to the spawn, and in the case of perch this is easily effected.

Men who are acquainted with the river know the spawning grounds, and after the perch eggs have been deposited, it is not difficult to cover them up with wire netting. But perch are accommodating creatures, and if open hurdles, within which withy wands or other twigs have been interlaced, are staked down in water about five to seven feet in depth, and surrounded by wire netting, the breeding fish will usually deposit their spawn upon the twigs, and there it will hatch out safe from swans and ducks. This has been done many times with great success in the Thames, in the Reading and Henley districts.

Perch can be introduced without difficulty into any water by collecting perch eggs from rivers or canals where these fish abound, and placing them on hurdles in their new abode and protecting them as before explained. In coarse fish streams the standard of size, beneath which all caught must be returned to the water, is all important. An excellent standard is in existence on the Thames, and it might be followed in any south country river.

In the north, where the fish run rather smaller, it would have to be modified.

Thames Standard.

Pike or Jack	18 in.	Grayling	12 in.
Perch	8 ,,	Bream	10 ,,
Chub	10 ,,	Carp	10 ,,
Roach	7 ,,	Tench	8 ,,
Dace	6' ,,	Rudd	6 ,,
Barbel	16 ,,	Gudgeon	4 ,,
Trout	16 ,,		

To preserve pike it is most desirable to prohibit trimmers and fishing either with live or dead gorge, methods which destroy every fish caught. In all streams, to defeat the pot-hunter, it is desirable to enact that no person may fish with more than two rods at one and the same time. Before this excellent rule, for which we were responsible, came into force on the Thames, we have known as many as ten rods to be used at one time by one fisherman, all laid out from the bank, and have seen five rods used from a punt by a person who was live baiting for pike.

There is a phase of this subject which does not obtain the attention it deserves. It is the question of food. In rocky trout streams and in many a Highland loch there is insufficient food and the result is a race of pigmy trout or other fish. Fresh water snails, weeds which are prolific in insect life, fresh water shrimps, and other fish food, may all be introduced. But the natural conditions of lake and river have to considered in each particular case, and the would-be improver of his fishery should take skilled advice before tampering with his water. One thing should be borne in mind, that there are very few streams or lakes which will produce a large number of large fish; it is generally a choice between a few large fish or many small ones.

JOHN BICKERDYKE.

CORACLES—The osier-woven, skin-covered basket of the Ancient Britons still survives on the Welsh rivers, more particularly on the Dee, in the shape of the Coracle, the fisherman's boat of those rapid streams. With slight variations of shape, even in modern times it may yet be described as a square basket with a seat across it, and at a little distance its occupant looks as if he had gone afloat in a washing tub. But no other kind of craft would so well suit the solitary angler on the rapids of the Dee or Severn as this odd-shaped vessel. With one hand wielding the paddle and the other his fly-rod, he drifts down the rippling shallows, shoots the boiling rapids and paddles gently along the still deeps. Then, when his fishing is over, he claps the Coracle upside down on his head and shoulders, and stalks back.

As a Coracle is so easily transported, either by manual power or on a donkey or pony cart, it is somewhat surprising that its use has not spread to Scottish moorland lochs and the smaller rivers. One man can propel it and fish from it at the same time, which is not usually the case with any other type of boat, and if it rains heavily he can land and use it as an umbrella. Its use is not confined to trout-fishing. It is constantly used for salmon-fishing, but in such cases it is advisable to land to play a fish, for a Coracle, having four sides instead of two, has four ways of capsizing instead of the two ways of the ordinary row boat. A Coracle may be made in a day, except for the drying of the tar or paint, and it would not be difficult to carry the necessary laths and a square of canvas already waterproofed to any outlandish place where a boat might be needed.

The dimensions of a Coracle are about as follows:—The square on the floor or water-line is four feet and the sides tumble in six inches, so that the square at the gunwale is three feet. The depth is thirteen inches; the square has of course rounded corners. Older Coracles had straight sides or a flare out on the front side, but the tumble-in type gives the most stability,

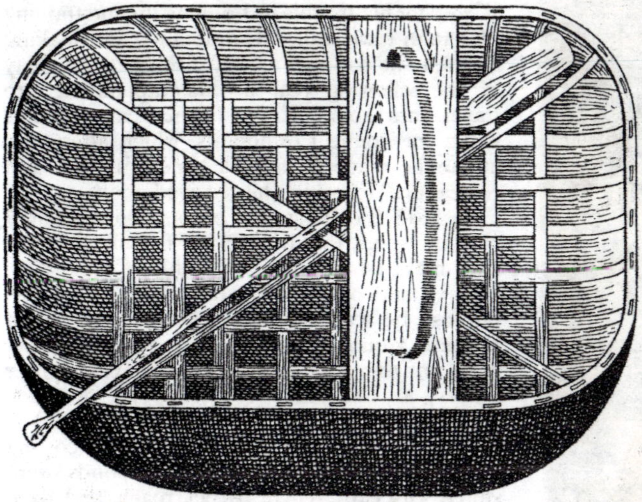

having a wider floor. The width of the gunwale square is limited by the fact that the occupant must sit in the middle and be able to ply his paddle over the side without leaning over. The bottom is flat and the draught only two or three inches.

To make the frame, get twenty long, clean laths, say eight feet long, by one inch and a half wide by three-sixteenths of an inch thick. Interlace ten across the other ten so as to form a lattice nearly four feet square, with the ends of the laths projecting about two feet. Bend these ends up to meet the previously prepared frame of the gunwale and fasten. Place a seat across from one side to the other and have some light floor-boards, and the frame of the boat is complete. Cover with canvas, and coat with boiling tar and pitch or, as in my own experience I prefer, good white lead paint made gray or brown in colour to match the boulders in the river. The single paddle is like the lower half of a flat-bladed scull, but very much lighter in make and is about four feet long. It is held in the hand midway, with the shaft braced against the outer side of the upper arm; the palm of the hand is towards the boat, and preferably the shaft should be grasped between the first and second fingers. The stroke follows the shape of a figure of eight, propelling the Coracle sideways, and is not easy to acquire at first. The efforts of the Sassenach to guide his Coracle, and prevent it from doing nothing but spin round have formed the subject of much amusing caricature in Wales.

In the shallows, of course, the Coracle may be stopped, retarded, or guided by pressing the paddle on the stones, and if the current is not too strong it may be worked from side to side of the river as it floats down, so that every part may be fished. It is essentially a craft which must go with the current on a river and with the wind on a lake, but it is so light that it is easily carried back to the starting point.

I have known a fisherman who thought nothing of walking ten miles up stream, with his Coracle on his back, for the purpose of fishing down.

Sometimes two persons use the Coracle, one paddling and the other fishing, usually a professional and a visitor; but to enjoy the true sport of Coracle-fishing, one should be alone.

G. CHRISTOPHER DAVIES.

CORACLES, INDIAN—These are made umbrella-shaped, 8 ft. across, 2 ft. deep, being a convenient size for fishing purposes. They are of split bamboo basket-work, covered with sewn ox-hide and without seat of any kind. Such a coracle, which can be easily carried by one man, and will comfortably hold two, is propelled by a paddle; and as it draws but a couple of inches of water, and will bear hard bumps against rocks, is invaluable for descending rocky rivers, floating buoyantly down many a rapid, apparently impossible of navigation. Large coracles of this description have been used for ferrying troops.

CORMORANT (*Phalacrocorax carbo*)—The Cormorant is a large sea fowl of dark green colour, looking uniformly black at a distance, weighing from seven to eight pounds, and characterised by a long straight beak strongly decurved at the extremity, a stiff rudder-like tail of fourteen feathers, and feet with all four toes united by a membrane. In this respect it agrees with another species of the same genus, which also inhabits the rocky portions of our coast, namely, the Crested Cormorant, or Shag (*P. cristatus*), a smaller bird, without the white patch on the thigh, and with only twelve instead of fourteen tail feathers. Both species breed gregariously in sea cliffs, on rocky islands, and occasionally in trees, after the manner of herons and spoonbills, forming a large clumsy nest of sticks and seaweed, in which are deposited four or five chalky-looking eggs. When taken young from the nest or captured soon after it has quitted it, by means presently to be described, the Cormorant is easily tamed, and may be taught to exercise its natural aptitude in taking fish for the pleasure of its owner.

The earliest description which the writer has met with of the sport as observed in China by

a European occurs in an English translation by R. Willes (from the Italian version first printed at Venice) of a Portuguese MS. by one Galotti Pereira, who, about the middle of the sixteenth century, was with others of his countrymen a prisoner in China. It occurs under the heading "Reportes of the Province China" in a small and rare quarto volume entitled *The History of Trauayle in the West and East Indies and other countreys lying eyther way towards the fruitfull and ryche Moluccaes.* By Richarde Eden, 1577. At page 253 we read:—"At the houre appoynted to fyshe, all the barges are brought togeather in a circle where the ryver is shalowe, and the crowes, tyed togeather under the wynges, are let leape downe into the water, some under, some above, worth the lookying uppon; eche one as he hath filled his bagge, goeth to his own barge and emptieth it, whiche done, he retourneth to fyshe agayne."

This was at Pekin, where the travellers in question saw no fewer than twenty barges so employed. A more satisfactory account of the practice may be found in Milne's *Life in China*, 1857 (p. 307).

It is most likely that the sport was first made known in Europe towards the end of the sixteenth century by the Dutch, who, besides being enterprising navigators and traders in the East, have in all ages been known as skilful falconers and great bird-fanciers. In 1609 Louis XIII., then a youth, witnessed this sport in the grounds at Fontainebleau, and in 1611 our own James I. had appointed "a master of Cormorants" in England. An entry in the "Issues of the Exchequer of that reign" shows that in April 1611 John Wood was paid £30 "for his trouble in bringing up and training of certain fowls called Cormorants, and making of them fit for the use of fishing." In May of the following year he was appointed "to travel into some of the further parts of this realm for young Cormorants, which afterwards are to be made fit for his Majesty's sport and recreation," for which he received another £30.

In 1618 the King had become so fascinated with the sport, that he decided to build a house and make some ponds for his Cormorants, ospreys, and otters at Westminster, and for this purpose he leased of Lord Danvers a piece of meadow ground, about an acre and a quarter, lying in the Vine Garden near Westminster Abbey, at the yearly rent of £7. A brick building was erected on this ground, at a cost of £100, and nine fish-ponds were dug, costing altogether another £40. These ponds were stored with carp, tench, barbel, roach, and dace (100 of each), and a sluice of elm planking was made to bring the water from the Thames. The total outlay incurred upon this, the first Westminster Aquarium, was £268, for which amount, in August 1618, the King gave an order upon the Treasury.

At Theobalds, also, his favourite hunting seat in Hertfordshire, and also at Thetford, in Norfolk, these birds were employed in fishing for the King's pleasure.

Of late years the sport has been revived both in England and France, thanks to the efforts of Captain F. H. Salvin and the late John Barr in this country, and to the Comte le Couteulx, M. Pichot, and M. de la Rue on the Continent.

Cormorants are not difficult to train, and do not require nearly so much care as hawks. They may be taken from the nest when they are ready to fly, or may be caught later in the year when fully feathered. The latter plan is preferable, for the birds have then had some experience in fishing, and are sure to be in good condition.

To catch them, it is only necessary to visit some tidal harbour wherein there are large posts set (to mark the river channel), on which Cormorants are fond of resting. A few strong gins, having the teeth bound with list to prevent injury, may then be set, unbaited, on the square tops of two or three of the favourite posts, each gin being attached to the post by a line with a float. It is easy to arrange with a fisherman to keep watch in a boat at a little distance; and as soon as a Cormorant alights and is trapped, it will come off at once into the water, and should be taken up as soon as possible. A cloth should be thrown over the back and wings, two corners being tied securely under the chin, and the other two corners under the tail behind the legs. The bird may then be tethered by the legs until brought ashore. While this operation is being performed, it should be held firmly, yet gently, by grasping first the back of the head and then the closed beak, care of course being taken to avoid a bite, which would be a very sharp one.

On getting ashore with two or three captures, the flight feathers of the left wing should be cut neatly with a large pair of scissors, and the birds turned into a loose box, or any outhouse from which they cannot escape, care being taken to lay down straw, tan, or sawdust, to prevent the breakage of the stiff tail feathers, which form so useful a rudder when in the water. Here they may be fed on fish, until such time as they can be forwarded to their ultimate destination. The training is commenced by putting soft leather straps or "jesses" on one or both legs, as with a hawk, to which a line is attached when the bird is first allowed in the water.

Capt. F. H. Salvin's Sub-Inspector.

It is taught (like a hawk) to come to the "the lure"—a tin box containing its food which is rattled every time the bird is fed—and may even be carried on the gloved hand like a falcon. A small leather strap being buckled round the lower part of the neck before the bird is allowed to enter the water, it is unable to do more than pouch any fish that it may catch, and has to come ashore to be relieved of its burden by its master, who rewards it every time for its obedience. After a little practice the line is dispensed with, and the bird soon becomes very docile, seeming fully to understand all that is required of it.

The Chinese method of fishing with Cormorants differs but little from that employed by English and French amateurs at the present day. In China, however, the birds, smaller than our *Phalacrocorax carbo*, and of a different species (*Phalacrocorax sinensis*, called by the Chinese *Leu-tze*), are carried on light shallow punts or rafts, and are commonly employed, not, as here, for amusement, but as a matter of business to supply the markets with fish.

J. E. Harting.

COURSING is one of the most ancient of field sports. King Solomon speaks of the greyhound as an example of what "goes well, and is comely in going." From the Greek historian, warrior, and philosopher, Arrian, who flourished in the second century of the present era, we gather everything worth knowing of coursing as practised by the people of his time. Many of the forms and methods of those days are still adhered to, though it is singular to note in Arrian's writings on the subject an entire absence of any code of rules or laws for gauging the merits of the competing greyhounds.

Although coursing was an undoubtedly popular pastime in the British Isles during the middle ages, it is some centuries later ere one discovers evidence of its being carried on with a due regard to the system and regularity that characterise the coursing of the present day.

The first authenticated code of rules for judging the work done by a brace of greyhounds in pursuit of a hare was compiled in the days of Queen Elizabeth. The title runs (probably a revised version): "*The Laws of the Leash or Coursing, as they were commanded, allowed, and subscribed by Thomas, late Duke of Norfolk, in the reign of Queen Elizabeth.*" These rules governed coursing until about the third quarter of the last century, when the sport, which hitherto had been confined to matches between braces of greyhounds, underwent a complete revolution.

Origin of Coursing Clubs—Clubs then sprang into existence, the first of these institutions being located at Swaffham, in Norfolk, with Lord Orford as its founder. There is a Swaffham Club at this present day, but it is only a recent namesake of the old association, though coursing over the very same ground. Coursing clubs quickly became the fashion, after the foundation of the Swaffham Club, and one of the earliest was Ashdown, in Berkshire, under the patronage of the then Earl of Craven. Successive owners of this incomparable coursing country have been actively identified with the sport, but the club

long ago dropped out of existence, whilst the splendid open meetings which followed—frequently lasting over a week—have almost dwindled away.

The numberless coursing clubs that at one time or other in the latter part of the last and in the present century were in existence, are, with very few exceptions, extinct. Amongst the oldest yet living may be mentioned the Altcar Club, the Ridgway Club, the Scottish National Club, and the North of England Club. The **Altcar Club**, established in 1825 by the then Earl of Sefton, has all these years enjoyed the privilege of using the fine lands of the Sefton estates, near Liverpool, and the present peer has for a long time been president. The **Ridgway Club** was founded some years later than the Altcar Club, and the membership of the two is at the present time, and has long been, identical. The ground coursed on is the splendid Clifton Hall estate, near Lytham, in Lancashire. The club owes its now historical name to Mr. Thomas Ridgway, its first president. Of the **Scottish National Club** it need only be said that, having passed through many vicissitudes in consequence of loss of ground, it is now apparently firmly planted on the Hoddom Castle estate in Dumfriesshire, through the kindness of Mr. Edward Brook, who takes an especial interest in its fortunes, although [illegible] courser himself.

In Ireland, where the instinct of sport is naturally keen, many old and influential coursing clubs of times past are now forgotten, not to omit the open meetings which for many years were held over the historical Raughlan and Derrymacash meadows of the late Lord Lurgan in county Armagh, and attracted crowds of sportsmen from every corner of the kingdom.

Laws of Coursing—Reverting to the laws that govern coursing, the old system of the Duke of Norfolk's time was pretty well done away with early in the present century; indeed, in 1828, the members of the Ashdown Park Club compiled a code of their own. Half a dozen years later a new set of rules was promulgated for general use by Mr. Thomas Thacker, who also introduced a yearly calendar of the sport. These latter rules were more or less in use until 1858, when it was universally agreed that coursing having become so popular in England, Ireland, and Scotland, the time had arrived when an association should be founded for its government on some such lines as the Jockey Club, which controls racing. Accordingly a small committee, consisting of Mr. Edward Marjoribanks, Mr. W. G. Borron, and "Stonehenge" (of *The Field*) was deputed to draw up rules for the establishment of the **National Coursing Club**. The first president was appropriately Mr. Marjoribanks, and on his death he was worthily succeeded by the

present Earl of Sefton. The National Coursing Club itself is composed of delegates from the different clubs, with a certain number of elective members. Meetings are periodically held during the year in London and Liverpool, at which all cases of complaint and appeal are considered and adjusted. With the founding of the National Club, coursing was at length put upon a business-like basis, as, though hitherto there had been rules for deciding the merits of the competing greyhounds' work, regulations for the mere conduct of a meeting had been almost unknown. As time rolled on the necessity for a systematic record of a greyhound's breeding and antecedents became most apparent, and in 1882 the **Greyhound Stud Book** was instituted, by means of which it is, in many instances, possible to trace back the genealogy of an animal to the last century; but, most important of all, no greyhound can be registered without a pedigree, and no greyhound is qualified to run in public unless its name appears in the "Stud Book" [*see* STUD BOOKS]. In these directions complete control has been acquired over coursing in the United Kingdom by the National Coursing Club, and it is a safe assertion that no field sport is more systematically conducted than is coursing at the present day.

The passing of the "Ground Game Act" in 1880 undoubtedly arrested the prosperity of coursing throughout the kingdom—indeed, in very many quarters it was feared that a crisis had come, and that the total extinction of the old pastime was but a question of a few years at the utmost. The effects of the measure were more especially and speedily felt in Scotland, meeting after meeting dropping out of existence through force of circumstances. A striking illustration of the extent to which coursing has fallen away over the Borders may be gathered from the fact that, whereas up to the year 1880 nearly a hundred days' running was customary during the six months' season, for years past no more than a dozen or fourteen days can be mustered.

In England and Ireland, however, the storm has been successfully weathered, and coursing farmers are strong enough in numbers to ensure a supply of hares for many a year to come, in co-operation, of course, with landed proprietors like Lord Sefton, Lord Anglesey, Lord Ripon, Lord Londonderry, Lord Massereene, Mr. Clifton, Lord Drogheda, Lord Craven, Sir Edmund Antrobus, and many others; while Scotland may still count upon the cordial assistance of Sir Robert Jardine, Bart., Sir W. C. Anstruther, Bart., and Mr. Brook.

Inclosures—The loss of so many estates to coursing through the operation of the "Ground Game Act" led to the substitution of a modified system of sport in the shape of inclosures, that is to say, a piece of ground was fenced round, and a thin cover formed at each end, from which imprisoned hares were coursed to the other by a brace of greyhounds. The first of these inclosures was at Plumpton, in Sussex, then followed Gosforth Park, near Newcastle-on-Tyne, Four Oaks Park, near Birmingham, and Haydock Park, near Liverpool, not to omit the Kempton Park racecourse. This drawing-room style of coursing was all the rage for a few years, and large sums were added to the entry money, whilst, as speed to the hare was the chief *desideratum*, people began to breed greyhounds accordingly, to the certain deterioration of the pure type of animal. Added to this, dishonest practices became too prevalent, which in the old-fashioned sport had been hitherto almost unknown. The end eventually arrived, for the true sportsman shunned the new-fangled invention and returned to his old love, with the result that every one of the afore-mentioned inclosures is now well-nigh forgotten. It is true that an inclosure was subsequently formed in Essex, and is still in operation; but it is under the management of a club committee, composed principally of members of the National Coursing Club. Moreover, the sport is as near perfection as can be desired, so that there is little comparison between it and the other places that have been named. In Ireland there are three or four inclosures, under responsible control; but in Scotland artificial coursing is unknown.

The Waterloo Cup—The Waterloo Cup has long been the chief prize of the coursing year, ranking, indeed, with the Derby of the Turf, and it has been copied in other countries where the sport has been introduced. Strange to say, its origin and beginnings were of the humblest character, and its promoter never could have foreseen its ultimate importance, though he lived to see the event one that it was the ambition of every courser to win. It was in the year 1836 that the proprietor of the Waterloo Hotel in Liverpool improvised an eight-dog stake, which he styled the Waterloo Cup, and it was run for on the Altcar estate of Lord Sefton, the home of the famous Altcar Coursing Club before referred to, and ever since it has been decided on the same ground. Appropriately, the founder of the first Waterloo Cup was the winner, and, better still, he achieved the distinction by nominating a greyhound, belonging to Lord Molyneux, called *Milanie*. Lord Molyneux was father of the present peer, so long connected with coursing. The year following its foundation the Waterloo Cup was increased to sixteen runners, and the year after to thirty-two, at which limit it remained till 1857, when it was made a sixty-four dog stake, and continues so to the present day. The entry money is £25 per greyhound, and the nominations, giving the right of competing, are usually arranged by a committee of members of the Altcar Club at the November meeting of that institution. The running takes place in February, when frost does not interfere, and, with a Waterloo Purse and Plate for the thirty-two and sixteen greyhounds beaten in the first and second rounds of the Cup respectively, the meeting is comfortably completed in three days. The stake partakes of an international character, though England, with the preponderance in nominations over Ireland and Scotland, necessarily possesses the best chances of winning the coveted prize. Since 1857 England has provided thirty-one winners, Scotland five, and Ireland the same number. For some years past a trophy has accompanied the winner's stakes in the Waterloo Cup in the shape of a collar, which is embellished with medals recording the names of the winners year by year. Since it was increased to a sixty-four dog stake, amongst winners of the Waterloo Cup no fewer than sixteen of the forty greyhounds were "named," that is to say, the owners were not the nominators, although the most particularly interested parties. Singular features of the Waterloo Cup are noted in connection with two consequently celebrated greyhounds, namely, Lord Lurgan's *Master M'Grath* and the late Colonel North's *Fullerton*, the former of whom was victor on three occasions, with a break of a year, whilst the latter actually divided with a kennel companion and then won outright three years in succession. The wonderful merit of these performances is strikingly apparent when it is seen that a greyhound has to defeat six opponents before it can be proclaimed the winner of a Waterloo Cup, not to omit the chance of getting extra courses in the shape of "undecideds." *Coomassie*, one of the smallest greyhounds ever known, was the winner in two successive years; but previously, when the stake was a "thirty-two," entailing five courses for the winner, *Cerito* was three times successful, with a break between the first and second occasions.

The Colonies—Here Coursing was introduced with more or less success. In Australasia (covering the great island continent, Tasmania and New Zealand), the sport was at one time exceedingly popular, the most influential men entering into it, regardless of expense, judging from the prices they paid for imported greyhounds. Of late years, however, interest in the pastime has declined, and the strongest and most influential clubs of fifteen or twenty years ago have ceased to exist; in fact, in Australia itself, coursing is now confined to the country districts. To South Australia must be given the credit of introducing the pastime to the "Greater Britain of the South." It was in the year 1867 that a few sportsmen were hunting kangaroo with greyhounds, when a wallaby (a smaller species of the marsupial) jumped up, and a very fine course resulted. A new arrival from England at once suggested the formation of a coursing club, which proved the forerunner of coursing as practised in this country, especially as the English hare had about that time been introduced successfully—too much so, as eventually turned out, for the farmer, for it breeds three or four times a year, with as many as four and five in a litter. Hares, in fact, in some of the colonies have been for years legally classed as "vermin." Emulating the old country, Waterloo Cups were started in South Australia, New South Wales, Victoria, and New Zealand. That in Victoria was for years conducted on precisely the same lines as ours, the stake and number of greyhounds being identical, and imported English dogs frequently were victorious, whilst the late Mr. George Warwick, the leading judge of his time, was engaged for a season. In addition, a National Coursing Club was founded, and subsequently a greyhound registration system followed. All these, however, are now merely matters of history.

The Continent—Some years ago, coursing, according to the English system, was introduced into Russia by the Grand Duke Michael, Prince and Princess Alexander Scherbatoff, and Count Stroganoff, the two latter of whom kept up kennels in England, and joined the principal clubs, and Count Stroganoff won the Waterloo Cup in 1894 with *Texture*, an English-bred greyhound that he had purchased only a few weeks previously in London for 110 guineas. This is one of the most striking exemplifications of the "luck" that is popularly supposed to surround Coursing. The Coursing in Russia takes place near St. Petersburg and Moscow, and the principal event is the Waterloo Cup, the peculiarity of which is the circumstance that most of the nominators run several greyhounds in their own individual names, and thus frequently "sweep the board." The Russian Waterloo Cup has generally been won by English-bred greyhounds; and an English judge and slipper are always engaged.

Coursing was experimented in France ten or a dozen years ago, on the inclosed system; but after one or two successful seasons it quietly died away, for reasons to which it is unnecessary to allude.

America—In the United States Coursing appears to have taken firm root, the one drawback being the many hundred miles separating the great centres of population from the prairie land in the west, where the running takes place. The National Greyhound Club's rules are almost identical with the English version; there is also a "Greyhound Stud Book," not to omit a Waterloo Cup. On the prairies the animal known as the jack rabbit abounds, and so game is readily at hand—in fact, it in every way tests to the utmost the qualities of a first-class greyhound.

The Judge.—A "good judge" is the *sine qua non* of a well-organised coursing meeting; and ever since the sporting papers commenced full detailed reports, their representatives have never hesitated to criticise what in their opinions was an error on the part of the official on horseback, or as in some countries, notably Lytham and Southport, on the ladder. In the last century, when matches between a brace of greyhounds were in vogue, the owner of each chose an umpire, and these two in their turn appointed a referee, in case of a difference of opinion. One of the earliest and best known judges of the present century was Mr. William Nightingale, whose heart and soul were in his work from the moment a couple of greyhounds were slipped. He was enthusiastic to a degree when he spotted a good dog, and equally the contrary with one of the opposite stamp. Following him was Mr. Anthony Dalzell, and then Mr. George Warwick, who in the zenith of his career once judged 105 days in a single season, frequently having to travel from the extreme south to Scotland, and *vice versa*, so as to be on the ground the following morning by nine o'clock or often earlier. Some big days, too, he accomplished, his record being 101 courses in a single day at Lurgan. If anything, Mr. Warwick's feats have been excelled by Mr. James Hedley, the leading judge of the present day, a born courser, so to speak, as his father was a keen follower of the sport on the Borders, and was wont to take the future judge out to meetings when quite a small boy. Suffice it to say that the nominators of no fewer than twenty-four Waterloo Cups have elected Mr. Hedley their judge, a striking testimony to his wonderful ability and unquestionable honesty. Next to him Mr. R. A. Brice's services are most in request, and then those of Mr. H. C. Fulwell and Mr. N. K. Wentworth.

Officials.—Indispensable officials to coursing meetings are the **slipper**, the **flag steward**, and the **slip steward**. The first-named must not only be an adept at handling the leash, so as to start each dog on equal terms, but he must likewise be a smart pedestrian (running as well as walking). The late Tom Raper (a Yorkshireman) was undoubtedly the most capable of his time, and since his day he has not been approached by the later generation. The flag steward's duty is to signal the judge's decision promptly, and, of course, correctly, as a single error on his part creates no end of confusion. Hence it is better that he should be an expert in the sport, and keep the competing greyhounds in his eye as long as they remain in sight. The slip steward also is a responsible official, it being his duty to see that the greyhounds are brought to slips in proper time, and in their proper turn.

W. F. LAMONBY ("SKIDDAW").

GREYHOUND CELEBRITIES—In treating of celebrities among greyhounds it is somewhat strange that we should find ourselves restricted to the last hundred years or so for any authentic information. For a record of names, not to speak of performances, we find ourselves at a loss till we come to the very end of last century, and even then the details are but meagre till we are well advanced into this century. It is true that quite at the close of the eighteenth century Mr. Mundy had a dog called Wonder, but this must have been a case of adult baptism, and the owner cannot have had the fear of the fines and penalties exacted by the keeper of the stud-book before his eyes. The dog was indeed a wonderful performer, and his blood in great fulness runs in all strains of the successful dogs of the present day. He was a grandson of a bitch belonging to King George III. Royalty is also still represented as widely by the descendants of a dog which belonged to

Princess Charlotte. They have in course of time combined with those of her royal grandfather's dog. It is believed that the blood of the Archbishop of York's black and white dog runs in the strain of the famous Bab at the Bowster, the best dog of modern days: a veritable mother in Israel, for there are probably few first-class dogs who cannot boast of being her descendants.

The first name which is handed down to fame is Lord Orford's Czarina. She was a wonderful bitch. She won forty-seven matches. Those were the days of match-making, when each owner vied in friendly rivalry with others of the same club. Stakes, as we have them, were scarcely known. This Czarina never was beaten.

Considering the length of courses in the old Swaffham Club, to which Lord Orford belonged, this was an exploit which means more than catches the eye at first sight. It is stated that she never bred till she was thirteen years old : a statement which savours of the mythical, for it is doubtful whether any greyhound has ever bred at that age in modern days. Certainly they have not bred anything good, whereas her progeny, Claret and Vengeance, were at the top of the tree. Lord Orford rode out to see her win her last match. The excitement caused by her victory was too much for him : he dropped off his pony and died. This happened in 1791.

Her grandson Snowball was even more celebrated. He found his "vates sacer" in Sir Walter Scott, a genuine sportsman, who entered heartily into the mysteries of a course, and from his famous lines ("'Twas when fleet Snowball's head was waxen grey") we can picture to ourselves the turns and doubles and wrenches, the struggle to reach the covert, the effort to take to the hill, and the fatal gap. Apart from this performance of Snowball in his old age, we have no record of his triumphs, but it is true, as Scott has it, that his race was triumphant in England and Scotland "o'er each meaner stamp." The date of his birth was about 1796. Mention has already been made of Wonder, who was born about two years later. He, possibly, was a dog of still greater excellence, but he lacked the necessary chronicler. However, he established the fame of "Mr. Mundy's breed." In those days each owner of a kennel jealously guarded the secrets of his harem, and all that transpired was that a dog was of such or such a breed. Mr. Mundy, Mr. Topham, Lord Stradbroke, Lord Rivers, Mr. Lloyd, Mr. Swan, Mr. Best, Mr. Hassall, Mr. Swinfen, and many others established a name for their blood, rather than for any particular dog ; but we can trace the union of the Snowball with the Wonder strains with excellent effect in Moorcock, Romp, Tiger, Tippoo and a younger Snowball. Mr. Hassall's Harold, one of the unbeaten heroes, was of this strain. About this time Mr. Goodlake's kennel was greatly in the ascendant, and its bright particular star was Gohanna. Mr. Goodlake was an enthusiastic courser : and it was possibly from a pardonable desire to embalm the "glories" of his breed that he undertook the compilation of the first stud-book, from which we now draw almost our only information. After a few years he evidently found the labour too great, and owners were so jealous of their breed that many years afterwards Thacker apologised for mistakes he had made by saying he would not venture on the impertinence of writing to the owners for information. The stud-book was discontinued, and a blank of about ten years follows, when Thacker started one on a larger scale : a work which under various forms has been carried on to the present day. Waterloo was the hero at that time. He was a dog of a peculiar colour, which varied so that sometimes he was described as dun and white, sometimes fawn and white, and sometimes brindled and white. Lord Eglinton bred him and challenged All England with him. Mr. Goodlake took up the challenge with his very good dog Gracchus. It was run off at Ashdown Park, where the hares are famous for their stoutness, and Waterloo won easily. In connection with his colour, in his letter of challenge, Lord Eglinton names his dog Waterloo, but excuses himself from giving his colour because of its well-known peculiarity. The blood of Waterloo still runs in the great family of Beacon and Scotland Yet, as well as in those which claim Fusilier as their ancestor.

With reference to this challenge, it may be remarked that more than once there was a challenge stake run off at Ashdown between North and South. Lord Sefton, Mr. Graham, Mr. Borron, the Listers, Mr. John Jardine were the chief representatives of the North, while Mr. Randell generalled the South, and was ever in the front himself. Stonehenge, in his book on *The Greyhound*, gives an account of several breeds—the Newmarket, Wiltshire, Lancashire, Scotch, and Yorkshire varieties—and no doubt in those days there was a distinct difference owing to the different style of coursing. At Newmarket and Swaffham and in Wiltshire, courses of from two to four miles were not rare. On the plains of Altcar a few hundred yards was the limit. In Scotland the running was more on the hill than in the vale, while in the northern counties the country was enclosed, and fallow or growing corn more often met with than grass, and then always in ridges. The want of communication and the jealousy of rival breeders helped the great law of the survival of the fittest. But just at this time Captain Daintree placed his grand dog, King Cob, at the service of the public. He was essentially a Newmarket dog. Strange to say Lord Stradbroke, who was a great supporter of Newmarket coursing, considered that the use of King Cob had poisoned his breed, and was glad to get rid of the produce. In this way Mr. Sharpe, of Hoddom, obtained his celebrated Queen of the May, and was rewarded by winning the Waterloo Cup with her son Hughie Graham. Soon after Mr. Sharp had got her, Will Nightingale was judging in Scotland. He was singing the praises of King Cob's stock, and some one told him that there was a King Cob puppy entered at the meeting. He laughed at the idea of a King Cob puppy being found so far north, but the moment he saw her run he called out, "That's a King Cob." The enterprise of Mr. James Hedley, the father of our famous judge, took Matilda Gillespie to King Cob from the border of Northumberland, and was rewarded by The Tollwife, who laid the foundation of Mr. John Jardine's unequalled successes. These two daughters of King Cob now live in the almost universal progeny of Bab at the Bowster, and that distinguished family of Ptarmigan and Gallant Foe, which was the glory of Northumberland and the champion race at Altcar. A year or two afterwards Sir James Boswell bred Jason, who was very successful both in the field and at the stud, notably with his son Vraye Foy, who again, through Egypt and Lopez, is represented by most of the first-class dogs of the day, another line of Jason being found in Herschel's pedigree. This, with The Czar, is characterised by Stonehenge as the "bulldog cross"; but Captain Daintree held that there was a bulldog strain also in King Cob, which makes it common to all greyhounds. About the same time appeared Mr. Sharpe's Monarch, whose dam was bought from a tramp. The bitch must have shown great quality and General Sharpe must have been a rare good judge, for her son has left his mark on the stud-book to the present day. And now we come to sound ground, for we have the bead roll of the winners of the Waterloo Cup to guide us and tell us something of the performances of those dogs whose fame still lives in coursing annals. And it is worthy of remark that though the Waterloo Cup began in a very small way by being only an eight-dog stake, and in its second year a sixteen-dog stake, and in its third, one for thirty-two dogs, yet the second and third winners and probably the first are still successful in their progeny, as they themselves were in their flesh, not only over the plains of Altcar, but all over the coursing world. The strains of Blue Bugle and of Emperor are still among the most cherished, sometimes perhaps unconsciously, by breeders of the present day. Emperor, indeed, failed himself in the deciding course, being beaten by a kennel companion, but two of his sons revenged his defeat, and his other successful descendants are legion. As Lord Sefton was the founder of the Altcar Club, as he brought in the best blood from North and South to improve the native greyhounds, it was but fitting and fortunate, not only that his bitch Milanie should head the list, but that in Senate we should have one of the most valuable lines in every modern pedigree. It is not without reason that the term "fortunate" is used. His father and mother were as well bred as could be, but perhaps not coming up to the Lancashire ideal of the trainer, that ideal being a sprinter, he was about to put them down, when the bitch came in season, and they were respited till the puppies were weaned. The produce was Oliver Twist, Senate, and Eastham. Contemporary with Senate in the North was Figaro at Newmarket, a son of King Cob; somewhat unfortunate himself, as was his sire, but the father of a host of dogs of the finest stamp. Among them were Mocking Bird, one of the handsomest bitches seen, Bedlamite, and Boreas. It may be noted here that all the progeny of Bedlamite were without exception black, while those of Boreas were of all colours. Weapon, Lablache, Gamechicken, Hurkaru, Music Master, and a host of others, including sisters of Mocking Bird, still testify to the permanent value of the merits of Figaro. Bedlamite was a small dog of 58 lbs. weight, but full of quality; his stoutness and cleverness were undeniable. He naturally became the favourite sire, especially in the South; but his blood survives to-day chiefly through Hopmarket, a daughter of the famous Cerito, and through Randell's wonderful bitch Riot, who was the grandmother of another public favourite in Mr. Haywood's Rebe. Riot was mated with the best dogs of the day, but her most successful son was Regan, the sire of Rebe by Barrator, himself a most extraordinary dog. Though he failed to have his name inscribed in the roll of successful dogs in the Waterloo contest, yet his style pleased the eye of all good judges; but what attracted most notice was the complete command which his master had of him. At a word he would lie down and take not the slightest notice of a hare passing close to him, or he would play at leapfrog with his master, or he would fly at and worry a man. Bedlamite's rival in the South was David, doubly a descendant of King Cob (but not through Figaro), and a grandson of Senate. It may be the combination of the Northern with the Southern race which eventually gave his family the pre-eminence; be that as it may, there is scarcely a pedigree of note which has not the name of David in it. The union of Bedlamite, through The Brewer, with Glimpse at Glory, a daughter of David, produced Gaudy Poll and a number of winners of the first class in the South.

Bedlamite was put to Flounce and produced Jacobite, probably the fastest dog of his day, but a very wide worker. Old coursers still talk of Jacobite, and of Belligerent, a grandson of Weapon a few years later as showing most wonderful speed. But while the line of Mr. Brundrit's dog has died out, that of Jacobite survives in the numerous families of Cardinal York, Picton, Forster's Meg, whose son Kingwater almost rivalled his sire in pace, and the great family of Lord Haddington's, which at one time swept the board.

The next which attracts attention is Cerito, one who ranks with Master M'Grath and Fullerton as thrice winner of the Waterloo Cup. In her case the Cup was only for thirty-two dogs. But when she was beaten in her second attempt, she succeeded in running up for the Altcar Stakes. She left one descendant, Hopmarket by Bedlamite. The family of Hopmarket by her union with Sharpe's fast dog Larriston, promised to carry all before them, but it has nearly dropped out of the front rank, the produce of Bit of Fashion, a most successful bitch, being the most conspicuous; but with the physical failure of Fullerton, the comparative failure of Young Fullerton, and the more complete failure of the rest, this family seems on the verge of extinction. It is worthy of remark that these three great winners, Cerito, Master M'Grath, and Fullerton, have all been more or less failures at the stud; while those who stand next in rank, Coomassie and Miss Glendyne, as dual winners, have met with no more success. Sackcloth, who followed Cerito, deserves more than a passing notice. Not only did he belong to Lord Sefton, but he had been to Amesbury, where he had won three courses in the beginning of February; then to Ashdown, where he won a fourteen-dog stake three weeks later, and the week after he won the Waterloo Cup; truly a magnificent performance and an undeniable proof of stoutness. The judgment of Lord Haddington, then Lord Binning, in breeding from him was properly rewarded in giving him a succession of winners, whose performances it was a pleasure to watch. Through Sackcloth and through Patent the line of Foremost, once a successful rival at the stud to Figaro, chiefly now exists; but the success of Greentick, their greatest descendant, spreads it far and wide. Larriston, a very fast dog by Mr. Sharpe's famous Liddesdale, ran up to him. Larriston was successfully mated with Hopmarket, and also with Mr. Hayward's Hopbine. The produce of the latter union was Rackety Hoppicker, the founder of Haywood's great successes, a strain not likely to die out, as it permeates all breeds. And now we come to the two last of the Waterloo Cups limited to thirty-two dogs, when Judge beat Scotland Yet, and Protest beat Judge, and Blackcloud won the Altcar Stakes—a collection of great names. No finer dog than Judge ever won the Waterloo Cup, and it is pleasing to remember that he won it for Sir Thomas Brocklebank, the best, the most respected, and almost the oldest supporter of the sport. Judge was most successful at the stud, and the cross between Canaradzo, a son of Scotland Yet the runner-up, and daughters of Judge was as much sought after as that between Herschel and Greentick in the present day. Scotland Yet was the sweetest of runners. She was a great favourite of Will Nightingale. It is said that in her last course he took off his cap (he could not see her beaten), and whispered to her trainer: "Draw her, Jimmy, draw her; she is not running to her form." She was of a beautiful shape, white, with a small patch of brindle. Most of her family took after her and introduced the white and brindled colour, which was for a long time the winning colour in the North.

The coming of this family was a distinct era in the history of the greyhound. They all had the same style of going; starting slowly, they stole along with the smoothest of action, and as they neared the hare they shot out and pressed it from the first with determined efforts to kill, but never throwing themselves out: a very winning and a very pretty style. Their stoutness was not a strong point, though Coorooran, one of the family, was noted for his lasting qualities in the old Dirleton country, where the hares were of the strongest, and a three-legged hare was known to try the mettle of the best of them. They were good killers and so, as a rule, made short courses. The family consisted of Canaradzo, who won the Waterloo Cup and was sire of King Death, who also won it and the Plate as well, Coorooran, Seafoam, Bugle, Dalgig, and Canopy, besides others who bred nothing of consequence. Seafoam was the sire of Lobelia, and Bugle the grandsire of Seacove, also Waterloo Cup winners. King Death was the sire of Cock Robin, who ran up to Master M'Grath, and of Chameleon, who was thought by some to have been the best bitch of modern days over the Altcar ground. Her two long undecideds with Gone, in Peasant Boy's second year, were recognised as an abuse of the power of the judge, and led to a change in that department. Cock Robin was grandsire of Misterton, and Chameleon the dam of Commerce, who had the worst of the scrimmage for the Waterloo Cup of 1879. Canaradzo is also represented in the descendants of Ptarmigan; Mr. Fawcett's splendid family from Fair Future have several strains of Canaradzo apart from one of King Death; Herschel has a line of Coorooran, and probably there are few winners who have not some of the family blood in them through Contango as well as other lines.

We have somewhat outrun our subject in treating of this great family. In 1857 the Waterloo Cup became a sixty-four dog stake. King Lear, a very elegant white dog with a little fawn about him, won it, and David ran up for the Purse. King Lear was scarcely a success at the stud; still, he was the ancestor of Muriel, and still lives in the stout-hearted breed of Sir Robert Jardine. Of David it is scarcely necessary to say much. In the South his stock carried all before them; in the North, if his puppies were not so successful in the first generation, they have happily combined with the strains of the country, and he takes rank with Canaradzo, Judge, Figaro, and their congeners as indispensable in a pedigree of the first class. Patent was probably his most successful son in the field and also at the stud, but now he is not so often met with as other sons, though in fact his blood appears in the pedigree of Greentick, whose great grandam Merrywife was by David his sire, out of Henrietta by Regan out of Lady Clara his dam, the grand lines of Barrator and Riot being thus thrown in.

The following years seem to have produced no dogs which live in our memory, though Lady Watford, the grandmother of both Brigadier and Master M'Grath, and Java the grandam of Bed of Stone and Gaudy Poll, were among the unsuccessful competitors of the Waterloo Cup. We then come to the era of Canaradzo and his family, the praises of which have already been sung, soon followed by the success of his son, King Death. That sterling good bitch, Rebe, showed her quality by twice running up for the Cup and dividing the Purse ; foreshadowing the even more excellent performance of Bed of Stone in winning successively the Purse, the Plate, and the Cup. And now comes a time when, for a few years, the form of the greyhound of the day was absolutely of the highest class. We will take the Waterloo contest of 1867. In the last eight of that year we find Master M'Grath, Lobelia, Brigade, Cock Robin, Charming May, and Patent Lever, Bab at the Bowster having been beaten by Lobelia the preceding round after an undecided. Each of these was equal to winning the Cup with the necessary luck. The next year the names of Bacchante and Cataclysm and that of Lady Lyons, the sensational conqueror of Master M'Grath, swell the list, and this period, this Augustan age, seems to end in a display of rockets in the shape of Bendimere, Cavalier, Waywarden, Cyclone, and that extraordinary bitch, Bed of Stone, who, through her one solitary son Bedfellow, has stamped successive generations with her hall-mark. Chameleon in the following year kept up the reputation of her parents King Death and Chloe, both being winners of the Cup in their day ; and the name of Smuggler appears, whose excellence, not appreciated at that time by Warwick, re-appeared as a halo of glory around that princess of her kind, the charming Miss Glendyne. Still the quality of the competitors seems to have died away from that time. Here and there a name appears which we mention with the greatest respect ; as, for instance, Gallant Foe, whose defeat afforded one of those rare instances when the crowd differed from Mr. Hedley ; Contango, that sire of sires, the worthy mate of Bed of Stone, being the son of Bab at the Bowster, perhaps the best greyhound of modern days ; Lord Glendyne, the grandsire of Miss Glendyne ; that sensational bitch Coomassie, possibly the smallest and the smartest winner of the Cup, whose pedigree unfortunately must for ever remain unknown ; Misterton, the winner of the Cup in a memorable year when on the second day the courses were run with two or three inches of snow on the ground, fatal in many cases to the fastest dog from the hare doubling back : the conqueror in a scrimmage, not a trial : the sire of the largest number of winners, and yet a strain to be avoided ; Princess Dagmar, one of the famous Ptarmigan and Gallant Foe family ; Snowflight, whose victory and defeat alike were full of incident. But few of these appeal to our memories as quite of the class of that wonderful time about five-and-twenty years ago. Not even Greentick, sterling and honest and unlucky greyhound as he was, the premier of stud-dogs, quite fulfils our ideal. It is not till we remember the exquisitely finished style of Miss Glendyne, and the resolute manner of Herschel, who would never be denied, that we have good grounds for not despairing of the quality of the breed. It was a thousand pities that a broken toe prevented Miss Glendyne from meeting Herschel, when we might have been treated to such another display as the never-to-be-forgotten struggle between Master M'Grath and Bab at the Bowster. It is true that Bit of Fashion divided the honour of her first Cup with Miss Glendyne, but in the opinion of most the one owed her forward position to good fortune, the other to merit. They were both by Paris, a brother of Princess Dagmar, and one of that brilliant family of Ptarmigan and Gallant Foe, which for a while had the monopoly of the Waterloo Cup as Herschel has now. Bit of Fashion has earned a higher fame in being the dam of Fullerton who stands pre-eminent among dogs as the winner or divider of four Cups, as much an idol of the public as Master M'Grath, and probably of the same class, as their owners carefully declined to subject them to that test of stoutness which appeals to every courser's heart, however much he may admire the speed which brings a dog first to the hare and the carefulness which keeps him in his place. The victories of Texture and Thoughtless Beauty produced two sterling good greyhounds, but there was in each case a slight flavour of luck which prevents them from taking the highest place unchallenged by the carping critic. Fabulous Fortune and his family promise to rival that of Ptarmigan and Gallant Foe, and yet in their case health or condition have shown them in such different colours that, much as we must admire their cleverness, their honesty and their resolution, they seem to bring the qualification of constitution into more prominence when we treat of the requirements of a greyhound of the first class.

There are so many varying circumstances which attend the success or failure of a dog that mere success in the field cannot be received as decisive evidence ; there must be an appeal for a new trial. A case in point is furnished by Mineral Water and Greentick. Twice they met ; twice did Mineral Water receive the verdict. At Gosforth the judge overruled the jury ; but an appeal to the stud book and the calendar leaves no doubt as to the merits of each dog. Mineral Water scarcely survives in any kennel but that of Sir Thomas Brocklebank, while Greentick has founded a dynasty.

Accepting the fact of a dog having transmitted his excellence to his posterity as a necessary confirmation of the verdict of the judge, and applying this criterion in examining into the claims of the dogs named in the foregoing pages, we must allow that, with one or two exceptions, they have all established their right to a place in the Valhalla of greyhounds.

Even this must be received with some reservation, for the union of a dog with a certain bitch may have met with phenomenal success, while his failure with others may have been just as striking. Witness the produce of Beacon and Scotland Yet, Ptarmigan and Gallant Foe. But with bitches it is altogether different. From circumstances beyond control, a bitch may not have been mated with the right dog, or the produce may have died, or she herself may have been short-lived; while during her running career she herself may have not been able to take part in the great contests of the season. Riot and Prizeflower, and perhaps Carlton may be cited as instances of the latter kind; while Cerito and Bed of Stone left behind them only one representative each in Hopmarket and Bedfellow—produce which alone were enough to place their parents in the highest class.

Most of these dogs had their characteristics and peculiarities. Fullerton comes first as the winner and divider in four consecutive contests for the Cup. He was certainly a fast dog, though his brother Simonian could always lead him; but among a crowd of mediocrities he stood forth as a giant. He was brimful of wisdom. With a competitor of the same class it might have been to his disadvantage; as it was, he expended it on the handling of the hare, which was a treat to see.

Master M'Grath comes next as the winner of three Cups. A small, shabby dog, called by some the Irish-terrier, he went like a bolt out of the slips, was as quick as a cat on his feet, and always dashing for a kill, which he seldom missed.

We will pass by Coomassie, probably the smallest winner ever recorded, as quick as lightning with the hare, and a deadly killer, an art said to have been brought to perfection by practice in killing rabbits on a farm, for she seems to have failed in stamping her quality on her progeny. And we come to Miss Glendyne, by some thought to have been the finest greyhound of modern days, good all round; and if she had not broken a toe it is more than possible that she might have kept the Cup at Shortflatt Tower till her nephew was ready to take her place. Then, passing over the family of Ptarmigan and Gallant Foe—viz., Paris, Palmbloom, Pathfinder, Peter, Prenez Garde, Princess Dagmar, Jester, and others, of whom it may be said that they were all big, fine, slashing dogs, carrying a good deal of flesh, with plenty of pace and cleverness, and not too fond of following their game if they could not kill—we take a great stride backwards to Canaradzo and his family, passing by the way that good hard dog Cauld Kail, a lightly made, wiry animal who could run in every country, but more especially on the hills, where he always managed to get the upper side, and if the hare disappeared over a knoll he ran all the harder to catch sight again, an intelligence he inherited from his famous grandam, Ladylike. This family of Beacon and Scotland Yet comprised Canaradzo, Coorooran, Canopy, Seafoam, Seapink, Bugle, and some others. They all had a peculiar style of stealing away with the smoothest of action, seemingly making a race of it with their opponent, but drawing out at the finish, rattling the hare about viciously, and quickly killing at a long shot.

The sire of Seacove, Strange Idea, deserves some mention. Seacove was a granddaughter of Bugle, brother of Canaradzo, with all the cleverness of the family but not the colour. Strange Idea was one of the winning produce of High Idea; fast and clever, with a peculiar manner of wearing their hares, which ran up points very effectively, they were yet always more dangerous to meet at the beginning than the end of a stake. And lastly, we come to Herschel, only half a winner, to the regret of all who respected his owner and felt what a tower of strength he presented to coursing in the light of a relaxation, not a business, to the genuine sportsman. Gladly would he have been hailed as the holder of the long-coveted prize, and quite as enthusiastically would the dog himself have been cheered on his complete victory. However, it was not to be. Misfortune followed him the following years, and he retired to the stud, where, if quality of produce be the test, he stands *facile princeps* in the pages of the calendar.

Some of the bitches who have been winners have been mentioned incidentally, but Bab at the Bowster deserves a second notice. Probably the best greyhound of modern days, she proved her excellence in all countries, over the plains of Altcar, on the hills of Lanarkshire, with the stout hares of Southport, and set her seal on her claim of precedence by producing Contango, Banrigh, The Admirable Crichton, and a number of others, whose blood runs in the veins of every successful greyhound of these days. The peculiar merits of Riot also should not be overlooked, especially in these later times, when the owner of Master M'Grath set the fashion of keeping his dog for one contest only in the season, an unsatisfactory proceeding, to put it in the mildest way, followed by the trainer of Fullerton. The record of Riot, on the contrary, shows us that she was running every fortnight or three weeks, weather permitting, for three seasons, giving a total of 84 courses run, of which she won 74, a fitting moral wherewith to end this dissertation on the celebrities of the stud-book. But perhaps a short account of two most exciting courses within the last thirty years may furnish a tail-piece of greater interest. The first of these two memorable courses was that between Herschel and Fullerton in 1889, in the last tie but one. What with a wet season, and water standing in pools, the hares were running very badly, only three or four hares escaping in the three days. Fullerton had the reputation of being a bad killer at home, but with the weak hares he took his share in the deaths. The courses, and especially his, seemed to be very short, so he was very fresh for his fifth course. Herschel, on the contrary, was lamed in his very first course; and on the second day, for his fourth course, he ran a hare single-handed from the Withins to Gore House Wood, and in coming back he got on two fresh hares, and ran them till he lay down exhausted. As a natural consequence, the next day he started very stiff from the slips, and Fullerton led him by three lengths, and put in three or four wrenches. Herschel then exchanged, and put Fullerton in possession, and then by a magnificent effort forced himself past, fairly took the hare away from him, wrenched two or three times strongly, seeming to leave Fullerton, and unfortunately killed.

The excitement of seeing the old dog, stiff and lame, fairly take the hare from the young and fresh puppy was intense, and many thought it was the finest performance of a brilliant career.

The other course was one which roused the feelings of the onlookers to a still greater extent. It was the deciding course for the Cup in 1869, fought out between Master M'Grath and Bab at the Bowster. The course was run on the farthest of the Hill House meadows, which is bounded by the road leading to the Withins. The crowd was standing on the embankment, the hare coming straight to them. A little knot of spectators was placed broadside on, near the road. The hare was driven from the other side of the main road, a beat which usually affords good hares. The slip was a perfect one, worthy of Tom Raper, that prince of slippers. Master M'Grath began as usual to draw out, but in a long straight run, parallel with the ditch, Bab at the Bowster gradually collared him, and as they neared the bridge a cry from that little band on the road arose, "The bitch leads!" and leading she was by half a length when the hare took the bridge. This was fatal to her; she had to go round, while Master M'Grath, with his wonderful quickness, was across the ditch on the inside like a flash. The hare doubled right back, and then there followed a long series of the quickest of exchanges, a treat indeed to see, when Master M'Grath, nearly at the place they had started from, drew out and made one of his dashing kills. Every one felt convinced that they had then seen the finest pair contest the final for the Cup in the finest style which it was ever likely for them to behold. The winners in these two courses undeniably stand out as the most successful in the contests for the Cup, and yet they both have turned out worthless at the stud, while the losers have distinctly conferred on the whole race of greyhounds those qualities which we all desire to see and strive after; the ualities whose praises have been sung in the foregoing pages with, it is to be feared, wearisome iteration, but certainly with heartfelt appreciation. No doubt not only pace but special quickness with the hare are called for at Altcar more than anywhere else. Master M'Grath and, we may add, Fullerton were dogs of this character, a shade above the dog-racing of the enclosures. But any one who has had the pleasure of seeing the coursing at Altcar at club meetings of late years will feel that stoutness and true running are absolutely necessary for success, and as the hare leads them a far from merry dance, the owners of the cracks must sigh in vain for the deadly jaws of the Canaradzo tribe.

W. ELLIS.

GLOSSARY.

Brace—A pair of greyhounds.

Bye—A course in which, owing to the withdrawal of its opponent, or to an odd number at the bottom of the stake, a greyhound has no one to meet. The first class of bye is called *accidental*, the second *natural*.

Collars—When two greyhounds of the same colour are coursing they are ordered to wear a red and a white collar respectively, the red being on the left and denoting the upper dog on the card.

Cote—An old coursing term, signifying that when two dogs start together, and one outruns the other and turns or wrenches, it be allowed two points, or three points if the hare be bent on the outer circle.

Division—When two or more greyhounds left in a stake divide either by mutual arrangement on the part of the owners, or compulsorily through bad weather or scarcity of hares.

Draw—Of the owner; to withdraw a dog. Also the classifying of the greyhounds prior to the running for a stake.

Enter—Of the trainer; to show the young dog its game for the first time, and to prepare it for coursing.

Exchanging—Of the greyhound; when the dogs alternately move the hare from her course, they exchange points.

Fence—Of the greyhound; the act of leaping over a fence or other obstacle.

Fewterer—The old term for *slipper* (q.v.)

Flag Steward—The official responsible for signalling the judge's decision, after a course.

Fleck—Of the greyhound; to snatch the hare and lose hold.

Form—The resting place of a hare.

Gaze-hound—The old term for hounds only able to follow game by sight, which were probably the ancestors, in large measure, of the modern greyhound.

Go-by—The starting of a greyhound a clear length behind his opponent, passing him in a straight run, and obtaining a clear length's lead.

Guarding—When two or more greyhounds are entered in a stake, the *bona fide* property of the same owner, the order of running is altered, so that they may meet other greyhounds, should they come together.

Hare Bearing—Favouring one of the greyhounds, after the slip. In Queen Elizabeth's time the term signified a go-by.

Home—A refuge for hares.

Law—The amount of space a hare is allowed to run after being put up before the hounds are slipped. In Queen Elizabeth's time the nominal distance was twelve score yards, but since the country has become more cut up, from sixty to eighty yards is the rule.

Leash—(1) The line used to retain the dogs until the order comes for slipping.

(2) Sometimes used as a term defining the whole practice and pursuit of coursing.

Long Dogs—An old term for greyhounds.

Lurching—Of the greyhound; running cunning, and leaving the most part of the work to its opponent.

Meuse or Muse, or Musit—(2) and (3) are obsolete. Gaps in the hedge through which the hare can escape.

Mob—To press a hare unfairly by the crowd.

National Coursing Club—The governing body of the sport, founded in 1858. In that year they drew up a code of rules, which, very slightly altered, is now almost universally observed.

No Course—A course which, owing to accident, or to shortness of duration, gives the judge no opportunity of deciding the comparative merits of the dogs.

Ns—An abbreviation of the word "names," indicating that a greyhound is entered by other than its registered owner.

Pot-hunting—Coursing in which the object is not to test the relative merits of dogs and game, or of dog and dog, but simply and solely to kill the hare.

Produce Stakes—A collection of puppies, usually entered before the commencement of the running season.

Puppy—A greyhound whelped on or after the 1st of January, of the year preceding the commencement of the season of running. See also *sapling*.

Rick—Old term for *wrench* (q.v.)

Sapling—A greyhound whelped on or after the 1st of January of the same year in which the season of running commenced.

Serving—Of the greyhound; when a dog turns his hare, and keeps his place for another turn, he serves himself; or, losing his place, serves his opponent.

Slipper—The official entrusted with the task of letting the dogs go when they have both fairly sighted the hare.

Slip Steward—The official responsible for greyhounds going to slips within the proper time.

Slips—The couples by which the two dogs are held whilst the hare is put up.

So-ho—The cry used to indicate a sitting hare.

Stud Book—The official registry of running and breeding greyhounds.

Trip—An unsuccessful effort to kill, which throws the hare off her legs, or the getting so close to the hare as to *fleck* (q.v.) her.

Turn—A sharp change of not less than a right angle in the hare's course when pressed by a dog.

Undecided Course—A course in which the number of points scored by the greyhounds is considered by the judge to be equal.

Unsighted, To be—Of the greyhound; to lose sight of the hare, either when slipped, or at any part of the course.

Waiting—Of the greyhound; lying behind an opponent, and never making an effort to get near the hare; in other words, waiting a chance to kill.

Wrench—A change of less than a right angle in a hare's course when pressed.

Bibliography—*Angling, Shooting, Coursing*, Robt. Lascelles (London, 1815); *The Courser's Manual*, Thos. Goodlake (Liverpool, 1828); *Continuation of the Courser's Manual*, Thos. Goodlake (1833, Simpkin); *The Courser's Companion*, Thos. Thacker (2 vols., 1834-5, Bohn 30*s.*); *Rules for the Decision of Courses*, Thos. Thacker (Longman, 1843, 2*s.* 6*d.*); *On Coursing* (Arrian) trans., W. Dansey, 1831 (Bohn, 31*s.* 6*d.*); *Thacker's Courser's Annual Remembrancer and Stud Book* (Longmans, 1842-58, 10*s.* 6*d.*); *The Coursing Calendar* (Ed. Stonehenge, now Allan-a-Dale, 1857 to date, *Field* Office, 5*s.*); *The Coursing Guide; or the Waterloo Cup Made Easy*, W. J. Bullock (Simpkin, 1873-74, 1*s.* and 2*s.* 6*d.*); *The Greyhound*, Stonehenge (Longmans, 1875, 15*s.*); *Sports and Pursuits of the English*, Earl of Wilton, pp. 155-78, "Coursing" (Harrison, 1868, 10*s.* 6*d.* and 5*s.*); *An Encyclopædia of Rural Sports*, D. P. Blaine, pp. 551-602 (Longmans, 1870, 21*s.*); *Country Sports, Angling, Shooting, Hunting, Coursing* (Ward and Lock, 1882, 1*s.*); *The Greyhound Stud Book*, David Brown and now W. F. Lamonby, 1882, &c. NOTE.—Vol. iii. pp. xxv.—lxiv. *Historical Sketch of Coursing*, 5*s.*; *The "County Gentleman" Coursing Guide* (*County Gentleman* Office, 1887, 1*s.*); *British Rural Sports*, J. H. Walsh (Warne & Co., 1886, 21*s.*); *National Coursing Rules*, 1894-5 (*Courier and Herald* Office, Dumfries, 1*s.* 6*d.*); *Coursing and Falconry*, H. Cox and G. Lascelles (Badminton Lib. Longmans 1892, 10*s.* 6*d.*); *The Hare*, H. A. Macpherson ("Coursing the Hare," by Chas. Richardson) ("Fur and Feather" series) (Longmans, 1896, 5*s.*).

CRICKET

CRICKET—Wherever Englishmen plant the Union Jack they are sure to set up the wickets as well. Other European nations have never taken kindly to the game, but the natives of many of the lands we have occupied have soon learned to appreciate its merits. In Samoa legislation has interfered to limit the pursuit of the game; in Fiji it is thoroughly acclimatised; some years ago a team of Australian aborigines—not in any way to be confounded with the crack Colonial elevens—visited England; a Zulu is said to be one of the best bowlers in South Africa; the Parsees of India have sent—and are eager to send once more—a team to try conclusions with us; and, finally, the crack bat of 1896 was an Indian prince. It is needless to add that Englishmen settled abroad have in no way shown themselves more English than in their enthusiasm for the national game, and the Australians in particular have proved that they are well able, if not to beat the best English sides, at least to make the most imperative demands on all their skill and resource.

The original popularity of the game was no doubt due to the amateurs who devoted themselves to its practice and extension; but it was only natural in the process of events that another class should spring up, consisting of men who have a large ability for the game, but neither the spare time nor the spare money necessary for its cultivation; and, as the keenness between counties and clubs increased, the paid services of this class were enlisted, till professional cricketers became the backbone of the game; and it is not too much to say that thousands of men are now earning a livelihood by means of cricket.

The Cricket Ground—The first requisite for the game is a place to play it on—a smooth and level sheet of grass. The match-inclosure varies in size, eight acres making a large ground and four acres a very small one; the shape is immaterial, though a circle, oval, square, or a broad oblong is the best; a long narrow strip is not very suitable. The turf requires most careful tendance, and should be firm and close, but not too close; coarse grass makes a very poor ground, and a spongy turf, with thick matted grass-roots, is not satisfactory. To keep the turf in order incessant rolling and mowing are necessary throughout the summer and early spring; weeds of every kind must be carefully eradicated, and the holes and bare places caused by the wear and tear of the game should be filled up as soon as a match is over. A well-appointed ground should be provided with two rollers, a heavy one of, say, about a ton or a ton and a half, and a lighter one of from 10 to 15 cwt.; the heavy one is for use when the ground is hard, and in the early spring, when the turf is soft but dry; on saturated turf a heavy roller is worse than useless, as it squeezes up the moisture to the surface. It is of course essential that a man should be kept whose business it is to look after the turf, the ground, and its accessories. The chief of these last is the pavilion, which should contain a members' room (large enough to hold a table at which at least twenty-five can have lunch at once), from which the game can be watched. Two dressing-rooms are also necessary, with lavatory accommodation. A bath is a pleasant luxury, but not a necessity. In front of the pavilion should be an inclosure, reserved for players, members, and their friends, while, in large clubs, seats are often provided on the pavilion roof. A private room should be reserved for the scorers, either in the pavilion or on some other part of the ground whence a perfect view of the game can be obtained, and special provision should be made for the "press" on any ground where first-class matches are likely to be played. Finally, the pavilion should, when possible, be built behind the line of the wickets. Two white screens should be provided, to be set up behind the bowler's arm so as to give the batsman a good sight of the ball; if these are made of wood and set on wheels, they can be shifted about when necessary; in this case they may be about 20 ft. long by 12 or 15 ft. high. If the screens are of canvas and re-erected for each match, 30 ft. would hardly be too long. Seats should be provided for the spectators, who are never allowed to intrude on the match-inclosure during the progress of the game. Water must be laid on, to be used in the preparation of the wicket, to which it is conducted by a long hose. A good lawn-mower is also essential, and a "telegraph," *i.e.*, a black board raised on a stand, to which white figures can be attached to show the progress of the game, which is done in three lines of figures; thus

75
3
19

would indicate in the top line that the batting side had scored in all 75 "runs," in the second that 3 men were "out," in the third that the last man "out" had scored 19 "runs." Two such boards are useful on a large ground, but one must always be close to the scorer's room or box. The figures on the top line are altered whenever ten runs are made, except when a man is "out", when the exact aggregate is posted. On large grounds a more elaborate system of "telegraphing" is adopted, and it may be added that the Australian system is somewhat different from the English, as the full score of each man and the analysis of the bowling is shown. At the side of the match-inclosure, part of the turf should be reserved for practice, and should be as carefully tended as the inclosure itself. Nets, the higher the better, are required for practice, and two long white coats should be provided for the umpires.

Paraphernalia—The cricketer's costume consists of trousers of white flannel (or serge, as less liable to shrink when washed), white shirt, and boots; the coat and cap are generally of flannel, and show the colours of the club to which he belongs; the boots are of white buckskin, or brown leather, with thick soles well studded with hobnails or set with spikes, to prevent him from slipping; in cold or wet weather a thick, knitted jersey—known as a "sweater"—is worn over the shirt. The chief implement which he carries about with him is his bat, as the ball and "stumps" are provided at the ground where the match is played, but for protection he requires "pads" (*i.e.*, padded guards for the legs), and gloves with the fingers backed with india-rubber to protect his hands. Thick socks prevent the feet from getting sore when the ground is hard. All these, together with his "flannels," should be carried in one of the bags made for the purpose. It is well to take two bats to a match in case one should break, and the wise man will also carry such odds and ends as scissors, sticking plaster, a roll of adhesive bandage, extra socks, handkerchiefs, shoe-laces, &c., in case of accident.

The Laws of Cricket—The Marylebone Cricket Club, with its headquarters at Lord's Ground, St. John's Wood, is the supreme legislative assembly as regards Cricket, and it is to the M.C.C. that cricketers look for the revision and alteration of the laws when necessary. Those laws, as at present received, are as follows:—

The Laws of Cricket.

As Amended by the Marylebone Club, 1884, 1889, *and* 1894.

1. A match is played between two sides of eleven players each, unless otherwise agreed to; each side has two innings, taken alternately, except in the case provided for in Law 53. The choice of innings shall be decided by tossing.

2. The score shall be reckoned by runs. A run is scored:—

   1st. So often as the batsmen after a hit, or at any time while the ball is in play, shall have crossed, and made good their ground, from end to end.

   2nd. For penalties under Laws 16, 34, 41, and allowances under 44.

Any run or runs so scored shall be duly recorded by scorers appointed for the purpose. The side which scores the greatest number of runs wins the match. No match is won unless played out or given up, except in the case provided in Law 45.

3. Before the commencement of the match two umpires shall be appointed; one for each end.

4. The ball shall weigh not less than five ounces and a half, nor more than five ounces and three-quarters. It shall measure not less than nine inches nor more than nine inches and one-quarter in circumference. At the

beginning of each innings either side may demand a new ball.

5. The bat shall not exceed four inches and one-quarter in the widest part; it shall not be more than thirty-eight inches in length.

6. The wickets shall be pitched opposite and parallel to each other at a distance of twenty-two yards. Each wicket shall be eight inches in width and consist of three stumps, with two bails upon the top. The stumps shall be of equal and sufficient size to prevent the ball from passing through, twenty-seven inches out of the ground. The bails shall be four inches in length, and when in position, on the top of the stumps, shall not project more than half an inch above them. The wickets shall not be changed during a match, unless the ground between them become unfit for play, and then only by consent of both sides.

7. The bowling crease shall be in a line with the stumps: six feet eight inches in length; the stumps in the centre; with a return crease at each end, at right angles behind the wicket.

8. The popping crease shall be marked four feet from the wicket, parallel to it, and be deemed unlimited in length.

9. The ground shall not be rolled, watered, covered, mown, or beaten during a match, except before the commencement of each innings and of each day's play, when, unless the in-side object, the ground shall be swept and rolled for not more than ten minutes. This shall not prevent the batsman from beating the ground with his bat, nor the batsman nor bowlers from using sawdust to obtain a proper foothold.

10. The ball must be bowled; if thrown or jerked the umpire shall call "No ball."

11. The bowler shall deliver the ball with one foot on the ground behind the bowling crease, and within the return crease, otherwise the umpire shall call "No ball."

12. If the bowler shall bowl the ball so high over or so wide of the wicket that in the opinion of the umpire it is not within reach of the striker, the umpire shall call "Wide ball."

13. The ball shall be bowled in overs of five balls from each wicket alternately. When five balls have been bowled, and the ball is finally settled in the bowler's or wicket-keeper's hands, the umpire shall call "Over." Neither a "no ball" nor a "wide ball" shall be reckoned as one of the "over."

14. The bowler shall be allowed to change ends as often as he pleases, provided only that he does not bowl two overs consecutively in one innings.

15. The bowler may require the batsman at the wicket from which he is bowling to stand on that side of it which he may direct.

16. The striker may hit a "no ball," and whatever runs result shall be added to his score; but he shall not be out from a "no ball" unless he be run out or break Laws 26, 27, 29, 30. All runs made from a "no ball" otherwise than from the bat, shall be scored "no balls," and if no run be made one run shall be added to that score. From a "wide ball" as many runs as are run shall be added to the score as "wide balls," and if no run be otherwise obtained one run shall be so added.

17. If the ball, not having been called "wide" or "no ball," pass the striker without touching his bat or person, and any runs be obtained, the umpire shall call "Bye;" but if the ball touch any part of the striker's person (hand excepted) and any run be obtained, the umpire shall call "Leg bye," such runs to be scored "byes" and "leg byes" respectively.

18. At the beginning of the match, and of each innings, the umpire at the bowler's wicket shall call "Play;" from that time no trial ball shall be allowed to any bowler on the ground between the wickets, and when one of the batsmen is out the use of the bat shall not be allowed to any person until the next batsman shall come in.

19. A batsman shall be held to be "out of his ground" unless his bat in hand or some part of his person be grounded within the line of the popping crease.

20. The wicket shall be held to be "down" when either of the bails is struck off, or, if both bails be off, when a stump is struck out of the ground.

The STRIKER is out—

21. If the wicket be bowled down, even if the ball first touch the striker's bat or person:—"Bowled."

22. Or, if the ball, from a stroke of the bat or hand, but not the wrist, be held before it touch the ground, although it be hugged to the body of the catcher:—"Caught."

23. Or, if in playing at the ball, provided it be not touched by the bat or hand, the striker be out of his ground, and the wicket be put down by the wicket-keeper with the ball or with hand or arm, with ball in hand:—"Stumped."

24. Or, if with any part of his person he stop the ball, which in the opinion of the umpire at the bowler's wicket shall have been pitched in a straight line from it to the striker's wicket and would have hit it:—"Leg before wicket."

25. Or, if in playing at the ball he hit down his wicket with his bat or any part of his person or dress:—"Hit wicket."

26. Or, if under pretence of running, or otherwise, either of the batsmen wilfully prevent a ball from being caught:—"Obstructing the field."

27. Or, if the ball be struck, or be stopped by any part of his person, and he wilfully strike it again, except it be done for the purpose of guarding his wicket, which he may do with his bat, or any part of his person, except his hands:—"Hit the ball twice."

Either BATSMAN is out—

28. If in running, or at any other time, while the ball is in play, he be out of his ground, and his wicket be struck down by the ball after touching any fieldsman, or by the hand or arm, with ball in hand of any fieldsman:—"Run out."

29. Or, if he touch with his hands or take up the ball while in play, unless at the request of the opposite side:—"Handled the ball."

30. Or, if he wilfully obstruct any fieldsman:—"Obstructing the field."

31. If the batsmen have crossed each other, he that runs for the wicket which is put down is out; if they have not crossed, he that has left the wicket which is put down is out.

32. The striker being caught no runs shall be scored. A batsman being run out, that run which was being attempted shall not be scored.

33. A batsman being out from any cause, the ball shall be "Dead."

34. If a ball in play cannot be found or recovered, any fieldsman may call "Lost ball," when the ball shall be "dead." Six runs shall be added to the score; but if more than six runs have been run before "Lost ball" has been called, as many runs as have been run shall be scored.

35. After the ball shall have been finally settled in the wicket-keeper's or bowler's hand, it shall be "dead"; but when the bowler is about to deliver the ball, if the batsman at his wicket be out of his ground before actual delivery, the said bowler may run him out; but if the bowler throw at that wicket and any run result, it shall be scored "No ball."

36. A batsman shall not retire from his wicket and return to it to complete his innings after another has been in, without the consent of the opposite side.

37. A substitute shall be allowed to field or run between wickets for any player who may during the match be incapacitated from illness or injury, but for no other reason, except with consent of the opposite side.

38. In all cases where a substitute shall be allowed, the consent of the opposite side shall be obtained as to the person to act as substitute, and the place in the field which he shall take.

39. In case any substitute shall be allowed to run between wickets, the striker may be run out if either he or his substitute be out of his ground. If the striker be out of his ground while the ball is in play, that wicket

which he has left may be put down and the striker given out, although the other batsman may have made good his ground at that end, and the striker and his substitute at the other end.

40. A batsman is liable to be out for any infringement of the laws by his substitute.

41. The fieldsman may stop the ball with any part of his person, but if he wilfully stop it otherwise, the ball shall be "dead," and five runs added to the score; whatever runs may have been made, five only shall be added.

42. The wicket-keeper shall stand behind the wicket. If he shall take the ball for the purpose of stumping before it has passed the wicket, or, if he shall incommode the striker, by any noise, or motion, or if any part of his person be over or before the wicket, the striker shall not be out, excepting under Laws 26, 27, 28, 29, and 30.

43. The umpires are sole judges of fair or unfair play, of the fitness of the ground, the weather, and the light for play; all disputes shall be determined by them, and if they disagree, the actual state of things shall continue.

44. They shall pitch fair wickets, arrange boundaries where necessary, and the allowances to be made for them, and change ends after each side has had one innings.

45. They shall allow two minutes for each striker to come in, and ten minutes between each innings. When they shall call "Play," the side refusing to play shall lose the match.

46. They shall not order a batsman out unless appealed to by the other side.

47. The umpire at the bowler's wicket shall be appealed to before the other umpire in all cases except those of stumping, hit wicket, run out at the striker's wicket, or arising out of Law 42, but in any case in which an umpire is unable to give a decision, he shall appeal to the other umpire, whose decision shall be final.

48A. If the umpire at the bowler's end be not satisfied of the absolute fairness of the delivery of any ball he shall call "No ball."

48B. The umpire shall take especial care to call "No ball" instantly upon delivery: "Wide ball" as soon as it shall have passed the striker.

49. If either batsman run a short run, the umpire shall call "One short," and the run shall not be scored.

50. After the umpire has called "Over" the ball is "dead," but an appeal may be made as to whether either batsman is out; such appeal, however, shall not be made after the delivery of the next ball, nor after any cessation of play.

51. No umpire shall be allowed to bet.

52. No umpire shall be changed during a match, unless with the consent of both sides, except in case of violation of Law 51; then either side may dismiss him.

53. The side which goes in second shall follow their innings if they have scored 120 runs less than the opposite side in a three days' match, or 80 runs in a two days' match.

54. On the last day of a match, or if a one day match, at any time, the in side shall be empowered to declare the innings at an end.

ONE DAY MATCHES.

1. The side which goes in second shall follow their innings if they have scored 60 runs less than the opposite side.

2. The match, unless played out, shall be decided by the first innings.

3. Prior to the commencement of a match it may be agreed that the over consist of 5 or 6 balls.

SINGLE WICKET.

The laws are, where they apply, the same as the above, with the following alterations and additions.

1. One wicket shall be pitched, as in Law 6, with a bowling stump opposite to it at a distance of twenty-two yards. The bowling crease shall be in a line with the bowling stump, and drawn according to Law 7.

2. Where there shall be less than five players on a side bounds shall be placed twenty-two yards each in a line from the off and leg stump.

3. The ball must be hit before the bounds to entitle the striker to a run, which run cannot be obtained unless he touch the bowling stump or crease in a line with his bat, or some part of his person, or go beyond them, and return to the popping crease.

4. When the striker shall hit the ball, one of his feet must be on the ground behind the popping crease, otherwise the umpire shall call "No hit," and no run shall be scored.

5. When there shall be less than five players on a side, neither byes, leg byes, nor overthrows shall be allowed, nor shall the striker be caught out behind the wicket, nor stumped.

6. The fieldsman must return the ball so that it shall cross the ground between the wicket and the bowling stump, or between the bowling stump and the bounds; the striker may run till the ball be so returned.

7. After the striker shall have made one run, if he start again he must touch the bowling stump or crease, and turn before the ball cross the ground, to entitle him to another.

8. The striker shall be entitled to three runs for lost ball, and the same number for ball wilfully stopped by a fieldsman otherwise than with any part of his person.

9. When there shall be more than four players on a side there shall be no bounds. All hits, byes, leg byes, and overthrows shall then be allowed.

10. There shall be no restriction as to the ball being bowled in overs, but no more than one minute shall be allowed between each ball.

INSTRUCTIONS TO UMPIRES.

THESE instructions, drawn up in 1892 by the Committee of the M.C.C., are intended as an appendix to the Laws of the Game.

FITNESS OF GROUND.

LAW 43.—At the commencement of a match, the umpires may be appealed to by either side as to the fitness of the ground for play.

Should they not agree, play will not commence until they are agreed.

In case of interruption from rain, as soon as the rain has ceased, the umpires shall, immediately, without further instruction, inspect the wicket, unaccompanied by any of the players, and decide upon its fitness. Should it prove unfit, they shall continue to inspect at intervals, until they decide that it is fit for play, when they shall call upon the players to resume the game.

The ground is unfit for play—when water stands on the surface, or when it is so wet, muddy, or slippery as to deprive the bowlers of a reasonable foothold, or the fieldsmen of the power of free movement.

The umpires are not to be biassed by the opinions of either side, still less are they to allow themselves to be influenced by the impatience of the spectators for a resumption of the game, and are not to be induced, by the public interest in a particular match, to declare the ground fit for play, unless they would consider that ground fit under any circumstances.

FITNESS OF LIGHT FOR PLAY.

The umpires may decide, on appeal, that there is not sufficient light for play. Should the light improve before the time for drawing stumps, they shall, without waiting for instructions, call upon the players to resume the game.

LAW 47.—An umpire is only justified in appealing to the other umpire when he is unable to decide, owing to his having been prevented from seeing the occurrence on which the appeal is based. He is not to appeal to the other umpire in cases on which he could give a decision, merely because he is unwilling to give that decision. If he be in any doubt, the principle laid down in Law 43, "That the existing state of things shall continue," shall be followed, and, in consequence, the decision should be in favour of the batsman.

LAW 48.—The special attention of umpires is called to

this law, which directs them to call "No ball," unless absolutely satisfied of the fairness of the delivery.

Umpires should not allow themselves to be unduly influenced by appeals from such of the field who were not in a position to form a judgment on the point appealed upon, or by tricks—such as throwing up the ball, on appealing for a catch at the wicket, without waiting for the decision. Umpires, being the sole judges of fair or unfair play, should remember that such devices are obviously unfair, and are not in accordance with the spirit in which cricket should be played.

By order of the Committee of the M.C.C.

June 20th, 1892.

Rules of County Cricket.

The following were established as the laws of county qualification, at a meeting held in the Surrey County Pavilion, Kennington Oval, on June 9th, 1873.

1. That no cricketer, whether amateur or professional, shall play for more than one county during the same season.
2. Every cricketer born in one county and residing in another shall be free to choose at the commencement of each season for which of those counties he will play, and shall, during that season, play for that county only.
3. A cricketer shall be qualified to play for any county in which he is residing and has resided for the previous two years; or a cricketer may elect to play for the county in which his family home is, so long as it remains open to him as an occasional residence.
4. That, should any question arise as to the residential qualification, the same should be left to the decision of the committee of the Marylebone Club.
5. That a copy of these rules be sent to the Marylebone Club, with a request that they be adopted by the club.

The county qualification was discussed at a meeting of the County Cricket Council, held in the Pavilion at Lord's, on December 10th, 1888. It was carried unanimously that:—

"For purposes of county cricket, county boundaries are not affected by the Local Government Act, 1888.

"During the two years a cricketer may be qualifying to play for another county under the residential qualification, he shall be allowed to play for the county for which he has previously been playing under that rule."

In consequence of the passing of this latter resolution the rules of county cricket have been modified by the addition of the words: "That a man can play for his old county during the two years that he is qualifying for another."

County Classification.

On the 20th of October, 1894, the Committee of the M.C.C., to whom the whole question of the classification of counties had been referred, made public the following scheme:—

Lord's Ground, N.W.
October, 1894.

The Committee of M.C.C. having at the request of the leading counties, prepared a scheme for regulating the county championship, and that scheme having met with the approval of counties concerned, the contest for the championship will in future be regulated by it.

The scheme as finally approved is as follows:—

Classification of Counties.

Cricketing counties shall be considered as belonging to first-class or not. There is no necessity for further subdivision.

First-class counties are those whose matches, with one another, with M.C.C. and Ground, with the Universities, with the Australians, and such other elevens as shall be adjudged "first-class matches" by the M.C.C. Committee, are used in compilation of first-class batting and bowling averages.

There shall be no limit to the number of first-class counties. The M.C.C. Committee may bring new counties into the list, may remove existing ones from it, or may do both.

The list for 1895, which still (1897) holds good, was as follows:—

Derbyshire	Kent	Nottingham	Sussex
Essex	Lancashire	Somerset	Warwicks.
Gloucestershire	Leicestershire	Surrey	Yorkshire
Hampshire	Middlesex		

The County Championship.

After the close of each cricket season the Committee of the M.C.C. shall decide the county championship.

It shall be competed for by first-class counties. No county shall be eligible unless it shall have played at least eight out and home matches with other counties, provided that if no play can take place owing to weather or other unavoidable cause such match shall be reckoned as unfinished.[1]

One point shall be reckoned for each win; one deducted for each loss; unfinished games shall not be reckoned.

The county which during the season shall have, in finished matches, obtained the greatest proportionate number of points shall be reckoned champion county.

This code, though frequently revised, is not perfect, but the interpretation of any law and the settlement of any question for which the laws do not provide, are left to the umpires, whose ruling is (or ought to be) cheerfully accepted by both sides. A few notes, explanatory of points in the laws, follow.

Law 3. [*See* Umpires, p. 239.] In ordinary games, each side provides an umpire and scorer, but only men of strict integrity and impartiality should be allowed to stand.

Law 4. The foundation of the ball is a cube of solid cork, wrapped round with layers of cork-shavings and very fine twine; over all is a tightly-sewn skin of reddish leather. A good ball will stand a great deal of knocking about, but bad ones soon lose their shape, in which case it is customary to allow a new one to be used, even in the middle of an innings.

Law 5. In the bat there is no relation required between the length of blade and handle; the blade is generally about 22 in. long, and the handle about 14 in., the full legal size being found inconvenient even for tall men. The blade is made of carefully-seasoned and selected willow, and the handle of numerous slips of cane glued together, with various patent additions to combine elasticity with strength.

Laws 6, 7 and 8. The following diagram will best explain how to "mark out the crease."

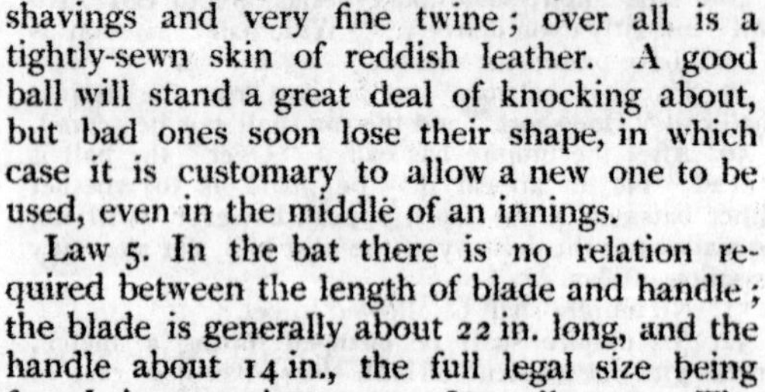

Fig. 1.—Scale of Creases.

The distance between O and P, O' and P' is 4 ft. PQ and $P'Q'$ are the "return creases,"

[1] In 1896 the number of out and home matches qualifying for the Championship was reduced to six, owing to the Australians' tour, and for 1897 the number has been fixed at seven.

and are of unlimited length; they are at right angles to *Pc* and *P'a*. The stumps are represented by *a*, *b*, and *c*; from *a* to *c* is 8 in., outside measurement of the wicket. *P'a* and *Pc* are 3 ft. long. The "popping crease" is so called because the bat is "popped" over it when the batsmen are completing a run; it should be made about 10 ft. long; the return crease should be at least 1 ft. long, as some bowlers are apt to get the hinder foot very wide.

Law 11. The umpire should call "No ball" *directly* the ball, wrongly delivered, has left the bowler's hand. [*See* Law 48B.]

Law 12. The umpire must *call* the "wide"; some men only signal to the scorers with the hand [*see* p. 239], thereby confusing the batsmen. [*See* Law 48B.]

Law 13. [*See* "One Day Matches," Law 3.] The ball is not "finally settled," if the batsman, having overreached himself in playing forward, has not entirely recovered his balance, the ball being in the wicket-keeper's hands. The wicket-keeper should not pretend to throw the ball to the bowler in the hope of tricking the batsman out.

Law 16. The case has occurred before now of an umpire calling—wrongly—"Wide," before the ball has passed the batsman; of the batsman hitting the ball, and being caught. Is he "out"? The equitable decision is that he *is* out: the ball was proved, by the fact that the batsman hit it, *not* to be "wide," whatever the umpire thought, erroneously, that it was going to be. In other words, the umpire's *opinion* was confuted by the batsman's *action*, and if the latter had hit the ball for six he would be very dissatisfied if the runs were disallowed.

Law 18. Note that a bowler may bowl a few preliminary balls at the side of the wicket, to get his arm loose.

Law 21. By "bowled down" is meant "if a bail be dislodged, and fall to the ground."

Law 23. "With ball in hand" means "with the ball in the hand of the arm that knocks off the bail." If the wicket-keeper—or bowler, in the case of a "run out"—takes the ball in his right hand, and knocks down the wicket with his left hand or arm, or *vice versa*, the batsman is "not out."

Law 27. "Wilfully strike" is interpreted to mean "strike with the intention of running," and hence if a batsman, having struck the ball a second time, with whatever motive, starts to run, it is assumed that he struck the ball "wilfully" a second time, and he is given out.

Law 30. The point of the rule is the word "wilfully"; the umpire alone can decide from the batsman's behaviour whether the obstruction was wilful, or accidental, or a legal effort to save his wicket, as provided by Law 27.

Law 34. "Cannot be recovered," *e.g.*, if it lodge in a tree or building; if it is hit into a pond or river; or if it be carried off by a dog; all of which things have occurred.

Law 40. To this law should be added: "or if the ball, hit by the striker, hit the substitute and then be caught."

Law 43. This law is not perfect, as it gives the umpires no authority as to how to act in the case of "unfair play," for a man cannot be given out and registered in the score-book as "played unfairly," though if a fieldsman by interfering with the batsman causes the loss of his wicket, the umpire can, on appeal, give the batsman not out.

As to the question of the fitness of the ground for play, *see* UMPIRES, p. 239.

Law 44. "Fair" means "such as to favour no particular bowler."

Law 45. This law was enacted to prevent sharp practice. The chivalrous behaviour of cricketers has seldom, if ever, made it necessary for the umpires to put it in force.

Single Wicket—This form of the game, at one time very popular and often played for large stakes, has now practically disappeared. It need only be remarked that if five men, or more, play against less than five antagonists, the numerically weaker side has all the privileges conferred by Law 9, while the other party is bound by the special restrictions of Laws 2, 3, 5, 6, and 7.

Instructions to Umpires—Some remarks on these instructions and on the duties of umpires in general, will be found on p. 239, under the head of **Umpires.**

Rules of County Cricket—These rules, together with the "Classification of Counties," and the regulations for "The County Championship," are subject to alteration from time to time, as necessity arises, especially with regard to the calculation of points. The system as printed has been in use during the year 1896, but it is possible that by the time these lines are read some new method of scoring points may be adopted, the system now in vogue not being entirely satisfactory.

How a Match is Played—Having discussed and commented on the rules, the next point is their practical application to the game, as played by experienced cricketers, and the most convenient method will be to describe, as briefly as possible, the ordinary procedure. When both sides have mustered on the ground, each will be under the charge of a captain, who will manage the side, arrange the order in which his batsmen are to go in, and the place each man is to occupy in the field. The captains must also arrange at what time lunch is to be taken, and at what time "stumps are drawn," *i.e.*, at what time play stops for the day. If the match-inclosure is restricted by the presence of a ring of spectators or is limited in size, hits to the ring or to the boundary might not get their full value, and hence a nominal value is assigned to them by arrangement between the umpires [*see* Law 44], this value being accredited to the batsman if he hits the ball to the boundary, or to the score if the ball travels there in the way of "byes" or "leg byes," under Law 17. It is the business of the umpire at the bowler's end to decide whether the ball has actually reached the boundary. The usual allowance for such strokes is four runs, but if the ball is hit clean out of the ground, six runs are generally awarded. Three runs should never be recognised for a boundary hit, for the following reason: it may happen that towards the close of a game, when time is precious, a good batsman may be partnered by a bad one; the bowler will naturally be anxious to bowl to the inferior player, and if he finds the superior player opposed to him, he can deliberately sacrifice three runs by sending a ball to the boundary, and as after a hit or bye for an *odd* number of runs the batsmen "change ends"—this will be explained hereafter,—the inferior player will have to receive the next ball bowled. This is also the reason why the batsmen do not change ends after a "wide" or "no ball" has been delivered.

The boundaries and the times for stopping having been arranged, the captains then—but *not* before—toss for the choice of innings, the successful captain having the privilege of taking the first innings for his side, or of ordering the others to bat first. As a rule it is wise to go in first [*see* p. 238]. The other side—the "fielding" side—then goes out to the ground; its captain appoints two men to bowl alternately from either end, and directs the others to take their proper places in the field, the umpires having preceded them to the ground. When all is ready, the two selected batsmen go to the wickets, having settled between themselves which is to receive the first ball.

And here a digression is necessary to explain the positions of the fieldsmen: their individual duties are explained later on, but it may be premised for the information of those who are not acquainted with the game, but who wish to become initiated into its mysteries, that the bowler is armed with the ball, and that his business is to try to get the batsman out in one of the various ways for which provision is made by the rules (Laws 21—30); that the fieldsmen endeavour to give him their best support, and that the batsmen, each in his turn, try with the aid of the bat to baffle their assaults. The duties of the umpires and scorers are explained on pp. 239 and 240.

It is impossible to lay down any final statement as to the positions taken up by the different fieldsmen, many circumstances combining to influence the judgment of the captain and bowler—who should always work in concert on this point—as to the best arrangement of their forces; the most important of these circumstances are the pace of the bowling; the condition of the ground, whether fast or slow; the ability of the fieldsmen, and the character, known or to be discovered, of the striker, who may be a consistent hard-hitter, an occasional hard-hitter—perhaps in a particular direction only—or a quiet and steady batsman. Nothing except experience can guide the authorities on this point, but it is the duty of captain and bowler to watch the style of every new batsman as he comes in, to see whether any special alterations should be made in the field (*i.e.*, in the fielding side) with a view to getting him out. With this preface a couple of diagrams are here submitted, giving the usual positions of the fieldsmen, first for a fast bowler, and secondly for a slow bowler, it being assumed in each case that the batsman plays a free and sound game, hitting bad balls severely and playing the good ones with a fair amount of freedom. It may also be premised that to hit a ball from eighty to ninety yards before it reaches the ground is a good free stroke, but not at all beyond the power of an average hitter. In Fig. 2,

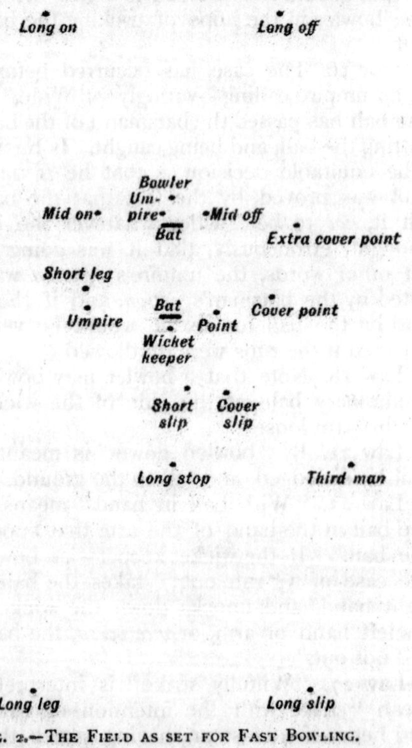

FIG. 2.—THE FIELD AS SET FOR FAST BOWLING.

then, the ground is supposed to be fast and in good order; the bowling is fast too, but not abnormally so; the batsman is supposed to be a free, clean hitter, but not of a phenomenal type; the fieldsmen are all supposed to be first-class. The side of the ground on the left of the bowler is known as the "*off*-side"; that on his right as the "*on*-side," or "leg-side." One umpire will be observed standing near the wicket at the bowler's end, the other in a line with the "popping crease," and about eighteen yards from it at the other end. The batsman A is about to receive the ball, while his partner B stands behind the popping crease at the other end. The distances of the fieldsmen from the wicket may be roughly reckoned as follows: "Long-off" stands at eighty yards; "mid-off," "cover-point," and "third man" at thirty yards; "point," "short-slip," and "cover-slip" at ten yards; the "wicket-keeper" is close to the wickets; "mid-on" is in a line with the bowler's wicket, and about ten yards from it. It will be seen that only ten men have places assigned to them, the reason being that the position of the eleventh man depends entirely on the stroke most favoured by the batsman A; any of the positions marked long-on, extra cover long-slip, short-leg, or long-stop, might well be occupied. Further, if the bowling is very fast or erratic, or the "wicket-keeper" is not very good, the latter may with advantage stand back about ten yards. [*See* THE WICKET-KEEPER, p. 236.] For slow and medium-paced bowling, a man at long on and extra cover is almost necessary, and cover-slip may be moved to one of these places with advantage, but beyond this it is hard to lay down laws as to the best allocation of the fieldsmen, for the character of the batting is the only thing that can guide the captain.

After this long, but most necessary digression, we pick up the thread of our story from the point at which the fieldsmen and umpires were imagined to be ready in their places, and the batsmen, having settled which was to receive the first ball, had proceeded to their respective wickets. Batsman A, on going to his wicket, begins by asking the umpire at the other end to give him "Guard," or "Block"; in other words, he holds up his bat in front of his wicket, the face towards the umpire, to ascertain whether his bat, as he holds it, is protecting his wicket from the bowler's attack. As the bowler may be either right-handed or left-handed, and may elect to bowl from either side of the wicket, this "guard" is somewhat important, for the batsman may be "out" (under Law 24) if he obstruct with his leg the passage of the ball to the wicket, and the position of his bat, relative to the position of the bowler, will help him to stand so as to keep his legs clear. The three stumps are known as the "leg," "middle," and "off" stumps; the one nearest to the batsman being the "leg-stump." The umpire, placing himself as nearly as possible where the bowler's arm will probably come, or in such a place as the fancy of the batsman may suggest, looks at the bat, held upright about a foot behind the popping crease, and informs the batsman what stump or stumps are hidden from view by the bat; the batsman, when he has found the desired place, either makes a scratch with a bail or his spikes, or hammers a small hole in the ground with the point of the bat, and the ceremony is complete. The batsman now knows what position he occupies relative to the bowler's arm; the umpire looks to see if every one is ready, calls "Play!" and the game begins in earnest. If the batsman hits the ball past one of the fieldsmen, and he and his partner run across from wicket to wicket, each getting inside the popping crease without being "run out" (Law 28), one run is scored; if the

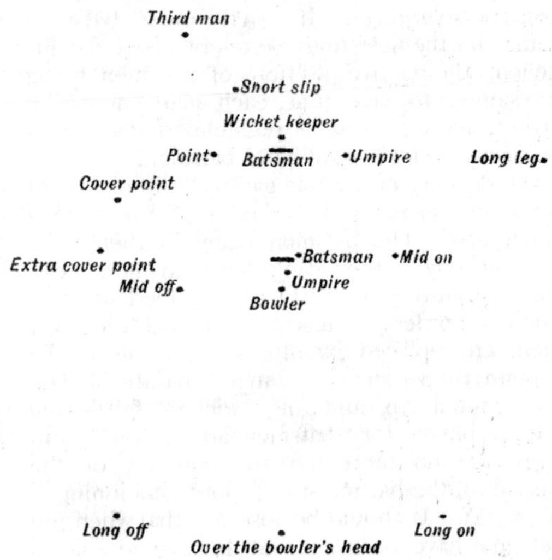

FIG. 3.—THE FIELD AS SET FOR SLOW BOWLING.
Scale, ½ in. to 22 yds.

process can be repeated, two runs, and so on. It may be observed that if an ***odd*** number of runs is made for a hit, batsman B will have to receive the next ball. When five balls have been delivered the umpire calls "Over!" A fresh bowler is deputed to bowl—this time from the other end—and the fieldsmen take up fresh places, but bearing the same relation to the position of the striker as before; but as we will suppose that the second bowler is a *slow* bowler, the position of the fieldsmen must be to some extent altered, somewhat as shown in Fig. 3. Here it will be seen that both third man and short slip have come several yards closer to the wicket; that point, cover-point, mid-on, and mid-off are at about the old distance from it; and that long-on is now permanent, both he and long-off being at ninety yards distance, more or less, according to the hitting powers of the batsman, on which also depends the position of the eleventh man, who may be placed at extra cover, long-leg, or over the bowler's head; if the last, long-on and long-off would probably move a few yards to their right and left. To save needless walking and waste of time some of the fieldsmen would occupy a fresh place when "Over" was called, but the wicket-keeper, point, mid-off, mid-on, and cover-point would cross over. Third man might fall back to long-on, and cover-slip to long-off. The original long-off would come up to third man, and the bowlers would probably field short-slip when not engaged in bowling; but it must be repeated that all these alterations depend on the capacity of the fieldsmen to fill each particular place, and of this the captain must be sole judge. If a left-handed batsman comes in, the field must be re-organised for his benefit, the relative positions of the men being the same; to save time, each man should be given a place as near as possible to that which he occupied for a right-hand batsman.

The history of a whole game is the history of two overs, so far as the routine of the game is concerned. The batsmen maintain their position as long as they can; the fieldsmen move across each time that "Over' is called, and the original bowlers, if unable to defeat the batsmen, are replaced by others according as the captain thinks such a change advisable. The runs mount up, and the "wickets fall"—the cricket phrase for "batsmen are got out"—till there are no more left to come in, or the captain of the batting side "closes his innings" (Law 54). It should be observed that when ten batsmen have been got out, the whole side is considered out, as although there is one batsman left who has not been defeated, still he must retire, as he has no comrade to remain with him. He is entered in the scoring-sheet as "not out." The innings being ended, the original batting side goes out to field, and their opponents proceed to bat, this going on alternately till the day or days assigned to the match come to an end, or the match is decided. No side, however, goes to the wickets more than twice in the same match.

Having dealt with the generalities of the game, the time has arrived to discuss its several points in detail—the batting, bowling, and fielding, and the best and recognised methods for acquiring proficiency in them; but first it must be premised that a first-class cricketer, or he who would be a first-class cricketer, must not devote his attention to one of these three sciences to the exclusion of the other two. The bowler, if any one, is allowed to specialise, but even the best bowler's value is largely discounted if he is unable to catch and field.

In first-class cricket, as played nowadays, "all-round mediocrity," is not valued very highly, but a man who is a first-class bowler and fieldsman, or a first-class batsman and fieldsman, will always find a place in a first-class side, and, to become either of these, careful, patient, and whole-hearted practice is the only royal road. There are no "short cuts" to good cricket, though on a few fortunate individuals the science of the game seems to have descended like a revelation; their probation has been comparatively short, and their ultimate success unbounded; these, however, are the lucky millionaires of the game; the ordinary mortal can only win his way forward by determination, patience, and practice. With this short preface, to which, short as it is, too much attention cannot be paid, the discussion of the best methods of attaining comparative perfection—absolute perfection is impossible—may now logically follow, and the first paragraph shall, as is usual in works on cricket, be devoted to the batsman, for batting possesses a fascination of its own, which appeals with especial vehemence to ninety-nine out of every hundred cricketers.

The Batsman—Little space is needed for a wicket on which good practice can be had; a level strip, 10 yards by 4, is ample; but it should be carefully rolled, mown, and cleared of weeds, and the wickets should be frequently shifted to avoid unnecessary wear and tear of the ground. The proper nets, which can be procured at any cricket warehouse, save an infinity of trouble and time, and with these, and a couple of boys to field, one bowler is quite sufficient, especially if two or three balls are provided. Allusion has already been made to the batsman's outfit, but one word of advice must be added: "Never, under any conditions, go in to bat without pads and gloves; the slowest and easiest ball may hit one on the knuckle and carry away a piece of skin, or may glance off the bat on to shin or ankle." A word may be useful as to the selection of a bat, but every batsman must find out what kind of bat suits him best, and choose accordingly. The weight varies from 2 lb. to 2 lb. 10 oz., but only a man of special strength can use the latter weight, and the former is exceedingly light, so that the average weight varies from about 2 lb. 3 oz. to 2 lb. 6 oz., and it is worth while remembering that, as a bat should be rubbed fairly frequently with unboiled linseed-oil to keep it from getting dry, it always increases in weight. Weight, however, is hardly so important as balance, a well-balanced bat, though heavy, being far more easy to wield than a light, but ill-balanced weapon. All the makers of the present day turn out excellent bats, of well-seasoned willow, so that a good bat is easily procured, of a clean straight grain, free from knots and blemishes. Every man must find out the kind of handle that suits him best; indeed, the patent handles are innumerable, but the larger the handle the greater is the leverage, and, consequently, the greater the ease in handling the bat. If on grasping the handle with the right hand, the end of the middle finger reaches the ball of the thumb, and does not overlap it, the handle will be of the right size; but on this point, as in the matter of weight, every man has his idiosyncrasy. The bottom of the bat should not be too thin, as when a ball is struck with the end of such a bat, the fingers are apt to be unpleasantly jarred; nor should the handle be too stiff. As a firm grip of the handle is essential, an india-rubber casing is useful if the palm of the hand perspires. One further word of advice is necessary—*choose a bat which is too light, rather than one which is too heavy.* Everything depends upon quickness, and while it is easy to move a light bat slowly, it is impossible to move a heavy bat (*i.e.*, a bat too heavy for one's strength) quickly. It is no bad practice to go through the motions of the various strokes in one's own room, a sort of drill routine, in which hand, leg, and eye take part.

Practice should always be carried out as far as possible under match conditions; the popping crease should be marked, and the batsman should be careful to take "guard" at the distance from the wicket which he finds most suitable to his style. As a rule the mark should be made about 3 ft., a bat's length, from the wicket; some men like to take it nearer to the crease, but the distance mentioned is long enough to obviate any danger of hitting the wicket, while the nearer one gets to the crease the greater is the danger of shifting the foot over it, and so running a risk of being stumped. But what one's custom is in a match, that must it be in practice.

Position—A correct position is very important, even though some men who are really fine batsmen adopt a very unorthodox pose. It must be firm, yet easy. The following instructions may help the beginner. Take "middle-and-leg" guard [*see* GLOSSARY] about twelve inches behind the popping crease. Set the bat lightly on the mark where the "block" is, the face towards the bowler. Place the toe of the right foot so as just not to touch the inner edge of the bat, and parallel to the crease; the foot will then be just clear of the wicket. Set the left leg about fifteen inches in front of the right, the toe pointing slightly towards the bowler, the two heels being in a line at right angles to the crease. The weight of the body should rest entirely on the right leg, not on the bat or the left foot; indeed, only the left toe need touch the ground, and that lightly. The right knee should be straight—this is most important—and the right leg as rigid as a bar of iron. The left shoulder should be brought well across the body in the direction of the bowler. The correctness of the attitude may be tested by lifting the bat and the left leg off the ground together; if the batsman can stand still without swaying, his balance is correct. The body must naturally bend over the bat, *but from the waist and not the knees*, and none of its weight must rest upon the bat. On the immobility of the right foot and the freedom with which the left moves, the batsman's success largely depends.

Even so simple a thing as holding the bat can be done in a wrong way. Grip the handle of the bat with the right hand about the middle; the grasp must be as tight as possible, and must never be relaxed. All four fingers must clutch the bat, the thumb resting just below them, the knuckles of the clenched fist being towards the bowler. The grip of the left hand must not be too tight; the knuckles are towards the batsman and the back of the hand towards the bowler, while the end of the handle rests in the palm, against the ball of the thumb, the handle being practically a prolongation of the left arm. Both the grip of the bat and the pose of the batsman should be carefully noted and practised in private, the bat being swung about in the direction of an imaginary ball. The various strokes mentioned hereafter may also be tried when the wrist and arm are familiar with the feeling of the bat, and it will soon be found that the right hand is the executive hand, and gives force to the stroke, while the left guides the bat, and may be called the "directive" hand, the importance of which will be seen in the next paragraph.

"How beautifully straight his bat is!" is a remark often made about a good batsman. As a matter of fact "upright" would be a more correct term than "straight," but "straight" is the almost invariable epithet, and this "straight bat" is the first thing to be mastered by the novice, as it is the primary essential for sound cricket, offensive and defensive. Only batsmen of special natural advantages can afford to play with a horizontal bat, and even they often lose their wickets in consequence. The bat, then, except for certain strokes which will be described, must be kept absolutely perpendicular, and it will be found by practice that the *left* hand is called upon to do this part of the work and to correct the vigour of the right hand. More will be said on this subject when "back-play" and "forward-play" are being dealt with, but for the present, attention may be called to Fig. 4, in which the batsman is standing in position ready to receive the ball. No criticism of his pose is necessary, except that his weight *appears* to be equally distributed on either leg, whereas the left should bear none of it. The "skeleton pads" he is wearing give, by the way, the best protection, and are cooler and lighter. If a left-handed bowler is bowling round the wicket, the left foot may be brought further across the wicket, and the left shoulder may follow it. The shoulder should always be over the foot.

Tabulating these remarks for convenience of reference we may lay down the following rules:—

I. Grip firmly with the right hand, less firmly with the left.

II. The right toe should be just clear of the wicket.

III. All the weight of the body should be on the right foot, none on the left foot or bat.

IV. Both knees should be kept straight.

V. The left shoulder should be brought well across the wicket.

VI. The bat must be kept perfectly upright for nearly all balls, always for those which are straight or nearly straight.

No spare moments will be wasted that are spent in lunging about with the bat, hitting at imaginary balls, straight and crooked; by this means the wrists will become supple and will learn to work together, a most important point. Two things, however, will be noticed—or should be noticed—first, that it is not easy to keep the bat upright even when the imaginary ball is straight; second, that the point of the bat naturally flies up, so that the ball, if struck, would be hit into the air, and the batsman run a risk of being caught out. With regard to the first point, the question of balancing the body on the right leg is all-important, as the left leg is then free to move in any direction, and it will be found that by advancing it in the direction of the supposed ball, the body going with it, the bat can be kept perfectly straight, and will meet the ball flush with its face. Further, by transferring the whole weight of the body from the right to the left leg at the moment when the ball and bat meet, the bat will receive a considerable share of that weight and impart it to the ball, the result being a much more vigorous stroke. But it must be especially remembered that under no circumstances (except as detailed

FIG. 4.

on pp. 222 and 223) must the right toe be allowed to leave the ground; as, if the toe is in the air, however little above the turf, the batsman is out of his ground, provided no other part of his body, or his bat, is properly grounded. By shifting the left foot, as described, it will be found that not only can the bat be kept "straight" for balls a foot or more outside the off-stump, but also that additional power can be put into the stroke.

To deal with the second point. It is difficult at first to reach far forward without raising the point of the bat and hitting the ball into the air. Some men, when playing forward, avoid this by turning the left wrist outwards as they lunge forwards, and bringing the back of that hand against the wrist of the right hand. The movement is very simple and soon becomes mechanical, but more will be said of this under "Forward-Play" (p. 221). The second and greatest aid towards "keeping the ball down," *i.e.*, preventing it from going in the air, is to thrust the left shoulder towards the direction of the ball as the left foot goes out, almost pointing the shoulder at the ball itself. This is not very easily described, but any good cricketer can make the matter clear, practically, in a moment, and even the novice may teach himself by following the instructions given.

Thus far it has been assumed that practice has taken the form of a sort of drill; now we may pass on to the moment of encounter, describing and explaining the various recognised strokes and the methods of making them. It may be premised that the bat should in all cases strike the ball and not be struck by it, and that the ball should be met, if possible, with the lower part of the blade, as thereby the "driving," *i.e.*, the propelling, power of the bat is utilised to the best advantage. As it will be necessary to use several technical terms connected with bowling, it will be convenient to explain them here, reminding the reader that the "off-side" is on the left of the bowler, and the "on-side," or "leg-side," on his right. When the ball "breaks" (*i.e.*, twists) from the off-side towards the wicket, it is said to "break back," when from the leg-side, to "break from leg." A "full pitch" is a ball which the bat meets before it touches the ground. A "yorker" (or "tice") pitches on, or within six inches of, the popping crease; a "half volley" from one to two yards in front of it; a "length-ball" from one to two yards further back still; and a "long-hop" pitches yet nearer the bowler. In the case of an exceptionally tall batsman with a long reach, a ball is a half-volley even if it drops somewhat shorter than the distance given, and this is one of the advantages which height bestows. Each different class of ball, it will be observed, has a fairly large range, depending on the reach of the batsman. More accurate definition is impossible, especially as a ball may be a half-volley on a fast wicket, which is a good length-ball on a slow one. Experience will be the batsman's best instructor on these points, and he should also study the article on "Bowling."

Most strokes are in the main either defensive or offensive, though many combine both qualities. It is clearly the batsman's first object to prevent the bowler from getting him out,

FIG. 5.

but there is no better way of doing this than by hitting the ball to the furthest possible distance. But as there are certain balls, which from their "length" (*i.e.*, the distance at which they pitch from the batsman) it is difficult, or impossible, to hit away, and as defence is paramount, they shall be dealt with from this point of view first. There are two classes of strokes, known as "forward-play" and "back-play," the original object of which is to stop the ball from hitting the wicket. Many fine cricketers hold that back-play is the foundation of good defence; others are equally vehement in their support of forward-play. The temperament and physique of the individual alone can decide which he will, as a rule, adopt; but the taller the man is, the better is he adapted for forward-play, as his reach gives him an immense advantage over a shorter player.

Back - Play — Fig. 5 gives an excellent illustration of the position for back-play. The ball has pitched rather short of a "good length" but is perfectly straight; the batsman has met it correctly, by drawing back his right foot, which his left foot follows, and by keeping a perfectly upright bat for the ball to encounter. The errors of the position are (1) that the bat does not appear to be *quite* straight, and (2) that if the left foot were more in front of the right, the batsman would run less risk of being "cut over" (*i.e.*, hit in the groin) if the ball broke back suddenly. It may be observed that this is one of the cases in which the right foot is moved, but it must be specially noted that it is still kept behind the popping crease. The illustration shows what may be called *quiescent* back-play, the pitch and rise of the ball not allowing the batsman to try to score off it, but a taller and more commanding man would have waited till he felt the ball touch the bat, and would then, by an instantaneous—almost electrical—movement of his wrists, have forced the ball away in front of him to some distance, instead of merely allowing it to drop against the bat, as in the plate. The position of the left elbow, cocked up in the air so as to keep the bat upright, should be noted; some batsmen exaggerate this position in their determination to play straight, and raise the elbow till it almost conceals the face; this, if a fault, is a fault on the right side.

Forward-Play—This style of play is adopted when the ball is pitched fairly close to the batsman, but is not so far up as a half-volley, which is the best ball to hit. Fig. 6 shows the position of the batsman at the supreme moment, when he has lunged out as far as he can reach, hoping to "smother" a somewhat over-pitched ball before it has time to rise or break. Observe that the left wrist has turned round, as explained on p. 220, that the left shoulder is pointed right at the ball, that the bat is perfectly upright, and that the point of it is kept back by the influence of the left hand, the left foot being advanced towards the ball, while the right toe is just on the ground. The weight of the batsman has been entirely trans-

FIG. 6.

ferred from the right leg to the bat and left leg, and if at the moment of transference the bat hit the ball, the latter will have been sent away at a considerable velocity. This description may sound very elaborate, but a few trials will prove that the position is easily attained, provided that the original balance is perfect and that the wrists work freely and easily together. The beauty of the whole stroke consists in the "timing" of the ball; and if the question is asked, "What is timing?" the only answer is that, "When the batsman times the ball correctly, the whole power of arms, wrists, and body is thrown into the bat at the precise instant when it meets the ball; at this instant the ball will probably be just passing the left leg." A blow is perfectly timed at boxing when the fist encounters the opponent's face at the exact moment when the arm has straightened out; and the same remark applies to cricket.

At this point the reader will naturally ask, "When am I to play forward, and when am I to play back?" As a definite answer is impossible, one must fall back on generalities, and say that, as a rule, on a fast wicket, a batsman of average height should play forward to all balls which pitch within two and three or, sometimes, four yards of the popping crease; for a shorter man to do so with effect, the ball must be closer to him, and *vice versa* for a tall man; but much depends on the temperament of the batsman, the pace of the bowling, and the condition of the ground. Some tall men persistently play back, and lose the advantage of their height; some small men habitually play forward, and by overreaching themselves cause the ball to drop lifeless from the bat. On a fast, smooth, true wicket the ball will not rise much higher than the top of the stumps, and a comparatively short ball may then be played forward; but if the ground be slow or rough, the batsman, being in a somewhat more strained position than he is when playing back, will be unable to adapt his stroke readily to the vagaries of the ball, and back-play will be his best resource.

Forward-play is the best way of meeting a fast bowler, as the ball has less twist on it than a slower bowler can produce. To play forward to slows is dangerous unless the ball can be "smothered" to a certainty.

A useful general rule is, "When in doubt, play forward on a fast wicket, and play back on a slow one." On a ground as fast as Lord's it is always a rule of thumb to play forward rather than back. On a fast, true wicket, on which the ball does not rise higher than the stumps, runs may be got fairly freely, even off straight balls, by both styles of play, the forward stroke, if well-timed, driving the ball hard in front of the wicket; while by back-play a skilful batsman can place the ball between the fieldsmen in front of the wicket, or by a well-timed turn of the wrist at the moment the ball strikes the bat direct it along the ground through the slips; but it is impossible to make back-play as powerful as forward-play, as it depends on the arms and wrists alone, the weight of the body lending little help.

The Drive—This, the most delightful of strokes, is the first genuine "hit" hitherto introduced, as the length-ball and long-hop, when straight, must be met by a stroke the primary object of which is defence. When, however, a ball is pitched nearer to the batsman than a length-ball, it becomes a "half-volley," and the batsman has a fine chance of making a big hit. To be bowled out by a half-volley is humiliating, to play forward and smother it is to lose a chance, to play back to it is probably fatal. The ball should be hit in front of the wicket with a good swing of the bat, the left foot being moved, as usual, in the direction of the ball, and when the stroke is correctly made, every muscle of the legs, back, arms and wrists seem to take part in it, and the ball flies off without an apparent effort. To time the stroke properly, the bat should meet the ball just as the latter is rising from the pitch. It adds force to the hit—besides enabling the striker to get to exactly the right spot—to jump in to meet the ball, even leaving one's ground and taking the risk of being stumped, if the ball is missed altogether. This is exactly what the batsman is doing in Fig. 7, which, however, does not show the position of the feet at the moment of impact. When the down-swing of the bat has brought it against the ball, the right foot will close up on to the left, and the whole momentum of the

FIG. 7.

body will be added to the swing of the arms and bat. One rule must never be forgotten: "Never jump out to drive a ball on the off-side." It is hard to keep the bat straight when the ball is, say, a foot wide of the off-stump; the chances of missing it are consequently greater, and the wicket-keeper has the easiest of opportunities.

To hit a half-volley all along the ground, the left hand must check the point of the bat so that it does not go beyond the left foot, but many batsmen in the exhilaration of the stroke let the bat complete its swing, and the ball soars away in the air in the direction of one of the "long-fields," who may, or may not, be able to catch it: the batsman has to take his chance of this, relying on the fact that it may be too far to the side of the fieldsman to be caught, or may fly fairly over his head; since, however, it is frequently hit to a distance of 100 yards before it drops, and has been sent by fine hitters as far as 170 yards, a little risk may fairly be taken. It is useful in practice to try to hit a straight half-volley straight back, either over the bowler's head or all along the ground to him. A crooked ball should be sent away on the same side as that on which it pitches. Probably more runs have been got off a half-volley than any given ball, and probably more batsmen have fallen a victim to its temptations, as not only may a fair hit be as fairly caught, but also any error of timing or any inaccuracy may send it high into the air.

FIG. 8.

The Cut—This is another beautiful stroke, which appeals to the experienced cricketer even more than the drive; the latter even the uninitiated can appreciate, as the sight of the ball sailing through space is easily "understanded of the people." The ball which the batsman cuts is more or less wide of the off-stump, and is generally short of a good length; indeed, many batsmen nowadays prefer to let the good-length ball go by, as the slightest error may send the ball into the hands of an expectant "slip." Figs. 8 and 9 show the batsman preparing to strike, and striking the ball. In making this stroke several of our canons are violated; firstly, the right leg is shifted so as to take the batsman across to the ball; secondly, the bat is used horizontally and not perpendicularly; thirdly, the weight of the body is a negligeable quantity, as most of the work is done by the wrists and forearm. It may help the reader who happens to be a fisherman, to tell him that what he does perpendicularly with a two-handed salmon-rod, he does horizontally with a cricket-bat. The ideal ball to cut is a long-hop, not too short, about twelve inches outside the off-stump. Directly the batsman realises the situation, out goes his right leg, which should touch the ground at about the same moment as the bat hits the ball, or even a moment before, the two wrists moving the bat with a sort of "flicking" movement, impossible to describe, so that the ball is struck just as it has passed the right foot. It is a stroke which must be seen to be imitated; but if all goes well, the ball will travel square with the wicket, just past "point's" left hand, or even further behind it, as a clever "cutter" can place the hit with much precision. If the ball rises much—is a foot higher than the wicket, for instance—it should be left severely alone, as a catch is very likely to ensue. The cut is one of the few strokes made *across* the path of the ball; in most instances bat and ball travel along the same path, but in opposite directions. The cut is a difficult stroke to acquire; indeed, some batsmen never get pro-

FIG. 9.

ficient at it, and endeavour instead to hit the ball, still with a horizontal bat, in front of the wicket. Such a stroke is often incorrectly called a "cut," but it is rather a species of "drive." Great care should be taken to "keep the ball down" (*i.e.*, hit it along the ground), and in such a way as to make it skim the surface without bounding too high. If any one finds a difficulty in "hitting" this particular ball, let him try "guiding it"; in other words, let him frame for the cut, and, as the ball passes the right leg, just lay the bat against it, without attempting to strike; the pace imparted to the ball by the bowler will hardly be checked, and many a run may be got by the stroke, while in process of time the man who has mastered this will master the cut, pure and simple, as well.

The Leg-Hit—A ball which is well pitched up and would, if left alone, hit the batsman's

Fig. 10.

leg, may easily be driven in front of the wicket to "long-on," or more squarely with the wicket; but when such a ball would pass just outside the legs a different kind of stroke is required, as the "drive" would be a physical impossibility. This class of hit is known as the "leg-hit," and it may be made even off balls which pitch straight for the wicket, or even on the off-side of it, but such strokes are not strictly orthodox, and demand special powers on the part of the batsman. They are dealt with under the heading of "The Pull."

In the present day most bowlers try to get the batsmen out by bowling tempting balls on the off-side for them to hit into the air, and the result of the increased accuracy of bowlers is that very few balls are sent up which pitch on or outside the legs; hence leg-hitting, pure and simple, is, for want of opportunity, almost a thing of the past, except in cricket of a somewhat inferior grade. Still, as it is given to few to reach good cricket without a long noviciate, and as the leg-stroke is as delightful to the striker as to the spectator, a more than passing allusion must be made to it. The "leg-hit" covers a large range, as shown by the position of "long-leg" in Figs. 2 and 3, and it is even more extensive than this, and the various modes of scoring off a leg-ball are too numerous for exact description. The cricketer will find them out for himself, but a few general hints may be helpful. A long-hop on the leg-side may be hit away square, with a horizontal bat, which is the most drastic method of treatment; or the batsman may simply hold the face of his bat at an angle of about 45° to the ball's direction and allow the ball to strike it, when the pace imparted by the bowler will send the ball away behind and to the left of the batsman. Such a stroke is known as "the glance" or "the glide" (Fig. 10). This stroke is made off a ball of any length; and to men who are not good *hitters* to leg it is invaluable, as the ball, if the bowling be fast and the stroke made with accuracy, flies away to the boundary like lightning. In this case it will be seen that the ball hits the bat, and that its course is deflected by it, but this is not "hitting," in any sense of the word. The proper "leg-hit" is made off a ball which may vary in pitch from a "good length" to a "full-pitch," and in direction to a distance of about three feet from the batsman's legs and outside them. The rule for the stroke is simple enough—"throw your left foot towards the ball, and hit beyond the left toe as the ball passes." If such a stroke be well-timed, and catches the ball as it passes the toe, a delightful hit will be the result; all the more delightful because the striker may put his full strength into the "smite," and need not trouble himself about the risk of being caught. The ball flies away square or fine according to the pace of the bowling, and as it travels *behind* the batsman he cannot usually do much to control its direction or elevation, but as the range of the leg-hit is so large, he may trust to the chapter of accidents to escape being caught; one thing is certain, that if the ball is struck fair, the fieldsman is not likely to catch it, unless he happens to be standing in exactly the right place, for the hit, being more or less a "blind hit" to the striker, will also be a blind hit to the fieldsman, as he cannot place himself for it with any certainty.

The "draw," being obsolete, is only mentioned here for the sake of completeness. Old-fashioned players used to meet a short-length ball coming straight to the leg-stump with the bat inclined, as for the "glance," the ball being deflected between the legs and the wicket; it was a risky stroke, though some batsmen made it effective.

The leg-hit as described is made with a more or less horizontal bat which "sweeps" the ball away; but the bat may be kept perfectly straight and the body perfectly straight, the ball being struck just before it reaches the striker, whose left leg is drawn up close to the right; the resultant stroke, if accurately timed, is one of the most brilliant that can be seen, but it requires a combination of strength and accurate timing and exact length which are not to be met with every day. When all these requisites meet, a huge hit is the result.

Leg-hitting is more or less a natural gift, and some batsmen never attain it; for them the most effective stroke is the old "Cambridge poke"; no attempt is made to *hit* the ball, but rather to push or guide it, in front of the wicket or behind it, according to the position of short-leg, if there is one.

The Pull—The term "pull" is applied to a stroke which is more practical than orthodox, and which brings a straight ball or an off-ball across the wicket to the on-side. It is dangerous to the batsman, inasmuch as it cannot be done with a straight bat; to the bowler, inasmuch as it is more or less unexpected, and usually sends the ball to an unguarded part of the field; but the batsman is more likely to suffer than the bowler, and consequently the stroke can only be recommended to a batsman of large experience, who is also blessed with a quick, sure eye.

General Remarks—The batsman's first object should be to defend his wicket; his second, to do what damage he can to the enemy by scoring runs. The two things may, however be reasonably combined, and a defensive stroke if played with determination and power, may, and often does, result in the acquisition of runs. Hence every ball within a certain limit should be played hard; the bat should meet the ball, and not be struck by it, though in the contest between the hand and head of the bowler and the hand and head of the batsman, the former often has the advantage, and the latter has to be satisfied with merely arresting the ball's progress. "Shooters" [*see* GLOSSARY] are rare nowadays, thanks to the ground-keeper's care, but if they come, the batsman must be satisfied to stop them, and it is well, when playing forward, to keep the point of the bat so close to the ground as to smother a possible shooter. "Yorkers" do not lend themselves to scoring; they must be watched carefully, and most men play them by chopping down quickly at the place where they are going to pitch; but by playing forward—perhaps the best method—they may generally be met on the "full pitch"; in any case the batsman should be content with merely stopping them.

In both back- and forward-play the bat and left leg should be so close together that the ball cannot pass between them.

One of the bowler's devices is to bowl about a foot outside the off-stump, keeping a good length, to induce the batsman to hit more or less wildly at the ball, and to hit it into the air. The best way to meet this artifice is to hit the ball fair and square in the middle of the bat, and when the batsman is well set this may be done with success, but experience will teach him that great care is necessary, and that there is a ball of a particular length which cannot be struck at without danger. This rule, however, is reduced to an absurdity by some men, who refuse to "let go" at anything between a long-hop and half-volley, and who, when the intermediate ball comes, merely step in front of the wicket so as to protect it with their legs in case the ball breaks back. This may be magnificent, but it is not cricket; it is a loss of opportunity to let any off-ball pass without an attempt at a stroke, save that one which, if straight, should be merely played, without an effort to force it away; at the same time, the best and safest way of meeting a slow, leg-break bowler is to get in front of the wicket—thereby defending it with the legs—and to sweep the ball round to the leg-side, always supposing that the ball pitches on that side.

The batsman should always be comfortably settled to receive the ball before the bowler begins to run. He should, directly the bowler is in position, rivet his glance on the ball and never lose sight of it till it has struck the bat. Too much importance cannot be attached to this habit of observation, and "Be ready in [illegible]" is an invaluable maxim. If the bowler is fidgety at the post and bowls before the batsman is quite ready, the latter should draw away and refuse to play the ball; if the wicket is hit, no harm is done. If spectators, or one of the fieldsmen, are behind the bowler's arm, they should be asked to withdraw, as they may catch the eye of the batsman and distract his attention, as well as interfering with his sight of the ball: but the umpire is bound to stand so as to get a clear sight from wicket to wicket, and the batsman has no right to demand, as many do, that he should stand out of the line of sight.

The art of running between wickets, without coming to a misunderstanding with one's partner, is indispensable. The rule is simple—the striker calls for all strokes in front of the wicket, his partner for all strokes behind the wicket. Some players make an exception to this rule in the case of a stroke to "third man," for the striker has a better view then of the direction of the ball than his partner; but even here the non-striker should have the right of calling the run, as his is the greater risk; but it is well to arrange with one's partner on going in, who is to call for the stroke. Directly a ball is struck the batsman

—whether striker or non-striker—whose business it is to call, should shout—sharply, quickly, and distinctly—"Come!" "No!" "Not yet!" as the case may be. It is well to add to the word "Come!" the number of runs that seem likely to be got for the stroke—*e.g.*, "Come one!" "Come two!" and the like; in fact, every information should be given to one's partner that may help him in running, but in all cases it should be regarded as a golden rule that the man who runs the risk of losing his wicket has the right of calling or refusing a run. If the non-striker has to call for a sharp run, he should be prepared to stop, as the striker may not be in a position, especially if his legs are far apart, to start at once.

The non-striker should always "back up," *i.e.*, should always follow up the ball for a yard or two towards the striker's wicket, so as to get a good start in the event of a possible run, but he must be careful not to leave his ground till he has *seen* the ball leave the bowler's hand [*see* LAW 35], nor to go so far that he cannot regain his ground in case the ball be driven straight back, for then, if he has not made good his ground and the ball, having first touched the bowler, hits his—the non-striker's—wicket, he would be run out. With a hard-hitting partner it is well not to "back up" too far, as there is a danger of being struck, if the ball is hit hard.

If a misunderstanding occurs between the batsmen when running, the one who has made the mistake should give way and allow himself to be run out, but there is a generous feeling among cricketers that the worse batsman should sacrifice his wicket in the interests of his side, even if the error is not his, and that the batsman who is "well set" should be the survivor.

The fieldsmen should be carefully watched by the batting side, both when actually batting and in the pavilion, to note and record which are good fieldsmen and good throwers, and which are left-handed men. If the ball goes to the "wrong" hand, a run may often be got; or to a man who is standing a long way from the wicket and has been noted down as a bad thrower.

Some batsmen are famous for "stealing" runs, (*alias* "running short runs"), when the ball is only hit a very short distance. This practice, it is true, often demoralises the fieldsmen, but usually does more harm to the batsmen, who run themselves out of breath and are very liable in the excitement of the moment to commit an error of judgment which results in the loss of a wicket. It is a bad speculation to risk a wicket for a run, and the worst way to get a run is to run out one's self or one's partner.

Every batsman should jealously inspect the condition of the turf at his wicket when an over is concluded. Fragments of grass and turf should be removed, as likely to make the ball "jump" or "shoot"; on a soft wicket the marks made by the ball should be gently tapped flat with the end of the bat; if the turf is very soft, it is a mistake to hammer it with the back of the bat, as such a process makes a pulp of the ground in the immediate neighbourhood. The process of clearing the ground of *débris* is known to cricketers as "gardening."

All superfluous "flourish" is fatal to good "timing"; such flourish may appear very graceful to ladies and such spectators as do not understand the game, but to the cricketer's eye it is not only a meretricious, but a dangerous ornament, especially when the wicket is "tricky"; and this seems a convenient opportunity for saying a word on the different conditions of the ground, and their effect on batting and bowling, for in the natural course of events what is good for the bowler is bad for the batsman, and *vice versa*.

The condition of turf which the batsman loves—and the bowler dreads—is produced by a succession of hot days on a smooth, level, close-shaven ground, on which the grass is not too thick. On such a wicket the bowler is comparatively powerless, as he cannot make the ball break to any appreciable extent; and it comes true and fast, never more than about a stump's height from the ground, so that the batsman need not worry himself about eccentricities of curve, but can, and should, play boldly forward at every ball which is not a long-hop. A thunder-shower may change the whole course of procedure, if the sun shines hot and bright when the tempest has passed. At first the ground, wet on the surface and hard underneath, gives the bowler no help—especially as the ball is wet, and his footing precarious—while the ball "cuts through" the wet surface, and comes up to the bat fast and easy: but when the sun begins to tell, and the wet surface begins to cake, then the batsman's troubles begin, and the ball "breaks," "shoots," or "jumps," like an animate fiend, and sound cricket is almost impossible. Under such conditions the batsmen should run a few risks to score runs quickly (in cricketers' parlance, "to force the game") while they have the chance, and the judicious captain will send in his hard-hitters, with orders to get all the runs they can in the shortest time. It is hardly incorrect to say that a side, which might be expected to score 400 runs on such a wicket as was first described, would be well satisfied with 120 on a caked and crusted wicket, affected by rain and sun. A soft wicket, especially if the grass is still wet, is an easy one, from the batsman's point of view. It is of course hard to make the ball travel on the slow turf, and the bowler may be able to make it break considerably, but it comes so slowly from the pitch that the batsman has no difficulty in watching its eccentricities, and runs come surely, if slowly. Probably there is no condition which delights the bowler's heart more than the "crumbly"—when a wicket, once hard and true, has begun to wear, and has a broken, dusty surface. At such times the ball gets a good grip of the crumbling surface, and not only dances about like an acrobat, but dances so fast that scientific cricket is difficult. Here, again, the batsman must realise the condition of affairs, abandon cricket "by the book," and hit out (not indiscriminately, but fearlessly and boldly) on the smallest opportunity. On this, as on the "caked" wicket, hay must be made while the sun shines, but whereas the "caked" wicket may recover, for the "crumbled" there is no hope.

It may be useful to remind the reader at this point that the remarks made about the batsman apply equally, but in a reversed sense, to the bowler. What is good for one is bad for the other, and as the contest is *à l'outrance*, each should make himself acquainted with the tactics of the other, so as to meet, and, if possible, defeat them.

The following paper, by K. S. RANJITSINHJI, *embodies some valuable hints on various points, the views of so practical and admirable an exponent of the game naturally commanding the cricketer's attention and interest.*

Batting.—A good and easy position at the wickets is highly important; by "good" being meant such a position as experience has shown to give the batsman the best chance of combating the bowling; by "easy," a pose which is in no way stiff or constrained, but allows the player to move arms, legs, wrists, and the whole body with readiness and freedom. As to the placing of the feet, sufficient has been said before (p. 219), though it may not be amiss once more to emphasise the importance of keeping all the weight upon the right leg when preparing to receive the ball. Any weight upon the left must delay, if only for a moment, that rapid advance of it upon which, to a large extent, correct timing must depend. As to the hands, the left hand should grasp the bat so near the top that the ball of the thumb rests against it, and the right hand should be brought up as close as possible, provided that the left be allowed to twist round without catching the glove, when the batsman plays forward. There is nothing that cramps the style more than a grasp too low down the handle, and the best that can then be expected is a dogged defence.

It is impossible to lay down general rules as to when back-play or forward-play should be employed. On this question it is hopeless to expect complete agreement, and all that can be done is to state one's own practice, without any dogmatic assurance that it is necessarily the best for all. It seems to me that the school of cricket that was supreme, roughly speaking, from 1875 to 1885, was too sweeping in its advocacy of forward-play, and looked upon back-play as a mere device for defence, instead of being, what it may often be, a most rapid and effective way of scoring. Of course, to a fast ball well pitched up, say, dropping six yards from the wickets, it is almost necessary to play forward, but to a batsman blessed with a good eye and supple wrists, the extra two or three yards, through which a short-pitched ball may be watched, give a very great advantage. In playing forward, one is compelled to trust to the judgment formed from the flight of the ball before it pitches, and the bat itself obscures the sight of sudden developments.

In playing back, one must be prepared to draw the right foot back freely and promptly. The absolute fixity of that leg is undoubtedly a golden rule for the beginner, but it is a mistake for the experienced batsman to regard it as a law which may in no case be broken. Let him, if resolved to play back, slide the right leg towards the wicket, *not* putting it in front of the stumps, and always remember to keep the bat and play the ball, *in front* of that leg. This will save him from all danger of hitting his wicket.

The cut is a stroke which is certainly not used to the extent that it deserves, and this for two reasons. The first is the modern habit of letting balls go by upon the off side that seem at all dangerous, without the least attempt to hit them. The custom has grown almost to an absurd extent, and bowlers, encouraged by the timidity of the batsman, send down unharmed ball after ball which ought to yield plenty of runs. As a general rule one may say, "Never let an off-ball pass without striking at it, if it be within anything approaching to easy reach." If the batsman step well across, and get fairly over the ball, he has every chance to score, and if it should bump, he has complete control of the bat, and should be able to avoid a dangerous stroke. One may often see a batsman let off-ball after off-ball pass his wicket, and then, at last screwing up his courage, hit one, precisely similar, to the boundary, a feat which he might have performed earlier with much advantage to his side.

The second reason of its rarity is the small attention that the majority of batsmen pay to the placing of the ball in the stroke. Most men are content to cut it square, or almost square, direct to the hands of point or third-man, who find little difficulty in dealing with it; but if a little more care were taken, and the ball struck a fraction of a second later, it would be quite as easy to steer it safely through the slips.

In leg-hitting, one of the chief things to remember, when a ball is coming upon or outside the legs, is that a long innings is a very exhausting business, and that it is a waste of energy to smite furiously at the ball, when a slight change of its direction will secure the object equally well. There is no more effective stroke on the leg side than the "glide" or "glance." To make it, put the bat well forward, not square with the course of the ball, but at an angle that will vary with the direction in which the ball has to travel after the stroke so as to avoid a fieldsman. Just as the ball touches the bat, a quick turn of the wrist sweeps it well away behind the batsman, and, in the stroke, the whole body should pivot upon the right toe, as in the conclusion of a golfing drive.

Some men have the dangerous habit of jumping round to a leg ball, instead of swinging upon the right leg; it is dangerous, because, when bowler and wicket-keeper understand one another, the former may deliberately send a ball up to the dancer upon the leg-side, and put him in great peril of being stumped while his right foot is in the air.

The "pull" also is a stroke which every batsman should learn, as there is none more demoralising to the bowler, and none more necessary to have at one's command when the wicket is very bad, for naturally, as this stroke sends the ball where it has no right to go, it finds a place where a fieldsman has no right to be, and therefore scores. At the same time, though an important stroke, it is most dangerous, and requires to be conducted, as all others, under rule. One may assume that any first-class batsman can pull a very short-pitched ball with ease and safety, and place it where he likes, and much the same applies to the full-pitch, unless it be very fast, but the difficulty arises when the ball is of a fairly good length. One should *never* attempt to pull a half-volley, for the risk of being bowled is enormous, but if the ball be a little short of it, and a pull be necessary, throw the left foot right across the wicket, and sweep the bat round the toe, taking especial care to keep the ball down.

There is perhaps a danger that batsmen may get too orthodox, and throw away possible chances of winning a game by a refusal to take any risks at all. As a general rule, especially if the wicket be bad, and not likely to improve, it is well to hit at almost everything. Three fours in five minutes, and then retirement, will do more to help a side than remaining at the wickets for an hour for ten, even though the difficulties faced and surmounted may have been enormous; for there is very little chance on a bad pitch of the bowlers getting tired out. There is, however, one moment at which the average batsman is a little too much inclined to force the game, and that is when a lob-bowler is put on, but there is no more reason for contempt than there is for the panic that he occasionally inspires. To every ball well pitched up the batsman may fearlessly walk out, take it on the full-pitch, if possible, and place it along the ground for a single or a two. If the bowler pitch them short, one may step back and gently place them where seems best; the only dangerous method is that which tries to secure enormous hits off every over.

If, however, the batsman should wish to make a big drive (and this applies to all bowling, not merely to lobs), by all means let him jump in to meet the ball, so as to get it on the half-volley. Some advocate the "fast-footed" style of hitting, but though this makes the risk of missing the ball slightly less, it is almost impossible, as the ball is met on the rise, to prevent it from soaring. It may go over the fieldsman's head, but the risk of giving a chance is great. By jumping in to meet it, the batsman hits the ball at the moment when it pitches, and, the body being well forward, he is less likely to get under it.

A word may be useful as to fielding at those difficult places, point and short-slip. Slip should never take his eyes off the ball, from the moment the bowler starts his run to the time when the ball is safely held. He should not attempt to watch the batsman at all. Point, on the other hand, if the bowling be fast, does well to draw conclusions, from the way the batsman is framing, as to the direction of the hit. Both should make every experiment possible in order to find exactly what distance from the wicket suits them best to stand. Many a man finds out that at a particular spot he can take the ball with fair certainty, but that if he stand a yard or two nearer, or further away, he is almost helpless. It is well to remember that the ball can only be caught by the *fingers*, as near the palm as possible, and that it should never be allowed to hit the palm, for from there, in all probability, it will bound off to the ground. In any case, let the hand be beneath the ball, and never try to grasp it from the top, or sideways.

K. S. Ranjitsinhji.

The following paper by F. G. J. Ford (*of the Cambridge and Middlesex elevens, and of A. E. Stoddart's Australian eleven*) *on "Left-handed Batsmen," may here be appropriately introduced.*

Left-handed Batsmen—The appearance of a left-handed batsman is always an aggravation to the fielding side, and his dismissal is generally greeted with corresponding signs of gratification. As will be seen hereafter, it is not so much the number of runs he makes, as the general effect he produces on the *morale* of bowler and fieldsmen, which influences the state of the game. The incessant and necessary change of position whenever an odd number of runs is made by a hit is as trying to the temper as it is to the physique, and as demoralisation, more or less temporary, is likely to follow, it is perhaps fortunate that these sinister cricketers are not numerous: they are certainly not beloved of the opposition. Among individuals the trouble and responsibility are most severely felt by bowler and wicket-keeper. The latter always seems to find an increased difficulty at his post, as a proof of which it is not uncommon to find him standing back for the left-hander, but close to the wicket for his companion, as the whole game has now become "wrong-handed" for him, and many a nick from the left-hander's bat is allowed to pass, when the right-hander might not have escaped. Even short-slip and point sometimes find it less easy to follow the ball as it leaves his bat. But it is the bowler on whom the chief difficulty falls. A special mental effort is required of him, created by the task of ridding his side of the obnoxious player. He is troubled in various ways. Accustomed to pitch the ball persistently on the off-side for a right-handed man, he has now to suit himself to the altered conditions, and to pitch the ball on the leg-side. Easy enough for a ball or two, no doubt, but when singles are being rapidly made, and the bowler has constantly to alter his tactics and the direction of his bowling, length and pitch are apt to suffer, to the benefit of both batsmen. Many right-handed bowlers cannot bowl over the wicket to left-handers, and they are seen bowling round the wicket to the one batsman, but over to the other. A left-handed bowler especially dislikes bowling to his left-handed opponent. The reason is simple enough. His favourite break-back is eminently liable to be "pulled," and to avoid this he will generally be found bowling over the wicket to the left-handed instead of round—a practice which is quite novel to him, and correspondingly difficult. To the best bowlers these difficulties may be comparatively slight, but it is not uncommon for a good captain to take a left-handed bowler off when a left-handed batsman comes in, often to the advantage of the latter's colleague. It is to such constant yet necessary changes as these that the left-hander owes his advantage—changes which help to demoralise the man and spoil his bowling.

A left-handed batsman enjoys a reputation for certain strokes as being peculiarly his own. In particular, he seems to have many more driving strokes—not *cuts*—that range between third man and extra cover, than have right-handers, due perhaps to the fact that a ball breaking away to the off is better adapted to this class of stroke than a ball coming in from the off. As left-handers for the most part meet right-handed bowlers who break back, they naturally get more practice for such strokes, and develop their talent in that direction accordingly. For off-driving purposes a right-hander certainly prefers a left-handed bowler, who makes the ball go away from leg to off, and similarly the left-hander loves medium-paced, right-handed bowling, which he meets so frequently, that constant practice thereat has made these off-strokes a prominent feature of left-handed play.

One service in particular the left-hander is specially adapted to lend his side, and that is the checking of the successful attack of the slow right-hand bowler who bowls with a strong break from leg. The right-hander who steps in to drive takes two risks—the risk of a "miss-hit," and the risk of being stumped, the chance being generally quite simple; but the left-hander, if he misses the ball, has a second line of defence to fall back upon, viz., his legs, and if the ball does come to the wicket-keeper, the chance, being probably on the leg-side, is neither very visible nor very easy.

Hence it is not merely the left-hander's score, but his mere presence, that fieldsmen resent, and should his stay be a long one, he may materially alter the course of the game. No side is quite complete without such a batsman, if he be of good quality, though there are not many first-rate left-handers to be found. It is politic to send one in to bat, *cæteris paribus*, if it is desired to spin out time; and, on the other hand, he should not be sent in, even if a fast scorer, when time is precious, as many valuable moments are lost during the necessary chopping and changing of the field.

F. G. J. FORD.

Bowling—An excellent and instructive paper on the subject will shortly be introduced from the pen of T. Richardson, the famous Surrey and England fast bowler, who was also a member of A. E. Stoddart's Australian Eleven. The questions of "length," "break," and "accuracy," are there exhaustively dealt with, but as the author dwells mainly, and naturally, on fast bowling, a few lines on other points may not be out of place.

Bowlers are classified (1) according to their action, as "Under-hand," "Round-hand," and "Over-hand" (the word "arm" is often substituted for "hand"); and (2) according to their pace, as "Fast," "Medium-paced," or "Slow." In "under-hand" bowling the arm is not raised above an angle of 45° from the body; in "round-arm" it must not be lifted more than 90°; if the arm is raised higher the bowler is an "over-hand" bowler. At different times legislation restricted and limited the height to which the arm might be raised; at present there is no limit save that imposed by Laws 10 and 48A.

So little is seen nowadays of fast under-hand bowling that the batsman who suddenly encounters it, is often "surprised" out. The real difficulty lies, not in the bowling itself, but in the meeting of it; the eye, accustomed to look up towards an upraised arm, does not at once accommodate itself to the altered conditions which suddenly require it to look down; consequently the golden rule already given of "Watch the *ball* from the moment the bowler begins to run" will be found invaluable. It is rarely met with except in rustic matches, where some village champion often defeats cricketers of a high class; as a matter of fact, he "surprises" them out, or they get themselves out by their own carelessness, or by contempt for the bowling. Most fast under-hand bowlers bowl a large proportion of "sneaks"—balls which seem to cling persistently to the ground, sometimes with an awkward curl or break. The best way to play them is to watch them well, to "place" them if crooked, and to play out or hit out with the point of the bat close to the ground. If they only bound once, they seldom rise more than half-stump high, and may be played with the utmost ease; if they are "many-bounders" hard forward play will always meet the case, the only risk being that of being caught by the bowler, or mid-on, or mid-off; judicious "placing" on the leg-side will secure many a run.

No slow bowling should be played "fast-footed"; in other words, the batsman should always be ready to step or jump in towards the pitch of the ball, *unless it be on the off-side* (*see* p. 222), but when "lobs" are introduced the batsman can do as much with his feet as with his hands. "Lobs"—slow under-handed bowling—are invariably terrible to the timid batsman, partly because a certain amount of humiliation is, without any reason, attached to a failure to cope with them; yet good lobs require as much care and pains as any bowling. In pace they should vary with every ball, and both leg-break and break-back—especially the former—are to be looked for, but, as bowled nowadays, they have seldom a great deal of spin, and should be met on one absolute principle—"hit them on the long-hop or the full-pitch." In the former case the batsman keeps himself back and "places" or "pulls" them; in the latter he runs out, and—does the same thing. To play forward is dangerous; to hit them on the half-volley is delightful, but entails a certain amount of risk. But in no point of cricket is so much individuality displayed as in the playing of lobs.

It may seem strange to have included the last two paragraphs under the head of "Bowling," but instructions to the batsman are in an equal degree instructions to the bowler, if they be read aright; consequently it will be the lob-bowler's aim to keep so sound and true a length and such a pace, as to induce or compel the striker to play forward. Nothing however should be so disconcerting to a lob-bowler as to be consistently placed past the fieldsmen for a single. A half-volley hit to the boundary should inspire him with hope, but a series of well-placed singles should convince him that his efforts are vain.

It may be added that a lob-bowler who depends, as most of his kind do, on the leg-break requires but few fields on the off-side; point, short-slip, and third man may be compendiously represented by a sort of third man, about six yards from the wickets.

We may now pass to the classification of bowlers according to their pace, premising that the words "fast," "medium," and slow," refer to the *general* pace of the ball as delivered. A "fast" bowler may bowl one "slow" and one "medium" ball per over, and a slow bowler one "fast" and one "medium," but the pace of three balls in the over will be "fast" in the former case, and "slow" in the latter.

For all questions connected with fast bowling, and for many questions associated with medium and slow, the reader is referred to the following paper by TOM RICHARDSON.

Fast Bowling—The fine batting and good wickets of the present day are doubtless the cause of the improved condition of modern bowling, but the acquisition of the art demands not only long and patient training, but a physical capacity and natural aptitude such as are not given to every man. Further than this, nerve, good temper, and pluck are quite indispensable. It is a question whether he who bowls well as a boy also bowls well as a man, as the attendant strain is certainly severe, but the writer certainly developed in youth some of the break and spin which have helped him to his later successes.

The first thing to learn is to bowl straight and to bowl a good length, and this power is probably natural and not acquired, though nature requires the assistance of perpetual practice. But the bowler, whether born or made, should cultivate or acquire a high action and a good swing of arm and body, as such a delivery will make the ball rise quickly and perpendicularly from the pitch; but the action must at all costs be easy and free, qualities which neither imitation nor education must allow to disappear.

For early practice nothing is better than to bowl, the arm raised as high as possible without strain, at a disc of paper, the size of a crown-piece, placed at the proper distance from the wicket. It is impossible to state exactly what this distance is, as it depends on the pace of the bowler and the nature of the wicket, to say nothing of the height and play of the batsman; but on a fast true wicket the bowler, if he be a fast bowler, should try to pitch the ball about four to five yards from the popping crease, *not less*, for a batsman of about 5 ft. 10 in. in height, the pitch being shorter or longer according as the batsman is tall or short, but to bowl, as some men do, about six or seven yards from the crease is to bowl with the idea of hurting, or at least frightening the batsman, which is contrary to the spirit of the game. If the wicket is slow or sticky the ball may be pitched at least a yard further up, as the rise is more abrupt. In the case of a slow or medium-pace bowler the ball should be pitched further up than it is by a fast bowler, to prevent the batsman from having time to step back and pull the ball.

Accuracy and length are the essentials of bowling, and till they are acquired break may be left alone, but for the first-class bowler a combination of the three things is absolutely necessary; so it is now assumed that the first two have been fairly perfected, and that the question of break and spin remains.

Break and Spin—A ball is said to break when, on touching the ground, it deviates sharply from its original line of flight. When it is delivered by a right-hand bowler and twists from the off to the leg, it is said to "break back"; when from leg to off, it "breaks from leg"; but a left-handed bowler's "break-back" twists, for a right-handed batsman, from leg to off. It will be observed also that the ball, delivered round the wicket, may, in its natural line of flight, which is not parallel to the line of the wickets, hit the stumps even if it does not pitch on a line drawn from wicket to wicket. This ball is said to "go with the arm," and a slight amount of leg-break is often combined with it.

A ball is said to have "spin" on it when it gains an acceleration of pace, not necessarily a variation of direction, on touching the ground. Such "spin" is generally a natural gift, due to a practically unknown peculiarity of delivery, and there are probably few men who can make any given ball spin at will.

"Break" is occasionally natural, but most frequently acquired, and it is caused by giving rotation to the ball as it leaves the fingers, the break-back being the most easy to acquire. In the following remarks the bowler is supposed to be right-handed. To make the ball break back, it must be made to rotate from left to right, which is in most cases effected by holding the ball with the fore-finger round the seam; at the moment of delivery this finger and the wrist turn outwards, *i.e.*, from left to right, so that the back of the hand is downwards after the ball has been released. Some men put this break on with the middle finger; indeed every bowler finds out his own best method, but the foregoing description will be a useful preliminary hint.

To make the ball break from leg, it must be held more in the palm of the hand, and the rotation must be from right to left. The third and little fingers produce the rotation and the hand turns over with the ball, the back of the hand being now uppermost. It may be added that accuracy with the leg-break is very hard to acquire.

It is most important that a bowler should be able to vary his pace, unobserved by the batsman. To do this, the action and run must be the same as before, but the ball should be allowed to drop back from the fingers into the palm, and the shoulder-blade restrained. The result will be a slower ball, but it must be tossed a little higher in the air and pitched rather farther up to complete the deception and induce the batsman to play forward to it and mistime it. This art of variation of pace is not easily acquired, but it is invaluable, especially when the batsman, having made a fine drive, can be induced to try to repeat the stroke on the deceptive slow.

The following are different balls which the fast bowler should have at his command.

(i.) The good-length ball, already explained.

(ii.) A very fast, short-length ball, just on the off-stump, or just outside it, often tempts the batsman to hit too hard at it, and, mistiming it, to hit a catch to the slips or wicket-keeper. Care should be taken not to bowl such a ball at the batsman's body.

(iii.) The "yorker" is most useful. Its exact pitch varies according to the batsman's height, but it may be said, generally, to pitch between the creases. No man can score off it with any certainty, though to the good batsman it presents no special terrors. Its chief merit is that it may catch him off his guard for the moment, with disastrous results. It is a capital ball to give a batsman when first he comes in, but as it entails special exertion it should only be bowled as a variation, in which its chief merit consists, and not continuously. Two variations of the "yorker" demand a word; cricketers know them as "the curling yorker" and the "running-away ball." Both of these curl in the air before touching the ground, the first from the off, the second from leg. The former occurs more frequently with a cross wind, the second when the wind is directly against the bowler. No bowler, it may be asserted, can bowl either ball at will, though base-ball "pitchers," who "chuck" or throw the ball, have ample command over the curve, while to some bowlers the "curl in the air," however produced, is natural; yet it may be positively stated that no bowler can make any given ball take this peculiar flight. If, however, the bowler, bowling with a cross or head wind, finds that a ball, well pitched up, seems to curve in the air, he should pursue his advantage, as such a ball is most perplexing to the batsman.

(iv.) The "full-toss," or "full-pitch," pitches right on the wicket, and is useful as a variation to keep the batsman on the alert and prevent him from settling down.

When once a batsman is "set," the bowler must try every device in his power, the head aiding the hand; least of all must he lose heart. No wicket is impregnable, and he must storm at the fortress till he brings about a capitulation, remembering for his comfort that many a bad ball gets a wicket. The bowler should at all times see that his fieldsmen are properly placed, and especially, if he be a fast bowler, short-slip and cover-slip; the former about three yards deeper than the wicket-keeper (who is supposed to be standing back), and a yard to his right; cover-slip is about a yard deeper than short-slip and a yard to his right. If a batsman is known to "cut" finely, third man may well field on the boundary, especially if the ground is hard.

To get the full value out of the off-break, the fast bowler especially should bowl over the wicket, but he should train himself to bowl on either side, as a variety; indeed many fast bowlers always bowl round the wicket to a left-handed batsman. Throughout this paper, it should be noted, the writer has had right-handed men in his mind.

The bowling of the present day is largely affected by the perfect wickets now provided, this perfection accounting in the main for the large scoring. They render the bowler's, and especially the fast bowler's, task hard indeed. Mere straightness, in consequence, is almost useless unless the bowler has some variations at his command. On the extraordinarily hard, true wickets which prevail in Australia, the fast bowler cannot be said to be a great success. He has to adapt himself to the changed conditions and bowl a much shorter length, owing to the greater speed with which the ball travels on to the bat, making what would be a good-length ball in England almost a half-volley, or at any rate one that lends itself to be driven. In England it is a hard task to bowl out good batsmen, but in Australia that task becomes herculean.

The paucity of really good bowlers compared with the number of first-class batsmen is a matter for surprise and regret. The reason is not far to seek, and may be found in the fact that much more pleasure is derived from learning to bat than to bowl, and in the case of amateurs the ball is almost neglected. With regard to professionals the fault lies not so much in the aspirants themselves as in the habit which prevails in many counties of having a "Colts' match" early in the year, when the weather is cold and the young players out of practice. Then, the match being over, and no one, as is natural, having distinguished himself, the "colts" are relegated to obscurity. The county which looks to the future, which keeps an eye on its recruits, which subsidises them by retaining them as "ground bowlers," and which supports a well-organised "second eleven," will surely reap its reward.

T. RICHARDSON.

Medium and Slow Bowling—The medium-paced bowler is a bowler of varied paces, a bowler who, in cricket language, "mixes them," that is, seldom bowls two consecutive balls of identical pace and length. If, however, he detects a weak spot in the batsman's defence, if he sees that a ball of a particular length and pace puzzles and perplexes him, he should give him that ball at least once an over, following it up with something of an entirely different nature, either much faster or much slower, but the alteration in pace must be concealed, as far as possible, at the moment of delivery. A slower ball may be delivered and its pace concealed by checking the arm at the instant before delivery; a fast ball by swinging the arm further back, the pace of the run and the usual action being kept as far as possible. Needless to say, the variations of pace must not follow a stereotyped sequence of order. It is a good variation to deliver the ball with the arm raised sometimes as high as possible, sometimes almost at a right angle with the body. If the bowler can make the ball break both ways, he would of course use the two breaks at different intervals, and it is well to vary the *amount* as well as the character of the break. To a new batsman the first few balls may well be bowled without any break at all; he may imagine that in the existing condition of the wicket the bowler cannot make the ball break, and an unexpected "break-back" may secure his wicket. A very useful ball, from the slow bowler's point of view, follows two or three break-backs which have pitched, at a good length, a few inches outside the off-stump. It should pitch at about the same length, have no break, and be somewhat faster, so as to conceal the absence of break; if the batsman fails to realise the situation, a catch at the wicket or in the slips is very likely to follow. In fact, to lay down a general maxim, it is good to make the batsman think that the bowler is mechanical and to induce him to be mechanical too. This effected, an unexpected motion on the part of the bowling-machine may have a very surprising result on the batting-machine. But the contest is one of brain *versus* brain, as well as of hand *versus* hand, and the better man, for the time being, will win. An important factor in the duel is the temperament of the contestants; there is the steady bowler as well as the steady batsman; the brilliant batsman finds his counterpart in the brilliant bowler. When two of the former type are in opposition, things rule dull for the spectators; when brilliancy meets brilliancy the whole game glows. Indeed, bowlers may be put, generally, into two classes: firstly, those who "pound away" on the principle that, "if you knock at the door long enough, some one is sure to open it;" secondly, those who are not capable of such machine-like regularity, but who make up for the want of it by an occasional flash of inspiration, by a ball that even the best batsman cannot meet. One essential every bowler who has any pretensions to the name must possess—a perfectly equable temper. It is desperately trying to have laid a trap for the batsman, to have lured him on to ruin, and to have led him to make the stroke that should have been fatal, and then to see the ball drop out of the fieldsman's hands; but it is at this moment that the philosopher must prevail over the man. No one is more mortified or more sad when a catch is missed than the erring catcher, but when the bowler adds to his mortification by a hasty exclamation of disgust, that fieldsman is spoilt for the day.

It is often very useful to change ends and to change from one side of the wicket to the other. The former variation is subject to the approval of the captain, but the latter should always be tried when batsmen are well set; consequently every bowler should accustom himself to bowl on either side of the wicket. Again, when the bowler has a good command of the ball and the break, no device is more successful than to bowl several balls with a fair amount of break, and another with just a little more twist; the ball that gets the wicket is the ball that just gets past the bat and does not just get past the wicket; hence a very little additional break may have the desired effect. If, however, the wicket is "caked" or "crumbled" (*see* p. 227), a change—for a "break-back" bowler—from "over" to "round" the wicket is often useful, as the ball is not so likely to miss both bat and wicket.

One maxim the slow bowler, and indeed the medium bowler, should lay to heart, viz., that a short-length ball seldom bowls a man, but that an over-pitched ball is often fatal, and that a series of half-volleys is more likely to succeed than a series of long-hops.

Above all things, a scrupulously fair delivery should be cultivated, free from all taint of suspicion of "throwing." To define the difference between throwing and bowling is most difficult, but the accompanying plates may supply a clue,

FIG. 11*a*.

as they are reproduced from photographs specially taken.

In Fig. 11*a* a "fair" delivery is shown; the arm is almost straight and swings with the body; in Fig. 11*b* it is bent at the elbow, and the elbow, instead of following the swing of the arm, is stopped at the body with a jerk, which

FIG. 11*b*.

stoppage and jerk are, in the writer's opinion, the essential points of a throw. It is right to add that what seems a throw to one man seems perfectly fair to another, and that bowling which seems unfair from one point of view (*e.g.*, from the side or back of the bowler) may seem perfectly fair from another, the batsman, strange to say, having often the worst chance of judging, owing to the "fore-shortening" of the arm.

It is most important that the bowler, directly he has delivered the ball, should hurry back to his wicket—always supposing that he is not called upon to field the ball or make a catch—so as to receive the ball when thrown up by the fieldsman, being careful to keep the wicket between the fieldsman and himself. With this in view all bowlers should practise how to "take" the ball and "put the wicket down" quickly and smartly. As the bowler's hands are unprotected, this may imply some hard knocks, and if the bowler knows that the fieldsmen are "backing up," he may, to save his fingers, let a hard throw go by, unless there is a chance of getting a wicket, for which purpose he must take any and every risk of being hurt.

An opportunity of running a man out under Law 35 occurs but seldom, but it may be watched for, and there is nothing unsportsmanlike—as some people hold—in exacting one's strict rights, to say nothing of the fact that the batsman who backs up too soon is taking an advantage of the bowler to which he is not entitled.

Finally, the bowler should not forget that he

has ten men to support him, and that there are more ways of getting a batsman out than clean bowling him. A hard hitter may be tempted to hit a half-volley into long-field's hands, or, in

FIG. 12.

trying his favourite drive, to mistime or miss-hit the ball. A man may have a special stroke for a particular ball; it is often useful to tempt him to try this stroke early in his innings, and before he is well set. But as the devices of the bowler are best learned by experience, the beginner will gradually acquire them for himself, but he should early accustom himself to note the style of the opposing batsman and to observe which balls seem to puzzle him, and which balls he plays or hits with ease.

Fielding—It is not given to every man to be a brilliant fieldsman, but as good fielding, both catching and "ground-fielding," is essential to any one who has even second-class pretensions, it should be carefully practised; there is no better practice than for four or five men to go out and to take it in turns to hit the ball either in the air or along the ground to each other. It is well to take out several balls, and to vary the distance between striker and fieldsman. It will soon be found that nerve and courage are necessary as well as agility and alacrity, and that the art of catching can be largely improved by practice. Nerve, activity, and accuracy are therefore essential—nerve for facing a hard hit, activity for getting to the proper place to stop it, and accuracy for returning it hard and straight to the bowler or wicket-keeper.

Catching—This should be practised at all distances from the striker, in every possible position relative to him, with both hands together, and with right and left separately. The fieldsman should carefully watch the batsman, as his motions generally give a clue to the direction of the hit; but short-slip and cover-slip should watch the bowler, as the ball when it comes to those places is seldom sent there intentionally, and the batsman's movements give no hint. No rules can be given for sharp, low hits to fieldsmen standing from seven to thirty yards from the wicket; each man will find out by observation and practice what method is easiest for himself, but a one-handed catch may well be received on the middle joint of the middle finger, when the other fingers will form a sort of cage to retain the ball; other men prefer to take it on the lowest joint. Again, it is sometimes useful with a hard-hit catch, far from the body, to try to break its force by knocking it up a little way into the air, but there is a distinct risk attaching to this process, unless practice has made the fieldsman an adept at it, and the catching of hard hits, which come to the hands like a flash of lightning, is more a matter of instinct than of instruction. Fig. 12 is a good illustration of a sharp, low catch as it comes to point or slip. In all catches it should be remembered that the ball should be allowed to strike the hand, which should then give with it slightly so as to break the force of its impact. Any "grabbing" at the ball is almost invariably fatal and is likely to knock the ball away. Long fingers and a lissom wrist are a great adjunct to good catching.

If the ball is hit high, the first thing is to

FIG. 13*a*.

judge the true course of its flight and the place of its descent, as naturally it seldom singles out the fieldsman. This "judging" must be instinctive and instantaneous, and must be followed by a rapid run to the place of descent, the fieldsman, if possible, getting to the place and steadying himself for the catch, which, if all goes satisfactorily, will be effected as in Fig. 13*a*, where the fieldsman has just caught the ball in the long-field. The sides of the hands are close together, thumbs uppermost, forming a sort of cup, and the wrists held close to the body so that the ball may be "hugged" (Law 22) if it jumps out of the "cup." The wrists should be allowed to give a little as soon as the ball is felt. Fig. 13*b* shows a one-handed catch in the long-field.

All these preliminaries are only occasionally possible, so the cricketer must accustom himself to rushing at catches at all sorts of distances from him and on all sides of him, holding them as best he can; and if there is any one maxim which should be writ large in his mind it is "Try for every ball hit towards you, whether in the air or along the ground." Many a wonderful catch has been made which the fieldsman never thought he could even reach, still less hold, but which he tried to reach and catch. Occasionally a few runs may thus be lost, but the chance of a wicket is worth a risk in runs, and even if the catch does not come off the fieldsman will have won the bowler's heart. When a catch is missed—as many catches are—the next thing to do is not to tear one's hair, but to throw the ball in; a man is occasionally run out by a sharp return from a missed catch; anyhow, the "hair-tearing" can wait. One more hint, "Never use one hand for a catch when both can *easily* be got to the right place"; but if a catch is nearly at arm's length from the body, it is sometimes easier to take it with one hand than with two. Experience is the only guide.

Ground-Fielding—If a ball is hit along the ground the first thing to be done is to stop it; but mere "stopping" is not sufficient; it should be stopped, and held, and thrown in without an instant's delay to bowler or wicket-keeper. The hand is the proper member to stop the ball with, but as the hand may be deceived, a second line of defence should be provided, viz. the legs. Hence, when possible, the fieldsman should stand full face towards the line of the ball, heels together—this is most important—and hands together in front of the heels. In short, the ball must be stopped at all hazards. But mere stopping is not always enough. If the ball is only moving towards the fieldsman at a moderate speed, and he remains stationary, it is clear that the batsman may have time to get a run, to avert which the fieldsman must not await, but meet the ball, dashing in at full speed, picking it up clean, and throwing it in. One attempt will convince the novice of the difficulty of doing all this when the ball is moving slowly. Augment the pace, and every difficulty is many times multiplied. The moral is, "Practise!" The beginner should, however, be warned against trying to be brilliant when, on the face of it, he can save the run without dashing in, as brilliant fieldsmen often lose runs by

FIG. 13*b*.

dashing at the ball and missing it, when "running" was the last thought in the batsmen's minds.

Throwing—Too high a value cannot be set on hard and accurate throwing, in which point many English fieldsmen, perhaps owing to the effect of a wet and chilly climate on the necessary muscles, are often deficient. The ideal throw comes into the wicket-keeper's or bowler's hands about six inches above the wicket; from a distance of thirty yards or less it should go straight from hand to hand; from longer distances it should be thrown on to the ground, but so as to be a *long-hop* to the receiver; any other "length" is very difficult to handle. From long distances it is a waste of strength to throw a ball high—a low, skimming throw is far more useful, and reaches the wicket quicker. The ball should be thrown, too, directly it is fairly in the hand, as a long preliminary "wind-up" is wasted time; the batsman, unable at once to judge the accuracy of the throw, dare not start when it is seen to be on its way. It is very useful to be able to hit the wicket, but only rarely should the experiment be tried. If the wicket-keeper knows his business, the time wasted in catching the ball and breaking the wicket is infinitesimal; if, however, time is very precious, the fieldsman may throw at the *top*, and the top only, of the stumps. Especial care should be taken to spare the bowler's fingers as much as possible.

A cricketer should be able to take any place in the field to which the captain may ask him to go, but after some experience he will probably find that some particular position suits him best, and to that place he should go whenever he has the opportunity. In case either bowler or wicket-keeper should miss the ball, or the ball go wide of him, at least two fieldsmen should be behind him to save "overthrows"; nothing shows want of organisation so much as bad "backing up"—a term, by the way, which is also used when a fieldsman passes the ball on from a throw from the deep-field which is too long for the original fieldsman's powers.

No special directions seem needed for special places in the field; some men will find that their quickness qualifies them for positions near the wicket, others that their powers of throwing and of judging long hits makes them good out-fielders, but for short-slip and cover-slip a few hints may be useful, as, especially to fast bowling, they are the most important men on the side, not excepting the wicket-keeper. From these two, then, especial vigilance is demanded; they must watch the ball—not the batsman, as other fielders should—from the moment the bowler begins to run, stooping down, hands to the front ready for action, in the crouching position of the wicket-keeper. Quickness of hand is more important to them than quickness of foot, and they should be able to catch well with either hand. No place in the field is more delightful or more difficult.

Wicket-Keeping—*The following paper by* M. C. KEMP (*Harrow, Oxford and Kent*) *well sums up the duties of this most important post, and should be carefully studied by those who wish to qualify for the arduous and thankless task.*

The Wicket-Keeper—No post, except the bowler's, is more important and more responsible than the wicket-keeper's, and by the end of the season he will generally have dismissed more of his opponents than any other two fieldsmen, with the possible exception of short-slip. To a keen and competent cricketer the charms of the position are many; the wicket-keeper is incessantly on the alert, he enjoys the finest view of the game, he can appreciate better than any one else the delicacies of the bowler's and batsman's art, and he can tell, as no one else can, whether the fieldsmen are in their right places. Hence it is the ideal place for the captain, and even if the two offices cannot be combined, the wise captain will generally consult his wicket-keeper as to any changes of bowling and the progress of the game generally. A wicket-keeper must be prepared to take some painful knocks; balls are hard and hands are soft. It is most difficult to judge the exact course of the ball, especially if it be deflected; a blow on the shin, rib, knee, or top of the thumb is both painful and disconcerting; batsmen do not always get out of the way of a rising ball in time to let the wicket-keeper do the same, and fieldsmen often throw the ball in most erratically. Still, as every team must have a wicket-keeper, and no cricketer must shirk a few hard knocks, every aspirant should try whether he possesses the needful quickness and accuracy of hand and eye.

The wicket-keeper's first duty is to get the batsman out, his second—subsidiary to the first, but quite important—to save runs in the shape of byes. Except when the bowling is remarkably fast, the skilful wicket-keeper may attain both ends by standing close up to the stumps, but to very fast bowling it is generally considered

FIG. 14.

advisable to stand about ten yards behind the the wicket, sacrificing the chance—which seldom occurs with really fast bowling—of stumping a man. When standing up, he should be so close to the wicket that he can easily touch it with his hands; his body should be mainly on the off-side, where most of the chances come, but his left leg should be just outside the leg stump, so as to stop any ball which may just miss it. If the ball is seen to be coming outside the batsman's legs, he must jump across like lightning, knees together, and hands at the height at which the ball may be estimated to come, as the batsman's body prevents a consecutive view of it. Some wicket-keepers stand entirely on the off-side, when they can implicitly trust the bowler's accuracy. The body must be bent—the wicket-keeper must stoop to conquer—till the eyes are a little higher than the wicket. The hands should be spread out, with the palms forward and well pressed back, so that the finger tips may be spared injury as far as possible. When the batsman plays forward there is always a chance that he will lift his right toe, if only for an instant, hence the wicket-keeper, so as to lose no time, must take the ball directly it passes the wicket and bring it like lightning up to the bails, or the precious moment may be lost. The bails should not be knocked off unnecessarily, but it is better to do so too often than too seldom. If the batsman touches the ball and also leaves his ground, the wicket-keeper must not neglect to break the wicket even though he has caught the ball, as the umpire may fail to hear or see the catch, and in that case "the second string to the bow" is invaluable. There is no chance of a "stump-out" if the batsman plays back [*see* BACK-PLAY, p. 221], hence the wicket-keeper will then be wise to take the ball well behind the wicket, which will give him a better chance of following its course and of saving his hands. He must learn to stand perfectly firm, never flinching except when a ball rises suddenly. When learning, a long-stop gives confidence, but he should be gradually dispensed with; leg-balls may be left severely alone by the beginner. If the hands get badly bruised, they should be rested at once, and above all things, after a long innings, they should be rubbed, while still warm, with St. Jacob's Oil or Elliman's Embrocation, which will prevent any bruises or soreness from becoming permanent. Appeals to the umpire should be made as seldom as possible, but then quickly and confidently, and only when the wicket-keeper is sure, or nearly sure, of the answer "Out!" The left hand should be well practised in catching and "grabbing" at balls, for which purpose Fives is an admirable exercise. When the ball is thrown in from the field the wicket-keeper should always stand so that the wicket is between him and the thrower, and the ball, as in stumping, should be taken, unless it is coming very slowly, *after* it has passed the wicket. Chances come so thickly to the wicket-keeper that the best men miss many, hence occasional failure must not produce discouragement, for coolness in spite of mistakes often enables a man to retrieve his blunders. If two men are running for a catch, the wicket-keeper should call out loudly, distinctly, and promptly, the name—nothing more—of the man who has, in his opinion, the best chance of securing it. Most wicket-keepers nowadays make their gloves sticky by artificial means, the better to retain the ball, to such an extent that a man has been seen to lift a ball off the ground without grasping it. Whether this is right or not, from a moral point of view, is a moot question, but it is generally done and no objections are raised. If, however, the gloves are *too* sticky the bowler will complain when he finds that the ball will not readily leave his hand. The practice is useful to wicket-keeping, but does not conduce to good bowling.

Too much stress cannot be laid on the necessity of taking care of the hands. No man who has to keep wicket in first-class cricket should risk his fingers by taking the same place in other matches. India-rubber finger-stalls worn inside the gloves are a great protection, both from bruise and dislocation, but some men hold that they interfere too much with the freedom of the fingers' action. Good pads are essential, but, if a bad bruise occurs on the leg, a batting-glove, inside the pad, is a very useful protection; and another useful guard is to have a thick piece of padding sown on to the inside of the pad, so as to protect the inside of the right knee—a most vulnerable point. Yet one more hint: if the ball is so badly thrown up—as it often will be—that it will reach the wicket-keeper on the "half-volley," he will find it almost impossible, or certainly very difficult, to handle it; as a last resort, he should let it hit his legs (knees and heels together), and so place himself that it may bound from his pads to the wicket. Finally, the wicket-keeper should always return the ball to the bowler as a gentle catch or long-hop; the bowler is bearing the burden and heat of the day, and it is sheer cruelty and bad policy to increase his labours by a crooked return, or a half-volley.

If the wicket-keeper or bowler has to run after the ball, the nearest fieldsman should at once hurry to the deserted wicket, in case there may be a chance of running a man out.

M. C. KEMP.

The Captain—As the captain who is chosen to manage a side in the field has, almost invariably, a voice in its selection, the two questions—management and selection—are here included under the same head.

The two best bowlers available should be chosen first, as attack is more important than defence. Next comes the best wicket-keeper who can be secured, and after them the three or four best batsmen—always supposing that they are good "fields"; for it must not be forgotten that a fine field always saves runs, though a fine batsman frequently fails to get them. This leaves five places to be filled up; two, at least, must be *good* change bowlers, who can also bat fairly well, and the last three vacancies may be given to men who can bat well and field well, regardless of their bowling powers; though probably one at least can "go on" at a pinch. When there is any doubt, a sure fieldsman who can bat fairly well should be selected over the head of a better batsman who is known to field badly, but it is no good sacrificing batting to moderate bowling. "If you can't win with four good bowlers, you can't win at all," is a recognised axiom. A lob-bowler is a useful addition to a side. So much for the composition of the team, which contains two bowlers, selected for their bowling only, and a wicket-keeper chosen merely to fill that post; two men who bat fairly and bowl fairly, the rest being all respectable fieldsmen, and some of them brilliant batsmen. With a side so composed the captain need not be afraid "to speak with his enemies in the gate."

Some remarks on the captain's duties preliminary to the call of "Play!" will be found on p. 216; but if he wins the toss, he has first to make up his mind whether he will send in his own side or his adversaries. The latter policy is rarely good. To take first innings implies that the ingoing side has the wicket when fresh, and that the other will have to play the fourth innings when the turf will be more or less cut up—a serious disavantage. To send the other side to the wickets implies that the captain is sure—nothing short of "sure"—that the ground will improve with time, and during the continuance of the game. The man who can feel thus positive as to his weather-wisdom has not yet been born; hence the writer's advice, notwithstanding what others may say, is, "Go in *always*, if you are lucky enough to win the toss." Critics may be wise after the event, but that means nothing. Special circumstances, too, may alter cases, but there are few occasions when it can possibly be a foreseen disadvantage to bat first.

In making out the "order of going in," the best batsmen should be sent in early, but a young player, a "colt," who is being played as a batsman, may well be sent in first, before the bowlers have got into their swing, as a good beginning will banish all nervousness. If two men are of equal merit, the one who can bowl should go in before the other, so as to give him a chance of a rest if he makes a long innings. The last few men, the "tail," may bat in a descending order of merit. The captain should always be on the spot, in case any point of strategy requires his presence, especially if his side goes in late in the day, and a wicket falls just before time, in which case it may be advisable to send in an inferior batsman in the waning light, so as to avoid, if possible, the loss of a more valuable wicket. But on this point experience—and all captains should be experienced—is the best guide. A left-hander may well be sent in early, as he is likely to destroy the equanimity of the field if he makes a long stay. Slow scorers, again, may be sent in before hard-hitters, if time is of no importance, but if the "game has to be forced," the hitters must have precedence, especially if rain has fallen on a hard wicket, and is followed by bright sunshine. Such a condition of things always implies a "caked" wicket in the early future, and the hitters must make their runs while the sun shines, but before it has ruined the wicket. If time is precious, a left-hander should not be sent in, as the incessant changes in the field waste time. The captain should see that a heavy roller is not used after rain, if its weight is likely to bring the water to the surface.

The captain's task is more arduous, and more severely criticised, when his side is fielding. He must of course assign to his men the positions which are known to suit them best, though these may be varied as the game proceeds. He should be careful to see that no man has an unnecessarily long journey between the overs, and that his bowlers are not required to run about in the field after their spell of bowling. A bowler must be spared all unnecessary exertion. All changes in the position of the fieldsmen should be made by the captain, but only after consultation with the bowler, or at his suggestion, if approved; but the captain of an eleven should be, like the captain of a man-of-war, an absolute autocrat. At the same time, he should so far veil his despotism as to consult with the bowler occasionally, and with the wicket-keeper always—or nearly always—as to any change of bowling which events have not rendered obvious. He must watch the score, and remember that it is generally better policy to change his bowling too often than too seldom, and that when one of the original, and presumably best bowlers has been removed, it is better to reinstate him as soon as possible, than to try another bowler, who is inferior. If the principle may be worked into a maxim, that maxim would run, "Trust to your best bowlers to get the wickets, and regard the others as mere reliefs"; at the same time, the willing horse must not be worked to death, and frequent but short rests will help the captain to make the most of his attack.

When two batsmen are well set, the captain's power of resource is tested to its uttermost; if a separation seems hopeless, he should try every bowler, however inferior, in turn, hoping that a stroke of luck may break up the partnership. This done, the best bowlers should be called to the attack once more, as if the inferior, though successful, bowler is allowed to continue, the newcomer will probably "get his eye in," and defy the most dangerous assault. A bowler sometimes sends down a succession of "maidens." Unless the batsman's defence is seriously taxed, this bowler should be changed; he is only helping the batsman to get set; but on this point the wicket-keeper should always be consulted, as he can see better than any one else if the batsman is really at his ease or not.

The captain should field near the wicket—if he can keep wicket, so much the better for his side—and he must set his men an example of hard work and cool temper; for the captain who shows signs of ill-humour, however slight, at any blunder on the part of his men, will never pull them together in the hour of distress. A word of sympathy with the man who has just missed a catch will restore the erring one's peace of mind, which a hasty ejaculation would have banished for the rest of the innings. To be a disciplinarian is one thing, to be a martinet is another; and this the captain need seldom be.

It would be easy to write for ever on the various qualifications required in a captain, and the various contingencies which may call for special qualities. The hints here given must be sufficient, with the *addendum* that only a cricketer of some experience should accept the post, unless it is forced upon him, and that only experience in the field and observation from the pavilion can teach him his multifarious duties.

The Umpires—The ideal umpire must be a man of wide experience, quick of eye, and prompt in decision. Needless to say, he must know the laws of the game thoroughly. The best umpires are generally first-class professionals, who have retired from active service and are known to be men of the highest integrity.

Umpires have no light task: they are the first to enter the field and the last to leave it; their attention is strained throughout to the uttermost; they get practically no rest, as probably one-half of the players do, except the interval for luncheon; and the points on which an instantaneous decision is necessary are sometimes most delicate, and a moment's inattention, resulting in a wrong decision, may have a very serious effect on the match. Nothing, then, is so wrong—to the writer's way of thinking, so suicidal—as an incessant series of appeals, or, worse still, an expression of ill-temper, when batsman or fieldsman is dissatisfied with the decision of a hard-worked official, who is presumably doing his very best to be impartial and accurate. Only those who have filled the post, however unimportant the match, can fully sympathise with its difficulties.

For the umpires' duties Laws 43–53 should be studied, and the "Instructions to Umpires," issued by the M.C.C., who also appoint the umpires for each match in the County Championship, each county nominating an umpire, who, however, is not allowed to officiate in a match in which that county takes part.

Five minutes before play begins the umpires go out to the wickets, taking the ball and bails with them. Their positions are described on p. 216; their first duty will be to give the batsman "guard" or "block" (*see* p. 217), standing for the purpose wherever the latter wishes. As the bowler delivers the ball, the umpire must stand so that he can see clearly down the line of the wickets, and watch the bowler's foot and hand (as best he can), in case he delivers a "no-ball." All doubtful catches will be referred to him; if he is unable to give a decision he must appeal to his colleague; if neither can decide, "the existing state of things continues," *i.e.*, the striker remains at the wicket. If the umpire is not *perfectly sure* that the batsman is out, he must give the verdict in his favour. He will be most frequently appealed to for a catch by the wicket-keeper, often the slightest touch on the edge of the bat, and in this case most good umpires agree that the eye must be convinced as well as the ear, for there are many things which may cause a "click" which *sounds* like the contact of bat and ball.

All cases of "leg-before," the hardest of all, come before the bowler's umpire, who must be absolutely convinced that Law 24 has been infringed before ordering the batsman out. It should be remembered that if the ball hit the leg first and the bat afterwards, the striker is out, provided that the ball has fulfilled the conditions required by Law 24. In deciding the question of "the fitness of the ground" (Law 43), the turf should be in a condition fair both to batsman and bowler, and the best umpires consider the ground fit for play after rain if the pressure of the foot brings no water to the surface of the wicket, and if the bowlers can get a footing.

The umpire at the striker's end has practically to decide only on a "stump-out," or "run-out," but as his colleague may appeal to him at any moment, he must never relax his vigilance.

Umpires have a code of signals by which they communicate with the scorers. Thus, a bye is signalled by holding up the hand; a leg-bye by touching or lifting the leg; a boundary-hit by waving one arm horizontally; and a wide by waving both. A no-ball and a short run, being loudly called, require no signal. The scorer answers and acknowledges signals by holding up his hand.

At every cessation of play the umpires should bring the bails away with them; at the end of the match, or of the day's play, they bring the stumps also; hence "to draw the stumps" means "to stop play for the day."

They should be careful to call wides and no-balls clearly and promptly; when a wide is only signalled the non-striker does not know whether it is a wide or not, and may consequently be at a loss whether to run a bye or not.

The Scorers—Each side usually provides its own scorer, and the two can thus keep a mutual check on each other. Strict attention to the game and to the umpires' signals, which should be promptly answered, is necessary, and care must be taken, when the full score is not shown on the telegraph, that each successive "ten" is promptly exhibited. The method of keeping the "analysis of the bowling" is perfectly simple, and a properly-printed score-sheet really explains itself. An imaginary extract is, however, given here, as a matter of completeness. When only one run is required to finish the game, the scorers are required by tradition to stand up.

Match played at..................on..............
between..................and..................

Batsman's name.	Runs as scored.	How out.	Bowler's name.	Total.
Jones...	11324114 ...	bowled	Robinson...	17
Smith .	....	c Thompson	Robinson...	0
Brown .	4144231114	c Johnson ...	Johnson ...	25
Stokes .	13	run out	....	4
Noakes.	13441	st Thompson.	Johnson....	13
Styles .	133241114	not out	....	20
Byes, 144; leg-byes, 12113; no-balls, 1; wides, 1				19
Total..				—

An extract from the bowling analysis might read as follows :—

Robinson ...... 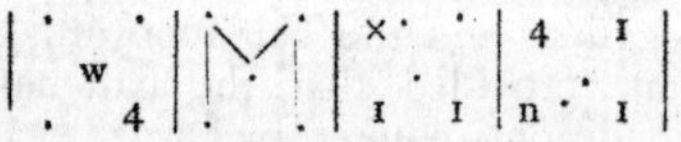

In the first over a wicket (w) was secured by the third ball, while the last was hit for four runs. The second was a "maiden," *i.e.*, no runs were scored by the batsman off it. The first ball of the third was wide (×), and the fourth of the fourth a no-ball (n). Only runs from the bat spoil a "maiden," none that are called or signalled, except boundary-hits. The bowler is credited with the wickets of all men whom he bowls out, and all who are caught, stumped, l.b.w., or "hit-wicket" off his bowling. If a batsman hits the ball on to his wicket, or it glances on to it off his leg, he is registered as "bowled," and the bowler gets the credit of the wicket. In the imaginary score-sheet Brown is "caught and bowled" (c. and b.) by Johnson, which is, however, entered in the score as shown.

Australian Cricket.—Between 1862 and 1878 four English elevens visited Australia, but whereas the first three sides only played against odds, with fifteen, eighteen, or twenty-two men to oppose, the team of 1876–77 played three matches on even terms, a win, a draw, and a loss being the result. This fact first opened the eyes of English cricketers to the possibility of international matches, though even in 1878, the date of the first visit of Australian cricketers to these shores, no match was arranged between the colonies and the mother-country; yet the sensational defeat of a fine M.C.C. team by the visitors gave some clue to their powers. It was in 1880 that the first Australia *versus* England match was played, and since that time the match has been a regular fixture. In 1893 two such "test-matches" were played, and in 1896 three. It is not surprising that England should have had considerably the "best of the deal," the results being, England twelve, Australia three, four having been drawn. In Australia the balance of success also lies with the old country, though few, if any, of the visiting sides can be said to have been absolutely representative of English cricket, while, from the methods in which such visits are arranged, the Australians have probably a better chance of getting a *nearly* representative side to visit England than England to visit Australia. In all, thirteen English sides have gone to Australia, and nine Australian elevens have come over to England, to the great advantage of both countries and of cricket in general.

To compare the cricket of the two countries would present no easy task, but it may be asserted generally that English batsmen, especially on slow and difficult wickets, are markedly superior to the Australian, that Australian bowling is slightly better, and Australian fielding and throwing distinctly better than the English, the last two items especially emphasising the fine qualities of the English batsmen. Each country has undoubtedly learned something from the other.

The following paper on Australian cricket is from the pen of F. G. J. Ford, *a member of A. E. Stoddart's Eleven, which visited Australia in 1894–95* :—

Cricket, as played in Australia, differs in a very marked degree from the game as played in England, and from various causes. Possibly the most remarkable feature of Australian cricket is the fact that from her limited number of players she has been able, from time to time, to put an eleven into the field fully capable of holding its own in home and home matches with representative teams of England; and such is her position at the present time. In spite of this, it seems very doubtful whether her second eleven would make anything like such a favourable comparison with the second eleven of England. But she is certainly stronger in this respect than she was ten years ago; for, particularly in the last few years, there has been a strong advance made in every colony, as is shown by the great increase of clubs and players, as well as by a remarkable improvement in the play, both "up-country" and in the big towns. It is true, however, that some five or six years ago there was a strange decline in the interest taken in the game. The old enthusiasm seemed to be wanting, and even the inter-colonial matches failed to arouse the keenness formerly associated with them. Possibly the non-success of the teams sent home just at that time had served to damp men's interest; possibly the slow style of play then coming into vogue wearied the public taste. Then, somewhat indirectly, the visit of Lord Sheffield's team in 1892 revived the cricket interest that had so long been latent. A sudden change was brought about by the victory of the Australians in the rubber of three representative matches that was played with that combination. One gratifying result of the revived interest is the appearance of a colonial team from Queensland, which, though scarcely a match at the present time for any of the other colonies, yet commands sufficient interest in the game to enable it to take its place with the others. A very strong evidence of this revival is to be found in the extraordinary excitement caused by the visit of Stoddart's team in 1895 and the recent return visit of the Australians to England. It is only natural that, in view of their paucity of numbers, the Australian teams should not have always maintained their highest standard, but however the strength may have varied, there has never been anything commonplace about Australian cricket. Individuals among her players have always stood out prominently in one branch of the game or another, and there are Australian names which, with one great exception, take no second place even among the greatest.

How does Australia train her men? There are no cricket nurseries such as we have in our public schools, where colts can take advantage of the advice of experienced cricketers, but the facilities for practice are numerous. Most of the cricket in Australia is played upon cement laid upon a brick foundation, with matting stretched over the whole, proper turf being a great rarity. Thus, in the rough land which lies outside the Sydney cricket-ground, there are several cement wickets laid down by the local authorities, where any one may practise, and this system has been adopted in other quarters to encourage men to learn to play. These cement and matting wickets, though apt to be fiery, are always true and fast, and the bowler can generally get a little work on the ball; also, when they begin to wear out, they can be repaired at a trifling cost; while, further, as they are quite independent of the weather, neither side can plead a "sticky wicket" as the cause of defeat. Again, wherever an open space can be found, a ground can be made fit to play on in a very short time; for a good wicket—which is mainly important—is a great compensation for rough out-fielding. Some grounds, such as the ground at Broken Hill, cannot boast a single blade of grass, but the brown undulating soil is rolled tolerably smooth, and a good cement wicket adorns the middle. In almost every up-country town a ground of this sort, with perhaps rough grass to field on, is to be found. The Adelaide Oval provides perfect wickets, but for fielding is open to improvement. The Melbourne and Sydney Clubs possess as fine turf grounds as exist anywhere, smooth as a lawn all over, and circular in shape. A white wooden paling or railing, three or four feet high, runs round them, and the crowd is never allowed to invade the sacred precinct. The wickets on these grounds are indeed the batsman's paradise—in fine weather. A peculiar black soil is used where the wickets are laid, which becomes as hard as adamant—so hard that even the making of a block-hole is often out of the question—and as true as a billiard-table. There are a few other turf grounds to be found; but the majority of cricketers have to learn to play on matting and receive their polishing at one of the great cricket centres. For the most part they learn to play by the light of nature, with the advantage of a very long summer and a possibility of practising nearly all the year round. To the former is probably due a certain absence of that finished style which we are accustomed to associate with cricketers who have been studiously coached in their youth—not that their skill in any way suffers thereby, but rather is the individuality disposed to be more strongly marked.

One great advantage that the Australians possess is that with their long summer they are able to play all their matches out to a finish; drawn games are almost unknown. It is the custom, too, at the Melbourne, Sydney, and Adelaide grounds to cover the wicket at night-time with a tarpaulin, so that neither heavy dews nor rain by night may unfairly handicap the batting side during the first hour's play in the morning. Every precaution then is taken that a match may be fought out on a hard wicket. And we may see in this the reason why the Australians enjoy a reputation for appearing at their worst on the slow, sticky wickets that so frequently occur in England. Still, on the whole it is a distinct advantage for the youth of Australia that they should receive the beginning of their cricket education on true and fast wickets; it is in this that they have the best chance of learning to play with a free, upright style and a straight bat, and to overcome the very natural fear of fast bowling. But this is not an unmixed blessing, as, from want of proper practice on wet and difficult wickets, an Australian side is especially liable to collapse if a match has to be played under these conditions. On the other hand, to these hard wickets is due that remarkable accuracy of length which the greatest Australian bowlers have shown us. By bowling constantly on them, her bowlers learnt what the English bowlers learnt from them—that great accuracy of pitch and subtle variations of pace are the deadliest weapons that a bowler can command. It taught them to exercise greater cunning and to acquire the art of making the ball spin and break even on perfect wickets, and this has always been a more prominent feature among Australian than among English bowlers.

There is at the present time, unfortunately, a strongly marked tendency among colonial cricketers of all classes to adopt a slow, "pottering" style of play. No doubt this development has arisen from the fact that, as all matches are played out to a finish and no economy of time is necessary, the batsman is apt to overvalue the cricket adage, "If you only stay at the wickets, the runs are sure to come." It is an excellent thing for every team to possess one or two players who can be relied upon never to take a liberty; no less is it ruinous to the interests of the team that *every* member should adopt these tactics, which have for the time being almost ruined one English county team, and if encouraged further may imperil Australia's reputation for producing brilliant cricketers, and sadly spoil her "winning brackets" in this country.

There is another external influence acting on the game in Australia which has never failed to make itself felt by the English teams when visiting the country—and that is the light. Visiting teams have invariably had to pay the penalty, particularly in the earlier matches of the tour, for being unable to judge the ball accurately in its flight through the air; and it is no uncommon thing for a deep field, expecting to bring off his catch, to find the ball pitch ten yards over his head, to the huge delight of the crowd. The tropical heat of mid-summer also proves a great trial to Englishmen, and so far affects the Australians themselves that the necessity of an interval for tea is recognised. On the other hand, when the Australians visit England, they in their turn suffer from the cold winds of our early summer, and their play must be affected thereby.

Another fact that may be noticed by way of comparison is that while one or two members of an English eleven will invariably be found to *jerk* the ball back to the wickets, *all* the Australians can throw, and for the most part with greater force and accuracy than our own players. Doubtless our climatic conditions are accountable for the number of strained arms that exist, but, generally speaking, the Australians have the reputation for being better in the field than we are; and, as it is true that they learnt the finer arts of batting from watching English cricketers, no less is it true that the Australians first opened our eyes to the value of smart fielding and hard accurate returns.

The minor cricket of Australia has a peculiarity of its own. Its matches, except when arranged to last for one or two days only, are seldom played out on consecutive days, but are carried on from Saturday to Saturday till they are lost or won. Fortunately the long summer allows of these club fixtures being easily finished in this manner, but a difficulty arises therefrom in that the players have to bind themselves from week end to week end, which involves some inconvenience; and many cricketers, being unable to pledge themselves so far in advance, are debarred from this class of cricket in consequence. Time is more precious, and there are fewer idle men in Australia than in England, so that working days cannot be set aside for cricket, except in the case of the most important matches.

Two more points alone require notice. The first is the almost universal fairness of Australian bowlers; their delivery—possibly two exceptions might be made—has always been most strictly orthodox, and "throwing" instead of "bowling" is an unknown, or almost unknown, offence. It would be good for English cricketers if we could say the same of all our bowlers, fast and slow.

Secondly, the question of umpires deserves a word. In the early days of Australian cricket, when professionals did not exist, and amateurs, with little more experience than a general knowledge of the rules, were pressed into the service, the umpiring was undoubtedly very unsatisfactory, both to the cricketers and the spectators; and as, in inter-colonial matches, each colony provided its umpire, and our system of selecting neutrals had not been adopted, disputes, cessations of play, and even miniature riots took place in consequence, while Australian elevens got rather a bad name for cavilling at the umpires' decisions. Happily this is now a thing of the past. Stoddart's men were unanimous in their praise of the fairness, impartiality, and ability of the Australian umpires; and with this brief allusion to what *has been*, the question may be relegated to its grave for ever. The disputes were doubtless due largely to the amount of public betting that took place on the grounds.

F. G. J. FORD.

ENGLISH TEAMS IN AUSTRALIA.

The following is a list of the years in which English sides have visited Australia, with the names of the captains:—

1862 Stephenson (H. H.).	1886-87 Shrewsbury (A.).
1864 Parr (G.).	1887-88 G. F. Vernon.
1873-74 W. G. Grace.	,, ,, C. A. Smith (Shrewsbury's team).
1876-77 Lillywhite (James).	
1878-79 Lord Harris.	1891-92 W. G. Grace (Lord Sheffield's team).
1881-82 Shaw (A.).	
1882-83 Hon. Ivo Bligh.	
1884-85 Shaw (A.).	1894-95 A. E. Stoddart.

AUSTRALIAN TEAMS IN ENGLAND.

1878 D. W. Gregory.	1888 P. S. McDonnell.
1880 W. L. Murdoch.	1890. W. L. Murdoch.
1882 ,, ,,	1893 J. McC. Blackham.
1884 ,, ,,	1896 G. H. S. Trott.
1886 H. J. H. Scott.	

County Cricket—From very early times, matches between rival counties were common, and attracted much attention and interest, and when in later years it became customary for certain counties, presumably the best, to put a regularly organised team in the field and to play home-and-home matches with others, it also became customary at the end of the year to analyse results, and to pronounce this county or that the champion county of the year. But as there was an absolute lack of system, it was practically the sporting newspapers which decided the championship, each more or less according to its taste, and no real importance was attached to the title. In 1873 the question of county qualification was raised and settled, and in 1888 a further rule was passed [*see* RULES OF COUNTY CRICKET, p. 214], but no definite "County Classification" was adopted until some years later, when, by tacit consent, certain counties were held to be "first-class," and to be the competitors for the championship, which is now awarded by the M.C.C. under the regulations then adopted. At that date, too, several new counties were admitted to the "sacred pale" of first-class. In 1896 a new system of awarding the championship was arranged experimentally, and it was left to the Marylebone Club to decide from year to year the number of inter-county matches which each county must play, if it wished to qualify for the championship. The whole system may be regarded as "rough and ready," but there is a general "roughness and readiness" about many of the regulations attached to the game which is possibly one of its charms, for, as all cricketers know, a thousand and one problems may be suggested for which the laws do not properly provide, or as to which the dispensers of those laws—the umpires—are not in accord. At the time of writing (1897) county cricket has proved an enormous attraction to the cricket-loving public; it has done much to popularise the game, and, in the absence of a visit from the Australians, ranks far above any other form of first-class cricket, the matches between Oxford and Cambridge, and the Gentlemen and Players not excepted.

In a work of this description it would be impossible to follow in detail the performances of different counties and their "ups and downs." A chart of the last fifty years would be full of interest, were it not for the desultory nature of the engagements before the whole question was formally taken in hand. Whether the scheme, as now arranged, is perfect, remains to be seen; it is certainly superior to the chaotic condition of things which existed till then. The following list of counties, which have been held to be "champions" in different years, can hardly be regarded (in the absence of definite rules, as was for some time the case) as final, but for the last ten years it may be considered absolutely correct, and to be founded, for earlier years, on the consensus of public opinion, as the methods of calculation have often differed, and the number of matches played by each county depended on its own sweet will.

1880. Notts.
1881. Lancashire.
1882. Lancashire and Notts, equal.
1883. Notts.
1884. ,,
1885. ,,
1886. ,,
1887. Surrey.
1888. ,,
1889. Surrey, Notts, and Lancashire, equal.
1890. Surrey.
1891. ,,
1892. ,,
1893. Yorkshire.
1894. Surrey.
1895. ,,
1896. Yorkshire.

W. J. FORD.

FAMOUS GROUNDS—**Cambridge**—For very many years the University has played its matches on the ground which was opened by F. P. Fenner in 1846, and which was known as "Fenner's," till in 1875 the C.U.C.C. leased the ground and added a handsome pavilion. In 1892 the club acquired the freehold. The match enclosure, about five acres, is covered with such beautiful turf that high scoring is the rule rather than the exception. The full size of the ground, now known as "The Cambridge University Cricket Ground," is about eight acres, and 10,000 persons can witness the game with ease.

Derbyshire has its head-quarters at Derby, a ground of eleven acres, seven of which are reserved for matches and three for practice. The pavilion and grand stand seat about 1,000, and there is every convenience for the public. The turf, though a little coarse, is grown on good clay marl and wears exceedingly well.

Essex has its ground at Leyton, where on a good gravel soil are eleven and a half acres of capital turf, eight and a half acres being reserved for cricket. There is plenty of accommodation for 20,000 persons, apart from the seats in the stands and pavilion.

Gloucestershire—The county ground is at Bristol, and comprises fourteen acres and a half of good sound turf, eight of which are reserved for matches. There is a fairly large pavilion and stand. Two county matches are played annually on the Clifton College and also on the Cheltenham College grounds, the latter fixtures forming the "Cheltenham Week." Both grounds are exceedingly good.

Hampshire plays two matches annually on the "Officers' Recreation Ground, Portsmouth," a ground famous for good wickets and high scoring, but the bulk of the matches take place on the county ground at Southampton, where there is plenty of room for cricket, and on the good, sound turf the average scoring is very high.

Kent distributes its matches among various towns, but the head-quarters of the county are at Canterbury, on the recently acquired St. Lawrence ground, where the famous "week," the progenitor of all similar weeks, opens on the August Bank-holiday. The ground, thirteen acres in area, half of which is devoted to cricket, is well-drained and dries fast; the turf is of the best. The ground can hold 14,000 spectators, including some 2,000 in the pavilion and stands. A "week" is also held at Tonbridge, on the Angel ground, a large and commodious enclosure of excellent turf. The Maidstone ground in Mote Park is somewhat small, and, though the turf is capital, the slope is so marked that the ground is hardly first-rate. County matches are also played occasionally at Beckenham, Blackheath, Catford Bridge, and Gravesend.

Lancashire plays all its matches except two on the famous "Old Trafford Ground," Manchester. The extent of the ground is ten acres, of the match enclosure six; stands, pavilion, and other buildings occupy the remainder. The pavilion is a reduced fac-simile of that at "Lords." The turf is admirable, though often very slow, owing to the rainy climate. One of the international matches is always played at Old Trafford. Two county matches are played on the Aigburth Ground, Liverpool, where there is a splendid pavilion and every facility for cricket. About eight acres out of eleven are set apart for matches.

Leicestershire—The county ground is in the Aylestone Road, and all county matches are played there. The ground, eleven acres in extent, is covered with good turf; and half of it forms the match portion. The pavilion and stand seat 1,500 persons, and there is seating round the ground for 1,500 more.

Lord's is the head-quarters of English cricket, and comprises about fourteen acres, with a match enclosure of six acres. There are seats for 7,500 spectators round the ground and for about 4,000 more in the stands and pavilion. From the clayey nature of the soil, the ground is as hard as iron after a succession of hot days, but after rain it is probably the most treacherous in England. [*See* LORD'S and M.C.C.]

Middlesex—All the home-matches of this county are played at "Lord's."

Nottinghamshire—The Trent Bridge Ground, Nottingham, is the home of the county's cricket. It is nine acres in size, six acres forming the match portion, and being covered with excellent turf. The new pavilion, built in 1886, holds some 3,000 spectators, and the ground is surrounded with terraces, provided with seats and roofed with canvas, for the convenience of the public.

Oxford—For many years the O. U. C. C. used a ground known as "The Magdalen Ground," and belonging to that college; the present ground was acquired in 1880. The total size of "The Parks" is about ten acres, of the match enclosure five and a half acres; the turf is sound and good under favourable conditions, but is apt to be tricky if the weather is unpropitious. As "The Parks" are public property, no admission fee can be charged, and consequently, when gate-money is required, matches are played elsewhere—on the Christ Church Ground, in the Iffley Road. The Pavilion accommodates about 600 persons.

Somersetshire possesses an excellent county ground at Taunton, with a fine sward of turf, which dries after rain more quickly than any ground in England. It is six and a half acres in size, accommodates 6,000 spectators in "the ring," and 1,000 more in pavilion, grand stand, and ladies' enclosure.

Surrey—In "The Oval," Surrey possesses a ground which in fame stands second only to "Lord's," in excellence second to none. Out of eleven and a half acres eight are devoted to match purposes, and the turf is remarkably fine and good. There are 3,250 members, 1,600 of whom who can find seats, while for the visiting public 3,000 seats are provided in the various stands. The ground belongs to the Duchy of Cornwall and is situated in Kennington.

Sussex—The County Ground is at Hove, Brighton, and is famous as being the easiest ground in England for batsmen. The turf is close and smooth; the ground is level and recovers with marvellous rapidity after rain. The total size is ten acres, six of which form the portion devoted to matches, but so fast is the turf that the six acres seem to shrink into four when the ground is hard. It is the paradise of batsmen and the terror of bowlers. Matches are also played on the good grounds at Eastbourne and Hastings, but the arrangements for the public are necessarily of a temporary character. The "Hastings Week," held in September, is a very popular and flourishing institution.

Warwickshire—The County Ground is in Edgbaston, a suburb of Birmingham. The size of the ground is twelve acres, of the match enclosure five and a half. There is a capital pavilion, with seats for 2,000 members, and for the general public raised accommodation is provided round the ring. The grand stand holds about 600 persons. The turf is close and thick, and the ground admirably level, but, as the ball does not seem to travel very fast, the ground does not lend itself to rapid scoring.

Yorkshire—Bramall Lane is the head-quarters of the Y.C.C.C., the ground being eleven and three-quarter acres in size, and the match enclosure taking up eight of these. The grand stand can seat 3,500 persons, and 30,000 can witness the cricket without inconvenience. Unfortunately the turf of late years has not been in the best condition, but, as special attention has been paid to it recently, it should now revert to its former excellence. One drawback to the ground is the bad light which prevails, when the wind blows from certain quarters. County matches are also played at Leeds, Bradford, Scarborough, Dewsbury, Harrogate, and Huddersfield. The "Scarborough Week," held in September, is a recognised institution, but is not an occasion for genuine inter-county cricket. The Headingley ground at Leeds provides about eight acres of playing surface, with pavilion and stand accommodation for 5,000 people, while fully 30,000 can witness the game in comfort, the turf being of the best quality. The playing area at Bradford is about six acres, the whole ground covering ten. The turf is second to none, the ground is most accessible, and some 30,000 people can watch the game simultaneously. The pavilion is spacious and contains all necessary comforts.

W. J. FORD.

RECORDS.

In January, 1897, the following were the "record" performances—

Highest total for one innings in a first-class match—
887 by Yorkshire *v.* Warwickshire (1896). In this match four men scored over 100 runs (one of them over 200); also a record for first-class cricket.

Highest individual score in a first-class match—
424, made in 1895 by A. C. Maclaren for Lancashire *v.* Somersetshire.

Highest aggregate in a first-class match—
1,514, made at Sydney in 1894, in a match between All Australia and A. E. Stoddart's English Eleven. This match lasted into the sixth day.

Highest aggregate in a three-days' match—
1,410, made in 1895 in a match between Sussex and Oxford University.

Highest individual score ever made—
485, by A. E. Stoddart (1886) for the Hampstead Club *v.* The Stoics.

Highest score ever made in a single innings—
922, scored by Carlton C.C. against Melbourne University in 1896. One higher total is recorded, but not properly authenticated.

Two hundreds in the same match have, in first-class cricket, been scored by—
W. G. Grace, in 1868, for South *v.* North of the Thames, 130 and 102 not out.
" " in 1887, for Gloucestershire *v.* Kent, 101 and 103 not out.
" " in 1888, for Gloucestershire *v.* Yorkshire, 148 and 153.
A. E. Stoddart, in 1893, for Middlesex *v.* Notts, 195 not out, and 124.
G. Brann, in 1892, for Sussex *v.* Kent, 105 and 101.
Storer (W.), in 1896, for Derbyshire *v.* Yorkshire, 100 and 100 not out.
K. S. Ranjitsinhji, in 1896, for Sussex *v.* Yorkshire, 100 and 125 not out, both these scores being made on the same day, a feat without precedent.

The largest number of runs produced by the partnership of two men in a first-class match is—
398, made by Gunn and Shrewsbury for Notts *v.* Sussex, in 1890.

The largest number of runs produced by the partnership of two men in any match is—
623, made by Captain Oates and Private Fitzgerald, in 1895, for Royal Munster Fusiliers *v.* Army Service Corps.

The longest stand made, in first-class cricket, for the first wicket is—
346, made by H. T. Hewett and L. C. H. Palairet for Somersetshire *v.* Yorkshire in 1892.

The longest stand made, in first-class cricket, for the last wicket is—
173, made by Briggs and Pilling, for Lancashire *v.* Surrey, in 1885.

The largest number of hundreds made in first-class matches is (1896) *one hundred and eleven*, made by W. G. Grace, the first being 224 not out, made in 1866 for England *v.* Surrey, and the last, 301, made in 1896, for Gloucestershire *v.* Sussex.

The furthest distance, properly authenticated, to which the ball has been hit before reaching the ground is 168 yards 2 feet. This was done at Brighton by C. I. Thornton.

COLOURS.

Cambridge University—Ribbon: light blue, on white straw. Cap: light blue. Blazer: ditto.

Derbyshire—Cap: blue cloth, embroidered with rose and crown in gold, within a shield, and words

Derbyshire County Cricket Club. Blazer: chocolate, pale blue and yellow.

Essex—Cap: dark blue, embroidered in red with shield, three seaxes, one over other. Blazer: ditto, embroidered over pocket.

Gloucestershire—Cap: dark blue, embroidered in buff, with "G" within a circle.

Hampshire—Cap: dark blue flannel, with Hampshire rose and crown.

Kent—Cap: dark blue, Kent horse embroidered in silver.

Lancashire—Cap: dark blue, embroidered with red rose. Blazer: dark blue, red rose on pocket.

Leicestershire—Cap: dark green, narrow red stripe, embroidered with fox. Blazer: dark green, narrow red stripe.

M.C.C.—Ribbon: three equal stripes, vermilion, canary, vermilion. Cap: equal stripes, vermilion and canary. Blazer: ditto.

Middlesex—None.

Nottinghamshire—Cap: Lincoln green, embroidered N.C.C.C.

Oxford University—Ribbon: dark blue, on black and white straw. Cap: ditto, embroidered O.U.C.C. Blazer: ditto, O.U.C.C. on pocket.

Somersetshire—Cap: blue, embroidered with white griffin.

Surrey—Cap: chocolate, embroidered S.C.C. For players in twelve or more matches, cap has two white stripes.

Sussex—Cap: dark blue, embroidered with county arms. Blazer: arms on pocket.

Warwickshire—Cap: navy blue, embroidered white with bear and ragged staff.

Yorkshire—Cap: medium blue, embroidered with white rose. Blazer: rose on pocket.

Glossary of Terms.

Analysis (Bowling)—The record of a bowler's performance during a game (*see* p. 240).

Average (Batting)—The record of a batsman's performances during the season. Calculated by dividing the total number of runs by the number of completed innings; in the case of "not out" the runs are reckoned, but the innings is not, *e.g.*,

	Innings.	Times not out.	Total runs.	Average.
Ranjitsinhji	55	7	2780	57·91

Here the total of 2,780 is divided by 48, *i.e.*, 55 minus 7.

Average (Bowling)—The record of a bowler's performances during the season. Calculated by dividing the number of runs scored off his bowling by the number of wickets captured, *e.g.*,

	Overs.	Maidens.	Runs.	Wickets.	Average.
Hearne, J. T.	2,003	818	3,670	257	14·28

"Maidens" do not affect the average.

Back-play—Playing the ball by drawing the bat backwards.

Back-stop = Long-stop (*q.v.*)

Bails—[*See* Wickets.].

Bailer—A ball which removes one or both bails without disturbing the stumps.

Ball—(i.) [*See* Law 4]. It consists of a leather casing, tightly stretched over a foundation of cork, &c.

(ii.) The bowler is said to bowl "an easy ball" or "a difficult ball" in the abstract, without regard to the material ball. The bowling of the ball is also called "a ball."

Bat—The implement used by the batsmen. The blade is made of willow, and the handle of cane or a combination of elastic substances.

Batsman—The man who uses the bat.

Block—(i.) A term sometimes applied to the "popping-crease" (*q.v.*).

(ii.) [*See* Guard].

(iii.) To play a ball without attempting to score from it.

Boundary—The limits of the match-inclosure.

Boundary-hit—A hit to the boundary (*see* p. 216).

Bowled—If the ball, bowled by the bowler, strikes the wicket, the batsman is bowled, and the wicket is also said to be bowled.

Bowling-crease—[*See* Law 7].

Break—A change of direction taken by the ball after touching the ground.

Break-back—A ball which, as delivered by a right-handed bowler, twists from "off" to "leg." With a left-handed bowler the ball breaks from "leg" to "off."

Bump-ball—A ball which after being struck by the bat strikes the ground before it reaches a fieldsman.

Bye—A run made when the ball has not touched the bat or person of the batsman.

C. and B.—Caught and bowled, (*q.v.*).

Call—To shout to the other batsman to run.

Captain—The manager of an eleven during a match.

Carry bat—To be "not out" at the cessation of play.

Catch—(i) To hold the ball, when hit, before it touches the ground.

(ii.) The holding of the ball, so struck.

(iii.) A man is described as a good or bad "catch" who generally holds or fails to hold such a ball.

Caught and Bowled—Caught by the bowler who delivered the ball.

Century—An innings of 100 or more runs.

Century (Double)—The making of two "centuries" in the same match.

Chance—An opportunity given by the batsman to the fieldsman to get him out.

Change-bowler—A bowler who is only invited to bowl when presumably better men have failed.

Change ends—To bowl from one wicket, having previously bowled from the other. [*See* Law 14.]

Clean bowled—To be bowled by a ball which hits the wickets without previously touching the bat or person.

Closure—Declaring an innings at an end. [*See* Law 54].

Colts—Young and untried cricketers.

Colts-match—A match in which one at least of the sides is composed of young and untried cricketers.

Country—To field or be caught in "the country" is to field or be caught at either "long-on" or "long-off."

Cover-point—A fieldsman on the off-side, somewhat in front of the batsman.

Cut—(i.) A stroke on the off-side made chiefly with the wrists (*see* p. 223).

(ii.) An adept at this stroke is called "a good cut."

(iii.) To strike the ball as described.

Cut-over—To be struck by the ball in the groin.

Cut up (the wicket)—To spoil the turf where the ball is likely to pitch, by running over it.

Daisy-cutter—The same as "sneak" or "grub." A ball pitched close to the bowler's foot, which runs along the ground without bounding.

Dead—The ball is "dead" when it is out of play. [*See* Laws 13, 34, 35, 41, 50.]

Declare—To close an innings. [*See* Law 54.]

Delivery—(i.) The method and action of the bowler.

(ii.) Synonymous with "Ball (ii.)" (*q.v.*).

Double wicket—The game as usually played.

Draw—(i.) To remove the stumps.

(ii.) To leave the game undecided.

(iii.) An undecided, or "drawn" game.

(iv.) An extinct stroke on the leg-side (*see* p. 224).

Drive—(i.) A hard hit in front of the batsman (*see* p. 222).

(ii.) To make such a hit.

(iii.) A bat "drives" when the ball flies easily off its face, without jarring the hands.

Ducks-egg—An individual score of 0.

Extras—Any runs not made from the bat.

Field—(i.) The match-inclosure.

(ii.) The fieldsmen, collectively or individually.

(iii.) To act as a fieldsman.

First-class Cricket—Cricket played between two sides, *both* of first-class rank as decided by the M.C.C.

It comprises the games between the selected Counties, the Universities, the Australians, and of the M.C.C. with any of the above. Certain other matches (*e.g.*, North *v.* South and Gentlemen *v.* Players) are annually included.

Follow on—A side "follows on" which, under LAW 53, has two innings consecutively.

Forward-play—Advancing the bat and foot to meet the ball (*see* p. 221).

Full-pitch or **Full-toss**—A ball which hits the bat or wicket without touching the ground.

Gardening—Clearing the pitch of stray scraps of grass or earth.

Get up—A ball "gets up" which rises abnormally high from the pitch.

Go with the arm—A ball "goes with the arm" when on touching the ground it goes across the wicket in the same direction as the bowler's arm swings (*see* p. 231).

Ground—(i.) The space behind the popping-crease, which is the batsman's "ground."

(ii.) The professionals, collectively, attached to a club, *e.g.*, "Surrey Club and Ground."

Ground man—The man whose duty it is to look after the playing area.

Grub—[*See* DAISY-CUTTER].

Guard—The place where the batsman puts his bat to guard his wicket.

Half-cock stroke—A forward stroke suddenly checked, so that the ball strikes the bat and is not struck by it.

Hands—An old term for "innings."

Hang—A ball "hangs" which rises unexpectedly slowly from the pitch.

Half-volley—A ball which is met by the bat the instant after it leaves the ground.

Hat-trick, Hat—A white hat used to be given to the bowler who got three batsmen out in successive balls, provided that they were bowled, stumped, caught, leg-before, or hit-wicket. A bowler who performs this feat is said to "get a hat," or to "do the hat-trick."

Hook—To hit the ball from the off-side to the on-side in the direction of square-leg.

Innings—The stay of a side or an individual at the wickets.

Late cut—A cut (*q.v.*) which sends the ball considerably behind the wickets.

Leather-hunting—Fielding.

Leg, Leg-side—The side of the wicket on which the batsman stands.

Leg-bail—[*See* WICKETS].

L.B.W.—Leg before wicket (*q.v.*).

Leg before wicket—[*See* LAW 24].

Leg-break.—A twist of the ball from the leg-side to the off-side.

Leg-hit—A hit to the leg-side, either square with the wicket or behind it.

Leg-stump—[*See* WICKETS].

Length—The distance from the batsman at which the bowler pitches the ball.

Life—If a fieldsman misses an opportunity of catching, stumping, or running out the batsman, he is said to give him a "life."

Lobs—Slow under-hand bowling.

Long-hop—[*See* SHORT].

Long-leg—A fieldsman deep on the on-side, behind the batsman.

Long-off—A fieldsman deep on the off-side, in front of the batsman.

Long-on—A fieldsman deep on the on-side, in front of the batsman.

Long-slip—A fieldsman deep on the off-side, behind the batsman.

Long-stop—The fieldsman who stands behind the wicket-keeper to save byes.

Lost ball—A ball hit away which cannot be recovered. [*See* LAW 34.]

Maiden over—An over from which no runs are scored off the bat.

Match—A contest between two sides.

Mid-off—A fieldsman on the off-side, in front of the batsman.

Mid-on—A fieldsman on the on-side, in front of the batsman.

Middle—Guard that covers the middle stump.

Middle and leg—Guard that covers the middle and leg stumps.

Mid-wicket—Another name for mid-on or mid-off.

No-ball—A ball improperly bowled. [*See* LAWS 11, 13, 16, 17, 48A and 48B.]

Notches—An old name for runs, which used to be scored by notches cut on a stick.

Not out—One batsman is necessarily "not out" in a double-wicket match. If the match is won by "wickets" [*See* WICKETS], two are "not out."

Off, Off-side—The opposite side to the "leg-side" (*q.v.*).

Off-bail, **Off-stump** }[*See* WICKETS].

Off the wicket—A ball not straight for the wickets.

One-leg—Guard that covers the leg-stump only.

Out-cricket—Bowling and fielding as opposed to batting.

Over—A series of five (sometimes six) balls delivered alternately from either end.

Over the wicket—Bowling so that the delivering arm passes over the wicket.

Overthrows—Runs scored after the ball has been thrown to the wicket-keeper or bowler but not stopped.

Pitch (i.)—The ground between the wickets.

(ii.) Synonymous with "Length" (*q.v.*).

(iii.) Almost synonymous with "to bowl." To make the ball strike a particular spot.

Place—To hit the ball intentionally out of a fieldsman's reach.

Play on—To hit the ball on to one's wicket.

Players—Professionals as opposed to amateurs.

Point—A fieldsman on the off-side, square with the wickets.

Popping-crease—[*See* LAW 8].

Pull—[*See* HOOK].

Return the ball—(i) To throw it to bowler or wicket-keeper.

(ii.) To hit it back to the bowler, especially used of a c. and b. (*q.v.*).

(iii.) A sharp straight throw is known as a good "return."

Return-crease—[*See* LAW 7].

Rot—The failure of several good batsmen in succession.

Round the wicket—The opposite to "over the wicket" (*q.v.*).

Run out (i) A batsman is "run out" who in trying to score a run or runs, fails to reach the popping-crease before the wicket has been struck. [*See* LAWS 2 and 49.]

(ii.) A hit is "run out" when the batsmen actually run all the runs gained by the stroke, no allowance being made for boundaries or "lost ball."

Score—(i) The record of runs made.

(ii.) The number of runs made by a side or individual.

(iii.) To keep the record of runs.

Scorer—The man who records the runs &c. (*see* p. 239).

Screens—Erections of canvas, or wood, to provide a white background behind the bowler.

Set—A batsman is "set" who has been in so long that the bowling seems easy and familiar.

Shooter—A ball which on touching the ground keeps very close to the turf, often with an increase of pace.

Short, Short ball, Short-pitched—A ball which pitches too far from the batsman for a good length.

Short-leg—A fieldsman on the on-side, square with the batsman or behind him but close to him.

Short-slip—A fieldsman behind the batsman, on the off-side, and close to him.

Silly—Applied to point, mid-on and mid-off, when they stand dangerously near to the striker.

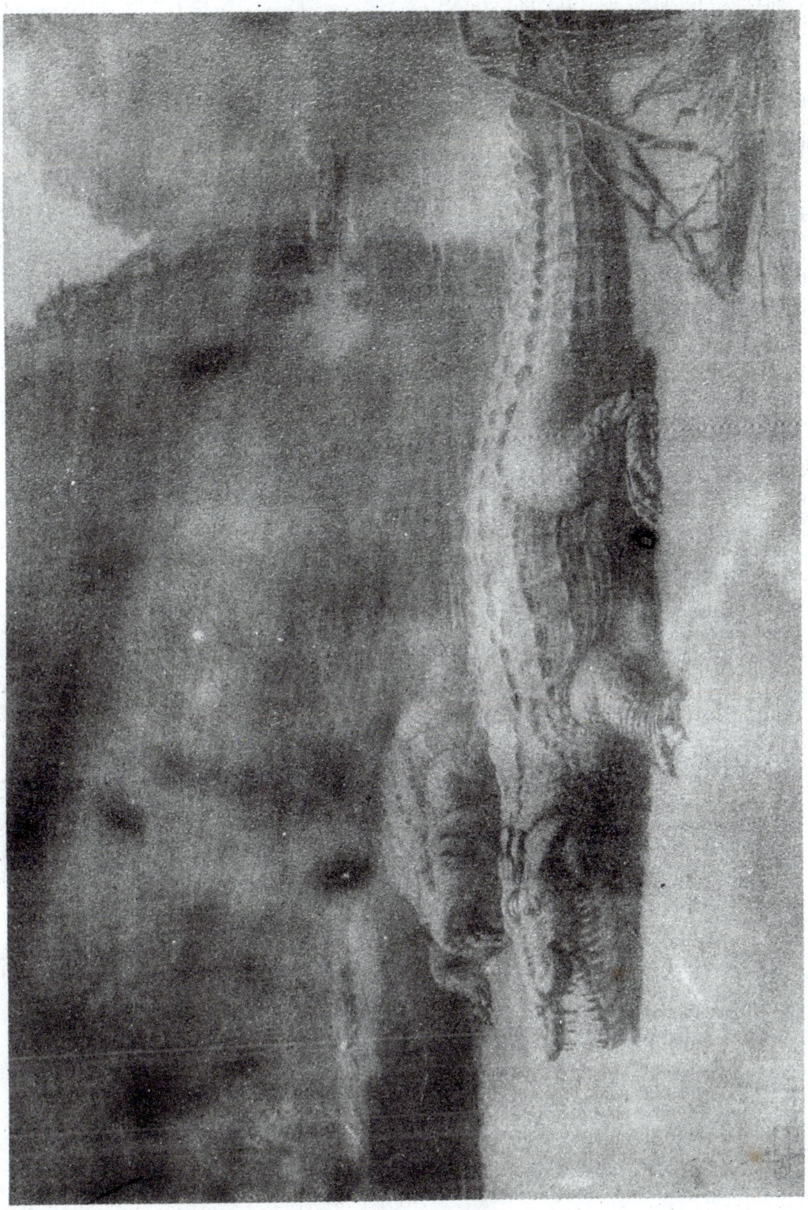

Single wicket—Cricket with only one batsman at the wickets. [*See* LAWS OF SINGLE WICKET.]

Skyer—A ball hit very high into the air.

Slog—To hit hard and indiscriminately.

Sneaks—[*See* DAISY-CUTTER].

Snick—To hit the ball with the edge of the bat instead of the face.

Spectacles—Two scores of 0, made in the same match by the same batsman.

Spin—An acceleration of pace acquired by the ball after touching the ground.

Spot—To bowl "on the spot" is to bowl a good "length" (*q.v.*). A bowler is said to have "found a spot," when he continuously pitches the ball on a broken patch of ground, which makes the ball break or rise unnaturally.

Square-leg—A fieldsman on the leg-side, square with the wicket.

Steal runs—To get a run for a hit, when no run seems reasonably possible.

Sticks—A colloquial term for the stumps.

Stump—One of the wickets.

Stump out—To get the batsman out under LAW 23.

Substitute—Under certain conditions [*See* LAWS 37 and 40] a batsman or fieldsman may have a man to represent him.

Swipe—Synonymous with "slog" (*q.v.*).

Tail—The batsmen who go in late, and are generally less skilful than their predecessors.

Talent-money—Money given to a professional as a reward for special success.

Telegraph—An apparatus for showing the state of the score (*see* p. 211).

Third man—A fieldsman on the off-side, behind the batsman.

Thrown out—Synonymous with "run out," provided that the fieldsman hits the wicket with the ball. The term is not used now in the score-sheet.

Tice—[*See* YORKER]. The term is obsolete.

Timing the ball—Hitting it at the precise moment when it can be effectively struck (*see* p. 222).

Trial-ball—An obsolete term. The first ball of an innings, from which the batsman could neither make runs nor be out.

Two-leg—Synonymous with "middle and leg."

Under-hand bowling—Bowling with the hand close to the body, and not raised level with or over the shoulder.

Wicket—(i.) One of the stumps or uprights.

(ii.) The ground between the stumps.

(iii.) The batsman is sometimes, by inference, described as a wicket, *e.g.*, "two wickets are down" means "two batsmen are out."

Wicket-keeper—The fieldsman immediately behind the wickets.

Wickets—(i.) The three uprights and the two bails which are laid on the grooves are collectively called the wickets or wicket. The stumps are known as the off, middle and leg stumps; the bails as the off and leg bails. [*See* LAW 6.]

(ii.) A side is said to win by—say—four wickets when the number of runs necessary to win the match have been got, and only six batsmen are out.

Wide—A ball so crooked that the batsman cannot reach it. [*See* LAWS 12 and 16.]

Willow—A colloquial name for a bat.

Win in an innings—To make more runs, in one innings than the other side makes in two.

Work on the ball—Identical with break.

Yorker—A ball which pitches far up; roughly speaking, between the bowling and popping creases.

Bibliography—*Cricket Scores and Biographies*, F. Lillywhite and A. Haygarth (Longmans, &c.), 14 volumes published, comprising matches from 1772–1878; *Wisden's Cricketers' Almanack* (Wisden), 34 volumes, from 1864; *Guide to Cricketers*, F. Lillywhite, 19 volumes, from 1848–1866; *Cricketer's Companion*, J. Lillywhite, 33 volumes, from 1865; *Cricket* (weekly), 15 annual volumes, from 1882; *Blues and their Battles from* 1827–1892, Wright; Perkins, *Scores at the Oxford and Cambridge Cricket Matches from* 1827–1889; Haygarth, *Public School Matches from* 1805–1852; Ellis, *Complete Record of all Cricket Matches between Charterhouse and other Public Schools*, 1850–1890; Guillemard, *Rugby School Cricket Matches*, 1831–1893; Mann, *Winchester College Public School Cricket Matches*, 1825–1890; *Gentlemen and Players*, 1806–91 (Wright); Pentelow, *England v. Australia*, 1877–1895; *Twenty Years of Gloucestershire Cricket*, 1870–1890 (Arrowsmith); *Lancashire County Cricket*, 1864–82 (Reynolds); Coplestone, *Record of Lancashire County Matches*, 1865–1881; *Nottinghamshire Cricket Matches from* 1771–1865 (Sutton); Spybey, *Nottinghamshire County Cricket Matches from* 1855–1877; Richards, *Nottinghamshire Cricket Scores and Biographies*, 1838–1892; Brown, *Short History of Nottinghamshire Cricket*, 1887; De Lugo, *Surrey at the Wicket*, 1888; Holmes, *Surrey Cricket and Cricketers*, 1896; Ewbank, *Sussex Cricket Scores*, 1865–1878; *Yorkshire County Cricket Club*, 1863–1893; *Scottish Cricketers' Annual Guide*, 13 volumes, 1870–1882; *Scottish Cricketers' Annual*, 17 volumes, 1881–1887; Hedley, *At the Wickets*, *New South Wales and Victoria*, 1856–1888; Moody, *Australian Cricket and Cricketers*, 1856–1894; *South African Cricketers' Annual*, 9 volumes, from 1889; *New articles of the game of Cricket, as settled and revised at the Star and Garter, Pall Mall, February 25th*, 1774, *by a Committee of noblemen and gentlemen of Kent, &c., to which is added the old laws as settled by the different Cricket Clubs* (London, J. Williams, 1775); Boxall, *Rules and Instructions for playing at the Game of Cricket*, 1790; Lambert, *Cricketers' Guide, or Instructions and Rules for playing the noble Game of Cricket*, 1816; *Laws of Cricket, as approved by the Marylebone Club*, 1828; Nyren, *Young Cricketers' Tutor*, 1833; Nyren, *Young Cricketers' Guide*, 1840; Denison, *Sketches of the Players*, 1846; Barden, *Illustrated Laws of Cricket, as revised by the Marylebone Club*, 1849; Fitzgerald, *M.C.C. Extracts from Minutes of Committee, from* 1826–1867; Alcock, *Cricket, a Record of the Game*, 1882; Christian, *At the Sign of the Wicket*, 1894; Daft, *Kings of Cricket*, 1893; Gale, *Echoes from the Cricket Fields*, 1871; Read, *Annals of Cricket*, 1896; Pycroft, *The Cricket Field*, 6th edition, 1873; Grace, *Cricket*, 1890; C. Box, *The English Game of Cricket*, 1877; E. Lyttelton, *Cricket* (All England Series), 1890; MacLaren, *Cricket* (Oval Series, 1896); Murdoch, *Cricket* (Oval Series, 1893); Steel and Lyttelton, &c., *Cricket* (Badminton Library, 1888); Small, *Canterbury Cricket Week, its Origin, Career, and Jubilee*, 1842–91; Bedford, *Annals of the Free Foresters*, 1896; Gibbs, *The Preparation of Cricket Grounds*, 1895; Dale, *Some Statistics of Cricket, or the Influence of Weather upon the Wicket*, 1891.

CROCODILE SHOOTING.—**Crocodiles**, of which there are a dozen species, are found in Africa, Southern Asia, North Australia, and tropical America. The chief difference between Alligators and Crocodiles is that in the former the fourth tooth in the lower jaw is received into a *sulcus* or *pit* in the upper jaw, and is invisible when the head is looked at from above, whilst in the Crocodiles the corresponding tooth is received into a *notch* in the upper jaw and can be seen from above. There are other differences, but they are of comparatively slight importance. There are only three Crocodiles about which sportsmen are likely to be interested. First, the **Gavial** (*Gavialis gangeticus*), which has a beak-like snout, and is found in the Ganges, Bramapootra and their larger affluents, the Mahanudi in Orissa, and the Koladyni River in Arrakan. It is a purely fish-eating species. Secondly, the **Mugger or Marsh Crocodile** (*Crocodilus palustris*), identical, but for its snout being somewhat shorter, with the African *C. niloticus*. It is found in tanks and rivers all over India and Ceylon and in Madagascar. In India it does not generally attack men, but instances are known there where they have been carried off by it; and in Africa, both on the Nile and the Limpopo (or Crocodile River), they are not only habitually man-eaters, but have been known to attack men on horseback, who have succumbed to the injuries inflicted. *C. palustris* is also a cannibal, and feeds freely on the remains of its companions, as related by Hornaday in his *Two Years in the Jungle*. The third species, the **Estuarine Crocodile** (*C. porosus*) is, as its name implies, chiefly found at the mouths of rivers but has been seen well out at sea. It is *par excellence* the man-eating Crocodile of the East. It is found in the Bengal rivers, sparingly on the West Coast, and curiously enough, not recorded as met with in any part of the Bombay Presidency. It is also found in Ceylon, Burma, and North Australia. It builds a mound of leaves and rushes, the fermentation of which hatches the eggs. It watches this nest, and will attack any one that comes near it. It has also been known to kill its congener *C. palustris*, from which it differs in having a narrower head, and two ridges on the skull converging towards the snout, and, in the adult, four instead of five teeth in the upper jaw, counting from the median line to the notch. This species is probably the largest of the Crocodiles, a specimen in the British Museum being recorded as thirty-three feet in length. The favourite haunts of all Crocodiles are on rocks and spits of sand left by the floods in rivers and tanks, and it is no use looking for them during the monsoon. They frequent the same spots year after year, so that any one living on the bank of a large river is certain, by taking trouble and occasionally anchoring the intestines of a sheep or pig, or tethering a dog close to the water, to get a shot eventually, which should prove fatal. The brain of a Crocodile is very small, but unless the bullet penetrates it, or the neck, where the spine joins the head, so that the animal is paralysed, it will, although mortally wounded, get into the water, and may not be recovered for twelve or even four-and-twenty hours.

The Crocodile of the Nile is now seldom met with in any numbers below the Second Cataract. Owing to the **Crocodile-bird** or **Zic-Zac** (*Hoplopterus spinosus*) giving the alarm, it is most difficult for the sportsman to approach sufficiently near to make sure of getting a deadly shot. On the Indian rivers, however, although an allied bird sometimes picks the teeth of the Crocodile, it rarely deprives the sportsman of a shot.

Method of Approach—The Crocodile, unless molested, is by no means wary, and will allow a near approach. The most satisfactory way is to be paddled in a canoe along the banks, or, if it is determined to be out for the whole day and the river is deep enough, in a boat with an awning over the stern sheets and manned by four men. It is useless to go out too early, as the Crocodile chiefly feeds during the night and only comes out to bask when the sun is pretty high; then they resort to the spits of sand or rocks, or lie on the banks sleeping, often with the jaws wide open, which gives them a curious appearance. On all the Indian rivers, unless the banks are rocky, the vegetation is luxuriant, the screw pine (*Pandanus*), high grass, and creepers with enormous roots abound, and these, with flotsam in the shape of logs of different sizes, make it most difficult to distinguish the quarry in spite of a good pair of binoculars and the sharp eyes of the crew. Slowly drifting down the stream, or carefully paddling up, you may at last see a beast worth shooting, or more probably one of the men will spot him. At a sign the boat is noiselessly rowed until it is opposite the sleeper, when, with luck and good shooting, a single shot secures him. Should, however, the shot not prove instantly fatal, although mortal, a reward to the boatmen will enable you to recover the beast, which has sunk and will not rise to the surface for at least twelve hours.

In estuaries the Crocodiles seldom come out to bask except at half or low tide, so that there is little or no use in going out when the tide is full.

EGYPTIAN CROCODILE. (*C. niloticus.*)

Best Weapon—In old days, when Crocodiles were plentiful and unmolested, many a magnificent specimen was secured with a No. 12 smooth-bore, which had the advantage of not being deflected by twigs. On the other hand, it is now universally allowed that fine shooting cannot be made with such a weapon at over thirty yards, and the most conservative of sportsmen have abandoned it. The best weapon would be a double ·450 Express, the bullet having a hollow of a smaller diameter than that used for soft-skinned animals, and a solid base. This would combine the shock caused by the expanding bullet with the required penetration. It must, however, be allowed that the ·303 Express, furnished with an approved expanding bullet, is fast replacing what sportsmen have hitherto considered the perfection of a sporting rifle.

H. R. P. CARTER.

[The natives of Ceylon catch Crocodile in the following manner. A piece of wood about an inch in diameter and fourteen in length is sharpened at both ends. A dozen strands of twine are made fast to the centre, their other ends being attached to eight or ten feet of rope with a wooden toggle at the other end. The bait is a dead dog, in the body of which the wooden stake is completely hidden. Several of these lines are set in the tanks infested by these creatures, and the native merely inspects from time to time until one of them disappears. He then follows the beast to some well-known landing-place, and by the aid of its track in the soft earth, finds it eventually caught by the rope and toggle in the dense undergrowth, and despatches it by a blow from an axe. Some more elaborate Crocodile tackle, with triangle hooks, swivel and steel chain, has recently been supplied to a sportsman in South Africa, but the report of its efficiency is not yet to hand.]

ALLIGATOR—The alligator seems so likely to be exterminated for the sake of his skin, that any account of shooting him may become ancient history in the comparatively near future. And save for the fact that the pursuit of the saurian takes one far from the tread of man, it cannot be said that the sportsman will have much to regret when *Alligator mississippiensis* is as rare as the wild camel of Spain or the buffalo. For beyond an ordinary acquaintance with the handling of a rifle, a boat, and the knife, the most enthusiastic alligator hunter cannot claim for his hobby that it exacts much skill, patience, or nerve. As an angler for pike and one who likes the sport, I would say that alligator shooting is a sport of about the same calibre. And more, the alligator himself is by no means dissimilar to *lucius esox*.

The alligator is to be found in many parts of the world. His habits and methods of capture do not appear to vary. The personal experiences with which I shall deal are such as may at present be enjoyed at almost any time of the year in the rivers, creeks, lagoons, and cypress swamps that pour their waters into or are supplied from the Gulf of Mexico, away down by the Ten Thousand Islands.

The equipment for an alligator shooting expedition is not complex. For a land journey one needs a mule wagon, containing a flat-bottomed folding-boat—any other keelless boat would do—a tent, mosquito nets, cooking utensils, small bore rifle, gun, rods, large gaffs, several bull's-eye lanterns, some skinning knives and skin preservatives, and any luxuries that are easily portable. A day's journey inland from almost any place on that portion of the Gulf Coast described will bring one to a lagoon, or pond, as they are called.

If travelling by boat or canoe, one will speedily be able to tell if one is going in the right direction. Provided an approach is made with comparative silence, the alligator will be found basking in the reeds, or in the mud, or, as often as not, floating with the stream, a portion of his head and his eyes just appearing. At the least sound he disappears in an instant. Like almost every creature of the forest and solitudes, he is quite harmless, unless wounded or aroused. And then beware his sharp, wolf-like fangs and lashing tail.

I can best describe the method of shooting him by an account of a recent expedition of mine. Having spent some days in getting ready our tents, cooking utensils, tinned and other provisions, canoes, rods, cast nets (for live bait), guns, rifles, revolvers, and other impedimenta, we started at dawn from a spot somewhat south of Caximbas Bay, heading direct for the Everglades.

Our little company set out in the chill that precedes the first glimmer of morning. In that region, where either rod or gun may be used every day in the year, we were busy at once. Breakfast had to be caught *en route*, and the simple and clumsy device of a piece of mother-of-pearl attached to an ordinary Jardine snap tackle, and trailed behind our boat in fashion now very properly illegal in the Thames, speedily resulted in what at home would have been considered a fair day's sport—one channel bass, glorious in his golden scales, one sheephead, two bone fish, and many groupers.

At six we came up with our advance guard, cried a halt, lighted our fire, and ate what in those climates should be the best meal of the day; and at night we came to the shores of one of the best alligator lakes the heart of hunter could desire.

We pitched our tent a hundred yards from the shore, and after dinner our guides took the canoes to the lagoon and launched them, and we looked to our lanterns and rifles.

Towards eleven, when the great wilderness

around us echoed with the myriad noises of a tropical night, when the fireflies were at their brightest, and the shooting stars reached right across the sky, it became time to commence our operations. First, we filled our belts with cartridges, then we armed ourselves with Winchesters and a long iron gaff, and finally we fastened round our palmetto hats a leather band which secured our lanterns.

That we should puzzle primitive four-footed creatures and paralyse all manner of fowl was not to be wondered at, for the effect of a number of human beings stalking through such surroundings in the dead of night with great beaming lanterns where their heads ought to be was startling even to the initiated onlooker. It was all new to us then, and we tingled with pleasurable excitement. Twice, as we made our way as noiselessly as possible, we stopped suddenly, involuntarily. Once to make way for something large, heavy, and cumbrous, yet active, that moved from us, and went rustling through the reeds into the distance, till with a splash it tumbled into water: it was an alligator, a big bull alligator. And again, when close by we saw two gleaming opals that came slowly towards us. But crash! on a sudden the deer had recognised its enemy man, and was off and away.

A minute more and we divided and took to the boats. We had already seen the effect of the beam of light on a deer, and we were now to witness something indescribably ghostly. We pushed silently and slowly on to the waters, one party taking the right side of the lake and the other plashing gently in an opposite direction. In the strange silence, broken by the noises of frightened birds and the occasional swirl of some rising fish, moments seemed hours, and at least one of the party thought that the sport would never begin. We had got what I imagined to be a hundred yards or so out into the lagoon when our guide turned slowly inshore, telling me to take up my station in the bow of the canoe. Rifle in hand I knelt. Following the directions of our instructor I flashed my light from side to side. When we got accustomed to the weight of the lantern and the darkness, it became evident that the fringe of the lake was jewelled with small, twinkling, and star-like orbs. "Them's 'gators, sirree."

Presently some of the twinkling lights came nearer, or we travelled nearer to them. "Wait till a pair gets as close as possible and fire between the widest pair you can see."

These, then, were alligators' eyes, and the widest pair would necessarily belong to the biggest Caiman. When the eyes had come quite close, "Crack!" I fired.

There was a splashing all about us, and the eyes disappeared. It was an anxious moment, and, as it proved, a disappointing one. For, though our guide tried to console me by the reflection that I had probably hit him in the body (they can carry any amount of metal) instead of between the eyes, I had my doubts. We searched the spot, our guide displaying a good deal of polite and unnecessary zeal, I thought, and in a minute or two resumed operations, for the bright orbs were re-appearing all around us.

BLACK ALLIGATOR (*Caiman niger*).

My next shot was more successful. Hit clean through the middle of the brain, the quarry convulsively lashed the water with his unpleasantly powerful tail. That night we came back freighted with a great store of skins, and to-day I have about me in many useful shapes abundant testimony to the efficacy of the simple plan of arousing the curiosity of *Alligator mississippiensis* by means of a bull's-eye carried in the hat.

This, then, is Alligator shooting *en battue*. One can, as I did, carry a rifle on fishing excursions and pot any particularly big specimen approachable.

I had read somewhere that at hibernating time the negro loves to catch the alligator, who falls an easy victim, and that the tail is considered a great delicacy by these native epicures. We tasted him, and though our negro friends are beyond criticism in their judgment of other people's melons and chickens; though they, and they only, can properly appreciate the true merits of opossum meat; yet we were fain to confess to our inability to agree with them in their estimate of this curious musk flavoured and fishy meat.

ALFRED C. HARMSWORTH.

CROQUET—History of the Game—There are not many phenomena in the history of games more curious than the fluctuations in the popularity of Croquet under its various forms. That it was ancient we know from a well-known cut in Strutt of a "curious ancient pastime, from which, I make no doubt, originated the game of billiards." A glance will show that it contains all the essentials of Croquet. Its immediate ancestor, Pall-Mall, the favourite sport of Charles II. and his courtiers, seemed as firmly grounded in public favour as any game could be, but yet it is mainly due to the accidental discovery in a ruined house of the malls and balls which were then used, that we are so much as able to establish the genealogy. It is true that the change is not small from the long straight course of hard-beaten earth, "dressed with powdered cockle-shells," and the "two high arches of iron," to the six or ten hoops upon a closely-cut lawn, but the fact of this development is not so curious as the darkness which hangs over the process. From Whitehall and the Court the pastime seems speedily to have departed, but it was kept up in Brittany, and was also a village game in the South of France. From neither of these, however, did it come back to England, but from Ireland, where it had been played, as was maintained, for an unknown length of time. Its popularity in England was immense, and between 1860 and 1870 it spread, not merely over the island, but over India and the Colonies. The general enthusiasm inspired Capt. Mayne Reid to declare that the game had become "the national pastime," and was "to be cherished as the tree of life"!

The reaction was speedy and complete. After 1875 the game fell away in importance; it became a laughing stock, and the butt of much clumsy jesting. One may fear, indeed, that, two or three years ago, some would have been irreverent enough to turn for an account of it to the article on "Obsolete Sports," but at present there is a distinct revival of interest in it. Many can now be found who confess, with some unnecessary protestations and apologies, that they not only play, but enjoy the game.

The danger that besets it is the lack of any central organisation to control and develop the game, and it may be hoped that the fresh interest in all that concerns the game may bear some lasting fruit. The All England Club of Wimbledon seemed likely to form the rallying point, but it was swept away by the irresistible fashion of Lawn Tennis.

Preparation of Lawn—The first thing needful is a stretch of level turf, where possible, of about thirty by forty yards in extent. Above all, one should guard against choosing a spot which, though fairly smooth [illegible] a steady slope in one direction. Rough [illegible] may be made smooth by diligent work wi[illegible] roller, but for such a general tendency there is no remedy. The roller should be *light*; a heavy roller tends to exaggerate the worst places, especially if used, as it is sure to be, when the ground is soft. A light roller, used constantly, and a well-oiled mowing machine are the only requisites. The grass must have help against invaders. Dandelions and daisies must all be pulled up, and the hoary plantain faced with especial energy. The roots of the last should be dug out with a pen-knife, and the bare space where its leaves have killed all vegetation, re-sown with grass seed in the autumn. There need be no fear of playing on the lawn when soft; a little breaking of the surface seems to strengthen the plant, and the roller soon restores the level, but all "divots" must be replaced at once.

Apparatus—The necessary apparatus is simple, consisting of two 1 in. posts 24 in. high, hoops of iron (varying in number from six to ten according to the setting adopted), and a mallet and ball for each player. The modern *Mallet* usually consists of an ash shaft some 33 in. long, fitted into a cylindrical head, whose length is 8 or 9 in., and diameter 3 in. The head should be of boxwood. Much ingenuity has been expended in contriving mallets of all varieties, which could never miss their aim. Some had looking-glasses fixed on them, which, if focused upon the object ball, secured a hit; others were provided with a leather tipped end, after the fashion of a billiard cue. Ivory was declared to be the very best material for a mallet, and many were actually made of it.

The *Ball* is made either of beech, or, better, of Turkey boxwood, and has a diameter of $3\frac{5}{8}$ in. The maximum number of players allowed by the rules is eight, and there are accordingly eight mallets and eight balls, each differently marked.

Arrangement of Hoops and Posts—The modern setting of the hoops is that known as the Championship or Six-Hoop plan (*see* Fig. 1), which has certainly all the elements of difficulty. Another setting that is sometimes adopted for the sake of variety, and presents several advantages, requires ten hoops, two of which are set crosswise in the middle of the ground to form a cage (*see* Fig. 2). The plan chosen must depend somewhat on the size of the hoops. The Championship hoops for gentlemen in 1872 allowed only $\frac{1}{8}$ in. margin for the ball on either side, whereas the hoops used in the original game were 15 in. to 18 in. wide at the base! Perhaps the best width for ordinary play is $5\frac{1}{2}$ in. to 6 in., which admits of a satisfactory cage.

The Game—Shortly put, the object of the player is to drive his ball through each hoop in its proper order, and from the proper side, and to touch the two sticks or posts, in the fewest number of "turns." A turn or break may consist of any number of strokes. After the first stroke, a player may continue, if he has by it run through his proper hoop or hit another ball. In the former case, he may again attempt either of the two feats; in the latter, he is obliged to

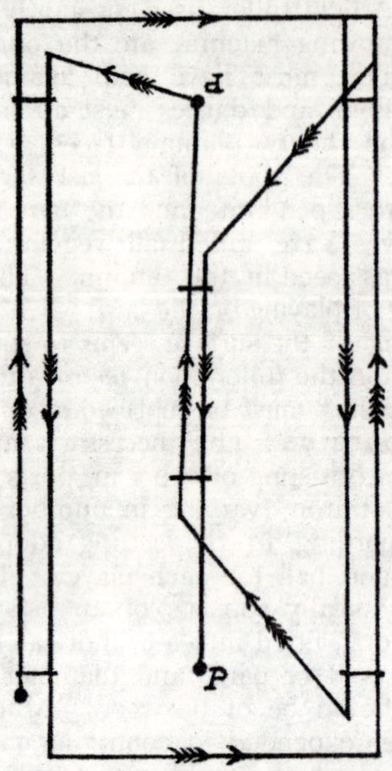

FIG 1

bring his own ball to that which has been hit, and after placing them together to hit his own in such a manner that both are moved. After

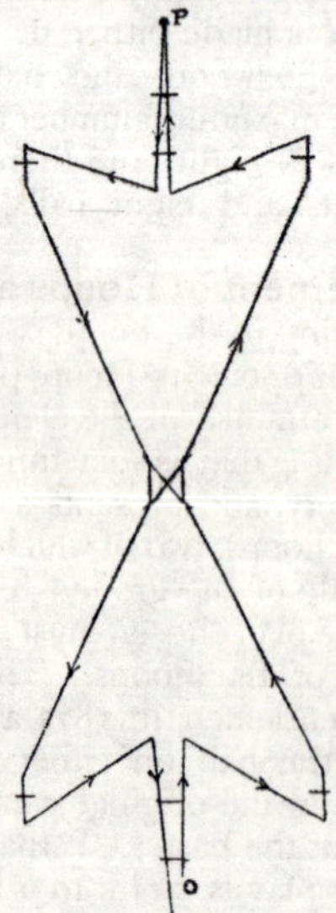

FIG. 2.

this he may again attempt to run through his next hoop, or to hit another ball, when the process is repeated. He may not, however, hit the same ball a second time, unless he has in the interval passed through a hoop in its proper order. Should he fail at any shot, the next player takes the turn.

It was, naturally, some time before the rules were satisfactorily settled, and the codes at first suggested were very complicated. Capt. Mayne Reid, for instance, required 126 rules with much explanation. In 1870, the Conference Code was issued, and that, with the slight modifications of the next two or three years, may be regarded as the standard authority. The most important amendment is that known as the Boundary Line Rule. By this, a player's turn comes to an end at once if he, in hitting the two balls placed together as above, drive either his own or the croqueted ball over the line that limits the Croquet Lawn. The effect of this is to prevent the player from indulging in smashing hits, which drive an opponent to the farthest end of the lawn, or which send his own ball flying over the boundary, to be replaced on the edge, within a yard or so of his partner. From the point of view of vigorous exercise, the game has perhaps been somewhat damaged, but it has gained much in delicacy and judgment.

The ideal form of the game requires four players, one pair playing against the other, or two players, each having two balls. These were the varieties adopted in the Championship games, when Croquet was universal.

Hints on Play—The golden rule of Croquet, as of Whist, is "Play to your partner's hand." It is useless to press on, making hoops, only to be obliged to come back and wait about for one's partner, who has been left behind, and subjected to the attacks of a united couple. So long as a pair can keep together, a game is never lost. Second to this is the warning, never to take an easy shot carelessly. The man who never misses a certainty is a far more dangerous opponent than the brilliant, but erratic player who brings off perhaps two long shots out of five, and who has often a yearning to leave his partner in the lurch in order to try them. Each must find out the position in aiming that best suits himself, but for a close shot there is no safer attitude (and few more inelegant) than to stand well over the ball, hold the mallet low, and swing it between the legs. Never *hit* with the mallet, nor should the hands grasp it, except in the "chop" stroke, very tightly. Let the arms swing quite freely, and it will be found, as in golf, that the work is done more effectively, and with a tithe of the exertion, if the weight of body and mallet is the main force applied.

There are two strokes to be used when the balls are to be croqueted which require and repay a considerable amount of practice. They are:—(1) The rolling, push, or follow-through stroke; and (2) the chop, screw, or stop stroke. In the first, the mallet must keep along its course at the same pace as the balls start, and there must not be the slightest checking at the moment of contact. Both balls will then run for a considerable, and for much the same, distance. In the "chop" stroke, on the other hand, the object is to move one's own ball as little as possible, and to drive the other well away. In this the mallet should, for once, be gripped tightly, and the ball hit as low as possible. The swing should be entirely checked at the moment of contact, if possible, not at the expense of the turf.

Remember always that however and wherever one's own ball is hit, *the direction* in which the other will tend to go is the line of the two centres produced.

It is perhaps necessary to remind the beginner that the next player must not be allowed to lie so close that he can take advantage of one's mistakes, but should be sent off, with due regard to the Boundary Rule, to the farthest possible distance.

There is no game in which judgment and strategy plays a larger part. Before each stroke one must instinctively ask upon which side of the object ball one would wish to be in case of failure, and play strength accordingly. Roughly speaking, it is well to play hard at an opponent, but gently at a partner, a rule that the partner at his next turn often finds to have been forgotten.

All the countless other devices of Croquet—the getting a "rush," *i.e.* hitting a ball with such force as to drive it into a favourable position for "taking two off"; finessing to the boundary when in difficulties, so that a partner may join one easily, and the distance make it not worth an opponent's while,—all these and their like can never be learned from books, but from hard work on the lawn. This one principle may, however, be again enforced, "*Play to your partner.*"

C. S. COLMAN.

GLOSSARY.

All England Croquet Club—The club was founded in 1866, and had its headquarters at Wimbledon. In 1871 it amalgamated with the National Croquet Club, and became the governing body of the sport. It conducted the annual contest for the championship every July, from 1869 (when the hoops were $7\frac{1}{4}$ in. wide) until its death. The A.E.C.C. succumbed to the popular enthusiasm for lawn tennis.

Ball—The balls are usually made of boxwood, and the proper diameter is $3\frac{3}{8}$ in., and the weight should be $14\frac{1}{2}$ oz. They are painted in various ways so that each player may distinguish his own without difficulty.

Bell—In old-fashioned settings of the hoops, a bell hung from the hoop or cap in the centre of the lawn, and no ball was supposed to have passed through it fairly unless the bell was rung.

Bisque—An extra stroke allowed to the weaker side in order to make the contest equal.

Blocked—To find a useless ball, or the *stick* (*q.v.*) in the way of a shot.

Booby—In early croquet a ball that misses its first hoop; now rarely seen.

Break—A sequence of successful shots at balls or hoops.

Cage—Two hoops crossed at right angles in the centre of the ground, as in the Eglinton Castle setting.

Climbing on the Scapegoat—Said by Captain Mayne Reid to be a technical term for "roqueing a ball into a better place for the player to croquet it, so that the roqueing ball may get in front of its own proper bridge, or obtain some other advantage of position." Equivalent to *rush* (*q.v*).

Clips—Thin plates of iron, variously coloured, and set upon the hoops which the respective balls were due to pass. They were found to increase the forgetfulness of players and abandoned.

Croquet—(1) The game itself.

(2) The act of hitting at the player's own ball when set against another which it has "roqueted."

(3) In the usual modern sense it may mean (*a*) the first hitting of a friendly or opposing ball; (*b*) the stroke upon them both when set together. *Roquet* is a term now very rarely heard.

Dead Ball—(1) A ball that has gone through all the hoops in their proper order and hit the stick.

(2) The ball of the last player, which has to wait longest for its turn to come again.

Dead Boundary Law—In 1872 the Conference Code made a rule for match play, which has been generally adopted, that if a player in croqueting the balls sent either of them over the boundary, he should at once lose the remainder of his turn.

Double Shot—Two balls lying so close together that if one be missed there is a very good chance of hitting the other.

Grand Round—The complete circuit of all the hoops up to the turning post and back again. Now rarely used.

Hollow Double—Two balls which lie near enough to one another to distract the aim, but not near enough to make the hitting of the one not aimed at likely.

Hong Kong, Off to—The old term for the driving of an opponent's ball from the croquet to the extreme corner of the ground. Also called driving it "up the country."

Hoops—The iron arches through which the ball must be driven. They have varied much in number and width. A book of instructions in 1867 recommended a width of 18 in., whilst the championship of 1872 was played with a width of hoop of $3\frac{3}{4}$ in. The best for ordinary play is 6 in. The number has varied from ten to six. [*See* SETTING.] The square-topped hoops are to be preferred to the rounded, which are a reminiscence of pall mall and the very early days of croquet, when the hoops were complete circles, "as round as a gong."

Jump Stroke—A stroke which takes the ball clear over another, which may be lying in the way of hoop or object ball. (Also called *Leap-frog stroke.*)

Loose Croquet—The striking of the player's ball when both are set together, without putting one's foot upon it. The form universally adopted now, but formerly only the privilege of the *Rover*, and termed *Roquet Croquet.*

Mallet—Consists of head and handle. The latter is now usually about 2 ft. 9 in. to 3 ft. in length, made of ash, and trimmed to an octagon shape at the top.

The head is cylindrical, generally of boxwood, though sometimes of lignum vitæ, 8 in. in length and 3 in. in diameter, the weight of mallet altogether being about $3\frac{1}{2}$ lbs.

Formerly the mallets were intended for use with one hand, and were very small and light. The heads were of all shapes—some like a barrel, some like a dice-box, some like pickaxes, and some actually trimmed to a leather-covered point like a billiard cue.

Pass Stroke—The hitting of the ball in croqueting so that both go about in the same direction, but the player's ball goes farthest. Really a foul stroke made by pressing the player's ball again after the opponent's has started.

Peg—[*See* POST.]

Player—The one whose turn comes next.

Post—The two sticks which have to be hit by each ball during the progress of the round. They should be 18 in. above the ground, and not less than an inch in diameter. Also called *Peg* and *Stick*, the last two being sometimes used as verbs, for hitting the post.

Roquet—The old and more correct term for hitting the ball off which croquet was to be taken. Now rarely used.

Roquet Croquet—[*See* LOOSE CROQUET.]

Rover—A ball which has passed through all the hoops in order, but has not hit the finishing post.

Rush—A position from which one can hit a ball and drive it into a more convenient position for making the croquet stroke proper. Hence to get a rush upon a ball is to put one's self in such a position.

Settings—The original setting had ten hoops. This was found too easy, and the Eglinton Castle setting with nine hoops, or eight hoops and a cage, was introduced (Fig. 1). Finally came the six-hoop or championship setting (Fig. 2).

Split Stroke—Taking croquet so as to drive the balls on courses nearly at right angles to one another.

Stick—[*See* POST].

Stop Stroke—Taking croquet so as to drive the object ball to a distance, but, by striking one's own ball low, to keep it near the original position. It resembles the screw shot in billiards.

Strike Out—To hit the winning post after passing through the hoops in order.

Take Croquet—After hitting a ball, to carry one's own to it, set it down touching, and then by hitting it, to send both in the desired directions.

Take Two Off—To take croquet in such a way that the ball not hit directly only just moves, whereas the player's ball closely follows the line of the mallet's swing.

Tight Croquet—The old method of taking croquet, which consisted in putting the foot upon one's own ball and driving the other by the shock of the stroke to the required spot. Now illegal.

Toll the Stake—Old term for hitting the post.

Tunnel—A very narrow hoop, or rather arch, of some length, said to have been used in the early days of croquet, but more probably only proposed.

Up Country—[*See* HONG KONG, OFF TO].

Wired—A ball is wired when one or both legs of a hoop are in the way of its effecting the shot desired, or in the way of an opponent who desires to hit it.

THE LAWS OF CROQUET.

1. **Mallets**—There shall be no restriction as to the number, weight, size, shape, or material of the mallets; nor as to the attitude or position of the striker; nor as to the part of the mallet held, provided the ball be not struck with the handle, nor the mace stroke used.

2. **Size of Balls**—The balls used in match play shall be $3\frac{5}{8}$ in. in diameter.

3. **Choice of Lead and of Balls**—It shall be decided by lot which side shall have choice of lead and of balls. In a succession of games the choice of lead shall be alternate, the sides keeping the same balls.

4. **Commencement of Game**—In commencing, each ball shall be placed on the starting spot. [*See* SETTINGS.] The striker's ball, when so placed and struck, is at once in play, and can roquet another, or be roqueted, whether it has made the first hoop or not.

5. **Stroke, when taken**—A stroke is considered to be taken if a ball be moved in the act of striking; but should a player, in taking aim, move his ball accidentally, it must be replaced to the satisfaction of the adversary, and the stroke be then taken. If a ball be moved in taking aim, and then struck without being replaced, the stroke is foul (*see* Law 25).

6. **Hoop, when run**—A ball has run its hoop when, having passed through from the playing side and ceased to roll, it cannot be touched by a straight-edge placed against the wires on the side from which it was played.

7. **Ball driven partly through Hoop**—A ball driven partly through its hoop from the non-playing side cannot run the hoop at its next stroke, if it can be touched by a straight-edge placed against the wires on the non-playing side.

8. **Points counted to Non-Striker's Ball**—A ball driven through its hoop, or against the turning peg, by any stroke not foul, whether of its own or of the adverse side, counts the point so made.

9. **Points made for Adversary's Ball**—If a point be made for an adversary's ball, the striker must inform his adversary of it. Should the striker neglect to do so, and the adversary make the point again, he may continue his turn as though he had played for his right point.

10. **The Turn**—A player, when his turn comes round, may roquet each ball once, and may do this again after each point made. The player continues his turn so long as he makes a point or a roquet.

11. **Croquet imperative after Roquet**—A player who roquets a ball must take croquet, and in so doing must move both balls (*see* Law 25). In taking croquet, the striker is not allowed to place his foot on the ball.

12. **Ball in Hand after Roquet**—No point or roquet can be made by a ball which is in hand. If a ball in hand displace any other balls, they must remain where they are driven. Any point made in consequence of such displacement counts, notwithstanding that the ball displacing them is in hand.

13. **Balls Roqueted simultaneously**—When a player roquets two balls simultaneously, he may choose from which of them he will take croquet; and a second roquet will be required before he can take croquet from the other ball.

14. **Balls found touching**—If at the commencement of a turn the striker's ball be found touching another, roquet is deemed to be made, and croquet must be taken at once.

15. **Roquet and Hoop made by same Stroke**—Should a ball in making its hoop, roquet another that lies beyond the hoop, and then pass through, the hoop counts as well as the roquet. A ball is deemed to be beyond the hoop if it lies so that it cannot be touched by a straight-edge placed against the wires on the playing side. Should any part of the ball that is roqueted be lying on the playing side of the hoop, the roquet counts, but not the hoop.

16. **Pegging out**—If a rover (except when in hand) be caused to hit the winning peg by any stroke of the same side, not foul, the rover is out of the game, and must be removed from the ground. A rover may similarly be pegged out by an adverse rover.

17. **Rover pegged out by Roquet**—A player who pegs out a rover by a roquet loses the remainder of his turn.

18. **Balls sent off the Ground**—A ball sent off the ground must at once be replaced 3 ft. within the boundary, measured from the spot where it went off, and at right angles to the margin. If this spot be already occupied, the ball last sent off is to be placed anywhere in contact with the other, at the option of the player sending off the ball.

19. **Ball sent off near Corner**—A ball sent off within 3 ft. of a corner is to be replaced 3 ft. from both boundaries.

20. **Ball touching Boundary**—If the boundary be marked by a line on the turf, a ball touching the line is deemed to have been off the ground. If the boundary be raised, a ball touching the boundary is similarly deemed to have been off the ground.

21. **Ball sent off and returning to Ground**—If a ball be sent off the ground, and return to it, the ball must be similarly replaced, measuring from the point of first contact with the boundary.

22. **Ball sent within 3 ft. of Boundary**—A ball sent within 3 ft. of the boundary, but not off the ground, is to be replaced as though it had been sent off, except in the case of the striker's ball, when the striker has the option of bringing his ball in, or of playing from where it lies.

23. **Boundary interfering with Stroke**—If it be found that the height of the boundary interferes with the stroke, the striker, with the sanction of the umpire, may bring in the balls a longer distance than 3 ft., so as to allow a free swing of the mallet. Balls so brought in must be moved in the line of aim.

24. **Dead Boundary**—If, in taking croquet, the striker send his own ball, or the ball croqueted, off the ground, he loses the remainder of his turn; but if by the same stroke he make a roquet, his ball, being in hand, may pass the boundary without penalty. Should either ball, while rolling after a croquet, be touched or diverted from its course by an opponent, the striker has the option given him by Law 26, and is not liable to lose his turn should the ball which has been touched or diverted pass the boundary.

25. **Foul Strokes**—If a player make a foul stroke, he loses the remainder of his turn, and any point or roquet made by such stroke does not count. Balls moved by a foul stroke are to remain where they lie, or be replaced, at the option of the adversary. If the foul be made when taking croquet, and the adversary elect to have the balls replaced, they must be replaced in contact as they stood when the croquet was taken. The following are foul strokes:—

(*a*) To strike with the mallet another ball instead of or besides one's own, in making the stroke.
(*b*) To spoon—*i.e.* to push a ball without an audible knock.
(*c*) To strike a ball twice in the same stroke.
(*d*) To touch, stop, or divert the course of a ball when in play and rolling, whether this be done by the striker or his partner.
(*e*) To allow a ball to touch the mallet in rebounding from a peg or wire.
(*f*) To move a ball which lies close to a peg or wire by striking the peg or wire.
(*g*) To press a ball round a peg or wire (crushing stroke).
(*h*) To play a stroke after roquet without taking croquet.
(*i*) To fail to move both balls in taking croquet.
(*k*) To croquet a ball which the striker is not entitled to croquet.

26. **Balls touched by Adversary**—Should a ball when rolling, except it be in hand, be touched, stopped, or diverted from its course by an adversary, the striker may elect whether he will take the stroke again, or whether the ball shall remain where it stopped, or be placed where, in the judgment of the umpire, it would have rolled to.

27. **Balls stopped or diverted by Umpire**—Should a ball be stopped or diverted from its course by an umpire, he is to place it where he considers it would have rolled to.

28. **Playing out of Turn, or with the Wrong Ball**—If a player play out of turn, or with the wrong ball, the remainder of the turn is lost, and any point or roquet made after the mistake. The balls remain where they lie when the penalty is claimed, or are replaced as they were before the last stroke was made, at the option of the adversary. But if the adverse side play without claiming the penalty, the turn holds good, and any point or points made after the mistake are scored to the ball by which they have been made (that is, the ball is deemed to be for the point next in order to the last point made in the turn), except when the adversary's ball has been played with, in which case the points are scored to the ball which ought to have been played with. If more than one ball be played with during the turn, all points made during the turn, whether before or after the mistake, are scored to the ball last played with. Whether the penalty be claimed or not, the adversary may follow with either ball of his own side.

29. **Playing for Wrong Point**—If a player make a wrong point it does not count, and, therefore (unless he have, by the same stroke, taken croquet, or made a roquet), all subsequent strokes are in error, the remainder of the turn is lost, and any point or roquet made after the mistake. The balls remain where they lie when the penalty is claimed, or are replaced as they were before the last stroke was made, at the option of the adversary. But if the player make another point, or the adverse side play, before the penalty is claimed, the turn holds good; and the player who made the mistake is deemed to be for the point next in order to that which he last made.

30. **Information as to Score**—Every player is entitled to be informed which is the next point of any ball.

31. **State of Game, if disputed**—When clips are used, their position, in case of dispute, shall be conclusive as to the position of the balls in the game.

32. **Wires knocked out of Ground**—Should a player, in trying to run his hoop, knock a wire of that hoop out of the ground with his ball, the hoop does not count. The ball must be replaced, and the stroke taken again; but if by the same stroke a roquet be made, the striker may elect whether he will claim the roquet or have the balls replaced.

33. **Pegs or Hoops not upright**—Any player may set upright a peg or hoop, except the one next in order; and that must not be altered except by the umpire.

34. **Ball lying in a Hole or on Bad Ground**—A ball lying in a hole or on bad ground may be moved with the sanction of the umpire. The ball must be put back —*i.e.* away from the object aimed at—and so as not to alter the line of aim.

35. **Umpires**—An umpire shall not give his opinion, or notice any error that may be made, unless appealed to by one of the players. The decision of an umpire, when appealed to, shall be final. The duties of an umpire are—

(*a*) To decide matters in dispute during the game, if appealed to.
(*b*) To keep the score, and, if asked by a player, to disclose the state of it.
(*c*) To move the clips, or to see that they are properly moved.
(*d*) To replace balls sent off the ground, or to see that they are properly replaced.
(*e*) To adjust hoops or pegs not upright, or to see that they are properly adjusted.

36. **Absence of Umpire**—When there is no umpire present, permission to move a ball, or to set up a peg or hoop, or other indulgence for which an umpire would be appealed to, must be asked of the other side.

37. **Appeal to Referee**—Should an umpire be unable to decide any point at issue, he may appeal to the referee, whose decision shall be final; but no player may appeal to the referee from the decision of an umpire.

Bibliography.—*Rules for the Game of Croquet*, G. V. H. (Bosworth, 1862, 2/6); *Croquet*, Capt. Mayne Reid (Warne, 1863, 2/6; *The Game of Croquet* (Cassell's Sixpenny Handbooks, 1866); *Croquet and Lawn Tennis*, Captain Crawley (Chambers' Useful Handbooks. 1866, 6/-); *Routledge's Handbook of Croquet*, E. Routledge, 1864 and 1867, 6*d.*); *Croquet Tactics*, W. J. Whitmore (H. Cox, 1868, 2/6); *Croquet: the Laws and Regulations of the Game*, J. Jaques (Jaques, 1864, 1865, and 1870, 1/- and 6*d.*); *Notes on Croquet, and some Ancient Bat and Ball Games*, R. C. A. Prior (F. Norgate, 1872, 3/6); *The Book of Croquet*, Arthur Lillie (London, 1872). *All England Croquet Club. Regulations for the Management of Prize Meetings*, 1870, 1871, 1873, and 1875; *Lawn Tennis, Croquet, &c.* (Ward and Lock, 1882 and 1890, 6*d.*); *Laws of Croquet*, B. C. Eveleigh (F. H. Ayres, 1893); *The Laws of Croquet.* Adopted at the General Conference of Croquet Clubs, Jan. 19, 1870 (De la Rue, 1870, 1871, 1873, 1894); *The Complete Croquet Player* (Oval Series), J. D. Heath (Routledge, 1896, 1/-; another ed. 1874).

CURLEW—[*See* SHORE SHOOTING].

CURLING is the most characteristic of Scottish sports, and in one form or other has been practised in that country for more than four centuries back. From some of the words found in the glossary annexed hereto,—such as Kuting, Rink. Bonspiel, Tee, etc.,—some have maintained that the game was introduced into Scotland from the Low Countries, but this inference from etymology is contradicted by historical facts, and there is little doubt that curling, in its origin as in its development, is peculiarly Scottish. Although now to be found in most other countries where ice abounds, there is always a Scottish ring about the game, and even more than golf, which has now spread over the world, it is regarded as a national sport, the title generally given to it by its devotees being—"Scotland's ain game." At first the game seems to have been a kind of quoiting on the ice, a stone rounded by some river[1] and weighing a few pounds being used, with a niche for the thumb on one side, and one for the fingers on the other. With a curving sweep from behind, the player pitched his large pebble, and the ice carried it to the tee or mark aimed at, the thrower making due allowance for the nature of the surface in delivering his shot. This was the Kuting-Stone or Pilty-cock period of curling. Next came the Giant, or Boulder age, when the curler took a large boulder or block from the river-bed, inserted a rough iron handle therein, and propelled it along the ice to the desired goal. The variety of weight and shape of stone during this period must have been infinite, for while 60 lbs. was about the minimum, we hear of some stones which actually weighed 200 lbs., and one is on exhibition which turns the scale at 117 lbs. Each player used one stone, and when the many-shaped boulders lay around the Gogsee or Tozee they must have had a motley appearance, and some of their owners must have been giants. About the middle of last century the curling stone was found in a more civilised shape, the formation of clubs for the purpose of enjoying the sport having a good deal to do with the improvement. By the end of the century the stones were all rounded with more or less precision, though some were still rather uncouth in appearance, and the variety of chiselling so great, that force rather than scientific accuracy ruled the play. The two most renowned curling clubs of last century were the Canonmills and the Duddingston clubs. As a proof of the national character of the game, it may be stated that in the Scottish capital the magistrates used to march in procession, headed by a band playing the *Curler's March*, to open the winter's sport on the Nor' Loch, where the Edinburgh curlers played before they were driven therefrom to Canonmills when the Loch was drained dry for city improvements. In the history of this popular pastime, the most important event was the institution in 1838 of the Grand Caledonian Curling Club, the object of which was to be a Curling Union, in which all clubs would be associated, and which, by representatives from all its clubs annually convened as a curling parliament, would regulate the laws of the game at home and abroad. This association or union has been most successful, and it may safely be said that no sport is so admirably supervised and regulated as Curling, a fact which is due to the admirable way in which the business of the head club is conducted.[2]

Curling, like golf, is not only ancient, but also royal. There are some shadowy traditions that several of the Stuart kings played the game; and the unfortunate Darnley, who was for a time husband of the still more unfortunate Queen Mary, is reputed to have been a curler. When the Prince Consort and her Majesty the Queen were on a visit to Scotland, they were initiated into the mysteries of the game by the Earl of Mansfield, then President of the Grand Club, and the Prince then agreed to become its patron. Soon after, the club received permission to wear the title "Royal," and as "The Royal Caledonian Curling Club" it has continued to preside over the sport. From its institution may be dated the great improvement that has made the game one of the most scientific, and required the development of the stones on such lines that they are now "things of beauty." By awarding medals for competition between clubs and districts, and by the great national gathering at Carsebreak for the Grand Match, in which the North of the Forth curlers meet those of the South in battle; by the recent institution of the International Match—England *v.* Scotland, and in a thousand other ways, the Royal Club has fostered and advanced the fascinating ice-game, and made it popular far beyond the borders of its home. Through the club's influence, the sport will, no doubt, become still more popular. There is certainly no manlier, healthier game, and the countries are fortunate in which it has been taken up and practised with enthusiasm.

Ice is, of course, the first requisite for curling. But the ice must be in good condition. Quality is of more importance than quantity. Frost being so fickle in our country, curlers have in many places had cement ponds laid out. With a few degrees of frost they can have a game on these by sprinkling water over the

[1] Hence the term channel-stone still given to the curling-stone.

[2] The present secretary of the club is Mr. A. Davidson Smith, C.A., and the offices are at 4A, York Place, Edinburgh. In the *Annual* published by the club may be found all information as to the laws of the game, literary contributions relating to it, and a list of all the associated clubs and their members.

surface, which immediately freezes. In this way play can be obtained when the natural ice is not strong enough. At various times and places, and at great expense, ice rinks have been constructed, where ice is made by an artificial process, and curlers and skaters can enjoy themselves all the year round in a handsome building, independent of the changes of the climate. In Canada, with the intense frost which there prevails, curlers have natural ice with covered rinks, and all the comforts which these are supposed to afford. But curling is best enjoyed in the open air, and is to be seen at its best when Greek meets Greek on some moorland loch surrounded by snow-covered mountains. The majority of curling clubs have ponds constructed so that there is no danger to the players from the depth of the water, should the ice give

FIG. 1.—A SCOTTISH RINK.

way. These have to be constructed by puddling the bottom with clay about 6 in. thick, and making embankments suitable to the depth. The cost is not great, and the up-keep of such ponds is also simple, so that to start a curling club need not be an expensive matter. Nor is the curler's outfit costly. He must have a Broom, or Kowe, to sweep the ice when directed, for sweeping is a most important part of the game; but the best brooms, made from the plant of that name, cost nothing, and if that cannot be had, two shillings will procure a broom of sufficient power. The curler's chief equipment is a pair of stones exactly matched. These range in value from 30*s.* to £5, and fancy prices are, of course, paid for fancy pairs. Each stone is fitted with a reversible handle and bolt, a good pair of handles being procurable for 10*s.* or 12*s.* 6*d.* The open or swan-necked are generally used, but a few use the closed oval variety. Curling-stones are named after the places where they are procured. The principal varieties now in the market are Ailsa Craig, Crawfordjohn, Burnock Water, Douglas Water, Crieff, Carsphairn, and Tinkernhill. By far the larger proportion of curling-stones now in use bear the name of Ailsa Craig, from which they are quarried, and cut into square blocks before being sent to the manufacturers to be rounded and polished. They are so hard that they best resist the effect of hard knocks, and in Canada they are preferred because the excessive frost does not affect them so much as softer varieties. In the home country, Crawfordjohn and Burnock Water are also very popular stones. It is important, however, that these should be boulders before being wrought into shape, for the quarried stones, owing to the blasting, are often *strained* and therefore liable to fracture; whereas the boulders, if well rounded, must have come through a long experience of grinding against each other until their flaws have all been detected and destroyed. By a recent resolution of the Royal Club, the maximum weight of the curling-stone (and handle) has been fixed at 44 lbs. From 40 lbs. to 44 lbs. is a suitable weight for the lead or first-hand player, while from 33 lbs. to 40 lbs. is appropriate for other players. The majority of stones will be found to be included between 35 lbs. and 38 lbs. (At Montreal, Quebec, and other places in Canada, where iron has to be used in place of stone, the usual weight is from 60 lbs. to 70 lbs.) Each stone has two sides, one for dull, the other for keen ice. The former is usually highly polished, and so curved that the stone runs on a pivot, thus getting easily through slush when the ice is "baugh" or soft; but in Canada, and in many cases at home, a small hollow about 2½ in. wide is scooped out, and the stone, running on the ring or rim of the hollow, is supposed to keep better hold of the ice. The dull side of the stone, which is used when the ice is keen, has a much larger concave or hollow, the diameter of the ring in this case ranging from 5 in. to 7 in. This gives the stone a better catch of the ice, and all leading stones should be thus concaved, that they may be able to keep their position in the "house." This side is not so highly polished as the other. No stone is allowed in play whose circumference exceeds 36 in., and its height must not be less than one-eighth part of its greatest circumference. Those who wish to provide themselves with stones and other curling requisites will find the names of manufacturers in the advertising pages of the Royal Club *Annual*, which costs one shilling, and may be had at the club's offices from the secretary. Before describing rink-play, which is the proper game of Curling, we may show the various parts of the game by "points," which are practised by curlers, and for which one day in the season is usually set apart. Just as a golfer might practice driving, lofting, and putting preparatory to a full game at golf, so the curler may learn his art by trying his hand at the various "points" which have been selected to illustrate the anatomy of Curling.

The following are *The Rules for the Point Game*, laid down by the Royal Club:—

1. Competitors shall draw lots for the rotation of play, and shall use two Stones.

2. The measurement of the Rink for Point Play shall be in conformity with the provisions of Rule 1 for Rink Play.

3. Two Circles, having a radius of 4 ft. and 7 ft. respectively, shall be drawn round the Tee, and a line through the centre of these circles to the Hog score.

4. Every Competitor shall play four shots at each of the nine following points of the game, viz., Striking, Inwicking, Drawing, Guarding, Chap and Lie, Wick and Curl in, Raising, Chipping the Winner, and Drawing through a Port, according to the definitions and diagrams here given.

5. In Nos. 2, 6, 8, and 9, and at *Outwicking* when played, two Stones shall be played on the right and two on the left.

6. No Stone shall be considered *without* a circle unless it is entirely clear of that circle.

NOTE 1.—No scores made in Local Competitions shall be reported in the *Annual* unless these have been conducted under the above Rules.

NOTE 2.—Much time will be saved if two Rinks be prepared lying parallel to each other, the Tee of the one being at the reverse end of the other Rink; every Competitor plays both Stones up the one Rink, and immediately afterwards both down the other, finishing thus at each round all his chances at that point.

The following is the diagram to be drawn on the ice before playing:—

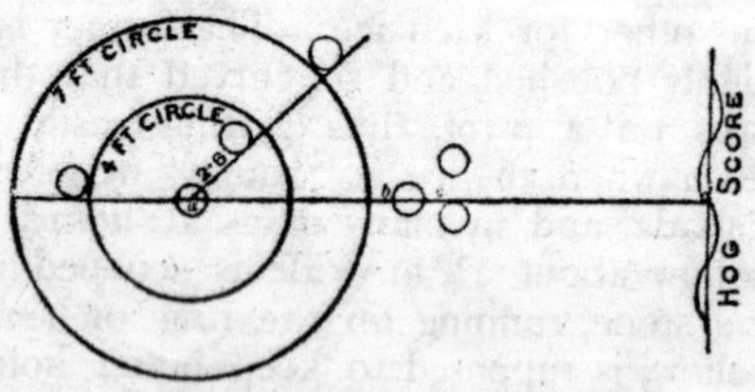

a–b=8 ft. a–c=10 ft. a–d=21 ft.

Placed Stones shown ● Played Stones shown ⊙

The various points and the values given for them in the point game are shown in the diagrams and definitions here given:—

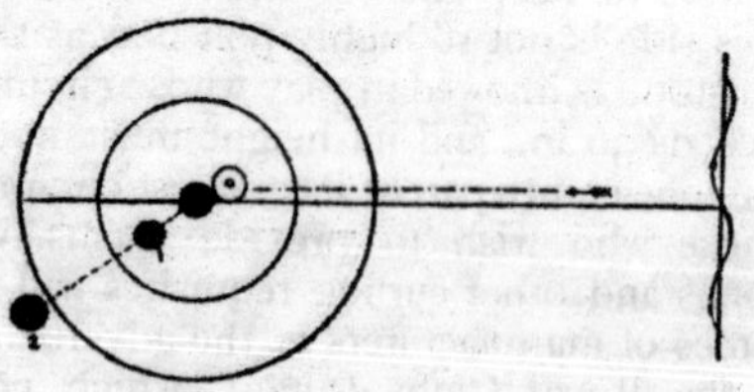

1. Striking—A Stone being placed on the Tee, if struck, shall count 1; if struck out of the 7-ft. circle, it shall count 2.

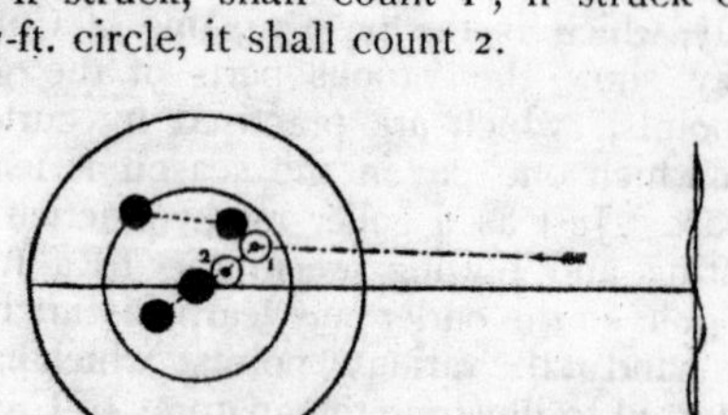

2. Inwicking—A Stone being placed on the Tee, and another with its inner edge 2 ft. 6 in. from the Tee, and its fore edge on a line drawn from the Tee at an angle of 45° with the central line, if the played Stone strike the latter on the inside, it shall count 1; if it perceptibly move both Stones, it shall count 2.

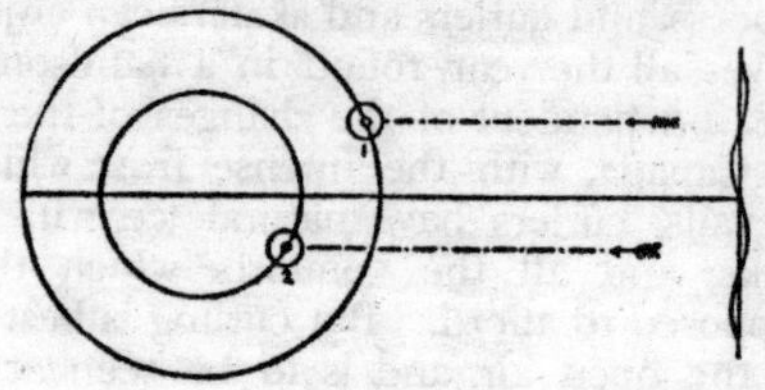

3. Drawing—A Stone being played, if the same lie within or on the 7-ft. circle, it shall count 1; if within or on the 4-ft. circle, it shall count 2.

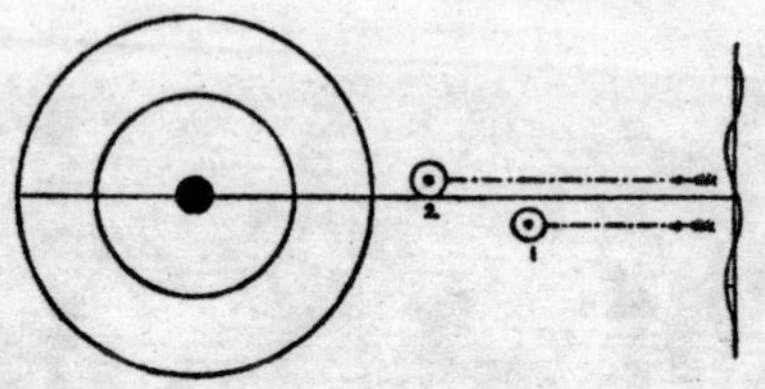

4. Guarding—A Stone being placed on the Tee, if the Stone played rest within 6 in. of the central line, it shall count 1; if on the line, it shall count 2. It must be over the Hog, but must not touch the Stone to be guarded.

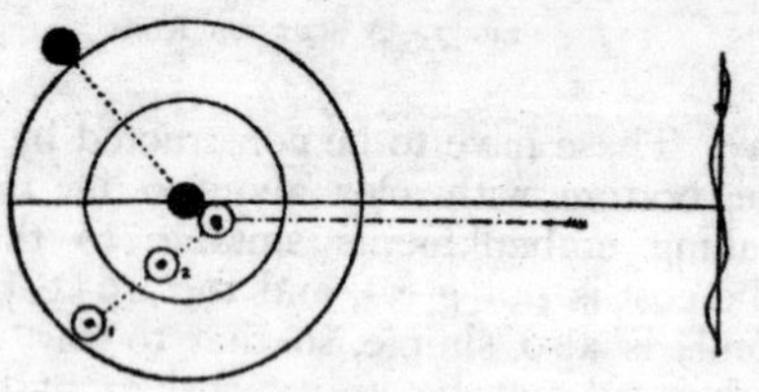

5. Chap and Lie—A Stone being placed on the Tee, if struck out of the 7-ft. circle, and the played Stone lie within or on the same circle, it shall count 1; if struck out of the 7-ft. circle, and the played Stone lie within or on the 4-ft. circle, it shall count 2.

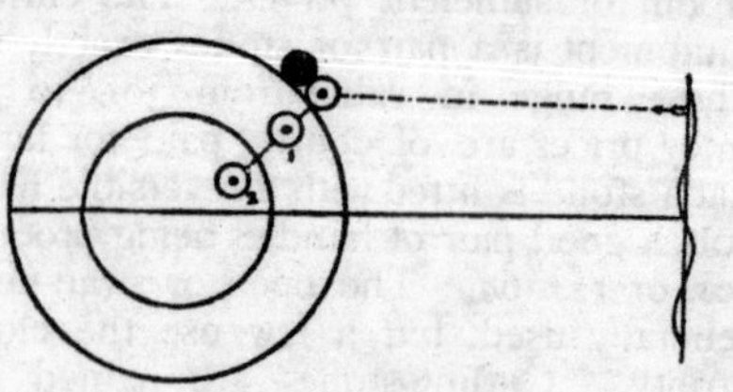

6. Wick and Curl in—A Stone being placed with its inner edge 7 ft. distant from the Tee, and its fore edge on a line making an angle of 45° with the central line, if the same be struck, and the played Stone curl on or within the 7-ft. circle, it shall count 1; if struck, and the played Stone curl on or within the 4-ft. circle, it shall count 2.

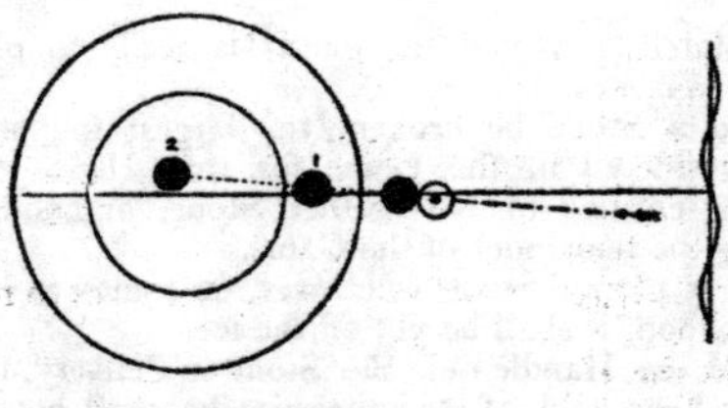

7. **Raising**—A Stone being placed with its centre on the central line and its inner edge 8 ft. in front of the Tee, if it be struck into or on the 7-ft. circle, it shall count 1; if struck into or on the 4-ft. circle, it shall count 2.

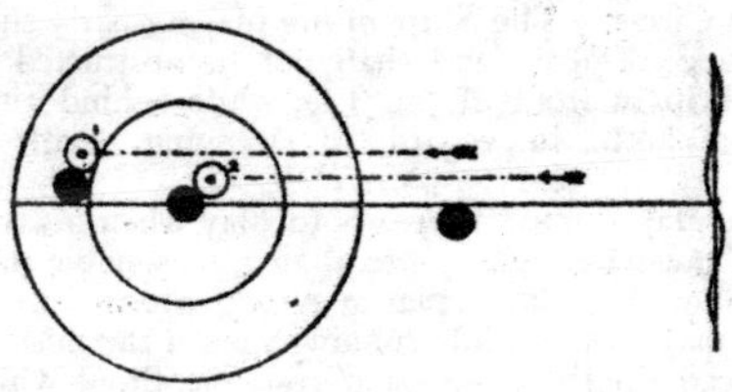

8. **Chipping the Winner**—A Stone being placed on the Tee, and another with its inner edge 10 ft. in front, just touching the central line, and half guarding the one on the Tee, and a third Stone being placed 4 ft. behind the Tee, with its inner edge touching the central line, but on the opposite side from that on which the guard is placed, if the played Stone strike the Stone placed behind the Tee, it shall count 1; if it strike the Stone on the Tee, it shall count 2.

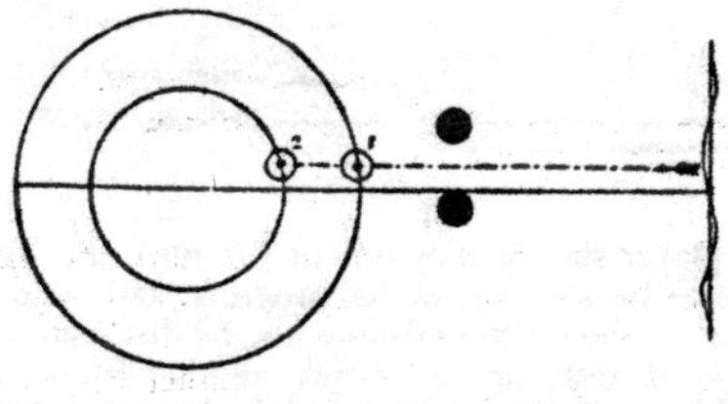

9. **Drawing through a Port**—A Stone being placed with its inner edge on the central line 10 ft. in front of the Tee, and another Stone on the opposite side and with its inner edge 2 ft. from the central line, if the played Stone pass between these two Stones without touching either, and rest within or on the 7-ft. circle, it shall count 1; if within or on the 4-ft. circle, it shall count 2.

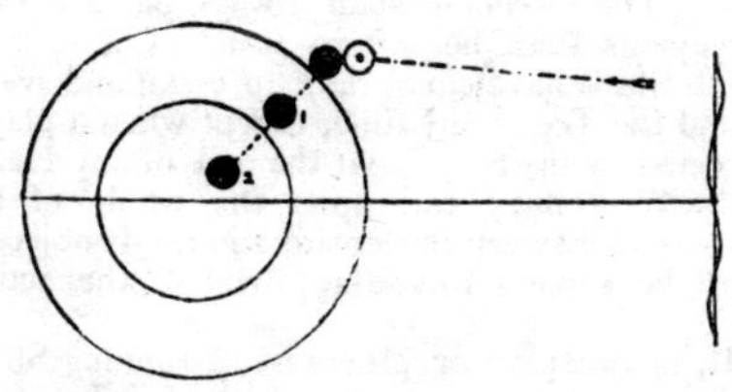

Outwicking—A Stone being placed with its inner edge 7 ft. distant from the Tee, and its centre on a line making an angle of 45° with the central line, if struck within or on the 7-ft. circle, it shall count 1; if struck within or on the 4-ft. circle, it shall count 2.

This point is only played in the event of two or more competitors gaining the same number of shots.

If the competition cannot be decided by these shots, the Umpire shall order one or more of the preceding points to be played again by the Competitors who are equal.

The point game serves a good purpose. It shows how difficult curling is; for while it is possible to score 72 at these 8 points, no one has ever done so, or hoped to do so. Twenty-five is accounted a good score, and medals, in the great majority of clubs, are won with scores under that figure.

These points, as we have indicated, are only the "bones" of curling. The living game is the rink-game. The word *Rink* has two meanings. In one case it is the team of four players.

FIG. 2.—A SWISS RINK.

When this rink is made up, with a skilled and tried hand as skip or captain, and three other trusty players under him, and three opponents under their skip are drawn against them in battle array, the contest begins. The rink is also the name for the field of battle itself. This has to be clearly drawn and defined, for it is not only the slippery nature of the field, but also its narrowness, that makes the curling fight so keen. The game is not allowed to go on "all over the place," but a small portion of the ice is taken up, scores and broughs or circles laid down, and limitations fixed which give intensity and excitement to the play. We must now proceed to give a diagram of the ground, or *Rink*.

The following directions comprise in brief the chief requirements of the diagram and conditions of the rink. It need scarcely be explained that the dark lines bounding the diagram are not to be drawn, and that rinks may be multiplied according to the extent of

the pond and of the match, without making any boundaries of that kind, sufficient space being afforded for each two rinks of players to have their game.

DIRECTIONS.

1. The Tees to be 38 yds. apart.

2. Around each Tee draw a circle having a radius of 7 ft.

[Inner circles may also be drawn.]

3. In alignment with the Tees, draw central lines to points 4 yds. behind each Tee.

4. Draw scores across the Rink at right angles to the central line, viz. :—

(*a*) The *Foot Score*—18 in. in length, 4 yds. behind each Tee.

(*b*) The *Back Score*—behind and just touching outside the 7-ft. circle.

(*c*) The *Sweeping Score*—across the 7-ft. circle and through each Tee.

(*d*) The *Hog Score*—Distant from the Tee one sixth part of the distance between the Foot Score and the further Tee.

N.B.—The length of the Rink for play is 42 yds. It may be shortened, but in no case shall it be less than 32 yds.

All measurements of shots shall be from the centre of the Tee to the nearest part of the stone.

during a Match, provided the player is ready to play when his turn comes.

6. Should a Stone be broken, the largest fragment shall be considered in the Game for that Head—the player being entitled to use another Stone, or another pair, during the remainder of the Game.

7. When a played Stone rolls over, or comes to rest on its side or top, it shall be put off the ice.

8. Should the Handle quit the Stone in delivery, the player must keep hold of it; otherwise he shall not be entitled to replay the shot.

9. Players, during the course of each Head, shall be arranged along the sides, but well off the centre of the Rink, as the Skips may direct; and no one, except when sweeping according to rule, shall go upon the centre of the Rink, or cross it, under any pretence whatever. Skips only shall be entitled to stand within the Seven-Foot Circle. The Skip of the playing party shall have the choice of place, and shall not be obstructed by the other Skip in front of the Tee, while behind it the privileges of both, in regard to sweeping, shall be equal.

10. Each player must be ready to play when his turn comes, and must not take more than a reasonable time to play. Should a player play a wrong Stone, any of the players may stop it while running; but if the mistake is not noticed till the Stone is at rest, the Stone which ought to have been played shall be put in its place, to the satisfaction of the opposing Skip.

Diagram to be drawn on the Ice and referred to throughout the Rules as the Rink.

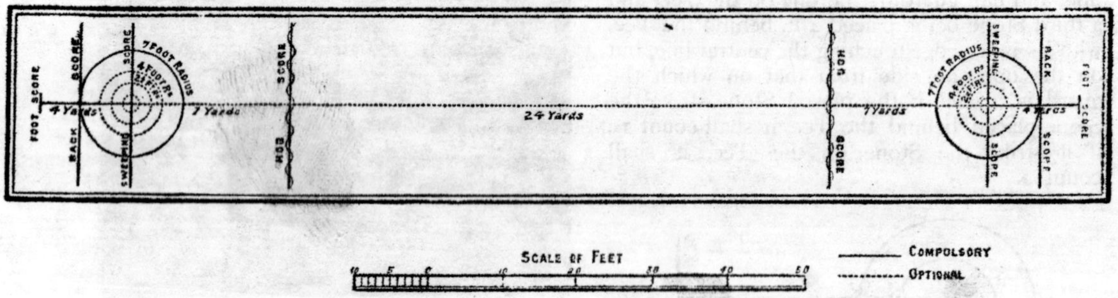

With the diagram and directions before us, we may now deal with the rules of the game as drawn up and recently revised by the Royal Club.

THE RULES OF THE GAME OF CURLING.

1. All Matches shall be of a certain number of Heads, or Shots, or by Time as may be agreed on, or as fixed by an Umpire at the outset. In the event of Competitors being equal, play shall be continued by all the Rinks engaged for another Head or Heads until the Match has been decided.

2. Every Rink of players shall be composed of four a side, each using two Stones. The rotation of play observed during the first Head of a Match shall not be changed.

3. The Skips opposing each other shall settle by lot, or in any other way they may agree upon, which party shall lead at the first Head, after which the winners of the preceding Head shall do so.

4. All Curling-Stones shall be of a circular shape. No Stone, including handle, shall be of a greater weight than 44 lbs. imperial, or of greater circumference than 36 in., or of less weight than one eighth part of its greatest circumference.

5. No Stone shall be substituted for another (except under Sections 10 and 14) after a Match has been begun, but the sole of a Stone may be reversed at any time

11. If a player should play out of his turn, the Stone so played may be stopped in its progress, and returned to the player. Should the mistake not be discovered till the Stone is at rest, or has struck another Stone, the opposing Skip shall have the option of adding one to his score and allowing the Game to proceed, or of declaring the Head null and void. If another Stone be played before the mistake is discovered, the Head must be finished as if it had been properly played from the beginning.

12. The sweeping shall be under the direction and control of the Skips. The player's party may sweep the ice from the Hog Score next the player to the Tee, and any Stone set in motion by a played Stone may be swept by the party to which it belongs. When snow is falling or drifting, the player's party may sweep the ice from Tee to Tee. The sweeping shall always be to a side, and no sweepings shall be left in front of a running Stone. Both Skips have equal right to clean and sweep the ice behind the Tee at any time, except when a player is being directed by his Skip. At the end of any Head, either of the Skips may call upon the whole of the players to clean and sweep the entire Rink. If objected to, this shall be subject to the approval of the acting Umpire.

13. (*a*) If, in sweeping or otherwise, a running Stone is marred by any of the party to which it belongs, it may, in the option of the opposing Skip, be put off the ice; but if by any of the adverse party, it may be placed where the Skip of the party to which it belongs shall

direct. If marred in any other way, the player shall replay the Stone.

(*b*) Should any played Stone be displaced before the Head is reckoned, it shall be placed as nearly as possible where it lay, to the satisfaction of the Skip opposed to the party displacing. If displaced by any neutral party, both Skips should agree upon the position to which it is to be returned; but if they do not agree, the Umpire shall decide.

14. No measuring of shots shall be allowed previous to the termination of the Head. Disputed shots shall be determined by the Skips; if they disagree, by the Umpire; or, when there is no Umpire, by some neutral person chosen by the Skips. All measurements shall be taken from the centre of the Tee to the nearest part of the Stone.

15. The Skip shall have the exclusive regulation and direction of the Game for his Rink, and may play last Stone, or any part in the Game he pleases, but he shall not be entitled to change his position when that has been fixed. When his turn to play comes, he shall select one of his players to act as Skip in his place, and take the position of an ordinary player. He shall not have any choice or direction in the game till he returns to the Tee as Skip.

16. If any player engaged in the Game shall speak to, annoy, taunt, or interrupt another, not being of his own side, while in the act of delivering his Stone, one shot for each offence may be added to the score of the party so annoyed.

17. If from any change of weather after a Match has been begun, or from any other reasonable cause, one party shall desire to shorten the Rink, or to change to another, and if the two Skips cannot agree, the Umpire shall, after seeing one end played, determine whether and how much the Rink shall be shortened, or whether it shall be changed, and his decision shall be final. Should there be no acting Umpire, or should he be otherwise engaged, the two Skips may call in any neutral Curler to decide, and his powers shall be equal with those of the Umpire. The Umpire shall, in the event of the ice appearing to him to be dangerous, stop the Match. He shall postpone it, even if begun, when the state of the ice is in his opinion not fitted for testing the Curling skill of the players. Except in very special circumstances, of which the Umpire shall be judge, a Match shall not proceed, or be continued, when a thaw has fairly set in, or when snow is falling and likely to continue during the Match, nor shall it be continued if darkness comes on to prevent the played Stones being well seen by players at the other end of the Rink. In every case the Match, when renewed, must be begun *de novo*.

18. Every Stone shall be eligible to count which is not clearly outside the Seven-Foot Circle. Every Stone which does not clear the Hog-Score shall be a Hog, and must be removed from the ice, but no Stone shall be considered a Hog which has struck another Stone lying in position. Stones passing the Back Score, and lying clear of it, must be removed from the ice, as also any Stone which in its progress touches the swept snow on either side of the Rink.

At the opening of the game the two skips take their place at the Boardhead to direct their players. Skip A having won the toss, calls on his "lead" to play. The lead "fits his tee," that is, gets himself into proper position on the crampit or iron footboard, which with its under-spikes fixed in the ice is prevented from slipping. A canny, or quiet, draw is expected from the lead, and it is better that his stone, when spent, should lie short of the tee, where it is in the way of promotion, than be past, when it is not likely to count. Skip B now has his turn, and he tries to get his leader to play a stone nearer the tee than his neighbour. So the game goes on. If either skip gets a stone into good position, he tries to get it guarded or protected by the next player. When the three on each side have done their parts the skips

FIG. 3.—A SKIP AT WORK.

then take the position of ordinary players, each being directed by his third or hin'-han' player. Very often the fate of the end or head depends on them, so they require to be cool and experienced players. The skips having finished, the "end" or "head" is counted. All stones that

FIG. 4.—A PLAYER FITTING HIS TEE.

lie within the 7-ft. ring are eligible for counting, and if one skip had all his shots so well played as to lie therein, while none of his opponent's are in the desired territory, he might actually score 8. This, however, is a rare occurrence in the game. Indeed, the game is best when it is a tussle for one shot at each end, and that depending on the last stone. Curling has been called bowling on the ice, but a true curler would call bowling a very feeble shadow of his favourite game. A stone is useless that does not reach the colly or hog score, and of no

FIG. 5.—HIS EYE ON THE SKIP.

value if it passes out of the parish, or 7-ft. ring. This confines the area of play, and calls for greater nicety of calculation than in bowling. The *twist*, which corresponds to the bias at bowling, is also a much more scientific action as seen in curling. The stone itself gives no assistance by an overweighted side as in the case of a bowl. By an elbow-in or elbow-out turn (which is really more from the wrist than from the elbow) a stone may be made to curl round a guard and find a winner, or to go straight to the tee when the bias of the ice leads away from it; the in-turn is made when the curl is to be toward the right, the out-turn when it is to the left. This is the acme of scientific play, and is seen to perfection on the Canadian rinks, where they have more practice and generally better ice than in this country. Without this power the player is at the mercy of the bias, and must content himself with such a "borrow" as will eventually lead his stone to the place aimed at.

Any ordinary match will give occasion for all the "points" formerly described being required. But others abound as infinite and varied as Cleopatra's charms. Some are of the quiet order. The player will be called on to "crack an egg," to "come snoovin down the howe and chuckle gently to the patlid," to "edge in to the fireside," to "smell the ring," to "cuddle into Grannie's wing," to "kittle up" one stone and let another "die" as his skip directs, to "pit doon a bit sidelin' shot on 'ither side the Wittyr'," and so on, all these directions being redolent of the home of the game. Or, as desperate diseases require desperate remedies, he may be asked to "come wi' a hair o' pith," and "cannon" or "redd the hoose"; he may be asked to "ride" out the winner or drive a "bullet" into him, or if things appear hopeless he may simply try "a thunderin' cast," and wait the result of rebutting, for strange things happen betimes in the parish when every way to victory seems barred. Only recently, in a match played at Edinburgh, one side were lying five shots, and the skip of the other side sent up his last stone in desperation and with all his might; when the air cleared, it was found that the five shots of the enemy had all been removed, and that his own side actually lay five shots!

It is essential in curling that implicit obedience be given by the players to the skip, and when they are not playing the members of a rink should all be on the alert, ready to sweep their utmost or to desist from sweeping, as the skip directs. Indeed, the importance of this part of the game can scarcely be over-estimated. "Keep your eye on the skip" is a good rule for the player when about to deliver his stone. Some hunker, others stand half erect. There is no certain rule. But a player who gets into position in the style of the Fig. No. 5, follows what appears to us the best plan for taking accurate aim and having complete power over the stone. As he elevates his body he raises the stone, and, stepping forward, he brings it down in such a gentle curve that it meets the ice without friction and has a good start in its career, which in curling, as in life, goes for much. Figs. 5, 6, 7, 8 are illustrations of various stages in the swing and delivery of the stone which may all be studied with advantage.

It is claimed for curling that it is the healthiest of all sports, giving "birr and smed-

FIG. 6—SOLING THE STONE.

dum" to the body at the season of the year when it is most needed. Also that it is the most democratic, for on the ice peer and peasant are equal, and Jack is even better than his master, if he can "guard" or "draw" or "wick a bore" in better style. Certainly no game is more sociable. It is not only that players meet with heartiest "grip" in these matches on the ice, but from time immemorial there has followed on the day's play the evening's diversion, when victors and vanquished meet to partake of "beef and greens," and fight their battles over again as the toddy goes round. Toasts and sentiments relating to the game are proposed, such as "The King and the Core," "The Courts of Just-ice," "The Land o' Cakes and her ain game o' Curlin'," "May we ne'er be a hog, when we should be in the hoose," "May curlers on life's slippery rink frae cruel rubs be free." Many clubs have also "courts," at which new members are "brothered" or "initiated." These courts are the occasion of many high jinks, the candidates being put through some extraordinary performances prior to receiving the "word" and the "grip." During the meeting fines are imposed for all kinds of factitious offences, and "the roupin o' the stoup," or sale

FIG. 7.—A GOOD DELIVERY.

of the box of fines to the highest bidder, closes the hilarious meeting. Dr. Norman Macleod and others have written spirited curling songs which help to make such meetings all the merrier.

Curling has not yet taken such a hold of England as golf. But it is gradually making way in the south, there being now forty English clubs in direct association with the Royal Club, which has 548 clubs in Scotland. The majority of the English clubs have combined to form an association of their own with its headquarters at Malton. Associated clubs are found in other places—Ireland 1, Canadian Branch 24, Newfoundland 2, New Zealand 7, Nova Scotia 2, Russia 1, Switzerland 2, United States 2. This list does not include all clubs, but only those directly under rule of the Royal Club. In the United States there is the Grand National Curling Club,[1] with twenty-five different local clubs under its care. Then, besides the Canadian clubs above noted, there exists the Manitoba Branch of the Royal Caledonian Curling Club,[2] which has no less than eighty-seven affiliated clubs, and which, in respect of the amount of play afforded each season, is perhaps the most favoured of all curling organisations.

Full information as to the evolution and science of curling will be found in *The History of Curling*, by the Rev. J. Kerr (Douglas, Edinburgh). *The Annual* of the Royal Caledonian Curling Club, from which we have been permitted to take the diagrams in this article, contains all rules and regulations as to the game. The Grand National Club, and the Canadian Branch above referred to, both issue *Annuals* with information of the same kind, in addition to lists of clubs.

JOHN KERR.

GLOSSARY.

Baugh ice—Damp or bad ice.

Beef and greens—The traditional dish at a curler's dinner.

Bias—Any deviation of the ice from the level.

Boardhead—The whole 14-ft. circle around the *tee* (*q.v.*). Also called HOUSE and PARISH.

Bonspeil—A curling match between two rival districts or parishes. To be distinguished from **speils**, which are properly, according to Christopher North, matches between members of the same society, or between a limited number of adversaries.

Borrow—The width of ice to be allowed for bias if a stone played without the twist is to find the mark.

Break an egg on—To touch another stone gently.

Brittle shot—An angular cannoning shot.

Broom cowe—[*See* COWE].

Broughs—Circles drawn around the *tee* to assist the players in deciding what stone is nearest. Outside of the circle of 7 ft. radius no stone can count.

Bullet shot—A stone played hard and straight in order to drive another from its position.

Cannoning in the technical curling sense is the driving of one of the guards (*q.v.*) upon the winner (*q.v.*) with such a velocity, and at such an angle that both go off the tee, whilst the player's stone, following on, takes the place the winner has left.

Channel stone—The old term for the stones used in curling, given to them because boulders found in the bed of streams were usually employed for the purpose.

Chap and lie—To drive a stone placed on the tee outside of the 7-ft. circle, but to remain within it oneself, and if possible within the 4-ft. circle. [*See* DIAGRAM OF RINK].

Chipping—Striking a stone, of which only a small part can be seen upon the exposed portion. Especially in the phrase "Chipping the winner."

Chuckle—To pass through a narrow opening between two stones, and then by a series of wicks from other stones, to reach the destination.

Coal score—[*See* HOG-SCORE].

Cockee—[*See* TEE].

Coiting—The earlier form of curling when the stones were without handles, and more nearly resembled "quoits," from which the word is probably derived. The term is still used for curling in Ayrshire. Also spelt **Kuting**.

Coll or Colly—[*See* HOG-SCORE].

Core—Old term for Rink (2) (*q.v.*)

Cowe or Kowe—A besom made of broom twigs,

[1] Secretary, D. Foulis 260 West 115th St., New York.

[2] Secretary, J. P. Robertson, 208 Edmonton Place, Winnipeg, Manitoba.

with which the ice is swept in front of an advancing stone if it appears to be going too slowly.

Crampit—Originally a plate of iron shod with nails, fastened to the boot-sole, now a plate fastened in the ice, upon which each player has to take up his position before delivering the stones.

Dam—A sheet of water confined for curling purposes.

Doupar—[*See* SKIP].

Draw—To play a stone up gently.

Drive—To deliver a stone with extra force in order to dislodge a winner or a guard, and drive it out of the house.

Driver—[*See* SKIP].

Drug ice—Soft or dull ice, on which the stones run heavily.

Dry—A seam running through a stone, and rendering it liable to break.

Edge in—To rub one stone gently upon another, so as to assist it slightly in changing its course.

End—[*See* HEAD].

Ettle—To aim at.

Fill the ice or port—To play a stone so as to block an opening which lay between two other stones, and thereby to guard a position previously obtained.

Fit the tee—To set the foot fairly upon the heel of the fixed crampit (*q.v.*) before delivering the stone.

Flee the ice—To deliver a stone in such a direction or with such force that it goes off the rink (*q.v.*) altogether.

Fore Han'—The player first in order on the side.

Gogsee—[*See* TEE].

Grannie's wing, to get under—To go from a stone lying in the way at an angle, and shelter behind another.

Guard—(1) A stone that lies in a direct line before another.

(2) As verb: to play such a stone.

Hack or Hatch—A hollow cut in the ice 4 yds. behind the tee, in which the player puts his foot to prevent it from slipping. An ancient plan still followed in some clubs in preference to the *Crampit* (*q.v.*)

Hair o' pith—*Lit.* "a trifle of extra force."

Handle—[*See* STONE].

Hands up—The command of the Skip (*q.v.*) to stop sweeping.

Harried—A side is said to be "harried" when, owing to the condition of the ice, they are unable to send their stones up to the tee.

Hatch—[*See* HACK].

Head—The portion of the game in which all the players have delivered their stones, and have counted the winning shot or shots.

Hin' Han'—The last player on a side, who also acts as *Skip*.

Hog—A stone which after delivery fails to pass the *Hog-score*.

Hog-score—A line drawn across the ice at a distance from the tee of one-sixth the length of the rink. Stones which do not cross it must be removed from the game. A wavy line is usually drawn over the same, in order to distinguish it from a crack.

House—[*See* BOARDHEAD].

Howe—The middle of the rink, which is hollowed by the passage of the stones.

Inringing—[*See* INWICKING].

In-turn—A twist given to the stone, which causes it to describe a curve to the right.

Inwicking—A stroke which reaches the tee, or object stone, by rebounding from the inside edge of another stone lying to the side. Also as verb. Also called **Inring** and **Wick**.

Kittle—(1) Adjective; of a shot, difficult.

(2) Vb. To work keenly, especially at sweeping.

Kowe—[*See* COWE].

Kuting—[*See* COITING].

Lie shot—Of a stone, to come and rest nearest the tee.

Mar—To disturb a stone while running, by accident or otherwise. If by one of the player's own side, the stone must be removed; if by an opponent, the stone must be placed to the satisfaction of the opposing captain.

Out-turn—A twist given to the stone on delivery, which causes it to describe a curve to the left.

Outwick—A stroke which hits a stone upon the outer edge and drives it towards the centre. Also as verb.

Parish—[*See* BOARDHEAD].

Patlid—A stone that comes to rest exactly upon the tee.

Piltycock—The original form of curling-stone, and really a large stone quoit, with depressions for fingers and thumb. Also called **Kuting-stone.**

Point Game—A variety of curling, in which each player tries in turn certain assigned shots, receiving marks in the measure of his success. The eight shots are: (1) Striking; (2) Inwicking; (3) Drawing; (4) Guarding; (5) Chap and Lie; (6) Wick and Curl in; (7) Raising; (8) Chipping the winner; (9) Drawing through a Port. The tenth shot, to be played in the event of a dead-heat, is outwicking.

Port—An interval between two stones.

Raising—Driving on a partner's stone in a straight line up to or near the tee.

Rebutting—A stroke delivered with full power, in order to clear the Boardhead as far as possible on the chance that it may be some help to a desperate game.

Red the ice—To drive off the guards by a strong shot, in order to lay open the tee or winner.

Ride—To deliver a stone with such force upon another as to drive the latter from the boardhead.

Rink—(1) The members composing a side, four in number.

(2) The area on which the game is played.

Royal Caledonian Curling Club—The governing body of the sport of curling. Founded in 1838 on the suggestion of an anonymous advertiser, it at once secured the allegiance of the various curling clubs, of which, in 1897, no less than 716 acknowledge its authority.

Shot—(1) The unit of scoring, each stone nearer to the tee than any opponent counting one. (2) The delivery of a stone.

Sidelin' shot—A stone lying on each side of the tee.

Skip—The captain of a side, who gives his men elaborate advice as to the play, and controls the sweeping. Also called **Director** and **Driver.**

Sole—(1) Noun; the base of the curling-stone.

(2) Verb; to deliver the stone on the ice.

Soop—Scottish command for "sweep."

Souter—To score a love game; not to allow the opponents to score, as certain souters (shoemakers) of Lochmaken are said to have done.

Speil—[*See* BONSPEIL].

Spend the stone—To play a wasted shot.

Stone—(*a*) Consists of an iron handle and a cheese-shaped mass of hard stone.

(*b*) It must not weigh more than 44 lbs. (the usual weight is 35 lbs. to 40 lbs.), nor measure more than 36 in. in circumference, nor be less than one eighth of its circumference in height.

(*c*) Material. The most popular material is blue Ailsa Craig, but even better formations are Burnock Water and Crawfordjohn. Other well-known varieties are Crieff Black, Carsphairn, Crieff Serpentine, and Tinkernhill.

Stones are now generally made with reversible soles, so that the sole may be used which is most suited to condition of the ice.

Striking—Hitting with a stone another placed on the tee with sufficient force to drive it out of the circle.

Stug—A shot gained by accident.

Sweeping—Clearing the ice with besoms. When snow is falling, sweeping may be practised from tee to tee [*see* DIAGRAM OF RINK], but in ordinary cases only from the nearest hog-score. The player's party only are allowed to sweep, unless an opponent's stone be moved, in which case the other side may sweep in front of that. The ice behind the tee may be swept at any time by either side. Sweeping must always be to a side, and no dust swept up may be moved forward or left in front of a running stone. [*See* Rule 16.]

Tee—A point in the ice,—the centre of the boardhead,—to lie as near as possible to which at the end of the head (*q.v.*) is the aim of each player. Also called **Tozee, Gogsee,** and **Wittyr.**

Tramp—Old name for the crampits affixed to the boots of players.

Tricker or Trigger—Pieces of iron shod with spikes, which could be fixed at any point of the ice

FIG. 8.—THE WINNER GOES.

behind the tee, and from which the player in old times delivered his cast.

Wick—[*See* INWICK].

Winner—The stone lying nearest to the tee at any particular moment in the game.

Wittyr—[*See* TEE].

Bibliography—*Songs for the Curling-Club held at Canon-mills*, by a Member (Edin., printed by J. Robertson, 1792, pp. 16); *An Account of the Game of Curling*, by a Member of the Duddingston Curling Society (Edin., "Correspondent" Office, 1811, pp. 46). [Written by the Rev. John Ramsay, the earliest hist. of the game]; *A Descriptive and Historical Sketch of Curling, &c.* (pp. 48, 1828, Kilmarnock, H. Crawford); *Memorabilia Curliana Mabensia* (Dumfries, John Sinclair, pp. 111, 1830). [The work of Sir Richard Brown, Bart., of Coalstoun]; *Essay on Curling and Artificial Pond-Making*, by J. Cairnie Largs (pp. viii. 144, Glasgow, 1833); *The Channel-Stane: or, Sweepings frae the Rinks*, series i–iv., 4 vols. (Edin., 1884, Ed. Capt. Machair); *Curling: The Ancient Scottish Game*, with illust. by C. A. Doyle, by James Taylor, M.A., D.D., F.S.A. Scot. (Edin., Paterson, 1887, 10*s.* 6*d.* and 5*s.*); *History of Curling*, J. Kerr (Edin., Douglas, 1890, 10*s.* 6*d.* and 31*s.* 6*d.*); *Skating, Curling and Ice Sports* (Badminton Lib.), J. M. Heathcote and C. J. Tebbutt (Longmans, 1892, 10*s.* 6*d.*).

CYCLING—

LEARNING TO RIDE—The balance of a bicycle is maintained by turning its front wheel towards the direction in which it is falling: in actual practice, of course, the tendency to fall is counteracted rather by the rider slightly inclining his body from side to side as required; but the first and more easily acquired method is that first to be attempted by the novice. If the prospective rider has not even an inexperienced friend to help him, he should procure a strong but antiquated and valueless machine, and lowering the saddle so that he can straddle the machine, and selecting a piece of road which has a very slight downward gradient, should throw one leg over the machine, seat himself, and, following the pedals round with his feet, do his best to put the above principle into practice. He should take care to keep the machine going fast enough to secure "steering way." The difficulty will at first be considerable, but he should remember that he can always save himself by sticking out a leg. As he progresses, he will discover how very slight is the force required for steering, and how great a bias the mere inclination of the body exercises over the machine.

Should he possess a friend who will help him his task will be easier; and it is to the latter that our instructions are best addressed. The assistant should hold the machine upright by grasping the saddle springs so that the learner does not know for certain whether he is not riding by himself, and, running with the machine, give it that necessary motion which the learner is apt to minimise. Except to help in starting, he should refrain from touching the handle-bars. The novice, when he has fairly mastered the balance, should again select a slightly downhill road, and holding the handles and placing his left foot on the step, should hop on the other till the pace attained admits of his straightening his left leg and balancing himself with his other leg hanging across the back wheel, while the machine runs by its own momentum. After a little more practice he will discover that from this position he can easily and without assistance lower himself forward into the saddle, which should, as we have said above, be adjusted very low, and commence pedalling. He should next learn to dismount: this is effected by waiting till the left pedal is at its lowest and throwing the right leg over the saddle and back wheel, meanwhile retaining his grip of the handles. He will thus alight standing on the left of the machine. He will soon discover that he can dismount with the pedals in any position. The practised rider will of course, in dismounting, throw as much of his weight as possible on to the handles, so as to minimise the strain on the frame caused by throwing it all on to the pedal.

BUYING A CYCLE—It is always best to avoid second-hand cycles unless you know their history, and they bear the name of a good maker.

We shall hereafter indicate the "points" which should be looked for in a good cycle.

The safest advice to give to a novice is a reference to one of the great firms, who, if they do ask a high price, at least have a reputation to uphold. By this we mean a reputation among practical and disinterested riders, not the proprietorship of a long list of "records" made by paid riders.

We cannot too greatly emphasise the statement that these records, the achievement of which has corrupted the whole tone of cycling as a sport, prove absolutely nothing. There is little to choose among the machines of the best makers, and the strings of records quoted in the advertisements only prove that a lot of money has, economically speaking, been wasted in the support of hired racing men.

The Dunlop and the Palmer are both good tyres: but does any one suppose that it is their speed, and not the length of purse of their makers, that can be gauged by the magnitude of their respective contributions to our list of records?

Still, in spite of what we have said, it is extremely risky for a novice to buy a cheap machine; it is better for him not to go out of the fashion, unless he does it under the guidance of an experienced friend. There are, however, a large number of local makers, who, using the excellent parts turned out by the Eadie, B.S.A., Perry, and other companies, can sometimes supply a really good and light machine at a price considerably below that of the big makers. The chief drawback to buying their machines is that, lacking the elaborate plant of the great firms—especially that for frame building—they are apt to fit their frames together untruly, and that, owing to their small capital, they cannot afford to throw aside defective work. The fact remains that some small makers can turn out uncommonly good machines.

In buying or ordering a cycle see further that it is fitted to your own personal requirements. Insist on having your frame of full height; state whether you want brake and mud-guards, and carefully specify your wishes in such details as shape of handlebars, material of handles, weight and gear of machine, throw of crank, and make of saddle and tyres. The novice will do well either to get a friend to see to these details, or, failing this, to furnish the maker or dealer with particulars as to his weight, length of reach, as well as the kind of work for which he intends the machine.

Local Agents—We strongly advise the purchase of well-known machines through local agents. It is a delusion to suppose that the casual purchaser can buy for less money on Holborn Viaduct than from a dealer in his own town. Moreover it is not well to be on terms of enmity with the local repairer.

Maker's Guarantees—The maker's guarantee usually covers all breakages (not the result of an accident) which occur within a twelvemonth. Saddle, chain and tyres are usually guaranteed by the manufacturers of those parts, who will generally make good defects.

Second-hand Machines—A second year's machine by a first-class maker, and in good condition, should be worth £10 to £14, a good machine of lower grade or less known make from £7 to £10. A fair number of good machines are advertised for sale in the cycling papers. Choose an advertisement that is business-like and to the point, *e.g.*, "1896 * * * * No. 1. Road Racer; 24 lbs. Dunlop, Carter, gear 72; 25 frame; £12"; this is evidently written by a cyclist for cyclists. Avoid advertisements which descant on the beauties of the plating and enamel, and still more those headed "*Beeston Humber pattern*"—a palpable attempt to persuade the buyer that he is getting a Beeston Humber when he is not.

It now remains to inspect the machine. If the owner consent, take it home and examine it at leisure. If, as is not unreasonable, he refuse, look first at the teeth of the back chain wheel; any wear will be most apparent here. If the backward side of the teeth is deeply worn, have nothing to do with the machine.

Next test the bearings; if they will not run freely without considerable side shake and seem tight in one place and loose in another, considerable and uneven wear is indicated. Try also whether the head can be correctly adjusted. Next inspect the frame for twists, and see that the wheels "track." This is easily done if the machine is on a boarded floor; if not, judge it by the eye, or by a straight stick laid along the frame. See that the wheels are true and the tyres in good order. Make sure that the chain wheels are in line; this is best ascertained by seeing that the teeth of the chain wheels do not rub against the side links. Test the frame for rigidity as prescribed on p. 273, and keep a look-out for uneven places in the enamel that may conceal a crack.

ROAD RIDING IN GENERAL—Too many beginners are under the impression that when once they have mastered the difficulties of steering, mounting and dismounting, their cycling education is complete. How general this fallacy is can be seen by looking at three out of every four cyclists one meets, who, while sufficiently expert at controlling their machines, are entirely lacking in that finish which stamps a good rider.

Position—First of all the machine must be properly adjusted. The saddle should be raised to such a height that when the pedal is at its lowest, the foot, with the heel well dropped, rests comfortably upon it, and the knee just misses being absolutely straightened at the joint; the centre of the saddle should be about ten inches behind a vertical line drawn through the crank axle. The handles should be about level with the saddle, so that when one is sitting upright the handles can just be grasped. Many fast riders ride with a shorter reach, a more forward position, and the handles lower than this, but, for a beginner, this is by far the best position. When the rider is reasonably expert he will discover for himself the position in which he can ride best; it is a great mistake to imagine that the same position must necessarily suit all cyclists.

Ankle Action—The great thing in cycling is to attain to an effective use of the ankles; if these be kept stiff, the power of each foot can only be exerted through a comparatively small arc of the circle described by the pedals. When the cranks are vertical the rider will find that there is a "dead point," at which he can exert no power whatever, and the impetus of the machine is alone carrying him on. To overcome this dead point is the aim of ankle action.

If the ankle be relaxed, it will be found quite possible so to incline the foot to the leg, that power may be exerted before this dead point with the rising pedal, and after it with the descending one, and the gain in efficiency is tremendous.

To this end the ball of the foot should rest upon the pedal: at the commencement of each stroke, before the pedal reaches the vertical, the heel should be dropped, and pressure at once applied to the pedal by a kind of clawing action; during the down-stroke the heel will naturally rise relatively to the rest of the foot, till when the pedal is at its lowest the heel is uppermost; a further clawing action will bring the pedal past this point till it is again well on the ascent; the foot should then be lightly lifted, without of course leaving the pedal, but so as not to impede its upward course, till just before a fresh revolution is commenced the heel is again dropped, and the process begun afresh.

With good ankle action much of the work is taken by the calf muscles, which will be largely developed, especially on the side and towards the front of the leg. Pulling at the handles will be almost entirely obviated when the going is easy, and minimised when it is heavy. The practised ankler will, for road riding at all events, be able to dispense with the uncomfortable "toe-clip." This contrivance, necessary for the safety of the racing man, is to be eschewed by the novice, as it militates against the attainment of a good action. Its later adoption is a matter of individual taste.

In riding, the body should be kept absolutely at rest; fidgeting and wriggling in the saddle, and any movement of the shoulders, should be especially avoided.

As he progresses, the rider will discover that steering is effected not so much by the hands as by a gentle inclination of the body; this he will pick up automatically as he grows in proficiency, and to this end he should practise riding "hands off," not as an end in itself (nothing looks worse than cheap "showing off" of this kind), but to perfect his steering.

Nursing the Machine—In no case is the difference between a good and bad rider more observable than on a rough road. In surmounting an obstacle a practised rider will not allow his weight to descend heavily on the springs of the saddle, but will minimise it by momentarily shifting some of it to the handle bars and pedals, thus distributing the shock over the whole machine.

Mounting—Very few light machines are fitted with steps. Mounting on such machines is effected by placing one of the pedals (usually the right) slightly in advance of the vertical, and, standing if possible on higher ground than the machine, *e.g.*, on the "crown" of the road, or best of all, on a friendly kerbstone, by throwing one leg over the saddle so as to rest on the pedal, then with one movement applying the pressure to the pedal, and sliding into the seat. This mount is at first difficult in crowded streets, and riders who do much traffic riding should certainly use a step, but it puts less strain on the machine than any other method.

Dismounting—Several kinds of dismount should be practised, as in crowded traffic there may not be room for any one given variety. Practise the pedal dismount on either side. A very useful way of getting off is to shoot back over the saddle, and alight straddling the back wheel; or more simple still, merely to remove one foot from the pedal and, as it were, step back out of the saddle. This method strains the machine least of all. Before trying these last two methods, make sure that you can straddle the back wheel with safety, and do not diminish your length of leg by bending the knees.

Sideslip—On greasy roads the wheels have a tendency to slip from under the rider: a certain amount of slip in the back wheel is immaterial, but when the front wheel slips the whole machine generally goes over. Corrugated tyres minimise this danger to some extent: but the best safeguard lies with the rider. "Funk" and nervousness are fatal. Keep on the "crown" of the road, sit still in the saddle, ride at an easy pace, pedal lightly and carefully, and avoid back pedalling; hold the handles lightly and give the machine its head; if it is necessary to turn, do so gradually; be prepared to save yourself if the machine really goes, but don't jump off wildly because you feel a twitch from the back wheel. Tramlines should be crossed as nearly as possible at a right angle.

Descending Hills—None but an expert rider should ride without a brake, but such an appliance should only be used in the last resort; it ruins the tyres, and, if applied to the front wheel, puts a great strain on the front forks, and promotes sideslip. Moreover, if the brake from any cause refuses to act, the rider is put more at the mercy of Providence than is usually deemed advisable. Therefore learn to check the machine by back pedalling. Pressure is applied by the feet to the rising pedal, using the ankles in exactly the opposite way to that advised for forward-pedalling. If you find that despite all your efforts you are being forced out of the seat, hold yourself down in the saddle by one hand. Do not back-pedal too suddenly, or you may break your chain.

Brakeless riders may improvise an excellent brake by applying the sole of the foot placed crosswise to the front tyre immediately behind the fork crown. If mudguards be carried, this must be done in front of the crown, but it is less effective.

Hill Climbing differs only in degree from ordinary riding; and in this direction good ankle action will be found indispensable. Purchase is gained by pulling at the handle-bars, not in jerks, but steadily. The best results are obtained by leaning forward over the handle-bars, but on a long hill a change of position is beneficial, and the rider may lean backwards, pulling steadily the while. Riding through deep mud and against a head wind come under the same category as hill climbing, but in the latter case it is absolutely necessary to lean forward in order to diminish the surface presented to the wind.

Gearing—The question of gearing from a mechanical point of view is discussed on p. 274. We need hardly explain that the higher the gear, the further the machine travels at each stroke of the pedals, and the greater is the force needed at each stroke to drive the machine. From this it will be apparent that for hilly country a very high gear is inadvisable; there is a limit to the amount of power which any rider can put into a stroke (*e.g.*, a machine geared to 1,000 could not be driven at all), and as one approaches this limit, the effect of the heavy work is very tiring. This is especially noticeable in hill climbing. The power required for each stroke is greater than on the level, so that a gear which might easily be propelled along a flat road, might become unrideable on a steep hill. Assuming that the high-gear machine succeeded in getting up, although the *total* power expended by its rider would, if measured in foot-pounds, be the same as that put forth by a low-geared rider, yet, by the near approach at each stroke to the extreme limit of his strength, the big-gear man would soon be exhausted, while his low-geared companion, pedalling faster, but always well within his strength, would be comparatively fresh.

Again, a heavy machine is harder to drive up hill, so that a heavy machine necessitates a comparatively low gear, while a light machine may be fitted with a higher one. On the other hand, below a certain point, additional ease of driving becomes inappreciable on a level road, while the foot has to be lifted in preparation for the stroke very much oftener; as this lifting the foot is all power wasted, an unduly low gear exhausts the rider without giving any compensating advantage. Therefore, shun too low gears equally with excessively high ones.

Speaking generally, powerful riders will ride high gears, and light active pedallers low gears, but it is by no means always true. There is no doubt, however, that the development of the muscles caused by practice enables an expert to use with advantage a gear far too high for a novice. Let the novice of ordinary strength, therefore, riding a machine which "stripped" weighs, say, 27lbs., confine himself within the limits of 60 to 63 (for ladies 6 inches lower). As he increases in skill and strength, he will find for himself what gear best suits him. We may add however for road-racing machines 68 to 76 is considered a medium, and anything over this a high gear.

Variable gears (See p. 276)—A good gear of this kind will be found valuable in a hilly district or for winter riding. It should, however, be remembered that *fast* riding uphill on a low gear is often as tiring as on a high one, hence, when the lower gear is switched on, the rider should be content to pedal no faster than with the higher.

Throw of cranks (See p. 274)—A long crank throw increases leverage, but necessitates the moving of the feet through a larger circle than a small crank, *i.e.*, it sacrifices speed for power. The normal crank throw is $6\frac{1}{2}$ inches, and for ladies 6 inches. A long-legged rider may, however, beneficially increase his throw up to 7 inches. (Much above this is a mistake.) A short legged one may go as low as 6 inches. An increase in throw may with advantage be coupled with an increase in gear, or *vice versa*. It is however inadvisable for a rider to change the throw of his cranks; having once found the right throw he should keep to it.

Pedals—Should be wide enough to take ordinary walking shoes if necessary. The use of rubber or rat-trap pedals is a matter of individual taste.

Handle bars—For average road riding we prefer flat handlebars well brought back, inclined at right angles to the head. For very fast work they are usually "dropped" or bent downwards. The meaningless upcurved handlebars that have recently come into use among beginners should be avoided; a flat handlebar may be raised to any desired position, and we need hardly say that unnecessary curves in tubing detract from its strength.

Cycling Dress—The best material for cycling garments of every kind is wool—wool throughout. For casual riding there is perhaps no very great risk in riding in a canvas shirt, but if there is any prospect of getting hot, the danger of catching cold is considerable. Woollen garments permit of the ready escape by vaporisation of the perspiration, and, being non-conductors of heat, keep the air within them at an even temperature; cotton, on the other hand, retains all moisture, and hangs, wet and chilly, on the body; being a ready conductor of heat, it at once exposes the wearer to all changes in the temperature of the air, besides permanently retaining perspiration in an unpleasant manner.

Firstly of underclothing. In summer a flannel shirt, preferably with a detachable flannel collar, is enough for any one. In winter this should be supplemented by a woollen vest and short drawers; omission of the latter in frosty weather tends to produce chaps and soreness.

The shape of cycling garments is mostly a matter of taste: for ourselves we prefer Norfolk jackets, which having no particular shape to lose may be suffered to lose it. No coat used for really hard cycling will retain its shape.

Numerous pockets are indispensable; the fit should be easy; the sleeves should not be too long; and it should always be possible to turn up the collar and button it closely over the throat. Waistcoats are a mistake; in cold weather sweaters and cardigans are preferable.

Knickerbockers should be fairly full, and may be made either with buttons or straps; if box-cloth "continuations" are worn, they should be wool lined. Knickerbockers should have a "hip pocket" to hold one's purse, as carrying anything in the ordinary side pockets when cycling is uncomfortable; the pocket is moreover liable to disgorge its contents. Cycling knickerbockers should all be double-seated *outside*; this requires an experienced cycling tailor, as, if it be unskilfully done, the seat rucks up into agonising wrinkles.

Stockings may either be worn short and secured by the buckle of the knickerbockers, or may be long enough to fold over, in which case the end of the breeches is secured to the leg itself and the stocking folded over it. Tight garters are to be avoided; the best are plain bands of broad elastic. A wool-lined cloth cap is the best all round head gear: in summer a felt "tennis hat" is even better.

Shoes should be of the orthodox cycling pattern: viz. rounded at the toes, flexible at the "waist," and with very low heels. The laces should be fastened by hooks all the way down and not by eyelet holes. In dry weather the variety which is attached by an ankle strap will be found satisfactory.

Many riders have the soles "clumped" and cut with slits for the reception of the plates of rat-trap pedals. Bars on the shoes are most uncomfortable for walking purposes.

THE RULE OF THE ROAD—The British rule of the road, which is the reverse of that obtaining in all countries except, we believe, in Bohemia, is to keep to the left or 'near' side when meeting traffic, and to keep to the right or 'off' side when overtaking it. To this rule there are two general exceptions: in overtaking trams it is usual to keep to the left, and in passing a led horse in either direction it is customary to keep to the side of the man leading it. Moreover a driver who is keeping to the left has prior rights to one who, in overtaking other traffic, is keeping to the right: the latter must fall back till the former has got through.

When two or more cyclists are riding together and meet a vehicle, or are overtaken by one, they should form single file, the rider on the off side falling behind the one on the near side. In overtaking traffic this procedure is reversed. If riding with a lady, however, the gentleman, who should be on her off side, should in all cases quicken his pace and take the lead, unless, of course, she expresses a wish to the contrary.

Special Laws affecting Cyclists—Cycles are carriages within the meaning of the Highway Acts, and are required to conform with its enactments, with the following additional provisions: (1) That between one hour after sunset and one hour before sunrise they must carry lighted lamps; (2) that in *overtaking* traffic they must "give audible notice of their approach by bell, whistle or otherwise." Without discussing the vexed meaning of the last word, we strongly advise all cyclists to carry loud-ringing bells. We need hardly add that cycles, in common with all carriages, are under all circumstances prohibited from using the footpath.

CYCLE TOURING—**Preparations for a Tour**—The first step to be taken by the prospective tourist is to join the Cyclists' Touring Club, which will furnish him with road books to nearly any civilised country, will equip him with all that he can desire in the way of garments, will defend him from the extortions of the innkeeper and the *douanier*, and generally keep a watchful eye on his well-being.

Do not start on a tour unless you are in good health and fair riding condition, which is soon attained by a few preliminary spins. Thoroughly overhaul your machine before starting; clean out the bearings with paraffin and carefully adjust and oil them. See that your frame and wheels are true, the spokes taut, and the brake fittings in order. Above all things do not start with a defective tyre; if the jacket show any signs of disintegration, buy a new one at once and use up the old one in subsequent home riding. A bad tyre is an intolerable nuisance on a tour. We need hardly add that it is inexpedient to tour on a new and untried machine, and most of all on a new saddle.

It is as well roughly to map out your itinerary before starting, especially with a view to the forwarding of parcels of linen, to be picked up on the way. The splendid road books of the C.T.C., or the humbler work of Mr. Spurrier (very accurate so far as it goes), will be found of service. It is as well to make an abstract of these and of the C.T.C. hotels in a note-book, to avoid carrying the actual volume.

Dress and Luggage—Touring attire should follow the rules for ordinary riding dress, and no aberrations from the standard of all-wool clothing should be tolerated. In the way of foot-gear, stouter shoes than usual should be worn; the ordinary light cycling shoe, though good for its purpose, offers feeble resistance to wet and mud, and will go to pieces if much walking is done. Spats are uncomfortable, but indispensable in muddy weather. They should be as thin as possible.

A light waterproof cape should never be omitted. The quantity of extra clothing carried on the cycle should be cut down to Spartan limits; a heavy kit turns a pleasure into a toil. It is, however, not necessary to carry more under-clothing than will suffice for two or three days, as fresh supplies can be sent to inns, post-offices and railway stations *en route*. We prefer the last; the first ties one down to sleep or eat in the house, which the hour of one's visit may render inconvenient, and post-offices keep shorter hours than railway parcel offices, the larger of which are nearly always open.

The irreducible minimum would seem to consist of two spare flannel shirts for evening and night wear (the former may afterwards be promoted to active service), one or two spare collars (say one flannel and one linen), two or three handkerchiefs, a toothbrush and a comb. Spare stockings, a hair brush, and shaving tackle come on the "margin of utility." The luxurious traveller who is contented to cumber himself may add to this list as his fancy dictates. Good soap, we may say, carried in a tin box or in a tobacco pouch, is conducive to comfort.

It is often our practice to stay several days at one place, and take long daily trips round about it; a complete change of clothes can then be kept at the inn, and afterwards forwarded to the next stopping place. This obviates the necessity of carrying any luggage on the machine. In any case, for very long tours, a complete change of clothes should be sent on by rail: after three weeks' constant use, any suit will stand in need of a thorough cleaning.

How to Pack the Luggage—A simple outfit may be packed in a large sheet of American cloth, rolled into a sausage-like parcel, and strapped upon handle-bar carriers; to omit these is a mistake, as the handle-bars alone do not afford a firm enough hold to avoid shifting and consequent friction, and the American cloth will rapidly be worn into holes. Large parcels should be carried on a "gridiron" carrier, such as the Cycloe, clamped to the head socket. Further parcels may be carried behind the saddle in place of the tool-bag, which may be strapped to the handle-bars or the top tube. Valises which fit into the "diamond" of the frame are to be avoided, as in these days of narrow treads they hamper the knees of the rider.

Tools—A larger assortment of tools should be carried when touring than when engaged in ordinary riding. In addition to the usual outfit of pump, spanners, oil-can and repair tackle, the following articles should be taken:—

A yard of stout copper wire in a hank; combined pliers and wire-cutters; screw-driver; spare nuts and washers; some strong whipcord; sheet rubber; extra large tube of solution; large piece of repairing canvas.

En route—Do not degenerate into a "mile-hunter"; remember that you are not a professional tourist and are not bound even in honour to get anywhere in particular. Riding too far or too fast leads to "fatigue fever" and sleeplessness. The best rule is not to ride at all after dinner. Over exertion in hill climbing is to be avoided. One may, when touring, walk unashamed up even moderate gradients.

We take this opportunity of protesting against the habitual use of coca and similar stimulants when riding; we have good medical authority for stating that they afford no real sustenance, and that their use, unless very occasional, is decidedly harmful. Chocolate, raisins, bananas, or meat lozenges are far preferable.

Maps should be mounted on linen; four miles to the inch is the handiest scale: use such as disregard county boundaries: "county maps" are an unspeakable nuisance, as well as being usually on different scales to each other. We always use Bartholomew's, which fulfil all these conditions, and can always be had at Smith's bookstalls.

Cost of Touring—Upon this point no hard and fast statement can be made: the cost will largely depend on the taste and means of the tourist: it is possible to tour comfortably on about ten shillings a day under the C.T.C. tariffs; generally speaking it will be found less expensive to avoid spending the night in large towns, where hotels are usually either expensive or uncomfortable, and to put up in the smaller market towns, in which the C.T.C. will usually possess the best hotel.

For those of narrower means the C.T.C. has appointed a cheaper class of houses, often very good, as well as Temperance Hotels, which are usually not under contract. But very often, especially in out-of-the-way places, excellent accommodation can be obtained at small village inns; it needs, however, a practised eye to pick out good ones; one may fare on an excellent supper and breakfast, and sleep between lavender-scented sheets for some three or four shillings, or one may eat rancid bacon off a dirty table-cloth among fumes of stale beer and bad tobacco, at the price of good hotel accommodation.

Continental Touring—The C.T.C. ticket will get your machine duty free into most countries; that body is also negotiating for reciprocity of membership with the Touring Club de France, the Deutsche Rädfahrerbund, and other foreign touring Clubs.

We can only offer brief and general advice:

for details the tourist should apply beforehand to the C.T.C. foreign Chief Consul.

More luggage should be taken than for home touring; in France the railway arrangements for parcels are good, but elsewhere the cyclist will do well to rely on himself. Most people nowadays know French well enough to get about; a pocket English-French-German Dictionary is very handy: it is useful to jot on the flyleaf the foreign equivalents for the principal parts of the bicycle.

CYCLING INSTITUTIONS — **The Cyclists' Touring Club** (Sec., E. R. Shipton, 47, Victoria Street, S.W. Subscription 5s. a year; 1s. entrance fee) was founded in 1878. It now possesses about 40,000 members, and is rapidly increasing. Its advantages include:—A system of excellent hotels of varying grades, which are found in nearly every town, and at which a discount may be obtained; to prevent misrepresentation the tariff is printed in the Club Handbook; a system of approved cycle repairers, and of official tailors who supply at a fixed tariff the excellent cycling garments approved by the Club; a unique organisation of local chief Consuls and Consuls, who will furnish, on personal or written application, information of every kind; the admission of members' machines duty free into most civilised countries; a monthly gazette, the most valuable to the general cyclist of all the cycling papers; a splendid series of British and foreign road books, the former incomparably superior to anything previously issued. The C.T.C. has also taken a leading part in asserting the rights of cyclists, and is always prepared to render assistance, legal and otherwise, in approved cases; it has also erected numerous danger-boards on steep hills, and has done much to keep road surveyors up to a sense of their duties. These latter objects are also the care of the N.C.U. (see below). A recent development of the C.T.C. has been the formation of district associations among local members for mutual intercourse; membership of these is, of course, purely optional. The C.T.C. is governed by a council, part of which, the representative councillors, are elected by postal vote of the Club, the remainder, the chief consuls, by cooptation.

The National Cyclists' Union (Sec., S. R. Noble, 57, Basinghall Street, E.C. Subscription, for clubs 10s. 6*d*. per twenty-five members; for private members 2s. 6d.) is the governing body of the sport of cycle racing, and, like the C.T.C., keeps watch over the rights of cyclists, and interests itself in the condition of highways and erects danger-boards. In this way there is much needless duplication of work and jealous competition between the two bodies; we look forward to seeing all matters affecting the public rights of cyclists dealt with by a joint board of both Associations.

The units of the N.C.U. are the clubs; these are divided into autonomous local centres, to which they return delegates; the centres, each according to its size, return delegates to a supreme federal body—the council. This appoints a general committee which deals with current business.

The Roads Improvement Association (Hon. Sec., R. Dudley Ward, 57, Basinghall Street), which has done excellent work in spreading among surveyors the true principles of road construction, is an offshoot of the C.T.C. and the N.C.U.

Cycling Clubs—The oldest English Club is the Amateur B.C. (chiefly a University club) which was informally founded in 1869, though the Pickwick B.C. (1871) was the first to start regular minutes. The Edinburgh Amateur B.C. dates from 1870, and the Surrey B.C. from 1871. The Oxford University Bi.C. was launched in 1873, the Cambridge University Bi.C. and the London B.C. (which is largely recruited from the Universities) in 1874. Dublin did not follow till 1877. The famous Stanley C.C., which organises the Stanley Cycle Show, counts from 1876, and the next year saw the formation of the Brixton B.C. Of the more modern organisations the North Road and Bath Road clubs were founded for road-racing, but still continue to flourish. Large and vigorous metropolitan clubs, largely devoted to path-racing, are the United Hospitals, London County, Catford, Polytechnic, Anerley, and Silverdale. Of country clubs, the Anfield B.C. 1879 (Liverpool), and the Speedwell B.C., 187[illegible] (Birmingham), are famous in history.

Cycle Shows—The Stanley Show, which is managed by the Stanley C.C., dates from 187[illegible] and till 1892 held the field undisputed; in that year was started the National Show, organised by a trade body. At one or other of these two shows, which are held independently in November and December, are exhibited the standard machines of all makers of any note as well as all the novelties intended for the coming season. The country towns have in many cases now formed shows of their own.

DETAILS OF THE MACHINE.

The modern rear driving bicycle consists of two wheels placed tandem-wise, and mounted in a frame of steel tubing, which carries the saddle and driving gear, and is hinged in front to permit of the front or steering wheel turning freely from side to side. The frame thus falls into two rigid portions—the "Front Frame," which carries the steering wheel; and the "Rear Frame," which carries the saddle, gear, and driving wheel. In Fig. 1 the names of the principal parts of the machine are given and distinguished by letters.

The Frame is made of steel tubes, inserted at their points of junction into hollow stampings or castings of metal, known as "lugs," and held there by brazing, and internally reinforced at these points by short pieces of tapered or serrated tube, known as liners.

The modern frame owes its strength to the fact that it

virtually consists of two triangles—the most rigid form that can be given to a frame of any kind. One of these has the back fork ends and the crank bracket for its lower corners, and the saddle at its apex, and thus bears the weight of the rider; the second has at its angles the seat lug, the crank bracket, and (theoretically) the point of junction of the upper and lower backbones with the steering socket. In practice, however, it is advisable to give greater length to the head or steering socket than would be possible with the above arrangement. Hence the front triangle of the frame becomes a quadrilateral, and the entire frame pentagonal. It would of course be possible to extend this principle of triangulation by joining the seat lug to the bottom of the head, and, in frames of over twenty-seven inches diagonal, the whippiness of the long tubes renders this advisable; in small frames it is not worth its weight.

The members of the frame are described in detail beneath the annexed illustration, but we offer the following general remarks.

The prevalent fashion of making the upper backbone at all costs horizontal is unfortunate; the length of the head should never be less than eight inches, and when

FIG. 1—THE MODERN BICYCLE.

A, front or steering wheel; B front rim; C, front tyre; D, front hub; E, rear or driving wheel; F, rear hub; G, front forks (the only visible portion of front frame); H, rear frame; K, crank bracket; L, front chain wheel; M, back chain wheel; N, chain; O, crank; P. pedals; Q, handle bars; R, handles; S, lamp bracket; T, brake lever; U, brake rod; V, brake spoon; W, seat pillar; X, saddle; Y, mud-guards; Z, mud-guard stays. The names of such parts as are not lettered in the above block are given under subsequent illustrations.

the short reach of the rider necessitates a short diagonal, the effect of keeping the upper backbone horizontal is to trench on the length of the head, and so injure the steering.

Three deviations from the general pattern deserve note—the Referee triple head, which is immensely strong; the Raleigh fork crown (shewn in Fig. 14), which appears to be no weaker than the usual type, and does not serve as a trap for mud and dust; and the Elswick lower backbone. This is duplicated, the two members being crossed as in Fig. 4 (6); the arrangement gives great stability to the crank bracket.

The chain stays are perhaps the most difficult part of the machine to design satisfactorily: they, especially the stay on the chain side, have to withstand the whole driving strain of the gear: the pull of the back wheel forward will, if the stays be weak, crample them or at least force them out of line (*see* page 274). The stays, therefore, have to be designed to resist this compressing strain, as well as the twisting strain on the crank bracket caused by pedalling. They should theoretically run straight from the very end of the crank bracket to the ends of the back wheel axle: but the necessity of securing clearance for the cranks without unduly increasing the "tread," or width apart of the pedals renders it necessary to bend them: they should always be bridged

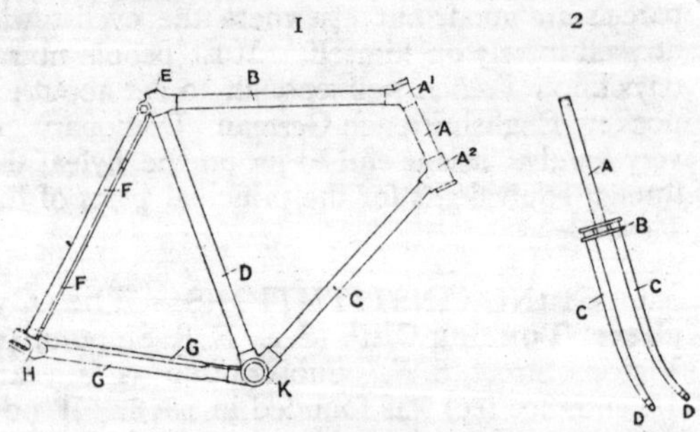

FIG. 2—THE FRAME.

1. *The Rear Frame.*—A, the head socket, described under Fig. 5. A1, the upper head lug. A2, the lower head lug. B, the upper backbone. C, the lower backbone. D, the diagonal. E, the seat lug. This is split, the two tips being forced together by a bolt so as to grip the seat pillar. F, the back stays (sometimes called the back forks): these are usually merely bolted to the seat lug by the bolt which secures the seat pillar: occasionally however they are brazed to the seat lug which is shaped accordingly. They should be connected by a strut above the back wheel. At their lower end they are often brazed into the back fork end, but are with equal frequency pierced for the reception of the axle, and are secured to the back fork ends by the fork end nuts. Stays which are thus secured by bolts at each end are called "swinging back stays." They are often made of D section or oval tubing to give increased clearance to the wheel. G, the chain stays or compression stays (sometimes known as the back forks) are brazed to the back fork ends and to the crank bracket: their importance is explained in the text. Like the above they are often made of D section or oval tubing. H, the back fork ends: these are solid and out of them is cut a slot broad enough to admit of the axle (which is secured to them by nuts and washers), and long enough to admit of sliding it backwards or forwards for the adjustment of the chain (see Fig. 8). K, the crank bracket is a shell of metal containing the crank bearings, the cups of which screw into it; its shape will be understood from Fig. 12; to it are brazed the lower backbone, diagonal, and chain stays.

2. *The Front Frame.*—A, inner Head-tube: this swings upon ball-bearings inside the head socket. It passes through and is brazed to the crown-plates. Fixed to it just above where it emerges from the crown is the lower half ball-race of the head (see Fig. 5). Its upper end is split and has an external screw thread, the object of which is explained under Fig. 5. B, the fork crown: this type, which is almost universal, is known as the double fork crown, from the doubling of the horizontal crown plates. In multicycles these are often triple. C, the front forks; these are tubular and usually flattened at the sides; D, the front fork ends are solid, and pierced for the reception of the axle.

across close to the bend. A somewhat better design is given in Fig. 3, where the bending of the stays is avoided.

Height of Frame is measured from the top of the seat lug to the centre of the brake axle. The seat pillar should never project more than two inches from the seat lug: nothing puts a more unfair strain on a machine than to subject it to the leverage of the weight of the rider at the end of a long stretch of saddle pillar. Hence a tall rider will require a frame of from twenty-seven to as much as thirty inches.

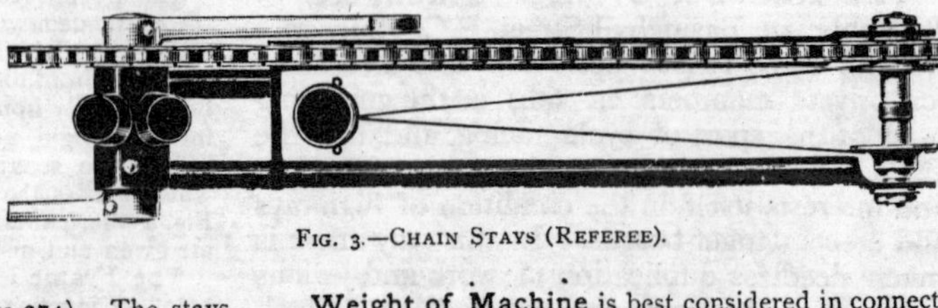

FIG. 3.—CHAIN STAYS (REFEREE).

Weight of Machine is best considered in connection with its most important constituent, the frame. It must be remembered that a cycle must be built strong enough not merely to sustain the weight of the rider, but also to withstand the strain of driving. A machine may answer the former end, yet may be so light (or have its weight so badly distributed) that the frame is twisted out of line at each stroke of the pedals ; not only is much force wasted through this undue elasticity, but the chain wheels may be set out of line and much friction of the chain result. Such a machine may run tolerably when the work is easy, but uphill, against the wind, or at high speed, it will be much inferior to a heavier, but more rigid, machine.

To test the rigidity of the frame in this respect, set the machine up, hold it firmly, and press with the foot on the downward pedal : the machine will in any case "give," but a little experience and comparison with a cycle known to be rigid will soon show the amount of spring legitimately to be expected. An unduly "whippy" machine should be let alone. A heavy rider will require a heavier machine than a lightweight, especially if he be also tall and require a high frame : the greater length of the tubes admits of more "give" than in a small frame, and the weight should be *more* than proportionately increased.

Speaking generally, we should say that an experienced rider of about 11 stone, who understands pedalling, may on ordinary roads ride a machine weighing, with road racing tyres and saddle, and without brake, mudguards, gear case, &c., 24 lbs. : light roadster tyres will add about 1½ lbs., a roadster saddle about 1 lb., a gear case 2 lbs., and brake and light mudguards over 2 lbs. more : a machine weighing with these accessories 33 lbs. is heavy enough for anyone up to about 14 stone : 36 lbs. ought to suffice even a very heavy weight.

The Frame of Ladies' Bicycles—As the great majority of the weaker sex continue to ride in skirts, the upper backbone has therefore to be moved downward sufficiently to give clearance for the skirts, and

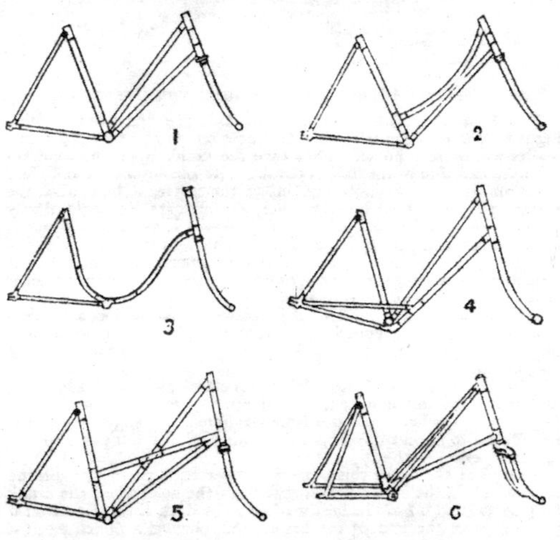

FIG. 4—FRAMES OF LADIES' BICYCLES.

this is done by carrying it (in either a straight or a curved form) from the top of the head to a point above the crank bracket, so that we get a frame like that shown in Fig. 4, Nos. 1 and 2.

It will be seen that while the crank bracket is strengthened in the same way as in a man's machine, the rigidity of the frame, due to its triangulation from fixed points, is entirely done away with. The diagonal, upper backbone, and head tube form a V or U, open at the top, which, when the front wheel is checked by any obstacle, tends to close up, thus putting a shearing strain on the junctions of the two backbones with the diagonal. Hence a curved upper backbone (see No. 2) is perhaps *slightly* preferable to a frame like No. 1, as towards its lower end it travels in an approximately horizontal line, and furthermore by its comparative elasticity tends to minimise the shocks received from the front wheel. A single tube frame like No. 3 is beneath serious notice.

Stronger and altogether better frames are No. 4, designed by Mr. C. W. Brown, the only drawback of which is its weight, and Nos. 5 and 6, made by the Raleigh and Elswick, respectively.

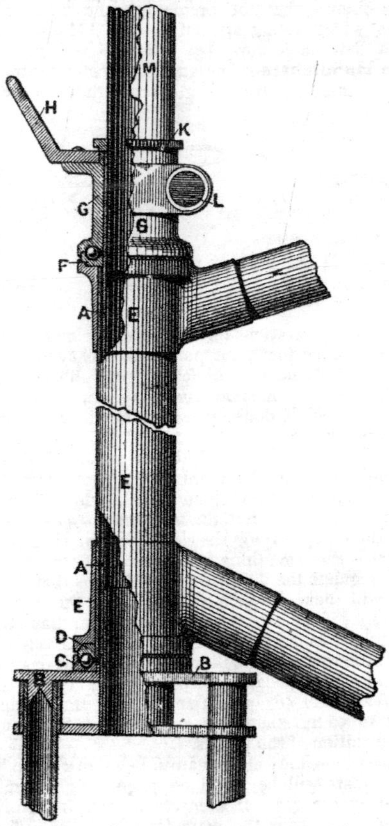

FIG. 5—THE HEAD (ENFIELD).

To put together—A is the inner steering tube ; round it, just where it emerges from the fork crown B, is fixed the lower half of a ball race C ; the balls are placed in position, and the complementary upper half D dropped upon them ; the steering socket E is slipped over A and lowered on to D ; into its upper end and round A is placed the lower half F of the upper bearing ; the balls are placed therein, and the clip G, in which is incorporated the upper half-bearing, is dropped on to them ; a milled or hexagonal ring K is then screwed over the inner steering tube and down on to the clip G so as to obviate any vertical play (in the Humber and most other machines, the lamp-bracket is first slipped over the tube and gripped between K and G. The variety shown above (H) is secured to G by a screw); the lower end of the handlebar M is slipped through K and G well into the steering tube A (at least an inch further than shown above); and, finally, the bolt at L is screwed up, thus compressing the clip G on to the steering post ; this is itself split at its upper end, and so grips the handlebar tube ; the entire arrangement is thus securely locked. Note.—In many machines the half-bearings D and F are permanently fixed into the ends of A.

To adjust the Head—Slack the bolt L and tighten or loosen K till the required adjustment is obtained. This is ascertained by grasping the handles, and pulling up and down on them, when any shake in the head will be felt (notice, however, that this is not due to the front wheel bearing). The head is correctly adjusted when it swings with perfect freedom, and there is no shake. If the head be unevenly worn a compromise must be effected, very slightly on the side of tightness. Such uneven wear is the result of neglecting the adjustment. Finally, again tighten the bolt L.

To raise or lower the Handlebars—Slack the nut of the screwed bolt L, adjust the handlebars as desired, always leaving at least a clear inch and a half remaining in the head tube to give a safe hold. See that the handlebars, clips, and lamp-bracket (if secured in this way) are quite straight, and tighten the bolt L.

The Head—The head of a bicycle is the hinge where the upright tube of the front portion of the frame, which rigidly connects the handlebar with the front wheel, swings on ball bearings inside the socket formed by the front tube of the rear frame.

The head should not be less than 8 inches long, measured from the top and bottom of its two end lugs. Its construction and adjustment are described under Fig. 5.

Steering Locks are valuable not only as securities against thieves, but for preventing the machine from moving when resting against a wall. Many machines have a detachable key, but this is a nuisance.

The Handlebars—The adjustment of the handlebars will be understood from Fig. 5 and their shape from

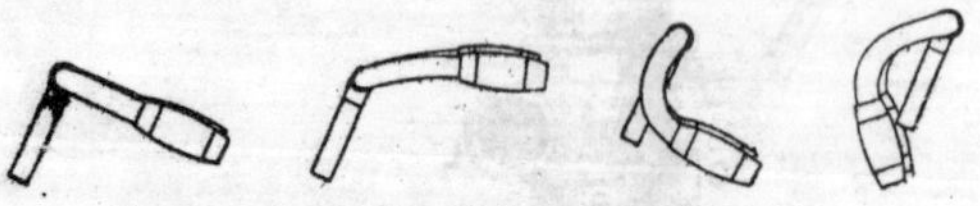

1 2 3 4

FIG. 6—TYPES OF HANDLEBARS.

1. Flat; 2. Raised; 3. Dropped; 4. Dropped and forward.

Fig. 6. Considerations on the respective merits of these patterns will be found on page 268. They are fitted at their ends with handles of felt, cork, rubber, horn, or other materials, which are usually cemented on; this should be carefully done, as a loose handle may come off and cause a bad fall.

The Driving Gear—Motion is communicated from the cranks through the crank axle, front chain wheel, and chain to the back chain wheel, which drives the back wheel and so causes the machine to move forward. Furthermore, by varying the size of the two chain wheels, or, what is the same thing, the number of teeth on each, we can regulate the number of revolutions that the back wheel will make to each revolution of the front chain wheel, *e.g.*, if the back wheel be 28 in. in diameter and the front and back chain wheels have respectively 16 and 8 teeth, the rear wheel will make two revolutions to each revolution of the pedals, which are equal to the revolution of a wheel 56 in. diameter: thus the machine is geared to 56 in., thereby covering 14½ ft. of ground at each revolution of the pedals.

Remarks on the relative advantages of "high" and "low" gears will be found on page 268; the rule for calculating the gear of a machine is to multiply the number of inches in the diameter of the back wheel by the number of teeth on the front chain wheel and divide by the number of teeth on the back chain wheel. Thus:

$$\frac{28 \times 16}{8} = 56.$$

If the machine be fitted with a gear case, measure the distance covered by it during one revolution of the pedals and divide by 3⅐.

The Crank Bracket and Bearing—The crank bracket is a tubular case or shell of metal forming a portion of the frame, and containing the ball bearings upon which runs the crank axle. [*See* BEARINGS, p. 277.]

The Crank Axle is a solid steel shaft of about ⅝ in. dia., fitted with cones for bearing purposes (*see* below). It carries at its extremities the cranks and, just inside one or other of them (usually the right), the front chain wheel.[1]

Tread—The tread is the distance apart of the feet in pedalling; it should, strictly speaking, be measured from the inside plate of the pedal, where it touches the side of the foot; in practice, however, it is measured between the outside of the crank bosses, *i.e.*, it is the length of the axle, and as crooked cranks are now obsolete, this furnishes a fair standard of comparison.

The tread may vary from 4¾ to 5½ inches on machines with clearance for gear cases; on racing machines we should place 4½ in. as the safe downward limit. With the absurdly narrow treads of some American machines, the narrow crank bracket cannot be stiff enough to resist the strain of driving, to say nothing of the disadvantage of the puny bearing necessary (*see* page 278).

[1] In the American "Columbia" the crank axle is lengthened and its ends bent to form the cranks; to admit of its removal it is divided in the centre, the two halves locking together.

The Cranks are bars of steel (usually rectangular in section) of from 6 to 7½ in. in length. At the end remote from the axle they are pierced with a hole for the attachment of the pedals (*q.v.*), and near the axle they broaden into a rounded end or boss. This is pierced with a circular hole to admit the axle, the end of which is flush with the outside of the crank. To secure one to the other, a keyway is cut transversely to the axle through both of them. Into this is fixed a tapering "cotter pin," which when driven home secures the crank in place; this keyway (as of course also the cotter) is circular in section with one flat side, so that the axle presents a flat surface on one side for about ⅜ in.

The distance from the centre of the crank boss to the centre of the pedal axle is known as the "throw" of the crank; in most old machines this was made adjustable by elongating the hole for the attachment of the pedal to form a slot (*see* Fig. 10, No. 2). For remarks on the subject of crank-throw see page 268. Directions for attaching and removing cranks are given under Fig. 7.

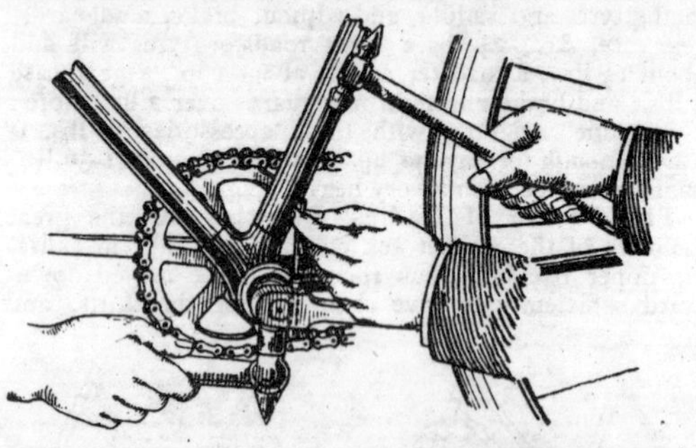

FIG. 7—METHOD OF DETACHING THE CRANK.

To attach the crank—Fit it on to the axle, pressing it in and twisting it round till it comes flush. If it goes on very stiffly a tap with a mallet will drive it home. Then turn the crank upon the axle till the flattened side of the axle is parallel with the keyway, and a clear way can be seen through, and insert the cotter. Then drive the cotter quite home with a hammer, taking care to hold firmly against the opposite side of the crank-boss a heavy mass of metal, *e.g.*, a large hammer or a flat iron. This will take the weight of the blow off the crank axle; if this precaution is neglected the axle and the bearings may be seriously injured. When the cotter is quite home, a washer is placed over the other end, which is provided with a screw, and a nut is screwed home against a crank.

This nut is only intended to prevent the pin getting loose, and any attempt to tighten the crank by it will only result in stripping its thread.

If the crank is found loose, drive the cotter tighter with a hammer and screw the nut home; if it still remains loose a new cotter is required. If, when the cotter is driven home, the length of screw is insufficient to permit the proper tightening of the nut put over the cotter an extra washer.

To detach the crank this process is reversed, a smart blow on the reverse end of the cotter releasing it from the hole, when the crank may be twisted off. The best method is to slack the nut so that it projects over the end of the cotter, and, placing a punch against the cotter, give it a smart blow; the nut will keep the punch in place. In emergencies, the nut thus projecting may be struck with the hammer; but remember that to hit the unprotected end of the cotter will ruin the threads, and the nut will not afterwards engage with them.

The Chain and Chain Wheels—The chain wheels must be exactly in line with each other, or else the teeth will not engage cleanly with the chain, but will rub against its sides, and a great deal of unnecessary friction and uneven wear will result. Much depends upon the degree of tension of the chain, as if it is too slack it may swing from side to side, and, refusing to engage with the teeth, may mount over them and work endless havoc with the frame, whilst, on the other hand, an over tight chain will greatly increase the friction of driving and will wear out the teeth. As the chain tends to "stretch," or rather to increase in length, owing to the wear of the rivets and blocks, means of adjusting it is necessary, and this is obtained by allowing the back wheel, and with it the back chain wheel, to be moved backwards and forwards in the back fork ends. The exact method of adjustment is described under Fig. 8.

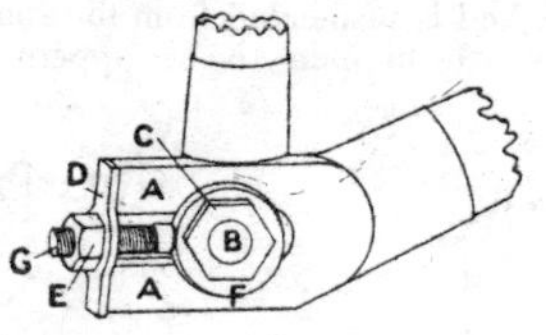

FIG. 8.—THE CHAIN ADJUSTMENT.

F is a plate pierced with a hole in its centre to admit the axle B; from one side of this plate projects a screw C, which passes through a cap D covering the tips of the fork ends A. Over this screw is screwed a small nut E, and when this is screwed up against the cap D it pulls the screw C, and with it the plate A and the axle C, further towards the tip of the fork ends, increasing the distance between the two chain wheels and so tightening the chain.

By slacking the nut, we allow the axle to be pulled a corresponding distance into the fork ends, and so loosen the chain. This process of course has to be performed separately for each side of the axle.

The method of adjusting the chain may be summarised as follows:—

The chain when rightly adjusted should show a very slight deflection from a straight line, in fact the very slightest that will allow it to run freely. This must be judged by spinning the wheel. If the chain is allowed to hang in a kind of festoon it, as we have said above, is highly dangerous. Roughly speaking, the ends of the cranks should have a quarter of an inch play.

To adjust the chain, slack the large nuts that held the axle in the fork ends; to loosen or tighten the chain, slack or screw up each of the small nuts E, taking care to adjust both sides equally. Half a turn of the nut will make a surprising difference; pull the axle home so that the small nut bears on the cap D, then see that the wheel is perfectly equidistant from both of the back stays; should it incline to one side, slacken that side or tighten the other, as accords best with the right adjustment of the chain. Then cautiously screw the nuts on the axle ends moderately tight, taking care in doing it not to force the wheels to one side; if the wheel remains still central, finally tighten the nuts, and lastly screw the small adjusting nuts well home. If you have cone adjusting hubs see that you do not disturb the adjustment of the back wheel bearing in loosening or tightening the fork end nuts (see page 277).

An ingenious variety is that adopted in the American "Crescent," where the rear axle is moved along the back fork ends by means of a rack and pinion, which allows of great precision of adjustment.

The Front Chain Wheel is now usually attached to the crank either permanently, or by screwing on to the crank boss, or in numerous other ways. The rim which carries the teeth is often made detachable, being secured by bolts to the spokes and hub, so as to admit of a ready change of gear.

The Back Chain Wheel takes the form of a ring and runs of a piece with the hub. Its size is an important point: in any case to encircle it the chain has to make far sharper curves than on the larger front wheel, and, the smaller the wheel gets, the sharper become the angles formed by the links of the chain. Of course the larger the back chain wheel the larger must the front one be, if we wish to keep the same gearing, and this places a limit to the size of the back chain wheel. Still, for road work even with a high gear an 8 tooth wheel should be the minimum; but a 9 tooth wheel runs far more easily, especially up hill, and with moderate gear (*e.g.*, up to 72) is not too large to be convenient. For gears up to 64 a 10 tooth is even better.

The Chain—The shape of the chain will be best understood by reference to the annexed illustrations (Fig. 9), to which is suffixed a description.

The distance between the central points of two similar links, *e.g.*, from A to A in Fig. 9, is called the *pitch* of the chain: it is nearly always one inch; the *gauge* of a chain is the breadth of the block. These definitions apply to all types of chain.

The type of chain in most general use is the "block chain" (*a* and *b*) in Fig. 9; the "long link roller chain" (*c*) is obsolete, but its descendants the "Osmond" (*d*) and "Twin Roller" (*e*) and (*f*) seem likely to become the chain of the future.

The Simpson Lever Chain is a production of the last two years. We must confess ourselves sceptical as to its

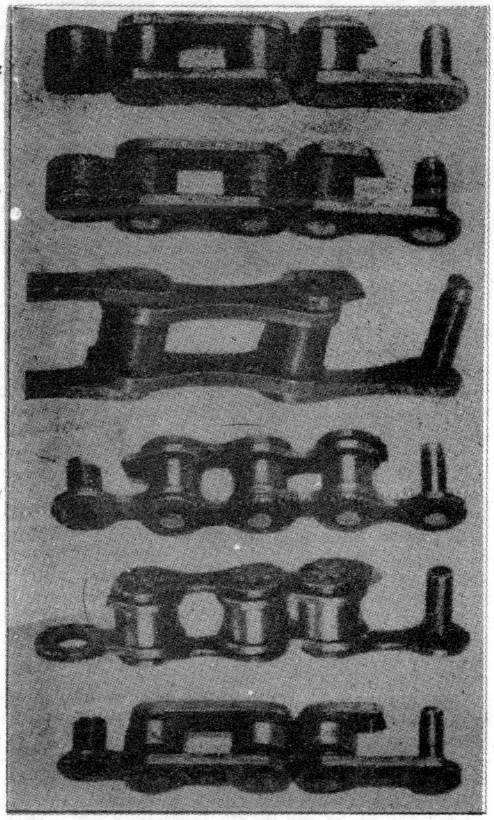

FIG. 9.—THE CHAIN.

a & b, the Block or Humber chain—These consist of alternating solid and open links: into the latter the teeth of the chain wheel engage, while the former, known as the "blocks," take the friction of the teeth. The blocks and "side plates," are held together by and move upon rivets which are either case-hardened as in the Eadie (*a*) or covered with a pen-steel shell or bush as in the Perry (*b*).

c. The Long Link (inch pitch) Roller chain is practically obsolete: it consists wholly of open links, the blocks being eliminated and the friction of the teeth taken by hard steel rollers which revolve on the rivets. This chain has only half as many turning points as the block chain: hence its links make much sharper angles with each other: the extra friction so caused more than compensates for the sweeter running of the roller as compared with the block.

d, The Osmond or short link roller chain (Perry) and

e and *f. The Twin-Roller* (Jos. and Alf. Appleby) have each as many turning points as the block chain, and have the advantage of rolling over sliding friction, as well as that all the parts in tension are of mild metal, and there are thus no hardened blocks to break.

To detach the chain—Get the screw bolt and nut on one of the gear wheels: remove the nut and unscrew the bolt (taking care not to lose them). The chain will then come apart.

To replace—Place the chain in position and bring the ends together on one of the chain wheels: thread the bolt through the side plates and block, screw it home and secure it with the nut: the last usually comes on the *inside*.

Chains in Gear Cases—Before removing the bolt secure the penultimate links with wire or string so that they can easily be recovered from the case: even if the chain is itself removed this method will serve much time in rejoining it: this should be done in the back chain wheel.

merits, and do not believe this chain to be superior to the ordinary type.

Attachment of Chain.—The chain is usually joined by a screw bolt and nut; the mode of attachment is explained under Fig. 9. A decided advance on this method of fastening is the Eadie connecting link, which explains itself at sight, and is more secure and gives less trouble than the ordinary bolt.

Care of the Chain—No machine that is habitually used on the road should be without a gear case. If you have no gear case, cover the chain with vaseline, or, better still, molten tallow (black lead is terribly messy), and do not wantonly interfere with any moderate accumulation of dust, which will form a protecting crust. When the chain gets too foul to run sweetly (as it will probably do after a bath of liquid mud) immerse it in paraffin for a night, and carefully work it about in the oil, paying attention to any stiff links; then replace it and lubricate as before. A dirty chain will often run tight and require re-adjustment, owing to grit getting under it and raising it from the gear wheels. Riders who do not possess gear cases will do well to keep a second chain for use while the first is in pickle. A dirty gear case should be cleaned out with paraffin.

Gear Cases we regard as indispensable for ordinary road use. There are many varieties, but they fall into two classes: rigid cases of metal or celluloid, and lace-up leather cases stretched on a metal frame; the former are infinitely superior for excluding dust and retaining oil, but the latter will keep off all the mud, and most of the dust, and can be knocked about with comparative impunity; this is detrimental to metal cases.

Metal cases, again, fall into two classes, fixed and detachable; in the former the central part of the case is soldered to the machine, access to the chain and chain wheels being obtained by removing a large plate in the front portion, and a quadrant-shaped section at the back. In the latter the whole case can be removed if desired; this, however, is a serious business, and is only resorted to in the case of an accident to the machine. On the whole, we incline to fixed cases, as being less likely to rattle and admit dust. The oil bath we hardly consider necessary: it suffices to keep the chain freely oiled—not a difficult operation.

Into the intimate structure of gear cases we do not propose to enter—the mechanical reader will find it out for himself; the unskilled rider will let it severely alone.

Variable Gears—Various attempts have been made to devise arrangements by which the gear of a machine may be changed when in motion, *e.g.*, lowered to ascend a hill, or to ride against the wind, or raised for opposite purposes. Considerations as to their value in use will be found on p. 268. Their chief drawback is their additional weight and complication. These are, however, reduced to a very small minimum by the "Reilly and Haigh" gear, which is fitted to the rear hub, and does not increase the tread. It has the further advantage that, when the high gear is used, the extra gear is not called into play, the back chain wheel acting in the usual way. The special mechanism is only used with the low gear when the slight extra friction does not so much matter.

The "Collier" is good, but reverses this principle, and is not so light or neat: the Linley expanding chain wheel (or Protean gear) is very clever and effective, but involves the necessity of a brake, as backpedalling is impossible.

The Pedals take the work of the feet, and consist of a metal framework, running with ball-bearings upon an axle, which is carried on the end of the crank. The frame may carry rubber blocks: or the feet may rest direct on the framework; pedals of the latter type are called rat-traps. The bearings are almost always cone-adjusting, and are of the type shown in Fig. 11. A dust-cap is not infrequently placed over the adjusting cone. This must be removed before the pedal can be adjusted.

All good pedals have the axle encased in light metal tube to exclude dust, and should be provided with oil-holes. Pedal bearings are particularly liable to get choked with mud, and require an occasional rinse out with paraffin.

Attachment of Pedals—This is described under Fig. 10.

The Wheels, which are nearly always shod with pneumatic tyres, consist of a hub connected by steel wire spokes with a rim of wood or metal.

The hub revolves on ball-bearings upon an axle held rigidly in the frame, thus receiving the weight of the rider and machine, and is suspended from the rim by means of the spokes which happen to be uppermost. This is

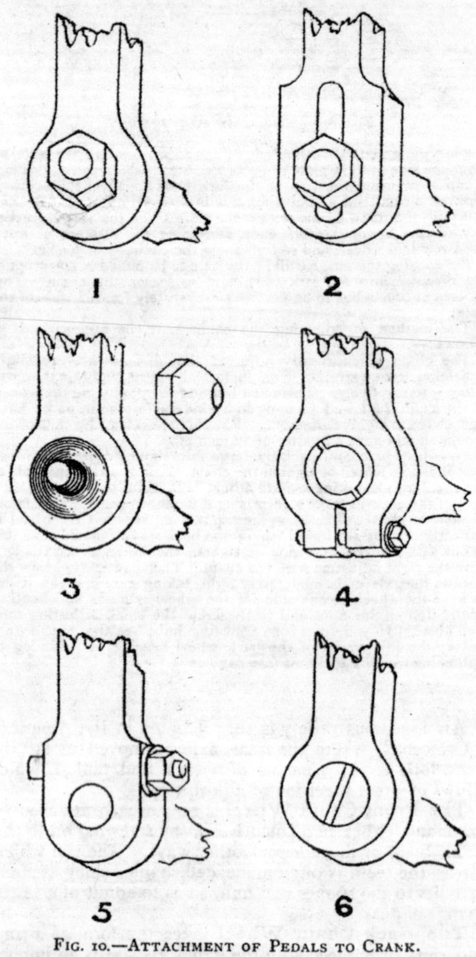

FIG. 10.—ATTACHMENT OF PEDALS TO CRANK.

1. Axle secured by ordinary nut; 2. The same with adjustable throw; both these methods are obsolete owing to the width of tread necessitated; 3. The nut is countersunk into a recess in the crank (Eadie); 4. Axle screws into crank, the ends of which are split and the "lips" clamped together by a screw bolt (Humber, Swift, B.S.A., &c.); 5. Axle secured by cotter just as the crank is itself attached to the crank axle (Premier); 6. Axle simply screws into crank (Scottish Manufacturing Co.).

termed a Suspension wheel, as opposed to an ordinary carriage wheel, the spokes of which are in compression.

But as the bicycle does not remain stationary, the spokes have yet another kind of strain to undergo. In the back wheel the whole of the driving power is applied to the hub, and thus communicated through the spokes to the rim and tyre. For this reason modern wheels are not spoked radially, in which case the pull on them would be at right angles to the direction of the spokes, and would tend to cause the hub to break away from them (to say nothing of the loss of power), but the spokes leave the hub at a tangent (or nearly so), and the pull is thus communicated from the hub to the rim along the direct line of the spokes. For this reason the tangent wheel, as it is called, is immensely stronger than the old-fashioned radial or "direct" wheel, which has long since passed out of practical cycling.

To proceed to details: the hub is furnished on each side with a flange, generally pierced transversely with holes for the reception of the spokes, which are headed, and, passing through the holes in the flange, take a sharp turn[1] and run to the rim, where they are screwed into a brass nipple: this nipple protrudes through the rim, but is prevented from passing through it by a broad flange, which bears on the hollow bed of the rim; the tension of the spoke is regulated by turning the nipple, the spoke being thus drawn further or less into the rim. Upon the correct tensioning of the spokes depends the "truth" of the wheel, the natural shape of the rim being of less importance than that imparted to it by the pull of the spokes. The intersections of the spokes are usually tied with thin wire, though the advisability of this is by no means certain. The spokes should be thickened (butt-ended) where they pass through the flange, as well as where they are threaded to screw into the nipple. The hub should not measure less than 2 in. between the spoke-flanges.

The intersections of the spokes and the rim often form only one row along the centre of the rim: it adds to the rigidity of the wheel if they are placed in two rows on either side of the centre.

Size of Wheels—Most machines are fitted with two 28 in. wheels; it is urged by some that a 30 in. front wheel gives better steering, but we scarcely think that it is worth its weight. Ladies' machines are often built with 28 in. and 26 in., or two 26 in. wheels.

Removing the Wheels—To remove the front wheel, take off the nuts and washers, and, pressing with the thumbs upon the hub, spring the fork ends one by one over the end of the axle. To replace it, reverse the process.

To remove the back wheel, take off the sliding end of the gear case; slacken the fork end nuts, when the axle and with it the nuts, washer, and chain-adjuster may be slid out of the fork ends. To replace it reverse the process, taking care to fit the chain-adjuster (*see* p. 275) well on to the fork ends.

Steel Rims—Steel rims are either hollow or solid: the former are lighter and more rigid, but decidedly more liable to permanent damages from stones and similar obstacles. The Westwood is a solid rim with the edges curled into small tubes and is peculiarly suited for wired-on tyres.

Wood Rims are best built either of segments of wood dovetailed into each other, or, as in the case of the Fairbanks, constructed of thin layers of wood with the grain running in different directions, and are covered with canvas; they are unsuited to detachable tyres, as the outward pressure of the jacket tends to splay the rim out with disastrous consequence. They are particularly liable to damage in detaching wired tyres. There is, however, undoubtedly a peculiar "life" in wood rims, and when built for tube tyres they are lighter than steel. Single-Tube Palmer, Morgan and Wright, and Woodstock tyres, are specially suitable for them.

In all cases wood rims should receive every three months a liberal coating of good varnish: this will greatly increase their powers of resistance to wet, and prolong their life.

Bearings—A bearing occurs where any part of a machine, which rotates, bears upon another part which does not rotate, or *vice versa*.

A ball bearing is one in which the two bearing surfaces, instead of running directly on each other, are separated by steel balls; thus instead of the friction of one level surface upon another we have only the friction of small points of these surfaces against the balls, and to a large extent rolling friction is substituted for sliding friction.

The most usual type of ball bearing consists of two cones affixed to the ends of an axle and resting upon balls, which themselves bear upon cups contained in the case of the bearing. These may be divided into two classes: *a.* where the cups are stationary, and the axle and cone revolve, *e.g.*, crank bearing of a safety; or *b.* where the axle and cone are fixed and the cups revolve, as in either wheel of a safety.

This distinction is, however, of no great importance, as with slight modifications any description of one type will equally apply to the other.

A more important distinction for our purpose is based upon the method of adjustment of the bearings. For a bearing to run freely it is necessary that the balls should not be so tightly jammed as to prevent their revolving, nor that the bearing should be so loosely put together as to admit of the balls running out of their proper circular track; to insure this it is necessary that we should have some means of regulating the distance between the cup and cone.

To attain this end we may move the position of either the cup or the cone, and the most convenient and accurate way of doing this is by providing one or other with a screw thread engaging with some other portion of the machine, which for running purposes is of a piece with it, and securing it to that portion by some locking arrangement.

We may accordingly divide ball bearings into two classes.

(*a*) **Cone-adjusting bearings,** in which one cone screws upon the axle, and the cups are fixed in to the case of the bearings.

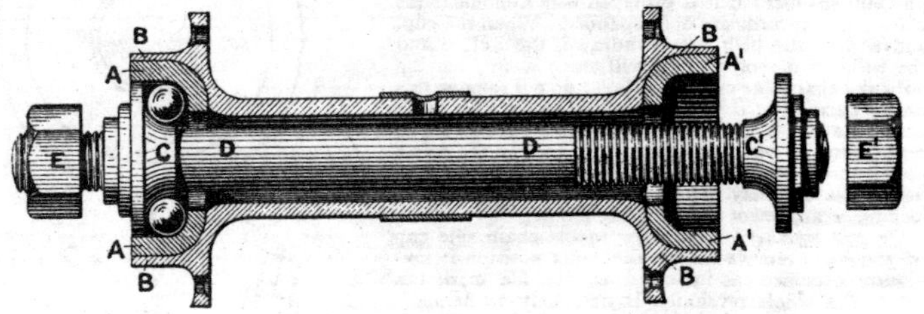

FIG. 11.—DIAGRAM OF CONE-ADJUSTING HUB (EADIE).

The cups A A' are fixed into the case of the hub B; in these are placed the balls, which are held in place by the cones C C'; of these C is of a piece with the axle D, but C' is free, working upon the threaded end of the axle to allow of adjustment.

To take the bearing to pieces—Remove the fork end nuts, slide or spring the wheel out of the forks and lay it on its side with the free cone C' uppermost. We can now unscrew the free cone C' and, holding the other end of the axle firmly in place, tip the balls out of the cup A'; place the hand under the cup A and remove the axle, when the opposite balls will fall into the hand.

To put the bearings together—Lay the wheel on its side with the cup A uppermost; put the axle D through the hub with the fixed cone C uppermost, place the balls in the cup, and let the cone C fall upon them; then, holding the axle firmly in place, turn the wheel over so as to rest on the end of the axle nearest to C. The balls may now be placed in the cup A' (the screwed end of the axle will keep them in place); lastly, screw the free cone C' down upon the balls; when it is screwed home the wheel may be set upright.

To adjust the bearing—When the wheel is in place, slack the nut E' (the opposite nut need not be touched), grip the flattened sides of the cone C' with the open spanner provided, and screw it up as far as it will go, then unscrew it about a quarter of a turn and screw up the nut E; take the wheel by the rim and see if there is any perceptible side shake in the bearing; if there be none, and the wheel runs freely, the adjustment is correct; if there be any perceptible shake, screw up the cone a little; if the wheel runs stiffly, slacken it off. It will be noticed that tightening the nut often tightens the bearing also, and for this allowance has to be made. If the proper spanner be not available, the cone may be turned by twisting a piece of string round it, taking the ends in the hands and pulling them tight. The cone may readily be forced round.

[1] In the "New Rapid" the flange of the hub is provided with small studs pierced at right angles to the width of the hub, and through these the spokes are inserted. This obviates the undesirable weakening of the spoke by bending, and is decidedly preferable.

(*b*) **Cup-adjusting** (commonly called **disc-adjusting**) **bearings**, in which the cones are immovably fixed to **the axle and** the cups (discs) screw into the case of the **bearing.**

FIG 12.—DISC- (OR CUP-) ADJUSTING CRANK-BEARING (CENTAUR).

A is the case or shell of the bearing and is called the chain bracket; B B, the cranks; C, the front chain wheel; D, the crank axle; E, one of the cones (of a piece with axle); F, one of the discs (or cups) fitted with "flat" to give grip to spanner; G, locking ring to lock disc against bracket. NOTE.—The above locking arrangement (though very good) is not of the usual type; see Fig. 13.

To take to pieces—The following directions apply primarily to the crank bearing, but with slight modifications apply also to the hub. Detach both the cranks (B B) and the chain wheel (see Fig. 7); undo the locking arrangements (in this case the locking ring G) and unscrew the left hand cup; if the cup adjusts by means of holes in its outward surface this is done with a pin-hole spanner; if it is provided with a shoulder (as above) use an ordinary open spanner. When the cup, and with it the balls, are withdrawn, the axle D and the balls of the other side will come away, leaving only the chain-side cup in position; do not remove this unless necessary; if you must do so, make a file mark across the case of the cup and the case of the bearing to make sure of your replacing it in exactly the same position; otherwise you will set the chain-wheel out of line. The cup may then be removed by undoing the locking arrangement and screwing it out.

To put together—First screw in the chain side cup (if you have removed it) to the exact position it previously occupied, as indicated by the file mark (an error of a whole revolution is not likely to be made and may be guarded against by counting the threads outside which, before removing the cup, lie outside the bracket). Lay the bicycle on its chain side, and put the chain end of the axle D through the cup (there is always more space outside the cone on the chain end of the axle than on the other). Drop the chain side balls into the cup and let the cone of the axle fall on them. Next very carefully turn the machine over, pulling on the chain end of the axle while so doing to nip the balls between the cup and cone to prevent them escaping; with the same object, when the machine is turned over, keep the opposite end of the axle supported.

Take the other cup: fill it with vaseline and place the balls in a ring inside it, taking care not to warm them or the cup, or the vaseline will melt; then very gingerly pass it upwards over the downward end of the axle and engage it in the threads of the bracket, screwing it home very gently, especially as the balls begin to approach the cone, or they may over-ride one another and jam.

When the cup is screwed home replace the chain wheel and cranks and adjust the bearing.

To adjust—Slack the locking ring G or its equivalent; apply an open spanner to the shoulder of the disc or cup F and loosen or tighten till an adjustment is made (see directions under Fig. 11).

If, as is usual, the disc has pin-holes instead of a projecting shoulder, turn it by inserting into the holes the prong of a "pin-hole spanner"; the crank-boss is usually an obstacle to the convenient accomplishment of this method of adjustment: only one firm (the Osmond Co.) wisely cut a semicircular piece out of the crank-boss to give clearance; but, in emergencies, the disc may be cautiously driven round with a long nail and a hammer.

The head bearing of the modern safety is of a different type, and is described under Fig. 5.

Before entering on the description of these two classes we may here remark that a bearing should have its ball races as far apart as possible; a narrow bearing is very ill-adapted to resist a one-sided strain, such as that experienced in the driving of a safety. Furthermore, power should be applied to the axle inside and not outside the ball races; if the pull of the chain comes outside the crank or hub bearings, the axle is clearly forced sideways by its leverage, and much uneven friction and consequent wear will result. Ideally, the driving should be central; as this cannot be effected, we must bring the front chain wheel well up to the bearing, and by "dishing" it, and causing its chain-ring to overhang the race, make the strain as near central as possible. This is well carried out on the Humber; in the case of the hub chain wheel (especially with disc hubs) it is easy to place the chain-ring well within the bearing.

(*a*) **Cone-adjusting bearings**—In the diagram of an Eadie hub (Fig. 11) it will be seen that by unscrewing the cone C′ we alter the relation not only of C′ itself to the cup A′, but that of the cone C to the cup A. When the required adjustment has been obtained, the cone C′ is fixed in place by screwing up the nut E, which drives the washer F against it.

(*b*) **Cup- (or disc-) adjusting bearings**—In these the cones are permanently fixed to the axle, and the cups screw bodily into the case of the bearing (*see* Fig. 12). It will be seen that the cup and cone respectively, necessarily face opposite ways to what they did in the

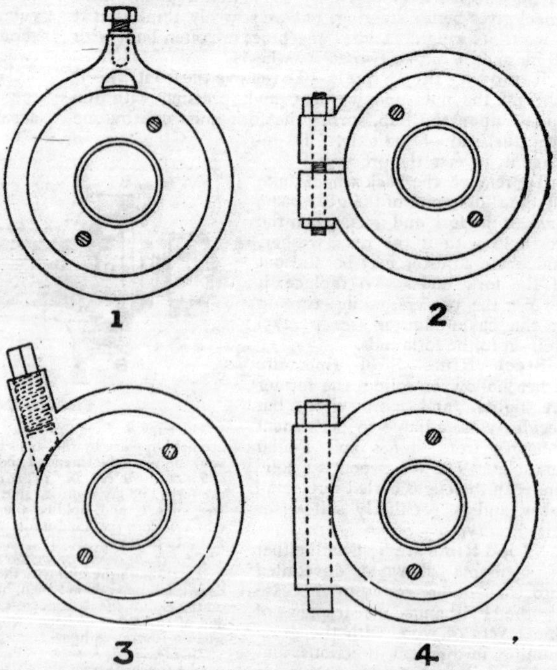

FIG. 13.—METHODS OF LOCKING THE CRANK-BEARING (CUP-ADJUSTING).

1. Set screw: acting on block at right angles to disc; 2. Split bracket; "lips" compressed by screw bolt; 3. Set screw acting on block pressing sideways on disc; 4. Cotter and nut. See also Fig. 12.

cone-adjusting bearing, and this has the effect of placing the ball races further apart. The locking arrangement too is quite different, and some difficulty has, in the case of hubs, had to be overcome in devising a satisfactory method of effecting this.

A description of the cup-adjusting crank bearing and hub is given, together with full instructions for their manipulation, under Figs. 12 and 13.

Comparison of the two types—We consider cup-adjusting bearings decidedly preferable. Firstly, they are more dust proof. In each type there is space for the entrance of dust between the cup and the coned axle: but in the cup-adjusting bearing this is only the size of the diameter of the axle itself: in the older type it is the size of the diameter of the whole cone, and this can only be mastered by complications in the way of dust caps, &c.; secondly, for the same reason, it is oil retaining, and, thirdly (in the case of hubs), the bearing can be adjusted without disturbing the fork end nuts and so possibly the chain adjustment. Fourthly, the same disc-adjusting bearing allows for the same length of axle a slightly greater distance between the ball races. There is, however, apart from these incidental advantages, absolutely no essential difference in the running of the two types, and a good cone adjusting bearing is far better than a bad specimen of the other.

Care of the bearings—As we have shown above, careful adjustment should be made when necessary: refrain, however, from tinkering with the bearings more than you can help, especially from taking them to pieces. Nuts which are always being tightened and slackened cannot be expected to hold. In fact, never touch any part of the machine unless it really calls for it.

The best way of testing the running of a wheel bearing is to put the valve of the tyre towards the top of the wheel, and see that its weight causes the wheel to oscillate backwards and forwards till at last the valve settles down at the very bottom of the wheel. The back wheel, even when the chain is in place, should oscillate several times, the untrammelled front wheel much longer. If the bearing is unevenly worn you will not be able to effect a perfect adjustment: make the best compromise you can, remembering that it is better to put up with a *little* shake in the bearing than to hinder the free running of the wheel: but if a worn bearing is run too slack the wear is only exaggerated. The just mean is to be learnt only by experience.

Oil the bearings with good oil (Rangoon oil or sperm with a little paraffin is best) say once in a hundred miles or so, and then but sparingly, don't slop the oil about, as it attracts dust: if, however, you find a ring of dust around the entrance to bearing it is better not to remove it, or at all events very rarely, as you are very likely to rub it in the bearings, especially if they are the cone-adjusting variety. Disc-adjusting bearings may be oiled more copiously, and much less often. If from any cause the bearing should become clogged, it should be slackened and paraffin injected: it should then be spun round, fresh paraffin being added till it runs out perfectly clean: the bearing should then be adjusted, left to run dry, and oiled. It is a good thing to have a hole fitted with a screw plug drilled in the bottom of the crank bracket for the escape of the paraffin. A piece of chenille lightly wound round the axle where it emerges from the bearing will go far to exclude dust.

The Step is usually a roughened prolongation of the left-hand back fork end nut, but is occasionally brazed on to the back stays.

The Brake—The back wheel brake (except the pneumatic variety) has long since been condemned by its cumbrousness, hence the brake is usually applied to the front wheel; though the effect of a sudden and violent application is very apt to drive back or even break the front forks, or to cause the machine to slip. Furthermore, pneumatic tyres seldom take kindly to the frequent use of the brake. For these reasons we would strongly urge readers to regard the brake as an appliance to be used only *in extremis*: back pedalling comes automatically to a practised rider, and can usually at ordinary speed be applied far more rapidly than any brake. Still, emergencies which call for a brake, though rare, are generally imperative; and none but really experienced riders will dispense with its use. The novice should, however, accustom himself to use it as little as possible, and should above all things eschew the immoral practice of "coasting" with the brake hard on—ruinous alike to machine and tyres.

The ordinary front wheel brake is applied to the tyre, and is fully described under Fig. 14.

Several effective brakes have recently been devised which are applied to the rim instead of the tyre.

The band brake consists of a band of leather, encircling a drum on the back wheel, which by means of an arrangement of rods is, when required, pulled into contact with the drum. It is powerful but extremely troublesome, being seldom entirely clear of the drum.

The Dolittle Brake is applied by backpedalling to the back wheel; once the brake is on, it remains so till the pedals are again pressed forward; it is a little difficult at first to master its use, but we can testify to its thorough efficiency.

FIG. 14.—THE BRAKE (RALEIGH).

To adjust—Slack the screw-bolt or set-screw which is half way down the telescopic brake-rod; put the brake-lever at such a distance from the handlebars that it can readily be grasped by the hand, and yet have space for effective action; put the brake-spoon about $\frac{1}{2}$ or $\frac{5}{8}$ in. clear of the tyre; then tighten the bolt or set-screw. When this is done, see that when the brake-lever is pressed home the tyre is effectually gripped.

The pneumatic brake consists of a suitably mounted rubber cushion, which is expanded by the pressure of air, applied by means of a rubber ball and tube attached to handlebars, and so grips the tyre; but there is yet considerable scope for its improvement.

The Seat Lug (see E in Fig. 2) is compressed by a bolt and grips the saddle pillar which slides into the diagonal of the frame: to adjust the height of the saddle, the bolt of the seat lug is slacked, the pillar raised to the desired height, and the bolt again tightened.

The Saddle Pin carries the saddle. It may consist of a single upright tube sliding into the diagonal of the frame and held there by the compression of the seat lug and having the saddle clipped to its upper end. More commonly, however, a second horizontal tube is brazed to it and carries the saddle, for which a backward and forward adjustment is thus obtained. Such pins may be T-shaped, or L-shaped; the latter are divided into "Forward L-Pins" and "Backward L-Pins," accordingly as the horizontal arm points forwards or backwards. The former are nearly universal.

The Saddle—The saddle normally consists of a pear-shaped piece of leather, suspended upon a metal framework: the sharp forward end is known as the "peak": the rounded rear end is rivetted to a plate called the "cantle," which is secured to the framework.

The most usual type is the "Hammock" shown upon the bicycle in Fig. 1. Here the framework consists of two or more long springs running from peak to cantle, and secured midway by a clip in the method shown in Fig. 15. The tension of the leather is regulated by a rather inaccessible nut just under the peak; the Brampton has a circular hole in the front of the peak for the insertion of a screwdriver—an excellent plan.

The "tilt" of the saddle is an important point; the

requirements of each rider vary, but we think that for a standard adjustment the peak should be about ¼ of an inch above the back of the saddle. Experiments should, however, be made until a comfortable angle is reached; the method of effecting this is shown in Fig. 15.

We are, however, strongly of opinion that the saddle and the spring should be independent of each other: *i.e.*, the saddle should have a perfectly rigid metal framework, and be bolted to the spring. In the hammock saddle when a jolt depresses the saddle leather, the peak obviously becomes more prominent, relatively to it. A rigid saddle never alters in the relative position of its parts and, once comfortable, is always comfortable. We have found the old "Brooks B. 20," with a "Salter" or "semi-Arab" spring, infinitely preferable.

Racing saddles should not be used on the road; they are always breaking and the absence of a spring to ease down the weight of a rider puts most unfair strain on the machine.

Of the numerous saddles in which the peak is eliminated we have no good to say; the absence of the peak makes the rider lose the "grip" of the saddle which

FIG. 15.—THE SADDLE CLIP (BROOKS).

To adjust the position—Slack the end nuts on the transverse bolt; the clip, and with it the saddle, may then be shifted to any position upon the L-pin; then tighten the nuts.

To adjust the tilt—Slack the nuts as before, when the saddle and springs may be swung bodily upon the bolt to any desired tilt; then tighten the nuts. In all cases see that the clip grips the spring wires in their centre; adjustment should not be obtained by sliding the wires along the clip.

NOTE—The above type of clip will fit either an upright or L-shaped pin.

is so essential to good steering; we consider them uncomfortable and dangerous.

Pneumatic saddles are now seldom used, excepting those kinds in which the pneumatic contrivance takes the shape of a pad *under* the ordinary saddle.

Mudguards—There is nothing to beat the ordinary steel guard: we have, we believe, tried every "detachable" guard on the market and found them all wanting, except perhaps the celluloid one with wire stays. Those abominations that are hung with strings from the back of the saddle can seldom be restrained from getting askew.

The ordinary mudguard is secured by screws or clips to the bridges of the back forks and back stays or front fork crown, and further supported by wire stays terminating in a flat ring which encircles the wheel axle and is secured by the fork end nut. Our only complaint is that they are almost always made too narrow (the "Swift" is an honourable exception), and that the stays should be secured to the fork by independent clips, so that they can be detached without disturbing the fork end nuts—always a thing to be avoided.

Multicycles, or cycles carrying two or more riders, have, owing to their speed, recently come into use for pacing and other purposes. Such of them as seat their riders side by side may be dismissed as mere fads: but where the riders sit one behind the other, it is evident that while their united power is available for the propulsion of the machine, the resistance of the air amounts to little more than that to be faced on a single. The tandem safety, *i.e.*, a safety for two riders one behind the other, is, however, the only representative of the class with which we need be concerned.

Tandem safeties, owing to the great length of the wheelbase, the great weight carried, and the extra stress

FIG. 16.—TANDEM FOR TWO MEN (SWIFT).

of driving the machine, should be built of far stronger parts than singles. Whippiness of frame is even more detrimental to the good running of a tandem than of a single, while the consequences of a breakdown are usually serious. More particularly the head and the front forks and crowns have to be specially strengthened: triple fork crowns are often used, and the forks are wisely duplicated; when this duplication is lateral the outer forks are often carried to the top of the head. The chains of tandems should never be placed on opposite sides.

The frames of tandems present great variety: the principle of triangulation referred on p. 272 should be fully carried out as in Fig. 16. When the machine is built to carry a lady before or behind, the difficulties of construction are greatly increased.

The steering on machines built for two men, or for a lady behind, is best left to the front rider only, the rear handles being rigidly fixed. Where the steering is coupled, the coupling rods should always be carried low down on the frame, so that the front rider is not shut in, as in the case where the handle-bars are connected by a straight swivelled rod.

Where the machine is designed for a lady in front, double steering is necessary, but there are several contrivances for gearing it down in favour of the rear rider, the front handle-bars being allowed only a slight movement, and the steering merely indicated to the front rider. We may, however, say that we consider that the balance of advantage rests with machines on which the lady sits behind (Fig. 17).

The adjustment of the parts of a tandem is, with the exception of that of the front chain, performed as with a

FIG. 17.—TANDEM FOR LADY TO SIT BEHIND (RALEIGH).

single. The adjustment of the front chain is best carried out by placing the front crank-bearing eccentric to the bracket (which is made very large): by turning the whole bearing in the bracket the tension of the chain can be adjusted.

OTHER TYPES OF CYCLE.

The Bevel-Geared Safety, an invention of some years' standing, has recently come into fresh prominence in the "Acatene." The crank axle carries a bevel-toothed wheel which drives a hollow shaft revolving on ball bearings upon what would otherwise be the chain stay, and this by a similar arrangement of bevel-wheels drives the back wheel. We do not anticipate that this will for serious riding oust the chain-driven safety: but for light work, especially in and about town, its neatness and the absence of both chain and gear case may bring it into some popularity.

Front Driving Bicycles—In these power is applied to the front wheel: one result of this is that the wheel is in a manner gripped by the feet, which thus to a great extent control the steering. In the early days of rear drivers, which then steered atrociously, this was a distinct gain: but in view of the present perfection of the steering of the prevalent type, we think it more of a drawback than otherwise, especially in the case of the smaller front drivers. Two types are extant:—

The Ordinary or High Bicycle, the name of which perpetuates the memory of its former glories. The front wheel is large, ranging from 60 inches down to 46 or so, and is not geared: the hub is of a piece with the axle, which revolves in two independent ball bearings placed at the fork-ends. Its most recent type, the "Rational Ordinary" has the front forks "raked," *i.e.*, sloped backwards from the vertical, the saddle well back, and the rear wheel of at least 24 inches, in place of the old-fashioned wheel of 16 inches or so. Such a mount, fitted with pneumatics, is perfectly safe, free from side-slip, never goes wrong, and will last for ever. The "Farringdon" is the only example of the type now on the market, but no better could be desired.

The Crypto is the only survivor of a numerous class of geared front-drivers. The gearing is by means of an arrangement of small toothed wheels of great ingenuity: the machine was originally made as the "Geared Ordinary" in size of from 40 to 46 inches; this was, however, soon abandoned in favour of wheels of from 34 to 38 inches: while the last two or three years have seen the introduction of the "Bantam" in which the driving wheel is only 26 to 32 inches.

We can say from long experience that the medium sized Crypto is a safe and comfortable mount, cleanly, free from side-slip, and never giving trouble. It is, however, while easier running than the Bantam, markedly slower than the Rear Driver: at a slow pace this inferiority is not very noticeable, but for fast or heavy work (*e.g.*, uphill) it is quite distinct. The Bantam scores over the medium sized F.D. in portability, weight, and decreased wind-resistance: the steering, however, is not nearly so good, nor is the machine so safe a mount. It is, moreover, difficult for a tall rider to get sufficient length of reach without resorting to an excessively backward position.

The Tricycle—It is with some regret than we have relegated this type of cycle to the "etceteras." It has many good points:—freedom from side-slip, and absence of the nervous strain always present, though not always consciously recognised, as the result of the need of preserving the balance of a safety. These reasons, with its ability to support itself, render it a good machine, not only for traffic riding, but for long distance road riding. Its inferiority to the safety is not, moreover, so marked as is generally believed, as till quite recently the performances of Mr. Bidlake and others upon it were not conspicuously inferior to those of their contemporary safety riders.

Accessories.

Spanners—All machines should be provided with spanners to fit each nut, and these should always be used in preference to an adjustable wrench.

Oil-cans—Cheap oil-cans are to be avoided—a really well-finished one is worth its cost.

Tool-bags should be large enough to enable the contents to be readily packed; here, again, cheap varieties are to be avoided.

Lamps—It yet remains to be shown that paraffin and benzine lamps are superior to the old-fashioned variety. Those made by Miller, Lucas, and Salsbury leave little to be desired. Excessively small lamps always give trouble. Sliding side-lights should be fitted, as they are the most air-tight and not liable to injury.

Bells—A loud bell is a distinct advantage. Repeating bells are preferable to single-strikers, but require careful manufacture.

Pumps—Short pumps are an insufferable nuisance: 18 inches is the best length. Aluminium pumps we have found light and quite efficient—more so than celluloid. It is a distinct advantage to have all the loose parts (*e.g.*, the rubber tube and nozzle) made to screw inside the pump: the aperture should be closed with a dust cap.

A foot-pump for home use is a most desirable possession.

Pump-clips—Hill's rubber pump-clips are efficient and cannot possibly cause rattle. Celluloid clips tend in time to loose their grip of the tubes which they encircle. Metal spring clips, lined with horn, and secured to the machine by means of a little solution, are thoroughly reliable.

Cyclometers—There are numerous excellent cyclometers on the market: but most of them will be found to register from 30 to 40 yards too much in the mile, owing to their not allowing for the flattening of the front tyre. Those which rotate with the hub or crank are quite unreliable at high speeds.

Pneumatic Tyres.

The reason of the superiority of the pneumatic over the obsolete solid and cushion tyres appears to lie in the following facts. Each successive portion of the tyre as it comes into contact with the ground is compressed by the weight of the rider, and when it is freed from the weight immediately flies back to its original form, and, pushing against the road, helps to propel the cycle, restoring to it nearly as much energy as was absorbed in its compression. A solid or cushion tyre absorbs just as much force in its compression, but owing to the relative sluggishness of rubber as compared with compressed air, fails to regain its shape with sufficient promptitude to push against the road and so be of service.

A fast pneumatic tyre is one in which the materials hinder as little as possible this "resilience" of the air. The other essentials of a good tyre are immunity of the rider from vibration, ease in repair, durability, and freedom from puncture.

The last of these is the least important; any ordinary puncture can be repaired in ten minutes, and as with the usual light roadster tyres puncture occurs but rarely, it is not necessary to cumber and retard the tyre with protective bands. Durability is a matter of using good material, and sufficiently thick rubber; while freedom from vibration and resiliency go together and are considered below.

Pneumatic tyres normally consist of three concentric layers, which, beginning from the inside, are:—

I. The air-tube, made of very slightly vulcanised rubber, and fitted with a valve. II. A layer of inextensible fabric to prevent the air-tube from bulging or bursting, and to take the strain of driving. III. A layer of more highly vulcanised rubber to protect the fabric from the road: it is usually thicker on the centre or tread than on the sides, and on racing tyres becomes a mere strip of rubber mounted on the fabric as a tread.

The second and third members are nearly always of a piece, and are together known as the "jacket"; in some tyres they interpenetrate each other, but are more usually fastened to each other in such a way that they can be separated if needful. They should preferably not be vulcanised but merely solutioned together, which greatly facilitates repairs to the jacket. In single-tube tyres all these members are more or less permanently fastened together.

Nature of the Fabric—It cannot be too strongly emphasised that it is by means of the fabric that the force of driving is communicated from the rim to the tread of the tyre and so to the ground: the rubber is only to act as a protection to the fabric; except on the tread, it takes none of the driving strain, and adds very little to the actual strength of the tyre.

Without entering into details we may say that the best results are obtained from a fabric which, like the "Flexifort" (Dunlop), Palmer, or Scottish, consists of layers of pendent threads running diagonally from edge to edge of the cover and not interwoven. This is called a "tangential" fabric because the pull travels lengthwise along the threads (as in a tangent spoke) and not across them; it has the further advantage of eliminating the friction and "sawing" action that takes place between threads of ordinary canvas.

The Rubber of the Jacket—It is essential that this should be of high quality: too many of the tyres on the market contain an abnormal amount of incorporated earthy matter, useful to a slight extent to give substance to the rubber, but beyond that point a mere adulterant. Good rubber may be known by the peculiar brownish mottlings which appear when the powdery sulphur has been cleared off.

Non-slipping devices—The jacket of roadster tyres is generally made with fluting or corrugations to prevent "side-slip." Such devices inevitably detract from the resilience of the tyre, especially when their effect is unduly to stiffen the jacket by rendering it too massive. Other jackets, where the corrugations are intermittent, (viz., in the form of isolated bosses, knobs, &c.) suffer severely from the use of the brake. We consider that the fastest and most effective device is that of scoring the jacket with a few deep flutings, the only drawback being the liability of the hollows to cuts and punctures. A slightly less effective, but more durable, type is when the tread is left plain and one or two bold ridges are placed on each side of it.

Non-slipping bands may be fixed with solution to smooth tyres, and afford the further advantage of saving them from cuts or punctures. On very flinty roads this is the only way to save the tyres: when badly cut the band may be replaced.

How hard to pump—The tyres should just show a slight flattening when ridden: for riders of about eleven stone, the finger and thumb of one hand should be able to make no impression on the back tyre and a very slight one on the front. Heavier riders should inflate rather harder, and *vice versâ*.

Classification of tyres—Pneumatic tyres may be classified under two heads:—I. Detachable tyres. II. Tube tyres.

In the former the jacket is a broad band, secured to the rim by its edges, the air-tube resting on the rim and being protected from it by a strip of tape: the latter present to the eye the appearance of a simple hose-pipe, and are usually cemented to the rim.

Detachable Tyres.

Method of repair—First of all inflate the punctured tyre as hard as possible, and examine its exterior for the puncturing body: unless the puncture be very small, a quick ear will often be able to locate the puncture by its hissing sound without further measures. In such a case only a small part of the jacket need be detached. If the spot cannot be detected it will be necessary wholly to remove one side of the jacket from the rim. First, however, apply the moistened finger to the valve to ascertain that the fault does not lie there.

Carefully clean the tyre, as the entrance of grit beneath the jacket is most destructive to both fabric and air-tube: then deflate it and detach one edge of the jacket (see below), in the case of the back wheel choosing the side furthest from the chain, so as to avoid greasing the air-tube: with the same object wind a piece of rag round the end of the hub. Pull the air tube from under the cover; it is not usually worth while to undo the valve and so remove it altogether from the rim. Cautiously inflate the tube so that it just feels plump to the hand: over-pressure will cause it to swell up and burst. A large puncture can then often be heard: if not, pass the whole of the tube in front of the lips, when a very slight escape is usually noticeable: test any suspected spot with the wet finger. Should this fail the whole tube must be passed under water (a small bowl will suffice) stretching each successive portion as it is immersed: the smallest puncture will be betrayed by a persistent stream of bubbles. If this is unsuccessful it will be necessary to remove the valve from the rim (*see* p. 285), replace it in the tube, re-inflate, and test the small remaining piece of tube round the valve.

Having found the puncture, mark it with an indelible pencil, carefully dry the tube for some distance round, and gently rub the surface round the puncture with a piece of sand-paper to remove the whitish deposit of sulphur on which no patch will stick. The sand-paper on a matchbox may be used; or the wetted head of a wax match will equally well remove the sulphur. Next, with a circular motion of the finger, apply round the spot a thin and even coating of rubber solution: leave this to dry, and cut a patch of sheet rubber, inclining the scissors so as to make a bevelled edge; clean the non-bevelled side with sand-paper or benzine and coat it also with solution. Allow time for it to set; it should be "tacky" to the touch, and up to ten minutes the longer interval the better: then apply the patch to the puncture, remembering that once the two solutioned surfaces have touched, the patch cannot be removed without cleaning off and beginning *de novo*. Press the patch firmly down, powder it with French chalk to prevent it from sticking to the jacket: it now only remains to replace the valve and air tube in the rim, and to attach the jacket. Before again inflating make sure that the air-tube is not "nipped" by the edge of the cover.

A very small puncture or a leak at the join of the tube, which escapes detection by the ordinary method, may often be roughly located by immersing the whole tyre, fully inflated, in a trough of water, when the escaping air will come through the neighbouring spoke holes.

If the hole in the air-tube be large, as in the case of a burst, the rubber patch should be covered by one of canvas applied in the same way. In the case of a long slit a little ingenuity will enable you to put a patch on the inside; this should be reinforced by another on the outside. For punctures under the valve canvas, cautiously peel off the canvas (using benzine or even rubber solution to free it from the air-tube), apply a patch, and again stick down the canvas with solution, allowing a short interval to admit of its drying. A leak at the inset of the valve usually arises from cutting of the air-tube; the valve must be inserted in a fresh place, and the original hole treated as a large puncture.

If, however, a section of the tube should happen to become hopelessly rotten, and patching is hopeless, it is sometimes advisable to cut away the affected portion and make a fresh join; in order to do this, fold back about $1\frac{1}{2}$ inches of one end of the tube, much as one might turn back the end of one's sleeves: coat this and the outside of the other end with solution, and when they are "tacky" lay one side of the folded end against the side of the other end; put the thumb inside one of them and press them well together; then very quickly unroll the rolled end over on to the other, pressing them well together, and taking care to avoid puckers. This operation requires nice manipulation and should not be attempted by a novice.

Butt-ended air-tubes—The whole operation of repair is greatly simplified by using in place of the ordinary endless air tube a butt-ended tube as shown in Fig. 18. In case of puncture the joint is undone, the valve nut unscrewed and the tube bodily removed from the machine, without the necessity of taking out the wheel.

The convenience of this is very great, nor does the contrivance perceptibly slow a roadster machine.

Puncture-sealing air-tubes appear to answer

satisfactorily for small punctures. When, however, they do leak, it will be found very difficult to locate the puncture, as a tube which leaks at high pressure may not do so at the low pressure necessary in testing by water.

Cuts and Bursts in the Jacket—Cuts which do not entirely pierce the rubber of the jacket should be cleared of all dirt by teasing with a splinter of wood: the sides of the cut should then be solutioned, and after an interval brought firmly together: a large hole may be plugged with cotton wool soaked in solution. This will prevent wet reaching the fabric and so causing it to rot. Cuts which reach the fabric and bursts (usually the result of a neglected cut) must be repaired from inside. Detach one edge of the jacket: with benzine or solution separate the fabric from the rubber for a short distance round the cut: then apply to the inner surface of the rubber an ordinary but large rubber patch to keep out water: after a wait, tenderly replace the fabric, and strengthen it with a good-sized patch of proper repairing canvas, applied in the same way as is a rubber patch to the air-tube. Dust with French chalk and replace the jacket. A really badly cut jacket should at the earliest opportunity be sent to the makers for repair.

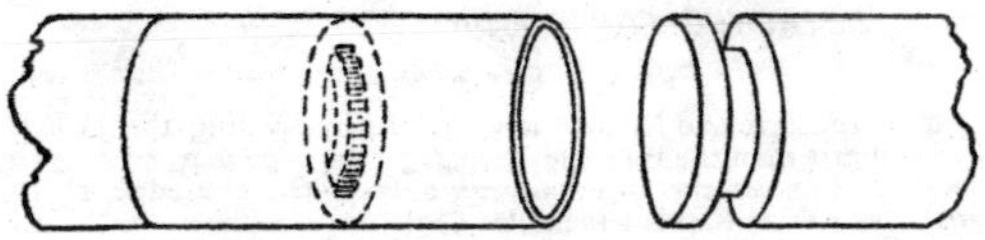

FIG. 18.—THE BUTT-ENDED AIR-TUBE (SMITH'S PATENT).

Dust blisters occur from the entry of dust into a neglected cut: it will often be found that the dust has worked between the fabric and the rubber: it should be carefully teased out and the cut filled up as described above.

CLASSIFICATION OF DETACHABLE TYRES.

Detachable tyres may be classified under two general heads. I. Tyres held in the rim independently of inflation. II. Tyres held in the rim by inflation.

Under the first head we include all detachable tyres which could be depended on not to leave the rim even if ridden deflated. For this reason this class is theoretically prefera le, though in actual practice the risk of an inflation-held tyre leaving the rim in the case of a sudden burst is but slight; such a tyre would take some time to work itself off. The inflation-held tyre is, however, subject to this drawback, that, if the jacket be carelessly attached to the rim, the air-pressure occasionally blows it off, though in the vast majority of cases it automatically drives it into its correct position.

A. Tyres held independently of Inflation are practically all secured to the rim by wires. The **Dunlop** is the most widely used of the class; the jacket carries along each edge an endless inextensible wire, which rests in a channel formed on the inside of the rim. These wires are smaller in diameter than the extreme edge in the rim, but larger than the diameter of its bed. Hence, if the wire be pressed well into the bed of the rim on one side of the tyre, it becomes no longer concentric with the rims, and its opposite side tends to rise over its edge, when it may be readily detached.

The great merit of the Dunlop, apart from its fabric, which is described above, is its absolute simplicity. It defies the novice to injure it. He can either get it on and off, or he cannot, but there is no middle course of imperfect attachment leading to disaster. To our mind its great drawback is that the working of the wire into the rim is in muddy weather a dirty process, which might be obviated by the use of that part of the Welch patent which relates to joining the wires by adjustable screw-blocks. Moreover, now and then a tightly fitting tyre will be found which is decidedly hard to detach.

The **Beeston** tyre is essentially the same as the Dunlop. It has however the ends of one of its wires bent and brought through the rim, to which they are attached by screws. For its racing and road racing varieties Flexifort fabric is used.

The Scotts' Standard, Woodley, Warwick, Ideal, and New Silvertown tyres present unimportant deviations from the Dunlop type.

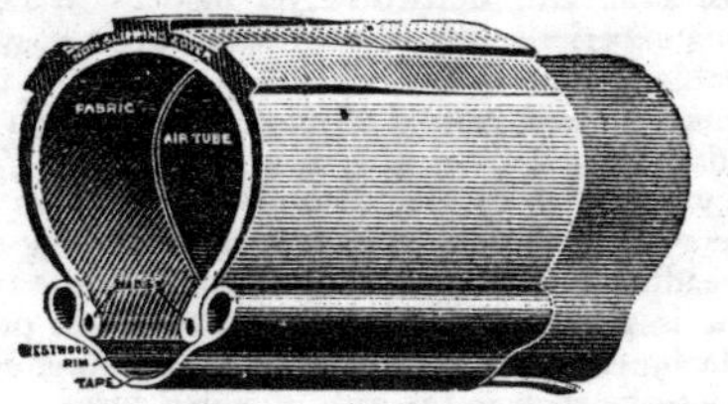

FIG. 19.—THE DUNLOP.

To remove the jacket, push the wire into the bed of the rim, beginning opposite the valve, and working it well down for nearly half its circumference by running the thumb along it. The wire will tend to rise over the edge of the rim in the neighbourhood of the valve, where a suitable lever (*e.g.*, a tyre-lever, the handle of a tooth-brush, or a claw spanner) is slipped under it, and its outward end forced well down towards the spokes till the wire comes over the rim. This generally happens with a slight jump. It should never be necessary to insert a second lever: this is characteristic of the bungler.

To replace the jacket, slightly inflate the air-hole and place it in position. Then beginning opposite the valve, place as much of the jacket as possible in the rims; if the wire beginning opposite the valve) be worked into the rim in the manner described above, the outstanding portion may usually be slipped over its edge with the fingers.

Before inflating, see that the jacket lies evenly in the rim, pulling it up and pushing it down when necessary; see also that the tube is not "nipped."

The **Detachable Scottish**[1]—In this tyre, by an ingenious arrangement described under Figs. 20 and 21, the circumference of the wires can at will be increased and the edge of the tyre readily slipped over the rim. This

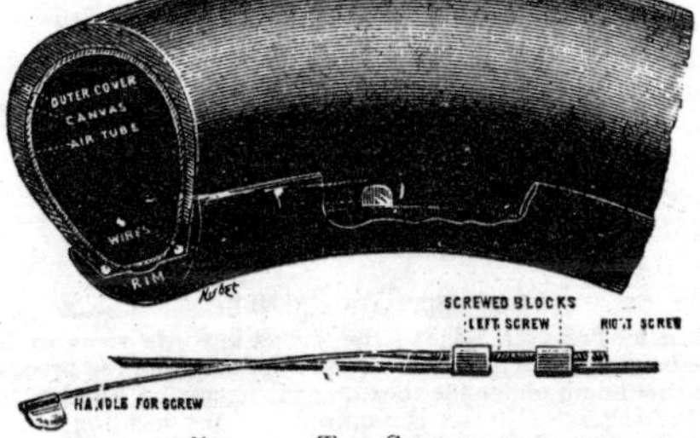

FIG. 20.—THE SCOTTISH.

In this case the wires are not continuous; their ends do not quite meet, and terminate each in a screwed block; through these blocks passes a separate wire which is, as will be seen from the illustration, fitted at one end with a right and left handed thread, and at the other with a small thumb-piece which serves as a handle. When the thumb-piece is unscrewed, the blocks recede from each other and the total circumference of the wired edge of the tyre is increased, so that it can readily be slipped over the rim; screwing up the thumb-piece causes the blocks to approach each other and makes the wired edge too small to slip off the rim. When not required the thumb-piece is tucked under the edge of the jacket, where it is securely held by inflation.

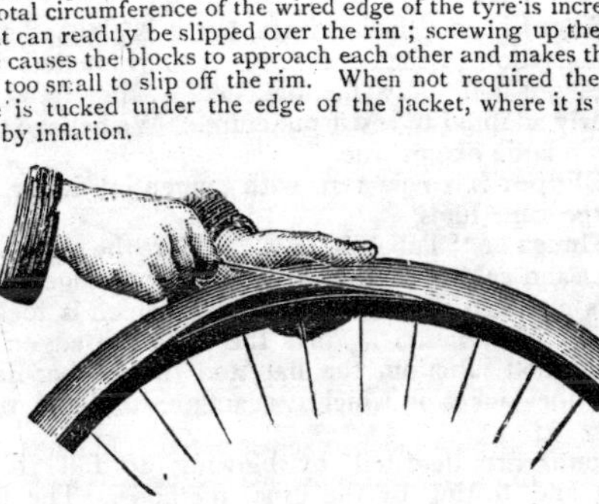

FIG. 21.—THE SCOTTISH.

To detach the jacket, deflate and look for the thumb-piece, the position of which should be marked on the rim; disengage it from the jacket and unscrew it five or six turns, when the wired edge may be lifted over the edge.

To replace.—Reverse the process, taking care that the blocks are screwed quite home.

[1] In spite of the fact that the adverse result of a patent action has caused the withdrawal of this tyre, we see no reason for omitting it, or modifying the opinion expressed above.

method of attachment by an adjustable wire we regard as the most promising departure yet made. We can say from long experience that this attachment is easy, quick and reliable, while, as the jacket has only to be touched in one place, repair can be effected without even soiling the hands.

B. Tyres held by Inflation—In this class of tyre the covers are made with stiffened edges forming on each side a beading which engages in a groove in the rim into which it is pinned or "clinched" by the air-pressure. The attachment and detachment of this class are considerably easier than in the case of wired tyres.

The **Clincher** is the oldest tyre of this class, and bears an excellent reputation; its best quality is fitted with tangential fabric.

The **Palmer** is made with the well-known Palmer fabric, which when applied to a single-tube tyre created

FIG. 22.—THE PALMER.

To detach—Press one edge of the jacket inwards so as to disengage the beading from its groove in the rim; continue the process by running the thumb under the beading till it can be lifted over the rim by the fingers. No tool is required. If the beading be rusted into the rim a little force may be necessary to detach it.

To replace—Lift the edge on to the rim, carefully tuck the beading into its groove, and inflate. Be careful not to nip the tube.

These directions apply to the whole class.

much sensation in 1894. It is a thoroughly good and fast tyre.

The **Bagot** is on Clincher lines, but it is claimed that the vulcanisation of the outer cover is so graduated that the sides are left very flexible, while the tread is particularly adapted to resist puncture. We believe that this is to a large extent true.

The **Clipper** is a new tyre with tangential fabric, on exactly the same lines.

The **Fleuss** or "Tubeless Tyre"—Here the air-tube is split open and vulcanised to the jacket; to one edge of the jacket is attached a flap of soft rubber which is locked by the act of inflation against the opposite edge: to ensure a good junction, the flap and the rubber-lined inside of the jacket on which it bears are anointed with soft soap.

Punctures are detected by blowing to full riding pressure and testing by the usual methods. The tyre when deflated is opened and patched on the inside. It is a clever device, but we do not believe that the "nuisance" of an air-tube is very widely felt. Moreover, should the tyre be cut through by a flint, we cannot see how the damaged fabric is to be reinforced with canvas, unless the rubber which lines the jacket be first peeled off, and this would be a serious operation.

The **Fleetwood**—The beadings, which are stiffened with fine crimped wire, are bent back into a hook-like section and engage in the inwardly recurved edges of the rim.

The **Woodstock** is explioted by the makers of the Fleetwood. The edges resemble those of the Fleetwood, but one of them is curved inward so as to engage with the other. The locking is thus independent of the rim.

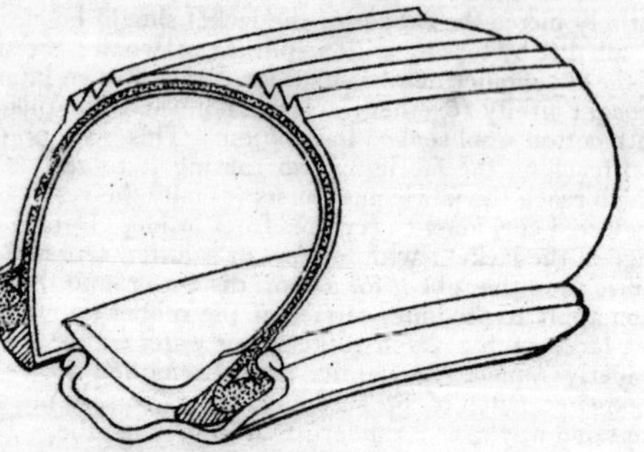

DETACHED FOR REPAIR

FIG. 23.—THE FLEUSS.

Inflate the tyre and locate the puncture by wetting the jacket. Clean all grit from the tyre and disengage the edge marked "open this side," in much the same way as a Palmer. The edge which carries the rubber flap is left in place.

Repair the puncture by placing a patch inside the jacket, and replace the jacket as in the case of the Palmer, pushing the rubber flap upwards, so that it is clear of the groove in the rim.

It is advisable from time to time to rub the two surfaces constituting the air-tight joint with soft soap.

The merit of this promising tyre lies in the absence of outward pressure on the rim. It thus shares with the tubular tyres the advantage of being well suited for wood rims, without the characteristic disadvantages of that class of tyre. It may be obtained with tangential fabric.

TUBE TYRES.

Tube tyres fall under two heads, single-tube and double-tube tyres: both are cemented into the rim. Owing to the absence of outward pressure from the tyre, they are well suited to wood rims.

A. Single-Tube Tyres—In the former all three layers of the tyre are vulcanised together so as to form a single tube: such tyres are nearly obsolete in England, the Boothroyd and the Palmer being the best known. Repairs are difficult and unsatisfactory, consisting:—I. Of the simple injection of solution into the puncture. II. The insertion into the puncture, by means of a kind of bodkin, of rubber threads covered with solution. III. The excision of the affected portion with an instrument like a cheese scoop, and the insertion of a rubber plug—a truly terrible remedy.

It is moreover difficult to make sure that a puncture has been repaired through the entire thickness of the tyre. The repair may extend only to its outer portion, so that the air gets through the unrepaired inner tube and forcing its way between the layers of the jacket, escapes by the numerous tiny cuts that are always to be found on the outside of a tyre which has been some time in use.

A hopeless single-tube tyre may be slit open at the valve and a butt-ended air-tube inserted: the slit being afterwards laced up.

It is sincerely to be hoped that American makers will not succeed in forcing this moribund type of tyre on heedless English buyers. Most American firms however are now fitting double-tube and detachable tyres.

B. Double-Tube Tyres—These differ from the single-tubes in having the air-tube distinct from the tubular jacket. There are only two important representatives of this class.

The Morgan and Wright Quick Repair Tyre—At the valve the inner surface of the jacket is slit for a short distance and laced up by means of eyelet holes, which are fended from the air-tube by an internal flap: through this aperture the air-tube, which has scarfed ends, may if necessary be withdrawn, the jacket being "crowded" off the rim at this point and afterwards re-affixed to the rim by "reviving" the cement with benzine or solution. This however is seldom necessary,

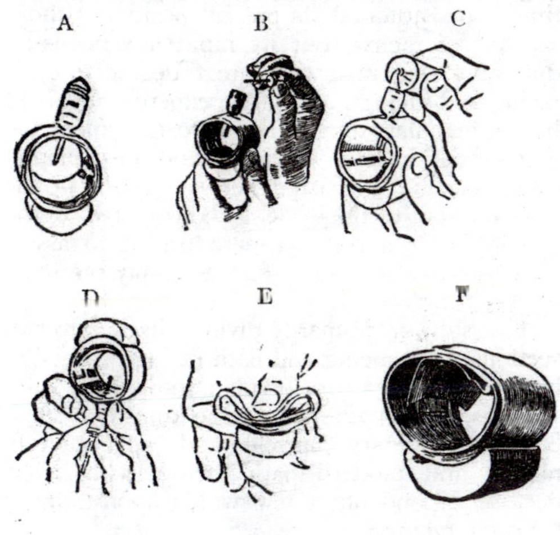

FIG. 24.—THE MORGAN AND WRIGHT TYRE.

To repair—Punctures are detected by blowing to full pressure, and wetting the jacket. When the puncture is found, keep the tyre at full pressure and force through the puncture the special injector supplied (see A); then unscrew the cap of the injector, thus withdrawing the needle-plug, leaving the nozzle still in the tyre: the air should then rush out. Fill, with the special solution supplied, the cup seen in C, and engage in it the screwed butt-end of the needle-plug; then turn the wheel so that the puncture is at its lowest point, and screw the plug home into the cup as in D; this will force the solution into the air-tube, where it will form a small pool around the puncture; next entirely withdraw the injector, and, again shifting the affected spot to the top of the wheel, press the thumb firmly on to the tyre, as in E; this will spread the solution over the air-tube and patching strip; slightly inflate the tyre and leave it for two minutes for the solution to set; then once more press the tyre in the same manner; this will cause the patching strip to adhere to the air-tube and the repair is effected (F). The tyre may now be blown to full pressure.

In finally inflating, the air between the air-tube and the jacket will find its way out through the cut in the latter, and may simulate a puncture. Should, however, this appearance persist, deflate the tyre and again press with the thumb to perfect the adhesion of the repairing strip. On no account insert the injector a second time, or the repairing strip will itself be punctured.

If the puncture cannot be found, or if it be necessary for any cause to remove the air tube, deflate the tyre, and tear it off the rim round the valve; undo the lacing, and tie round the scarfed end of the tube remote from the valve a piece of cord sufficiently long to encircle the wheel with a bit to spare, taking care not to mutilate the rubber. Then simply pull at the other end of the tube till the whole is withdrawn, and only the string left in the jacket. The tube may now be repaired in the usual way (see p. 282). If time admits, it is a good plan to use the opportunity to undo all the injection repairs, by cautiously pulling away the patching strip where it adheres to the bottom of the tube, and repairing them in the ordinary manner. We thus start afresh with the whole of the repairing strip again available for future use.

To replace the tube, rub it with French chalk and blow some into the jacket; then, by pulling the string, it is again drawn into position. See that the ends overlap neatly, and before lacing up make sure that the canvas flap is in place, or the lacing will chafe the rubber. Warm the cement on the rim, or, better still, moisten it with benzine or rubber solution, force the tyre on to the rim, and inflate.

To repair cuts in the jacket, make a slit in its inner side, mend in the usual way, and finally lace up the slit, fending the air-tube from the lacing by a piece of canvas. Then cement the tyre down.

as the air-tube is provided with a broad strip of repairing rubber attached to its side by light ligaments. Repairs are executed by the method described under Fig. 24.

The drawbacks to this tyre are: I. That a second puncture *in the same spot* can only be repaired by removing the air-tube. II. That in the event of a deep cut in the jacket an incision has to be made in its inner surface, the cut repaired, the incision laced up, and the tyre again cemented down. For this reason it is unsuitable for flinty roads; but on good roads it gives little trouble. Its great merit is that it can be safely used with wood rims (p. 277) and a very light wheel thus made.

The New Scottish is the only British representative of the class. It is secured to the rim by a flat band of steel, adjustable as to size by an adaptation of the method described under Fig. 20.

The repair of punctures is as with the Morgan and Wright. The tyre is deflated, and solution injected between the air-tube and the jacket, which is lined with unvulcanised rubber. The solution is spread by pressure and left to get sticky; finally a twist to the tyre puts the punctures in air-tube and jacket out of line; then by a second pressure the two are stuck together, and the repair effected.

VALVES—The valves of English detachable tyres are all twisted into the air-tube in the same way. The exact method is described under Fig. 25.

To insert the Valve in the Air-Tube—Cut in the air-tube a circular hole, slightly smaller than the diameter of the body of the valve A; stretch the hole and slip through it the head, which may be lubricated with a touch of solution. Take a diamond-shaped patch of fine fabric, cut a small hole in the middle, pass it over the valve, and with the usual precautions solution it to the tube B. Let it set thoroughly, and slip over the valve the plate C; screw down on to it the nut D, taking care that the plate is longitudinally parallel to the tube; do not screw the nut D so tightly as to mutilate the rubber. Put the valve through the rim E, secure it with the lock-nut and washer G and F, and lastly fit in the plug H.

a. The '94 Woods—The body A is provided half way down with a shoulder; into this fits the plug H, which is guided into it and prevented from revolving by two small projections at its top fitting into two nicks in A. The plug C is furnished with a shoulder, sloping the reverse way to that in A. H is traversed by a channel to admit the air, which turns sharply towards the bottom and emerges from its side. A thin tube of rubber K fits somewhat tightly over its lower portion, covering its shoulder. A cap L, screwing on to A, forces this shoulder against the shoulder at B, the rubber making an air-tight joint.

The valve is not unscrewed for inflation; the incoming air forces up the rubber tube at D, but as soon as the pressure from without ceases the rubber resumes its position and no air can escape from inside.

Care should be taken in screwing up the cap E not to cut the rubber between the two shoulders. Leaks occur from this and the perishable nature of the tubes, which have to be renewed from time to time. The old one is pulled off, and a new one carefully worked on.

b. The '96 Woods is similar, except that the shoulders are dispensed with, and the air-tight joint made by a rubber washer between the plug H and the body A. It is lighter than the old valve, makes a smaller hole in the rim, and there is no risk of cutting the rubber tube.

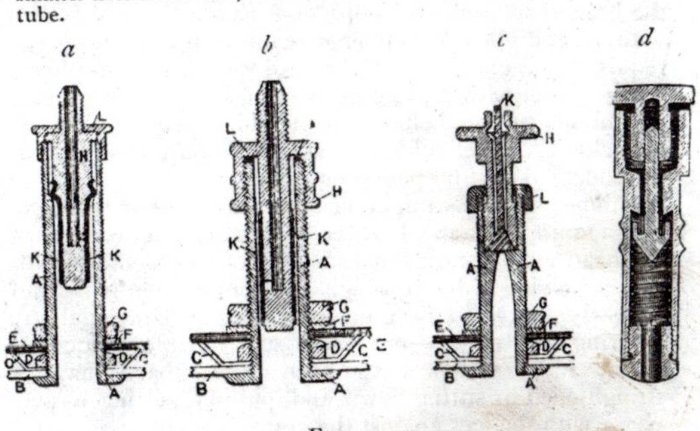

FIG. 25.

c. The Lucas—The body A is threaded internally, and has a shoulder half way down; into it screws the plug H, which carries inside it the pin K; K terminates downwards in a cone, the downward ends of H are chamfered off internally to fit it. The conical end of K has its base resting on the shoulder of A; when H is partially unscrewed air may be forced between it and the conical end of K; the air, attempting to return, only forces these coned surfaces into close contact, though in practice a slight regurgitation takes place; when inflation is completed H is screwed down and a positive joint made between it and K as well as between K and A. The screw cap L is merely to prevent the plug from being inadvertently withdrawn; it must be screwed off before H can be removed.

To inflate, unscrew H as far as it will go, afterwards again screwing it up; to deflate, unscrew H, and with the nail press down K.

Should the valve leak, clean it with methylated spirit.

d. The Morgan and Wright is similar in principle to the Lucas, though it depends entirely on the contact established between the rubber cone and the body of the valve. To take it to pieces screw out the bottom plate, when the coiled spring and conical-ended pin may be withdrawn. To deflate, press down the pin.

The leading English valves are the 1894 Woods, the 1896 Woods, and the Lucas.

Of the two Woods valves we rather prefer the '94, though it necessitates a large hole in the rim. There is, however, little to choose between them.

The Lucas valve is made entirely of metal, and is therefore not affected by climatic conditions which to some extent influence the rubber air-tight joint of the Woods, nor has it to contend with the naturally perishable nature of that material; on the other hand, the rubber of the Woods is easily replaced, while a rusty or grit-choked Lucas is not easy to put right. The Lucas is decidedly the easier to inflate, but has to be unscrewed for the operation.

We also give an illustration (*d*) of the Morgan and Wright valve, which is somewhat similar to the Lucas, except that it has a rubber plug.

MISCELLANEOUS—**Care of the Machine**—Cycles should be kept in a dry place not subject to extremes of temperature (this for the sake of the tyres). After use a machine should have the bulk of the wet mud promptly removed to avoid rust, though it is better to defer thorough cleaning till it is dry: a rag damped with paraffin should then be used, obstinate clots being touched with a drop of the liquid; water is to be avoided.

In wet weather the plated parts, excepting of course the handlebars and the outside of the cranks, should receive a thin coat of vaseline; this will collect dust, but no harm will be done to the machine. Plating is best cleaned of rust by hard rubbing with paraffin and polished with chamois leather or Selvyt; it is speedily ruined by harsh, gritty soaps which are so useful for many domestic purposes.

Breakdowns—Full directions for dealing with the normal ailments of cycles and tyres are given *passim* in the description of machines.

In cases of serious damage it is best, assuming that the machine is rideable, to let it alone till a skilled repairer can be secured; an infinity of harm may be done by unskilled attempts to true frames or wheels.

A broken spoke may usually be neglected for a short time. Should the wheel lose its shape, bend the ends of the broken spokes into loops and secure them together with several plies of copper wire or string, securing the required tension in the former case with a pair of pliers, in the latter with a piece of wood used as a tourniquet, and finally sprung behind the neighbouring spokes. A "buckled" wheel will occasionally resume its shape if the indented part be pulled outwards.

Frames may be straightened by a side pressure of the foot against the crank bracket, by passing iron bars down the head socket or diagonal, and so forcing them straight, or by passing a bar through the frame lengthwise and crosswise so as to bear on both head and diagonal and levering it straight—but these are terrible remedies. Front forks which have been driven back may be straightened by sitting down and pulling, getting a purchase with the feet against the crank bracket.

Broken tubes or forks may be strongly tied to splints of wood hollowed to receive them, the wire or string being tightened by wedging. Broken handlebars may be replaced by a stick lashed to their remains. Bent pedal pins are best dealt with by removing the frame of the pedal and riding on the base pin. Bent cranks may be cautiously straightened in a vice: attempts to put them right when on the machine will result in worse mischief. Broken chains may often be patched up with copper wire. Broken balls should be at once removed from the bearing; on emergencies, when this has been done, the machine *may* be ridden, but it throws an unfair strain on the bearing.

H. GRAVES.

N.B. I wish to express my sincere thanks for assistance rendered in the preparation of this article by Messrs. A. B. Evans, H. J. Swindley and F. R. Fowke.

CYCLE RACING—Cycling has many claims on the community outside the race path, and it is quite conceivable that it might in course of time have attained its present position without the aid of racing, but its rapid advance is indubitably due in a very great degree to cycle racing and racing men. The experience gained by the manufacturers in their efforts to meet the demands of the latter for lighter and consequently faster machines assisted very materially in the improvement of the cycle, as constructed for the ordinary user, and it is a mere truism to assert that the roadster of to-day is simply the racer of yesterday.

The subject primarily divides itself into two sections, road racing and path racing, whilst the latter may be again divided into three sub-sections, early path racing, the transition stage between ordinary bicycle and safety-bicycle racing, and modern path racing, with, as a necessary pendant, a few words upon training for cycle racing.

Road Racing was of course the original form of the sport. All the early velocipedes were made for use upon the highways, and as the claims made for the new machine were based upon the facilities which it offered for rapid locomotion, it was only natural that many of the very earliest efforts made to attract the attention of the public, and to interest them in it, took the form either of rides against time, or of actual races upon the road.

The story of the advent of the first French bicycle in London, and its exploitation in Charles Spencer's gymnasium by Mr. Rowley Turner, has often been told. Mr. Mayall was present at the unpacking of the crate when this strange *jouet d'enfant* from Paris made its first appearance. He learnt to ride it, and early in January 1869 was fired with a great ambition, and started from Clapham for Brighton, but was compelled to give up, completely exhausted, at Redhill, no less than 17¼ miles from his starting point, and return to town by train. After more practice he, in company with Rowley Turner and Charles Spencer, made a second attempt in the following February; and though his companions fell by the way, he succeeded in reaching Brighton alone in about sixteen hours. The feat was the subject of some public comment at the time, but as some three weeks later the brothers Chinnery *walked* to Brighton in eleven hours and twenty-five minutes, the advantages of the new steed, as demonstrated by Mr. Mayall's heroic efforts, were considerably discounted.

Between 1869 and 1874 a number of steadily improving performances were recorded in the public press. In 1871 Messrs. R. King, H. N. Custance, and J. C. F. May, of the still existing Amateur B.C., were probably the first bicyclists to ride one hundred miles inside twenty-four hours on the road, journeying from Amesbury to Stonehenge and back to London.

Charles Spencer, who made the essay with Mayall in 1869, together with G. Hunt, C. Leaver, and William Wood, journeyed in June 1873 from London to John o' Groat's, some 700 miles, in fifteen days, the performance evoking considerable interest; whilst William Wood in August of the same year rode to Brighton and back, 104 miles, inside eleven hours. H. Stanley Thorpe also put in some good rides; but perhaps the individual ride which did the sport most good at this juncture was accomplished in May 1874, when the Hon. Ion Keith Falconer rode from Bournemouth to Hitchin, piling up the mileage to 135 miles, and, which was more to the point, writing a very full account of the journey for the *Field*. This attracted a vast amount of attention, and stimulated a large number of other bicyclists to essay long distance rides. Amongst the names of men who accomplished big feats in this direction should be mentioned those of H. E. Kearley, A. D. Butler, Frank Smythe, W. E. N. Coston, F. E. Appleyard, Wat Britten, H. Blackwell, jun., and many more of less note.

By this time racing on the road was often held in an informal manner, the development of pace followed, and the road racing side of the sport grew with great rapidity. On one occasion a twenty-four hours' contest, organised by a firm in the trade, started and finished at Anderton's Hotel in Fleet Street, the chosen course being to Bath and back, and in due season clubs were formed, and a series of such contests arranged. The great North Road and the level stretches of highway branching from it became the scenes of highly interesting contests which at first were of a very sporting and purely amateur character. The arrangements were carried out by large batches of honorary officials, and the events attracted the attention of many riders apart from those actually engaged in them as competitors. The former were distributed over the country, checking the racing men at appointed spots, guiding them over the chosen routes, attending to their general welfare, making the pace if necessary, and in every way promoting their interests with impartial enthusiasm. Many splendid performances were accomplished on these occasions. F. Snook, G. P. Mills, J. H. Adams, T. R. Marriott, F. T. Bidlake, M. A. Holbein, T. A. Edge, and, *facile princeps* at the game, F. W. Shorland, with many others, put their names upon the pages of the road record book. The attention attracted by these contests, and the very full reports published by the sporting as well as the cycling press, caused the popularity of this phase of the pastime to grow exceedingly. The winner of a big road race not only secured great credit to himself but gave a widespread advertisement to the machine he rode, and as a natural consequence the trade appeared upon the scene, the friendly character of the assemblies gradually disappeared, things became more business-like, pacing was supplied, tandems and often larger multicycles swooped down in shoals upon the highways, and some riders unquestionably allowed themselves to be subsidised by the makers of the machines they rode. To crown all, the pneumatic tyre came along, increasing the speed at which the competitors and their pacers dashed along the highways, so that road-racing on cycles, which at one time created only mild excitement in the towns and villages through which the riders passed, developed into a serious danger and became an intolerable nuisance. The fact was only tardily recognised by the supporters of this form of cycle racing, after stringent measures to suppress it had in many districts been resorted to by the police authorities.

From time to time feeble revivals occur, but the doom of road-racing is sealed. Yet, ere it passes away, it is well to recognise how immense were the services which in its earlier stages it rendered to the sport. The great rides from Land's End to John o' Groat's, the twenty-four hours' races, and the many established records, advertised and emphasised the claims of the cycle to be recognised as a new factor in the matter of locomotion; nor should the world ignore the large number of enthusiasts who worked to establish cycling in the position it holds to-day. The inestimable benefits derived from the road-racing side of the sport should not be forgotten now that its abuse has made it impossible any longer to encourage its continuance.

Path-Racing — Long before the period when the abuse of road-racing led to action by the authorities to enforce its discontinuance, cycle racing upon prepared paths in enclosed grounds had become very popular. The athletic developments of the late sixties had given rise to a vast interest in athletic sports, and innumerable meetings were being held throughout the country, the running races taking place upon specially prepared cinder tracks, or upon grass courses staked out upon suitable stretches of turf; and in due season races upon bicycles were promoted as interesting additions to the sports' programme. This introduced the bicycle to the notice of a large number of people who would not otherwise perhaps have had an opportunity of seeing it at its best, for the men who raced upon these courses were of necessity masters of the machines they rode, and bicycle racing soon became very popular.

It was at such a meeting, held in Dublin, at the Lansdowne Road grounds, in October 1875 that Mr. W. P. Blood, one of the earliest of the Irish racing men, covered the mile in three minutes and eighteen seconds, the first fairly well authenticated performance over that distance on record; whilst in 1876 F. L. Dodds, a promising member of the Cambridge University Bicycle Club, rode 15 miles 1480 yards on the Cambridge track in one hour. Prior to these feats some short distance performances, more or less well authenticated, had been put in upon the road; but from 1876 onward all the records for short distances were made upon the track, with the exception of one or two down-hill straightaway mile times accomplished on the road for purposes of advertisement in 1895.

These paths were all level, or approximately so, and surfaced with cinders or some similar material. "Dirt tracks" they would be called in American phraseology to-day. They were unbanked, and in some cases the corners were very sharp, but nevertheless some splendid feats were accomplished upon them on the high machine, specifically known as the *ordinary* bicycle.

Amongst the men who, down to 1879, made records on the Ordinary, may be specially noted the Hon. Ion Keith Falconer, whose marvellous two miles' time withstood many assaults on the parts of later flyers; and the result of such performances was an increased interest in the sport, and its rapid growth in public estimation. Finally came the phenomenal performer, destined to awaken a far wider and more active interest, in the person of the late Herbert L. Cortis. Cortis was not only an excellent bicycle rider; he also possessed the gift of judgment, and rode with his head as well as his legs. No less than four times did he lower the one mile record, covering that distance in 2 minutes $52\frac{1}{2}$ seconds and 2 minutes $47\frac{1}{5}$ seconds in 1879, and in 2 minutes $43\frac{1}{5}$ seconds and 2 minutes $41\frac{3}{5}$ seconds in 1882, the last figures remaining unbeaten until 1885, and being then surpassed by Mr. M. V. J. A. Webber by one-fifth of a second only. Cortis was the first man to cover twenty miles in the hour, a feat which he would have accomplished in September 1880 but for a fall in the nineteenth mile, as at eighteen miles he was well inside even time; but on the old Crystal Palace track, on the 27th of July 1882, he covered 20 miles 300 yards in the 60 minutes, a few days later riding twenty-five yards further in the same time on the Recreation Ground track at Surbiton. His many feats, without doubt, assisted materially in increasing the interest taken in cycling; and they may even now be regarded with wonder, when the machines, the tracks, and the methods of training which obtained when they were accomplished are considered and compared with the machines, the tracks, and the training of the racing cyclists of to-day. There are many people who still consider Cortis's twenty miles in the hour as good a performance as has ever been accomplished on a bicycle.

Many good men followed in Cortis's steps, notable among them being M. V. J. A. Webber, C. E. Liles, P. Furnivall, F. P. Wood, R. H. English, G. Gatehouse, J. H. Adams, and last but not least F. J. Osmond, whose feats upon the Ordinary bicycle over all distances made him worthy to be compared with Cortis at his best, especially in his wonderful powers of handicap riding. His 2 minutes $28\frac{4}{5}$ seconds for a mile at Paddington in 1890 marked the zenith of Ordinary cycle records at that distance, whilst B. W. Attlee's 21 miles 180 yards in 1891 was the high-water mark for one hour, and the long series of tall champions on tall machines was finally closed in 1892, when the last Ordinary championships were run.

The safety bicycle, so called, was first introduced in a practical form by J. K. Starley. The idea, embodied in the rear-driven cycle of to-day, of employing as a medium of propulsion a chain or band, appears to have originated with Mr. Henry Bate, but to Mr. Starley is due the credit of making the first practical machine of the type. Many makers followed his lead, and it was not long before the rear-driving safety found its way on to the racing path. In 1885 H. E. Laurie rode 21 miles 125 yards in the hour upon it at Long Eaton. In the following year the Union added Safety Championships to its list of fixtures, and Osmond at his best on the Ordinary was riding when the rear-driver began to establish itself as a racing cycle. Ordinary *versus* Safety matches were arranged at several meetings; but the Ordinary men usually won, probably because they possessed the experience which is of such great importance in actual racing, and the merits of the two types were discussed at considerable length, until the advent of the pneumatic tyre. This was better adapted, for many obvious reasons, to the safety than the Ordinary, and the former naturally rose rapidly in the favour of the racing men, so that the users of the high machine became fewer year by year.

The noticeable improvement in speed which followed was not only due to the tyre. The racing men of the post-Ordinary days were drawn from a much larger field than in the earlier times of racing. To succeed in the old days certain physical advantages were almost absolutely necessary. A man had to be big, and gifted with long legs, ere he could propel and master the larger wheels, 58 or 60 inches in diameter, which told most effectively upon the path. Possibly not one hundred men out of a thousand possessed the physical qualifications, and scarcely ten per cent. of that limited number had the other qualities necessary to develop a champion; whereas, with the system of gearing up applied to the Safety, every man of the thousand could ride and master his racing machine; and, the field for selection being larger, the fitting survivors were more numerous, and the chances of finding a phenomenon were vastly increased.

Nevertheless the early winners on the Safety bicycle were often old Ordinary riders. They possessed experience and racing knowledge, and, as a natural consequence, they scored. Amongst them may be noticed such riders as H. H. Sansom, R. J. Mecredy, P. W. Scheltema Beduin, and

F. J. Osmond, all old Ordinary bicycle racing men prior to the advent of the Safety. The men who practically started racing on the Safety failed at first when in competition with older riders; but they did well in record attempts, and amongst them may be mentioned H. E. Laurie, R. A. Lloyd, W. C. Jones, H. Parsons, and R. L. Ede.

Despite the number of racing men who had come to the front on the Safety, no one man singled himself out as clearly above his confrères until the arrival from America in 1892 of A. A. Zimmerman. This rider provided the phenomenal development which had been looked for for some time. He took a long time to get fit, but suddenly jumped into form, and showed himself practically invincible, especially amongst men whose form he knew. His few defeats after he once got fit, as, for example, that which he suffered at the hands of Verheyen, at Berlin, were simply due to his holding unknown competitors too cheaply, and also to his failing to allow for the ease with which a rider may be shut in upon European tracks, which are narrow compared with the wide sweeps of American courses. Since Zimmerman's first visit many other foreign riders have come to England to compete, and a number of fine riders have been developed at home.

Any attempt to enumerate the men who have performed great feats upon the rear driver would be an overwhelming task.

The National Cyclists' Union, which organises and conducts these championships, has been properly termed the Jockey Club of cycling, for it discharges towards the racing side of the sport exactly the functions which the Jockey Club discharges as regards horse racing.

The Union, with a view to securing greater control of the racing path, has adopted a licensing scheme; and every cyclist—amateur or professional—expert or novice—who desires to race, must first ask for a permit and undertake to obey the rules of the Union.

This course is a direct result of the more liberal reading of the Amateur Definition, which was one of the first reforms instituted by the Union; and to the Union belongs the credit of being the first body ruling amateur sport to erase from its definition of an amateur what is known as the "Mechanics' Clause." Up to the date of the Union formation the Amateur Definition excluded from the amateur ranks the "Mechanic, Artisan, and Labourer." The new definition enabled any man—whatever his position in life—to be an amateur if he chose to submit to the rules. Of course so wide a gate admitted some who should not have been admitted, and this has necessitated the Licensing Rules. These rules, which permit the governing body to deal with an individual case, are clearly to be preferred to a definition which absolutely barred whole classes of the community without discrimination.

It may be well to add that although the racing work of the Union is more showy, it also does a great deal of other and useful work in the interests of the genuine road rider and the tourist.

Training for cycle racing falls very much within the lines of training for any other athletic sport, with one marked and important exception. The running man, whatever his distance, necessarily carries his own weight, and as seven pounds extra weight will stop a horse, it is quite easy to understand that the flat-racing athlete gets rid of every ounce he can spare. Often, in practice, he contrives to divest himself of a pound or two too much, as a natural consequence going weak, and probably failing in the contest for which he has prepared himself. With the cyclist this necessity and the dangers it involves do not exist; for just as it is easier to wheel a heavy weight in a four-wheeled truck than to carry it on one's shoulders, so the few pounds of extra weight on the form of a cyclist, being wheeled rather than carried, make little material difference to his progress; and it is this point that requires to be borne in mind when anything in the nature of training is undertaken.

The systems and methods of the modern school of trainers differ entirely from those of the old-time trainers of athletes. New ideas have been introduced into the art of training, and in no section of sport have they found wider expression than in training for cycle racing. This expression takes the form of a separate régime for every individual athlete, the individual's capacities and capabilities being considered in the course and extent of his training,—a very great change from the time when the trainer put every aspirant for honours on the racing path through exactly the same preparatory programme, a programme which, whilst occasionally successful with certain men, more often ended in the break-down and collapse of those submitted to it.

Until recently the athletes who came to this country from America underwent a much more intelligent and consequently successful course of training than was practised here; but experience keeps a hard school, and quite a number of English professionals are now under as careful and successful a system as any of their competitors.

The error into which most young riders fall is not too much, but too fast work. If we take a line from the course pursued in training horses for racing in great events we cannot go very far wrong; and no one ever heard, for example, of a horse in training for the Derby being sent the full distance every day at top speed throughout the whole of the season preceding the big race. Yet plenty of young cycling amateurs, when making their first essays on the path, ride themselves out night after night in training, not to mention two or more severe races on the Saturday, with perhaps a mid-week meeting in between. What wonder that after a time they go stale, even if they do not suffer more ill effects from so drastic a course of treatment?

The men who successfully take part in cycle racing are the men who, within certain limits, take most care of themselves in training. Suppose such a one to have time and opportunities for training. His work, if he be of ordinary build and average fleshiness, will come out somewhat as follows. In the early part of the day, after some sort of a meal—for it is very unwise to ride on an empty stomach—he should repair to the track, and, studiously keeping his rate of speed down within moderate limits, ride for half an hour, in sufficient clothing, simply as a pipe-opener. During this half-hour's ride, when sprinting should be rigorously avoided, he may study the various points of position on the machine, ankle work, steering, and so on—in other words he may essay to acquire "form." He will improve faster if he be coached from time to time by an experienced friend who will watch him on the track. Once let a man acquire a good style, a comfortable position, and an easy and effective ankle action, and if he possess the qualities needful to develop pace, his pace will unquestionably assert itself. So this easy canter, this half-hour's spin, is really of quite as much importance to his ultimate success as the faster work which follows later. The young rider should finish with a careful rub down, properly administered by a competent attendant; and, if he has to go to business, in the usual course of things he will do well to take a shower bath, so as to guard against cold.

The day's business done, he may return to the track in the afternoon or evening, and take another short turn upon it, and upon this occasion he may for the moment discard form and style and put in one or two short sprints with the view of acquiring speed, and the mastery of his machine at a great pace. But here again a caution is necessary. It is highly inadvisable that his sprints should involve very hard work. They should be as a rule over a distance of about one hundred and fifty or two hundred yards, and before the wind for preference. In fact they should be calculated to give the rider the "knack" of speed. They will not in the ordinary course provide the muscles necessary to maintain great speed over relatively long distances. These are, for the most part, grown and developed during the slower and easier spins of the morning exercise; but it is well to bear in mind that the rider should not omit, from time to time, to run a trial against the watch, and force himself at top speed over something more than a fast quarter, and to engage in actual competition as often as he can within reason.

The adoption of this programme is very sure to cause the average amateur, in time, to develop whatever powers he really possesses. Then comes the time when it is worth his while to engage the services of a professional trainer. The professional trainer of to-day is, or ought to be, a very different being from the gentleman who held that position in the past. In his hands the rider who under a proper régime has secured a certain measure of success, may look for increased improvement, because there comes a time when a man will show but little advance unless an experienced attendant is constantly with him throughout the later stages of his training.

Diet is another point in which much alteration has taken place, and again within certain very clear lines the severity of the old rules has been very materially relaxed. A cyclist in training may eat and drink any plain viands or liquors which do not disagree with him—in moderation of course, and should be careful to take daily some amount of vegetables, and, in small quantities, fresh fruit.

G. LACY HILLIER.

BICYCLING FOR WOMEN—Only a few years ago bicycling was looked upon as a pastime quite unsuited to women. The tricycle was used by a few who felt they needed more vigorous exercise than could be obtained by walking or playing a quiet game of croquet, and were unable to provide themselves with the more expensive luxury of a saddle-horse. The advent of the drop-framed safety rendered cycling not only possible but pleasurable; and, with the addition of dress-guards, mud-guards, and pneumatic tyres, bicycling was brought within the reach of all. To-day it is the means by which health is restored and recreation afforded to an ever-increasing number. To many it is simply a pastime, such as was before afforded by tennis or croquet; but to others it is the only means of obtaining pure country air without the fatigue of long walks or the expense and trouble of a long railway journey.

It is curious that, despite the inherent love of sport which most Englishwomen possess, they should have been behind both the Americans and the French, who have set the fashion in wheeling. Now that we have discovered its charms we shall be slow to give it up, even when the present somewhat exaggerated craze for it has ceased.

Hygienic Aspects—With few exceptions the medical profession at first adopted an attitude of extreme caution with respect to cycling for women, regarding it with distrust, and discouraging it in every possible way; but now there is a distinct reaction in its favour, and only a few of the obstinately blind are found in opposition. There is no doubt that the bicycle has brought health to many a nervous, overwrought woman. All depends, of course, on the common sense displayed by the individual. The ordinary rules governing women's health must be applied in this, as in all other cases, unless serious injury is to result; but certain other regulations are also necessary for those not accustomed to sustained exertion. Experience is the school in which all of us must learn wisdom, and the pioneers of cycling have suffered many ills from the want of it. Their suffering has brought knowledge which is valuable to others who have followed in their steps. A system of diet and clothing which is perfectly suitable to a person putting no strain on her lungs or heart, whose muscles are soft and undeveloped, and whose skin has only responded to the enervating relaxation of heated rooms, is not only inappropriate but extremely dangerous to the cyclist.

The old axiom, that what you eat does you less good than what you do not eat is a safe one to apply; and if a woman wishes to do good work and profit by it both mentally and physically, she must resolutely turn from useless foods, which are incapable of replacing the waste caused by such active exercise as she obtains on her bicycle.

The rider must study her own idiosyncrasies, and never drive a willing constitution beyond its powers. Whatever women borrow from their capital of nerve force is only too apt to reduce their income of health for life. Bearing this in mind, women may derive enormous benefit from a form of exercise which increases the circulation, strengthens the muscles, develops the chest, relieves the lower limbs from the dragging weight of the body, and enables us to obtain far more fresh air than our powers would otherwise allow. No woman should ride if she has any serious weakness, except with great caution, and the permission of a doctor who not only understands her constitution but who has also made a special study of cycling in all its phases.

The different forms of hysteria, sick headaches, anæmia, and neuralgia, as well as imaginary ills, are specially benefited by this exercise. In the case of girls earning their own living and confined all the week in places of business, certain cycling clubs instituted on their behalf are a great boon. The members are taken in parties to various places of interest, and during their holidays pleasant tours are arranged.

Dress—The question of dress comes next in importance. Anything tight on any part of the body is quite inadmissible, and wool next the skin is absolutely necessary to prevent chills, with their manifold evil consequences. The wearing of the skirt is still a much debated question. England has never encouraged the extremely unbecoming attire worn by many French cycling women, and it is to be hoped never will. The skirt, if properly cut, helps to conceal the ugly action of the knees and legs, and never need be a cause of danger if fastened down by elastic straps, and not made too wide or too long. Of course, for professional riders, and women who cannot afford a well-cut skirt, knickerbocker costumes are the only alternative; but, for those who ride only for pleasure, a smart tailor-made skirt and coat (or blouse in warm weather) is the most suitable costume.

A woman's cycling dress should be, in the first place, practical—that is, composed of materials which do not suffer from rain or dust and will stand a certain amount of hard wear. The skirt should be about two and a half yards wide and gored, so as to fit closely round the hips, and put into the waistband in such a manner that it will be easy to arrange it so that it falls equally on either side of the machine. A moderately tight-fitting jacket looks neater than one of the loose "sac" shaped coats. Attention must be paid to the arm-holes, which should be large and easy, while the sleeves are best loose, but not so large as to flap in the wind. The important point about the head-gear is that it should fit well on the head so as not to be loosened and disarranged by every gust of wind, and that it be neat in appearance and not trimmed with flowers or feathers.

General Advice in Riding—In choosing a bicycle care must be taken to suit it to the height of the rider; adjustment of saddle and handle-bar being most important. The rider should sit erect, but not stiffly, and should, when once able to mount in the proper manner, have the saddle as high as can be comfortably ridden, as this gives greater power over the machine. A rider should always practise mounting and dismounting on either side, and be ready in case of accidents to put out a foot and so save herself from falling. As to the distance which a woman can safely ride, all depends on the special circumstances of the individual, the age at which she began to learn, her strength and constitution. While some can cycle seventy miles without fatigue, and can keep up a speed of thirteen miles an hour, others must limit themselves to a modest ten or twelve miles at eight miles an hour. Hill-climbing is a serious source of injury to many, and must be attempted with caution. For all, and especially for those who ride in skirts, coasting is dangerous. If any part of the dress should catch in the quickly revolving pedals a serious accident is likely to result. Racing is on all accounts to be deprecated for women.

On returning from a ride every article of clothing should be changed at once. After sponging the skin with hot water, followed by a cold douche and a thorough rubbing, fresh dry under garments should be put on. These rules strictly observed, all chills will be avoided, and the most delicate can derive nothing but advantage from an action of the skin which is one of the good effects of sustained exercise.

Cycling in Traffic is a vexed question; many consider it better for the weaker sex to abstain from doing so, but the matter really depends on the skill, nerve, and judgment of the rider. A woman who cycles in the streets of the metropolis or any other large city must learn the police regulations which prevail, and conform to them. She must not suppose her sex excuses her from doing exactly the same as others. Any act of courtesy on the part of cabmen and other drivers of vehicles should be acknowledged. A woman who has driven herself in town will naturally have an acquaintance with traffic, which will prove valuable to her as a cyclist, and will be aware that it is wiser in the long run to keep a whole skin and sound limbs, than to shave and scrape through narrow places at the risk of her life, and to the annoyance of other people. It is far easier and very often quicker to dismount and walk across a difficult crossing. There is nothing clever in wobbling about in the midst of a block of carriages and omnibuses, and causing drivers to use language which, though not pleasant for the ears of ladies, is perhaps excusable under the circumstances.

The numerous clubs which have been lately started for cycling women of all classes, have given them the opportunity of becoming expert riders, and also of seeing, during their club runs, remote parts of the country which are difficult of access in any other way. There is no doubt that, taken altogether, cycling has been one of the greatest blessings given to modern women. We can now scarcely realise that in years gone by delicacy was considered interesting, and that many girls would then have regarded it almost an insult to be called robust. That time has happily passed, and it behoves every able-bodied woman to look to it that she may be able to prove her strength and capabilities. For this purpose exercise of every sort in moderation and in the open air is necessary, and cycling will in future form an important part in her athletic education.

SUSAN, COUNTESS OF MALMESBURY.

DAB (*Pleuronectes limanda*).

MEASUREMENTS, ETC.—Length of head 4¾ to 5, of caudal fin 5⅔, height of body 2⅔ in the total length. *Eyes*—the lower slightly anterior to the upper, diameter 5½ to 6 in the length of the head, ½ to 1 diameter from the end of the snout, and separated by a narrow osseous ridge. Lower jaw prominent: the maxilla, which is as long as the orbit, extends to beneath the first third of the eye. *Teeth*—a row of about 22 closely set, lanceolate on the blind side. *Fins*—the dorsal commences above the middle of the upper eye, the rays gradually increase in length to about the centre of their number (37 to 40) when they commence decreasing in height: the fin does not reach the base of the caudal, leaving an uncovered space equal to about ½ the height of the free portion of the tail. Pectoral as long as the post-orbital portion of the head. Ventral not joined to anal. A small spine, directed forward, at the commencement of the anal fin. Caudal slightly rounded. *Scales*—on coloured side with ctenoid margins, those between the eyes and on the cheeks smaller than those on the body. A row along each dorsal and anal ray. *Lateral line*—smooth: at its commencement it has a semi-circular curve above the pectoral fin, while it sends a branch over the occiput. *Intestines*—three or four short cæcal appendages. *Colours*—brownish, with some cloudy markings and spots: dorsal and anal fin, with whitish margins. Occasionally white spots are seen on the coloured side of the body.

Day's *Fishes of Great Britain and Ireland*, vol. II., p. 32.

DACE (*Leuciscus vulgaris*).

MEASUREMENTS, ETC.—Length of head 5¼, of caudal fin 5½, height of body 4¾ in the total length. *Eyes*—situated slightly above the centre of the depth of the head, diameter ¼ of the length of the head, 1½ diameters from the end of the snout, and also apart. Suborbital ring of bones narrow. Body oblong and somewhat elongated, sides compressed. Cleft of mouth rather shallow, the posterior extremity of the maxilla reaching to almost beneath the front edge of the eye, lower jaw shorter than the upper. *Teeth, pharyngeal*—somewhat hooked at their extremities, 5, 2 – 2, 5. *Fins*—dorsal commences about midway from the front edge of the eye and the base of the caudal fin; the length of its base equals about two-thirds the height of the longest undivided ray, which equals three-fourths of that of the body below it: its last rays half the height of its front ones; upper edge of fin concave. Pectoral inserted in the lower fourth of the depth of the body, as long as the head excluding the snout, and pointed. It does not extend much more than half-way to the base of the ventral, which latter is inserted on a vertical line beneath the first few rays of the dorsal, and does not reach the anal. Front edge of anal in the commencement of the last third of the distance between the margin of the eye and the base of the caudal fin, the length of its base equals three-fourths of the height of its front rays. Caudal rather deeply forked. *Scales*—four rows between the lateral-line and the base of the ventral fin, where an angular one exists. *Lateral-line*—slightly concave, continued to the centre of the base of the caudal fin. *Colours*—bluish along the back, silvery white upon the sides and beneath. Dorsal, pectoral, and caudal fins tipped with black: the ventral and anal have merely a slight tinge of red or yellowish.

Day's *Fishes of Great Britain and Ireland*, vol. II., p. 181.

DECK SPORTS—Our survey may reasonably begin with **Deck Quoits**, for this pastime is at least as ancient as the century, and was played in the old ships of the line when Nelson won his laurels. Many generations of British tars have killed time with it, and thousands of travellers have sought the sport to destroy the monotony of long, uneventful days in mid-ocean. The game, as now played, admits of various methods of scoring according to the fancy of the players, but the practical part is only capable of three variations.

The quoits may be flung from a chalked line or mark—(1) at a peg, over which they must fall to score; (2) to a target of circles, of different values, chalked upon the deck; or (3) into a bucket. In the last case the range is much increased; but **Deck Quoits** proper, with a peg as mark, is a difficult game, not indeed admitting the science and variety of real quoits, but none the less requiring plenty of skill. Four or five yards is quite far enough from the peg for beginners; and even at this range they will probably be much astonished to find how lengthy a task is the compilation of a dozen "ringers." The peg should stand about eight inches off the deck, and the quoits, which are made of stout rope, usually have a circumference of about sixteen inches. This, however, varies much with the fancy of the mariner responsible for their construction. The golden rule for all deck sportsmen is to win favour with a boatswain, and he will introduce them to the carpenter, upon whom much depends. As a ship's game, **Deck Quoits** is far removed from the first rank. Much practice, patience, and determination are necessary to play it well—qualities which no man ever yet brought to bear upon the game or ever will. Great accuracy is necessary to get on the peg, even at short range, and, with a high wind blowing and the ship lively, scoring becomes slow, and a good length almost impossible to keep.

Bull is another ancient pastime, which has this interest: that it may be considered a ship's game pure and simple, while most other nautical amusements are adapted or developed from a sport or exercise proper to *terra firma*. Bull seems to have been born and bred on the wave. The materials are a scoring-board about a yard and a half square, and quoits made of lead cased in leather. These should be somewhat larger than a crown piece; and they are flung from the hand to the board at any range agreeable to the players. Upon the scoring-board, which is covered with tarpaulin, are painted twelve squares with the numerical value of each written therein. The numbers range from 10 to 100, rising in each case by ten at a time, and the "100 square" lies at the top of the board between two unnumbered compartments of similar size. These two top corners contain either a capital letter **B** or, if the designer of the board was an artist, the representation of a bull's head. The concern is laid upon the deck, and its upper end propped up so as to slope the whole slightly. There are two methods of playing. By the first, a definite game—say of 1500 up—may be played. But the number must be exactly scored, and if a player passes "game" in his last hand and totals—perhaps 1540 instead of 1500—he is not out but must throw 40 in his next innings to reduce the score to "game." In attempting to do so he may very possibly fall below the necessary total; in which case yet another hand must be played until the exact number of 1500 is shown. Thus, though a man be leading by 1000 points, it by no means follows that he will win. If either player throws a **B** or **Bull**, or fails to hit the board altogether, everything scored in that hand is cancelled. The better and more popular game is known as "going round the board," a feat accomplished by throwing first 10, then 20, and so forth to 100. The left **B** is next played, and the right **B** completes half the game. The return journey is thrown in reverse order: from the right **B** back again to the 10 square. In this variety no penalty attaches to a miss, but a **B** thrown out of turn cancels the hand. At both games any quoit overlapping a line between the squares is ignored in the score

The vitality of Bull is remarkable. It has not very much to commend it, and I never met a man who spoke of it with common respect, yet who has travelled in a passenger vessel which lacked a battered Bull-board amongst its resources for the idle traveller? Ladies, it may be noted, derive some pleasure from the sport, but before certain new games presently to be described, Bull must be doomed.

A better game is **Deck Croquet**, wherein a wooden disc is substituted for a ball, and weapons which may be described as a cross between a golf and a polo club take the place of mallets. The hoops can be arranged according to the facilities afforded by the ship, and a game involving plenty of skill is the result. **Shuffle-board and Deck Billiards** resemble the last-named pastime in some degree, though the "cue" for both sports is peculiar to itself, being a flat piece of wood fastened to the end of a broomstick, and having a half-moon shaped disc cut out of it to fit the quoit. These games, however, are now dying out before the greater attractions of one in some measure sprung from them. This infinitely better sport will presently meet the attention it deserves, for in my opinion it is the best ship's game ever yet invented.

Cricket as played at sea may be good fun on a big ship. The tethered ball variety is feeble sport and soon palls upon the most enthusiastic, but the bigger game, on a cocoa-nut matting pitch, with nets spread from awning to rail, can be played with pleasure and profit. Upon the "Castle" liners there is plenty of good marine cricket, and these great vessels carry special herring nets which, when rigged, give a very considerable practical pitch even with room for fielding. The Australians usually play a little cricket in mid-ocean on their way to this country, though it must be admitted that the highest professional praise won for the game is not great. They hold the sport is good enough to kill time, but deny that as practice for cricket it has any value. By way of a curiosity I may note that I have seen **Association Football** played aboard ship; but the game cannot be recommended.

Of the usual **Gymkhana** as practised on ship-board, much might be said, and the possible events may be multiplied *ad infinitum* according to the ingenuity and energy of those responsible for the sports. The programmes of course vary, but from a dozen different ones it is possible to pick a series of athletic items which shall embrace every physical qualification of skill, speed, pluck, and strength in the performers, and of interest and amusement for the lookers-on. In a programme of this sort the promoters should be careful to arrange at least a couple of contests exclusively for ladies.

The following dozen or more events are always popular and never fail to command good entries.

Tug-of-war is a great marine pastime, and affords wide scope for a variety of different matches on any big passenger ship. The different classes of travellers may pull against one another, and against the ship's crew, or officers. An excellent contest is assured if every contingent on board enter a picked team of five men; and on a 'liner' the result should be a fine struggle contested by at least six or eight teams. I remember a Tug-of-war when the betting was all one way and yet the weaker team managed to hold its own in a manner as gratifying to itself as inexplicable to its opponents. The lighter men were unable to make the least impression on their foes, and yet the team backed to win, do all they could, did not budge the enemy a yard. Then it was found that the end of the rope behind the ultimate losers had been carried round the corner of a deck-house and made fast to a bollard by some enterprising sportsman. That mainstay denied them, the rout of the losing men was speedy and complete. The rules governing Tug-of-war are almost too well known to need repetition. A handkerchief is tied round the centre of the rope, and the rival tuggers take their places at equal distances from it. Upon the deck a chalk line is marked; the umpire adjusts the handkerchief on the rope exactly above it; and upon the word being given it is then the business of the rival teams each to drag the other over the line. The best of three tugs usually decides a match and, given a big entry, a "singles" Tug-of-war is also good sport. Sailors, it is to be remarked, possess a considerable advantage over average landsmen at Tug-of-war. They know exactly how to hang on to a rope with the greatest possible effect, and with their naked feet they have the knack of winning a closer grip on the deck than any land-lubber, despite his lawn tennis or gymnasium shoes.

Cock-fighting has not much to commend it from the performer's point of view, but a "main" will always command a good audience, for it is laughable to watch. Into a ring chalked upon the deck, and having a diameter of about three yards, the rivals are placed, having first been trussed in the approved manner. "Trussing" consists in seating the bird on the ground, then putting a walking stick under his knees. Beneath the stick his elbows are also linked, and he is bound firmly in this position. That a man thus crooked into a ball has not much fight about him is clear; but in the extreme helplessness of the combatants such fun as **Cock-fighting** possesses is to be found. The rivals are placed toe to toe, and the first to get the point of his boot fairly under his opponent's promptly topples the helpless foe over in a heap. He will probably fall pretty hard on the back of his head, and the winner's next task is to roll, shove, or hustle the prostrate "cock" out of the circle. In this endeavour he sometimes loses his own centre of gravity, in which case both performers are set up again to renew the struggle—if they have not had enough of it.

Slinging the Monkey or **Bowline Stretching** is another sort of horseplay very amusing to the spectator. The performer must allow himself to be triced up by the legs with ropes. He then swings head-downwards clear of the deck, which his hands are just able to reach. He is now given a piece of chalk and the game consists in his efforts to draw or write upon the deck. He may be directed to represent a pig or indite a love-letter at the fancy of his tormentors, and his efforts to accomplish the required task, especially if the ship is rolling free, are entertaining enough—to the looker-on. No man, however, "slings the monkey" twice.

Many of the ordinary fixtures at an athletic meeting can be happily carried through on a big ship, but you must order your Sports according to your craft. Thus only the shortest Sprint is possible, even on a big deck, and then no more than two runners should compete in each heat and ample room be allowed behind the tape. **Long** and **High Jumping** are both practicable, the latter especially so. A bundle of engineer's waste makes good material to alight on.

The **Hop**, **Step**, and **Jump** is similarly a capital sport; and no nautical Gymkhana is complete without a **Sack Race**; a **Wheel-barrow Race**, with human wheel-barrows; and a **Potato Race**, in which the spoil is scattered along the deck in fixed positions and has to be transferred, one potato at a time, to a bucket.

For ladies the **Egg** and **Spoon Race** is always popular, and the **Needle-Threading** competition not less so. The former is sufficiently well known: the latter generally requires the assistance of the sterner sex at the turning point of the race, where the needles are threaded. Here a man to each lady runner stands with a needle, and the competitors, as they reach the crucial point of the race, produce a piece of thread which each carries and pass it through the needle—a feat requiring delicate skill even in fine weather.

The **Obstacle Race** is the grand event of a

Gymkhana aboard-ship, and of this sport it may be said that a vessel usually offers a finer course than could be imagined or devised ashore. Jack is an absolute genius in such matters, and with the skipper's permission he will turn you out a course with complications and difficulties bristling at every few yards. And he will also teach you how to negotiate it. Swinging life-buoys or barrels, to be climbed through; a water jump, to be fallen into (for Jack takes very good care that C. B. Fry himself could not get over); floured sails, to be crawled under; hanging nets to be climbed—these are a few of the problems set for solution in an **Obstacle Race**, and such an encounter has this charm, that the whole course is within easy sight of the spectator.

The latest arrival among ships' games is a pastime patented in the autumn of 1896 by Messrs. P. B. Cow and Co., of Cheapside. Their original intention was to produce an athletic pursuit capable of being played within the narrow limits of the smallest garden, but "Spiropole," as the game is called, has now found its way to sea, and, under the alternative titles of **Tether-ball** or **Do-do**, took its first cruise last September in Messrs. Donald Currie and Company's new liner "Dunvegan Castle." The game may be contested by two or four players who take up sides, the partners facing one another at the four corners of a square chalked upon the deck. In the centre of this figure rises a stout post, ten feet high, and from the summit there hangs a tennis ball fastened by a strong cord. The players, who are armed with small wooden racquets, serve or strike off alternately, and the object of the game is for a player or players to wind the string holding the ball completely round the post. One side strike to wind it from their right to left, and the opposers attempt the reverse, which means that each side is bent on getting the string wound in an opposite direction to the other; the side finally completing the spiral scores a point, and the game is usually nine up. Only the ball must be hit by the racquet and should a player strike the cord, and thus foul the ball, his opponent will restart the game by taking the ball in hand and hitting off anew; but the cord must not be unwound from the position it then occupies. Should a player strike the ball over the line, or whilst it is in the adversary's court, the Umpire (and an umpire is very necessary) must add one point to the side which is thus unfairly assaulted. **Tether-ball** must be seen to be enjoyed, and played to be thoroughly appreciated. The wild vagaries of the flying ball, the futile efforts of the strikers to take it "on the wing," and the various comic surprises incidental to the sport cannot easily be described.

Last numerically, and to my mind first in importance, comes the game before alluded to as perhaps the best ever played aboard a ship. **Marine Golf**, though a ghost of the real pastime, is worthy of widest consideration as a sport at once novel, varied, and interesting. Much of course depends on the nature of your ship and the good-nature of your skipper, but given decks of reasonable size and an easy-going commander, who offers no objection to "putting greens," excellent sport is a certainty. The necessary materials are extremely simple. A round disc or quoit of heavy wood about 4½ inches in diameter takes the place of a ball and, instead of a club, a fairly heavy walking-stick with a flat head, or handle, is used. The holes may be either a spot of chalk, to be covered by the disc, or a circle, about half as large again as the disc, into which it has to be played. Hitting will be found useless, and the stroke for drive, approach or put alike is a drag or push. On a smooth deck, with the wind behind you, a disc can be pushed 40 yards, which is a much longer stroke than any "links" save those on the biggest steamers would admit. For driving, the best position is to stand with both feet slightly in front of the disc; in putting, one foot in front and one behind produces the most satisfactory results. Unlike golf, the position of club and ball with regard each to the other being happily assured before the stroke is made, it is better in the act of striking to fix the eye on the distant spot where it is desired to bring your disc. "Links" may be much diversified so as to give opportunities for a variety of strokes and the display of much skill. The "cannon" is admissible, and sometimes a hole, which can only be played direct in two, may be achieved with a single shot by a cannon off bollard or grating edge. Such shots carry their special danger, and the loss of a "ball" by falling into the sea means a penalty, to be fixed according to the fancy of the players. In hole matches the hole is of course lost if the disc goes overboard; in matches by score two strokes should be the penalty. Holes soon get their own names, as on links ashore. One hole which I well remember was named the "Devil." It lay behind the mouth of a coal bunker and its proper number was theoretically three, but a man thought himself lucky to hole out in four. It was a heart-breaking hole in times of head-wind, for the effect of driving at a big wind when playing marine golf is peculiar. The disc in such a case promptly gets up on its side, stops dead, and then starts with the wind and rolls aft, its career being a spectacle of horror, terminating either in the scuppers, many yards behind the place from which it was originally struck, or in the sea.

A pitching ship generally means a head-wind and tribulation, both going out and coming in, to the marine golfer; but in beam seas, with the ship rolling not unreasonably, the perfection of the game may be seen.

At such times it is possible to reach directly

holes not so approachable on an even keel, and the most beautiful curved shots "round the corner" can be made.

Your disc of course takes a bias from the angle of the deck and will perform graceful and invaluable feats if you only keep your eye on the ship as she rolls, and wait for the right moment. I have seen astounding performances thus brought off, and holes made in one, by a combination of perfect strength and a sloping deck, that until the achievement were always voted threes.

Marine golf is rapidly developing its own terminology. To be "scuppered" is a condition of affairs which speaks for itself to anybody who knows a ship; while a "coal-bunkered" player can also be imagined without difficulty. The frequency of the "stimey" is rather a nuisance at the game, and the best rule is to make the player whose disc is nearest the hole strike first whether it be his turn or not.

A beauty of the game is the variation in condition of the "greens" and consequent unexpected difficulties in "putting." It might be supposed that a deck of bare boards was incapable of much change as to surface, but this is not so. Climatic conditions make tremendous differences, and a "green," so keen under bright sunshine that the shortest and slowest of puts goes too far, will, on a grey day, be as slow again; while if there happens to be any spray coming aboard the difficulties are still further increased, for you never can be sure in a wet place whether the disc will "drag" or "slide." In putting, the danger of a foul shot is as great as in pushing at billiards, and rules have yet to be made concerning the contact of disc and club over strokes of a yard or less. Indeed, the game is worth a complete code of rules, and when once taken in hand by a well-regulated golfing mind it should speedily eclipse all other pastimes afloat. I have witnessed its infancy, and unhesitatingly predict for it a phenomenal career.

Doubtless human ingenuity and high spirits bred of sea breezes, have, between them, produced many another excellent device for killing time on the ocean; but in my experiences, than those mentioned, I have observed no other sport, or pastime, worth recording or of a sort to make just claim to a place upon this page. Many of the games here set down are sufficiently trivial, but they serve to lessen the monotony of long days circled by the rim of the sea.

EDEN PHILLPOTTS.

DECOYS—A decoy is a contrivance for taking wildfowl, introduced from Holland; hence the name, from the Dutch *eend*, duck, and *kooi*, cage. The earliest method of capturing ducks in this country, as described by Willughby (1678) and other authors, was by driving them into tunnel nets at a time of year when the young birds were unable to fly, and the old ones were moulting. This plan, which was in vogue as early as the reign of King John, and gave rise to litigation in Lincolnshire in 1280 and again in 1432, was found to be so destructive that in Henry VIII.'s time (1534) an Act of Parliament was passed to prohibit it. In the subsequent reign of Edward VI. (1551) the law was altered by protecting the eggs instead of the birds, and this protection was afforded to certain species of wildfowl, as well as game, by what is now known as the principal Game Act of William IV. (1 and 2 Will. IV. c. 32), which is still in force.

Another method of duck-catching, which, like "driving," has long become obsolete, was by means of a wire cage, which was worked with cords and pulleys and lowered on to a platform in the water, to which the birds were enticed by feeding. An example of this contrivance may be seen at Hardwick Hall, Derby, and a plan of it is given in Sir R. Payne Gallwey's *Book of Duck Decoys*, 1886 (p. 71). In this volume may also be found a description of a so-called "trap-decoy" (examples of which exist at Haughton, Park Hall, and Ossington in Nottinghamshire) whereby the fowl are captured "by lowering a trap-door at the entrance to the pipes after they have entered them for food placed therein."

The ordinary wildfowl decoy, however, as now generally understood, is worked neither by "driving" nor "trapping" but by "enticing" the birds up a wide-mouthed "pipe" (as it is termed), partly by means of a small dog, trained for the purpose, towards which they are attracted by curiosity, partly by means of decoy ducks which come at a call to be fed at the mouth of the pipe, and gradually lead their wild companions into it. Once within the pipe their retreat is barred by the decoyman, who, showing himself behind them, causes them to rush up the pipe into a bag-net at the further extremity, where they are then easily captured and killed. It is generally asserted, on the authority of Sir Henry Spelman (*Posthumous Works*, ed. Gibson, vol. ii. p. 153), that this method of decoying wildfowl was introduced from Holland by Sir William Wodehouse in the reign of James I. However this may be, the decoy constructed in 1665 by Charles II. in St. James's Park is apparently the first made in England on the Dutch plan, of which any account has been preserved. In that year, John Ogilvy, described as "Master of His Majesty's Revells in the Kingdom of Ireland," published a little book entitled *The Fables of Æsop paraphrased in Verse*, in which is a curious woodcut representing a decoyman taking fowl from the end of a pipe-net, by the side of a pool wherein the mouths of two pipes are shown. Sir R. Payne Gallwey, who has reproduced this engraving in his work on Decoys above mentioned (p. 9), is of opinion that "this is the earliest sketch of a decoy and its pipes, as now used, in existence." In this, however, he is mistaken, for earlier engravings of the subject may be found, not only in the *Venationes Ferarum Avium*, &c., of Antonio Tempesta, 1605, and in the *Aucupationis multifariæ Effigies* by the same artist, 1639, but in a still earlier collection of engravings drawn by Bol and engraved by Philip Galle, 1582. (See *The Zoologist*, 1886, p. 382.)

Those who are of opinion that decoys in England are amongst things of the past may be

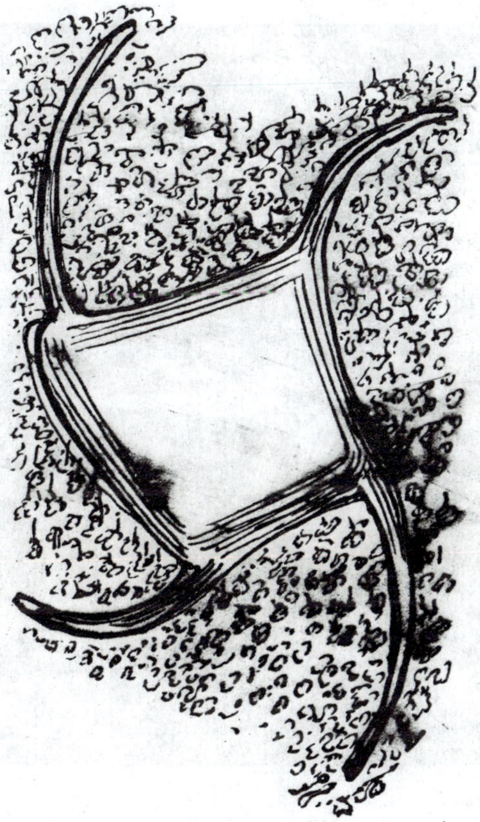

Plan of a Decoy Pool.

surprised to learn that at the present day there are about forty still in use in England, and three in Ireland, while at least 140 others are known to have existed formerly, and to be now dismantled or out of repair. The counties in which the greatest number of decoys once existed were, as might be expected from their proximity to the coast, Essex (29), Lincolnshire (39), and Norfolk (26). For the fourth place, Somersetshire vies with Yorkshire, each having possessed at one time no less than fourteen decoys in active operation. The reclamation and cultivation of the fens, the enclosure of waste land, the formation of railways, and the great increase in the number of shooters have each and all contributed to ruin decoys; while the large numbers of wildfowl which are brought by steamer and rail from Holland and other parts of the Continent every winter, render it less than ever necessary for the owners of decoys in this country to incur the expense of maintaining them. Moreover, in counties where game is strictly preserved for the purpose of being killed

Plan of a Decoy Pipe.

by shooting parties during the winter months, "decoying" is out of the question, since absolute quiet must prevail within sight and sound of the decoy pond, or no ducks will stay to be caught.

As regards the construction and management of a decoy, we have only to imagine a pool of a few acres in extent, lying in a quiet, out-of-the-way spot, far from any high road, and if surrounded by trees all the better. Marshes by the sea, especially on the East Coast, are found to be most favourable for such a purpose, since fresh-water pools in such situations at once attract foreign fowl coming in from the sea on their first arrival.

Having selected the pool, the next thing to be done is to cut the "pipes," as they are termed, up which the ducks have to be decoyed. These "pipes," which may vary in number according to the extent and shape of the pool, are simply net-covered ditches of a peculiar shape, something like a cow's horn, that is to say, wider at the end nearest to the pond than at the other end, and gently curving throughout their entire length. The reason for having several such "pipes" to a decoy is that the fowl may be taken when the wind, no matter from what point of the compass, is blowing down the pipe towards the pond. The reason for making the "pipes" curved is that, if they were straight, and the ducks could see the further end, they would at once suspect a trap, and never enter them.

Three, four, or five such pipes are cut, and are arched over at intervals with hoops of wood (or iron, if expense be no object), over which is stretched a strong netting, tapering gradually towards the far end of the pipe, and terminating in a sort of bag or purse, in which the fowl are eventually taken. As it is absolutely necessary that the decoyman should be concealed from view of the ducks on the pool, a series of screens, made of reeds and set one behind another in echelon, is fixed at intervals along the side of each "pipe." With a few tame ducks, taught to come at a whistle to be fed, a few handfuls of grain, and a small fox-coloured dog, the decoyman is ready to begin operations.

Selecting his "pipe" according to the direction of the wind, he throws a handful of grain over a screen into the pipe, and whistles. The wind carries the grain towards the mouth of the "pipe," the tame ducks come eagerly to feed, and the wild ones, getting an occasional mouthful as the grain drifts by them or towards them, gradually discover that the nearer they swim towards the mouth of a pipe the more plentiful does food become. Unsuspectingly they enter the wide mouth, so wide as to convey no suggestion of a trap, and then the decoyman's little dog comes into play. Taught to dodge in and out of the reed screens to fetch a piece of bread or biscuit, he shows himself momentarily to the ducks in the pipe, and disappears when returning to his master. Wildfowl are eminently curious, and their curiosity proves

THE DECOY POOL.

fatal to them. They behave towards the dog exactly as cattle would do—so long as he retreats from them, they follow him. Perhaps from his colour they take him for a fox, their common enemy, and fancy they are driving him away. At any rate, they follow him up the pipe until, having passed the first reed screen, they are virtually cut off from the rest of the flock. At this juncture the decoy-man shows himself to the ducks in the pipe, though not to those on the pool. He makes no noise, but merely waves his arms; and the frightened fowl, afraid to return past him to the open water, instantly rise on the wing and fly up the pipe, following its curve in the vain hope that it will lead to freedom. Instead of that, however, it leads to the bag-net, from which one by one they are taken out to have their necks adroitly twisted.

Mouth of a Pipe.

Such, briefly stated, is the *modus operandi*. The whole business is conducted so quietly that the wildfowl on the main water are never alarmed, and time after time the bag-net is filled and emptied.

In hard winters, when there may be several hundred ducks upon the pool in a day, great execution takes place if the decoy-man knows his work and has a good dog.

At a celebrated decoy at Ashby, in Lincolnshire, as many as 113 ducks have been taken at one time, and 248 in one day.

The following is a list of decoys at present existing in England, Wales, and Ireland. There are none in Scotland.

Bucks—Boarstall, near Thame.
Derby—Hardwick Hall, near Chesterfield.
Dorset—Abbotsbury, near Dorchester.
Essex—Bradwell Marsh, Tillingham Marsh, and Old Hall, Tollesbury.
Glamorgan—Park Wern, near Swansea.
Gloucester—Berkeley Castle.
Hertford—The Hoo, near Welwyn.
Lancashire—Hale, near Prescot.
Lincolnshire—Ashby, near Brigg.
Montgomeryshire—Lymore Hall, near Montgomery.
Norfolk—Westwick, near North Walsham; Southacre, near Swaffham; Wretham, Didlington, and Merton, all near Thetford.
Northampton—Aldwinckle, near Oundle; Borough Fen, near Peakirk.
Nottingham—Haughton, near Walesby; Park Hall, near Mansfield; Ossington, near Tuxford.
Pembroke—Orielton Park, near Pembroke.

Shropshire—Oakley Park, Broomfield, near Ludlow; Sundorne Castle, near Shrewsbury.

Somerset—Sharpham Park, near Glastonbury; Shapwick, near Sedgemoor; King's Sedgemoor, near Walton.

Suffolk—Iken, near Saxmundham; Chillesford, near Saxmundham; Orwell Park, near Ipswich; Nacton Heath, near Ipswich; Fritton, near Lowestoft.

Surrey—Virginia Water.

Sussex—Firle, near Lewes.

Warwick—Packington Hall, near Coleshill.

Wilts—Hampwork, near Downton.

Yorkshire—Hornby Castle, near Bedale; Thirkleby Park, near Thirsk.

Breast-wall screens—[*See* SCREENS.]

'Coy—The fowler's abbreviation for Decoy.

Decoy-ducks—Birds which are daily accustomed to be fed by the decoy-man in the pipe (*q.v.*), and therefore swim up without fear, followed by the wild ones. They are usually half-bred wild ducks.

Dog-jump—The low fence between two screens, over which the dog works. Usually about two feet six inches high, and of like width.

Draught of pipe—That portion of the pool which narrows to a bay at the entrance to a pipe (*q.v.*).

Drift—An attempt to draw the fowl up the pipe.

Elbow—The point at which a pipe curves.

Head-show—The spot at which the decoy-man

END OF A PIPE.

In Ireland at the present time there are but three decoys in working order, viz.:—

Cork—Longueville, near Mallow.

Kilkenny—Desart House, near Kilkenny.

Queen's County—Kellyville, Maryborough.

TECHNICAL TERMS USED BY DECOY-MEN.

Accommodation Tufts or Reed Edges—Small clumps of reed allowed to remain in front of the pipes (*q.v.*) for fowl to rest on.

Back Screens—[*See* SCREENS.]

Back-wing-landing—[*See* LANDINGS.]

Bank (*v.*)—Said of ducks coming to rest on the sides of the pool.

shows himself behind the ducks, in order to drive them further up the pipe into which they have been lured.

Hoop—The curved rods of wood or iron which span the pipe like arches and support the netting.

Landings—Smooth banks at the mouth of the pipe on either side; that on the inner curve being termed the *back-wing-landing*, that on the outer curve the *breast-wall-landing*.

Leading birds—Wildfowl that have been accustomed to rest in the decoy, and which, though not likely to be caught, are useful in attracting others.

Paddling—A flock of fowl on the water.

Pipe—The long curving net-covered ditch up which the fowl are induced to swim. The average dimensions are:—Height at mouth, fifteen feet; width, twenty-seven feet, gradually diminishing towards the end of the tunnel-net (*q.v.*). The average depth of water is eight to twelve inches, so as to hinder the fowl from diving back. Length, about eighty yards. Birds which swim up under the netting are said "to pipe."

Piper—The dog whose actions attract the notice and curiosity of the fowl and allure them up the pipe; usually a small spaniel, but any little dog of a bright colour may be taught the work if intelligent.

Purse-net—[*See* TUNNEL-NET.]

Reed-edges—[*See* ACCOMMODATION TUFTS.]

Rising of the Decoy—The flight of the ducks from the pond about twilight when they leave for the marshes to feed during the night.

Screen—Fences of reed erected by the side of the outer edge of the decoy to conceal the decoy-man. Of these there are three kinds. (1) The *breast-wall screens*, two in number, covering the landing at the mouth of the pipe, eighteen feet and twelve feet long respectively. (2) The *working screens* round which the dog works, eleven in number, and ranged "in echelon," connected by the dog-jumps. The working screen nearest the mouth is usually about twenty-eight feet long, the others about twelve feet each. (3) *Back screens*, which conceal the fowler when running back to the mouth of the pipe. Of these there are three, each thirty feet in length. All screens should be about six feet high.

Stale birds—Fowl that have frequently visited the decoy, but have lost interest in the actions of the dog.

Tunnel-net, bag-net, or purse-net—The net at the extreme end of the pipe into which the fowl are eventually driven. It is detachable from the main portion of the net, and is usually about fifteen feet in length.

Yackoop—The dog-jump (*q.v.*) between the breast-wall screens (*q.v.*).

For hints as to the construction and management of a decoy the reader may be referred to the following bibliography.

J. E. HARTING.

Bibliography.—Lubbock, *Fauna of Norfolk*, 1845; second ed. 1879 (Jarrold, 6/-); Folkard, *The Wildfowler*, 1859, 1864, 1875, 1897 (Longmans, 12/6); Southwell, *Norfolk Decoys*, in *Trans.* Norf. and Norw. Nat. Soc., vol. ii., 1879; Davies, *Norfolk Broads and Rivers*, 1883 (Blackwood); Payne-Gallwey, *Fowler in Ireland*, 1882 (Van Voorst, 21/-); Payne-Gallwey, *Book of Duck Decoys*, 1886 (Van Voorst, 25/-); Harting, *Wildfowl Decoys in Essex*, in *The Essex Naturalist*, vol. ii., 1888.

DEERSTALKING—This sport as now carried on in the Scottish Highlands is one that has changed but little since guns and rifles, bullets and villainous saltpetre first made their appearance on the hills; the weapons themselves have been improved, and have been coupled with the later advent of the telescope or spy-glass, but these are the only alterations that have taken place in the manner of carrying on the sport. The space placed at my disposal will not permit a discussion of the political or economical aspects of the deer forests, or the sport provided by each individual one; moreover, for the purposes of this work such a treatise would be unnecessary, and out of place, but those who are greatly interested in the doings of stagland will find in my books, *Deerstalking* and *The Deer Forests of Scotland*, further information on the subject. In this article I propose to confine myself to trying to tell the novice how best to carry on his sport, so that he may acquit himself creditably on the never-to-be-forgotten day of his first stag.

First, then, comes the rifle, and undoubtedly the single-barrel small bore of the present day is ousting from its pride of place the deerstalker's old friend, the double-barrelled ·450. The Mannlicher ·256, and the Government ·303, adapted for sporting purposes, are the weapons of the future. With good reason too, for they are very much less expensive, have greater accuracy, no recoil, no smoke, less weight, and, where more than two shots require to be fired in quick succession, they are much speedier to use than our old friend the double-barrelled express. Provided, then, that the ammunition be of the right kind, and the cartridge made so as to *ensure* the "mushrooming" of the bullets, these small bores with their six cartridges, one in the barrel and five in the magazine, are at the present time the very best the deerstalker can carry. Moreover they are made so well that they will put a ball into a three-inch bull's eye at 100 yards. But whatever sort of rifle be used, on no account take one to the hill that has not stops to it, for there is nothing more dangerous to all concerned. As to the rifle sights, there are various descriptions in use, all of which are good; the most common is the V sight, and the more obtuse the angle of the V, the easier it becomes to use this sight for stalking purposes. Then there is the Layman sight, the bar sight, and the "nick" sight, and one of the four is generally used by the deerstalker. The V sight has far the largest number of patrons, but it is easier to shoot with a "thick" sight of this description than a "thin" one. Cut A will show best what is meant by a "thick" sight, set exactly for a shot at 100

A B

yards, while cut B will explain what is meant by a "thin" sight set right for a hit at a similar distance.

Now, most men will find it easier to use sight A than sight B. Each will be "good" for a kill at from 80 to 120 yards, between which distances the greatest number of shots at deer are delivered. At nearer ranges, say from 70 to 40 yards, the A sight must either be seen much finer, if aiming at the heart, or held as in the cut and directed *well underneath* the heart. Now, in the B sight, in taking a shot at close quarters and aiming for the heart, the foresight, *to ensure a bullseye*, *ought to become well-nigh invisible*, and this is something very difficult to remember and put into practice in the excitement of a stalk. The light is often bad, and the shooter, longing to see a little more of his mark, raises his head, thereby making the thin sight into a thick one. Then he has the mortification of hearing and seeing his bullet smack on the stones, or cut up the peat, quite true in direction, but *just over* the back of his quarry.

Those who are purchasing rifles, or who are not making good shooting with the one they possess, will do well to try the various sights in use, for peculiarity of vision and the distance of the back sight from the eye will often make a vast difference to those who are not doing well with the rifles they are using. Personally the writer could never shoot well at deer with either of these sights. He then tried the bar sight, which the annexed cut explains.

The inverted V is made of platinum, and the foresight of white enamel. For liberty of vision and quick aiming the writer has found this beat all other sights. Its very formation ensures, unless the shooter have "stag fever," that it be held straight; and the sight thus held (though one may, as with other sights, easily shoot under or over a deer through misjudging the distance), it is quite impossible to perpetrate the atrocity of "haunching him," so often occurring when the V sight is used, and not kept perfectly upright. The "nick" sight speaks for itself,

the nick above the inverted V of ivory or platina being exactly filled by the fore-sight at 100 yards. This sight, however, is not nearly so quick and ready to the eye for moving shots as the bar or the obtuse V sight.

The pleasantest spy-glasses to use are made by Ross, of New Bond Street, and, if money be of no great account, "the gentleman," as distinguished from the stalker, is advised to fit himself out with an aluminium one for his own special use. The difference in weight between that metal and bronze is well worth considering in a long day's tramping over the hills.

The power of a spy-glass is determined by the length of draw; for this reason binoculars are of but little use to the deerstalker, for if made with tubes of sufficient length to give power enough to distinguish a "royal" from a six-pointer at over a mile, they are so bulky to carry, and so liable by a chance blow to have the two tubes knocked out of the exact parallel, that, as far as the Highlands are concerned, binoculars are only used when a telescope is not to be had.

Rifle and spy-glass both being in readiness, let the deerstalker take the hill, clad in the most suitable coloured raiment for the ground over which he is to pursue his sharp-eyed quarry. It is as well to gain previous information on this subject, but if none is attainable, then the Black Mount, or Mar, "mixtures," or a light coloured "Lovat" will be nearly sure to be suitable. Colour is not of extreme importance unless it becomes, as is frequently the case, necessary to creep across a stretch of peat, or rock, or heather in full sight of a herd of deer only about five hundred yards distant. On attempting such a ticklish movement, the forester may often be seen to exchange his own coat with the ponyman or gillie, should either of them chance to be wearing one harmonising better with that special bit of ground.

Wear flannel shirts, and, if the ankles are sound, stout and well-nailed shoes with spats are better than boots. Stand fast to the old-fashioned knickerbockers instead of wearing the modern and smarter-looking knicker breeches, which do not permit of free play to the calf or the tendons under the knee. Have all pockets made to button up, which will often save the loss of pipe or tobacco-box, &c., for when it comes to slithering down a steep hillside at best pace, the coat pockets are usually nearer to one's ears than to that part of the body they are intended to cover. A neutral-tinted macintosh of medium material, cut like a covert coat, but looser and more roomy, is the best sort of wrap to take to the hill. It weighs but little, is easily carried, will be sure to keep both back and chest dry, and does not get appreciably heavier by the absorption of rain. Should your host place a forest pony at your disposal to carry you to and from your stalking ground, never on any pretence gallop it, for these ponies are, as a rule, entirely grass-fed, and are therefore in no condition for such violent exercise, and are easily made broken-winded. These animals can always be relied on implicitly on the darkest of nights, and however bad the track may be, if the rider will but trust them, he is sure to be brought safely home. With regard to personal condition, if plenty of golf and lawn-tennis has been played during the summer months, and hill-walking be not an entire novelty, most shooters will find themselves fairly fit at the commencement of the season, while each day on the hill will make them more so. The Swiss Alpine guides have a very good maxim, and recommend one "to start as if one never meant to get to the journey's end." Sound advice too, for there are many who find the first hour's walking the most fatiguing of the whole day. Therefore when, soon after setting out, a long and steep hill has to be negotiated, stop to admire the view the moment nature warns that too great a strain is being placed on the pumping powers of the heart. Many a good man has seriously injured himself by trying to "live" with a practised and well-trained walker during the ascent of a high and severe hill. I have on several occasions seen tall heavy men of splendid physique quite beaten, and distressed to actual sickness, if out of condition, towards the end of a long day when all chance of sport was over, as dusk came on and there remained a bad ten miles' tramp to the lodge.

In mounting a very steep hillside of rolling stones or "screggans," it will be easier and quicker to ascend crabwise, with feet and body at right angles to the slope of the hill. Also, should it happen, when making a dash down a steep hill to cut off moving deer or a wounded beast, that a slip be made, and the shooter begin to roll, then let him turn instantly on his face and stick the toes into the first thing they meet, which will usually bring him safely to an anchor.

Sometimes during September the weather is so close and hot, even on the high hill-tops, that the heat and hard work tend to make the stalker very thirsty, but in such a case let him not stop and take a cup of water at every spring. Resist the thirst, and by degrees it will vanish, or if very done up, kneel down at the first spring to be met with, and, holding the head low, let the attendant pour cold water over the nape of the neck, which will be found a wonderful refresher. If your own flask contains anything more stimulating than cold tea (that abomination!) carry it in your own pocket, for it is extraordinary how unfortunate some flask-bearing gillies are, for when carried in their pockets the very best made ones *will* leak! Carry a white pocket handkerchief; it will be useful for signalling to ponyman or gillie, and may also be further utilised to pin on your stalker's back during a tramp home across country on a dark night. Such signal being once hoisted, keep pretty close to it, and pull up short if it vanishes, when the chances are it will be seen reappearing from a burn or a hole into which the bearer has fallen headlong. A stout birch or hazel stick some eight inches longer than the Piccadilly type, will now complete the stalker's outfit. Should he wish to cut notches in this stick for every stag killed, why, it is a harmless amusement; but it is subject to the temptation, often overpowering, to cut a notch for an escaped and wounded stag, "sure to die" across the march.

It goes without saying that deer must be stalked up wind or on a side wind, so that they cannot get the scent of the stalkers. The actual distance at which deer will take the scent of a man varies according to the force of the wind and the conformation of the ground; when it is blowing fairly hard, it is certainly not safe to pass within a mile of a herd; and I once saw deer in a gale take the scent of a man and a pony (a stronger smelling animal than a man) fully a mile and a half off. As a rule, deer move up wind as they feed, and when alarmed, provided there are no adjacent sheep fences to head them, though they may gallop off down wind, they will surely circle round and eventually head up it. It should be borne in mind that the air currents in a narrow glen always move up or down it, although the true wind may be blowing directly across it; indeed the eccentricities of the wind are numberless, and it is a matter of daily occurrence to see masses of low-lying vapour rolling up with the wind to meet others advancing at a higher level from an entirely opposite direction. Therefore, when nearing deer, if there is a shifty wind which there is every reason to distrust, pull out the spy-glass, and try to make out which way the grasses are blowing at the point you wish to gain. Then, guided by the result of your observations, finish the stalk as promptly as possible.

In the middle of the day, deer usually lie down and will sometimes so remain for two or three hours, and nothing is more vexatious than passing such a period some hundred and fifty yards from them. The temptation to take a lying shot becomes very great, but it is far better not to do this, for deer are very easy to miss in such a position. A sharp shower will be nearly certain to cause deer to rise, so that they may shake the wet off them, and thus a ducking is often welcomed by those who have been lying a long time within shot. Thunder also frightens deer very much, and will frequently cause a stampede of several miles. If on a steep hillside, the biggest stags are usually nearest the base of the hill, with the smaller stags and the hinds above them. When lying in a position like this, most of them will be looking straight down hill, and of course, if there is a strong wind, they will be on the sheltered side of the valley. Then deer are nearly unapproachable; to get in from up wind and below is hopeless, while to attempt a down wind stalk, trusting to the force of the gale carrying one's scent right over the deer, is well-nigh as desperate, so that when deer are in a place of this sort, it is wiser to wait and watch their movements or to pass them undisturbed and look for others in more favourable places. Unless suspicious, or disturbed by grouse, fox, raven, &c., deer rarely look up hill, and for this reason it is always better to stalk down hill, and if the wind permits, manœuvre so as to get the sun at your back and in their eyes. In strong sunshine, with a dress suitable to the colour of the ground, a good stalker can take great liberties. In large herds, sentinel work appears to be deputed entirely to the hinds, and though the sight of neither hind nor stag is *marvellously* sharp, both are uncommonly quick at detecting any movement at close quarters. Deer startled early in the day will be apt to shift their ground further afield, and even when settled down again, will be far more restless than those disturbed at feeding time in the afternoon. Again, on fine calm days they will not move nearly so far as on cold days, with a strong wind blowing. Indeed, in very high winds, deer play fanciful tricks, and will start suddenly of their own accord and dash off full tilt for a mile or two for no discernible reason. On such days, unless the wind is in exactly the right airt for the ground, it is far wiser to stay at home and leave the forest quiet. In fine warm weather, the big stags will mostly be on the highest hills, and on wet stormy days on lower ground. They are sharply observant of other creatures, and if grouse, fox, or other creatures have been disturbed by man, they know it at once, though if either one or the other is moving for its own convenience, they do not display the least sign of alarm.

About the beginning of the last week of September—the 26th is the precise day known as the "day of the roaring"—the stags commence to bellow and seek the hinds.

To me the roar has always seemed to be more of a love-sick than an angry sound, and although I have had many years of stalking, it has never been my good fortune to witness a combat *à l'outrance* between two big stags. That they do so fight is undoubted, and instances are recorded where the bodies of two stags have been found with horns locked together. I have at this period of the year seen many smart skirmishes in the forest, and often had a laugh at the quick way in which the lesser or weaker stag would find discretion the better part of valour, and turn tail after the exchanges of a few rounds had assured him of his antagonist's superiority. Many friends who have been associated with deer forests for years tell me that they also have never witnessed any duel to the death, and I am of opinion that encounters of this sort are few and far between. As the rutting season begins, the stags start on their travels, in search of hinds, wandering singly or in small companies, and as long as the wind keeps in one quarter, they will travel up it to very great distances. In fact, at this period, and with the wind in any one particular airt for a month or so at a stretch, a not very large forest may become almost denuded of its best stags, during all of which time the lessee will be gnashing his teeth with vexation, for he will know that there are sure to be sharp eyes on the look-out across the march. At this season also stags will travel by water as well as by land, for they are bold, strong, fast swimmers, and think but little of swimming a mile.

In starting out for a day on the hill let the "gentleman" make sure for himself that cartridges, coats, flask, lunch, pipe and tobacco are all with him, for in many parts of the Highlands it is thought to bring bad luck to turn back for anything after having once made a start. Especially let him see after his own cartridges, for I have known several instances of ·500 bore cartridges being taken out for a ·450 rifle, and the discovery not made until many miles from home with deer in sight!

As soon as the stalking party reach the first spying-place, out come the glasses, and the novice will not find it such a simple matter as it sounds, to search a corrie thoroughly. The best spying position is to lie nearly flat on the back with a rock or hillock to support the shoulders. Draw up the knees, fix the glass firmly against the inside of the left leg, and it can be held perfectly steady even in a high wind. Practice alone will make an adept at "picking up" deer, but absolute immovability of the glass is the first thing necessary to ensure success. It is as well to learn to use the glass with both eyes, and the ability to do so being acquired, then use the left eye if spying shortly before expecting to shoot, which does away with any fear of the shooting eye becoming "dazed." To use the left eye will feel very awkward at first, but practice will soon overcome that sensation.

When deer are lying quite still in broken ground, the beginner may often have the exact spot pointed out to him, and yet be wholly unable to find them. As soon as a shootable stag has been found, the novice must perforce put himself in his stalker's hands, but after a few shots and careful watching of the *modus operandi* he should be allowed the satisfaction of finishing the last two or three hundred yards for himself. Even in that short distance he will find himself making many errors and losing much valuable time in reaching a position, from which he may find it necessary to retreat, whereas if it had been left to the stalker he would, from his better knowledge of the ground, have been able to go straight to his quarry. Those few minutes gained often make just the difference between an easy shot and a difficult one, or perhaps no shot at all; nevertheless, the "gentleman" will have had more sport and fun if he takes the lead when nearing his quarry, and even if the worst come to the worst, and he put the stag away, that will be a lesson for a future opportunity. No great harm is done, and anything is better than being led about all day even by the best of foresters. To me it is quite wonderful how few sportsmen there are who stalk for themselves; and personally, were I able to rent a forest supposed to be good for, say, fifty stags, then I would rather kill but ten, alone and unaided, than the full allowance with the assistance of the professional stalker. There can be no doubt about it that many stags are missed by novices, through the stalker being the leading man at the critical moment of taking the shot.

When crawling uphill or on level ground, always advance head first; but in creeping downhill, let the feet go first; in very flat crawls, punt yourself along with the elbows, and be careful to keep the legs straight to the ground, for somehow or other in a creep of this sort they have a determined tendency to "cock up" and throw themselves above the level of the head. When crawling, hold the rifle across the body, keep close to the stalker if he is in front, and be *sure* to keep as *low as he does*, for one who knows his business will often only be an inch or two out of the view of

the quarry. It is unfair to him if you, by keeping a few inches higher, let the deer into the secret just at the end of the sport. With regard to this crawling or creeping, simple as it sounds, and painful as it often is, there is a right and a wrong way of doing it. Do not move as if "playing at bear" with children, for in that style, your tail will be a good bit higher than your head, which is a sight that deer will not stay long to admire. Keep nearly flat; place the hands far in front and well apart; stretch the legs at nearly full length; turn out the feet, and then, with knees barely touching the earth, you will acquire a crocodile-like motion to which you will soon get used. When moving in this way *the eyes*, with the exception of the very top of your head, become the highest parts of the body. As to "stag fever," neither whiskey nor advice will cure it; and the best remedy is a course of a few downright bad misses. In getting up to deer never crawl *over* a boulder or hillock or anything to bring you into the sky-line—creep *slowly round* all such obstacles, and you will rarely be detected.

We will now suppose the novice and the stalker are within shot of a good stag; they have crawled, slithered, run, waited, and done all that was possible to outwit their quarry, and the next minute will decide whether all their toil and trouble has been in vain. It is small wonder that anxiety should take possession of the shooter, for up to this time all responsibility has been with the stalker. He has done his work right well; and now will his "gentleman" follow the good example? In taking a first shot, remember you *must* at least show your head. Nor need you be afraid to do this, for it is impossible to make a good hit without fully seeing the object aimed at. But beginners are often so afraid of being detected that they will try to aim through heather or long grass. Very slowly, without any jerky, quick movement, bring the eye into sight of the quarry: and then, if the stag is standing broadside on, put the rifle-sights on the inside of his nearest foreleg; raise them slowly till they meet the body, and squeeze the trigger gently when you "see brown." This was the maxim of the late Colonel Campbell, of Monzie, and there was no one in all Scotland more able to give good advice on such a matter. Do not fire at deer standing end-on or facing you, but bide your time, and they will usually offer a fair chance. In shooting downhill, sit up by degrees; plant the heels firmly in the ground and rest *both* elbows on the thighs. Your rifle will be in vice-like rest, and far more steady than if only *one* elbow were rested. In uphill shots, seek for a big stone or tussock against which to rest the rifle, and put the left hand between the rifle and the rest, for if it be of stone there will be a "jump," and the bullet will not speed truly.

In firing at walking, trotting, or galloping deer, practice alone will tell how far to hold in front; and, in the event of a miss, be careful to note where the bullet struck. As a rule, at about one hundred yards, shoot right at a walking deer, for the bullet goes so quickly that even if it strike an inch or two behind the heart it will be fatal. At a deer trotting slowly, fire at the point of the shoulder; but at one stepping out at a good pace, just see daylight in front of him and then pull. For a stag galloping as fast as he can, from two to three feet may be "borrowed," and I think all shots at moving deer are better taken off the shoulder than from a rest. In downhill shots, the aim should be a little under the heart; but in uphill ones, it should be rather over. In all shots, the cheek should be kept *well glued down* to the rifle-stock. If a long run has been made, and the firing and halting point are reached almost simultaneously, and exertion has reduced the shooter to panting, the rifle will be held more steadily if it is aimed and emptied in the few seconds between exhaling and again inhaling. No stag should be fired at if over two hundred yards away; but when the light is good, and he is broadside-on, he should be killed at that distance. The directions of the late Lord Lovat for judging the distance at which a deer stands from the shooter are so good and so accurate that, in the interests of my readers I cannot refrain from quoting them. Says Lord Lovat:—"Up to eighty yards the deer's eye is to be seen distinctly; at one hundred yards the shape of the eye is no longer discernible, but only the dark line is visible. Up to one hundred and fifty the ears are plainly to be seen, but at two hundred they are well nigh invisible; so, unless the ears are distinct, it is better not to fire."

If you miss with the right barrel, do not empty the left in a hurry; take time to steady yourself, and then seize the first fair chance. Should that not present itself, it is better not to fire at all, for it is of very little use "loosing off" at deer end-on to you; but if you are unable to resist the temptation, then pitch the rifle-sight quickly in the centre of the horns directly above the top of the skull, and pull as if taking a snap-shot with a gun. Such a shot rarely comes off, but if it does the deer is killed stone dead, and all risk of "haunching" him is avoided. Should both barrels be emptied in vain, then, in the name of all that is sportsmanlike, do not sit down and open fire at random and as fast as you can blaze away. After missing with both barrels, keep as much concealed and as quiet as possible, but load again instantly in case the deer take a circle and offer *really* good second chances. If a beast drop to the shot, get up to him at once and as soon as possible, but reload before starting, and be *careful to put the stops on.* If the ball has gone high and just grazed the spine above the heart, but without breaking it, the stag will fall as if stone dead, and then in a few minutes he will recover himself and be gone. Nothing can be more vexing than to witness this resurrection while the shooter is yet a good way off, for the chance then offered will almost certainly be an end-on shot, which usually results in a miss and the loss of the beast.

Now and again it happens, when stalking near the march and spying into Naboth's vineyard, that Naboth himself may be spied coming in pursuit of his deer. Then, if he has not seen you first, it is as well to sit down quite hidden and watch his proceedings, for if he has deer in front of him, he may possibly blunder and send them to you.

Perhaps the prettiest shot that can be given to a novice, and also one of the easiest, is cutting off deer feeding up wind, the *détour* of the stalker being so timed that, keeping a side wind, he arrives at the desired spot only a minute or two before the deer come feeding past it. A perfect knowledge of the ground and of the pace of the deer can alone insure success in this description of stalking, for if any one unaccustomed to it makes the attempt he is nearly sure to arrive at the selected spot *after* the deer have passed by, for when feeding they progress at a much greater rate than they would appear to. When this manœuvre is well carried out, it is most fascinating, for the shooter will be nearly certain to reach the firing-point hot and even breathless, but he has just sufficient time to settle himself comfortably and get a good rest, and then, while his blood is still "up," the deer pass slowly by. Hand and eye have had no time to grow nervous, and both combine to do him good service as he presses the trigger.

There is usually a mutual understanding known as "stalkers' law" on the marches of adjoining forests. The rule is that either party, finding deer on his own ground, but so close to the march that they cannot be stalked except by crossing it, may come over on to his neighbour's ground sufficiently far to hide his cap while crawling on hands and knees. At the same time it is best never to follow an injured beast across the march, and the usual plan is to send a letter to the owner of the adjoining ground, to tell him of the wounded one, and ask that his foresters be enjoined to keep a look out for it.

When a deer is palpably hit but recovers himself, remain hidden. Keep still and turn the glass on to him and try to see where he is wounded. He will be nearly certain to make for water adjacent to good cover, where he will hide himself, and if you can see him do this he should go to the larder, for he is usually an easy stalk when in such sorry plight. It is extraordinary how close a badly wounded stag will lie, and how cleverly, and in how small a hole he will conceal himself. When the surface is broken by watercourses and precipitous gullies overgrown with bracken and old heather, he will lie so close that he may easily be passed over. Therefore, if he has vanished in such sort of ground, every bit of it should be carefully searched, and often he will start to life within a few yards. Nothing is more annoying than to lose a good beast through not making a sufficiently close search at the moment, and then perhaps ten days later to come upon the spoilt carcass, likely enough not twenty yards from the very line taken when searching for him. It sometimes happens that a deer unsights you the moment the shot is fired. If he does, get as fast as may be to some spot commanding a view of the flying herd. If the stag fired at is not with them, he will, more often than not, be found lying dead, or so badly hurt as to be incapable of flight. A not very severely wounded stag, if he detect your approach, is nearly certain to become a lost one, for he will not rest again until he has gone a great distance, and rendered pursuit almost hopeless. If a stag be struck in such a way that he cannot rise and is yet very strong and full of life, especially if he is sitting up and has the use of his fore-legs, be very careful about getting within reach of his horns, for he will stab viciously and make furious efforts to avenge himself. Once only have I seen a wounded stag actually charge. He was hit high in the back (as it afterwards turned out, the spine was chipped but not broken), and as I ran with rifle in one hand, knife in the other, to give the *coup de grâce*, I plunged up to my hips in a bit of green and very soft ground when but fifteen yards from him. Turning my back to him to extricate myself, a yell from the stalker warned me only just in time to put in a snap shot, for the deer had regained his legs and with a furious rush was coming full tilt for his destroyer. He fell with his nose nearly touching me.

In shooting at deer brought to bay by a dog, great care must be taken that the neck of the deer and the dog are not in the same line, and, with an active dog bounding about in front of the deer's head, one will often be obliged to wait some minutes ere a safe shot can be delivered.

In most forests any stag scaling sixteen stone clean,—that is without heart or liver,—is reckoned a really good one, and it is very rare for a hill stag to exceed twenty-one stone. Wood stags often top this weight, and the heaviest red stag about which I have ever been able to get absolutely authentic information, was shot in the forest of Glenmore on October 2nd, 1877, by the present Lord Greville while on a visit to the late Earl of Stamford. It was a wood deer of eight good points and weighing *thirty-three* stone quite clean.

Stags usually stay with the hinds till they are three years old, when they quit the nursery and go off to join their big brothers in the high hills. One of the most remarkable features of stag life is the extraordinary rapid growth of the horns. These are usually shed some time in the month of March, and by the end of July are again fully grown, though covered with velvet. A healthy six year old beast will in about four months shoot out some *twelve feet* of horns, for, measuring all the points of a royal head which I once laid low, I found that the total length of horn came to 140½ inches. During the month of August the velvet is shed and the horns begin to appear in all their wild and beautiful outlines, and this period having been reached, the stag is now fair game for the stalker and his gentleman, and should either of them have derived pleasure or profit from the perusal of this short essay I shall indeed be flattered.

AUGUSTUS GRIMBLE.

Bibliography.—*Forest Sketches: Deer Stalking and other Sports in the Highlands Fifty Years Ago* (Edmonston and Douglas, 1865, 15/-); *Deer Stalking and other Sports in the Highlands Fifty Years Ago*, Wm. Scrope (Edin., 1865); *Encyclopædia of Rural Sports*, Blaine (Longmans, 1870, 21/-); *Handbook of Deer Stalking*, Alex. Macrae (Blackwood, 1880, 3/6); *On the Grampian Hills*, F. F. Whitehurst (Tinsley, 1882, 7/6); *The Still Hunter: Practical Treatise on Deer Stalking*, T. S. Van Dyke (New York, 1882, 10/6); *Days of Deer Stalking in the Scottish Highlands*, Wm. Scrope (1838, 1st ed.; Hamilton, 1883, 12/6); *Sport: Fox Hunting, Deer Stalking, &c.*, W. Bromley Davenport (Chapman, 1885, 21/-, 6/-, 3/6); *Shooting*, Lord Walsingham and Sir R. Payne-Gallwey (Bad. Lib. 2 vols., Longmans, 1886); *Deer Stalking*, Aug. Grimble (Chapman, 1886, 6/-); *Rural Sports*, "Stonehenge" (Warne, 1886, 21/-); *The Moor and the Loch*, J. Colquhoun (Blackwood, 1888, 26/- and 21/-); *Short Sketches of the Wild Sports and Nat. Hist. of the Scottish Highlands*, C. W. G. St. John (Hamilton, 1888, 4/6); *Out-of-Door Sports in Scotland*, "Ellangowan" (W. H. Allen, 1889, 7/6); *Sportsman and Naturalist's Tour in Sutherlandshire*, C. W. G. St. John (Simpkin, 1891, 4/6); *Deer Stalking in the Highlands of Scotland*, H. H. Crealock (Longmans, 1892, 126/-); *Forays among Salmon and Deer*, J. Conway (Morison, Glasgow, 1893, 4/6); *Deer Stalking*, in "The Red Deer," Fur and Feather Series, Cameron of Lochiel (Longmans, 1896, 5/-); *Scotch Deerhounds and their Masters*, G. Cupples (Blackwood, 1894, 30/-); *Highland Sport*, Aug. Grimble (Chapman, 1894, 42/-); *The Deer Forests of Scotland*, Aug. Grimble (Kegan Paul, 1896, 50/-).

DEERSTALKING IN THE CAUCASUS

—The sportsman who wishes to add to his numerous trophies that of a Caucasian stag, must make up his mind that deerstalking in the Caucasus differs entirely from deerstalking in the Scotch Highlands, where the beginner usually gets his first shot. By the Caucasus is meant more particularly the Kouban district, which extends, northwards of the main range, between the Black Sea and the Rostov-Wladikavkaz Railway; for in this part, undoubtedly, are to be found the finest heads and largest animals of the kind. There everything seems in their favour: rich Alpine pastures above, long healthy grass below, dense virgin woods with tall fern undergrowth, and sunny glades in their midst, deep valleys with precipitous timber-covered cliffs on either side, and clear trout streams flowing at their bottom.

The reader can easily understand the complete difference between Scotch and Caucasian stalking. In Scotland, after a luxurious breakfast, you start, generally on horseback, with an experienced stalker at your heels, and sometimes with numerous gillies behind with luncheon baskets and deer-saddles; in the Caucasus, accompanied by half-wild natives, with a bit of bread and cheese in your pocket, starting from camp before sunrise and generally on foot, you have to toil up steep ravines for hours through dense underwood, through wild blackcurrant or raspberry bushes, stopping now and then to take breath, and to look up at the coveted ridge which seems as far from you as when you started. Then, picking yourself up, you continue your acrobatic performance over huge fallen trees that have been lying there for years and years, and into which you plunge knee-deep until, utterly exhausted, you reach a spot whence you "may" hear one of those magnificent calls which make your heart leap for joy! In Scotland your pony brings you to the high grounds, whence you begin spying and usually very soon discover several herds grazing on the other side of a corrie; you only have to pick out the best head, and sometimes wait till they feed towards an easier spot. If you score a miss, you generally get a second chance on your way home. In the Caucasus, owing to forests covering the greater part of the ground, telescopes are hardly of any use, and field glasses come in much handier. On reaching the timber line, or some place below it, you unsling your rifle, which has been seeming to you an eighty-ton gun, and finally sit down to listen. You may lie there the whole day without hearing a single call; or if you do, the stag may be at such a distance that you cannot possibly get back to camp before nightfall. If the animal is within reach, you may try the stalk and get within a hundred yards of him, yet never see him, for if a stray whiff of your wind (wind being very shifty in the Caucasus) reaches his nostrils, you will probably not catch sight of him at all; bending his head back so as to keep his antlers well out of the way, he will sneak off through the bushes without the slightest noise, as if he were not larger than a fox. I have been myself within thirty yards of a roaring stag, the wind as I thought being steady, and yet I could neither see him nor hear him go. Motionless I waited for a good hour after he had stopped calling, thinking he was still close at hand, while he was perhaps already miles away. My hunter, whom I had left some way off, told me afterwards that he had seen the animal come out of the brushwood in a crouching position, with his horns laid along his back, and make off in this manner till he probably thought himself safe, when he suddenly galloped away. On the other hand, the finest trophy obtained in the autumn of 1895 by one of our party was a twenty-one pointer (span 58½ in., girth between bez and trez 8 in., rosette $11\frac{1}{2}$ in., length along outer curve $44\frac{1}{2}$ in., length of brow antlers 21 in., weight before cleaning $21\frac{1}{2}$ puds, *i.e.* 53 st. 4 lbs.), killed while asleep at the distance of twenty yards! Another one that year, also a very good head, was bagged in the same way.

The Caucasian stag is a most capricious beast; in some seasons, as I was told by native hunters, he will not call at all, in others he will scarcely stop roaring the whole day, excepting between 1 and 3 p.m. during the greatest heat. One year, as I myself can testify, stags would not call properly, *i.e.* they would only call every half hour or so; the weather being very fine, the natives suggested that it was owing to the intense heat. Gradually the temperature changed from day to day until the ground was everywhere covered by a couple of feet of snow. Stags, nevertheless, did not improve their calling. We left the hills that year on September 28th, and

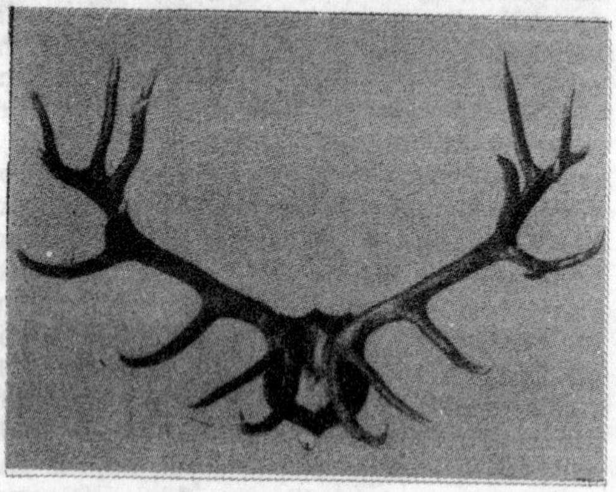

A Record Head.

very likely they began after our premature departure. Another curious fact I noticed one year was that although the roaring was fairly good at one of our early camps, for four or five days afterwards not a call was to be heard, although the weather was as settled as could be wished. Eventually they began again, but nobody could account for this interval of silence. From this it will be apparent that deer-stalking in the Caucasus can only take place during the rutting time, which usually lasts a month, beginning from the middle of September, although, according to the difference of seasons and other unknown factors—to the moon, as natives often say,—it may begin earlier, or end later. I have occasionally tried wandering about the woods in search of stags while they were not calling, and although numerous fresh tracks were to be seen everywhere, such as twigs and young trees stripped of their bark, or places where they had been scraping, although even the strong scent emitted during the rutting-time was perceptible, I never had the good luck to come upon one in this manner.

In winter, deer come down from high ground in search of food, sometimes to the vicinity of Cossack villages, where they are unsparingly slaughtered, hinds and all, by native hunters, who at that time of year have no other occupation, and are continually on the look out for them. They feed on the meat, make straps of the hide, and sell the horns, or convert them into dagger handles. An average of ten roubles (£1 sterling) is what they can get out of a stag, and for that sum many an inhabitant of the Caucasus would not mind dismissing his neighbour.

At the present time the localities where stags are most numerous are in the preserves of His Imperial Highness the Grand Duke Sergius Mikhailovitch, son of the Grand Duke Michael, formerly Viceroy of the Caucasus. His shooting grounds stretch over an area of 400,000 acres, taking in all the country north-westwards of the larger Laba, the main range being its boundary to the south. The sportsman would therefore have to look eastwards towards Mount Elbruz in the numerous parallel valleys of the Kouban tributaries. Unfortunately, unless strict measures be shortly taken, and game laws reinforced, deer will rapidly decrease, and perhaps soon entirely disappear, in the unpreserved grounds of the Caucasus.

While out in the Kouban district last year, I had ample opportunity to convince myself of the abundance of poachers, who mostly come over the main range from the Black Sea side, and deliberately shoot every animal that comes within range of their rifle; in fact I do not exaggerate when I say that I found nearly as many tracks of hunters in the woods as I did of stags. A friend of mine actually stalked a herd of Ibex simultaneously with one of those poachers who was approaching the same herd from a different direction, and eventually got the first shot. Government foresters themselves, buried as they are in those wilds, have the right of shooting any beast they come across for their living, and, distances being out of proportion to their number, they cannot possibly stop unlawful proceedings. Moreover, with the view of encouraging horse and cattle breeding in the Caucasus, an Ukase of the Emperor has given natives the right, in consideration of a small tribute, to turn all their horses, sheep and cattle, during the summer months on to the Alpine pastures. At the head of every valley a large brown patch on the grass denotes the presence in the neighbourhood of a few thousand sheep and several shepherds, who not only make noise enough with their songs, but also bring their wretched guns and occasionally wound an animal, which goes away to die, perhaps at some distance. This being the case, the stags are evidently frightened out of their wits by the noise and constant traffic, and consequently will only roar—if a few grunts can be called roaring

—at night time, taking the greatest precautions, and ceasing before 4 a.m.; in the daytime not a sound is to be heard from them. I noticed this fact in the autumn of 1896, when we camped six weeks in the hills during the best time and never got a single shot, but of course it may have been an exceptionally bad year. I have remarked that as a rule during the rutting-time Caucasian stags are most likely to be found in glades just under high wooded ridges, or among willow trees on the timber line; but I have also often heard stags call low down by the streams, or half way up steep banks of ravines.

Shells, tin horns, and other instruments are frequently used for calling stags, though natives never employ anything but the dry stems of large *Umbelliferæ*, from which they cut a short thick cylinder, and with it imitate very successfully the stag's call.

Excepting on the Grand Duke's grounds, where a numerous staff of "jägers" strictly protect the game from incursions of poachers and keep down vermin, including bears, of which they destroy an average of seventy a year, stags are growing very scarce, and the sportsman who succeeds in getting two or three shots during the whole rutting season, may consider himself fairly fortunate. But then he may obtain a trophy of which he may be justly proud! As already stated, the largest and finest heads are to be found in the district about Kouban. There are said to be large deer in Daghestan, but I have never seen a really good head that was procured there. I have shot a good twelve-pointer to the south of the main range in the Borjom District, but there can be no comparison with our Kouban trophies of 1895, amongst which, for instance, six out of seven heads measured above 45 in. in length and above 7 in. in girth between bez and trez tines, most of them being 14 and 16 pointers. These were shot in the Grand Duke's preserves. The keepers told me that in winter they often see herds of from 15 to 20 head lying on the snow, 24 pointers being not uncommon amongst them, and the size of the antlers of unusual dimensions.

I always rely on the experience of native hunters to judge a stag by his voice, and am inclined to believe that they are rarely mistaken. What I noticed was that loud, frequent calls seldom denote heavy old animals, while low deep grunts, cautiously delivered and hardly perceptible at a great distance, are generally emitted from the throat of a "royal." Locating the sound, especially of the latter, which is singularly ventriloquial, is not an easy task. It requires a great deal of practice and knowledge of the ground, every boulder changing the direction of the sound. Moreover, Caucasian valleys being very deep, with steep lateral hollows, and very precipitous cliffs, the echo is naturally greater and more apt to puzzle one. I have several times been a victim of this deceit. I remember once, after a hard day's crawling through fallen timber, towards evening I suddenly heard a loud challenge, at what I considered a hundred yards below me; so crept down cautiously in the direction of the voice! As I approached, the calls seemed to come from further and further till they completely ceased. Having reached the bottom of the ravine and the place being clear of trees, I looked around me, but seeing no signs of stag, and light growing dim, I was about to give up the chase, when up started a fine old beast twenty yards off, from behind a thick stump.

My companion explained to me that this stag had been probably standing when his voice had seemed so near to us, after which he lay down behind the stump; this was enough entirely to alter the direction of the sound and make us think that he had gone at least 500 yards away.

The inhabitants of those parts of the Caucasus are either Cossacks, Russian settlers since the Caucasian War, or regular natives belonging to different tribes; all Mahommedans having been for centuries under Turkish dominion. When passing through a village your guide will unfailingly say, either "This is a Cossack Stanitza" (village) or "This is an Asiatic one," meaning that it is inhabited by Russians or by Mahommedans. This classification of natives in two groups is plainly marked by a difference of language and altogether different customs and mode of living. These peculiarities are pointed out in order that the sportsman who intends to camp-out in the hills for a month may see the necessity for choosing reliable companions. "Asiatics" are undoubtedly the laziest and most unwilling creatures imaginable, but on the other hand they are better mountaineers than the Cossacks, and make up the contingent of native hunters. The dilemma may be solved by taking out Cossacks for camp work and Asiatics for hunting, although you can never be sure that they will not refuse to follow you. On our last trip we actually had to hire a cook for our Asiatic staff, otherwise they refused to go. These fellows being inveterate thieves, precaution should be taken to keep one's goods constantly under key. Their ponies are considerably better: as durable as can be, accustomed to hard mountain work, the deepest ridges being accessible to them. Their regulation load is 200 lbs., though their proprietors never cease to grumble, insisting that they are too heavily laden. One rouble (2*s.*) a day for a man, and as much for each horse, is what I have generally paid, though, to judge by their satisfaction, it is probably too much; the same fee for the hunters with an occasional tip at the end according to behaviour. One man usually leads two ponies; our attempts to make them take three ponies each were unsuccessful—in fact we were nearly induced last year to mount the men, the district "Ataman," or chief, having told us that they would never consent to go on foot!

From London *via* Vienna eighty hours will bring you to Odessa, whence ships sail twice a week or more to Novorossisk, and another eight hours will carry you to the Rostov-Vladikavkaz Railway, whence one can branch off for the hills at Armavir, Nevinomisk, or any other station in the neighbourhood. There are plenty of villages at the foot of the hills where one can find some sort of lodging, and ponies may be obtained everywhere. The best stalking grounds beyond the Grand Duke's preserves are the Urup and Zelentchuk Valleys up to the main range, though they will probably be preserved within a short time. The sportsman will then have to try the valleys eastwards, viz. the Teberda and Aksaout Valleys, which hold not only stags, but also Ibex, especially towards the sources of their tributaries, such as the river Marko and others.

Regarding the battery to take out, every sportsman has of course his own ideas on the subject. It is impossible to point out why a Mannlicher is better than a Mauser, or the latter worse than a ·300 Express. Some prefer one pattern, some another. For my part I have invariably taken out with me a pair of Purdey's ·303's, double barrelled and hammerless (which have proved very useful at long ranges), as well as a ·450 magnum Express for stags.

I have never been able to make up my mind to shoot the large Caucasian stag with a ·303, and yet it is beyond doubt that, if hit in the forepart, the stag will fall as well to a ·303 bullet as to a ·577 one. The ·303 has the advantage of a flat trajectory and therefore possesses greater accuracy—and long shots are often required; yet I cannot help thinking that it is too small a bore for so large an animal. For Chamois, Ibex, or Mouflon, it is an invaluable weapon, the ·450 magnum doing well for deer.

In conclusion I may observe that although sport may be difficult, game scarce, and autumn weather showery and cold, it is nevertheless a most enjoyable trip, if only patience be rewarded by some fine Caucasian trophy.

E. DEMIDOFF PRINCE SAN-DONATO.

DOGS—Although much ingenuity has been displayed in endeavouring to prove the origin of the domestic dog from various crosses between so-called wild dogs, wolves, foxes, &c., the matter is still one of supposition. The dog (*canis familiaris*) is a natural development, and the varieties were produced primarily by accident, by selection, by the surroundings under which they have lived, such as climate, food, training, &c.; and latterly by selection only. All facts and researches prove that in various parts of the world and in various ages, different species or varieties of the wild *canidæ* were gradually brought into a state of domestication, and therefrom the dog, as we know him now, has been developed—a process which has taken many thousand years to perfect.

Only **Sporting Dogs**, or such as are used for the purposes of giving amusement to their owners, or for providing them with food, are dealt with here; and no doubt this "sporting division," if it may be so called, is much older, and dates much further back, than such animals as are used for pets, even than those which have been trained to guard the flocks, or used as beasts of burden, as food, or in the many other duties in which they have been found valuable. Primeval man had his dogs, semi-wild creatures no doubt, but they assisted him in the chase which was to provide him with food. When more domesticated, they were taught to guard the sheep and cattle. At the present time it may be noticed that in the uncivilised countries the dogs still remain semi-domesticated; at the same time they more closely resemble what the original dog must have been than do any of the varieties of the canine races of Great Britain and of other civilised countries.

The original dog was somewhat wolf-like or fox-like in appearance. He had a close, woolly, weather-resisting coat. By cultivation and by a change of living, this coat gradually changed until it became almost smooth. At the same time pace was developed in order that the wolf and the stag could be caught; and to obtain this pace and power a gradual evolution took place, so that in some of the more civilised countries the dog became hound-like, or similar in shape to the modern greyhound. Thus, most of the Assyrian sculptures, which are three or four thousand years old, represent dogs of this type. Some few are stronger and more massive, bearing a resemblance to the old English mastiff strain and that of the German boarhound. The longer-coated dogs are an unnatural development, caused by crossing and inter-breeding from the smooth dogs which have had a tendency to grow long hair. These long coats are purely of such manufacture; in many cases they are not sufficiently close to be weather-protecting, but are rather ornamental than useful. The natural weather-resisting coat was, and still is, close, thick, soft, and more like flannel in appearance, and to the touch, than anything else. This kind of coat will be developed on any smooth-coated dog kept in a cold damp kennel, or allowed to sleep out and rough it as his progenitors had to do. The *Hounds*, which include such dogs as hunt on the ground and do not feel for the taint of scent in the air, are perhaps the most important group, and many varieties of them have been produced in various countries.

Cropping—This is cutting the ears of dogs in order that they may stand erect in a point, or entirely removing the ears on an animal used

for fighting purposes. Happily this cruelty, seldom perpetrated upon sporting dogs, has been discontinued in this country. It however prevails elsewhere. In 1895 Robert Carling and his wife were sentenced to a term of imprisonment for cropping an Irish terrier; and following this the Kennel Club decided that no dog, if cropped after March 1895, can win a prize at a show under their rules. So far as Irish terriers were concerned a similar rule had, at the instigation of the Irish Terrier Club, been passed, the date being after December 1889.

Dew Claws—These may be removed or allowed to remain; they are however unsightly and liable to be troublesome to the dog when working. They occasionally appear upon the front legs as well as upon the hind ones. In their removal a pair of strong, sharp scissors are required, and the operation is best performed when the puppy is about three weeks old and suckling on the dam, whose tongue will soon heal the sores.

Docking or Tail Cutting—It is the custom to shorten the tails of certain dogs in order to prevent injury thereto when they are hunting in coverts and thick undergrowths. The spaniels and German griffons undergo the operation, which ought to be performed in early puppyhood, when a fortnight old, when with the dam. The hair should be turned back, and about one-half the tail taken off with a pair of sharp scissors. The practice once obtained of biting off the tail with the teeth.

Dog Clubs—Dog clubs were formed to look after the interests of the dog, especially in so far as their show career is concerned. The first Club was the *Kennel Club*, established in 1874. It seeks to occupy in the kennel world a similar position to that occupied by the Jockey Club with relation to the Turf. The entry fee is five guineas, and the annual subscription five guineas. It publishes annually a stud book, monthly a journal called the *Kennel Gazette*, and besides its ordinary members has "Associates," who are admitted at a much reduced fee. The latter are not allowed the advantages of the Club house. The Kennel Club holds a show each year, and every dog exhibited thereat, or at any other show in which their rules are enforced, has to be registered, the fee for which is one shilling. Mr. S. E. Shirley, Ettington Park, Stratford-on-Avon, is the president of the club, and Mr. W. W. Aspinall, 27 Old Burlington Street, London, W., the secretary. There are also the Scottish Kennel Club, the Irish Kennel Association, and the Ladies' Kennel Association. The two first-named have no particularly distinguishing feature, but hold shows annually. The last also arranges a show at which only ladies can exhibit. It has a Club house at 5 Great St. James Street, Bedford Row, London, a monthly magazine called the *Ladies' Kennel Journal*, and it looks after the interests of all dogs with which ladies are concerned. Mrs. Stennard Robinson is the secretary. Then there is the old-established National Society for the Improvement of Sporting Dogs, whose headquarters are at Shrewsbury, and which holds field trials annually. The more recently formed International Pointer and Setter Society is conducted on much the same, though perhaps on more inclusive, lines. Most varieties of the dog have specialist clubs, some one, others more. The Fox Terrier Club (which publishes monthly the *Fox Terrier Chronicle*), the English Setter Club, the Irish Setter Club, the Spaniel Club, the Sporting Spaniel Club, the Deerhound Club, the Beagle Club, the Irish Wolfhound Club, the Borzoi Club, the curly-coated Retriever Club, the Dandie Dinmont Club, the Scottish Terrier Club, the Welsh Terrier Club, the Irish Terrier Club, and the Airedale Terrier Club are the most important. There is also an Association of Bloodhound breeders. The subscriptions vary in amount from five shillings to twenty-one shillings annually. The oldest of the specialist clubs for sporting dogs is that for Fox Terriers, which was instituted in 1876, whilst the youngest is the Sporting Spaniel Club, established early in 1897. There is also an American Kennel Club and similar establishments in France, Russia, Germany, Belgium, and in other continental countries.

Field Trials—These are trials instituted for the improvement of sporting dogs—pointers and setters in particular. Retriever trials were run at Vaynol Park in 1871–2, but have since been discontinued. In America, beagle and spaniel trials take place, but here they have not yet been tried. Field Trials for pointers and setters are amongst our most important sporting functions. In 1896 five such meetings were held, viz., by the Kennel Club, by the National Association, and by the English Setter Club in the spring over partridges; by the International Pointer and Setter Society, and by the Irish Setter Club in the autumn over grouse. The first four of these are, at any rate, likely to be continued annually. The work done by the dogs on these occasions is generally of high class — nose, pace, natural ability, training, staunchness, style, quartering and beating out the ground, game-finding, and general behaviour being taken into consideration by the judges who make the awards. The first Field Trial meeting ever held in this country took place in April 1865, over Mr. W. H. Whitbread's Bedfordshire estate at Southhill. In 1894 an autumn meeting was held over the late Mr. Heywood Lonsdale's shootings in Scotland, and with this exception all the field trials have taken place either in the Midland or Southern counties, in Ireland, or in Wales. Similar gatherings are held on the Continent and in America.

Licenses—In England, Scotland and Wales

the license for each dog is *7s. 6d.* Puppies under six months old, dogs used solely for the purpose of tending sheep and cattle on a farm or owned by shepherds, and such as are used by blind persons for their guidance, are exempt, but application for exemption has to be made to the local authority. In Ireland each license is *2s. 6d.*, and in the Isle of Man one guinea.

Muzzling—The Board of Agriculture and local authorities have the power to issue compulsory orders compelling all dogs to be muzzled, under certain penalties. When such orders are issued, they are only in force in that locality in which the authority has jurisdiction; but the Board of Agriculture can issue an extended order, which takes precedence over anything local. Other local orders may be issued, the most important of which makes it compulsory for each dog to wear a collar upon which the name and address of his owner is legibly inscribed. A system of registration has been adopted in Glasgow, where each dog has to be licensed, and when the license is obtained, a metal tablet is purchased which bears a number corresponding with that on the license. This tablet has to be worn on the dog's collar. At the time of writing this (1897) some alteration in the general licensing system of dogs appears to be pending, but so far the "regulation" wire muzzle is required. In districts where the muzzling order is in force, exemptions are made with regard to hounds and to other dogs when actually being used in sport.

Registration.—The Kennel Club has adopted a system of registration; the fee is one shilling per dog, for which the owner is entitled to select a name not already appropriated, and this is duly published in the *Kennel Gazette*, the official organ. No dog can compete at any show held under the Kennel Club rules unless it has been previously registered. There is an additional fee of 2s. 6d. to pay when the owner of an already registered dog wishes to change its name. A bitch lent for breeding purposes has to be duly registered with the Kennel Club, the fee for this being 5s.

Shows—Since their first institution at Newcastle-on-Tyne, June 28—29, 1859, when there were sixty entries, dog shows have become an institution in the land. The first show was confined to pointers and setters; a leading show at the present day may have anything from a couple of hundred to four or five hundred classes, and include upwards of seventy varieties of the dog. Birmingham has always held a great show, and it is the oldest of modern fixtures, having been established in November 1859, and held annually ever since. It is called the National Show, and a win thereat is considered the blue ribbon of the canine world. Equal to Birmingham, and even larger, is that show held by the Kennel Club, which now seems to be fixed at the Crystal Palace, Sydenham. This club has now held shows of its own since June 1873, at the Agricultural Hall and elsewhere. Until 1895, it was the custom for the Kennel Club to hold two shows annually. Edinburgh, Manchester, Liverpool, Darlington, Brighton, indeed almost all our large centres, hold or have held exhibitions of dogs, whilst private individuals have been successful in a similar manner. Mr. C. Cruft, at the Agricultural Hall, Islington, by liberal classification, has obtained enormous entries. The greatest number of dogs ever "benched" at any show was at Islington in 1863, when, with only seventy-three classes provided, 1,678 entries were obtained. Many of these entries included braces of pointer and setter puppies; couples and three couples of hounds, harriers and foxhounds, swelling the total number of dogs to about 2,100, a record which has not been reached since, although the classes are now more than quadrupled. In those early days no dog was allowed to compete in more than one class; now the arrangements are such that exhibitors are encouraged to enter one dog in as many classes as possible. The entry-fees are higher now than then, and with the exception of challenge cups, which are not for open competition, the individual prizes are lower than formerly, although more of them can be won. Another important show is that for foxhounds, harriers, and beagles, annually held in summer at Peterborough. Some of the specialist societies arrange shows of their own, those under the auspices of the Fox Terrier Club being the most important, and that body has held one or more shows annually since its establishment in 1876. Other clubs, not wealthy enough to run their own specialist gatherings, give extra support to the more comprehensive exhibitions. It may be estimated that about four hundred dog shows are held in the three kingdoms annually, many of them, however, of but local interest, whilst others take place in connection with the district agricultural societies.

Trimming or Faking.—This is a common but dishonest practice performed on a dog to make it appear better than it actually is. So far as sporting dogs are concerned it is confined to the removal of the coat by plucking when it is too heavy, curling and pulling curly coated retrievers, wetting the coats of the latter and singeing, rubbing, or in other ways "doctoring" a pointer's tail in order to make it look finer and smaller than nature had intended it. Cases have been known where tails have been "nicked," or cut underneath to make their carriage more perfect, and it used to be the custom to cut underneath the ears of some terriers in order that they might "drop" in the fashion required. When the latter is required now, plaisters and weights are used when the dog is young, and being continually worn give the ears a downward carriage. There are special rules of the Kennel

Club which deal with this matter, and they make cutting, singeing, damping, oiling, plucking, &c., disqualifications.

Hounds.

Beagle—The beagle, though varying much in size, is, generally speaking, the smallest of our hunting hounds, and is divided into many varieties. There is the "Kerry Beagle," a large black-and-tan hound, which has been kept for many generations near Killarney and in other parts of Ireland. The only pack now existent is that of Mr. Clement Ryan, of Emly, co. Tipperary. The Kerry Beagle is not unlike a miniature bloodhound, and is generally from 22 inches to 24 inches in height at the shoulders.

The beagle proper is usually hound-marked and "blue-mottled," the latter a very pretty colour; it should not stand more than 15 inches in height at the shoulders. In addition to the Kerry Beagle already alluded to, there are some smaller hounds of about 14 inches, black-and-tan in colour; there are others, very rare, fawn or wheaten in colour, with hard wiry coats. When classes are provided for beagles at our dog shows, they should be sub-divided into such as are between 12 inches and 15 inches in height, and those below 12 inches. The smaller sizes are known as rabbit beagles, and from time to time very pretty specimens from 9 inches and upwards in height have been produced. The terms "toy" beagles and "sleeve" or "pocket" beagles ought not to be used, the latter originating from a story that a few generations ago it was customary to take beagles to the meet in the pockets of the master and hunters, whilst it has been (also erroneously) stated that Queen Elizabeth had a pack of beagles which could be carried in a glove. The beagle, which has a stud book provided, ought to be built on the lines of a miniature foxhound, and whilst the majority are smooth coated, there is also a rough-coated variety. In the United States and Canada the beagle is more popular than in this country, and competitive working trials are often arranged, in which perhaps a score of little hounds take part. (*See* Hunting.)

Bloodhound—This hound, also known as the Sleuth hound, is the largest of all the variety which hunt by scent, the male varying in weight from 85 lbs. to 110 lbs., the female from 95 lbs. to 100 lbs., their respective heights at the shoulder being from 25 to 27 inches and from 23 to 25 inches respectively. His colour is black-and-tan, brown (or liver-coloured) and tan, sometimes flecked with white or with "badger-coloured" hairs. The nature of the bloodhound is kindly and sympathetic, by no means of that ferocity which his name implies, and which seems by common consent to have been ascribed to him. He makes a nice companion, and is far less ferocious than almost any of the big dogs — Newfoundlands, St. Bernards, Mastiffs, &c. His progenitor may have been the Lymer of Gaston or the Talbot of other earlier writers. Originally intended to hunt the larger game—the stag and such like—he was trained to hunt man, and by a continual process of selection he now naturally does the latter. An ordinary sporting puppy will commence to hunt hares, rabbits, &c., but a blood hound puppy's natural bent is to hunt man—a stranger, and not his master, as other young dogs will do. To this faculty he, no doubt, owes his bad reputation, which is gradually being removed, for when he has "hunted his man" to "tree" or elsewhere, he will not worry him to death, as has been said, but either runs up to him to be fondled, or "bays" him—*i.e.*, stands back and barks. The hounds which were said to hunt slaves in the Southern States of America were foxhounds and not bloodhounds, and the former on scent are much the more ferocious of the two. Extraordinary stories are told of

Bloodhound.

the bloodhound's capacity for hunting the line of a man, on whose scent he has been laid, through crowded thoroughfares. He cannot do this, and therefore as an aid to the detection of criminals in busy centres he is useless. In country places he may be used with advantage by the police to assist in the capture of poachers, burglars, and other law-breakers, for, being laid on the scent, even if it is several hours old, he can generally make it out, though should it be too much foiled by others crossing it, or by cattle, sheep, and horses, the hound is at a loss. He used to be employed on the borders against robbers and other offenders, and has been tried unsuccessfully in London and the provinces in cases of murder. In crossing with other hounds he has been found useful, inasmuch as he has improved their olfactory organs and made their voices more melodious. A good bloodhound, when properly trained, ought to be able to hunt what is called the "clean boot"—*i.e.*, hunt a man who has not had his boots smeared with blood or any concocted ingredient. About seven years ago several "bloodhound trials" were run in London, near Boxmoor, Dublin, &c., the quarry being men or lads; but although so far successful. they did not seem likely to serve any useful purpose, so were discontinued, and have not been revived since. Packs of bloodhounds have been used for stag-hunting, the last of these being Lord Wolverton's, who, about twenty years since, hunted the "carted deer" with them in Dorsetshire. At present the bloodhound is mostly valued as a show dog and as a companion, but he will always be found useful as a cross with other sporting dogs when it is sought to improve the size, nose, and voice of the latter. It is interesting to note that, although in ears, wrinkles, head, and other "fancy" points the bloodhound has been much improved of late years, this has not been done at the expense of other more important attributes. In April, 1897, an association of bloodhound breeders was formed in London, with the object of popularising the variety, especially so far as using it for the detection of criminals is concerned. In certain States of North America bloodhounds are kept in connection with the penitentiaries or gaols, to assist in the capture of escaped prisoners.

Brach (*Brache*, *Rache*)—This name, now obsolete, was by early writers used to describe a hound or any dog which hunted by scent. Sometimes it was applied to a bitch or female hound, but appears to have been given also somewhat indiscriminately to hounds in general. The earliest appearance of the name appears in the Arthurian Legend of Sir Gavaine and the Green Knight (1340). "Braches bayed therefore and breme (loud) noise made." In *Household Expenses* (1467), "a young brasch of halfe yere holde." Caxton *Emydos* (1490), "Theyr braches, retches and bloodehoundes." Carew (1594), "A brache to hunt and bring the game to his hand." Markham—Count. Content.(1611), "When your bratche is near whelping you shall separate her from other hounds," and in his *Gentleman's Recreations* the same writer says, "brach, a mannerly name for a bitch hound." Shakespeare makes several allusions to the brach: "Brach Merryman, the poor cur, is imbost;" "Couple Clouder with the deep-mouthed brach;" "I had rather hear Lady, my brach, howl in Irish;" "When Achilles' brach bids me:" "Hound or spaniel, brach or lym." Caius describes brache or rache as the "shee" sex. In border history the brach was known: "In Gillsland was that Brachell bred, Sikyr of scent, to follow him that fled." Again: "But this sleuth brach," both evidently in allusion to the bloodhound of that day. Jameson, in his Scottish dictionary, defines brachell as a hound employed to discover and pursue game by scent. In Spencer's well-known ballad "Gelert" we have: "And many a brach and many a hound obeyed Llewellyn's horn." Perhaps "poetic license" allowed him to use the word to signify another dog than a hound. Other writers have recognised in the brach the beagle and harrier.

Deerhound—This extremely fine hound, so nearly allied to the greyhound, is often erroneously called the staghound. He is the Scottish deerhound pure and simple, sagacious, intelligent, and in his rough affection and somewhat rugged appearance anything but uncharacteristic of his country. Probably the earliest mention we have of the Scottish deerhound appears in Hector Boece's History of Scotland, a peculiar work, inasmuch as, originally written in Latin, and printed in France 1526-7, it was translated into English by royal command in 1531. Here a story is mentioned that certain Picts went to hunt with the King of Scots at Craithlint. The hounds of the latter so proved their vast superiority to those of the former that the Picts were astonished. To console them the king presented them with both dogs and bitches of the best strains, but, not being contented therewith, the Picts stole one of the king's favourite hounds. The thieves were chased and overtaken; a great fight took place, in which a hundred Picts were slain and threescore gentlemen of the other side, besides a great number of commoners; and of the latter it was said that they had not known what the fight was all about. The hound was recovered. The Scottish nobles have from that time to the present carefully preserved their strains of deerhounds, which were originally used for the purpose of aids in

DEERHOUND.

deer-stalking and in coursing deer. Deer-coursing is not followed now, and retrievers and collies are used in most forests in preference, as disturbing the ground less, and not being so liable to drive the deer out of bounds. At present, it is doubtful whether there are in all a dozen forests where the deerhound is kept for purely sporting purposes, and some recent statistics obtained show that, out of sixty forests, Scottish deerhounds were used only in about seven. The hound will, however, survive, if only as a purely fancy dog and as a companion, for he is good-tempered, handsome, and sensible, and, when brought up and trained to live in the house or in the stable, no dog is more faithful, and his noble bearing and dark-coloured almond-shaped eyes are always objects of admiration. Of late, Englishmen have paid greater attention to the improvement of the deerhound so far as appearance is concerned, and in all cases when Scottish kennels have been dispersed by auction in London, Englishmen have secured the plums. Prices have ruled small, and at a recent auction a number of well-bred and good-looking deerhounds brought little more than a number of mongrel terriers would have realised, a grand old stud-hound of great character failing to attract a higher bid than a solitary one of a sovereign. This was at the sale of the Duke of Buccleuch's hounds at Aldridge's, London, in 1895. The deerhound should in colour be either brindled in various shades, or blue or fawn, even inclining to red; white is detrimental, though a little is often found on the chest and feet. Occasionally white deerhounds have been produced, or at any rate very pale fawns, but a purely black specimen has not come under notice. The brindles are considered best, and are perhaps most attractive, but many persons prefer a fawn dog, a hue which somehow or other appears to enhance the elegance of the outline of the hounds. The very large and heavily made dogs are not desirable, as, though they may be better able to hold a stag, they are much more liable to cut themselves on the rocks and loose stones than are the lighter hounds. A good male specimen should not stand more than 30 inches at the shoulders, a bitch a couple of inches less; a dog may weigh between 80 lbs. and 90 lbs., a bitch from 70 lbs. to 80 lbs. These figures are taken from well-known specimens of the modern hound which have secured leading honours at our chief shows. Many stories are told of the endurance of the Scottish deerhound; he can run on scent as well as by sight, and is mute in the chase, but when his quarry is brought to "bay" the hound opens, and by his baying or barking attracts his master, who soon gives the *coup de grâce* to a noble stag. At all well-regulated shows with any pretensions to comprehensiveness, classes for deerhounds are provided; but for some reason or other, which can only arise from the vagaries of fashion, he is not a popular dog, and where a St. Bernard approaching perfection might be sold for anything between £200 and £500, a deerhound of equal merit would not realise more than from £50 to £100, and nearer the former figure than the latter.

Foxhound—It has been said that the foxhound has been so carefully bred as to be at the present time the most perfect specimen of the canine race extant. That he is the most valuable no one will deny. He is built in a manner which ensures speed and stamina, and in both respects he cannot be excelled. He is not often seen on our show benches, though when classes are provided for him he is sure to attract attention. There is a foxhound show held at Peterborough each year, which is largely attended; and there representatives of the leading packs are always to be seen. A dog hound weighs from 70 lbs. to 80 lbs., whilst a bitch weighs from 60 lb. to 70 lb. As to the value of a pack of foxhounds, great variation is found. Squire Osbaldiston's pack was sold at Tattersall's in 1840 for 5,219 guineas, whilst the Haydon in 1884 went for 15 guineas; but these are the extremes. A lightly made foxhound is specially bred in the north of England, where it is used for "trail-hunting." In various parts of the world the

FOXHOUND.

foxhound has been introduced. In the United States it is popular, in Canada likewise. The Virginian hound is less heavily built than our foxhound, has longer and more pendulous ears, and certainly inclines to the bloodhound type. (*See* HUNTING.)

Greyhound—There can be no doubt that the greyhound is the oldest variety of hound which we possess, and the many sculptures which have reached us from the East prove his very ancient lineage. The greyhound was probably introduced into this country when the "Scoto-Celts settled in Scotland and Ireland from Europe." There is a MS. drawing extant of a Saxon with two greyhounds and his henchman, date about the ninth century. Since that period it has altered less than any other family of the dog in type, however it may have improved in pace. The greyhound is one of the most graceful and elegant varieties of the canine race, but he is seldom used as a companion, and seems out of place on the benches at our dog shows, where, however, classes are usually provided for him. As a rule the best and speediest greyhounds are not the most elegant in shape, and thus it often has happened that the cleverest animal in coursing is beaten in the ring by a very inferior performer. Greyhounds vary much in colour and marking, brindles, fawns, reds, blacks, blues or slate, with more or less white, being the usual colours. Greyhounds entirely white are rare. (*See* COURSING.)

GREYHOUND.

Harrier—This hound may be said to be a connecting link between the foxhound and the beagle, the modern type resembling in appearance the former rather than the latter. The harrier was the *Leverarius* of Caius and of other early writers, and was used to hunt the hare. Of late years, owing to the scarcity of "ground game" in some districts where it formerly abounded, the harrier hunts the "carted deer" and the fox. There is an old-fashioned Welsh harrier which in the principality hunts the fox, the hare, and the otter, bearing a reputation for nose and care in working out a cold scent which is not excelled by any other hound. It is generally marked or coloured in the orthodox foxhound style, but there is also a strain of black and tan harriers. (*See* HUNTING.)

Irish Wolfhound—A great deal has been written about the Irish wolfhound; he has had admirers and traducers. The latter with a good deal of reason urge that the last of his race became extinct when the last Irish wolf was destroyed, the former say he still survives in all his purity. The modern Irish wolfhound is undoubtedly a cross between the Great Dane and the Scottish deerhound; he is by no means uncommon now, and is useful in hunting big game, whilst he can also do his duty satisfactorily in the Scottish deer forests.

Otter Hound—In many particulars this is one of the most interesting of the varieties of the hounds, and appears to be one which we can pretty well call our own. He is a rough, or hard-coated hound, whose hair should be close, piley underneath, and thoroughly weather and water resisting, for the work of the otter hound is of the hardest and most exacting character. Then the constitution must be thoroughly sound and strong. Some modern otter hounds show a distinct cross with the bloodhound, and it is not uncommon to find in the same litter of puppies one that will be blue, gray, and tan in colour, hard and wiry in coat, and fit to win on the bench; whilst another of the litter may be almost smooth-coated, and a half-bred bloodhound in appearance. Some of our leading dog shows provide classes for otter hounds, and their noble appearance, good temper, and animation give them a popularity exceeding that of most other dogs. (*See* OTTER HUNTING.)

Stag Hound—The modern stag hound is merely a foxhound entered and used for the purpose of hunting either the wild or "carted" deer. The name is often applied, but very wrongly, to the Deerhound. (*See* HUNTING.)

Welsh Hounds—There are two varieties of Welsh hounds, one of which partakes of the harrier in size and character, the other resembling the foxhound in size and appearance. Both are, however, rough or hard coated, the hair being hard and crisp, close, and water and weather resisting. The most desirable colour is tawny red, mixed with black and grizzle hairs, and white; others are marked like ordinary foxhounds, and black-and-tans are not uncommon. Some of these Welsh hounds are extremely fine animals, and it is to be regretted that the race has been on the decadence for many years; recently some inquiry has been made for them, as masters of hounds have found them extremely useful in otter hunting. They cast on their own account when at a loss better than the modern foxhound, can hunt an old drag more correctly, and, if slower, are more painstaking, and throw their voices more freely than most of the cracks of our best hunting countries.

OTTER HOUND.

SHOOTING DOGS.

Pointer—Though a comparatively recent introduction into this country, this dog is now one of the most popular of our sporting varieties.

The date of its first appearance here, although not exactly known, was somewhere about 1720, at the time when shooting on the wing was coming into vogue. It is said that one Baron Bechill, who lived in Norfolk, had the earliest pointer, which he brought from Spain. At any rate, for a long time they were known as Spanish pointers, and from what we have been told they were thicker set and clumsier in build than is the modern pointer. They were useful in finding game and had good noses, but were said to tire soon. At the same time there were other pointers in France, some of which were no doubt from time to time brought over to this country. Then Colonel Thornton (Thornville Royal) crossed the Spanish pointer with the foxhound, and is said to have improved the strain exceedingly. From this combination of Spanish, French and foxhound blood has sprung the handsome animal of the present day. Sidney Gilpin, the eminent animal painter, was commissioned to take the portraits of Pluto and Juno, two of the gallant Colonel's best animals, and it is said that they remained on point for an hour and a quarter whilst they were being sketched. Colonel Thornton had another celebrated dog called Dash, which he sold to Sir Richard Symons for champagne and burgundy valued at £150, a hogshead of claret, a gun, and another dog! Then the Earl of Lauderdale, the Duke of Kingston, and other noblemen had celebrated strains of pointers, and Daniel Lambert, so renowned for his obesity, had some black pointers, which bore a great reputation. Later, Mr. Webbe Edge, of Stretley, near Nottingham, gave great attention to breeding pointers, and produced that which was once so widely known as the Edge strain, which, however, is now lost. Some of the blood, nevertheless, remains, and Mr. Edge having nothing but those that were liver and white in colour, such became the most popular, and remain so to this day. Sir R. Garth, Q.C., Mr. J. H. Whitehouse, Mr. Moore, Lord Chesterfield, Lord Derby, Sir R. Goodrich and others formed a connecting link between what may be called two generations, and later came Mr. R. J. Lloyd Price, and Mr. Pilkington, who secured "plums" at Mr. Garth's sale in 1874, where eight brace of pointers realised 490 guineas, £150 for the seven year old dog Drake being the top figure. With the introduction of field trials and dog-shows, pointers and other sporting dogs improved in quality and increased in quantity. Judges were not so particular as to colour, and now, so long as a dog works well, he may be black, black and white, orange and white, lemon and white, or liver and white, and of late we have found dogs of any and all of these colours running successfully in public competitions. On the show bench the liver and white, and different shades of lemon or orange and white do best, although black and whites, and even blacks, sometimes win. In size the pointer varies considerably, and seventy or eighty years ago it is said that the Earl of Lauderdale had a strain which did not exceed 30 lb. in weight. At the present time, at the leading shows they are divided by weight, dogs and bitches 55 lbs. and 50 lbs. weight and over being the large size, and below those standards the small or medium sized. The pointer is easily trained to point or stand game, while in America and Canada he is trained to retrieve. He is as popular on the Continent as in this country. A hot climate suits him better than it does the setter, and he can run longer without water than the latter variety.

POINTER.

Retrievers—With many sportsmen the retriever is considered to be the coming dog, as, in the many cases where grouse and partridge are "driven" or "walked up," a retriever is more useful than pointer, setter or spaniel; besides, he is a good all-round dog for a shooting man. There are two varieties of the retriever proper, the curly-coated, which may originally have been produced from the Irish water spaniel or the poodle; and the flat or wavy-coated, which is no doubt a cross between the Labrador dog, the collie and the setter. Black is the prevailing colour of each, though in the first-named variety liver or browns are not uncommon, and black and tan are sometimes seen. Of the flat-coated variety, liver-coloured specimens are unusual, though puppies of that hue are sometimes produced from black parents. The older variety is the curly-coated retriever; indeed, until a comparatively recent date, say twenty-five years ago, the flat-coated variety was hardly known, and in the first volume of the Kennel Club stud book he is classified with the curly coats; but now it is rapidly forcing its cousin from public favour. Harder in mouth, not so amiable in temper, nor so companionable as the flat-coated variety, the curly-coated retriever chiefly depends upon its popularity as a wild-fowl dog, and as a winner on the show bench. He is the hardier and pluckier dog of the two, but requires the greater amount of work to keep him in proper subjection.

Although the flat-coated retriever has had many detractors, he could scarcely have flourished and reached such a popularity as he has done, were he not a sound, good, and useful dog for all kinds of work. No doubt there are soft, unpersevering animals of the variety, indeed we have met with such, but they are the exception. As water dogs they are certainly not equal to the curly coats, but in nose, faithfulness, fondness for retrieving, and beauty, they cannot be excelled. In purchasing a retriever, particular attention ought to be paid to the dog's appearance, which should be kindly, sagacious, and sensible, for his work repeatedly requires more intelligence to do it properly than that of other sporting dogs. The light-coloured "gooseberry-eyed" specimen, with sinister, sour expression, ought to be at once discarded, and should on no account, if kept, be used for breeding. The brown, or liver-coloured, curly-

RETRIEVER.

coated retrievers are known in different localities as the Norfolk retriever and as the Irish retriever, but there is no reason to believe that they are particularly connected with either place. The Labrador retriever originally came from Labrador, where it was more or less scarce, and of late it has been impossible to procure specimens with which to strengthen the family of the present flat coats. The Duke of Buccleuch has, it is said, a pretty pure strain of the variety in his kennels in Scotland. The Russian retriever, introduced to this country in the early days of dog shows, was a huge beast of the poodle type, wearing long ringlets qualified to hang up any dog in a thicket of gorse and furze. The Chesapeake Bay dog is a strong cross-bred retriever used a great deal in America for wild-fowl shooting; he is usually brown or somewhat mixed in colour, has a semi-curly coat, is very hardy, and a powerful, strong swimmer. A useful working retriever may weigh anything between 45 lbs. and 65 lbs. according to the sex and the purpose for which it is required.

Setter—There are three varieties of this dog, viz., the English setter, the Gordon, or black and tan setter, sometimes called the Scottish setter, and the Irish setter. The first named is black or blue and white, orange and white, black tan and white, lemon and white, and liver and white in colour: the Gordon, as its name implies, is black and tan, and the Irish is usually red—sometimes red and white. There have been strains of black English setters, but they do not appear to have survived, and the colours alluded to certainly predominate at the present day. Until recently the setter was known as the spaniel, a name which is still applied to it in some country places. In 1814 William Dobson of Eden Hall published a work on training the spaniel and the pointer, and by spaniel he meant setter. The dog was used as far back as the sixteenth century for the purpose of assisting to take game by means of nets, when it was called the "sitter" or "setter" because it crouched down. Even earlier than this, a dog, which was no doubt not unlike our modern setter, had been trained to find partridge and quail, which were flushed and then killed by falcons. The oldest painting of a setter of the modern English form is one by Albrecht Dürer, who died in 1528. It illustrates St. Hubert, and in one corner of the picture is an excellent representation of a black, tan, and white dog of the modern type. In the time of James I. no man was allowed to keep a "setting dog," unless by himself or wife he owned land to the value of £10 per annum, or to £30 per annum if only of life interest. There is extant the copy of an agreement dated 1685, whereby one John Harris, was to be paid thirty-one shillings for training a "spaniell bitch named Quand to sitt partrages, pheasants, and other game." Since these early days many changes have been made in the *English* setter, the improved edition of which was introduced by Mr. E. Laverack early in the fifties. He tried various crosses with different strains, which he mostly obtained in the north of England, the result being handsome dogs which could win on the bench as well as do hard work in the field. In 1872 Mr. Laverack published a book on the setter, which he dedicated to Mr. Purcell-Llewellin, who continued and improved the breed. After Mr. Laverack's death the strain became so mixed that at the present day, although there are many good setters, such a thing as a "pure Laverack" is unknown. The colours were blue and white ticked, which he called blue Beltons, from a village in Northumberland, and orange and white, or liver and white, all more or less heavily ticked or flecked. Mr. Llewellin still keeps his own strain, guarding against an out cross of any sort; thus the family likeness is preserved, and the habits and methods of working peculiar thereto are maintained. The English setter is one of the handsomest of sporting dogs, good tempered and kindly, is easily trained to shoot over, and often retrieves naturally, a faculty which is not encouraged in this country. Many good dogs have gone to America and to the Colonies at high prices, one being sold for £230, and quite recently £100 was given for another, and £200 for a young dog not twelve months old. Still, the English setter does not realise so much money as some less useful varieties of the dog. The weights vary somewhat, dogs being from 48 to 60 lbs. in weight, and bitches from 40 lbs. upwards. The *Gordon*, or black and tan, setter, was first introduced to the public from Gordon Castle in Banffshire, the Highland seat of the Dukes of Richmond and Gordon. It was possibly originally produced early in the present century from a cross between an ordinary setter and a bloodhound. Many of the original Gordons were black, tan, and white in colour, but by careful crossing the white became entirely eliminated and a Gordon to-day should be black and tan, although a little white on the feet and on the chest is allowed. In this country he is not a popular dog, and more specimens are to be found in America and on

SETTER.

the Continent than here. *The Irish Setter* is much more popular, and during the past twelve years has come more prominently before the public than he had done before. He is a red dog, or red and white, with a certain character of his own, rather lighter and more elegant in build than either of the varieties already alluded to. History does not tell where the Irish setter came from, and he was not known as such much before about 1830, when he was red and white, and it was not probably until twenty years or more later that whole red became the fashionable colour. The loss of the white was certainly not an improvement, as the entirely red dog is very difficult to see on the moors, so much so that he is often used with a white collar or handkerchief around his neck to make him more easily distinguishable against the dark background of rock and heather. As a dog to shoot over, the Irish setter cannot be excelled, and if a little headstrong and difficult to train, when thoroughly broken he is untiring, and can certainly go longer day after day over the mountains and bogs than either the Gordon or the English variety. His scenting powers are quite equal to those of any other dog of the kind, and his pace and style are likewise high class.

RAWDON B. LEE.

Spaniels—There are four varieties of field spaniels, irrespective of the Cocker and the Irish Water Spaniel; these are the Clumber, the Sussex, the Black, and the any-other-colour. All of these have certain points in common, having very long bodies in comparison to their height, short legs and perfectly flat coats, the points in which they differ being the formation of the head, the colour, and, as regards the Clumber, in the size. A dog called a spaniel was known in this country 400 years ago, for it is mentioned (by the legendary Juliana Barnes) in "The Bokys of Hawking and Hunting," 1486. From this animal the setter is supposed to have been produced, but it is scarcely probable that there was very much resemblance between the spaniel spoken of in the fifteenth century, and that of the present day. The use of the spaniel, according to Nicholas Cox in his *Gentleman's Recreation*, published in 1677, was as an assistant in hawking, by springing and retrieving game. The same writer also alludes to shortening the tails of spaniels, a custom which still obtains, but not for a similar reason. At that time the fallacy prevailed that the cutting of the tails of spaniel puppies was a preventive against worms. The tail of the spaniel is now docked in order that he may be enabled to work amongst briars and thick underwood without its becoming lacerated. The spaniel mentioned by Cox is probably that from which all the present varieties of land spaniels have sprung, not excluding the toy spaniels, as, with regard to the latter, it is a matter of history that the Blenheim spaniel, which has now lapsed into a pet dog, was at one time used for covert shooting. It is, however, unfortunately the fact, that the improvement in appearance of the field spaniel to meet the requirements of the show-bench has been accomplished without consideration for his working qualities; fancy points are held in greater favour than some that are considered much more important by sportsmen, and prizes have been given to dogs with forelegs so badly shaped as to render them almost incapable of work.

The *Clumber* spaniel, white in body, with lemon markings on the head and ears, weighs from 45 lbs. to 65 lbs., according to sex. He is massive in build, with long body, short legs, and strong bone, a large head, of medium length, with heavy brows and deep stop, the flews being well developed. The eyes are dark amber, slightly sunk, and showing the haw. The ears are large and vine-leaf shaped and hanging slightly forward, the hair straight, the feather not extending below the fleshy part of the ear; the coat long and dense, heavy feathering behind and on the legs, the stern not carried higher than the line of the back. It is a defect for the colour on head and ears to be orange, the lighter the shade the better. In the field, a well-broken Clumber spaniel is a very useful dog; working about 20 yards in front of the gun at a steady trot, he does not give tongue, and can be trained to drop to hand, wing, or shot, and will retrieve. He is a slow dog, but does not "tire." Clumber spaniels are sometimes worked in teams of a few brace, when they take the place of beaters. This dog takes its name from "Clumber" near Worksop, one of the seats of the Duke of Newcastle, the breed having been introduced from France into this country by an ancestor of the present Duke, who lived about the middle of the last century.

The *Sussex* spaniel is not so large nor massive as the Clumber, the distinguishing feature of the variety being its rich golden liver-colour. Here again is a short-legged dog, with great length of body, well ribbed up, and with muscular hind quarters; his coat is rather hard in texture, dense underneath, and perfectly straight, feathering moderate, that will allow a willing dog to work in the thickest covert of briars and brambles. The head is a modification of the Clumber's, the brows being not so much overhung, the skull moderately long and wide, with an indentation in the middle and a full stop. The eyes dark hazel, fairly large, not showing the haw overmuch; the muzzle square, and lips somewhat pendulous; the nose liver, the ears fairly large and lobe-shaped, coated with straight silky hair, and free from fringe at the tips; tail carried the same as the Clumber and docked. He is hardy, busy, reliable as a worker, and sticks close to his game. He gives tongue when on the line of scent, but is not over noisy; he will retrieve, and is tender-mouthed. The Rosehill strain, which is considered to be the most pure, takes its name from Rosehill Hall, Brightling, near Hastings, where the late Mr. Fuller kept the variety for over fifty years, and used his dogs for beating the large woods and plantations in the vicinity of Brightling and Heathfield.

The *Black* and *any-other-coloured* spaniels are a much more modern production than either the Clumber or the Sussex. When all black he is a particularly handsome animal, in which length of body and shortness of legs with enormous bone are again produced to exaggeration. In head he differs from the Clumber, or the Sussex, inasmuch as it is longer and narrower; the skull is, however, well developed, the occipital bone being prominent, the ears longer and set lower, with more feather. As with the Sussex, the feet should not be too small, and should be protected with short hair between the toes; rather more feathering is, however, admissible below the hocks. The eyes should not show the haw.

FIELD SPANIEL.

The "any-other-colour" include black and tan, liver and tan, liver, black and white, and liver and white, with black-roan, and liver-roan. Admirers of these dogs claim for them that they are reliable workers with the gun, but they are probably seen to more advantage on the show bench, and may be taken as a sound example of what can be done in the matter of breeding "for show points." A variety of this spaniel is known as the Norfolk spaniel, but it is pretty well distributed throughout the British Isles and is by no means confined to the county from which it takes its name. It is liver and white in colour, inclined to be curly in coat, or at any rate wavy, and is higher on the legs and a more active, useful dog for sporting purposes than the ordinary black spaniel.

The *Cocker* is a particularly active little dog, and differs considerably in shape from the black spaniel. He must not weigh more than 25 lbs., and is shorter in body, and comparatively high on the legs in comparison with his size; the muzzle is not so square as in the other spaniels, and the frontal bones rather more prominent, showing plenty of room for brain power; the stop rather more decided; the ears, set on low, are fine in texture and do not extend beyond the nose when laid in that direction. The dog is well clothed with long silky hair, which must be straight or wavy—no postive curls or ringlets; the coat flat or wavy, and soft in texture. In colour he is the same as the black, or any-other-coloured field-spaniel. He is a merry and busy worker, specially smart in driving game from a gorse covert or other rough place.

The *Irish water-spaniel* is a dog in every respect the antipodes of any other of the varieties of spaniel, excepting only an animal known as the English water-spaniel, of which sight has now been lost, but which, when in existence, might be considered a link between the curly-coated liver-coloured retriever and the Irish water-spaniel. The early history of the Irish water-spaniel is such that no authority has ventured to say much about his origin ; all that is known about it is that there were at one time two, if not more, varieties in the north and south of Ireland, and that the type recognised in the south has been taken as the modern one. About the same height as a retriever, in colour he is rich liver with a puce shade. He has the appearance of a strong and dashing dog, with quaint and very intelligent expression, the quaintness being emphasised by the peculiar topknot which falls between and over the eyes, and hides a capacious skull, which is somewhat domed. The face is long, square in muzzle, and perfectly smooth ; the nose liver in colour ; the coat consists of short crisp curls all over the body, and round and down the legs to the feet, which are large and round. The inside of the hocks to the ground should, however, be smooth in a specimen of absolutely perfect coat, and there should be but little hair on the tail, which is thick at the base, somewhat short, and tapering to a point. Amber eyes are admissible, but

IRISH WATER SPANIEL.

when they are a soft brown, the expression of the face is greatly improved. The ears, which are long and set on low, are abundantly covered with wavy hair, the feather reaching at least 3 inches below the flesh on either side ; the whole measures from 24 to 26 inches. He is an excellent water dog, and particularly good for work on wild fowl in marshy ground, but next to useless in covert on account of his coat. Instances have been known where he has been taught to set game, and back like a pointer or setter, but they have been very rare ; indeed, his capacity for retrieving is his primary qualification.

TERRIERS.

The **Airedale Terrier** is the largest of the terrier race, and is a most useful animal to those who can only keep one dog for sport. Originally produced from a cross between the otter hound and a terrier, less than thirty years ago he was to be seen in the northern counties of England (but more generally in Yorkshire), with hound-like ears, and other characteristics of the hound. At that time he went by various names, the "Bingley terrier" and the "Waterside terrier." During the last twenty years, however, since he was given an entry in the Kennel Club's Stud-book, he has settled down as the Airedale terrier and, by careful selection in breeding, all the hound properties have been eliminated, and he is now essentially a terrier. An important feature is his very hard wiry coat, in which respect he has vastly improved during the past few years, as previously, where one with the correct coat was to be seen, half a dozen others with long, silky, and sometimes woolly, coats, or quite smooth ones were to be observed. There should be no ruggedness about the coat, which must lie close and straight ; the hair about $1\frac{1}{2}$ inches long all over the body. The colour is also peculiar, inasmuch as the hair on the back is black at the ends and gray close to the body, and this is the explanation of the badger grizzle coat that is desired in this variety. To the unpractised eye the dog appears to be black in body, with tan thighs, head, legs, chest, and ears, and in many cases he really is black, as the dual tint does not appear on the back and neck of every specimen. In this connection it may be mentioned that, when the puppies are born, they resemble the smooth black and tan terrier in coat and colour, and have dark heads ; but as they develop, the black leaves the head, and gives place to a deep tan, and the hair on the back gets longer and harder. Many litters of puppies on this account have been destroyed as soon as whelped, on the supposition that they were only dark-coloured mongrels. Forty-five pounds is the weight for a dog, and rather less for a bitch, but many prize-winners do not weigh quite so much. The head is long and very strong about the jaw, with little or no stop, the skull flat, the ears small and set well forward, lying close to the cheeks, the eyes small and dark with a keen expression. His bone is strong for his size, and he is a particularly active dog, with very straight legs and well set up feet.

The Bedlington Terrier—This dog takes his name from Bedlington, a village in Northumberland, in which locality the miners have kept him for many years. It has erroneously been stated that he was brought from Holland by a weaver, the mistake arising through his having had at one time, as his greatest supporter, a Mr. Taprell Holland. A more correct supposition is that he was bred from some other varieties of the terriers, to suit the requirements of the pitmen who wanted a speedy and active dog which could catch a rabbit as well as kill rats and other vermin, and would be useful for dog racing. He is a particularly wiry animal, more slender in build than any other of the terriers that are used for sport, can go a great pace, and is very plucky when occasion requires; in fact his disposition to fight, and jealousy of temperament with other dogs, has had something to do with his not becoming a very popular favourite. Another reason for his not having taken a high place in public estimation is that, before he can be exhibited in the show ring, he is often subjected to a considerable amount of trimming. In appearance he is somewhat delicate looking, but in this respect belies his looks, as, although a dainty feeder, he is hardy enough.

The Dandie Dinmont Terrier has peculiarities in conformation which are not to be seen in any other family of the terrier. These consist of a long body, short legs, and a head which appears to be abnormally large, partly owing to the topknot and moustache with which it is adorned. There is no doubt that the Dandie Dinmont terrier owes much of its prominence in public favour to Sir Walter Scott, who in *Guy Mannering* introduced the character of Dandie Dinmont with his pepper and mustard terriers. It had, however, existed long before 1814, when *Guy Mannering* was written, and was well-known about the borders of England and Scotland, but from whence his peculiar shape was derived no one has been able to discover. Still, there is evidence that in the last century the north country farmers, vermin killers, and others kept a hardy race of short-legged terriers, which assisted in hunting the otter, and were strong enough to kill a fox in its earth. Beside his long body, the dog has a decided arch in his back, which is considered one of the chief characteristics of the variety; his legs, although short, have immense muscular development, the chest being well let down between them; the hind legs are a little longer than the fore and are set rather wide apart. His head, surmounted by a topknot of silky hair, which also appears between the eyes, is strongly made and large, this extra growth of hair being lighter in tint than the body colour.

The Fox Terrier—There are two varieties of this terrier, the smooth and the wire haired. This dog, although but a comparatively modern production in its present state, is the most popular specimen of the canine race in England, and its development is fostered by a most flourishing club. There is also a journal which devotes its entire influence to its interests, and a special Stud Book, besides a publication entitled *The History and Description, with Reminiscences, of the Fox Terrier*. Although the fox terrier, as it is seen to-day, white in body with black and tan, or tan markings, or entirely white, has only been known about 100 years, there is indisputable evidence that a terrier spoken of as an earth dog, and used for going to ground to fox or badger, was known upwards of 300 years ago, and probably much earlier. From this dog the modern fox terrier has sprung, and by judicious selection in breeding the smart little dog, as we see him in the present day, has been produced. It is, however, difficult to fix the time when the fox terrier assumed the colour in which he is now

Fox Terrier.

recognised, for even at the commencement of this century and earlier there were fox terriers black and tan in colour as well as others with a great deal of white about them. It is to be supposed that, as it was the custom for each pack of foxhounds to be accompanied by one or two terriers, the idea suggested itself that a hound-marked terrier would be more desirable for the purpose required, and that recourse was had to a cross with a small hound, probably a beagle, to get the required markings. This seemed evident in the terriers that were to be seen about twenty years ago, from their large ears and full eyes. The occupation of the fox terrier, in his more immediate connection with hounds, is now gone, since foxes are less frequently dug out than formerly, and the new school of masters of hounds has dispensed with his services. With the loss of his vocation, some of that indescribable expression which denotes a readiness for any sort of rough and tumble work that may come in his way has departed, and he may be now looked upon rather as an ornamental than as a working dog, more suited for the show bench than going to ground to a fox; indeed, as regards the latter, he is often too big for the purpose. His popularity commenced some thirty years ago, since which time he has greatly increased in value. A dog that could previously have been purchased for from ten to twenty guineas soon mounted up to three figures, and as much as £400 has been given for a single specimen.

The Irish Terrier—It is just twenty years since the Irish terrier first obtained recognition in the Kennel Club Stud Book, and then there were only nineteen entries in the section apportioned for it. The total of about one hundred and forty in 1896 will give some idea of the advance in popularity it has made. When the first show of Irish terriers was held in the Exhibition Palace at Dublin in 1874, they were quite a mixed lot, some with long bodies, short legs, and soft fluffy coats, some brindle, and only a few, of red or sandy colour, showing the character that is recognised in the present day. But shortly after this a good terrier was found in Killiney Boy, from whom have been bred many of the best Irish terriers that are now to be seen. It is generally admitted that he is a plucky dog, ready to kill any kind of vermin, but as a rule too large to go to ground. He is fond of water and will fetch and carry. For several years after he was first introduced into England it was the fashion to cut his ears, which made him look particularly sharp, but in 1888 a rule was passed by the Kennel Club, acting on the suggestion of the Irish Terrier Club, that no "cropped Irish terrier born after December 31st, 1889, could compete at shows under their rules." At the present period a cropped Irish terrier is never seen at a show of any importance. In popularity this dog is only second to the fox terrier, and it is very much to the credit of those who have given their attention to the race, that such an uniformity of type has been obtained, considering the short time that he has been in the hands of breeders. The most desirable colours are bright red, wheaten, or sandy, the first-named for preference. No white on the head or body is admissible, with the exception of a small spot on the chest which is to be seen at times in most self-coloured dogs. His coat is hard and wiry in texture, not so long as to hide the outlines of the body, and straight and flat. The head is long, with flat skull, and but little stop. There should be no fringe on his ears. In shape he resembles the fox terrier, but he is built on larger and more racing lines. His tail, which is carried gaily, but not over the back, is generally docked. Twenty-two pounds is a good weight for a dog, and twenty pounds for a bitch, and any deviation from these figures should be in the lighter direction.

The Scottish Terrier—This is believed to be the oldest family of terriers in Scotland, although until recently he had not been so prominently brought forward as the Skye terrier, from the fact of his having been chiefly kept in the Highlands for killing vermin and hunting foxes amongst the rocks in the mountains, where hounds were never seen. Until about the year 1874 he was spoken of as the Skye terrier, but owing to a newspaper controversy in which the advocates of the two varieties each claimed a right to the title, it was arranged that the longer-coated dog should be called the Skye, and the shorter the Scottish terrier. From that period the latter has become very much the more popular, and has been largely introduced into England. It was, however, some time before he settled down as the Scottish terrier, having been called respectively the Aberdeen terrier, the Scots terrier, the Highland terrier, the Cairn terrier, and the "Die Hard," the last-named appellation remaining with him, as so thoroughly representative of his character. He was introduced to us with a serious defect, inasmuch as he had bent forelegs, a malformation claimed by some Scotsmen as a sign of purity of breed. This has to a great extent been rectified, and other improvements have been made in him; he is now not so long in body as formerly, and is of little value if his ears are not tightly pricked, notwithstanding that at one time, semi-erect ears were quite as generally seen; he is a game, hardy-looking terrier, very sturdy in body, on short legs, with great bone and substance, and immense teeth for so small a dog.

The Skye Terrier—The Skye Terrier is more suitable for a companion or house dog, and to kill a rat when occasion requires, than for the more serious work of exterminating foxes and other large vermin, for which he was used in days gone by. As a matter of fact, the coat, when quite perfect, is so long that its owner cannot do the duties of a terrier, even if he could see through the hair over his eyes, which is often so thick as almost to prevent his being able to detect anything in front of him. This, however, is not a natural state of things, and is only brought about by the greatest care and attention, in order to gain success on the show bench. This abundance of coat would soon disappear if the animal were called upon to do any work. As mentioned in connection with the Scottish terrier, which was probably the original Skye terrier, these dogs with very long coats are comparatively a modern production, but there is a family of terriers in Scotland which has the characteristics of the one under consideration without the superfluity of hair.

The Welsh Terrier—The Welsh Terrier is quite a recent introduction, for ten or a dozen years ago it had scarcely ever been heard of outside the Principality. However, when once he made his appearance he quickly found friends, and is now one of the most popular terriers we have. In appearance he has very much altered since a club was formed to look after his interests in 1886, for from a short-headed cobby dog with large eyes, he has been transformed into a smart terrier built much on the lines of the "old English black-and-tan terrier" that has existed in England for many years, but which, since the advent of the Welsh terrier, has almost become extinct. In fact, it is probable that the Welshman owes much of its improvement to the English dog which it has supplanted, for when classes were first made for it at the Birmingham and other shows, several of the winners were old English black-and-tan terriers, pure and simple; and when the Kennel Club gave it an entry in the Stud Book, the classification was for Welsh, or old English wire-haired, black-and-tan terriers. This arrangement did not suit the admirers of either variety, and separate clubs were formed for each, that for the Welsh with success, the other proving a failure. The result was that two years later the members of the Welsh Terrier Club succeeded in persuading the Kennel Club to remove the name of the old English terrier altogether from its connection with the Welsh terrier. There is not wanting proof, however, that a terrier, of the description of those that were first introduced as Welsh terriers, has existed in the Principality for upwards of a century.

FRED GRESHAM.

There are several other Families of Terriers which, if they cannot claim, like the foregoing, to be of any recognised variety, have yet proved themselves excellent for sport. In fact, in almost every district one hears of some terrier or other which has made its name famous in connection with the badger, fox, and otter. These surely deserve some notice, when it is considered that they more generally than not are covered with scars which tell of hardships that they have endured, of sharp encounters in which gameness alone has saved them from premature death. There is the Sealy Ham terrier, so called from the seat near Haverfordwest of the Edwardses, in whose family, it is said, the variety has been kept for nearly a hundred years. These are short-legged and long-bodied, not unlike the wire-haired fox terrier as regards colour, coat, and character of head, but more sturdy, and weighing rather under than over 18 lbs. The late Captain Edwards is said to have been particularly proud of the working capabilities of his dogs, frequently tried with badgers, otters, foxes, and polecats. Perhaps more interesting are the Border terriers, which are met with in Northumberland, and other of the northern counties, and for which is claimed an earlier existence than the Dandie Dinmont and Bedlington terriers, which also hailed from the same locality. They obtain their name of Border terriers from the fact that they were frequently used and bred in the country hunted by the Border foxhounds. The favourite colour for them is red, or black and tan. The services of these terriers, which follow hounds regularly, are often called into use, and they are sent into most dangerous places amongst rocks and peat moss drains, from which they sometimes do not return, so determined are they in the pursuit of their quarry. At Calliper's, near King's Langley,

BORDER TERRIER.

Mr. J. H. B. Cowley has a valuable strain of terriers, short-legged and long-bodied, marked like our fox terriers, but, unlike the latter, kept entirely for work. They excel in going to ground after fox or badger, in which business they are mostly employed.

RAWDON B. LEE.

OTHER VARIETIES.

Whippet—This is a dog originally produced by crossing with a terrier and greyhound, sometimes with the Italian greyhound. It is now a distinct variety, which breeds true to type, and in fact is a "pocket edition" of the ordinary greyhound. He may weigh anything between 10 lbs. and 25 lbs., not larger than the latter weight, and any colour is allowable. The Whippet is much in request by the lower middle classes for running purposes, either to course rabbits, or to take part in short distance races, the usual course being 200 yards. The competitors are handicapped according to their height or weight. A dog 20 lbs. weight has been known to cover the full distance of 200 yards in 12½ seconds. The sport is very popular in Lancashire, Yorkshire, and in the north of England, but the attempts to bring it into prominence in the southern counties have not been altogether successful. The competitors run on a cinder path, and are started by a pistol. On the mark they are held by a friend of the trainer; the latter runs in front of the dog up the course dangling a pigeon's wing, a towel, or anything attractive to encourage the dog; and the judge at the goal decides each race promptly and expeditiously. In coursing matches rabbits are used, twenty-one or thirty-one trials being run, the kill only scoring. In the large handicaps of this kind each dog runs from three to five rabbits with his opponent, and it will be seen that stamina as well as pace is required in a Whippet to be a champion at rabbit coursing. In some districts the Whippet is known as the Snap Dog.

There are several other varieties of sporting dogs that have been imported into England, which, although used in their native countries with the gun or for hunting purposes, have very little or no vocation here. One of the most prominent of these is the **Basset hound**, which, some twenty years ago, Mr., now Sir, Everett Millais, Bart., was instrumental in introducing into the country. The Basset is hound-marked, very low on the legs for the size and length of his body, and he is somewhat like the bloodhound in head and ears. The chest comes well down between the forelegs, which are heavy in bone, and incline inwards from the elbow joint to the fetlock and then outwards to the end of the toes. He has the appearance of a good-sized hound on very short legs. When used for hunting they go in packs, the followers being on foot. The Basset has a capital nose, and a rich, full cry, but it takes a pack some time to pull down a hare, occasionally from two to three hours, and then it must be in an open and fairly flat country, where there are no large fences nor stone walls. There are two varieties known in this country, the smooth, the more popular, and the rough or wire-haired, known as the Basset-Griffon.

The **Dachshund** is a native of Germany, where he does the work of a terrier, and is particularly good at going to ground to fox or badger. He is said to resemble the old Turnspit, which in days gone by was used by cooks to turn the spit when joints of meat were being roasted. During the last twenty or thirty years he has become very fashionable as a companion, but when occasion requires he will hunt the line of game as well as the Basset-hound. He also has a long body with short legs, and is crooked in his forelegs, but is smaller and differs in colour, inasmuch as he is generally black and tan, chocolate and red, though a few are dappled. He is usually smooth-coated, and his skin is particularly soft and velvety to the touch. Wire-coated and long-haired dachshunds are sometimes seen, occasions of their being produced from smooth-coated parents not being unusual.

The **Great Dane**, under which denomination is included the Boarhound, German Mastiff, and Tiger Mastiff, is an unusually powerful dog that has hunted the wild boar in Germany and other European countries, and is generally to be seen with cropped ears. He is somewhat like the English mastiff, but more slender in build and taller. At one time he appeared likely to become fashionable as a companion, and was taken up as a favourite by ladies and others; but his popularity was not destined to continue, and although a considerable number are kept in the country he has certainly lost ground. He cannot be kept under proper control, objects strongly to the muzzle, and, now that the Kennel Club has forbidden cropping, he is bereft of much of his smart appearance.

The **Borzoi** or **Russian Wolfhound** is another dog which has been introduced to us with a great reputation as a hunter of wolves, but he again, after receiving considerable attention for a few years, appeared to be losing his influence, for, like all other dogs that hunt their game by sight, he is given to chasing little dogs and soon disposing of them. However, a Borzoi Club has been formed, a special show of the variety held, and he seems to be regaining favour. He is one of the most beautiful of the canine race, and is highly appreciated in Russia; his elegant proportions, expressive face, attractive colour, and silky coat all combine to give him a most aristocratic appearance. In his own country a perfect wolfhound must run up to a wolf, collar him by the neck just under the ear, and, with the two animals rolling over, the hound must never lose his hold, or the wolf would turn round and snap him through the leg. Three of these hounds hold the biggest wolf powerless, so that the men can dismount from their horses and muzzle the wolf to take him alive.

The **Persian Greyhound** is another of the race of Greyhounds, and he is usually yellow-fawn in colour and very symmetrical in build. His chief peculiarity is the distribution of the coat, which is longer at the sides of the body and down the legs and thighs than it is on the back; the ears, which lie flat to the head, are heavily fringed. He is about the size of a small greyhound.

Somewhat of the same type is the **Rampur hound**, but quite smooth in coat, and without the arched loin that is such an important feature in the greyhound; he has large ears, in this particular partaking of the nature of the fox-hound, but very few of his breed have been seen in this country.

The **Griffon** (French), resembling the German wire-haired pointers, which takes the place of a setter in some parts of the Continent, has also found a home in England. He cannot be better described than as like a small otter-hound, possessing the intelligent expression and fine type of head of that hound, but in colour he is usually a liver-roan, and has a shorter and more wiry coat; his tail is shortened to half its natural length. He is steady with the gun, and will point game and retrieve, but he is not a wide ranger.

The **Norwegian Hound**, of which a considerable number have been imported, is a particularly active dog, dark blue-grey, peculiarly shaded, in body colour, with lighter hue of the same on legs and chest. He is not unlike the Esquimaux dog in shape, with prick ears and tightly-curled tail, but is somewhat smaller. His chief duty in Norway, his native country, is to hunt the elk, the bear, and even capercailzie and such "small deer," and it is said he displays extraordinary sagacity in the various departments for which he is specially trained.

FRED GRESHAM.

DISEASES OF DOGS.

In dealing with this subject, it must be understood that allusion is only made here to simple ailments that can be treated without the assistance of a veterinary surgeon. The most formidable malady which confronts the kennel owner is undoubtedly *distemper*, which, as a rule, attacks dogs in their early youth, before they are twelve months old. There is a very general belief that every dog must have distemper at some time of its life, but this is a mistake, for distemper, being a contagious disease, cannot be contracted except by contact with an infected dog or substance—*e.g.*, the clothes of a keeper who has attended a sick dog, a box in which it has travelled, or anything of like nature. The symptoms are loss of appetite in the first instance, followed by a falling away of the muscles of the face, and eventually a discharge of mucus from the eyes and nose, accompanied by a temperature of over 100. In the incipient stage, before the disease has pronounced itself, it is always safe to give a dose of castor oil, consisting of a dessertspoonful to a tablespoonful, according to the size and age of the patient. In the event of this failing to bring back the appetite, recourse should be had at once to a veterinary surgeon.

The various forms of skin diseases are generally amenable to treatment if attended to promptly. There are two descriptions of *mange*, the sarcoptic and follicular. The former is the more easy to cure, and its presence may be detected by the dog continually scratching itself; a bath composed of one part of some disinfecting fluid to forty parts of water, or a mixture of two parts of olive oil with one part of paraffin oil and half a pound of sulphur, well rubbed into the skin, will kill the parasite and eradicate the disease. Follicular mange is not so easily dealt with, as the parasite is buried beneath the skin, but by continually dressing with the paraffin mixture at an interval of from ten to fourteen days a satisfactory result may be obtained. Eczema, which is not a parasitic affection, will generally yield to similar treatment, if accompanied by mild aperients and afterwards by simple tonics. Arsenic is sometimes necessary, but the latter should not be given except under medical instructions. Very little skin disease will be experienced if the bath is freely used, for by that means the skin is kept clean, and fleas and other insects—a source of continual irritation to dogs in warm weather—are destroyed. There is, however, no better mode of dispersing fleas than to rub a small quantity of pyrethrum powder into the coat.

Canker in the ear may be detected by a continual shaking of the head, more particularly after a slight pressure of the hand upon the ear. In an advanced stage, the head will be held on one side, with one ear hanging lower than the other. For this complaint there are fortunately several remedies, for what will cure one dog may be of little benefit to another. One part of liquor plumbi to two parts of soft water; boracic acid dusted into the ear, or the same mixed with oil; a tablespoonful of methylated spirit in a pint of water, will all be found effectual for one or other of the cases that may occur. Another simple and excellent application is a lotion consisting of five grains of alum, one drachm of vinegar and one ounce of water, but, before applying either, the ear must be carefully cleaned with warm water and a soft sponge. Any liquid that is poured into the ear should be luke-warm.

All dogs are very liable to pick up *poison*, which is so often carelessly, and almost criminally, laid about for the destruction of mice, rats, and other vermin. If you suspect that your dog has obtained poison, and a veterinary surgeon or chemist is not at hand, empty the stomach by administering the simple emetic, lukewarm water, and, this done, give milk and white of eggs, or boiled flour and milk, or butter, lard, fat, or olive oil. However, if tartar emetic or sulphate of zinc is handy, give a dose of either in preference to the luke-warm water. Castor oil administered later on is useful, and if exhaustion is apparent, brandy, wine, or strong beef tea ought to be given to the patient. Arsenic, phosphorus, and strychnine are the most common "rat-poisons," the effect of strychnine being marked by frequent contraction of the limbs and cramps. Arsenical poisoning may, as a rule, be detected by swelling and violent pains in the bowels, accompanied by purging, feverishness, and unnatural thirst. The symptoms of poison by phosphorus take the form of peculiar listlessness and giddiness, vomiting, and an aroma from the mouth not unlike the smell of garlic or of lucifer matches. Although cases of poisoning of this kind must be alluded to here, it is always best to obtain skilled professional advice as soon as possible. [*See* VETERINARY WORK.]

There are a few simple rules with regard to the management of dogs which should always be borne in mind by the kennel-man or by the master. Grass is an important factor towards promoting the health of dogs; the first remedy which nature dictates to him for any sickness is a blade from the greensward. Attention to sanitary arrangement and the ventilation of kennels are likewise of primary importance, whilst regularity in feeding, a continuous supply of pure water, clean, dry bedding and benches, and sufficient exercise will not only add to the dog's comfort but maintain him in the best possible condition.

BREAKING AND TRAINING.

Different views are held by breakers as to the best mode to adopt in training young pointers and setters for shooting purposes. A prominent owner of field trial winners, when commencing to handle his puppies, allows them to chase birds as much as they like to begin with; his opinion being that the more they do so, the greater is their anxiety to hunt for and find them. In fact, he says that the most successful dogs that he has owned have all been broken in this way, and that those puppies which are too much schooled at first do not develop sufficient dash, will not range wide enough, and in the end become potterers. When his puppies begin to show signs of pointing, he makes much of them, and they soon give up their bad habit of chasing and are easily make steady at point. He does not use the check cord, nor, except on very rare occasions, does he have recourse to the puzzle peg. Two things that add greatly to the facility of breaking young sporting dogs are, first, that they be bred from parents that have good reputations as workers, and secondly, that they have confidence in their owners. To obtain confidence they should be constantly in their presence, for the puppy that accompanies his master on all possible occasions will soon find out what he is wanted to do; thus all the earlier lessons, such as teaching him to drop to hand, to keep to heel, and being held on, are easily acquired. A perfectly raw puppy can easily be taught to down charge in a few hours without the use of pegs, spike collars, or any other of the contrivances that are used by some breakers. Take your pupil into a large field, some distance from home, put him down on his belly, and hold up your hand, at the same time continually repeating the words "Down charge." Walk a few paces backwards from him, and when he gets up to follow you, as he will do at first, take him back and put him down again. By such means he will soon drop to hand when desired, and it will take only a few lessons to teach him to keep to heel, if a little kindness is shown and encouragement given. Having once taught the puppy to drop to hand, and keep to heel, two most important rungs of the ladder have been climbed, and the first lessons in obedience have been instilled. Some breakers choose the spring of the year, when birds are paired, to make their young pointers and setters perfect at point, but there are objections to this, inasmuch as there is no possibility of killing a bird to them, and rewarding them for any special good work that they may have done. Some drilling must of course be done in the spring, but it is better to give the finishing touch at the latter end of August or the beginning of September. The loss of a few days' shooting may be the result, but this will be amply recompensed in the greater proficiency that the dog will acquire. When, however, field trials are in contemplation, the work must all be done in the early spring. In the present day, when so little covert is to be met with, it is absolutely necessary that pointers and setters should be free rangers. During tuition they should be encouraged to take wide beats, but the whistle must always be used when they get to the fence, and so they are taught not to break field. For the first two or three times when birds are flushed, the inexperienced puppy will most probably chase them as far as he can see them. This should not be interfered with, except by the whistle when the fence is reached. On the puppy's return, however, he should be dropped to hand at the place where he started to chase, this to be done with a view to teaching him to drop to wing. When holding him on at the commencement of a beat, care must be taken to give him the wind, for it is very unlikely that even the most perfectly broken animal will find birds when the wind is against him, how much less then is it probable that a novice can do so. If this principle be steadily adopted, the dog will in due time seek the wind himself.

The endeavour must always be to encourage the young dog by rewards and flattery to use his brains as well as his nose, for without this combination no pointer or setter can be a perfect birdfinder. A golden rule in connection with tutoring puppies is not to do too much with them at one time, and always, if possible, to take them home after they have done a meritorious action, at the same time letting them know that you are pleased with them. Now supposing that the puppy has learnt all the minor details of breaking, will quarter his ground properly, does not break fence, will drop to hand, wing, and shot, is steady at point, and is obedient to whistle and word of command, his education is still a long way from being complete. He must yet be taught to back, and he may be gun-shy, though that fault is more frequent with dogs that are kept shut up in kennels than with those that more or less have their liberty and become accustomed to all sorts of unusual sounds. If there is the slightest inclination to be gun-shy, the endeavour must be to make the offender aware that the sound of the gun will not hurt him, but rather that it is associated with something from which pleasure is to be derived. All sorts of plans have been adopted to accustom young dogs to the sound of the gun, some men even firing off a pistol a short distance from the kennel just before feeding, while another method is to couple the puppy to an old dog which is perfectly steady to shot. Some offenders in this direction will gain confidence after a few birds have been killed to them, and not again show any nervousness, but in the case of a puppy a gun should not be fired over him unless a kill is certain, when he will probably be so pleased with the result as to become reconciled to the sound. If a dog is decidedly gun-shy, it is only waste of time to try to cure him. When teaching a puppy to back, it is desirable that he be taken out with a well-seasoned and perfectly steady dog. On seeing the latter make a point, the youngster may back of his own accord, or he may run in, and either flush the birds or take the point, or possibly may not take any notice whatever. Should he not behave properly, the handler must wait until he can get the puppy behind the pointing dog and then put him down, but if, after this has been repeated a few times, there is no improvement, the check cord and peg must be brought into use. Before being pegged down the puppy must have been accustomed to being tied up, or he will struggle to get free, and all the time that has been bestowed upon his training will probably be thrown away.

A bad habit which some dogs contract when being worked as one of a brace, is following close on the heels of their companion, which very often perplexes the leading dog. This under any circumstances is most objectionable, and is unpardonable in an adult pointer or setter, but puppies can sometimes be cured of it. False pointing is another fault; this is the result of overtraining, but it is often a sign that, although the dog knows his work, he has not a good nose and has no confidence in himself, or, like blinking, it may be brought about by fear of punishment. One of the most important attributes in a pointer or setter is that he should carry his head high when in quest of game, and if he goes with his head low, the puzzle peg may be used, but this requires great care in adjusting. Some breakers commence by using the check cord, but there is no doubt that to a certain extent it cramps the action of the wearer; nevertheless, if a puppy persists in declining to point, or back, or in chasing fur, it must be used. In districts where there are plenty of hares there is not much difficulty in making a dog steady to fur, but when they are not often met with, some live rabbits may be turned down, and the pupil put through his lessons with the check cord and peg.

These instruments are next to a necessity in training a retriever, in fact, it is only the most thoroughly broken dogs of this breed that can ever be taken out without a check cord or lead. A retriever puppy, like young pointers and setters, may be taken in hand as soon as he has outgrown his puppy habits, which may be any time between five and ten months old. As a rule there is not much difficulty in teaching him to fetch and carry, his early tuition commencing with a glove or a soft india-rubber ball. It will greatly facilitate matters in this respect if a reward is ready for him in the shape of a piece of meat or other dainty when he is having his lessons. Then, as to dropping to hand, the same tactics must be employed as those already described for pointers or setters. You next want him to hunt on his own account, and this may be done by hiding the ball and encouraging him to seek for it; he will have partly learnt this lesson when seeking for the ball that he had seen thrown and that had rolled out of sight. Here again he must be rewarded on completing his task, and also when he is obedient to whistle. With the check cord you can make him keep to heel, and then there is only one more accomplishment for him to acquire before he is ready to be entered on game, and that is to take to water freely. Most dogs, if they have not been forced when puppies to go in against their will, are fond of the water, more particularly retrievers, which inherit the liking for it from the Newfoundland or Irish water spaniel. If, however, there is any difficulty in persuading the dog to enter the water, choose a warm day, and place a ball, a piece of biscuit, or anything that he likes, close to the edge of the stream, then a little way in, and so on until he has to swim for it. He must be well rewarded when he has brought it, if the ball has been used.

That a retriever should not mangle his game is most important, and he should carry it in his mouth alive without injuring a feather or disturbing a hair. At the same time it is dangerous to let a puppy begin by retrieving a wounded bird, and it is better to drop the dog and knock the bird on the head first than to run the risk of the former giving it a nip, and so laying the foundation of a bad habit. Should a runner be lost in a fence, after the puppy has had plenty of time to try to find it, a dead bird should be placed somewhere near the spot, and the reward given in the same way as if the lost bird had been found. It is not unusual for an untutored retriever to attempt to make a meal of his find;

under these circumstances there is used an instrument called a retriever bit, which is in the shape of the letter U and lies on the dog's "grinders," preventing his mouth from shutting. This, like the spike collar, is an expedient only worth trying when the puppy to be experimented upon promises in every other respect to make a perfect retriever. Game should be retrieved quickly, and when there is any hesitation in this respect the dog becomes subject to suspicion. He would most likely eat the bird if he thought he could do so without being found out. A puppy should not be allowed to retrieve fur until it has been well broken on feather. Spaniels may be taught to drop to hand and shot in the same way as pointers and setters, but, as it is a *sine qua non* that they should not hunt out of gunshot, the check cord is necessary in breaking them, if they are to be quickly got ready to enter upon game. Clumbers, more particularly, are worked in teams; when they are first handled, the man in command should have another person with him to act as whipper-in to teach them to answer quickly to the whistle. With this assistant present, the principal need not carry a whip, and, as his companion does all the rating, the spaniels are more willing to hunt close to him. The peg will be required to break them from chasing, but with unruly spaniels it is sometimes the custom to put a belt or collar with a few pounds of shot in it round their necks, or to put a bandage on one of their hind legs. Then, in order that the guns may be able to discern in what direction the dogs are working when they are beating thick coverts, bells are sometimes attached to their collars. A well-broken spaniel that will keep within twenty yards of the guns, and retrieves, is a very useful dog to shoot over, either when hunted in a team or singly, whether the variety be a Clumber, a Sussex, a Field, or a Norfolk. The Irish water spaniel requires much the same tuition as the retriever. [*See also* SHOOTING.]

RAWDON B. LEE.
FRED GRESHAM.

GLOSSARY.

Blaze—A white mark up the face.

Brisket—The front of the chest.

Button Ear—An ear which falls over in front, concealing the interior, as in fox-terriers.

Cat Foot—A short, round foot, with high and well-developed knuckles.

Chest—The whole body of the dog from the brisket to the belly.

Couplings—The length between the tops of the shoulder blades and the tops of the hip-joints.

Cow-hocked—Having the hock-joints (*q.v.*) turning inward as a cow's, and almost touching.

Crest—The upper ridge of a dog's neck. Usually applied to sporting dogs such as the setter.

Cropping—Trimming off part of a dog's ear with the object of bringing it nearer to a conventional standard of beauty and making it stand erect and pointed. Cropping is not allowed in this country, it being discontinued in 1895.

Dew Claw—A rudimentary toe or claw found occasionally upon the inside of the lower portion of the fore and hind legs of all breeds, but especially upon St. Bernards.

Dew Lap—Pendulous skin under the throat.

Dish Faced—Having the nose higher at the tip than at the *stop* (*q.v.*).

Docking—The practice of cutting or shortening a dog's tail.

Drop-ear—The same as "*button-ear*."

Elbow—The joint at the junction of the arm and fore arm, close to the body.

Enter—To train a dog to his future work.

Feather—The fringe of hair on the stern, ears and back of the legs. Sometimes used of long hair generally.

Flag—The name of the tail in some breeds, especially Setters and Retrievers.

Flews—The overhanging lips of the upper jaw.

Frill—The feather or hair under the neck or throat of a long coated dog—especially in a setter.

Hare-foot—A long, narrow foot, carried far forward. Contrasted with Cat-foot.

Haw—The inside eye-lid, which is plainly seen, reddened by exposure to the light; most apparent in the Bloodhound.

Height of a Dog—The perpendicular distance from the top of the shoulder-blade to the ground.

Hocks—The joints between the *pasterns* (*q.v.*) of the hind legs and the upper part of the leg.

Hucklebones—The tops of the hip-joints.

Knee—The joints between the pasterns of the fore legs and the upper part of the leg.

Leather—The skin of the ear, most generally used when speaking or writing of the bloodhound.

Level Jawed—Epithet given to a dog whose teeth meet evenly, and whose jaws are never *Overshot* (*q.v.*) nor *Undershot* (*q.v.*).

Overshot—Having the upper teeth in advance of the lower. An excess of this characteristic is said to make a dog **Pig-jawed**.

Pad—The thickened protuberance on the sole of a dog's foot.

Pastern—The lowest section of the leg, from the foot up to the knee or hock, according as it may be of the front or hind-leg.

Pily—Epithet of a coat consisting of two kinds of hair, the one soft and woolly, the other long and wiry.

Rose-Ear—An ear which folds at the back, and whose tip falls away backwards, exposing the interior.

Rounding—Trimming a hound's ears in order to protect them from being torn by gorse, &c.

Shoulder—The top of the shoulder blade, the point from which the height of a dog is measured.

Stern—The tail of a sporting dog, especially of a Fox-hound.

Stifle—The joint in a dog's hind leg next to the buttock; the hip joint.

Sting—Epithet applied to a tail which tapers to a fine point.

Stop—The indentation just in front of the eyes, between the skull proper and the nasal bone. It is most prominent in Bull-dogs, Pugs, and short-faced Spaniels.

Top-knot—The long hair on the top of the head of an Irish water spaniel or on any other dog.

True Arm—The upper part of the foreleg, contrasted with the lower, which is also known as the fore arm.

True Thigh—The upper part of the hind leg.

Tulip-ear—An ear which stands erect; this ear is not desirable in any variety of sporting dog.

Undershot—A dog is undershot when the lower teeth project in front of the upper ones. This deformity in a terrier is absolute disqualification in the prize ring.

Wire-haired—Epithet of a coat in which the hair is coarse and harsh. Commonly used to distinguish the long-haired varieties of dogs that are usually smooth-coated, even when the hair is not rough.

Bibliography.—*Dogs of the British Isles*, Stonehenge (Horace Cox, 1886); *The Greyhound*, Stonehenge (Longmans, Green and Co, 1875); *The Dog in Health and Disease*, Stonehenge (Longmans, Green and Co., 1875); *British Dogs*, Dalziel (L. U. Gill, 1884); *Book of the Dog*, V. Shaw (Cassell and Co., 1881); *Dog Breaking*, General Hutchinson (John Murray, 1865); *The Scientific Education of the Dog for the Gun*, H. H. (Sampson Low and Co., 1890); *Modern Dogs of Great Britain and Ireland*, *Sporting* Varieties, 2 Vols., *Non-Sporting*, 1 Vol., *The Terriers*, 1 Vol., Rawdon Lee (Horace Cox, 1896-7); *A History and Description of the Fox Terrier*, Rawdon Lee (Horace Cox, 1896); *Dog Diseases*, Dalziel (L. U. Gill, 1896); *The Dog: its Management and Diseases*, Woodruffe Hill (Swan Sonnenschein and Co., 1886); *The Whippet, or Race Dog*, Lloyd (L. U. Gill, 1894); *The Scottish Deerhound*, Bell (David Douglas, 1892); *Scottish Deerhounds and their Masters*, Cupples (Blackwood and Sons, 1894); *The Dogs of Scotland*, Thomson Gray (Mathew and Co., 1891); *Our Prize Dogs*, C. H. Mason (Forest and Stream, New York, 1888); *Kennel Secrets*, Ashmont (New York, 1892); *Dog Law*, Manson (Clowes and Son, 1893); and *The Dog in Poetry*, C. M. Leonard (David Nutt, 1893). There are also Stud Books, including those of the *Kennel Club*, published annually since 1874 (Horace Cox); *Fox Terrier* Stud books, published periodically (L. U. Gill); *Fox Hound* Stud books published regularly since 1864 (Bolton); *Harrier and Beagle* Stud book, published annually since 1891 (Waterlow and Sons); and *The Greyhound* Stud book, published annually since 1882 (Horace Cox).

DORY (*Zeus faber*).

MEASUREMENTS, ETC.—Length of head $2\frac{3}{4}$ to 3, of caudal fin, $4\frac{1}{2}$, height of body $2\frac{1}{4}$ in total length. The greatest thickness of the body equal $\frac{1}{5}$ of its height. *Eyes*—high up, one diameter in the post-orbital length of the head. Head as high as long. Mouth very protractile, its cleft oblique, the maxilla being nearly perpendicular when it is closed, and not reaching backward to beneath the eye: lower jaw the longer, and terminating posteriorly in two spines. Opercles spineless. Scapular region ridged in the adult, and having some spines in the young: some also at occiput. *Teeth*—finely cardiform, present on the jaws and vomer, but not on the tongue or palatine bones. *Gill-rakers*—few, short, and finely spinate. *Fins*—first dorsal almost continuous with the soft portion; its spines rather strong, gradually increasing in length to the fourth; the interspinous membrane is externally prolonged into filaments of varying lengths, while at the base of each spine is an outwardly-projecting spinous process. Second dorsal increasing in length to its third quarter, and armed along its base with from 7 to 10 spines on a bony plate, each of which consists of two portions: the largest, curved and broad, is directed somewhat backward, while the shorter portion is produced outward and a little forward: its rays unbranched. Pectoral short. Ventral as long as the head, and having, in the young, a spinate base: a double ridge extends from the fin to the vent, armed with eight lateral spines on either side. The anal spines and rays are similarly armed to those of the dorsal fin. Second anal spine the longest, and somewhat the strongest. Caudal rounded. *Scales*—not imbricate, a few along the cheeks. *Lateral-line*—descends in a gentle curve from opposite the upper edge of the eye to above middle of the anal fin, from whence it proceeds direct to the centre of the base of the tail. *Viscera*—stomach rather large, the narrow pyloric portion encircled by numerous cœcal appendages, which in some cases are branched. *Air-bladder*—elongated, with the appearance of a slight constriction in its posterior fourth, while a rounded muscular body exists in its anterior fourth, from which passes a tendon. On opening the air-bladder, its lining membrane is found to cease at the commencement of the last fourth of the organ, and here it forms a very low valve. In the interior of the upper half of the air-bladder is a narrow, vermiform, red gland, of a semi-circular form. *Colours*—olive grey, with a yellowish tinge, and usually yellow wavy horizontal bands. In the middle of either side, just posterior to the pectoral fin, a circular or oval black spot, surrounded by a narrow yellow ring. Fins grey; in some examples the ventrals are nearly black; in others, two rather dark horizontal bands pass along the dorsal and anal fin.

Day, *Fishes of Great Britain and Ireland*, vol i., p. 139.

DRIVING—From the earliest times the "harness horse" has been of vast use to mankind both in war and in peace. He drew the chariots of the ancients, and he is the pleasure horse of to-day, but notwithstanding the time which has elapsed since the horse was first a draught animal, it was not until the first decade of the present century that driving upon any recognised system came to be practised. So soon as wheeled vehicles came to be driven at any pace, it was discovered that various details became of importance, and that things which had never before been regarded as material were not without weight. This was in the days when coaching began to be a science; vehicles were built of less weight; lighter horses were used; the stage coachman improved in social status, and consequently in appearance, and the result was that definite rules for driving were observed. In fact, the whole code for driving arose out of the custom of four-horse driving, and it is a curious circumstance that no early treatise on driving is to be found.

Whether the reader adopts the style here recommended, or any other, he must be prepared to encounter many different opinions. Many persons are given to say that so long as one or more horses can be driven in safety, the observance of sundry minor rules is of no consequence. It is not well, however, to fall in with this theory. Now that sport and pastimes are receiving so much attention, the value of a "coach" is universally admitted. The self-taught rowing man, cricketer, equestrian, boxer, or what not, seldom or never achieves a success. If there be two ways of doing a thing, the self-taught man generally adopts the wrong method. In driving, as in other pursuits, not a little depends upon the observance of rules which have been laid down, not merely for the sake of insisting on some arbitrary system, but because they have been found to be productive of certain advantages. Take, for example, the way in which a man sits and holds his reins. Nothing is more common than to see a driver sitting on the very edge of a seat, his legs tucked under him, and the reins held in the tips of his fingers, a combination which renders his position unsafe, and prevents his having any real control over his horse or horses; so that, to start with, the seat on the box, and the holding of the reins are important matters.

For the purpose of the present article it must be assumed that the reader has some elementary knowledge of driving; he must, too, refer to the glossary for the names of the parts of the harness and carriage. During a novice's early attempts at driving, the reins will have been handed to him in the course of a drive, while he is seated beside his instructor; but after some time he will start himself, and in this connection he must be warned not to mount a vehicle without first taking the reins in his hand, unless he has dismounted and handed the reins to some one else to hold during his absence from the driving-seat. To mount without reins is to court accident, as, should the horse start before the driver has the reins in his hand, an immediate smash may take place. Again, if it be necessary to put passengers in the vehicle before the driver is up, an attendant should stand at the horse's head the while, nor should he move under any consideration until the driver is in his seat and gives the signal to start.

DRIVING A SINGLE HORSE—**Holding the Reins**—The first and second fingers of the left hand are placed between the reins, the left, or near side rein being uppermost, that is to say, over the forefinger; the right, or off side rein is then between the second and third fingers. Many persons are seen driving with the forearm and wrist quite straight, and the thumb pointing to the front, while the reins are held near the tips of the fingers. This is wrong. The arm should not be held straight at the side of the body, because then the right hand cannot readily be brought to the assistance of the left

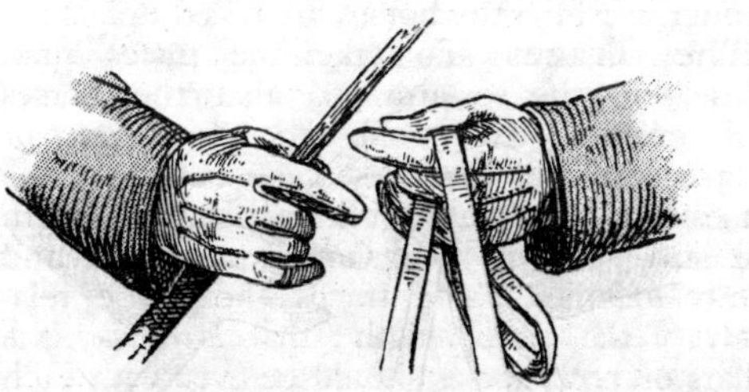

REINS FOR SINGLE HORSE.

without swaying the body about. The forearm should be carried across the body, so that the hand is opposite the waistcoat buttons. The wrist, instead of being perfectly straight in continuation of the forearm, should be very slightly bent, and the reins, instead of being at the tips of the fingers, in which position the driver has no power over his horse, should lie at the roots of the fingers, and, with the wrist bent as directed above, the top rein will lie just over the lower knuckle of the forefinger. The back part of the reins will then be in the palm of the hand, and from the beginning the novice should accustom himself to press the third and fourth fingers on the reins, by which means they will be prevented from slipping. When driving a single horse, this pressure of the third and fourth fingers on the palm of the hand is not absolutely indispensable, but it will be good practice against the time when an attempt is made to drive tandem or four horses, as in both these cases the fingers must be pressed down to prevent slipping. With the reins held as directed, there will be a sense of strength and firmness which will be entirely lacking when the reins are at the finger tips.

The left hand must not, of course, touch the body, or there will be no power to stop the horses, nor must the hand be held right away in front, as delicacy of handling would then be impossible, and the arm would quickly tire. The position must be easy, but the exact number of inches which should separate the hand from the body cannot be laid down; from six to eight inches will probably be found somewhere near the mark for the generality of people with ordinary horses.

Management of the Reins—It stands to reason that no horse can be driven with one hand alone, except on a country road where no other vehicles are either met or overtaken, and then only when the horse goes so temperately as not to require the assistance of the right hand. The latter will from time to time be needed. The second, third, and fourth fingers, may be placed between the reins, and the hand may grasp them in front of the left; two fingers (the first and second) may be placed on the right rein to aid in holding the horse, or either rein may be grasped with the right hand when about to turn a corner. The proper way to grasp a rein with the right hand is to put the little finger up against it, and take it with the full hand. For example, suppose it becomes necessary to take up the right rein, the right hand should be placed a few inches to the front, more or less, according to the amount of force judged to be required, and slipped in between the reins. The elbow is at the same time allowed to leave the right side, and when the rein is grasped by the right hand the line of the knuckles will be nearly parallel to the reins. If the left rein be taken up, the action will be the same.

One thing there is which beginners and self-taught drivers are frequently guilty of doing, but which never should be done. When they bring the right hand to the assistance of the left, especially on the right rein, they are very much given to pulling the rein out of the left hand. The reins thus become of unequal length, and if the right hand were removed the horse would immediately be guided to that side on which the rein was tightest. It is extremely difficult to avoid doing this, but the beginner should ever be on the watch, and should remember that in all circumstances the reins must ever be of equal length in the left hand. If by any chance one of them should be drawn out, it must immediately be slipped back again. The firmer the third and fourth fingers are pressed upon the rein in the palm of the left hand, the less easy will it be to draw out either rein with the right hand. Another thing to be remembered is that, so far as is possible, the left hand should be kept still and in the same position, but more will be said on this point when we come to the driving of four horses. In speaking of keeping the left hand still, beginners may be warned against indulging in that most uncoachmanlike and reprehensible practice of jerking the reins, "jobbing" the mouth as it is called, to make the horse quicken his pace. Anybody having any choice in the matter will never buy a slug, or, if he do chance to become possessed of one, will get quit of him at the earliest opportunity, for there is no pleasure in driving a horse of that kind. Still, his mouth must never be jerked, for the habit once acquired is very difficult to forget, and to "job" the mouth of a free-going, high couraged horse is to spoil him. If one finds one's self behind a sluggish animal he must be driven up to the bit by means of the whip.

The embryo coachman will, as he acquires proficiency in driving, hear a good deal about hands; and, although this estimable quality cannot be treated of in few words, the beginner will do well to remember that some advance will have been made if he never use more force on the reins than is absolutely necessary. It is far easier to observe this rule when driving than when riding. When on horseback the rider's balance may be disturbed by any sudden motion of the horse, and, if he find himself in company, the horse may begin to pull a little, which may induce the rider to pull at him. When driving, however, there is considerable security on the box seat, and there is seldom or never occasion to clutch at the reins as unfinished performers in the saddle are apt to do. The coachman should never leave slack rein out. The reins should be gathered up so that with each stride of the horse a slight tug at the reins may be felt, that is to say when a temperate horse is driven; and none other will be driven by a tyro. But even if he be somewhat impetuous, care should be taken that no greater pressure should be put upon the horse's mouth than will suffice to hold him. The driver must give and take with his horse, "dropping his hand" as the phrase goes, when the horse gives him the opportunity, and restraining him when inclined to go too much ahead.

Closely allied to the management of the reins is the use of the legs in driving. They should not be tucked up under the body, with the driver standing on his toes, so to speak; nor, on the other hand, should they be thrust out so as to bring the toes against the dashboard. On the position of the feet when there is no dashboard, the reader is referred to the remarks on driving four horses. The driver should sit well on his seat, and not on the front edge of it, and the legs should be just so far out that the whole of the foot from the heel to the toe is on the footboard; the latter, in fact, should be to the coachman what the stretcher in a boat is to the oarsman. No one can row properly with the arms alone, neither can he drive; the feet and legs must lend their assistance.

The Whip—(See remarks on driving four horses).

DOUBLE HARNESS—The directions given above for driving a single horse apply in the main to the management of a pair. The manner of holding the reins is the same, and the remarks concerning the right hand apply equally in each case; but of course two horses are more difficult to drive than one, because the coachman has to see that both horses share the work equally. In the case of a single horse, he alone has to draw the vehicle, and every indication given to him by his driver determines whether the passage round corners, or between two vehicles, can be made with safety or not. Two horses, on the other hand, cannot be said to be driven unless each does his share towards accomplishing the work. This is partly a question of harnessing, and partly a question of coachmanship. It is an old, but very true, saying that a pair of horses well put together are half driven, and the proper harnessing of two horses is really a more difficult task than driving them.

In double harness there are three things to be taken into consideration when putting a pair together—the adjustment of the traces, the adjustment of the coupling reins, and the manner in which the horses are poled up.

The Traces—To take the traces first. These must be so arranged that the horses work evenly. Every one who drives a pair for pleasure will of course take care that the horses match tolerably well in point of length and size, so that they should work well and evenly together. The traces should be relatively of the same length; that is to say, the collars of both horses should be even with each other; both horses should be as near their work as possible, but not so near as to cause the action of the hind legs to be interfered with by

Splinter Bar.

the splinter bar. How to put the horses to a vehicle will be best learned by watching some competent person, and asking him to explain the distance which should separate the haunches and backs of the horses from the splinter bar. The traces, once correctly adjusted, should never be touched, and if the horses do not work together, it is the coupling reins which must be altered and not the traces.

The Reins—If the reins of pair-horse harness be examined, it will be seen that they are composed of four pieces. There is one long rein, called the draught rein, which has a buckle halfway in its length, the buckle being (when the rein is in use) at that point which is in the

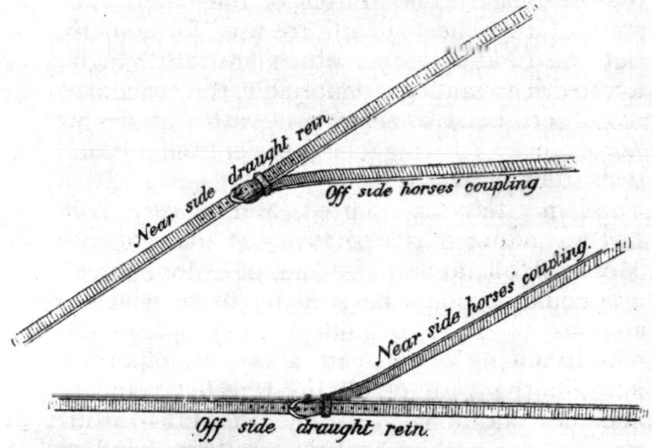

carriage behind the coachman's hands. The ends of this draught rein are buckled to the outside of the bit of each horse, that is to say, one end is buckled to the outside (left side) of the left or near side horse, and the other end to the out side (right side) of the right, or off horse. As it is perfectly clear that two horses could not be driven in this fashion, coupling reins, or couplers, have been designed to give the coachman the necessary control over his horses. Holes are punched in the draught rein at some little distance from the hand part, and from each side of the draught rein runs the coupler, the rein which is fastened to the inside of the bit of each horse. The illustration will make this clear.

It will be seen that, when the right or off draught rein is pulled, both horses will receive the indication to turn to the right; the off horse will feel the indication through the medium of the draught rein, and the near side horse through the pull on his coupling; while, if the left rein be pulled, the draught rein acts on the near side of the near horse, and the off horse receives his hint how to turn from the action of the coupling rein, which runs from the near side draught rein to the near side of the off horse. Here, it may be noted, that if the direction be given to take up or let out the near or off horse's coupling, the coupling which runs from the opposite draught rein is indicated. The near horse's coupling runs from the off side draught rein, and the off coupling from the near side draught rein.

At first sight, the adjustment of these coupling reins would seem to be a very simple matter, but really it requires a good deal of judgment to put a pair of horses properly together. It is seldom, unless great trouble and expense have been incurred, that two horses are found with precisely the same freedom, and consequently the coupling reins must be so adjusted that while the freer horse is restrained, the slower has more freedom. The effect of letting out a coupler is to tighten the draught rein, to take up a coupler is to slacken the draught rein; and when one horse is slower than the other, that which is less free should generally be put on the off side, where he can with greater convenience be gently touched with the whip.

Coupling Up—In double harness the horses are attached to the carriage by the traces and the pole-chains or pole-pieces, the latter being wide leather straps. Stage coaches, private drags, mail phaetons, and T-carts, in fact, all carriages which are presumably driven by the owner, have pole-chains, while broughams, victorias, landaus, and all carriages which the coachman drives have pole-pieces. Both pole-chains and pole-pieces are fastened to the pole-head, and, when the horses are put to, either chain or piece passes through the kidney link of the harness. The chain is made secure by putting the hook at the end through one of the links of the chain; the pole-piece by the ordinary buckle arrangement. Within the last year or two, the Kipling pole has been invented. It differs from the ordinary pole-head in that the pole is altogether shorter, reaching no more than an inch or two in front of the horses' chests, and from the end two metal curved arms turn right and left, so that the attachment is very much shorter than either pole-chain or pole piece. Several advantages are claimed for it, one of them being that there is no projecting pole to run into other vehicles; while it has been urged in its favour that with it the horse can hold back the carriage, and can turn more easily than when the ordinary pole is employed. New inventions, however, in the matter of harness and carriage fittings make their way but slowly into popular favour, so it remains to be seen whether this will ever come into anything like general use.

Any one buying a carriage for two horses, especially a second-hand affair, should be most careful to have the pole examined by an expert to see if any fault can be observed. A broken pole almost invariably means a frightful accident, although the brakes now almost universally attached to carriages may render valuable assistance; still, with the pole broken, there are absolutely no means of checking its progress, unless the horses be going uphill, in which case the pole would seldom break. From time to time, the pole should be examined by some competent person, and no consideration should induce any one to drive with a pole that is defective, or with any makeshift contrivance.

TANDEM DRIVING—The theory that the driving of two horses tandem fashion arose from hunting men desiring to take on their own hunter in economical fashion and putting him leader, may be at once dismissed as groundless. A far more reasonable theory is that as four horses were used to draw a four-wheeled vehicle, the idea occurred to somebody that both the team and the vehicle might be divided, and that two horses might be of as much service to the dogcart as four were to the coach or travelling chariot. In the main particulars, the rules for four-in-hand driving hold good for tandem, but in the harness there is some difference. The wheeler in the tandem wears the same harness as the ordinary dogcart horse, but the leader's pad is of a lighter description, being as often as not on the same pattern as that for double harness. For attaching the leader, several plans have been adopted. It was once the custom to have eyes on the shafts, to which the leader's traces were fastened; but this was a most reprehensible practice, for if the leader started, he at once pulled the cart on to the wheeler. Another plan is to have eyes attached to the tugs of the wheeler's traces, and to these the hooks of the leader's traces are fastened. There is very little to be said against this plan, the only objection in some people's eyes being that there is a rather large scope of trace between the wheeler and the leader; and, in the case of an unskilful coachman or an unwilling leader, the front horse may get his legs over the traces should he hang back. The next matter is the bar—a sort of imitation of those used for four-in-hand work. A short chain is attached to the harness, and this chain supports the bar, which is connected by a short strap with another one, having a hook at each end, to which the leader's two traces are attached. This unquestionably looks smarter than the ordinary long traces, but a leader so equipped should be driven by a very skilful coachman. The traces are very much shorter than on the other plan, and, unless the wheeler be very well in hand and kept back, it is an easy matter to drop the leading bar upon the leader's hocks, and thus cause him to kick should he be that way inclined. Lately, however, what is called the continuous trace has been invented, in which one trace is made to serve the purpose of both leader and wheeler. In theory it answers, I believe, exceedingly well, but in practice the objection is that you cannot put on a leader just when you want him without changing the trace; whereas, if the same metal eyes be affixed to the tugs of the wheeler's traces, one horse can be driven at pleasure. The leader, by the way, should have what are called loin-straps, that is to say, a strap crossing the loins, with a loop at either end; and through these the traces pass to keep them from dropping unnecessarily to the ground. These should never be omitted, for a leader whose traces are slack from the hames to the end is apt to become very unmanageable.

The Tandem Cart—In olden days it was by no means uncommon to see two horses, fastened tandem fashion, drawing a four-wheeled vehicle. This, however, is a very unsightly arrangement, and there is besides a useless waste of power, for although tandem-driving is very good fun and excellent practice for driving four-in-hand, there can be no possible doubt that two horses harnessed abreast do more work than two placed one in front of the other. All sorts of two-wheeled carts are used for tandem, but the best are those which are rather high; for, to drive a tandem comfortably, the coachman requires to be at some little elevation above his horses, just as driving four is easier from a coach than from a lower vehicle. A few years ago a Tandem Club was started, and a very nice cart was adopted as a pattern. It was built by Messrs. Holland and Holland, of Oxford Street, and could no doubt be seen by those who are anxious to start a tandem in proper style. The balancing of the cart, always an important item in the case of all two-wheeled vehicles, becomes additionally so when a tandem is attempted, for nothing looks worse than a tandem with the points of the shafts pointing towards the sky, while the groom on the back seat has to hold on like grim death to keep his position. The greatest care, therefore, is necessary in the adjustment of the back band, and of course in the arrangement of the seats. The weights should not press unduly upon the horse's back, but at the same time there should be no more than just sufficient play in the shafts to keep the vehicle level. This will always be found a matter of difficulty, as, if the coachman be light, and the groom heavy, the weight must of course be brought more forward, while, if the coachman be a heavy man and the groom a feather-weight, the back band will have to be rather shorter, so as to prevent excessive play of the shafts. The novice may be warned that neither the adjustment of the seats, nor the tightening or letting out of the back band, will accomplish all that is desired. There must be a compromise between the two, and it will take some little time to learn how a cart should be properly balanced, because the weight of each person riding in it has more or less effect upon the arrangements of the seats, and, of course, upon the tension of the backband.

The Leader—Tandem driving with a bad leader is indeed a sorry business; in fact, it may be doubted whether the best tandem coachman could drive with a bad leader, and consequently every pains should be taken to secure a suitable horse. Before the horse makes his first appearance in front, it is as well to give him a little preliminary training, and this may conveniently take the form of driving him in a field with a pair of long reins. He should be encouraged to go straight without having any weight to draw, as when descending a hill the leader in a tandem has of course nothing to do, and very little more when travelling on the flat. If a horse be walked about, and will go straight until an indication be given him to turn right or left, the chances are that he will turn out a satisfactory leader, and if his trainer be an active man, who can run 400 or 500 yards at a time, the horse will be more likely to turn out well. When first harnessed to the cart, it may be well to have a man to run by his head for a short time, but special care must be taken to have the wheeler well in hand, so that in the event of any vagaries on the part of a new leader the vehicle may be at once brought to a standstill. If he should be given to shying or turning round, the sooner he is replaced by another the better, for there is no pleasure in driving an ill-sorted pair.

Driving—For the method of holding the reins and managing the whip, the reader is referred to the section on driving four-in-hand, but he may be warned that the handling of the

Reins for Tandem.

reins is more difficult in a tandem than on a coach, because there is no spread. All four reins run nearly parallel, consequently to pick up the near or off leading rein, or one of the wheel reins, requires greater nicety than in the case of four, when the angle is greater. Should the leader happen to turn round, or land the driver in any trouble, the wheeler should be immediately turned round after him. It will be almost useless for the novice to attempt to get the leader into position again, for as fast as he pulls him from one side he will probably go to the other, but, if the wheeler be turned round, both horses will be in line, and a fresh start will be made. In consequence of the difficulty, already referred to, of picking out any particular rein in tandem driving, sundry other methods of holding the reins have been suggested. Some tandem coachmen drive with what is called a full hand, that is with a rein between each finger; others again hold the hand as in riding, with the leader's reins outside and the wheeler's in, but neither of these, nor sundry other methods, obtain the sanction of coachmen, and those who drive tandem are therefore recommended to adopt the ordinary four-horse style, as by so doing they will be more at home in driving four horses than if they adopt a different method for each team.

The portioning of the work in a tandem is a matter of nicety. On the flat the leader is really required to do no work; his traces should readily shake, and of course when going downhill he should be taken back an inch or two, so that by no possibility could he jump into his collar and pull the wheeler down. It is bad enough if the wheel horse falls in a four-wheeler when going downhill, but in a tandem the result is likely to be still worse, and, unless care be taken in the respect above mentioned, the chances of coming to grief are just double, because the wheeler may fall, either by treading on some loose stones or from some other cause, or he may be pulled over by the leader when he might otherwise keep his feet, and this will suggest that the pace downhill may be slightly slower, at any rate when a novice is driving, than if he were in charge of a single horse only. It is when going uphill, be the incline ever so slight, that the leader in a tandem becomes of real use. He may then be called upon to ease the wheeler. If the gradient be but gentle he need not be allowed too much play; but when a steeper hill is met with, he may be allowed to do a good share of the work, and the position of the wheeler's collar should tell the coachman what share the leader is bearing in the draft of the vehicle. On other occasions the leader should be nursed, for driving a tandem with a tired leader is not a pleasurable occupation. For the same reason, too, no slug should be driven in the lead. A slow wheeler may be kept up to his work with a double thong, but if he be free and the leader a slug, the wheeler will be constantly annoyed by the sound of the point of the thong passing him. Mention of the whip reminds one that the coachman would do well to practice hitting his leader on both sides, for if he hit him on the right side only he will be very much abroad, should he attempt to drive four horses, when he tries to touch the near leader. To hit him neatly is a somewhat difficult operation, but more can be learned in five minutes by verbal instruction than by whole pages of writing.

Turning a corner with a tandem also requires some nicety. Supposing the coachman desires to turn sharply to the left the pace must of course be slackened, and the greatest care taken to keep the wheeler from following the leader too quickly. Every one who has ridden in a hansom cab knows how the drivers of these vehicles cut their corners, and if the indication be given too soon to the leader, and the wheeler follow him, it is easy to see that the vehicle will go on to the curb, or against any post that happens to be in the way. The coachman should see well round the corner before he attempts to turn; the leader should then be pointed as for four-in-hand driving, and the opposite wheel rein should be kept tight to prevent the wheel turning too quickly. In driving through a carriage gateway, or into an inn-yard, especially if the road be not very wide, very careful management is required, and before attempting to make a turn, the tandem should be taken as far as possible to the opposite side of the road, so that as wide a sweep as possible may be taken.

DRIVING FOUR-IN-HAND—Some of the remarks made in connection with tandem driving apply with equal force to the handling

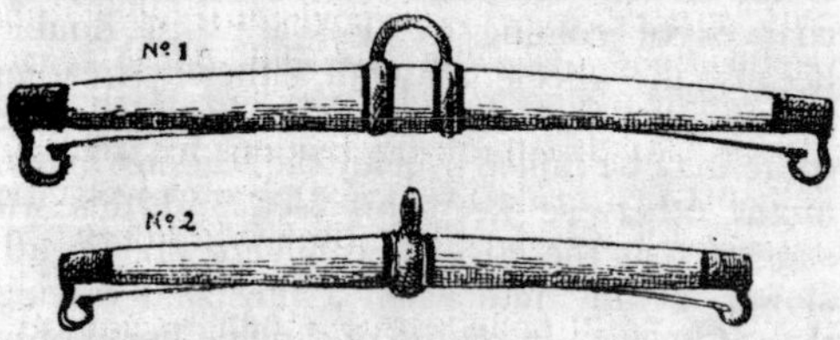

1. Main Bar.
2. Leader Bar.

of four horses, the team being really nothing more than two tandem teams placed side by side. The tandem may be the more "tricky" team to drive, but of course it stands to reason that four horses present more difficulties than do a tandem, for the simple reason that there are four horses to watch, to hold, to guide, or to urge forward instead of two, while it must not be forgotten that a great deal more strength is required to drive four.

In holding the reins, the near side leading rein is on the top of the forefinger of the left hand, the off leading rein being between the first and second fingers. The near wheel rein is also between the first and second fingers but underneath the off lead-rein, and then the off wheel rein lies by itself between the second and third

Pole.

Pole Hook.

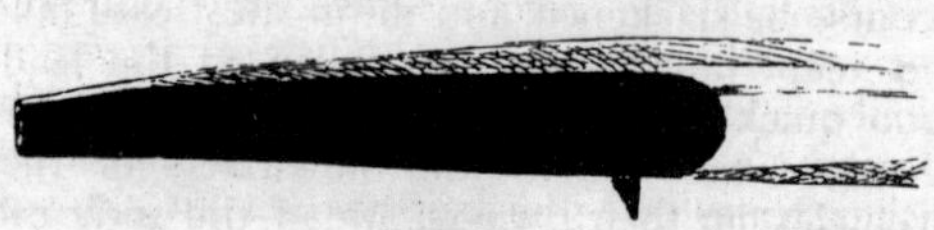

Pole End.

fingers, so that there are two reins between the first and second fingers.

At the top of the pole is a hook, to which is fastened the main bar, while at each end of this bar is a hook on which the leading bars hang, each horse having a bar to himself. As in the case of other kinds of driving, the early lessons will of course be received from an instructor, who will hand the reins to the beginner, but the proper method of mounting may be at once explained. The reins will be found tucked away by the pad, and the coachman, taking the leaders' reins in his right hand, places them as already directed on each side of the first finger, the wheelers' reins coming beneath them. All four reins should be drawn nearly as tight as they will go without causing the horses to move, and, with the right hand, a little slack is given to the two off reins, the whole being then transferred to the right hand, the same fingers dividing them as before; the coachman mounts to the box, and changes the reins from the right to the left hand.

The coachman being seated (remember, his toes must never project over the footboard), the next thing is to start. This is apparently a simple operation, yet one which is attended with great difficulty, and not in one start in fifty does practice coincide with theory. Theory says that the wheelers must start the coach, for if the leaders come into their collars they are very likely to break a bar, yet as a matter of fact it is not always easy to make the wheelers start first, and if they do, there is just a chance of their driving the pole into the leaders' quarters, in which event one or both of them may kick, and lead to a complication.

It may at first sight seem to be an easy matter to stop this by shortening the leaders' reins, so that, should they start first, they may at least be unable to get into their collars; but if this plan be tried, and the wheelers do not start quickly enough, the leaders, as soon as they feel the bit, will probably come back towards the wheelers. Plenty of scope, therefore, should be allowed the horses at starting: and the best must be made of the attempt, but most coachmen will confess that in starting they are not always able to act up to their principles. When the horses are once in motion, a final adjustment of the reins can be made, and then it will be seen at what length they should be.

After some practice this will be found out, but at first, in fact, for some little while, they will generally be too long, and will require to be shortened. Very many of the old coachmen simply shorten all four by catching hold of them with the right hand behind the left, and pulling them through gently, adjusting the length of each rein by pulling it singly from behind; but this is, by the majority of modern coachmen, held to be the wrong way. Instead, the right hand is put forward to take hold of the leading reins to draw them back and shorten them, while the lower fingers draw back the wheel reins to the proper length, and place them over the third finger, the leading reins being then replaced.

Any minor alterations which may still be necessary are effected by gently pushing the reins through from the back, for it is a canon of driving that no rein should be shortened from the back, except, perhaps, the bottom one, or when all four require pulling back together. At the same time, there are plenty of men who follow the old plan of shortening their reins from behind.

Whatever may have been the case with driving tandem, any one attempting to drive

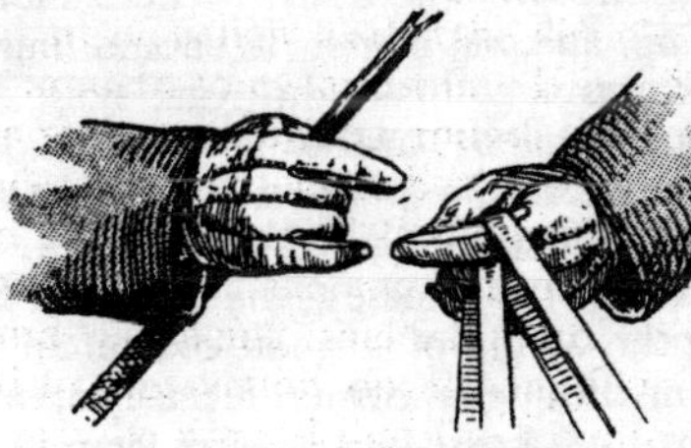

Reins for Four Horses.

four-in-hand will find that for some time the reins are given to slip, the off lead and near wheel reins, which lie between the same fingers, being the greatest delinquents. This will generally cause the horses to go unevenly. The wheelers may be to the right and the leaders to the left, but they can be instantly put straight by taking hold of the two middle reins, the two that will be easier to handle, and pushing them back through the fingers. Should these two reins have been hauled tight, and the other two allowed to slip, the easiest way to get the team straight is perhaps to pull out the two middle reins, which will then enable the others to act. After that, all four should be shortened at once, and the outside reins will, or should, be *in statu quo*.

The presence of an instructor is absolutely necessary to any one who desires to drive properly, and the position of the hands will be one of the greatest difficulties the beginner has to contend with. His tendency will be to get his hand too far forward, in which case he will be thoroughly tired in less than five minutes, for he will be doing what is analogous to holding a weight more or less at arm's length. On the other hand, if his hand be too close to the body he will not be able to check his horses. A good plan is to let the elbow joint rest on the hip bone and be kept there, care being taken to keep the arm well to the side. This may give a little stiffness to the position, but it will help to keep the hand in the proper place, and the coachman should remember that whatever he does with his reins, whether he shortens them, lengthens them, or pulls either the one or the other, the left hand must always be kept still. This sounds easy enough in theory, but in practice it is exceedingly difficult, and it takes a long time thoroughly to acquire the proper habit.

Another difficulty the beginner has to contend with is that he will be at a loss to know the exact amount of force he is using. The weight of the reins is of course considerable, and, as the coachman sits higher than in a phaeton or dog-cart, it is naturally more felt. Still, as a kite string is not straight from the kite to the hand, so the reins are not perfectly straight from the terrets to the coachman's hands, except when in the act of pulling up, and therefore the coachman need not think he is necessarily doing wrong because the reins shake a little. In driving four, as in driving one, he should just gently feel the horses' mouths, always supposing they do not need any greater amount of restraint, and it will not be until after he has made several attempts at handling four horses that he will know when he is succeeding in doing this.

In turning corners it is easier to turn to the left than to the right, for the simple reason that the near leading rein is more easily found and grasped than the off, while it is also simpler to catch hold at once of the two off reins than of the two near ones. The plan generally adopted in turning a corner is, in the first place (we will suppose a turn to the left is to be made), to draw the horses to the right before approaching the turn, and, while the coachman is doing this, it will be a convenient time to tighten the off wheel rein a little, so that when the wheelers see the leaders turn they may be prevented from following too quickly. When it is judged that the time has arrived for turning, the right hand is placed on the top rein (the near lead) several inches in front of the left hand, more or less according to the sharpness of the turn to be made, and drawn back to the left hand, while the thumb should grasp the rein just in front of the point at which the right hand seizes it. This makes the top rein loop under the thumb, the effect being to shorten the near lead rein by the number of inches which intervened between the left hand and the right. The leaders are brought round, and, as they make the turn, the right hand is placed on the off reins to hinder the wheelers, who should turn in the tracks of the leaders, from coming round too suddenly. The whole team should not, as is so often seen, cut the corner. To turn to the right the process is reversed. The off leading rein is looped, and the two near reins are seized by the right hand in order to check the suddenness of the turn.

To seize the two near reins, however, is not so easy as holding the two off side reins. The right hand must be put forward outside the reins, which must be grasped with the whole hand, and not merely with a finger or two. Here it may be pointed out that great care should be taken when pulling either of the reins, singly or in pairs, to draw them in a direct line to the body, and neither to the right nor to the left. For instance, in making a turn to the left, the two off reins should not be drawn to the right, but up to the buttons of the waistcoat.

A good deal of judgment is requisite in fairly dividing the work between the horses. In the case of a beginner the leaders, if at all inclined to be free, will do the bulk of the work, and when the leaders are doing too much, their traces will be tight, while those of the wheelers will be slack, and the collars will be hanging more or less loosely on their necks. The remedy for this is to shorten the leaders' reins, but, again it must be repeated, without allowing the left hand to fall forward. When ascending a hill the leaders may be allowed to do plenty of work, but in going down hill they should do none. In the ordinary way, with a good coachman, it is scarcely necessary to shorten the leaders going downhill, as, when the leaders come back and the reins are slipped through together, the normal position will hold good, and the leaders' traces will shake, or, in the language of the road, the leaders will be taken out of draught.

Pulling up, too, requires some little care. A beginner, even when driving the most perfectly broken team, will seldom or never have his wheelers quite so much under control that the slightest motion of his hand will serve to pull them up. He will generally find that at the best he has his wheel reins a little too long; consequently, when he expects his horses to stop they will not be receiving the necessary amount of pressure on their mouths. When approaching the gate or other point at which it is desired to stop, the embryo coachman should look at his reins and see whether they are at the proper tension, while a slight attempt may at the same time be made with the same object. If any of them are too slack, they should be pushed up gently through the fingers, and then the distance should be judged when to commence the operation of stopping. This should be accomplished very gradually by all coachmen, but especially so by the beginner, for nothing looks worse than what is known as a bad pull up.

The wheels of the vehicle should not be driven right into the gutter, nor should the coach be stopped several feet from the kerb, while to pull up a yard or two ahead of the proper place is an indication that the horses are not properly in hand. In all kinds of driving, but especially in four-in-hand work, a very great deal can be learned by the eye, and to sit on the box-seat of a drag or coach, when a good coachman is at work, gives ample opportunity for watching his every movement.

The Use of the Whip—In the hands of a coachman the whip is an article of the greatest value, but in the hands of an inexperienced and rash person it is a source of fruitful danger. A cardinal rule with every one who drives, whatever be the number of horses, should be never to use the whip at all without strict necessity, and in the hands of the beginner it should be strictly confined to causing a horse to accelerate his pace. It should not be grasped like an umbrella, but, when not wanted to touch a horse, it should lie on the thumb, under the fingers, steadied by the third and fourth fingers, an arrangement which leaves the first two fingers free to assist the left hand with the reins when necessary. This is the way to hold a whip, whether it be for two horses or four. To use it, it is with the generality of horses sufficient to draw it lightly over the body. There should be no flicking, and of course it should never be allowed to crack or make the least noise. Nor should any horse in harness be struck under the flank, or towards the quarters, a blow thus given being likely to cause him to kick.

In driving two horses, the whip is found useful in the hands of a good coachman as an aid. If in turning a corner, let us suppose to the left, the off horse hangs away from the turn and does not come round with his companion, a gentle touch over the shoulder causes him to flinch from the lash and take the required direction, while sometimes, if the near horse turns too quickly, a slight touch on his near shoulder will cause him to take things more leisurely. In driving two horses great care is necessary to hit the right horse and not the one which is already doing the bulk of the work. This sounds but a truism, but it is only after some little practice that one learns which horse it is that requires to be roused, even though it be but a little. In short, one of the obvious directions for the use of the whip is, use it as little as possible.

In tandem and four-in-hand work, the whip will be a sad difficulty in the hands of a beginner, and he should practice catching it most assiduously on foot, and have nothing to do with it while driving. It is not possible to give any lucid explanation of how a whip should be caught; all that can be done is to give a few broad hints. The thong of the tandem or four-in-hand whip is about double the length of the crop, but, when caught, the double thong is about the length of a pair horse whip. The point of the thong, that is to say, the thin end of it, is taken in the hand, which grasps the whip just below the thumb ferrule, about seven or eight inches up the whip. The crop should be held nearly, but not quite, horizontal to the ground, the elbow being at some distance from the right side of the body, and the knuckles pointing directly upwards. The next step is that three motions have to be made simultaneously. The knuckles should be brought vertical to the ground, the elbow should be dropped, while at the same time these motions will cause the crop to take a nearly vertical position, and while these are being made a slight circular movement should be given to the thong from left to right.

As the crop becomes perpendicular to the ground, the thong is thrown upwards, while the aforesaid slightly circular action causes it to catch about three or four inches below the quill of the whip; but it will be found that that portion which is round the stick coils two ways. About the centre it should be drawn out with the left hand, brought down into the right hand, and the point should be turned two or three times the reverse way round the whip, just below the thumb ferrule. This will keep the point of the lash from getting free. The description is soon given, but the attainment of the art is, to most people, exceedingly difficult. There must be no hitting at the thong with the crop, nor must the quill be held downwards, and the thong coiled round the stick. The whip will always be a difficulty until the art of catching it can be done instinctively, without either looking at the whip or thinking about it. In using it, care must be taken not to uncoil it when touching the wheelers, and, when hitting the off side leader, the point must touch him under the bar. The near leader must also be hit under the bar, but this exceedingly difficult operation cannot be taught in print. The coachman must be shown by a competent instructor, and he must be content to sit either on a vehicle or on a pair of steps, and practice half an hour at a time for a good many days before he succeeds in making even a moderate success of the trick.

Brakes and Skids—It has long been debated whether a brake on a two-wheeled vehicle is an advantage or not. Of those who have tried them, some assert that, when descending a hill, the use of a brake in a dog-cart or similar vehicle tends to throw extra weight on the horse's back, while others are just as loud in its praise. To some extent the matter rights itself, because for a country in which precipitous hills are found a two wheeled carriage is not suitable, for, if the horse does fall, the chances are greatly in favour of a serious accident. Without therefore saying more than that it is, on the whole, better to have a brake on a dog-cart than not, because it need not be brought into use unless absolutely required, the statement may fearlessly be advanced that the fitting of brakes to carriages with four wheels is an unmitigated blessing to both horses and coachman.

In the olden days, when roads were bad, a hill was really less dangerous than it is now, for the soil was generally rather "woolly," *i.e.*, loose, and so the wheels bit well into the ground and the vehicle was thereby retarded; while, if the road chanced to be a hard one, there was generally some loose soil at the side for the benefit of the vehicle going down hill. Prudent persons used to skid when about to descend a hill which was at all steep in proportion to the weight of the vehicle, but in the stage-coach days, when opposition was rife, they did not always trouble to skid, and many an accident resulted in consequence. It was a great boon when the patent skid was invented. This worked on an arm, to which was attached a chain with a leather hand-piece, and in the leather was a hole which went over an iron button within reach of the coachman's right hand, thus keeping the arm up and the drag off the ground. The coachman needed no assistance in putting on the skid; he merely pulled the leather off the button, lowered the arm gently, and the pan dropped just in front of the wheel. At the foot of the hill the coachman backed his horses and hauled the whole affair up again. Then came the patent brake, which, in a crude form, had been used years before on the trucks on some of the Northumberland mines. Several kinds are in the market, but it is best to adhere to the pattern in general use, in which the brake is put on by drawing the handle back, and taken off by releasing it from its notch and allowing it to come forward.

To use the brake properly, some little knack is required. In a light vehicle, if put on suddenly to its full power, a distinct and disagreeable jerk is experienced. In the case of horses suddenly bolting—underneath a railway bridge, for instance, as an unseen and unexpected train dashes along overhead — applying the brake suddenly cannot be helped; but when used at ordinary hills it should be put on gently at first. This will always be possible if the hill be taken, as it should be, in good time. Brake or no brake, the pace should be slackened as the crown of the hill is approached, and care should be taken that the horses are well in hand; but this does not mean that they should be violently pulled or held so tightly as to confine them unnecessarily. The exact moment for putting on the brake depends upon the fall of the ground, and must be left to the driver's discretion; but it should be at the spot where the ground begins to fall to the hill. Always go slowly off the crown of a hill, for if the horses once get the better of the coachman, he is scarcely likely to stop them before reaching the bottom of the hill.

The brake, though an excellent friend, can be made too much of. It is not wanted at every trifling gradient, and after a horse has been toiling uphill or drawing on the flat it is a relief to him to use some other muscles by getting out of draught—that is, doing no work. But if the brake be put on for every little descent, the wheels will be retarded, and the horse will have to draw the carriage just as though he were going uphill. At the same time, in order to be safe, an inexperienced person will require the brake far more often than will a finished coachman. The actual steepness of a hill alone will not decide whether the brake is to be used, and how much of it. In the first place, the weight of the carriage must be considered. A T-cart could be driven at a good trot, where a well-laden coach would be skidded. Secondly, the state of the road has to be regarded. On an ordinary country road, after much rain, the ground will be so soft as to lend great assistance to the coachman; but in dry weather, if the road be hard, more brake will be required, while, on wood or asphalte, the smoothness of the surface and the absence of all bite increase the need for the brake. When you have to stop to make a call or enter a shop, put on the brake; it will help to keep the carriage still, while, if the horse does walk away, the noise of brake and wheels grinding together will give you notice of the fact. (Always see that the brakes are in good order and do not need reblocking.)

Save in very hilly countries, skids are not often used with light vehicles. They are merely lifted off the hook and placed straight in front of the wheel, and the chain should be so adjusted as to allow of the pan lying perfectly under the wheel. Before the skid is taken off the vehicle the latter must be backed, and the novice may be warned not to catch hold of the pan itself in his attempt to lift it to its hook. If the hill be long and the pace a trot, the iron becomes far too hot to be touched by the hand.

W. C. A. BLEW.

GLOSSARY.

Axle—The rounded ends of the *axletree*, a timber running transversely beneath the carriage. Upon these the wheels revolve, the bearings being enclosed in the axle box. In the *Collinge* axle this box is secured upon the arm by two nuts screwed right and left.

Axletree—The pin which passes through the middle of the wheel upon which the circumvolutions are performed. Axles are of two kinds—Collinge's and the mail coach pattern.

Backband—A broad strap or chain passing over the saddle pad of a cart or carriage horse, used to support the shafts.

Bars—The timbers to which the leaders' traces are attached in tandem, unicorn, or four-in-hand teams.

Bearing Rein—A fixed strap which is fastened at one end to the bridle, at the other to the hook on the saddle pad. By its means the horse is prevented from dropping its head, and is made to appear more showy, and is said by some drivers to be better under control. A more severe form is known as the *Gag bearing rein* or *Gag*. This strap is first attached to the headpiece, then taken through a swivel on the bridoon and then goes to the hook on the pad.

Bellyband—A broad strap attached to the shafts of a vehicle by the saddle pad, and passing closely beneath the body of the animal drawing it.

Billets—Short straps used to connect the various parts of the harness.

Bits—The steel contrivance attached to the bridle inserted in the horse's mouth, to which the reins are attached. Bits are of many patterns, but for all practical purposes they may be divided into few classes. The only snaffle used for harness horses is the ring snaffle, which has two rings at each end. To drive double ring is to buckle the reins to both rings. To drive single ring is to buckle the rein to one ring only, so that when the rein is drawn it acts through the other ring; this is a severer form. Of curb bits there are the Liverpool and Buxton patterns. The former has a mouthpiece which shifts up and down; it has its advantages, but is liable to pinch a horse's lips. The Buxton was invented by an amateur of that name. The ports are of different heights, and of late years bits with india-rubber mouthpieces have been used.

Blinkers—Leather flaps placed by the side of a horse's eyes in order to prevent him from seeing anything except what lies straight in front. Also called *winkers*.

Body Roller—The band or girth fastened round a horse's body on the top of the clothing.

Boot—The receptacle for parcels or luggage on a coach, underneath the seats of guard and coachman.

Boot-tread—The iron step on the front boot used in mounting the fore part of a coach.

Bore—A horse is said to bore when he gets his head down and leans on the bit, and as a consequence on the coachman's hands.

Box—The seat upon which sits the driver.

Box Seat—For which an extra charge is made. The seat next to the coachman.

Brake—(1) A block of wood or iron faced with leather or india-rubber pressed by a lever at will upon the tyre. Its application to coaches was devised by a Mr. Tongue about 1824. Its original name was a "Coach Retarder," but long before that some contrivance in the nature of a brake had been used on trollies in coal-mines. (2) A large, high-set four-wheeled open carriage, with a straight body, and a cross seat in front for the driver.

Breast Harness—A form of harness adopted occasionally, which does away with the collar and gives the horse a breast-strap instead to work against.

Breeching is connected with all the harness upon a horse's hind quarters, which consists of the *crupper*, a divided strap which is s[illegible]ced over and behind the horse's tail; the *crupper d*[illegible]cting this with the saddle. The *breeching* is the [illegible] passes round behind the horse, and helps him [illegible]g and stopping a carriage.

Bridle—That part [illegible] harness which is put upon the horse's head. It c[illegible]s of a long strap or *cheekpiece* running down the horse[illegible]ad, to which are fastened the *blinkers* by the eye, the *headpiece* running behind the ears and the *bit* in the horse's mouth. The *noseband* goes round the head above the nostrils. The *browband* or *frontal* passes from the top of the cheekpiece around the forehead, and the *throatlash* from the same point passes round beneath.

Bridoon or Bradoon—The separate snaffle bit to which in harness the bearing rein is attached. In the case of saddle horses the bridoon is another name for the snaffle of a double bridle.

Browband—[*See* BRIDLE.]

Cavesson or Cavezon—A noseband put upon a horse's nose in order to wring it if he be obstinate or unruly during the process of breaking him in. It may be made of iron, wood, or leather.

Chaunting or Chanting—Originally the singing of a horse's praises above its worth; hence generally the cheating of a purchaser of horses.

Cheekpiece—[*See* BRIDLE.]

Cheek of the Bit—The portion outside a horse's mouth.

Chin-groove—The groove in the chin of a horse wherein the curb chain lies.

Clicking—The noise made by the heel of a hind shoe striking against the fore shoe. It is also called *Forging Foot* when trotting.

Coaching Club—Founded in 1870, through the instrumentality of Mr. G. Goddard, under the presidency of the Duke of Beaufort. Hyde Park is fixed for the first meet and, of late years, the Horse Guards parade for the second.

Cockeye—A slang name for the loop at the end of a trace, by which it is attached to the carriage or to the bar.

Collar—A roll, heavily padded with straw and covered on the outside with leather, which is passed over the horse's head and rests closely upon his shoulders. To it are attached the hames and traces, along which the draught acts.

Collar of Whip—A metal band around the handle of

the whip, at the point, usually about 7, 8, or 9 inches from the end, where it balances easily. Also called *thumb ferrule.*

Coupling Reins are the crossed inner reins which run from the *draught rein* (*q.v.*) of one horse to the inner side of the other. A horse's coupling is that rein which runs to the inner side of his bit. Hence to alter the near horse's coupling is to take up or let out the rein on the other horse's draught rein.

Crossing Traces is the device of fastening the inside trace of one leader to the inside bar of his partner. The practice is resorted to with the idea of keeping the bars even when one horse is freer than the other.

Crupper—[*See* BREECHING.]

Curb—A chain or strap used for rendering a bit more powerful. It passes under the lower jaw and is fastened to the upper branches of the bit. The curb-rein forces it powerfully against the jaw.

Dash Board or **Splash Board**—A board or leather apron, which is placed in front of a vehicle and over the wheels to prevent mud from being thrown up, either by the heels of the horse or by the rotation of the wheels.

Dock—To cut off the end of a horse's tail with a view to the improvement of its appearance. This is now declared to be cruelty, and punished by fine or imprisonment.

Double-thong—*Verb,* to hit the wheelers with the thong of a four-horse whip when "caught."

Noun, when the whip is not required for the wheelers.

Drag—A coach kept for pleasure and not for the carriage of passengers from place to place. Also the skid or slipper is sometimes called the drag.

Draught Reins—The outer rein of each horse, contrast with the *Coupling Reins.*

Dumb Jockey—A wooden contrivance fitted on to a horse's back ; from its arms are india-rubber and leather reins. It is used for mouthing young horses.

Felly—The rim of a carriage wheel, usually composed of curving sections of wood, into which the spokes are run and secured.

Fillet-strap—An ornamental strap lying across the back of the horse between the saddle pad and the *Hip-strap* (*q.v.*). This part of the horse is itself sometimes called the *Fillet.*

Foot-board—The sloping board upon which rest the feet of the coachman and box-seat passenger.

Fore-carriage—The under part of the coach to which the fore-wheels are attached.

Forehead-drop—An ornamental strap hanging down from the browband over the horse's forehead.

Four-in-Hand Club—Formed in April, 1856, under the presidency of the Duke of Beaufort, the secretaries being Mr. J. L. Baldwin and the Hon. L. Agar-Ellis. The number of members is limited to fifty. The Club holds two parades a year, the first at the Magazine in Hyde Park, and later on the Horse Guards' Parade at six o'clock in the evening preparatory to driving to the Crystal Palace. This second meet is held on Thursday —firework night at the Palace.

Futchells—Longitudinal pieces of timber between which the pole fits.

Hames—Curved pieces of wood or metal which are fixed upon the collar and have attached to them the traces.

Hammercloth—A cloth covering the driver's seat.

Hand—The unit of a horse's measurement. Equivalent to 4 inches.

Hand-pieces—That part of the reins which comes to the hand of the coachman.

Hang off—Of the horses, to pull sideways from pole or partner.

Head-piece—[*See* BRIDLE].

Head-stall—Any arrangement of straps or cord which encompasses the head, whether it be a bridle or a halter.

Hip-strap—A strap passing over a horse's hindquarters and fastened on either side to the *Breeching Body.* Also called *Quarter-strap.*

Jibbing—Moving restively sideways or backwards.

Jobbing—The letting out on hire of carriages and horses.

Kicking—The old term for the custom of guards to ask travellers for a tip or special fee. Also called *Shelling.*

Kicking-strap—A stout strap hanging loosely behind the horse's hind-quarters and preventing him from throwing up his heels.

Kidney-link—A link on the hames of the horse's collar to which the pole-chains are fixed.

Lamp-irons—The irons projecting from the body of the coach and fore boot into which the coach lamps are placed.

Lapping traces—Passing the inside trace of a leader round the inside trace of his partner and taking it back to his own bar.

Leaders—The two front horses in a four-in-hand are called leaders, and referred to frequently as "before the bars."

Leading-bars—[*See* SWING-BARS and WHIPPLE-TREES].

Lock—Of the wheels ; to jam, either accidentally in turning, or intentionally by a *skid* (*q.v.*) or hook and chain attached to the felly. A vehicle which can be turned round sharply like an omnibus or brougham does not lock ; but if an attempt be made to turn a coach in a narrow road it locks, *i.e.* the wheels catch the body.

Lozenge—The slang term for a circular piece of leather with a hole in the centre to fit round the mouth-piece of the bit and having a slit from circumference to centre which enables it to be slipped over the bit. It is used for horses which bear away or *hang off* (*q.v.*).

Main-bar—The cross timber fixed to the pole-head, from which hang the *Swing-bars* or *leading bars* (*q.v.*).

Martingale—A strap which passes from the bridle under the collar and is fastened to the bellyband. It is intended to prevent the horse from throwing up his head.

Milling—Old term for kicking in horses.

Nave—The centre of the wheel, from which the spokes radiate.

Near side—The left-hand side of the road, vehicle, horses, or driver.

Nicking—Making an incision at the root of a horse's tail in order that he may carry it higher.

Noseband—[*See* BRIDLE].

Offside—The right-hand side of the road, vehicle, horses, or driver.

Opposition point—Keeping a strain on the right reins when turning a corner to the left, and *vice versa,* in order to prevent the horses from turning too soon and not leaving room enough for the carriage.

Pad—A light form of saddle, used in some sets of harness.

Perch—The pole connecting the fore and hind part of a carriage.

Pickaxe team—A team consisting of two wheelers and one leader. Also called a *Unicorn* team.

Point—To give the leaders an intimation by the reins that they are about to turn a corner.

Pole—The longitudinal timber that is set between the wheelers, to which they are attached by the *Pole-chains* or, in some kinds of vehicles, by *pole-pieces.*

Pole-head—The metal fitting to the front end of a pole which carries the pole-chains or pole-pieces.

Pole-hook—The hook at the top side of a coach pole on which the main bar is hung.

Pole-pieces—Wide leather double straps which in broughams, victorias, and some other description of carriages are used instead of pole-chains. They run from the pole-head through a kidney-link in the harness. It is by means of the pole-chains or pole-pieces that horses in double harness are enabled to "hold" a carriage when descending a hill, and to stop it.

Poling up—Adjusting to the proper length the pole-chain or pole-piece.

Postilion—A driver who rides at the same time. If there be four horses he rides the near leader, and a driver on the box the wheelers; if a pair he drives both from the near horse.

Pull—Of the horse; to be always straining heavily on the reins whatever the pace.

Quarter-strap—[*See* HIP-STRAP].

Rearing—To stand erect, or to attempt to stand upon the hind-legs.

Reins—The straps, usually about an inch broad, fastened on either side of the horse's mouth, and carried back over the harness to the driver's hand.

Road cribbage—A game much played in old coaching days in which opposing parties took different sides of the road and scored points according to agreement for various selected natural objects such as cows, sheep, pigs, &c. Also called *Road Game* and *Road Piquet*.

Roller-bolts—The four protuberances on the splinter-bar over which the loops of the traces of horses in double harness are slipped.

Roughing—Altering a horse's shoe in slippery weather in order to give it a firmer hold of the ground.

Saddle—In driving, a pad laid across the back of a horse. The backband runs over the top, and the shaft tugs are supported from it, the bellyband running from the same point underneath the horse. The reins run through rings upon the top of it.

Shafts—The bars between which a horse is fastened to a carriage.

Shelling—[*See* KICKING].

Shooter—A name given to coach guards in the olden time. Various reasons have been given for the appellation, but the real origin is a matter of doubt.

Shouldering—(1) Of the horse, pushing sideways upon pole or partner. (2) Of the guard and coachman, picking up short-distance passengers on the road whose names were not entered on the way-bill, and whose fare was therefore secured by the guard for himself and the driver. Such passengers were called "*Shoulder-sticks*." At the dinners given by the great coach proprietors to their guards and coachmen a standing toast was "Shouldering—but don't let me catch you at it."

Shy—To spring suddenly either sideways or backwards from fear, or from excess of spirits.

Skid or Slipper—An iron shoe with flanges retained by a chain from the perch or axle, which fitting under the hind-wheel prevents its revolving. Now practically superseded by the brake except for very steep hills.

Snaffle—A bridle with a light bit and unprovided with a curb.

Splinter-bar—The transverse timber to which the wheelers' traces are affixed.

Split quarter-strap—A variety of the hip or quarter-strap, in which the strap is divided about half-way down the horse's side, and attached to the breeching in two places.

Spring—Of the coachman; to put the horses to a gallop.

Stage—The distance travelled by one team of horses.

Stops—Hooks upon the shafts which prevent the harness from slipping forward.

Surcingle—A girth which passes under the saddle and keeps some object, such as a blanket or sheet, tightly upon the horse's body.

Swing-bars—The transverse timbers swinging from the main-bar (*q.v.*) to which the leaders' traces are affixed. Sometimes called swingle-trees.

Tandem—Two horses driven, not side by side, but one in front of the other.

Terrets—The loops or rings upon the saddle pad through which the reins pass.

Throatlash—[*See* BRIDLE].

Top ferrule—[*See* COLLAR OF THE WHIP].

Trace—The stout straps passing from the collar to the splinter-bar along which the horse's draught acts.

Tugs—Stout loops of leather, depending from the saddle pad, through which the shafts are inserted. Also called shaft tugs or shaft loops.

Under carriage—That part of the coach which supports the body.

Unicorn team—[*See* PICKAXE TEAM].

Wheelers—The two horses attached directly to the coach, and next to the driver.

Winkers—[*See* BLINKERS].

DUCK SHOOTING—One hundred years ago the bulk of the wild fowl exposed for sale in English markets came from the Eastern counties and Somersetshire, and were taken in decoys. Since then, the gradual extinction of their old haunts, and the increase of population, have brought about, as regards season and locality, changes in the habits of the fowl, which have to be met with new methods of pursuit and capture, so that now the vast majority of ducks killed in the season in the British islands are shot with the gun.

In the first period, the killing of wild fowl was practically the work of a few; now, through the great increase of both professional and amateur sportsmen, it has become open to the many.

The ancient goose and duck gun, once such a common feature in the farmhouses of the maritime marshes of the Eastern counties, is extinct, except in museums. As we remember it, it had an extraordinary length of barrel and a flint and steel lock, yet these old rough-stocked pieces had a history. We would their chronicles had more fully survived, for they would have completely thrown into the shade the much-vaunted records of modern sport.

Roughly speaking, contemporary duck-shooting may be divided into three parts. First comes shooting with staunchion guns, in single or double-handed gunning punts; this is by far the most certain method of getting birds; at the same time it is one requiring the greatest amount of exercise, forethought, and skill, with exposure in all weathers, to say nothing of frequent disappointments and risk of life. Then there is shooting "at flight"—that is, at dusk, when ducks get on the wing and leave their resting-places for their feeding grounds on land or along the muddy shores of tidal estuaries, river-flats, and foreshores. This is a very ancient habit, for in the days of decoys the fowl always rose in a body in the evening and spread themselves over the adjoining lands. Our forefathers called this flight the "rising of the decoy," and the daily event was accentuated by the roar of wings, heard miles away, on a still evening in the dreary fens of the Eastern counties.

Thirdly, ducks may be shot by day, either by driving on preserved water or along the coast in severe weather, or by following open streams or drains at early dawn in districts where they are known to resort when the weather is very hard. In this latter case, duck-shooting can be followed not only in the day but on light nights, by visiting the spring-heads and open waters so long as they continue unfrozen. The results perhaps are not always equal to expectation, but we have always found the fascination of these

lonely wanderings in an Arctic solitude, and beneath the silent midnight heavens, a quite sufficient return for a comparatively small bag. Two guns at most are admissible, for the creaking of frozen snow on a still night can be heard by the quick-eared birds at a great distance. Even two shooters are apt to exchange ideas, and we have always done best alone.

Since the passing of the "Wild Birds' Protection Acts," there has been a very gratifying increase both in numbers and extension of range of several of the most valued species (as regards food supply) of ducks nesting in Great Britain. This is notably the case with the Mallard, Teal, Gadwall, Shoveler (and probably the Pintail), Wigeon, Tufted-duck, Pochard, and Sheld-duck. Of these, the first six are surface-feeders, obtaining their food on land and water without diving, and, as a rule, frequenting fresh water. The Wigeon is more often a coast feeder. These are all desirable in a culinary sense. The Pochard, Tufted-duck, and Golden-eye are expert divers, and these also feed much on fresh waters, and are valuable as food. The true sea-ducks, all expert divers, as the Scaup, Long-tailed duck, Eider, and the two Scoters, rarely leave the sea, and their flesh is worthless. The Sheld-duck is also valueless as food, although the eggs are considered a delicacy. The quality of a duck's flesh is dependent on its food, and even the best vary much according to the district they come from.

The ranks of home-bred birds are increased greatly in the later Autumn by immense arrivals from the Continent, coming from countries both northerly and easterly of Great Britain. Of these the Wigeon is the most common, and makes the best return to those who use a punt, for it flies in dense companies of hundreds and thousands, and, as the tide rises, they crowd the higher banks and elevated spots as long as these remain uncovered, so that, with luck and good management, 70 to 100 may be gathered after a shot. Taking into consideration the perfection of modern appliances, the bags of the present are far less than formerly. Punts one hundred years ago were either floating coffins or lumbering tubs, carrying a swivel-gun with its muzzle elevated like a telescope. Mr. Lubbock tells how an old man, who had the run of Breydon Water, with a piece destitute of any trigger-guard, which he called "Old Peggy," killed 83 fowl at a shot.

A modern punt may take either a single or double-barrelled breech or muzzle-loader, with a charge of 6 to 8 oz. of powder and 2 to 2½ lbs. of shot. A gun designed by Sir Ralph Payne-Gallwey had an oval bore, with major axis parallel to the water, so as to throw and scatter a lateral belt of shot.

Sportsmen differ as to the best gun for flight shooting. We have tried all sorts, and never found anything better than an ordinary 12 bore, 7½ lbs. weight, with 3½ drachms of powder, and 1¼ oz. of No. 4 shot—left hand barrel choke. With a heavier weapon, the weight becomes a burden to the flesh. When ducks come to their feeding-grounds they invariably fly against the wind. On calm, still nights they pass too high for a shot; a strong wind at the back of the shooter and against the ducks offers the best chance, particularly if the gun faces the light in the west. The time of passage is very limited, fifteen minutes to half an hour. If you want to kill, do not fire at your birds as they come, but sideways, high, and after they have passed. On a recent occasion on the Holderness coast, on an evening when ducks flew low and slow against a strong wind, a young farmer killed eighteen couple within half an hour, only desisting because his barrels got too hot. At this sport a steady retriever is required, or half the birds will not be gathered. Much disappointment will be saved by finding beforehand the places where ducks come to feed.

Mallard, Wigeon, and also Scaup come up from the sea at dusk to the muddy foreshores of bays, estuaries and tidal rivers to feed on the sea grass (*Zostera marina*), of which they are immoderately fond. It is a common practice amongst coast-fowlers to sink a barrel, or, better still, to dig a hole in the muds, deep enough to cover the shoulders of the shooter; a flat piece of board should be fixed for a seat, and the hole can be made quite comfortable, if lined with a piece of matting. A full moon is the best, with a slightly overcast sky. We have had excellent sport, but of course some nights are blanks.

Large numbers of Mallard, Teal, Tufted-duck, and, in a less degree, several other species, are bred on private waters in Great Britain. Their greatest enemy, when the broods are hatched, is the pike. The ducks are shot in the autumn after they have been joined by immigrants from the Continent. Thanks to the "Wild Birds' Protection Acts" the abominations of what used to be called "flapper-shooting" are at an end. With legitimate sport in the proper season, these sanctuaries afford excellent shooting. Discretion is necessary not to overshoot, otherwise the fowl would be driven to seek a quieter retreat. Permanent shelter-screens are placed round the ponds or lakes in the best places for guns. The ducks, when disturbed, rise in a body, perhaps 800 to 1,000 on the wing, at once; these soon break into small flights and spread in every direction, but after a short interval reappear at their old haunt by twos and threes and give excellent shots. We know of one such preserve of one hundred acres, with about ten acres of ponds, where 500 to 600 ducks may always be seen. It is shot lightly, from 100 to 200 head annually. The home-bred ducks are as a rule less wild, and heavier and finer birds than the foreigners;

practically, too, they spend their lives in a state of semi-domestication.

Out of thirty-one species—ducks and mergansers—included in the British *avi-fauna*, sixteen must be classed as residents (*i.e.* they have nested, more or less), three are winter visitants, and twelve occasional.

Ducks can rarely be approached at sea by sailing-boats, that is by going directly for them, but a skilful boatman, who is well up to the work, will often enough bring his craft within shooting distance. Duck shooting has many phases, and some of the Continental methods of pursuit differ materially from those of England. Sometimes, as on the great lakes of Sweden, the bow of a boat is masked with green branches and allowed to drift slowly down into the vicinity of the fowl, till the concealed sportsmen can open their battery. Ducks are also tempted within reach by decoy birds, or excellent imitations of the same. In America various schemes are employed to attract ducks within range, and numbers are shot from concealed boats, tubs, and artificial islands, as well as by combined boat attacks. In every case, however, the design is the same, to make a bag.

The literature of duck shooting would form a library in itself, from the classic works of H. B. Daniel, Hawker, and Folkhard to the inexhaustible files and pages of *The Field* newspaper, where every point connected with wildfowl shooting has again and again been threshed out. To those interested in the subject and wishing to increase their knowledge, information will be found to the most minute details in Sir R. Payne-Gallwey's *The Fowler in Ireland*, and in his *Letters to Young Shooters*, third series; also in Mr. Abel Chapman's *Bird Life of the Border*, and in *The Art of Wild-fowl Shooting*, all works excellent of their kind.

JOHN CORDEAUX.

DUNLIN—[*See* SANDPIPER].

DUIKER—The **Duiker**, or **Duikerbok**, (*Cephalopus mergens*), *Puti* of the Bechuanas, *Impunzi* of the Matabele, is a small antelope, standing some 26 inches in height, found singly or in pairs all over South Africa, as well as in Nyasaland, Angola, and other localities. Besides the common duiker, other varieties are to be found in various parts of Africa. The duiker frequents by preference bush, or thin forest, where scrub and covert are plentiful. It is, however, common enough in open country, wherever patches of bush occur. And in the deep, jungly kloofs of the mountain ranges it is also abundant. The duiker falls more often to the shot-gun than to the rifle, and, at fairly short range, succumbs readily enough to a charge of No. 2 shot. It is a shy, wary little beast, and has a habit of squatting and diving among the coverts it frequents, and its name, which, rendered from the Dutch, signifies diver or ducker, explains very aptly its somewhat sneaking, furtive attributes. In colour this antelope varies a good deal, the coats of individuals, even in the same locality, running through the whole range of hues between greenish and yellowish brown. A yellowish or reddish brown, tinged with green or gray, is the more common. The male carries short sharp horns not exceeding $5\frac{1}{2}$ inches in

DUIKER.

Ht. at shoulder, 26 in.; Av. length of horns, $4\frac{1}{2}$ in.; Max. length, $5\frac{1}{2}$ in.

length. The female is hornless. A tuft of hair between the ears is very characteristic. The duiker is frequently shot by the gunner when in pursuit of game birds. It has plenty of pace and staying power, and stands well before fox-hounds. In Natal a small bright bay species is found (*C. natalensis*), known as the Natal red-buck, the male and female of which both carry horns. The flesh of the duiker is moderately good eating.

H. A. BRYDEN.

EEL. (*Anguilla vulgaris.*)

MEASUREMENTS, ETC.—Lower jaw the longer; length of head $2\frac{1}{3}$ to $2\frac{3}{4}$ in the distance from the snout to the origin of the dorsal fin, and from $3\frac{1}{2}$ to $3\frac{3}{4}$ to the commencement of the anal fin. Body cylindrical as far as the anus, posterior to which it becomes more and more compressed. Lips broad and fleshy (*latirostris*), or narrow (*vulgaris*); the maxilla extends backwards to beneath the middle or hind edge of the eye. *Eye*—rather small, diameter 8 to 12 times in the length of the head; about $1\frac{1}{2}$ to 2 from the end of the snout $1\frac{1}{2}$ apart. *Teeth*—cardiform in the jaws and vomer. *Fins*—the dorsal commences far behind the head as already observed. The anal arises about the length of the head behind the origin of the dorsal fin, and a little in front of the middle of the total length. *Scales*—small ones under the epidermis and imbedded in mucus. *Colours*—variable, generally dull olive along the back, and white or yellow along the abdomen, fins darker than the body, except the first third of the anal. Among the outward signs by which a male eel may be recognised, says O. Hermes, is a very striking metallic or bronze colour.—Day's *Fishes of Great Britain and Ireland*, vol. 2, p. 242.